# The *The* BEST PLACES TO KISS in SOUTHERN CALIFORNIA

## BONNIE STEELE

EDITION 5

SASQUATCH BOOKS
SEATTLE

Printed in the United States of America
Published by Sasquatch Books
Distributed by Publishers Group West
14 13 12 11 10 09 08 07 06 05      6 5 4 3 2 1


Cover and interior design: Stewart A. Williams
Cover photograph: © Royalty-Free/CORBIS
Interior maps: GreenEye Design
Project editor: Kurt Stephan
Copy editor: Karen Parkin
Proofreader: Laura Gronewold
Indexer: Michael Ferreira

ISBN 1-57061-406-7


Sasquatch Books
119 South Main Street, Suite 400
Seattle, WA  98104
(206) 467-4300
www.sasquatchbooks.com
custserv@sasquatchbooks.com

# CONTENTS

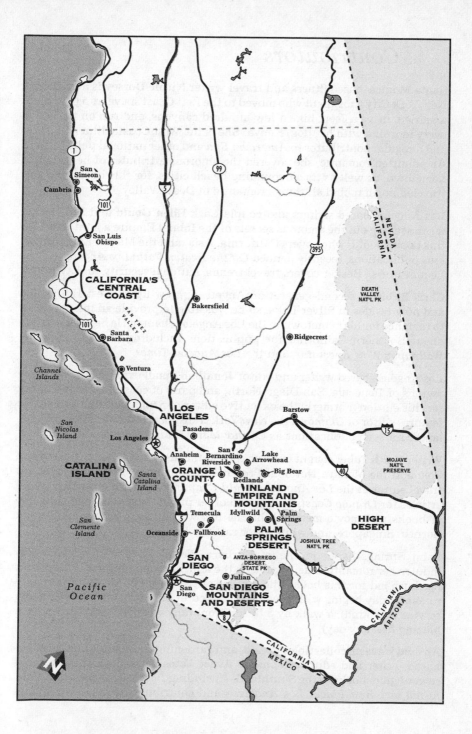

# Contributors

Santa Monica–based fitness and travel writer **Nicole Dorsey** is a contented New York City transplant who moved to the Left Coast six years ago to plant a garden, drive a Jeep, hike a few hundred canyons, and run on the beach every morning with her dog, Kenya. She is the West Coast editor of *Fitness* and a regular contributor to *American Spa* and other national publications. An admitted romantic, she covered the amorous attributes of her adopted hometown, as well as its surrounding beach cities, for this book. She also traveled north to find all things romantic in Death Valley.

Los Angeles–based writers and couple **Lark Ellen Gould** and **Bill Becker** made seeking out the amorous secrets of the Inland Empire a joint effort for this book. Gould, who covers California, Asia, and the Middle East for various publications, recently penned *Off the Beaten Path: Los Angeles* (Globe Pequot Press). Becker covers travel trends, national security, and aviation.

**Chris Rubin**, a second-generation Angeleno, grew up in West Hollywood and now resides in Silver Lake, so he was able to provide an insider's tour to romance for his hometown in the Los Angeles chapter. He has also written about Southern California for publications including *Travel + Leisure, Wallpaper, Wine Spectator*, and the *Los Angeles Times*.

Los Angeles–based writer and editor **Jonathan Small** explored the romance regions of Temecula, San Diego North, and parts of coastal Orange County for this edition. Formerly the executive editor of *Stuff* magazine and senior features editor of *Glamour*, the New York transplant is now a full-time freelancer for such publications as *Cosmo, Marie Claire, Maxim*, and *Redbook*.

Writer **Keith Tuber** sought out romance in the high desert regions of Joshua Tree and the Mohave National Preserve for this book. A former assistant travel editor at the *Los Angeles Herald Examiner*, Tuber has written travel articles for *Orange Coast, Valley*, and other publications. An avid collector of books and movie memorabilia, he has won awards for his articles on Borneo, Singapore, and whitewater rafting.

Palm Springs–based journalist **Barbara Wernik** savored the chance to indulge her romantic side, exploring the alluring community of Julian with her husband for this book. The mother of two says her idea of a perfectly romantic day begins with breakfast carried in on a tray (anywhere), a spa service (any kind), a walk by a beach front (any weather), and dinner by a blazing fire (any day).

An avid traveler, collectibles hound, and gardening enthusiast, Los Angeles–based writer and editor **Stephanie Avnet Yates** has edited and authored several guidebooks to the Southland—including *Best Places Southern California* and *Best Places Los Angeles*—and contributes to various regional publications and Web sites. This California native believes the Golden State is best seen from behind the wheel of a little red convertible (with husband Bryan along for company), and happily took to the road to explore the romantic regions of Catalina Island, the Central Coast, Palm Springs desert resorts, and San Diego for this book.

As the editor of this book and *LA Brides* magazine, Los Angeles–based writer and editor **Bonnie Steele** knows a thing or two about Southern California's romantic regions. She contributed her amorous insights to the Los Angeles, Orange County, and Northern San Diego chapters. Also a contributor to *Best Places Los Angeles* and *Best Places Southern California*, Steele serves as the editor of *Valley* magazine.

## Acknowledgments

Thanks to the Sasquatch Books team, who helped guide this book smoothly through the production process. Acquisitions editor Terence Maikels provided great insight, endless enthusiasm, and infinite patience throughout this consuming project. The thorough work of project editor Kurt Stephan and copy editor Karen Parkin also proved invaluable. Thanks also to designer Stewart A. Williams, proofreader Laura Gronewold, and indexer Michael Ferreira. And, a big thanks goes to the writers who contributed to this book, providing their personal takes on the Southland's most romantic spots.

# About Best Places® Guidebooks

**PEOPLE TRUST US**. *Best Places*® guidebooks, which have been published continuously since 1975, represent one of the most respected regional travel series in the country. We are proud to have incorporated the best-selling *Best Places to Kiss* guidebooks into our publishing series. This fifth edition (our first) of *The Best Places to Kiss in Southern California* has earned a special place in our hearts and aims to do the same in yours. Our Best Places to Kiss reviewers know their territory. They have your romantic interests at heart, and they strive to serve as reliable guides for your amorous outings. The *Best Places to Kiss* guides describe the true strengths, foibles, and unique characteristics of each establishment listed. *The Best Places to Kiss in Southern California* specifically seeks out and highlights the features of this region that harbor romance and splendor, from restaurants, inns, lodges, and bed-and-breakfasts to spectacular parks, pristine beaches, and romantic drives. In this edition of *The Best Places to Kiss in Southern California*, couples will find all the information they need, including the best times to visit a place for the most privacy, where to find the most intimate restaurants, which rooms to request (and which to avoid), and how to find each destination's most romantic activities.

**NOTE:** *The reviews in this edition are based on information available at press time and are subject to change. Romantic travelers are advised that the places listed herein may have closed or changed management and, thus, may no longer be recommended by this series. Your romantic feedback assists greatly in increasing our accuracy and our resources, and we welcome information conveyed by readers of this book. Feel free to write to us at the following address: Sasquatch Books, 119 S Main St, Suite 400, Seattle, Washington, 98104. We can also be contacted via e-mail: bestplaces@ sasquatchbooks.com.*

# Lip Ratings

The following is a brief explanation of the lip ratings awarded each location.

| | |
|---|---|
| ❤❤❤❤ | *Simply sublime* |
| ❤❤❤ | *Very desirable; many outstanding qualities* |
| ❤❤ | *Can provide a satisfying experience; some wonderful features* |
| ❤ | *Romantic possibilities with potential drawbacks* |
| UNRATED | *New or undergoing major changes* |

# Price Range

Prices for lodgings are based on peak season rates for one night's lodging for double occupancy (otherwise there wouldn't be anyone to kiss!). Prices for restaurants are based primarily on dinner for two, including dessert, tax, and tip, but not alcohol. Peak season is typically Memorial Day to Labor Day; off-season rates vary, but can sometimes be significantly lower. Because prices and business hours change, it is always a good idea to call ahead to each place you plan to visit.

| | |
|---|---|
| $$$$ | *Very expensive (more than $100 for dinner for two; more than $250 for one night's lodging for two)* |
| $$$ | *Expensive (between $65 and $100 for dinner for two; between $150 and $250 for one night's lodging for two)* |
| $$ | *Moderate (between $35 and $65 for dinner for two; between $85 and $150 for one night's lodging for two)* |
| $ | *Inexpensive (less than $35 for dinner for two; less than $85 for one night's lodging for two)* |

## Romantic Highlights

The Romantic Highlights section of each chapter guides you to the most romantic activities in each region. These include pursuits that are intimate and relaxing for couples, such as strolling to a lighthouse, taking an easy guided kayaking tour, or enjoying an alfresco lunch. It is our firm belief, however, that during any romantic getaway, doing away with the notion of an itinerary (and, of course, sleeping in!) is part of the fun. In Romantic Highlights, the establishments or attractions that appear in boldface are recommended and addresses and phone numbers are supplied. Every attempt has been made to provide accurate information as to an establishment's location and phone number, but it's always a good idea to call ahead.

## Lodgings

Many romance-oriented lodgings require two-night-minimum stays throughout the year (especially on weekends); during some holiday weekends or high-season periods, this requirement may be extended to three nights. It is a good idea to call in advance to check the policy at your lodging of choice. In the spirit of romance, popular family lodgings are mostly not included in this guide; however, some accommodations included do allow children, particularly those over age 12. Many of these have safeguards for your privacy, such as separate breakfast times (one seats children, the other is adult-only) or detached suites for those traveling with children. If having a kid-free environment is critical to your intimate weekend away, call ahead to find out an establishment's policy. For more information about where to find pet-friendly rooms, see the pet index at the back of this book.

## Indexes

In addition to the index of pet-friendly accommodations mentioned above, this book also features a wedding index. Organized by region, this index lists romantic lodgings with facilities able to accommodate wedding parties of at least 50 people. (Since, after all, one of the most auspicious times to kiss is the moment after you exchange wedding vows, we felt this was a good idea.) Additionally, all restaurants, lodgings, town names, and major attractions are listed alphabetically in the back of the book.

# Credit Cards

Many establishments that accept checks also require a major credit card for identification. Note that some places accept only local checks. Credit cards are abbreviated as follows: American Express (AE); Diners Club (DC); Discover (DIS); MasterCard (MC); and Visa (V).

> *"As usual with most lovers in the city, they were troubled by the lack of that essential need of love—a meeting place."*
>
> **—THOMAS WOLFE**

# ♡ The Fine Art of Kissing

**THIS IS THE FIFTH EDITION OF** *The Best Places to Kiss in Southern California*, and we are proud to be publishing this book in a new, improved format that provides better-than-ever coverage of the most romantic destinations in the Southland. This expanded edition includes features that are entirely new for the *Best Places to Kiss* series, including a "Romantic Highlights" section in every chapter that covers the most romantic activities in each region. In addition, we have added maps and detailed access and information sections and have greatly expanded the coverage of Southern California's most alluring lodgings and restaurants. As always, our research is enthusiastic, our investigations thorough, and our criteria increasingly more restrictive. We gather numerous reports from local and traveling inspectors before recommending a magical place to share closeness and private moments. We highly value our mission as one of the few travel books to review romantic properties with a candid and critical eye, and we treasure the feedback from readers who report that our reviews offer a breath of amorous fresh air.

With its year-round great weather and diverse geographic regions, Southern California offers so many romantic possibilities that compiling a list of the best places to kiss was more about narrowing down the most amorous options. From the village of Cambria in the north to the flawless scenery that surrounds San Diego, alluring settings are everywhere in Southern California. While some romantic choices may be obvious—like the sun-swept beaches and endless charm of Laguna, the snowy peaks of Lake Arrowhead and Big Bear, or the languid luxury of Palm Springs—true love can also blossom in unexpected Southland spots. For example, a day of fun and frolic at Disneyland or a raucous night of live country-western music and two-stepping in the middle of Joshua Tree can be the stuff that cherished memories are made of. It all depends on your definition of romance.

Any travel guide that rates establishments is inherently subjective—and *Best Places to Kiss* is no exception. We rely on our professional experience, yes; we also rely on our reporters' instincts to evaluate the heartfelt, magnetic pull of each establishment or region. Whether or not we include places is determined by three main factors: setting, privacy, and ambience. Setting is quite straightforward, referring simply to location and view, but the latter two categories deserve some clarification. In regards to privacy, our preference is for cottages and suites set away from main buildings. Such locations allow amorous couples to say or do what they please without fear of being overheard or disturbing others. However, many truly wonderful bed-and-breakfasts and hotels require sharing space; in these cases, we look for modern soundproofing techniques, as well as expert innkeepers who know how to provide guests with a sense of intimate seclusion. We also applaud the notion of private breakfasts, whether delivered straight to your suite or served at an intimate table for two in the dining room.

Ambience is the final major criterion, and it includes a multitude of factors. Intimate environments require more than four-poster beds and lace pillows, or linen-covered tables set with silver and crystal. Ambience requires features that encourage intimacy and allow for uninterrupted affectionate discourse, and relates more to the degree of comfort and number of gracious appointments than to image and frills. We also keep an eye out for details such as music, fresh flowers, and candles. Ambience is also created in part by innkeepers, and if you are traveling for a special romantic occasion, we highly recommend informing them in advance. With notice, the best innkeepers take extra care to ensure that an especially intimate ambience welcomes you and your loved one. They can also inform you of any "special occasion packages," which might include chilled champagne, breakfast in bed, and special touches during turndown service, such as dimmed lights and your beloved's favorite music playing in the background to set the right romantic mood.

If a place has all three factors going for it, inclusion is automatic. But if one or two of the criteria are weak or nonexistent, the other feature(s) have to be superior before the location will be included. For example, a place that offers a breathtakingly beautiful panoramic vista but is also inundated with tourists and children on field trips would not be featured. A fabulous bed-and-breakfast set in a less desirable location might be included, however, if it boasts a wonderfully inviting and cozy interior that outweighs the drawbacks of the location. It goes without saying that we consider myriad other factors, including uniqueness, culinary finesse, cleanliness, value, and professionalism of service. Luxuries such as complimentary champagne and handmade truffles, or extraordinary service, are noteworthy extras and frequently determine the difference between lip ratings of three-and-a-half and four. In the final evaluation, keep in mind that every place listed in this book is recommended. When you visit any of the places we include here, you should look forward to some degree of privacy, a beautiful setting, heart-stirring ambience, and access to highly romantic pursuits.

## LOS ANGELES AND ENVIRONS

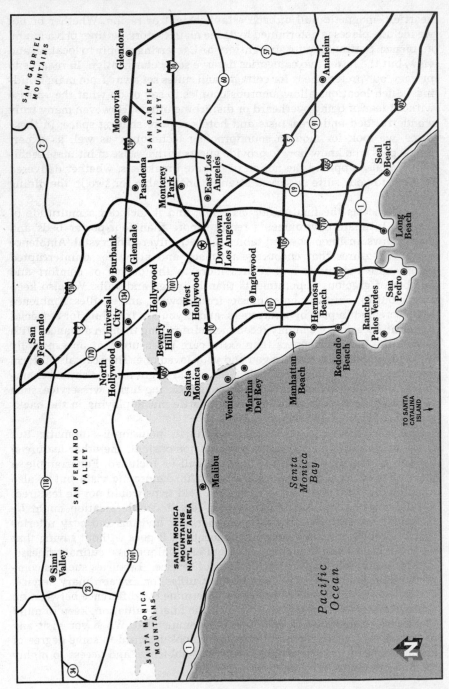

*"You are always new. The last of your kisses was
ever the sweetest...."*

—JOHN KEATS

# ♡ LOS ANGELES AND ENVIRONS

Think of Los Angeles and the first images that come to mind are likely to be beaches and sunshine, palm trees and convertibles, movie stars and Hollywood landmarks. All those are here, and much more. More like a collection of cities than just one big metropolis, Los Angeles spans from downtown to the Westside and the beaches to the Valley. Within this huge, sprawling city, there are more things to see and do—scattered over a variety of locales—than anywhere on the planet. With the Santa Mountain Mountains separating the L.A. Basin from the Valleys and the Pacific Ocean to the west, Los Angeles offers a diverse landscape for lovers, and amorous activities run the gamut from sightseeing and cultural offerings (museums, plays, concerts) to endless shopping and outdoor recreation (hiking, biking, sailing).

Because Los Angeles is so spread out, couples are going to need a game plan—and a car—for exploring the City of Angels. If you're dreaming of carefree days frolicking on the beach, make Santa Monica or one of its surrounding cities your home base. To the south, Long Beach and its environs also offer miles of coastline but are best known as the home of the *Queen Mary* and the Aquarium of the Pacific. If shopping, dining, and sightseeing are on your agenda, the ultrachic enclave of Beverly Hills or the flashy Sunset Strip in West Hollywood provide plenty of glitz and glamour. Downtown is the city's cultural center, with the Walt Disney Concert Hall, the Museum of Contemporary Art, and the Music Center. And, finally, over the hill, which in L.A. lingo means the San Fernando Valley and Pasadena, you'll find the city's most popular attraction, Universal Studios Hollywood, as well as the historically charming Old Town Pasadena.

However, be warned that since Los Angeles sprawls over miles of high-priced real estate, the two of you are going to have to endure some traffic to get from shopping on Rodeo Drive to romping on the sandy shores of Malibu. Planning ahead to be in transit during off-peak driving hours is helpful but not guaranteed. So when you're inching down the 405 trying to make a dinner reservation that started 10 minutes ago, just remember at least you are with the one you love.

1

# NEAR THE BEACH

## ROMANTIC HIGHLIGHTS

There is no more glorious stretch of coastline in the United States than the nearly endless miles of seashore that extend from Malibu to Redondo Beach. These white-sand beaches are chock-full of clandestine coves, warm tide pools for shell collecting, world-class volleyball tournaments, surfers galore, seasonal whale watching and—let's not forget—some of the most romantic spots for kissing.

**Santa Monica** serves as the perfect hub for exploring the Los Angeles beach communities. Featuring the broadest beach on the coast, this is surely a city for lovers, especially if you want to stroll hand-in-hand. The famous **Santa Monica Pier** (at the foot of Colorado Ave, off Ocean Ave) houses carnival-like games, roller coasters, an antique carousel, and plenty of touristy street performers. After riding the rides, the two of you can grab cotton candy or a corn dog and sit at the end of the pier watching the salty old fishermen bait their lines. Or, start your stroll at the **Third Street Promenade** (three blocks east of the beach, between Broadway and Wilshire), an outdoor haven for shoppers, hordes of tourists, and lovers taking in the sights. Cool stores such as Z-Gallerie and Restoration Hardware stretch on for six city blocks along this outdoor promenade, or head indoors at **Santa Monica Place** (at 4th St and Broadway; 310/394-5451; www.santamonicaplace.com), which has high-end retailers such as Williams-Sonoma and Arden B.

One of the most romantic drives in the Southland is along **Pacific Coast Highway** (PCH) heading north to Malibu. This beach-rich community—sinfully rich, in fact—has some of the best waves on the Pacific, so make like Frankie and Annette (in her yellow polka-dot bikini) and hit maybe the ultimate spot, aptly named **Surfrider Beach** (adjacent to the Malibu Pier). Here, you'll watch dolphins frolic 50 yards offshore, while surfers shred perfect waves, and seagulls caw overhead. California law protects public access to beaches—all are welcome—but access points are sometimes hidden, especially in Malibu's high-profile residential areas. To stroll onto a stretch of shoreline along this posh coast (short of hopping Steven Spielberg's fence), look for the small brown "To Beach" signs with white lettering. Beaches are open from sunrise to sunset (several are open until midnight) and most charge a parking entry fee. Metered street parking is also available, so stock up on quarters.

As you cruise up the coast, stop in at the low-key **Malibu Country Mart** (3855 Cross Creek Rd) for a quick bite and maybe even a little shopping. These 25 redwood buildings with simple green awnings attract many of the area's local celebrities who reside behind the gilded gates of the nearby **Malibu Colony**. Keep your eyes peeled for such regulars as Pamela Anderson watching her kids on the playground or Mel Gibson sipping on an iced blended mocha.

When it's time to eat, stop for a casual meal at **The Reel Inn** (18661 Pacific Coast Hwy; 310/456-8221) or **Gladstone's Malibu** (17300 Pacific Coast Hwy; 310/573-0212), two unfussy seafood restaurants near the beach, to throw back a bucket of clams or a glass of Chablis and watch the waves crash on the shore.

Long before the movie stars moved into beachfront mansions, the residents of this area were Chumash Indians. Artifacts of their era are displayed in the **Malibu Lagoon Museum** (23200 Pacific Coast Hwy; 310/456-8432), which sits just next door to a national historic site called the **Adamson House** (310/456-8432). Set on 13 lovely beachfront acres, this 1929 Moorish–Spanish Colonial Revival residence showcases the lavish use of tiles produced by Malibu potteries between 1926 and 1932. It's a truly romantic spot to stop and picnic under a palm tree, watch the waves break, or stroll along the sandy shore.

Heading south on PCH, traffic often grows impenetrable just past Santa Monica, and the rolling beaches give way to cityscapes and **Venice Beach**. This artists' enclave is home to an eclectic boardwalk, **Venice Ocean Front Walk** (beachside between Venice Blvd and Rose Ave), where the two of you can walk, ride, or skate past **Muscle Beach**—maybe the world's only 100 percent outdoor gym—which features hot dog stands, sarong shops, street vendors selling everything from silver jewelry to henna tattoos, hippie musicians, and skateboard parks.

Once in tie-dyed Venice, explore the little neighborhoods around Main Street and Abbot Kinney Boulevard, where artists-in-residence open their galleries and stores to onlookers. **Lily's French Café and Wine Bar** (1031 Abbot Kinney Blvd; 310/314-0004) features an outdoor patio that doubles as a Parisian garden. Sip 1 of 55 wines by the glass, order a decadent brunch of fluffy French toast or a hearty omelet, and enjoy the fresh ocean air.

When you need to tune into each other and tune out of the rampant tourism, drive west along Washington Boulevard (which separates funky Venice from glitzy Marina del Rey) and turn onto any one of the narrow streets that bottom out right at the ocean. You've now come to the famously photogenic **Venice Canals**, named by Venice Beach pioneer Abbot Kinney after his inspirational stint in Italy in the late 1800s. Here, a treasure trove of beachfront condos, cool coffee shops, and, above all, a huge and unrestrained beach await lovers.

Farther south, **Marina del Rey** is the center of all things nautical. Want to board a sailboat and hit the high seas with your special someone? Couples can sign on for a chartered sail or rent their own boat at **Bluewater Sailing** (13505 Bali Wy; 310/823-5545).

Past the marina, the tiny seaside hamlet of **Playa del Rey** begins the start of what is known as the South Bay, made up of such cities as **Manhattan**

3

**Beach, Hermosa Beach,** and **Redondo Beach.** Mainly residential communities, these charming beachfront cities provide couples with surf shops, bistros and cafes, and beach-chic boutiques (some are even affordable!).

When you've had enough of public consumption, you and your significant other may retreat to a well-deserved romantic hideaway or stroll across a sunset-worthy shoreline. After all, the precise beach with the perfect somebody can provide the ultimate in comfort, romance, and luxury.

## Access and Information

**Los Angeles International Airport (LAX)** (310/646-5252; www.lawa.org) is served by most major airlines and sits near the beach, just south of Marina del Rey. Once in Los Angeles a car is a necessity, and on a sunny day there's nothing better than driving with the top down, so you may want to consider renting a convertible. Depending on traffic, Santa Monica can be reached from the airport in a matter of minutes by taking the 405 Freeway north to the 10 Freeway west, which eventually turns into Pacific Coast Highway. PCH then winds its way up and down the coast through Los Angeles's beach cities. From the 405 Freeway, visitors can also travel west on Highway 90, which leads to Marina del Rey.

For more information, contact the **Santa Monica Convention & Visitors Bureau** (800/544-5319; www.santamonica.com). Its Palisades Park **walk-up center** (1400 Ocean Ave; 10am–5pm) is located near the pier.

## Romantic Lodgings

### THE AMBROSE HOTEL
**◐◐**

*1255 20th St, Santa Monica / 310/315-1555 or 877/AMBROSE*
Set on a quiet residential street in Santa Monica, this intimate boutique hotel combines Craftsman-style architecture with an Asian aesthetic to create a hip and cool, yet relaxed, neighborhood hotel. A lush Asian-inspired Zen garden with a serene pond welcomes couples as they arrive for check-in. While the Living Room and Fireplace Library stocked with plenty of interesting art books make up the lobby area, most guests spend their time exploring Santa Monica or enjoying quiet moments in the small, inviting guest rooms. Italian linens, a complete TV/CD/DVD set up, limestone bathrooms stocked with Aveda products, and a tempting minibar chock-full of everything from herbal tonics to high-end chocolates make it easy for lovers to stay put in their rooms. However, a small, well-equipped gym is available for those who feel they really need to get in their daily dose of cardio. A complimentary continental breakfast, complete with Starbucks

coffee, is served each morning in the Living Room area. And guest parking under the building makes it possible for lovers to not worry about feeding the meters and focus on more important things—like spending quality time together.

**$$–$$$** *AE, DIS, MC, V; checks OK; www.ambrosehotel.com.* &

---

## BARNABEY'S MANHATTAN BEACH
🌑🌑

*3501 Sepulveda Blvd, Manhattan Beach / 310/545-8466 or 888/296-6836*
Couples will feel like they've made a trip to jolly old England when they check in for a stay at this European-style inn nestled around a lush, flower-filled courtyard and patterned after grander 19th-century hotels. After an extensive recent renovation, each of the 128 rooms is individually decorated with noteworthy antiques, fancy flea market finds, brass lamps, distinguished artwork, and lace curtains, creating a romantic Victorian feel. The lobby and communal areas are magnificently furbished with elegant Victorian-era furniture, and each cozy room (some are definitely on the small side) features a one-of-a-kind hand-carved headboard with a lavish down comforter and whisper-soft linens. Many rooms offer private balconies overlooking the pretty wisteria-draped courtyard, and these rooms seem quieter, so couples in search of a little peace may want to request one. Other amenities include free airport shuttle, a small fitness center, a complimentary morning newspaper, and a heated outdoor pool and Jacuzzi. Best of all, the inviting hotel is only a short walk to the beach (along a tranquil, flower-strewn jogging path); bicycles are available for couples who want to pedal to the coastline for a ride along the shore. For those romantics who prefer to stay strictly indoors—there is no ocean view, mind you—the inn offers in-room video games, computer modems, and a selection of books . . . or the two of you can always figure out a way to entertain yourselves.

**$$–$$$** *AE, DC, DIS, MC, V; no checks; www.barnabeyshotel.com.* &

---

## CASA DEL MAR
🌑🌑🌑🌑

*1910 Ocean Wy, Santa Monica / 310/581-5533 or 800/898-6999*
Pull out your platinum card and spray that Binaca blast because long, deep, and drawn-out smooching is an absolute must-do activity at Casa del Mar. Considered Santa Monica's grandest beach club in the 1920s, this stately brick building sits directly on the sand (two blocks from the Santa Monica Pier) and contains some of the most graceful guest rooms in town—129 in all. Because of the hotel's U shape, most rooms feature ocean views, and they're furnished with sumptuously made beds, chaise lounges, hand-painted armoires, flowing draperies, wooden Venetian blinds, and opulent marble baths with deep hydrotherapy tubs for long soaks. After a massive renovation in 1999, the eight-story hotel boasts Renaissance Revival public

rooms (with velvet and bronze furnishings) in stunningly rich shades of gold, emerald, blue, and apricot. Its luxurious lobby doubles as the coolest cocktail lounge in town, where the two of you can sit in a dimly lit alcove and sip champagne while watching the chic crowd. Afterward, head to dinner in the hotel restaurant (Oceanfront), featuring fine California cuisine, large fan-back chairs, and unobstructed ocean views. Specializing in fresh seafood, Oceanfront is open for breakfast, lunch, and dinner every day, as well as brunch on weekends. By day, the two of you can hang out at the large outdoor pool and terrace garden, visit the spa for a couple's massage, or hit the well-maintained fitness center. By night, take a moonlit beach stroll or check out a movie from the hotel's DVD library and snuggle with your sweetie. After all, this place is so gorgeous, you'll want to make the most of your stay.
$$$$ *AE, DC, DIS, MC, V; no checks; www.hotelcasadelmar.com.* &

## CHANNEL ROAD INN BED AND BREAKFAST
◐◐◑
*219 West Channel Rd, Santa Monica / 310/459-1920*
Built in 1915 by Texas oil baron Thomas McCall, this fully restored fourteen-room B&B offers generous-sized rooms with firm queen- or king-sized beds, goose-down comforters, sleek fixtures, and spacious private bathrooms, some with whirlpool tubs. Oversized framed windows are draped in billowy, gauzy fabrics, but only one or two large rooms have ocean views. Located one block from Santa Monica beach in rustic Santa Monica Canyon, this small hotel is also adjacent to the famous Santa Monica Stairs (all 128 of them), where exercisers march to the beat of their own sneakers, up and down all day long. If you can bear the thought of really venturing out for a breath of fresh air—and we don't blame you if that seems impossible—explore nearby Will Rogers State Historic Park, the Getty Museum, or the famed Santa Monica Pier—then return to the inn for a sensuous soak in the outdoor Jacuzzi. Turndown service includes plush white robes, homemade cookies, fresh fruit, and flowers. In the morning, wake up and smell the roses—literally—and then dig into a hearty breakfast assortment of croissants, breads, muffins, fruit, and baked eggs served in the dining room or outdoor patio. (If breakfast in bed sounds more enticing, simply request delivery to your room, which may just inspire another kiss or two.) And you can work it all off by hitting those stairs next door.
$$$ *AE, MC, V; checks OK; minimum stay required during holiday weekends; www.channelroadinn.com.*

## THE GEORGIAN HOTEL
◐◐

*1415 Ocean Ave, Santa Monica / 310/395-9945 or 800/538-8147*
Originally opened in 1933 as an exclusive seaside getaway for Hollywood
royalty (think Howard Hughes and Bugsy Siegel), "The Lady," as the Georgian was commonly called, harkens back to the days of 1930s glamour and
makes for a romantic, old-fashioned holiday. Certainly modern amenities
abound (including an in-house health club, a multi-lingual staff, pay-per-
view movies, 24-hour room service, valet parking, and Internet service), but
when you recline on the art deco veranda across the street from the Pacific
Ocean, you and your sweetie will feel like you're living in a kinder, more
gentrified decade. (Of 84 spacious rooms, about half have oceanfront views,
so be sure to request one.) Lovers will be charmed in the authentic 1930s
Speakeasy restaurant, which serves gourmet breakfasts to guests only. After
a recent multimillion dollar renovation, the historic hotel has reached landmark status, and today you can still ride the mahogany-paneled elevator to
a turquoise or canary-yellow silk-striped room chock-full of fine antiques.
Don't be surprised if you're out on the veranda one sultry evening, drinking
champagne and unwinding with your significant other, when you see the
ghosts of The Lady's former regulars (Rose Kennedy, Carole Lombard, and
Clark Gable). Simply raise your glass, offer a toast, and know this is one
prime kissing opportunity.
$$$ AE, DIS, MC, V; no checks; www.georgianhotel.com.

## THE INN AT PLAYA DEL REY
◐◐◖

*435 Culver Blvd, Playa del Rey / 310/574-1920*
It's difficult to find a truly tranquil setting within a 10-minute drive of
notoriously chaotic LAX, but there is one—and it's a beauty. This New Eng-
land–style gray-and-white beach inn is located in Playa del Rey, Spanish
for "Beach of the King," but this bed-and-breakfast was built facing a
350-acre bird sanctuary known as the Ballona Wetlands, not the sand. The
inn features a stylish communal living room with a well-stocked library,
binoculars, and bird guides for bird-watching lovebirds. A wall of French
doors invites guests to an outdoor rear patio, where they can take off their
shoes and observe the colorful boats drifting by in the distant harbor. Each
of the inn's 21 rooms faces the wetlands and all are beautifully appointed
with eye-catching wall coverings, four-poster beds with thick down quilts
and pillows, and distressed pine and rattan furniture. Couples may want to
check into a View Suite, which features a two-sided fireplace in the bath-
room next to a bubbling oversized two-person Jacuzzi tub, which also casts
a heavenly glow on your pillowy bed. A complimentary full breakfast and
late-afternoon drinks and hors d'oeuvres are included. Bicycles are pro-
vided for enjoying the nearby bike path, but you may never want to leave

the inn's inviting deck. However, a small rose garden with a private hot tub lures lovebirds out back for a late-night soak.

$$$ *AE, MC, V; checks OK; www.innatplayadelrey.com.* &

## LE MERIGOT BEACH HOTEL & SPA

*1740 Ocean Ave, Santa Monica / 310/395-9700 or 888/539-7899*
Reminiscent of the fine hotels on France's Côte d'Azur, this stylish beach hotel blends European elegance with the laid-back coastal style of Southern Cal. The peach-hued hotel, done in alabaster marble and harlequin floral upholstery, has 175 guest rooms and sophisticated suites, each featuring the hotel's signature Cloud Nine Bed, made with Frette linens and fluffy down duvets and pillows. If that's not enough to lure couples for an amorous outing, giant marble bathrooms and generous views of both the Santa Monica Mountains and the lush coastline are sure to seal the deal. A stunning outdoor swimming pool is the perfect setting to while away the day in the Santa Monica sunshine with the one you love. And nothing's more romantic than getting a couple's hot-stone massage in the 6,500-square-foot spa. Alas, the caravan of summer tourists may occasionally put a damper on spontaneous kissing around the common areas of this hotel, but take heart: this celebrity hangout has plenty of spots for an intimate and serene moment. A sunset cocktail in Le Troquet lobby bar is the perfect prelim for a moonlight beach stroll, or make a reservation for a romantic meal in the hotel's Cezanne restaurant, which serves Cal-French cuisine in an elegant setting. Open for breakfast, lunch, dinner, and weekend brunch, the stylish eatery utilizes farm-fresh ingredients from the local farmers' market to create such specialty dishes as horseradish-crusted salmon with baby leaf spinach, and veal medallions with wild mushroom shallot sauce.

$$$ *AE, B, DC, DIS, MC, V; no checks; minimum stay required during holiday weekends; www.lemerigothotel.com.* &

## LOEWS SANTA MONICA BEACH HOTEL

*1700 Ocean Ave, Santa Monica / 310/458-6700 or 800/235-6397*
As you might expect of an oversized oceanfront hotel (350 rooms), the prices are high, the interiors are cavernous, and the service is solid and professional at this beachside landmark. What might surprise you, though, is that after a big remodel in 2001, a California casual ambience has overtaken this once generic hotel, and guest rooms nicely outfitted with oversized furnishings, thick comforters, and sand-colored fabrics and wall coverings offer a clean, sleek design that's downright inviting for romance. Lovers step into the airy four-story glass atrium lobby and are transported to a vacation hideaway. Regardless of what the concierge might tell you, the most intimate rooms are not the splendid, one-bedroom suites. Instead, choose one of

# Beachfront Property

For couples dreaming of a *From Here to Eternity* moment, unfortunately there aren't many beaches in the Southland where you can enjoy a little privacy. However, you can still find a stretch of sand to spread out your blanket for a little romantic oceanfront rendezvous: you just have to know where to look. **Point Dume Beach** is one such place. Surrounded by golden palisades and dotted with overflowing tide pools, Point Dume is not so remote that you will be the only ones around, but it's a heck of a lot more private than camping out by the Santa Monica Pier, and the surf is far less populated than at better-known Zuma Beach to the north. The only reason for the small numbers here is the remoteness of the area; access to this locale requires some degree of surefootedness and the desire to walk about a mile. Once you're reveling in the gorgeousness that is Malibu, head farther north on Pacific Coast Highway to Westward Beach Road. Turn left and follow the road to its end at the parking lot below Point Dume. From the southern end of the parking lot, head out across the sand and look for a well-marked trail on the left. On a clear day you can see large portions of the rugged coastline, as well as Catalina Island floating in the middle of a calm, measureless blue sea. Be patient and wait for sunset, when the sky will stage a stunning performance for just the two of you, and don't be surprised to see whales breaching on the horizon. The evening air can become chilly at the beach, so bring a sweater or cover-up if you plan to catch a glimpse of that fiery, hot-pink sunset. After so much tranquility and beauty, returning home will be much harder than you think. **Paradise Cove** (28128 Pacific Coast Hwy, next to the Paradise Beach Cove Café) is another beach where you can actually find a spot in the sand to enjoy a little private time. Because this small beach framed by cliffs on both sides is private, you and your sweetie can curl up on the sand with a bottle of wine (public beaches do not allow alcohol). You'll also find showers, barbecue pits, and picnic tables. Take Pacific Coast Highway north past illustrious Pepperdine University to Paradise Cove Road. Turn left toward the ocean and follow the small signs. While it's $15 for beach-goers to park, nearby **Paradise Cove Beach Café** (310/457-2503) shares the same parking lot, and you don't have to pay the parking fee if you're going to eat at this thong-and-sarong local haunt. Supermodel Cindy Crawford has been spotted here, and it's just south of where Jennifer Aniston and Brad Pitt's hush-hush wedding ceremony took place. Bartenders recommend the Paradise Dream, a perfect blend of rum and coconut crème served in a coconut shell. After two of these, you'll be ready for a little beach blanket bingo, if you get the drift. Before heading out for a beach adventure, call the **California State Park Service Malibu Sector** (310/457-8185) for information on beach closures and water quality. —NICOLE DORSEY

the ocean-view rooms that are a little larger than standard but simply dazzling with balcony seating for two. The hotel's elegant restaurant, Lavande, overlooks the beach and the Santa Monica Pier, and serves well-prepared simple fare like salads, pastas, fish, and grilled meats. In addition to breakfast, lunch, and dinner, Lavande offers a bountiful Sunday brunch buffet. Be warned that after a feast of this dimension (shellfish, crepes, French toast, steak and eggs—you name it), it may be slightly difficult to kiss—or even to breathe—until you unbuckle your belt. The well-appointed 6,000-square-foot fitness center and spa, with yoga and Pilates classes, can certainly help with that. Or simply grab a couple of chaise longues and camp out by the oceanfront pool.
$$$$ *AE, DC, DIS, MC, V; checks OK; www.loewshotels.com.* &

## MALIBU BEACH INN
🐾🐾
*22878 Pacific Coast Hwy, Malibu / 310/456-6445 or 800/4-MALIBU*
This exclusive resort is Malibu's only luxury oceanfront hotel and has gasp-for-breath views and excellent personalized service. The boutique-style inn was designed to create the feeling of being in your own private beach cottage, each with a balcony that's mere feet from the crashing surf below. From your alcove, witness panoramic scenes from Point Dume to Palos Verdes, perfect for sailboat and surfer surveillance all day long. Complimentary beach chairs are provided so the two of you can while away the day making googly eyes at each other on the nearby beach. The inn's picturesque peach stucco exterior and imported Mexican tiles are evocative of the famous missions that once dotted California's coastline. Each idyllic room (there are only 47) comes with an array of little luxuries, including a Mexican-tiled bathroom and plush robes; most rooms feature Mexican-tiled gas fireplaces as well as Soft Tub Jacuzzis for two on oceanfront balconies, so couples can take a soak while the waves crash on the shore just below. A light complimentary breakfast is served in the oceanfront lobby that adjoins the charming outdoor terrace. There aren't any restaurants on the premises, but there are several tasty options nearby, like Marmalade Café.
$$$–$$$$ *AE, DC, MC, V; no checks; minimum stay required during holiday weekends; www.malibubeachinn.com.* &

## PORTOFINO HOTEL AND YACHT CLUB
🐾🐾
*260 Portofino Wy, Redondo Beach / 310/379-8481 or 800/297-0144*
Located on a plush and private peninsula on King Harbor, this contemporary hotel lures lovers looking for an oceanfront hotel with a yacht-club feel. The main level has panoramic views of the Pacific Ocean from Palos Verdes to Catalina Island, and the lobby features a light-filled atrium lounge, floor-to-ceiling windows, and a large, welcoming marble fireplace. Overstuffed

couches look out at the breathtaking scenes—from sunsets and sailboats to dolphins and pelicans—framed in the floor-to-ceiling windows. Comfortable but modest-sized guest rooms are on three floors (they get nicer as you head upstairs), decorated in French country-style furnishings that mix modern plaids with richly hued florals and cheerfully upholstered furniture. Every room has a private balcony, distinctive artwork, and either ocean or marina-side views, and is fully equipped to meet the needs of those on a blissful romantic getaway—from thick towels, toiletries, and complimentary coffee maker to an outdoor pool, fitness center, and Internet dial-up service. The best rooms in the house for romance measure 600 square feet and have Jacuzzi tubs, king-sized beds, and spacious sitting areas. When the two of you have worked up an appetite, head to the steak and seafood joint downstairs called Breakwater, the white-tablecloth waterside setting that offers the relaxing sounds of a jazz band on the weekends. Overlooking the tranquil Portofino Marina, the 180-seat indoor/outdoor eatery serves breakfast, lunch, dinner, and an outstanding brunch on Saturdays and Sundays: try the apple-pecan French toast or the steak and eggs Benedict with sautéed mushrooms and tomato Hollandaise sauce. All of King Harbor is within walking distance.
*$$$ AE, DC, DIS, MC, V; checks OK; www.hotelportofino.com.* &

## THE RITZ-CARLTON MARINA DEL REY
✪✪✪

*4375 Admiralty Wy, Marina del Rey / 310/823-1700 or 800/241-3333*
Of all the hotel chains across the country, the Ritz-Carlton is perhaps the most consistent when it comes to style, elegance, quality, and service. Couples can expect to find all the distinctions that the Ritz-Carlton is known for—luxurious amenities, spacious marble bathrooms, and conscientious kid-glove treatment—at this Marina del Rey outpost. Spectacularly set harbor-side at the world's largest man-made marina, this luxury hotel lures robust lovers with the promise of an elegant, restful retreat where they can hang out by the pool, enjoy the spa, play a game of tennis, rent a bike for an oceanfront ride, or simply sit back and enjoy the setting. Guest rooms are small, but most feature private balconies with divine ocean or marina views. The Lobby Lounge and Terrace Bar is a plush place for cocktails and high tea for two. For higher-end dining, lovers can reserve a table at the French-Asian–inspired Jer-ne restaurant, where stark white walls are softened by rich hardwood floors, and a teak wood terrace offers unobstructed views of the picturesque harbor. Restaurant specialties include dim sum, a daily bento box, Kobe carpaccio, and New York strip steak. Couples can make the most of the setting for breakfast, lunch, and dinner.
*$$$$ AE, DC, DIS, MC, V; no checks; www.ritzcarlton.com.* &

## SHUTTERS HOTEL ON THE BEACH
🌸🌸🌸🌸

*1 Pico Blvd, Santa Monica / 310/458-0030 or 800/334-9000*
Some hotels just ooze sophistication and panache, while others dazzle with
another kind of pizzazz altogether: romance. Shutters is all of the above.
With its Martha's Vineyard vibe, this gray clapboard hotel achieves an ambience that could only be described as informal luxury—with a steep price tag.
Inside the casual-chic lobby, fireplaces cast a warm glow on conversation
pits, and a big balcony offers amazing ocean views, making it possible for
couples to find plenty of nooks and crannies worthy of a romantic interlude.
Guest rooms have a sunny country-club setting, with lots of sailcloth, rich
walnut furniture, tasteful fixtures, whirlpool tubs (complete with rubber
duckies), bright fabrics, high ceilings, and floor-to-ceiling shutter doors that
open to the ocean breeze. Nighttime storybooks offer a fun touch for turndown service. (You can read a little tale to your sweetheart before bedtime.)
Small balconies are a little close together but, all in all, this is one of the best
city escapes on the water. Downstairs is Pedals, a casual restaurant serving
simple salads, sandwiches, pastas, and fresh seafood that provides outdoor
seating so the two of you can get a tan while you sip Bloody Marys during
brunch. Open for breakfast, lunch, dinner, and weekend brunch, Pedals is
mere steps from the famous Strand bike path where people run, skate, and
flirt all day long. Upstairs, the hotel's formal eatery, One Pico (see Romantic
Restaurants), is open every day for dinner and provides a sophisticated setting for couples to dine on fine seafood and chops. The hotel recently opened
a new six-room spa, One, featuring treatments with the Ole Henriksen
Face/Body product line.
**$$$$** *AE, DC, DIS, MC, V; checks OK; www.shuttersonthebeach.com.* ♿

## THE VENICE BEACH HOUSE
🌸

*15 30th Ave, Venice / 310/823-1966 or 800/695-8284*
Lovebirds looking for a little edge to their romantic getaway may want to
check into this traditional B&B housed in a large 1911 blue frame house one
block from the wacky part of Venice Beach. The interior is simply but comfortably decorated, and most rooms are bright, attractive, and casual. Some
of the rooms have new floral furnishings, and plush carpet has been added
throughout, which is a welcome improvement. Homey and laid-back, the
Venice Beach House is a respectable choice, but only five of the nine rooms
have private baths, so amorous adventurers should book early to request
one. Couples who want to snuggle by a wood-burning fireplace should check
out the Pier Suite, which features mix-and-match antiques. A handsome
garden surrounded by sheltering shrubs makes the yard a calm retreat from
the crazy Venice Ocean Front Walk. Lovebirds who prefer their romance
with a view should book somewhere else, but you really can't beat the price

at this quirky hotel. If beach property, a relaxing atmosphere, and hearty breakfasts are high priorities, then this inn is one place where you two can curl up on a couch and call it "home" for a night or two.
$$ *AE, MC, V; checks OK; www.venicebeachhouse.com.* &

## THE VICEROY
❤❤❦
*1819 Ocean Ave, Santa Monica / 310/451-8711 or 800/622-8711*
One very long block away from the beach stands a fashion-forward hotel almost too terminally cool for its own good. Thanks to the hip hoteliers of the Kors Hotel Group, the theme is snooty British Colonial meets breezy So-Cal mid-century modern, done almost completely in bright white and apple green. The hotel's huge, dazzling lobby doubles as a massive cocktail bar (perfectly called Cameo, as in "It's time for your cameo"). Once through the decadent lobby, you'll find 163 boldly designed guest rooms—laid out studio-style, as a one-bedroom suite or as a presidential suite—with Frette linens, marble tubs, large vanities, and generous sitting areas. Couples will want to request a room with an ocean view, since only half the rooms face the Pacific. (You'll really need to be on one of the top floors to actually spy the Pacific.) Guests come more for the scene than seclusion. Private cabanas ring two petite swimming pools outside, creating a cozy setting for a little poolside smooching. Viceroy's all-star eatery, Whist, is as classic and clever as the four-person card game for which it's named. Open for breakfast, lunch, dinner, and Sunday brunch, Whist serves familiar dishes with sophisticated twists for breakfast, creative salads and sandwiches at lunch, and dinner selections that include honey-coriander duck breast and sea bass with lentils. Choose from a table, banquette, or lounge-style alcove seating in the restaurant, with its dramatic display of English china set against a green-mirrored wall. If you're in the mood for a little pampering, request in-room spa services, or if you're snuggling in a cabana, staffers from local day spa Fred Segal are happy to trot over and perform a poolside mani-pedi or foot massage. Not too shabby.
$$$-$$$$ *AE, DC, MC, V; no checks; www.viceroysantamonica.com.* &

# Romantic Restaurants

## BEAU RIVAGE
❤❤❤
*26025 W Pacific Coast Hwy, Malibu / 310/456-5733*
If you're longing for an affectionate rendezvous, this is the place to share a Mediterranean-style meal on the flower-packed patio, complete with a fountain and iron tables and chairs. The entryway is strung with whimsical lights year-round at this pretty French-inspired beachside eatery, inviting

couples into a restaurant that oozes romance. Located across the street (Pacific Coast Highway) from the sea, the dining room offers sweeping views of the ocean's tidal comings and goings. A fireplace flanked by Italian oil paintings and plate-glass windows showcases the sensuous sea in the main dining room. Order from the appetizing menu that proposes pricey pastas, an irresistible rack of lamb with fresh mint jelly, medallions of venison with red wine and watercress mashed potatoes, and tasty risottos. For a truly special occasion, book a table in the walk-in wine cellar, where red-letter dinners are served for 12 people or fewer. Beau Rivage is particularly provocative at Sunday brunch—perfect for a little afternoon flirting, so take your time and chew slowly.

$$$ *AE, DC, DIS, MC, V; no checks; dinner every day, brunch Sun; full bar; reservations recommended; www.beaurivagerestaurant.com.* &

## THE BOTTLE INN
◐◐

*26 22nd St, Hermosa Beach / 310/376-9595*
A local favorite, the Bottle Inn consistently garners awards for best Italian food, most romantic restaurant, and, especially, best wine list. Owner Silvio Petroletti has been honored with *Wine Spectator* commendations for several years running. The restaurant is cozy, quiet, and friendly, located several blocks from the loud, bright center of town. Its rather dated, vaguely European decor has remained unchanged since the Bottle Inn opened in 1974. Surprisingly, it still works—largely thanks to the expert kitchen and exceptional wine list. Lovers in search of a special setting may call ahead for the privilege of dining in the wine cellar. The menu is classic Italian with such favorites as veal piccata, chicken cacciatore, osso buco, fettuccine bolognese, minestrone soup, and seafood risotto, all expertly prepared. Start off with the signature toasted Italian focaccia topped with mushrooms, prosciutto, and zucchini, with béchamel, fontina, and melted mozzarella cheese. For dessert the house-made cannoli is a treat, though you may want to order two, as it's so good, you won't want to share.

$$ *AE, MC, V; no checks; lunch Mon–Fri, dinner every day; beer and wine; reservations recommended; www.thebottleinn.com.*

## CAFÉ DEL REY
◐◐◖

*4451 Admiralty Wy, Marina del Rey / 310/823-6395*
This marina-front restaurant creates fashionable fusion cuisine better than most places on the Westside. The grand 3,000-bottle, temperature-controlled display wine cellar at the pleasant restaurant entrance, and an exhibition kitchen area in the dining room, add attention-grabbing dimensions to this rather laid-back local staple. Couples who love seafood will appreciate the fresh fish, which is skillfully prepared with Pacific Rim fusion elements.

For example, appetizers like a smoked salmon sushi roll, shrimp sashimi salad with papaya-cucumber medley, and Chesapeake Bay soft-shell crab tempura are all winning starters. Innovative entrées include pan-seared black truffle John Dory with wild mushroom risotto, pecan-crusted rack of lamb, and the frequently ordered oven-roasted seafood tower (with halibut, shrimp, sea scallop, lobster, and lemongrass lobster sauce). Desserts are noteworthy, especially if the raspberry napoleon brûlée is featured. Arrive early on Sunday to nab a table for the standout brunch. The two of you can watch the boats bob up and down in the marina outside as you stuff yourselves silly.
$$$ *AE, DIS, MC, V; no checks; lunch, dinner every day, brunch Sun; full bar; reservations recommended; www.cafedelrey.* ঙ

## CHEZ MELANGE
◐◐

*1716 Pacific Coast Hwy (Palos Verdes Inn), Redondo Beach / 310/540-1222*
You want Asian, but your partner's dreaming of Moroccan chicken with Middle Eastern condiments. What to do? Make a reservation at Chez Melange, which presents a mélange of dishes, moving seamlessly between Cajun and Japanese to Chinese and Italian—regardless of its Francophile name. Located inside the modest Palos Verdes Inn (a no-nonsense beach motel), this neighborhood eatery has a menu that changes daily and reflects all that's fresh and in season, especially the sushi and raw bar offerings. There are always interesting pastas, a brilliant grilled vegetable plate, and at least one Asian entrée on the menu, including a threesome of savory meats (think rabbit cooked three ways). Desserts are out of the ordinary, too. A house fave is the coyly dubbed Mélange a Trois, consisting of crème brûlée, pot au chocolate, and a small caramel custard. You can even have a romantic gesture placed on the menu, since it's printed out on the computer daily. When you make a reservation, the hostess asks if it's a special occasion (birthday, anniversary, proposal), and when you arrive your table is decorated with confetti, and the honoree is presented with a personalized free dessert of brownie à la mode. Could this chocolate treat be a great place to present a big diamond ring?
$$ *AE, DC, MC, V; no checks; breakfast, lunch, dinner every day; full bar; reservations recommended; www.chezmelange.com.* ঙ

## CHLOE
◐◐◑

*333 Culver Blvd, Playa del Rey / 310/305-4505*
Sure, Playa del Rey has nice beaches, but it's never offered much of a dining scene . . . until now, that is. Run by owners Jeffrey Osaka and Christian Shaffer, this tiny restaurant offers couples a beach-chic setting to sample such tasty fare as roasted veal bone marrow with morels, succulent Angus

sirloin with artichoke and potato hash, or sautéed monkfish with shrimp and baby clams. The menu changes monthly to make the most of fresh seasonal ingredients, and the chef bakes his own brioche daily. While the restaurant only offers seating for about 30, lovers can pull up a stool for an intimate meal at the bar and sample from the restaurant's top-notch wine list. For special occasions, check out Chloe's upcoming schedule of wine dinners, presented in a private room that seats 40.

$$$ *AE, MC, V; no checks; dinner Mon–Sat; beer and wine; reservations recommended; www.chloerestaurant.com.* ら

## CINCH
ぴぴ

*1519 Wilshire Blvd, Santa Monica / 310/395-4139*
Take a talented chef, give him his own Asian-fusion restaurant, add a whimsically designed front room, drizzle the results with attentive service, and you've got Cinch. As with most Dodd Mitchell–designed hot spots (Dolce, Le Dome), this stunning restaurant and lounge reflects a devotion to earthy elements. The cavernous front room features glossy rock walls, sculpted water fountains, and jagged white-quartz candleholders on each table. The electric blue–lit bar is perfect for nerve-wracking first dates. The interior is quixotic and airy (not too crowded). For couples staying for dinner, request a downstairs table for optimal people watching—even though decibel levels can be challenging. The menu offers a mix of French- and Japanese-inspired dishes, including sushi, wok-seared halibut, and a lobster ravioli starter that's all-out excellent. But save plenty of room for dessert, as Cinch turns out stellar sweets for sweethearts. Fuji apple pie with Tahitian vanilla bean ice cream, chocolate pudding with poached pears, or brioche bread pudding with banana-caramel ice cream are the perfect way to top off an amorous evening.

$$$ *AE, DC, MC, V; no checks; dinner every day, late-night snack bar Sat–Sun; full bar; reservations required; www.cinchrestaurant.com.* ら

## FLEMING'S PRIME STEAK HOUSE AND WINE
ぴぴ

*2301 Rosecrans, El Segundo / 310/643-6911*
From the darkened (but welcoming) entryway to the stylish decor and genial service, this classic steakhouse may serve top-drawer chops, seafood, and indulgent desserts, but couples come for the beef. All-American appetizers like French onion soup, an adventurous cheese plate, or breaded Brie served with red jalapeño pepper jelly and sliced apples start meals off with panache. When it comes to the main course, lovers stick with hearty selections like tender bone-in rib eye, New York strip steak, an extravagant veal chop dripping with béarnaise sauce, a palate-pleasing lobster tail, or grilled swordfish. Excellent à la carte side dishes include steamed spinach,

creamed corn, or the restaurant's signature onion rings. And, there's one divine wine list, which offers 100 vinos by the glass, from $5 to $15. The list changes frequently—twice weekly, in fact—and primarily features vintages produced by small, boutique wineries in California, Oregon, and Washington. Guests are also encouraged to experiment with different flavors by combining flights of three 2-ounce tasters, exploring different types of Cabs or Zins or varietals from Down Under. What a good excuse to toast true love three times!

$$$ *AE, MC, V; no checks; dinner every day; full bar; reservations recommended; www.flemingssteakhouse.com.* ♿

## GEOFFREY'S MALIBU
❤❤❤❤

*27400 Pacific Coast Hwy, Malibu / 310/457-1519*
Oh my, there is something completely decadent about sitting atop an ocean-front cliff with nothing to do but gaze into the horizon, make eyes at your soul mate across a linen-cloth table, and order lip-smacking delicacies from a wait staff who happily attends to your every food-based whim. Make an early-evening reservation in time to watch the sun setting and waves rolling onto the deserted beach, not too far below your table. Then, if the mood strikes, order Geoffrey's Cal-American cuisine favorites—though the menu changes seasonally—including day boat sea scallops with Hudson Valley foie gras, a rich seafood pasta, or the coriander-crusted albacore tuna steak. Among the irresistible desserts, their house special stands out from the sugary crowd: a chilled lemon soufflé. For most extraordinary occasions, ask to be seated at an open-air table tucked between twin palm trees outside, which will make you feel like you're vacationing on the Italian Riviera. Most couples venture to Geoffrey's for the picture-perfect view, and the staff has tearfully witnessed hundreds of marriage proposals here.

$$$ *AE, DIS, MC, V; no checks; lunch Mon–Fri, dinner every day, brunch Sat–Sun; full bar; reservations required; www.geoffreysmalibu.com.*

## IL BOCCACCIO CUCINA ITALIANO
❤❤

*39 Pier Ave, Hermosa Beach / 310/376-0211*
Food equals love, in case you haven't already heard. That must mean that love runneth over at this family-run neighborhood gem. Daily blackboard specials include hard-to-find European fish, seasonal meats, so-fresh seafood, prime meats, and homegrown produce. For lovers who aren't on the South Beach Diet, the handmade pastas are a dream. (Live a little and forget your no-carb requirements for one romantic evening.) Oil paintings cover almost every wall, and a lively, award-winning wine list provides the perfect vintage to accompany your meal. Crispy fried calamari with red and green piquant sauce, fresh mussels steamed with white wine, or the imported

parma prosciutto are the perfect way to start off any meal. Homemade lasagne, tagliatelle with smoked bacon and Belgian endive sauce, spaghettini with cuttlefish and squid in ink, or grilled sausages will make the two of you feel like you're dining at your Italian grandmother's house—or the Italian grandmother you always wish you had. And if you have the slightest bit of room left after feeding each other these no-less-than-delicate morsels, don't miss the sensational espresso-soaked tiramisu.

**$$** *MC, V; checks OK; dinner every day; full bar; reservations recommended; www.ilboccaccio.com.* &

## INN OF THE SEVENTH RAY
❂❂❂

*128 Old Topanga Canyon Rd, Topanga Canyon / 310/455-1311*

This is one of those really rare places where the setting and the ambience are in perfect harmony; the restaurant simply seems to merge into the green rolling countryside. Situated next to a flowing creek, this otherworldly restaurant looks like a grand old church from the 19th century, complete with strolling cats, wildflowers, and towering pine trees. Inside, you'll find an eclectic collection of rustic rooms with wood-framed windows, and each dining room (there are several small interconnecting ones) has a vaulted wood-beamed ceiling and a brick fireplace that floods each table with golden warmth. On a clear day, ask to be seated on the large outdoor patio next to the creek, so the two of you can ingest the fresh air as you sample the inn's healthy, gourmet food with an accent on vegan fare. (Think lush salads and freshly baked breads for starters.) Fear not carnivore lovers: High-protein meat dishes are also available, including a free-range organic roast chicken and a grilled filet mignon of naturally raised beef. Weekend brunch is a must, featuring a variety of salads, quiche, organic cereals, and chicken, fish, and vegetarian dishes. On the way out stop in the bookstore, which specializes in astrology, organic gardening, and alternative health books.

**$$** *AE, MC, V; no checks; lunch, dinner every day, brunch Sun; beer and wine; reservations recommended.* &

## JOSIE
❂❂❂

*2424 Pico Blvd, Santa Monica / 310/581-9888*

A roaring fireplace, heavy tables, and two low-key dining rooms painted an arresting artichoke green color create a romantic, rustic, and welcoming setting at chef Josie Le Balch's eatery. There may be a low-key buzz of affectionate chitchat here, but diners aren't packed in close enough to overhear everyone else's conversations. Each evening, this cheerful chef prepares progressive American dishes with French and Italian influences, made with the freshest ingredients from the local farmers' market. Couples are greeted with a complimentary individual quiche then have the option of moving on to such starters as a fantastic cheese plate or baked pear and endive salad. Main courses change regularly, but butter-roasted monkfish or fish *tagine* with preserved lemons are both delicious choices. Sweethearts with a sweet tooth will love the dessert list, which is nearly as long as the dinner menu. These fantastic finales include chocolate–peanut butter lava cake and sticky pecan pumpkin pie. The food is so good that the two of you may even want to sign up for Josie's Sunday afternoon cooking classes.

$$$ *AE, DC, MC, V; no checks; dinner Mon–Sat; full bar; reservations recommended; www.josierestaurant.com.* &

## MELISSE
❤❤❤❤

*1104 Wilshire Blvd, Santa Monica / 310/395-0881*
When a special occasion calls for a special place, reserve a table at Melisse, which is sure to make your romantic night a culinary showstopper. The creation of Josiah Citrin, this ultra-upscale establishment decorated in a French Provençal style is a serious restaurant for couples who demand service on fine china and linens—and don't mind paying for it. The dreamy French-California menu offers overwhelming choices. Appetizers run from sweet pea ravioli or sophisticated foie gras with caramelized cherries to a stunning warm mandarin tomato soup poured around a centerpiece of icy tomato sorbet. Main courses are so tempting, it's hard to choose between such selections as pancetta-wrapped John Dory with a shellfish ragout, free-range chicken with fava beans, salmon with leeks, and rack of lamb with zucchini flowers. If the two of you really want to splurge, you can't go wrong with the chef-composed prix-fixe menu, which features perfect wine pairings on request. Cheese lovers will definitely want to sample a selection from the European-style cheese cart. The formally dressed staff is practiced, well trained, warm, and discreet, and will make the two of you feel like royalty.

$$$$ *AE, MC, V; no checks; lunch Wed–Fri, dinner every day; full bar; reservations recommended; www.melisse.com.* &

## MICHAEL'S
❤❤❤

*1147 3rd St, Santa Monica / 310/451-0843*
Neighboring Third Street Promenade may conjure up images of crowded bars and embarrassing street entertainment, but just a single block from all the activity is this perennial dining pearl. Still going strong after 25 years, this California classic is four short blocks from the beach and has the most romantic patio for outdoor dining in town. Rich, butter-toned walls lend a feeling of warmth to the restored private residence, and an impressive art collection featuring works by David Hockney and Jasper Johns are

displayed throughout the dining area. While romance is key, food is also a priority at Michael's (though some detractors may claim it's lost its edge), and the presentation will enhance a memorable dining experience. Villeroy and Boch china and Christofle silver create the backdrop for artfully presented nouvelle surf-and-turf cuisine, such as roasted spiny lobster tail with grilled zucchini ribbons, marinated pork tenderloin, and seared California squab and foie gras. The menu changes bimonthly, and an impressive wine list ensures that you'll always have a fine vintage to accompany your meal. Save room for one of the seductive desserts, then sit back with your special someone and watch the twinkling stars overhead.

$$$-$$$$ *AE, DC, MC, V; no checks; lunch Tues–Fri, dinner Tues–Sat; full bar; reservations required; www.michaelssantamonica.com.* &

## ONE PICO
♥♥❤

*1 Pico Blvd (Shutters on the Beach), Santa Monica / 310/587-1717*
Consistently rated as one of the best hotel restaurants on the beach, this respectable California-style dining room at Shutters on the Beach (see Romantic Lodgings) boasts a large fireplace, an amazing ocean view, and a menu filled with classic American fare. Mussels with spicy coconut and lemongrass broth, house-smoked salmon with warm corn cakes and crème fraîche, a hearty rack of lamb, and Alaskan halibut with tomato and fennel salad are sure to win over your palate as you win over each other's hearts. Show up in time to sip a cocktail on the outside balcony while the sun sinks into Santa Monica Bay and the lights come alive on the Santa Monica Pier. It's enough to make your hearts flutter. There's live music seven nights a week in the lobby bar, so the two of you can enjoy a drink from the inventive cocktail and martini menu while you listen to the musical strains of a yet undiscovered piano man. But if you're lucky, maybe he'll even play your special song.

$$-$$$ *AE, MC, V; no checks; lunch, dinner every day, brunch Sun; full bar; reservations recommended.* &

## SADDLE PEAK LODGE
♥♥♥♥

*419 Cold Canyon Rd, Calabasas / 818/222-3888*
If you've had your beach fix and yearn to explore the rugged mountain canyons just east of Malibu, the Saddle Peak Lodge offers a completely different and wild experience. Whoever designed this rambling wood-beamed uber-rustic hideaway must have grown up mesmerized by "Bonanza." The building itself is a huge, sprawling log cabin that ascends four stories along a rocky point in the middle of nowhere. Inside, there are imposing stone fireplaces, rough-hewn oversized furniture, and interesting Western motifs almost everywhere you turn. If the weather permits—especially on warm

Sunday afternoons for brunch—do sit outside on the rugged stone patio with its trickling waterfall. Executive chef Warren Schwartz, renowned for his culinary artistry with elk, buffalo, deer, wild boar, quail, and partridge, offers a host of game specialties and delectable alternatives for seafood lovers and vegetarians. Standouts include buffalo tartar with mustard aioli, roasted elk tenderloin, seared New Zealand salmon with fingerling potatoes, and cooked-to-perfection wild striped bass. Be warned: this remote location has no streetlights or marked signs, so nighttime driving isn't just dark, it's pitch black.

**$$$$** *AE, DC, MC, V; no checks; dinner Tues–Sun, brunch Sun; full bar; reservations required; www.saddlepeaklodge.com.* &

---

## VALENTINO
●●●◖

*3115 Pico Blvd, Santa Monica / 310/829-4313*
Valentino is like the arms of an old lover who feels comfortingly familiar but who still makes you tingle all the way down to your toes. A local fixture for 25 wonderful years, this darkly romantic eatery keeps on getting better and better and better. But this old comfort doesn't want to be taken for granted. In fact, chef-owner Piero Selvaggio has made a point of making sure his flagship eatery still surpasses other Italian restaurants in the United States like a Ferrari in the fast lane of the *autostrada*. Selvaggio imports the finest ingredients from around the world, from the purest olive oils to the best white truffles. Three intimate dining rooms and the glass-enclosed patio are awash in earth tones of rust and brown, creating the perfect setting for you and yours to sink into the lovely fabric-covered chairs, sample from an internationally praised wine list (go crazy and order a rich Barberesco or Chianti), and savor an elegant Italian meal. Beef carpaccio, fresh grilled fish, tender veal, duck ragù, and seafood risotto are Valentino standouts, as are the clams and sweet garlic pasta, and potato and spinach gnocchi with walnut sauce (all homemade, of course). For dessert, warm chocolate cake with mascarpone gelato gets the vote every time. The service is gracious and a night at Valentino's is always memorable. Now, that's amour!

**$$$–$$$$** *AE, DC, MC, V; no checks; lunch Fri, dinner Mon–Sat; full bar; reservations recommended; www.pieroselvaggio.com.* &

# LONG BEACH AND ENVIRONS

## ROMANTIC HIGHLIGHTS

Located just 20 miles south of Los Angeles, Long Beach is California's fifth-largest city and home to 5½ miles of sandy beaches, as well as massive Long Beach Harbor, which serves as the primary port for Los Angeles. Just north of Long Beach, beautiful Palos Verdes Peninsula—also known as "PV"—sits at the southern crescent of Santa Monica Bay and is largely an affluent residential enclave, with miles of breathtaking coastline looming tall over the ocean. To the south of Long Beach, the charming community of Seal Beach has a reputation as Southern California's last great beach town. All of the above cities offer an oceanfront setting where couples can soak in the Southern California sunshine, breathe the fresh ocean air, and point their compass toward romance.

Long Beach is perhaps best known as the site of the permanently docked **Queen Mary** (located at the end of the I-170; 562/435-3511; www.queen mary.com). Once the world's largest and most luxurious Atlantic ocean liner, today the ship welcomes visitors who come to see the romance and splendor of a different era, when the idol rich made the crossing amid vast teakwood decks, priceless interiors, grand salons, and lavish staterooms. While there are a number of guided tours, including the Ghosts & Legends tour, which details current sightings of the ship's deceased visitors, couples would do best to stroll this splendid vessel at their own pace on a self-guided one. Don't forget to head out to the grand ship's front bow and have a *Titanic* moment with your special someone.

The city's other main draw is the impressive **Aquarium of the Pacific** (100 Aquarium Wy; 562/590-3100; www.aquariumofpacific.org), where you and your sweetie can come face to face with a variety of denizens of the deep—from sharks and sea lions to jelly fish and sea horses. Built in 1998, this wonderfully presented aquarium features some 550 species from three major regions—Southern California and Baja, the Northern Pacific, and the Tropical Pacific—many displayed in three-story-high tanks that make you feel like you are really catching a glimpse of undersea life.

Lovers in search of a little culture will want to check out the **Long Beach Museum of Art** (2300 E Ocean Ave; 562/439-2119; www.lbma.com), set in a grand old mansion on a waterfront knoll. While the historic setting is stunning, art lovers will appreciate the museum's collection of 20th-century European modernists, post–World War II art from California, and a large video art archive. At the nearby **Museum of Latin American Art** (628 Alamitos Ave; 562/437-1689; www.molaa.com), spend the afternoon strolling the galleries of the only museum in the West to focus exclusively on the contemporary art of Mexico as well as Central and South America.

If music is more your thing, the two of you can make like Julia Roberts and Richard Gere in *Pretty Woman* and spend the evening at the **Long Beach Opera** (Carpenter Performing Arts Center, California State University, Long Beach; 562/439-2580; www.lbopera.com). This small, focused company presents two operas in June and a third in the fall, as well as special museum performances other times of the year.

From high art to high octane, lovers feeling the need for speed may want to plan their Long Beach visit in April when the city hosts the **Toyota Grand Prix** (562/981-2600; www.longbeachgp.com) and hundreds of racecars zoom through the streets. Okay, it may not exactly be considered an amorous outing, but perhaps you can follow up a day at the races with a romantic stroll in the quaint neighborhood communities of **Belmont Shores** or **Naples**, both just east of downtown Long Beach. The prewar bungalow-lined streets of Belmont Shores—known locally as "the Shore"—are in sharp contrast to the harbor district's industrial energy. East Second Street and East Broadway bisect this beachside village and provide hours' worth of strolling among antique and collectible shops, cafes, and boutiques. Here, an increasing number of high-profile retailers like Gap, Banana Republic, and Jamba Juice happily coexist alongside old-style hardware stores, barbershops, and delicatessens. During the summer months, wander out to the end of the **Belmont Pleasure Pier** and the two of you can get a cone from the seasonal ice cream stand. Nearby, Naples is a man-made island community of picturesque canals, boardwalks lined with million-dollar homes, and tiny sandy lagoons where couples take in the scenery and dream about what it might be like to call one of these seaside palaces home.

To the north of Long Beach, the Palos Verdes Peninsula offers a magnificent display of nature. The rugged cliffs are usually dotted with beautiful wildflowers, and waves rushing against the bluffs form foamy whitecaps as they break. Hiking trails meander along the hilly coastline and offer spectacular views of the coast all the way to Malibu. The **Malaga Cove trail** (from I-405, exit at Hawthorne Blvd, take Hawthorne to Palos Verdes Blvd, and turn west) allows you to walk down a semisteep incline; at the bottom, you'll find some large rocks that provide the perfect place to sit and snuggle. This is a very private and secluded spot to watch the sun set into the Pacific Ocean.

Lucky lovers may spot a whale or dolphin off the coast while snuggling in Malaga Cove, but those who want to almost ensure a sighting will want to visit Palos Verdes's annual **Whale of the Day Festival,** held the first Saturday of every March, at **Point Vicente Interpretative Center and Park** (31501 Palos Verdes Dr, Rancho Palos Verdes; 310/377-5370). While the two of you are on the lookout for migrating whales, you can take a lighthouse tour, stroll through the arts fair, or sneak away for a quiet moment and watch the waves crashing on the cliffs below.

Couples who prefer flora and fauna to a shoreline visit can head to **South**

# Two if by Sea

There's something about gliding through water and romance that goes hand-in-hand, whether it comes in the form of an old-fashioned riverboat paddlewheel, a historic tall ship, a Venetian gondola, or, of course, a big honking yacht.

**Gondola Getaways** (5437 E Ocean Blvd; 562/433-9595; www.gondola getawaysinc.com) offers Old World boating right in the heart of Long Beach. Authentic Venetian gondolas cruise the narrow canals and waterways of Naples Island, next to the resort area of Belmont Shores. These narrow waterways (pollution free, by the way) are remarkably secluded and lined by architecturally unique homes and crisscrossed by brick footbridges. As you arrange yourselves in the gondola, you are handed a warm blanket to snuggle under. A basket of bread, cheeses, and salami is provided, as well as glasses and an ice bucket; it's up to you to bring the beverage of your choice. A gondolier gently guides the boat through the beautiful canals, accompanied by classical music. Nighttime cruises are especially romantic, as the moonlight spreads a golden mantle over the water. Reservations are required at least a week in advance.

Lovers can also cruise Long Beach Harbor when they book passage on the **Grand Romance** (100 Aquarium Wy, Dock 4; 562/628-6000; www.grandromance.com), a 122-foot paddlewheel riverboat that departs from the Long Beach boardwalk right behind P. F. Chang's. The two of you will enjoy beautiful views of the city as you cruise along the shoreline and stroll the main deck hand-in-hand. On weekends, there's a musical revue, "American Melodies," on the main deck, or you can play Agatha Christie and take part in Murder Mystery events on the third deck. Hungry cruisers can enjoy lunch or dinner on board at Duke's Riverboat Steakhouse, or simply sit back and listen to music from the riverboat's classic calliope while you watch the giant paddlewheel churn through the ocean waters.

Nearby Rainbow Harbor is where the tall ship **American Pride** (714/970-8800; www.americanpride.com) is docked. While couples can tour the historic ship, it's more fun to enjoy this three-masted, 130-foot schooner while experiencing the romance of the high seas. Couples boarding the ship for a day sail can raise and lower the eight sails and take a turn at the helm. It's the perfect chance to show who's Master and Commander of your relationship.

However, if the two of you would rather just sit back and enjoy the scenery (as well as each other's company), **Harbor Breeze Yacht Charters & Cruises** (Docks 2 and 6 in Rainbow Harbor; 562/432-4900; www.longbeachcruises. com) takes passengers out on the water to enjoy a 45-minute narrated seaside tour onboard the 85-foot **Kristina**. During whale-watching season, it's a great opportunity to spot these migrating giants of the sea. Even if the two of you are just gazing out at the calm water, the flames of love are sure to be fanned by this seafaring adventure. —BONNIE STEELE

**Coast Botanical Garden** (26300 Crenshaw Blvd, Palos Verdes Peninsula; 310/544-6815), which is set on 87 flower-strewn acres. Stop by **Lisa's Bon Appetite** (3511 Pacific Coast Hwy, Torrance; 310/784-1070) or **Marmalade Café** (The Avenue Mall, 550 Deep Valley Dr, Rancho Hills Estates; 310/544-6700) and pick up all the makings for a picnic lunch, then spend the afternoon lingering by the lake or strolling hand-in-hand through the stunning grounds. It's a wonderful way to enjoy the beautiful outdoors, for which Long Beach is best known.

## Access and Information

Long Beach, Palos Verdes, and Seal Beach sit on the coastline just south of Redondo Beach and north of Orange County. All are best accessed by car, but it's easiest to reach Long Beach, which is traversed by the 405 Freeway, 110 Harbor Freeway, and 710 Freeway (which eventually turns into Shoreline Drive in downtown Long Beach). Hard-to-reach Palos Verdes isn't off a major freeway, but can be accessed from Pacific Coast Highway. Turn west onto Palos Verdes Boulevard, which will take you into the hills along the coast. Seal Beach is best accessed from PCH, as well.

**Long Beach Transit (LBT)** (562/591-8753; www.lbtransit.com) provides the local **Passport Shuttle,** which transports visitors around the downtown area for free and charges a minimal fee for transportation to Naples and Belmont Shores. Also a part of LBT, **Aquabus** shuttles passengers to points around the harbor for a small fee.

**Long Beach Airport** (4100 Donald Douglas Dr; 562/570-2600; www.lgb .org) is a pleasant alternative to LAX (310/646-5252; www.lawa.org) and is served by five major airlines, including JetBlue Airways, American Airlines, America West Airlines, Alaska Airlines, and Horizon.

Visitor information and maps of the area are provided at **Long Beach Area Convention & Visitors Bureau** (1 World Trade Center, Ste 300; 562/436-3645 or 800/452-7829; www.visitlongbeach.com).

## Romantic Lodgings

### BEACHRUNNERS' INN
◗

*231 Kennebec Ave, Long Beach / 562/856-0202 or 866/221-0001*
Location, location, location is the draw of this 1913 Craftsman-style B&B in Belmont Heights. Set just three blocks from the beach, the cozy five-room inn lures couples in search of modest accommodations within walking distance of the sandy shoreline. Five funky guest rooms, each with a private bathroom and TV/VCR, welcome beach-bound lovers. The Laguna Room,

with its blue-and-white striped walls and homey quilt, is the inn's biggest space, including a shower and full bath. For those who long for lots of light, the Kennebec Room offers plenty of windows to fill your love nest with sunshine. Couples can snuggle in to large wingback chairs in front of a fireplace in the living room or head out back to the inn's Jacuzzi for a long and lovely soak. Bikes are also available if the two of you feel like taking a spin along the coastline. Each morning from 7am to 9am, a complimentary continental breakfast is served in a cheery yellow breakfast room that looks like it could be the domain of June Cleaver.
$$ *MC, V; no checks; www.beachrunnersinn.com.*

## DOCKSIDE BOAT & BED
🌢🌢🌢

*316 E Shoreline Dr, Long Beach / 562/436-3111*
This unique B&B lets lovebirds spend the night at sea without even having to lift anchor. Moored at Dock 5 in Rainbow Harbor, four different boats—ranging from *Archangel* (a 38-foot Bayliner motor craft) and *Whimsy* (a 44-foot Pacemaker motor yacht) to *Desiree* (a 40-foot Mainship Sedan Bridge motor yacht) and *Me Wen Ti* (a 50-foot authentic Chinese junket ship)—offer floating overnight accommodations. Nautical-minded sweethearts have the run of their vessel; each includes a master stateroom with a queen-sized bed; slightly cramped bathroom (with a stall shower); and galley with microwave, coffeemaker, and fridge for storing romantic essentials like champagne, strawberries, and chocolates. Couples can toast their night at sea on the deck, enjoying marvelous views of the nearby Aquarium of the Pacific, the *Queen Mary*, and the twinkling lights of the harbor and the city beyond. TVs with VCRs and stereos with CD players provide entertainment after the sun has set, but it's also an easy walk to nearby Shoreline Village or trendy Pine Street for dinner or a nightcap. Or simply stay onboard and snuggle up down below, letting the gentle rocking motion of the water lull the two of you to sleep. In the morning, a basket heaping with muffins and fruit, a carafe of orange juice, and a newspaper are delivered to your yacht. It's the next best thing to breakfast in bed. However, forget about sleeping in. You'll be up with the seagulls.
$$$ *AE, DIS, MC, V; no checks; www.boatandbed.com.*

## HOTEL QUEEN MARY
🌢🌢

*1126 Queens Hwy, Long Beach / 562/435-3511*
Couples can relive the romance of an Atlantic crossing when they book one of 365 staterooms for the night on the *Queen Mary*. However, these once-lavish quarters aren't *that* exceptional when compared to today's contemporary hotels. Few modern amenities have been added lest they destroy the ship's historic authenticity. The idea is to enjoy the novelty of features like

original porcelain bathroom fixtures, walls paneled in tropical hardwoods with intricate art deco detailing, and the historic charm that pervades each hallway and well-walked deck. Quarters vary widely; try to splurge on a first-class or deluxe stateroom with an ocean view. The *Queen Mary* features a full complement of restaurants and bars. Sunday's champagne brunch, an overwhelming orgy including ice sculptures and a harpist, is served in the ship's Grand Salon, the original ballroom so lovely it's worth the price of admission alone. Don't miss the Observation Bar, a chic art deco cocktail lounge with panoramic views, and dinner at Sir Winston's (see Romantic Restaurants) can be an event in itself. On site are numerous shops and the ship's own spa, with full spa services.
$$–$$$$ *AE, DIS, MC, V; no checks; www.queenmary.com.*

## HYATT REGENCY LONG BEACH
🖤❿

*200 S Pine Ave, Long Beach / 562/491-1234 or 800/233-1234*
Adjacent to the Long Beach Convention Center, this high-rise hotel may cater primarily to business travelers, but there are plenty of amenities to tempt traveling lovebirds, too. The 17-story hotel boasts waterfront views from many of its 522 guest rooms, allowing couples to look out on the bobbing boats in Rainbow Harbor, and after a recent renovation in 2003, comfortable accommodations feature a sunny California coastal decor. While an outdoor pool and whirlpool surrounded by 5 acres of lushly landscaped lagoons, an exercise room, and preferred tee times at a nearby golf course may be wonderful distractions, lovers who have trysting on their minds may want to check into a room on the Regency Club floor, where complimentary snacks and extras like bathrobes, turn-down service, and a concierge can make your romantic sojourn special. In the morning, the two of you can wander down to the lobby and get your coffee and pastries from Perks Coffee Pantry. Simple breakfasts, lunches, and dinners are served every day in Tides, which specializes in California cuisine. With the hotel's convenient location in the heart of Long Beach, there are plenty of restaurants, shops, and night spots just a short walk away. And the shoreline is a mere quarter mile away, should the two of you feel like strolling hand-in-hand on the beach.
$$$–$$$$ *AE, DC, DIS, MC, V; no checks; www.longbeach.hyatt.com.* ♿

## LORD MAYOR'S B&B INN
🖤

*435 Cedar Ave, Long Beach / 562/436-0324 or 800/691-5166*
This elegant Edwardian home was built in 1904 and belonged to Long Beach's first mayor, Charles H. Windham, who earned his unofficial title of "Lord Mayor" from a group of British beauty contestants visiting the seaside resort. In 1988, after a sensitive restoration that earned a National Trust

for Historic Preservation award, innkeepers Laura and Reuben Brasser opened this charming bed-and-breakfast. The main house offers five guest rooms, each with 10-foot ceilings and carefully chosen antiques, high-quality linens, and heirloom bedspreads and accessories. Each room boasts a private bath cleverly re-created with vintage fixtures; some have claw-footed tubs. All the rooms are upstairs and utterly charming; three open onto a wooden deck overlooking the back garden, including the romantic Hawaiian Room with its ornately carved wedding bed and island memorabilia. A sun porch overlooks the street, and the entire house radiates warmth with original wood floors, a Vermont granite hearth, and vintage clocks whose gentle chiming enhances the historic ambience of the inn. More rooms are available in three less formal adjacent cottages—the Garden House, Apple House, and Cinnamon House—also dating from the early 20th century; they offer a private option for couples seeking seclusion. Lovers will appreciate the expansive homemade breakfast that is served each morning in the main house's dining room.

$$ *AE, DIS, MC, V; checks OK; www.lordmayors.com.*

## THE SEAL BEACH INN AND GARDENS
🌸🌸

*212 5th St, Long Beach / 562/493-2416 or 800/HIDEAWAY*
Located only a block from the beach, this restored vintage inn resembles an Old World country lodge. The 24 artistic rooms, including 13 suites, are uniquely decorated with antiques and collectibles—from wrought-iron railings to ancient statuary. Lacy curtains, wall tapestries, and unusual linens demonstrate the care and attention given to every detail. Couples on a quest for a blissful sojourn may reserve the alluring Primrose Room, which features a gas-burning fireplace, raspberry-flowered wallpaper, a coffered ceiling with a deep purple inset, and a bathroom with a Jacuzzi tub for two. The Azalea King Suite also seduces with a bright pink floral theme, a canopy bed covered with white flouncy gauze, and a Roman soak tub in the bathroom. Outside, the beautiful flowers and plants form a visual feast, and an 8-foot frescoed fountain from Paris stands guard over a lush patio adjacent to the kidney-shaped swimming pool. A lavish buffet breakfast is included, and tea, wine, and cheese are served in the evenings. When a chill sets in, the Tea Room's mammoth gas-burning fireplace is the place to get cozy with the one you love. Gourmet picnic baskets can be prepared upon request.

$$$ *AE, DC, DIS, MC, V; checks OK when reserving a month ahead; www.sealbeachinn.com.* ⚄

## TURRET HOUSE BED AND BREAKFAST
🌺🌺

*556 Chestnut St, Long Beach / 562/624-1991 or 888/4-TURRET*
As career flight attendants, Brian Pforr and Jeff Wilkins know a thing or two about hospitality, and they are making use of that knowledge as owners and hosts of this meticulously restored Victorian-style B&B, which caters primarily to a gay and lesbian clientele. The 1906 home boasts five guest rooms, each decorated with a different theme. Sea-loving lovebirds can check in to the *Queen Mary* Room, with its blue walls and artifacts from the ship's sailing; couples with wanderlust may want to reserve the Vagabond Room, decorated with travel mementos from the owners' trips to faraway places. The Turret Room has five leaded glass windows and 12-foot ceilings that complement the inn's namesake turret, and the Dreamcatcher Room is all soothing earth tones that are sure to induce a dreamy romantic sleep. However, the inn's most alluring suite may be the Provincetown Room, complete with a four-poster antique bed, a carved-wood dresser, and French doors that lead to a private balcony where you and your betrothed can breathe in the fresh ocean air. Each guest room has a wood-burning fireplace and a clawfooted tub and shower to add to the amorous ambience. Mornings begin with a complimentary breakfast served in the formal dining room; for lovers who feel the need to get in a workout, free passes to nearby Gold's Gym are provided.
*$$ AE, MC, V; no checks; reduced rates Sun–Thurs; www.turrethouse.com.*

# *Romantic Restaurants*

## DELIUS
🌺🌺🌺

*3550 Long Beach Blvd, Long Beach / 562/426-0694*
For couples who aren't lucky enough to have a friend that hosts dinner parties with seven-course gourmet meals, there's Louise and Dave Solzman's Delius. Since 1996, this intimate restaurant has been serving just one seating each evening, offering a prix-fixe dinner according to a menu that changes weekly and reflects British-born chef Louise's excellent culinary sense. Once the two of you enter the richly furnished, Victorian-flavored lounge and dining rooms, heavy velvet draperies enclose you in intimate surrounds, where tables are set with a full complement of flatware for each course and stemware for every carefully chosen wine. Cocktails are at 6:30pm and dinner begins at 7:15pm. The multicourse extravaganza includes hors d'oeuvres, soup, appetizer, first course, entrée, fruit and cheese, and dessert. Menus have featured crab-and-shrimp-stuffed zucchini flowers, sautéed halibut on penne pasta with porcini sauce, rosemary-and-feta-stuffed filet mignon, grilled chicken with Indian mango chutney, and chipotle crab cakes

with ginger-cilantro butter. A harpist who entertains on Fridays only adds to the romantic ambience. Delius also offers a plush wine bar for a quick bite. It opens at 4pm and serves tasty appetizers like homemade soup, Stilton apple fritters, and beef broccoli wontons.
*$$$ DC, DIS, MC, V; checks OK; dinner Tues–Sat; beer and wine; reservations required; www.deliusrestaurant.com. &*

## LA RIVE GAUCHE
◐ ❦

*320 Tejon Pl, Palos Verdes Estates / 310/378-0267*
Set in quaint Malaga Cove just off the main street in Palos Verdes, La Rive Gauche is an attractive place for candlelit dinners and leisurely romantic conversation. On a lovely evening, ask for a table under a tree on the outside patio, and the two of you can hold hands by the moonlight while you dine on traditional French fare that's big on fresh fish and light, flavorful sauces. Inside, a pianist plays nightly, and you can request your sentimental favorite to ensure that the evening lives on in your memories. Escargot, pâté, foie gras, and a creamy potato-leek soup start the meal off on a classic note. For the main course, try the duck with orange sauce, well-seasoned rack of lamb, or delicate John Dory. There's no happier ending to this romantic meal than with Grand Marnier soufflé and two forks. Order a selection from the diverse wine list, and you have all the makings for a wonderful night.
*$$$–$$$$ AE, DC, DIS, MC, V; no checks; lunch Tues–Sun, dinner every day; full bar; reservations recommended. &*

## LASHER'S
◐ ◐ ❦

*3441 E Broadway, Long Beach / 562/433-0153*
Set in a converted 1920s bungalow with mahogany wood trim and custom moldings, this cozy neighborhood restaurant offers classic American fare in a comfortable setting. If the weather is chilly, couples can cuddle up at a table by the fireplace and warm up with a bowl of Lasher's award-winning smoky New England clam chowder. On a beautiful day, request a table on the outdoor patio amid the flowers and fresh herb garden, which is harvested regularly for use in the kitchen. Crab cakes, cranberry-glazed meatloaf, prime steaks, and roasted chicken coq au vin–style, served with addictive lumpy mashed potatoes, are among the menu highlights sure to tempt you and your betrothed. Just be sure to save room for the restaurant's dreamy Key lime pie or the white chocolate bread pudding served with two chocolate sauces. An impressive Sunday brunch features four different types of eggs Benedict.
*$$$ AE, DC, DIS, MC, V; no checks; dinner Tues–Sun, brunch Sun; beer and wine; reservations recommended; www.lashersrestaurant.com. &*

# THE MADISON RESTAURANT & BAR
◐◐◐

*102 Pine Ave, Long Beach / 562/628-8866*
Set in one of Pine Avenue's most stunning historic buildings, this elegant 1920s-style supper club offers the grand experience of fine dining in a majestic setting reminiscent of opulent ocean liner dining salons. Coffered mahogany walls, gilded ceiling beams, sparkling oversized crystal chandeliers, and enormous two-story windows framed with rich brocade draperies provide the backdrop for a romantic night of dining. Originally a bank and more recently a private club, the 1890s building has been beautifully restored and features a lavish mahogany bar, where several nights a week you and your sweetie can dance to the sounds of a live band. The Madison serves exceptional dry-aged beef broiled and accompanied by à la carte sides like buttery garlic potatoes, tender asparagus hollandaise, and perfectly seasoned creamed spinach. You'll find some grand old dishes like oysters Rockefeller and beef Wellington on the menu, too, and lavish preparations of lobster tail and salmon (with mussels and clams). And there's no shortage of drink selections here. Lovebirds can order a bottle of vino from a great wine list, sample one of more than 15 different martinis, or choose from 30 single-malt scotches.
$$$ *AE, DC, MC, V; no checks; lunch Mon–Fri, dinner every day; full bar; reservations recommended; www.themadisonrestaurant.com.* &

# NICO'S
◐◐◖

*5760 E 2nd St, Long Beach / 562/434-4479*
Located on beach-chic Naples Island, this dark and sexy two-tiered restaurant has all the makings of a great date-night dining establishment. Couples can canoodle in cozy banquettes and survey the scene at this happening eatery owned by Christy Bono (daughter of the late Sonny Bono). Beautifully presented food sometimes looks almost too pretty to eat, especially starters like the shrimp cocktail martini and the grilled vegetable tower stacked with buffalo mozzarella and drizzled with basil oil. However, once you watch entrées like osso buco with creamy polenta, house-made pumpkin ravioli, New Zealand rack of lamb, and chicken with whole grain mustard sauce whiz by your table, the two of you will be so hungry, you'll have to dig in. Awarded *Wine Spectator's* Award of Excellence for its impressive wine list, Nico's is sure to offer a selection that will please your palate.
$$$ *AE, DC, DIS, MC, V; no checks; dinner every day; beer and wine; reservations recommended; www.nicosrestaurant.com.* &

# THE REEF
🦪🦪

*880 Harbor Scenic Dr, Long Beach / 562/435-8013*
There are not many restaurants in the Los Angeles area where you can dine in a Victorian setting, next to a glowing fireplace, with a spectacular view of the city lights reflecting off the calm water. The Reef is such a place. This restaurant is large but cozy, with overstuffed sofas in the entryway, a downstairs cafe, and an outdoor veranda dining area directly overlooking the harbor. Each intimate booth is surrounded by bookshelves, lantern candles, and small antiques. For even more privacy, request a booth upstairs near the back. The menu emphasizes California-style fish, prime beef brought in from the Stock Yards Meat Packing Company in Chicago, pasta dishes like creamy lobster carbonara, and a tasty Key lime chicken. But, the atmosphere is really the romantic selling point here.
*$$–$$$ AE, DC, MC, V; no checks; dinner every day, brunch Sun; full bar; reservations recommended; www.specialtyrestaurants.com. &*

# SIR WINSTON'S
🦪🦪🦪

*1126 Queens Hwy (onboard the Queen Mary), Long Beach / 562/435-3511*
This formal dining establishment onboard the *Queen Mary* gives couples a chance to dress up and pretend they are dining in a different era, when Atlantic crossings and writing letters instead of e-mails were the norm. Request a window seat for panoramic views of the coastline, then sit back and order from a menu that's made up of mostly continental classics. Lobster claws or portobello mushroom salad are winning starters that easily can be shared. Beef Phyllo Sir Winston, beef tenderloin with foie gras wrapped in a flaky crust and drizzled with merlot sauce, is one of the restaurant's signature dishes. For lovers who believe love handles don't necessarily add to romance, healthy choices like broiled swordfish are also available. An extensive wine list and the attentive service ensure that your evening will be special.
*$$$ AE, MC, V; no checks; dinner every day; full bar; reservations required; www.queenmary.com.*

# SIXTH STREET BISTRO
🦪🦪

*354 W 6th St, San Pedro / 310/521-8818*
When you want to add a little spice to your love life, start with a Mediterranean-style meal at this casual neighborhood bistro. Ceiling and wall murals of the grape harvest, woven copper light fixtures, and an exposed brick wall create a cozy, contemporary setting for couples who want to sit close in a comfy booth and share such tapas selections as grilled grape leaves, Roman-style olives, and spicy fire shrimp. Hungry sweethearts craving more

than just these small-plate selections can choose from a variety of pastas, gourmet pizzas, and entrées like filet mignon with hazelnut sauce or the restaurant's specialty of seafood paella for two, chock-full of fresh shellfish and chorizo. On a warm night, lovers can sit on the lovely outdoor patio and sip a selection from the impressive wine-by-the-glass list. And, when the restaurant is featuring live flamenco guitar music, the romance factor definitely heats up.

*$$–$$$ AE, MC, V; no checks; lunch Tues–Fri, dinner Tues–Sun; beer and wine; reservations recommended; www.sixthstreetbistro.net.* ⟨

## THE SKY ROOM
💗💗💗

*40 S Locust Ave, Long Beach / 562/983-2703 or 866/759-7666*
Designed to look and feel like a swanky New York penthouse, this retro supper club harkens back to the elegance of Hollywood's Golden Age, and it's all too easy to imagine Bogey and Bacall sipping martinis at the bar, or Astaire and Rogers hoofing the evening away on the dance floor. Set on the top of the former Breakers Hotel (which today is a seniors' residence), this art deco restaurant first opened in the 1930s and has hosted Elizabeth Taylor, Charles Lindbergh, Clark Gable, Cary Grant, and many others. Determined to bring back the glamour and mystique of the original room, owner Bernard Rosenson combines classic and contemporary, offering couples California-French cuisine, a superb wine list, and stunning 360° views of Long Beach Harbor. Piano music is featured during the week, and a seven-piece orchestra plays jazz and swing each weekend. Start with Russian beluga caviar (1-ounce with condiments), then move on to paella for two (with clams, prawns, and black mussels), Kobe beef with marinated portobello mushrooms, and such classic fare as Atlantic salmon with beurre blanc or succulent beef tenderloin. After dinner, hit the dance floor for a slow dance with your sweetheart. The experience will take your breath away (not to mention a few Benjamins).

*$$$–$$$$ AE, DC, DIS, MC, V; no checks; dinner Mon–Sat; full bar; reservations recommended; www.theskyroom.com.* ⟨

# IN TOWN

## ROMANTIC HIGHLIGHTS

There's so much to see and do in Los Angeles, it would be impossible to cover the town in one big romantic swoop. Besides, the magic of L.A. lies not in any one particular site or attraction, but in just being here, absorbing its diverse and overwhelming atmosphere. Depending on your mood, the two of you can visit museums, take a hike in the canyons, peruse the tourist attractions on Hollywood Boulevard, shop the streets of Beverly Hills, or just hang out at a sidewalk cafe and enjoy the almost-always perfect weather. Just follow your whim, and it's sure to be a memorable day in La-La Land.

Lovers with stars in their eyes can gaze at the stars on Hollywood Boulevard's **Walk of Fame** (Hollywood Blvd between La Brea Ave and Vine St, then along Vine down to Sunset Blvd). Along "the Walk," the names of luminaries and super-luminaries in the film, radio, and television industries are commemorated by stars set in the polished mauve granite sidewalk. Sure, it's a touristy thing to do, but it's a Hollywood landmark that couples may want to experience at least once in their lives. While you're at it, check out the cement-cast hand- and footprints of some of Hollywood's most famed celebs in the courtyard of **Grauman's Chinese Theater Complex** (6925 Hollywood Blvd; 323/464-6266). The two of you can see if your hands or feet are the same size as such greats as Clark Gable, Humphrey Bogart, Marilyn Monroe, Michael Douglas, and Mel Gibson. The site of numerous Hollywood premieres—both past and present—this beautiful landmark is still a public movie theater, too, so you can even catch a flick after checking out this Tinseltown site. Just next to the theater is the **Hollywood & Highland** entertainment complex (6801 Hollywood Blvd; 323/960-6070; www.hollywood andhighland.com), which boasts shops like Luxe Lingerie (323/464-1188) and Studio (323/464-7072), as well as restaurants like Wolfgang Puck's Vert (323/491-1300), and the famed Kodak Theatre (323/308-6363), which hosts the Academy Awards each spring, as well as theater and musical events. Be warned: this glitzy complex is more of a tourist trap than a local's hangout, and the crowds of out-of-towners can easily quash the mood for romance.

While Hollywood & Highland may be a fun place to browse, the streets of Beverly Hills are where you'll want to flash the gold card and maybe pick up a gift for your betrothed. Designer brands reign on fabled **Rodeo Drive** (between Santa Monica and Wilshire Blvds). **Barneys New York** (9570 Wilshire Blvd; 310/276-4400), **Saks Fifth Avenue** (9600 Wilshire Blvd; 310/275-4211), and **Neiman Marcus** (9700 Wilshire Blvd; 310/550-5900) make up what's known as the area's **Golden Triangle**. However, high-end boutiques line Rodeo and its neighboring streets, making it possible for you to browse, window shop, and even smooch as you stroll hand-in-hand past the enticing shops. Be sure and check out engagement stones and wedding bands—whether or not you're even that serious—at **Tiffany & Co.** (210 N Rodeo Dr; 310/209-1994; www.tiffany.com). You'll find a full range of fine jewelry and gifts, something for any occasion, romantic or otherwise. If it was good enough for Audrey Hepburn, it should be good enough for you.

Lovers can also go on a spree at **The Grove** (bordered by 3rd and Fairfax Sts, Los Angeles; 323/900-8080 or 888/315-8883; www.thegrovela .com), an outdoor shopping complex that's set along a cobblestone street

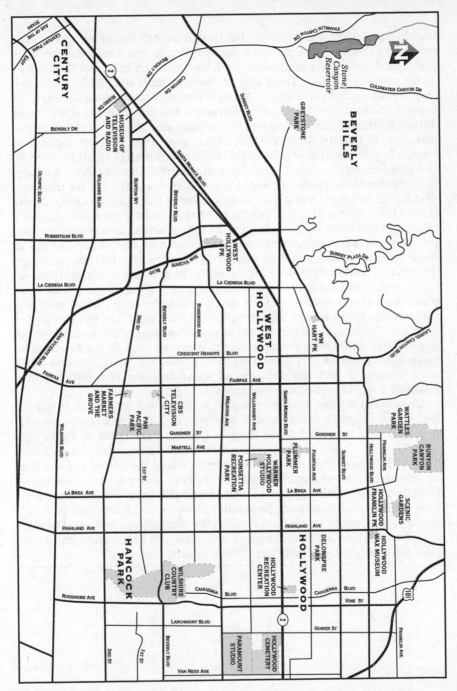

that looks straight out of Disneyland, with an old-fashioned trolley that transports shoppers up and down the promenade and a water show set to music that feels like a mini-Bellagio. Stop for lunch in one of the Grove's many restaurants, like **The Farm of Beverly Hills** (323/525-1699; www .thefarmofbeverlyhills.com) or **Morel's** (see Romantic Restaurants). Or browse the stalls of the historic **Farmer's Market** (323/933-9211; www .farmersmarketla.com) at one end of the mall, stopping for authentic Mexican fare at **Loteria Grill** (323/930-2211) or gourmet cheeses, tapas, and French fare at **Mr. Marcel** (323/934-3113; www.mrmarcel.com).

From finding treasures at the shops to admiring the treasures of others, Los Angeles has a number of world-class museums that offer the ideal setting for an amorous outing. Not to be missed is the stunning **Getty Center** (1200 Getty Center Dr; 310/440-7300; www.getty.edu) perched high on a hillside overlooking Los Angeles. The $1 billion art enclave made up of five two-story pavilions constructed of stone, glass, and steel is as beautiful as some of the priceless artworks displayed inside, which include paintings, illuminated manuscripts, drawings, sculptures, decorative arts, and photography. A perfectly manicured garden in the center of the complex is the ideal place to steal a smooch from your special someone or to just sit back and contemplate the beauty of the surroundings. On a clear day, you can see the Southern California coastline from the scenic vantage point, which is worth a visit itself. Other outstanding local art museums include the **Los Angeles County Museum of Art (LACMA)** (5905 Wilshire Blvd; 323/857-6000; www.lacma.org) and the **Museum of Contemporary Art (MOCA)** (250 S Grand Ave; 213/626-6222; www.moca-la.org).

On a beautiful day, though, you and your sweetie may want to get out and enjoy the great outdoors, and you won't even have to leave the city to take a hike into the hills at **Runyon Canyon Park** (2000 N Fuller Ave; 213/473-7070). Just a few blocks north of Sunset Boulevard, where Fuller dead-ends, iron gates open to a lush canyon where the two of you can hike up any of several serpentine mountain trails in this quiet rural setting. A favorite spot of local dog owners who want to let their pets off-leash for a little exercise, this lush park feels miles away from the city, and when the two of you ascend to Inspiration Point at the summit, you may want to mark the moment with a big kiss. Then look out on the city below and contemplate your next romantic outing in the City of Angels.

# Access and Information

Los Angeles is primarily served by **Los Angeles International Airport (LAX)** (310/646-5252; www.lawa.org), which is about 30 minutes from downtown or Hollywood. Once you're in town, a car is the best mode of transportation. However, the **Metropolitan Transportation Authority (MTA)** (800/266-6883; www.mta.net) runs buses, subways, and a light rail system that traverse the city. **Amtrak** (800/USA-RAIL; www.amtrak.com) trains arrive and depart from downtown's **Union Station** (800 N Alameda; 213/624-0171).

For more information on the area, contact the **Los Angeles Convention and Visitors Bureau (LACVB)** (800/366-6116; event hotline 213/689-8822; www.lacvb.com). Although the LACVB will provide information on the various cities-within-a-city that make up the L.A. metropolitan area, each separate municipality has its own dedicated visitors services. The **Beverly Hills Visitors Bureau** (239 S Beverly Dr; 310/271-8174 or 800/345-2210; www.bhvb .org) and the **West Hollywood Convention and Visitors Bureau** (8687 Melrose Ave, #M-26; 310/289-2555 or 800/368-6020; www.visitwesthollywood.com) are two that will be particularly helpful.

# Romantic Lodgings

## THE ARGYLE
🐞🐞

*8358 Sunset Blvd, West Hollywood / 323/654-7100 or 800/225-2637*
The Argyle has what few other places in town can claim: an authentic art deco pedigree. Built in 1929, the 15-story hotel was once an apartment building and home to such stars as Bugsy Siegel, Charlie Chaplin, Errol Flynn, and John Wayne. Today, it lures lovers who are aficionados of the 1920s to its 64 elegantly furnished guest rooms. Oval scalloped beds, deco-tiled bathrooms, and credenzas that electronically lift the TV at the touch of a button provide couples with a sensual appeal. Splurge on a suite and the two of you will enjoy separate living and dining rooms, second bathrooms, whirlpool tubs, and/or steam showers. Because standard rooms are small, the suites are preferable, but only because of space; all the other heart-stirring details are the same. The Argyle's restaurant, Fenix, attracts couples who want to enjoy the sunset views on the terrace—complete with its famed plaster palm trees—overlooking the city and the lap pool. Open for breakfast, lunch, and dinner, the stylish art deco restaurant specializes in New American fare such as chopped salads, spring rolls, tuna served three ways (grilled, pepper seared, and as a spicy tuna handroll), crispy whole catfish, and pork tenderloin with roasted cauliflower.
*$$$$ AE, DC, DIS, MC, V; checks OK; www.argylehotel.com.* ♿

## BEVERLY HILLS HOTEL & BUNGALOWS
◍ ◍ ◍ ◍

*9641 Sunset Blvd, Beverly Hills / 310/276-2251 or 800/283-8885*
Elizabeth Taylor chose this swank site for most of her many honeymoons, and that was before the owner shut it down for a couple of years in the early '90s and pumped more than $100 million into renovating the entire property. Rooms are larger and colors are more vibrant, but it's essentially the same old place—which is exactly how longtime fans, including countless Hollywood luminaries, wanted it. The 203 large, lavishly adorned rooms, suites, and bungalows are done in a plush late-deco style and offer the perfect romantic hideaway. Each room at the legendary "pink palace" has been elegantly appointed with warm colors, patterned fabrics, and original art. All feature comfortable sitting areas, walk-in closets, attractive beds with Ralph Lauren linens, and full entertainment centers with TVs, VCRs, and CD players (an extensive video and CD library is available for couples who want to create the right mood). Many rooms also offer terraces, wood-burning fireplaces, and separate entrances. The spacious, luxurious baths are done in pink marble and Italian granite. If you can afford to splurge, choose one of the 21 bungalows scattered throughout the winding gardens. The privacy and romance of these bungalows make them ideal for a tryst. The 12-acre grounds, which include the famous pool with its cabanas and tennis courts, are lush and overgrown. Couples who want to be pampered should check out the hotel's intimate La Prairie Spa. The hotel's Polo Lounge serves everything from breakfast through late-night suppers and offers both indoor and outdoor seating. Famous as a spot where Hollywood deals are made, the restaurant serves salads, pastas, and entrées like grilled ahi and New York steak. The Fountain Coffee Shop is still a favorite for lovers in search of a quick breakfast, or a lunch or early supper of burgers, salads, or ice cream treats from the old-fashioned soda fountain. Open from 2pm to 11pm every day, The Sunset Lounge (see Romantic Restaurants), adjacent to the lobby, serves a wonderful traditional afternoon tea, available with or without champagne. But, you'll want champagne to toast your time at this timeless hotel.
$$$$ *AE, DC, MC, V; no checks; www.beverlyhillshotel.com.* ♿

## CHATEAU MARMONT
◍ ◍

*8221 Sunset Blvd, West Hollywood / 323/656-1010 or 800/242-8328*
Chateau Marmont has been a legendary Hollywood hideaway since 1929. The romantic possibilities here are just too enticing to ignore. Modeled after a Loire Valley castle, this hip hotel perched above the Sunset Strip boasts sumptuous furnishings, wood-paneled walls, and beautiful throw rugs that transport you to that elegant locale. No two of the 60 antique-filled accommodations—which run the gamut from standard rooms to bungalows—are

# *Music of the Night*

There's nothing like a little music to spark the flames of love, and there are numerous places in Los Angeles where lovers can appreciate an evening of music and romance.

During the summer months, spending the evening under the stars listening to live music with the one you love at the **Hollywood Bowl** (2301 N Highland Ave; 323/850-2000; www.hollywoodbowl.org) is the ultimate amorous outing. Couples are encouraged to bring a picnic basket chock-full of gourmet goodies and wine to enjoy while taking in concerts that range from classical (the Bowl is the summer home of the Los Angeles Philharmonic) to contemporary (think Harry Connick Jr., Sting, and even Radiohead). Box seats near the stage provide an ideal setting for love to blossom under the stars, but it's also romantic to sit high up on the lawn and snuggle under a blanket. The Bowl recently upgraded its famed shell to improve the venue's acoustics, but a night here is more about ambience and tradition than a perfect sound.

Los Angeles's new **Walt Disney Concert Hall** (111 S Grand Ave; 323/850-2000; www.musiccenter.org/wdch) is where you'll find perfect acoustics. The stunning, new $274-million concert hall in downtown Los Angeles was designed by Frank Gehry and serves as home to the Los Angeles Philharmonic. The modern architectural masterpiece took years to complete and today is perhaps one of the hottest tickets in town, seating 2,275 concertgoers. Whether you choose to see the Philharmonic, or to get a seat for a Los Angeles Master Chorale concert, it's sure to be an event.

Friday evenings most of the year, hundreds of people descend on the Times Mirror Central Court at the **Los Angeles County Museum of Art** (5905 Wilshire Blvd; 323/857-6000; www.lacma.org) for first-rate—and free—jazz from 5:30pm to 8:30pm. In summer, the balmy nights and late-setting sun provide the perfect backdrop for sensuous tunes. You can call for a monthly calendar of scheduled appearances or check the Web site. The museum shop and galleries are open until 9pm, and drinks and a light supper are available from the museum cafe, now in the hands of the Patina Group.

Or, make a night of it and take in a show at the **House of Blues** (8430 Sunset Blvd; 323/848-5100; www.hob.com) in West Hollywood. This funky Cajun-style music venue, bar, and restaurant offers a relatively intimate setting to check out big-name performers like The Strokes and the Psychedelic Furs. Reserve a table at The Porch restaurant for dinner before the show, and you can avoid the line out front prior to the concert.

Other outstanding concert venues in the Los Angeles area include the

*Continued on next page*

restored deco revival–style **Wiltern Theater** (3790 Wilshire Blvd; 213/380-5005) and the **Greek Theater** (2700 Vermont Ave; 323/665-1927), an outdoor venue set high in the hills of Griffith Park.

—BONNIE STEELE

alike. A few bedrooms have garden views; the suites and bungalows feature full kitchens and dining rooms, and some have direct access to the outdoor brick-decked pool. Who knows—the two of you could end up in the same room Clark Gable shared with a paramour in times past. The gorgeous lobby is the ideal place to curl up on a couch with your sweetie and enjoy a nightcap or people watch. While this is unquestionably a chic celebrity hangout, the funky hotel lacks any air of pretension. A discreet staff caters to your every whim, and a small, intimate dining room serves breakfast, lunch, and dinner inside or in the splendid garden.
$$$$ *AE, DC, MC, V; no checks; www.chateaumarmont.com.*

## FIGUEROA HOTEL
⬡⬡
*939 S Figueroa St, Los Angeles / 213/627-8971 or 800/421-9092*
This 1920s gem, with touches of Spanish and Moorish architecture, is a funky retreat in the heart of downtown, with most of the area's key places (including the Staples Center and the Convention Center) within walking distance. Soaring stenciled beamed ceilings in the lobby lead to a rear patio bar and mosaic-tiled pool, the site of many celebrity parties, including one hosted by musician Peter Gabriel. Couples can check into one of the reasonably priced guest rooms, carefully decorated in a Southwestern Gothic theme, where terra-cotta sponge-painted walls, wrought-iron beds, Indian cotton draperies, and Mexican-tiled baths create an exotic cheap-chic love nest. Rates are reasonable as rooms are not as luxe as some of downtown's finest, but the location is tough to beat. Not looking to stay? Just stop in for a drink and get a glimpse of what Los Angeles looked like 80 or so years ago.
$$ *AE, DC, MC, V; no checks; www.figueroahotel.com.* &

## FOUR SEASONS HOTEL LOS ANGELES AT BEVERLY HILLS
⬡⬡⬡⬡
*300 S Doheny Dr, Los Angeles / 310/273-2222 or 800/819-5053*
The Four Seasons chain has a well-deserved reputation for first-rate service, and that's certainly the case here. Valets whisk your car away and a bellman opens the front door before you can even reach for it. Inside, the marble lobby is awash in fresh flowers. Turn right, and you're headed to the bar and restaurant, where the two of you may want to scan the faces carefully as you're likely to pass a virtual who's who in music and film as

you stroll through. Pastel-hued guest rooms are luxurious, with fabulously comfortable beds, and most have French doors, pleasing views, and all the luxurious amenities you could ask for. There's a full-service spa, complete with a couple's treatment room for the ultimate in togetherness, or the two of you can lounge by the lushly landscaped pool on the fourth-level deck, with its half dozen cabanas. Complimentary limo service within a 5-mile radius can transport the two of you to the nearby shops on Robertson or perhaps an elegant dinner at one of the area's top restaurants. Or, stay at the hotel for an evening at Gardens restaurant, which is an ideal spot for an intimate gourmet dinner. Tables are set discreetly apart in a number of small, attractive rooms, where couples can dine on a Cal-Mediterranean menu. Open for breakfast, lunch, and dinner, Gardens also boasts a magnificent Sunday brunch spread. Order a couple of mimosas, then sample the fresh seafood, salads, waffles, egg dishes, and pancakes. And, if the two of you really gorge yourselves, you can always head to your room upstairs for a midmorning nap. The adjacent bar specializes in martinis but also has great wines by the glass, and don't overlook the tray of gourmet nuts brought with your drink of choice.
$$$$ *AE, DC, DIS, MC, V; no checks; www.fourseasons.com.* &

## HILTON CHECKERS
◐◐
*535 S Grand Ave, Los Angeles / 213/624-0000 or 800/423-5798*
Located in central downtown Los Angeles, this small, gracious luxury hotel looks strikingly European on the outside, and that same classic design is reflected in the beautiful lobby and guest rooms. Luxury suites, decorated with a beige, taupe, and cream color scheme, come with silk canopy beds, fireplaces, intimate sitting rooms, and separate dining areas. Oversized beds, attractive linens and wall coverings, and all the amenities, including a selection of 50 movies, may tempt you to stay in. But Checkers has other lures, including a stunning rooftop spa and pool and a romantic walkway between the hotel and the nearby Central Library grounds. After a day spent exploring nearby museums, the two of you can review your outing in the Lobby Bar over the formal tea service. In early evening, this is also a good place to sip a cocktail and nibble on complimentary hors d'oeuvres before enjoying a gourmet dinner at elegant Checkers Restaurant (see Romantic Restaurants). Rates are reduced on the weekend, and some local transportation is provided.
$$$$ *AE, DC, DIS, MC, V; no checks; www.checkershotel.com.* &

## HOTEL BEL-AIR

❤❤❤❤

*701 Stone Canyon Rd, Los Angeles / 310/472-1211 or 800/648-4097*
Hotel Bel-Air is where everybody wants to stay in Los Angeles—some
people just don't know it because they haven't yet seen its stunning Mission-style architecture; 11 overgrown acres strewn with lush bougainvillea,
azaleas, and birds-of-paradise meandering stream; and signature swans.
For all those reasons and so many more, it may well rank as the very best
place to kiss in the entire Los Angeles area. Guest rooms are understated,
decorated with luxurious French country–style furnishings, and many have
wood-burning fireplaces, balconies, and private patios. Glass doors draped
in soft, billowy fabrics frame the private entryways to some of the bun-
galow-like suites. Even the standard rooms are fairly plush and inviting,
and the setting oozes charm and refinement. The restaurant and adjoining
bar/piano lounge are formal and handsome, yet they also feel soft and
inviting, as if nestling close and whispering sweet nothings were also part
of the menu. On a nice day, there's nothing more romantic than dining in a
cozy booth on the restaurant's bougainvillea-draped patio, which overlooks
the swan pond. In the evenings, the cozy dining room provides an intimate
setting for romantic dinners, featuring basil-crusted salmon or succulent
rack of lamb. Couples celebrating a special occasion may want to reserve
Table One, a hand-carved pine table set in a private room that overlooks the
action in the kitchen through a giant picture window. Numerous benches are
sprinkled throughout the beautifully manicured grounds, and the elegant
patio surrounding the outdoor swimming pool is a great spot for lunch. The
Bel-Air is a five-star experience by most standards; by ours, it's a four-lip
extravaganza. The setting alone is well worth the price. At the very least, the
two of you should drop in for a drink in the inviting bar, where the fireplace
is always lit. Just remember that jackets are required for gentlemen.
$$$$ *AE, DC, DIS, MC, V; checks OK; www.hotelbelair.com.* &

## LE MONTROSE SUITE HOTEL

❤❤❤

*900 Hammond St, West Hollywood / 310/855-1115 or 800/776-0666*
From the outside Le Montrose looks like an urbane, residential apartment
building. Inside, it is an attractive, well-run all-suites hotel with amenities
that make it one of the better places to stay in greater Los Angeles. Each
spacious suite features a gas-burning fireplace, settee, and tile bathroom
with a large glass-enclosed shower, giving couples plenty of room to make
themselves at home. Up on the roof, couples can lounge by a wonderful
swimming pool and a whirlpool spa with sweeping, unobstructed views. The
rooftop tennis court provides the same vista. A charming, petite restaurant
on the main floor serves relaxing breakfasts and intimate lunches and din-

ners for guests only. The food is surprisingly good, but the atmosphere and privacy are even better.
*$$$ AE, DC, DIS, MC, V; no checks; www.lemontrose.com.* &

## LOEWS BEVERLY HILLS
◐◐

*1224 S Beverwil Dr, Beverly Hills / 310/277-2800 or 800/421-3212*
This property has gone through a number of owners, finally settling in under the Loews flag. Located at one end of an affluent neighborhood, the hotel offers a central setting for lovebirds looking to stay on the Westside. Its 137 rooms are spread over a dozen floors, and many have fabulous—and romantic—city views, easy to enjoy with private balconies. Some touches remain from previous incarnations, but they blend nicely into an elegant property. Beds are costly and comfortable Tempur-pedic, and other nice touches include granite vanities, private balconies, and a well-stocked minibar. The small, inviting lobby boasts a warming fireplace and an outdoor patio awash in color, which lures lovers to hang out and people watch. A small pool welcomes couples in search of the sun, though its close proximity to busy Pico Boulevard can be distracting. Loews Beverly Hills's restaurant, Lot 1224 (310/772-2999), offers American flavor with rustic Asian and Mediterranean accents in a setting defined by warm, rich woods and a color scheme embracing night sky blues and ochre reds. It's the perfect place for the two of you to unwind with a cocktail after a day of shopping on nearby Rodeo Drive.
*$$$ AE, DC, DIS, MC, V; no checks; www.loewshotels.com.* &

## MAISON 140
◐

*140 Lasky Dr, Beverly Hills / 310/281-4000*
Once owned by silent film star Lillian Gish, the East-meets-modern property was completely redesigned by Kelly Wearstler, who has decorated some of the top homes and hotels in and around the City of Angels. It's an intimate, 43-room boutique hotel, European in style, and Wearstler went over the top on this one, ranging from black hallways to brightly colored (if smallish) guest rooms with a stunning blend of chinoiserie textiles and wall coverings, original 1930s details, 1960s-modern accents, and luxuries like Frette linens, CD players, and kimono-style robes. Couples will appreciate the perfect location—tucked behind the Peninsula Beverly Hills hotel in the heart of this posh city. Before a night on the town, sip cocktails with your sweetie in the hotel's seductive lounge, Bar Noir (whose signature cocktail is the champagne-and-Chambord French Kiss). In the morning, a complimentary continental breakfast is served.
*$$$ AE, DC, MC, V; no checks; www.maison140beverlyhills.com.*

## MILLENNIUM BILTMORE HOTEL LOS ANGELES
♦♦
*506 S Grand Ave, Los Angeles / 213/612-1575 or 800/245-8673*
Built in 1923 and renovated in the 1980s to re-create the original aura of
Renaissance Italy, the Biltmore aims to be as grand as any palace in Europe.
Towering ceilings, arched doorways, and painted murals that are a feast for
the eyes make this gorgeous 683-room hotel the ultimate lovers' hideaway.
Indeed, if this L.A. landmark is good enough for a host of U.S. presidents,
globe-trotting royalty, and numerous celebrities—including the Beatles—
it's good enough for the two of you. Guest rooms are elegantly furnished
and include all the amenities you'll need for a romantic getaway. Even if
you only tour its immense gilded halls and stop briefly to sip a brandy in
the stunning Gallery Bar, with its gorgeous terra-cotta tile, the Biltmore
is well worth the trek downtown. Don't miss the underground gym, with
its Roman-style pool that looks straight out of Hearst Castle. For a lovely
afternoon tea, the Rendezvous Court, crowned by a three-story ceiling and
surrounded by potted palms and a large fountain, is one of the best spots in
town. Couples craving Japanese specialties like yellow tail ceviche or pan-
fried oysters on the half shell can make a reservation at Sai Sai, which is
open for lunch and dinner every day. However, if the two of you are craving
simple American cuisine, the hotel's Smeraldi Restaurant serves breakfast,
lunch, and dinner in a pretty dining room. As the Biltmore caters to weekday
business travelers, weekend rates for couples are greatly reduced for deluxe
accommodations.
$$$$ *AE, DC, DIS, MC, V; checks OK; www.millennium-hotels.com.*

## PENINSULA BEVERLY HILLS
♦♦♦♦
*9882 Little Santa Monica Blvd, Beverly Hills / 310/551-2888 or 800/462-
7899*
Located in the heart of Beverly Hills, this refined, stunning hotel is clearly
a bastion for the local and international movers and shakers of the movie
industry and the world of politics—as well as true-blue lovers looking for
the ideal retreat. Without question, this is the ultimate in deluxe hotel
accommodations. Every floor has its own private valet, and each room has
its own call button to summon service. Need some more ice to chill the
champagne? Simply hit a button and your wish is granted. Done in lavish
French Renaissance style, the 196 guest rooms are large and luxury laden,
with bedside controls for everything (lighting, climate, "Do Not Disturb,"
and so on), big Italian marble bathrooms, VCRs, and Bose radios. The most
coveted guest locations are the villas with private entrances. Garden pathways lead you to these lavish accommodations, which feature private terraces, spas, and fireplaces (sigh). A 3,500-square-foot spa offers a menu of
pampering treatments and a state-of-the-art fitness center. There is even a

Rolls Royce available for complimentary lifts to Rodeo Drive and Century City, or for rent by the hour if the two of you want to go off on a tour of your own. The hotel's restaurant, the Belvedere (see Romantic Restaurants), is enchanting for almost any meal. Even if you aren't a guest at the hotel, consider having afternoon tea in the Living Room (see Romantic Restaurants), which boasts a stunning locale for tea for two.
$$$$ *AE, DC, DIS, MC, V; checks OK; www.beverlyhills.peninsula.com.* &

## RAFFLES L'ERMITAGE BEVERLY HILLS
🌸🌸🌸🌸
*9291 Burton Wy, Beverly Hills / 310/278-3344 or 800/800-2113*
Oversized, luxurious guest rooms tricked out with high-end electronics and fabulous European sheets attract couples to this Japanese-inspired hotel. Each of the 124 rooms is superbly decorated with tailored silk, Berber carpeting, and custom maple furniture, including low-platform beds and an armoire to hide the 40-inch TV, CD/DVD player, Bose tuner and speakers, and more. And gigantic bathrooms with soaking tubs, a shower for two, cotton and terry-cloth robes, and lots and lots of towels are a dream. However, it's the kind staff's stellar service that makes a romantic stay here all the more memorable. A rooftop fitness center and a small, lovely pool with cabanas provide couples with a relaxing spot to enjoy the Southern California sunshine. Or, pampering is always a possibility at the Amrita Spa. Jaan (see Romantic Restaurants) is a stunning setting for a memorable meal. The Writers Bar just off the lobby provides well-spaced chairs and sofas so couples can enjoy a little privacy while sipping cocktails.
$$$$ *AE, DC, MC, V; no checks; www.lermitagehotel.com.* &

## THE REGENT BEVERLY WILSHIRE HOTEL
🌸🌸🌸🌸
*9500 Wilshire Blvd, Beverly Hills / 310/275-5200*
Julia Roberts checked into this grand hotel in *Pretty Woman*, and Warren Beatty made this place his personal love nest for years, back when he was single and still in his prime. The lobby is grand, with massive amounts of marble, and the bar and restaurant in the main building are very nice, but it's the 395 guest rooms here that excel. Set in two wings—each with its own style—the hotel boasts the traditional elegant Wilshire Wing and the more contemporary Beverly Wing. Both feature beautifully appointed guest suites, perfect for a weekend with your special companion. Furniture and bedding are above the norm, and the bathrooms are much larger than most—even by luxury standards. The marble floor and counters frame a bathtub built for two, a separate glass shower stall built for a small crowd, and a lovely vanity area for après-bath primping. All this comfort, combined with superb service, makes for an extraordinary getaway. Best of all, Rodeo Drive is a just a romantic stroll away. The elegant setting in the Dining Room is the perfect

backdrop for leisurely breakfasts and romance-inducing lunches and dinners that showcase the chef's panache for California cuisine.
$$$$ *AE, DC, DIS, MC, V; no checks; www.regenthotels.com.* ᵭ

## ST. REGIS LOS ANGELES
❤❤❤

*2055 Ave of the Stars, Los Angeles / 310/277-6111*
Formerly the tower of the adjacent Century Plaza Hotel, the St. Regis Los Angeles got a spiffy makeover and its own identity a couple of years ago. Modeled on the legendary New York hotel, this five-star-level property is all about luxury and romance. Guest rooms are large and provide couples with traditional-goes-contemporary decor. California king beds dressed with Frette linens have bedside controls for everything, and VCRs, DVDs, and CD players provide lovers with all the extras needed to hole up for a night or two of romance. If the two of you do decide to venture downstairs, the hotel has its own lounge, the St. Regis Bar, inspired by the Manhattan property's legendary King Cole Bar, complete with its own mural, *The Dancer*, depicting a flamenco dancer, over the 30-foot-long bar. The main restaurant, Encore, has been a work in progress, but lately has seemed on track under a new chef. Couples can dine at the lush outdoor patio or in the elegant dining room; breakfast, lunch, and dinner are served Monday through Saturday, and Sundays feature a brunch menu until midafternoon. A classic European spa, a view-endowed health club featuring plasma TV screens, and fully wired poolside cabanas round out an impressive list of amenities sure to entice couples in search of romance.
$$$$ *AE, DC, DIS, MC, V; checks OK; www.stregis.com.* ᵭ

## WYNDHAM BEL AGE HOTEL
❤❤

*1020 N San Vicente Blvd, West Hollywood / 310/854-1111 or 877/999-3223*
The Bel Age tries very hard to be a formal luxury hotel, and in some regards it succeeds, but essentially it is a very nice, slightly pretentious hotel. The lobby and hallways are decorated with interesting pieces of original artwork. From the rooftop sculpture garden and pool, which feature panoramic vistas of the city below, to the vine-trellised courtyard filled with massive, modern wood carvings, couples will find much to appreciate in addition to the extra-large gray, navy, maroon, and gold guest rooms at this all-suites hotel. In smaller rooms, the bedroom area is separated from the living room by a raised platform edged with a wrought-iron banister. Each room is attractively appointed with a pillow-top mattress dressed with plush bedding, a TV with a VCR—in case you and your sweetie want to stay in for movie night—soft lighting, and a marble bathroom with plenty of counter space. If a culinary tour de force is part of your romantic itinerary, you would do well to have dinner at the hotel's Diaghilev (310/358-7780). This

ultraexpensive, ultraposh dining room serves a unique blend of French and Russian cuisine that is sheer perfection. Soft classical music, deftly played on a harp and grand piano, creates a sentimental atmosphere all evening long. But the food is the true seduction here, so be prepared. Ten20 Piano Bar doubles as a casual breakfast and lunch spot every day, with sweeping views of the city, and on Thursday and Friday evenings, the bar also comes alive with the sounds of live music.
$$$ *AE, DC, DIS, MC, V; checks OK; www.wyndham.com.* &

# *Romantic Restaurants*

## AOC
♥♥♥
*8022 W 3rd St, West Hollywood / 323/653-6359*
Fifty wines by the glass and delicious finger foods from around the world provide all the makings of a truly sensual meal at Suzanne Goin and Caroline Styne's casual eatery. The pair, who also own and operate Lucques, opened this hotspot to indulge some of their passions—like fine meats and cheeses and the many wines available by carafe. Here, couples can sup on cheese-stuffed dates wrapped in bacon or "small plates" menu items, including lamb skewers and Manila clams. It's gourmet finger food, and the fun is enhanced when the two of you order a few different wines to see how they pair with the various dishes. An entire menu page is devoted just to cheeses; don't leave without sampling at least a few. Tables are close together, so there's not much personal space, but everyone seems to have a good time here, and that in itself can fuel romance. While it's fun to people-watch downstairs, the quieter upstairs section of the restaurant is more conducive for an amorous evening.
$$$ *AE, DC, DIS, MC, V; checks OK; dinner every day; beer and wine; reservations recommended; www.aocwinebar.com.* &

## ASIA DE CUBA
♥♥
*8440 W Sunset Blvd (Mondrian Hotel), West Hollywood / 323/848-6000*
If you and your sweetie believe a romantic night is being where the action is, make reservations at Asia de Cuba, the main restaurant at the Mondrian Hotel. Dining as entertainment has been perfected here, as well as at other Asia de Cuba branches in New York City and London. It's like a party every night, with young Hollywood turning out, clamoring for tables at the very back by the windows that look down on the sparkling city below, or outside under the Land of the Giants–sized tree pots that mark the restaurant's portion of the patio, adjacent to the pool and the famous Sky Bar. While the setting is sexy, the cuisine is a mix of Asian and Cuban flavors and

ingredients. Prices are high but portions are substantial, and the flavors are fabulous, especially on dishes like *ropa vieja* with shredded duck, Hunan whole wok–crispy fish, and grilled mojito-glazed strip steak Other favorites include *tunapica* (tuna tartare) and pan-seared ahi, barely cooked, then sliced and served over wasabi mashed potatoes. For dessert, there's *cielo de coco,* a dense, white coconut cake topped with caramelized bananas, with caramel sauce on the bottom and a dollop of *dulce de leche* ice cream, and The Latin Lover, a chocolate mousse cake with white coffee anglaise. Do as the Cubans do and order a mojito, made to order with rum mixed with lime, sugar, and fresh mint leaves. It's the perfect accompaniment to spice up your night.

$$$ *AE, DC, DIS, MC, V; no checks; breakfast, lunch, dinner every day; full bar; reservations recommended; www.chinagrillmgt.com.* &

## BASTIDE
🌸🌸🌸🌸

*8475 Melrose Pl, West Hollywood / 323/651-0426*

Lovers longing for the sophisticated setting of a posh Paris restaurant can enjoy the next best thing at this exclusive eatery. Bastide brings back French dining with attitude. It's not that they're unfriendly, it's just that they're a little strict. Couples can make a reservation for one of two seatings (6pm and 9pm), and there's absolutely no corkage (bringing your own wine). But no one complains because the wine list is 100 percent French, the sun-kissed cuisine of chef Alain Giraud's native Provence is so delicious, and the setting is so magical that you'll instantly know you're in for a special meal. Set in a quaint bungalow with several small rooms painted in soothing pastel colors, Bastide offers a variety of settings. Most romantic are the front patio with its lush vertical garden and the atrium off the kitchen, weather permitting. Giraud changes his menu with what's available, and he's one of the very top chefs in town, so you can't go wrong with anything coming out of his kitchen. Couples can choose from one of three tasting menus, or just let Giraud choose for you. Rack of lamb with black olive sauce, foie gras terrine, and crab and melon cannelloni were among the offerings one particular night, and they were delicious.

$$$$ *AE, DIS, MC, V; no checks; dinner Tues–Sat; full bar; reservations recommended.* &

## THE BELVEDERE
🌸🌸🌸

*9882 Little Santa Monica Blvd (Peninsula Beverly Hills), Beverly Hills / 310/788-2306*

Located in the Peninsula Beverly Hills (see Romantic Lodgings), this elegant dining room boasts a picture-perfect setting for a romantic meal. However, the serious and sophisticated mood is lightened by chef Bill Bracken, who lets his outrageous sense of humor loose with playful menu selections. Couples can order "TV dinner"–style meals, which faithfully replicate the look of those thankfully forgotten dishes, but elevate the food within to gourmet level. And while his cuisine ranks high on every local list, he's not above indulging in culinary nostalgia, such as macaroni and cheese, a guilty pleasure spruced up with truffles. But make no mistake: It's serious dining here, and in an elegant setting. Tables are well spaced for privacy, and service is practically invisible—there when you need it, nowhere in sight when you don't. There's a substantial wine list, and the staff here knows the topic well, down to presenting the proper glass for any wine ordered. Order a glass of bubbly, sit back on the overstuffed banquette, and toast to the fine meal to come.

*$$$ AE, DC, DIS, MC, V; no checks; breakfast, lunch, dinner every day; full bar; reservations recommended; beverlyhills.peninsula.com.* &

---

## CAFÉ DES ARTISTES
● ●

*1534 N McCadden Pl, Hollywood / 323/469-7300*
In a city known for its slick, chic interiors, Cafe des Artistes is like a breath of fresh air for those in search of easygoing, rustic, yet genteel dining. The rough-hewn country interior, tucked inside a simple Craftsman-style house, is modest and lovely, with only a handful of tables in the dining area. But the shady, overgrown patio, with romantic seating cloistered beneath abundant foliage, is where everyone wants to sit most of the year. During either lunch or dinnertime, you and your special someone will find the same atmosphere and the same delectable French Provençal menu selections (ranging from steak or ahi sandwiches on foccacia bread and giant salads to pastas and such French fare as chicken paillard and duck leg confit). And, rare for Los Angeles, the kitchen stays open late, so the two of you can savor a late-night snack together.

*$$ AE, DC, DIS, MC, V; no checks; lunch Mon–Fri, dinner Mon–Sat; full bar; reservations recommended; www.cafedesartistes.info.* &

---

## CHECKERS DOWNTOWN
● ●

*535 S Grand Ave (Hilton Checkers), Los Angeles / 213/624-0000*
Set in the Hilton Checkers, one of downtown's most tasteful hotels (see Romantic Lodgings), Checkers Downtown is one of the city's most romantic getaways for both atmosphere and fine dining. The elegant yet comfortable interior is decorated in muted greens and tans. Tables are widely spaced, or you can choose to sit à deux in a velour-backed banquette for a leisurely, romantic meal. Many of the dishes on the eclectic California-style menu have an Asian influence, and all are delicious. Cold appetizer favorites include tiger prawns and Pacific yellowtail sashimi; entrées such as grilled

beef tenderloin with yams and pecan cake and New Zealand rack of lamb with rösti potatoes are succulently sensational. Couples can enjoy a pre-show dinner here, with complimentary transportation to the nearby Music Center.
$$$ *AE, DC, DIS, MC, V; no checks; breakfast, lunch, dinner every day, brunch Sun; full bar; reservations recommended; www.hilton checkers.com.* &

## DAR MAGHREB
🟡🟡
*7651 Sunset Blvd, Hollywood / 323/876-7651*
Belly dancing may not be everyone's ideal, but those who enjoy the sensuous movements and the rhythms of the music will no doubt be seduced at Dar Maghreb, a lovely Moroccan restaurant just off Sunset. Built like a traditional home in that exotic part of the world, this place entices the senses on many levels. The inside is adorned with tiled mosaics and fountains. Couples sit down to a seven-course prix-fixe dinner, which starts just after a server pours warm water over your hands—your utensils for the evening. The two of you will feast on exotic foods, eaten with your fingers, from chicken to lamb, and sink back into satiny pillows, allowing the seductive music to soothe your senses. While the belly dancers perform, allow yourselves to be pampered in a style once reserved for sheiks and caliphs.
$$$ *DC, MC, V; no checks; dinner every day; full bar; reservations recommended; www.darmaghrebrestaurant.com.* &

## DOLCE RISTORANTE & ENOTECA
🟡🥂
*8284 Melrose Ave, West Hollywood / 323/852-7174*
Ashton Kutcher is just one of the many Hollywood investors who have given this place its patina of celebrity. But the real star may be designer Dodd Mitchell, who transformed the once stodgy space into something ready for its 15 minutes of fame. Sure, the clock may be ticking, but don't tell that to the throngs of young people who flock here nightly. Everybody looks good in this room, where flames flicker behind the bottles in the bar and the tables are dressed in black leather. Couples can start with such enticing appetizers as prosciutto with dried figs or delicate beef carpaccio, and then move on to a main course that runs the gamut from pastas and risottos to fresh fish and grilled steaks. The wine list is nothing less than stellar. But, an evening at Dolce is not really about the food, is it?
$$$ *AE, MC, V; no checks; dinner every day; full bar; reservations recommended; www.dolceenoteca.com.* &

## ENOTECA DRAGO
✿✿❀

*410 N Canon Dr, Beverly Hills / 310/786-8236*
Couples can drop in and grab a seat at the bar or make a reservation if they
want a table at this very Italian wine bar and restaurant from one of L.A.'s
very best Italian chefs, Celestino Drago. You'll dine on authentic goods from
Italy under a vaulted ceiling surrounded by regulars who flock to Drago's
dining establishments. Feed each other delicious finger foods, like fried
olives and fried parmesan drizzled in balsamic vinegar, or dig in to hearty
Piedmontese steaks—your mouth won't believe they're low fat, but your
heart will know the difference. Pizzas, pasta, fish, and fowl are all delicious
and can be accompanied by any of 50 Italian wines by the glass or in various
sampling flights. And, if the two of you stop in for lunch, try the perfectly
grilled panini. For real privacy and romance, ask for a table in the upstairs
room, which is often reserved for private parties.
**$$** *AE, DC, DIS, MC, V; no checks; breakfast, lunch, dinner every day; full
bar; reservations recommended; www.celestinodrago.com.* &

## FOUR OAKS RESTAURANT
✿✿✿❀

*2181 N Beverly Glen Blvd, Los Angeles / 310/470-2265*
Once a private home, this restaurant boasts one of the loveliest settings in
Los Angeles. Tucked against a hill in rustic Beverly Glen Canyon, this cot-
tagelike residence offers many seating areas, both inside and out. Several
intimate rooms flow naturally, one into the other, though the tables are a
tad too close for kissing comfort. Weather permitting, the outdoor patios
are exceptionally lovely sites for dining. Inside, ask to be seated by the
rustic fireplace and you'll be assured an evening of romance. The food is a
five-star celebration, from such starters as Russian caviar or lobster spring
rolls to main courses like sesame seed-crusted Scottish salmon, roasted
Culver duck, and whisky-marinated pork tenderloin. Five- and seven-
course tasting menus are available for hungry couples that want to sample
a variety of chef Peter Roulant's selections. Service can be a little iffy, but
this setting is so beautiful, the two of you won't be in a hurry to get your
check.
**$$$$** *AE, DC, DIS, MC, V; no checks; lunch Tues–Sat, dinner Tues–Sun,
brunch Sun; full bar; reservations required; www.fouroaksrestaurant.com.*
&

## GRACE
✿✿

*7360 Beverly Blvd, Los Angeles / 323/934-4400*
There's a certain tranquility to dining at Grace, the elegant restaurant from
chef Neal Fraser, despite the crowds that pack the place from early evening

to late night. Couples can choose from more than the typical L.A. menu's offerings, with options including tenderloin of wild boar; a delicious, gamey saddle of rabbit wrapped in bacon; and a vegan entrée so colorful that heads turn as it goes by. Lovers can cozy up at a muted orange banquette in this sophisticated modern setting and order wine from a list that avoids the obvious choices and offers interesting alternatives—and is then poured into fine Riedel stemware. Fun menu selections like trios of fish and flights of soup make dining here a culinary adventure. After all, where else can you order a gourmet jelly doughnut for dessert?

$$$ *AE, MC, V; no checks; dinner Tues–Sat; full bar; reservations recommended; www.gracerestaurant.net.* &

## IL CIELO
●●●
*9018 Burton Wy, Beverly Hills / 310/276-9990*
With its many patios making for one of the loveliest settings in town, Il Cielo is often described as L.A.'s most romantic restaurant. Modeled after owner Pasquale Vericella's country home in Sorrento, this gorgeous Italian eatery is all about amour. From the vine-cloaked patio in front to additional alfresco seating on the side, all embroidered with trellises and flowering plants, this intimate, elegant hideaway provides lovers with an ideal locale to savor robust Southern Italian cuisine, from house-made ravioli to whole striped sea bass stuffed with fresh herbs. Inside the small building, once a private home, is the kitchen as well as wooden tables, a glowing fireplace, and hand-painted ceilings that make the interior as fetching as the exterior. A star-filled summer night would be well spent at this rare, inviting Italian spot. And it's no surprise that it's in constant demand for weddings, engagement dinners, and other special events.

$$$ *AE, DC, DIS, MC, V; checks OK; lunch, dinner Mon–Sat; full bar; reservations recommended; www.ilcielo.com.* &

## JAAN
●●◖
*9291 Burton Wy (Raffles L'Ermitage Hotel), Beverly Hills / 310/385-5344*
The modern room at this fine dining establishment in the Raffles L'Ermitage hotel (see Romantic Lodgings) is lovely—circular, with a domed ceiling—and the culinary creations, offered on both the regular menu and seasonal tasting menus, are just as pleasing to the eye as that special someone sitting across from you. Entrées—like Kobe beef tenderloin, arctic char, and the eatery's $45 salad chock-full of everything from lobster and ahi to foie gras and truffles—ensure that you and your betrothed will enjoy a special meal. Add to that unusual and beautiful china, elegant flatware, superior stemware, and gorgeous flower arrangements, and you have the ingredients

for a superb evening out. On warm nights, dine alfresco and enjoy the faint sounds of trickling water from the patio's fountain.

*$$$ AE, DC, DIS, MC, V; no checks; breakfast, lunch, dinner every day; full bar; reservations recommended; www.lermitagehotel.com.* &

## KENDALL'S BRASSERIE & BAR
🕸🕸

*135 N Grand Ave (Music Center), Los Angeles / 213/972-7322*
Located on the ground level of the Music Center in what was once Otto's Bar, this charming restaurant is a convenient place for a romantic meal before or after a concert or play, if you aren't planning to go big and make a reservation at Patina. (Kendall's is, however, also run by Patina restaurateur Joachim Splichal.) It is necessary to reserve ahead, and we recommend requesting one of the comfortable semicircular booths. Terra-cotta tile floors and white linen–draped tables make for a warm setting for a simple French meal. Start with such appetizers as a seafood platter from the raw bar or the tasty beet and prosciutto salad. Rotisserie chicken with crisp *pommes frites* and pan-seared salmon with mashed potatoes are among the main course highlights, and dish of the day selections include such traditional French fare as coq au vin on Mondays and roasted rack of veal on Saturdays. The menu even highlights entrées that can be served fast for couples rushing to make a show.

*$$ AE, DC, DIS, MC, V; no checks; lunch, dinner every day; full bar; reservations recommended; www.patinagroup.com.* &

## L'ORANGERIE
🕸🕸🕸🕸

*903 N La Cienega Blvd, Los Angeles / 310/652-9770*
Widely regarded as the finest and most expensive French restaurant in town (and undeniably among the most attractive and romantic), L'Orangerie is the type of place that attracts lovers celebrating a special occasion. Indeed, it's the perfect setting for popping the big question or celebrating an anniversary. Still going strong after more than 25 years, the restaurant welcomed the recent arrival of a new chef has reinvigorated the kitchen with his fresh take on classic French cuisine. Every detail in this opulent fine-dining establishment is invariably perfect, from the massive floral arrangements in the bar and the dining room to the Limoges china and the Riedel stemware. While everything on the menu is beautifully presented and top quality, couples may want to try the nightly six-course prix-fixe Menu Royale, which changes regularly but might include a main course of Kobe beef, rotisserie veal chop with morels, or grilled tuna with clams. If you and your sweetie aren't up for a complete dining experience, try sampling from the new bar menu, which includes a sampler platter with such delicacies as one egg with Serge caviar, and house-smoked salmon and rosval potatoes

with crème fraîche and chives. The wine list features 500 selections from France and the United States.

$$$$ *AE, MC, V; no checks; dinner Tues–Sun; full bar; reservations recommended; www.orangerie.com.* &

## LA BOHEME
❍❍

*8400 Santa Monica Blvd, West Hollywood / 323/848-2360*

An unlikely mix of Left Bank Paris and Tuscan country, this impressive, almost Gothic, space is filled with romantic possibilities. A massive stone fireplace, towering wood-beamed ceilings, and balcony seating create a magnificent setting, and striking crystal chandeliers and immense windows add elegance and light. Couples can ask to be seated in one of the handsome crimson-draped wood booths, where sweethearts will enjoy extra privacy for a blissful dinner featuring entrées such as yellow fin tuna tataki, crispy skinned New Zealand red snapper, Aurora Angus rib eye, spring pea risotto, and linguine with grilled tiger shrimp. Desserts are suitably decadent, from warm Valrhona chocolate cake to butterscotch pudding complete with whipped cream, English toffee, and a shortbread cookie. It's as sweet and delicious as true love.

$$$ *AE, DC, DIS, MC, V; no checks; dinner every day; full bar; reservations recommended; www.laboheme@global-dining.co.jp.* &

## LA CACHETTE
❍❍❍

*10506 Little Santa Monica Blvd, Los Angeles / 310/470-4992*

Chef-owner Jean Francois Meteigner runs this romantic restaurant with his wife, Allie. He opened it a decade back, after a 10-year stint at L'Orangerie. Provence is the inspiration for this casually elegant place, but the cuisine covers all of France, with a strong dose of California, evident in the lightness of the dishes. Meteigner long ago moved away from butter and cream in favor of olive oil, vegetable stocks, homemade vinegars, and emulsions. He's most famous for his white truffle oil, which he sprinkles on a seafood salad and splashes on endive with walnuts. (Like it? Purchase a bottle and use it at home.) Waiters with French accents purr the daily specials into your ear, and it's always advisable to follow their suggestions. You can't miss with such specialties as Marseilles bouillabaisse or braised lamb shank. For the most romantic table, ask for a seat in the Den, the quieter back room, or sit under *Les Amoureux,* a sexy Man Ray lithograph.

$$$ *AE, DC, MC, V; no checks; dinner every day; full bar; reservations recommended; www.lacachetterestaurant.com.* &

## THE LITTLE DOOR
⚫⚫

*8164 W 3rd St, Los Angeles / 323/951-1210*
An L.A. hot spot that's so "in" it can't be bothered with a sign, this exclusive French-Mediterranean restaurant, with many polished French servers, is nearly as dazzling as its celebrity roster. Ensconced behind heavy wooden doors—which are anything but little—the main dining area is actually a romantic canopy-covered courtyard, lit mostly by candlelight. The sounds of the gurgling fountain and the heavenly aromas coming from the kitchen make you long to be in love and bring that special someone here. The Little Door uses organic produce whenever possible and turns out a menu of popular regional favorites such as delicate tuna tartare, flavorful pistou soup, grilled salmon steak, sautéed scallops, and lamb *tagine* with peaches and almonds. Wine lovers are wowed by the extensive selections, many offerings available by the glass.
*$$$–$$$$ AE, MC, V; no checks; dinner every day; beer and wine; reservations required.* &

## THE LIVING ROOM
⚫⚫

*9882 Little Santa Monica Blvd (Peninsula Beverly Hills), Beverly Hills / 310/551-2888*
What could possibly be more elegant and civilized than afternoon tea? Pamper yourselves by indulging in each other's company along with delicious tea, delicate sandwiches, and fresh-baked scones. The Living Room in the Peninsula Beverly Hills (see Romantic Lodgings) is unsurpassed for this pleasure. A harpist's lyrical melodies soothe and refresh your senses as you sit in plush couches and overstuffed chairs reminiscent of a kinder, gentler era. Beautiful place settings do perfect justice to the unfolding courses. The complete Royal Tea consists of a glass of champagne, fresh strawberries and cream, finger sandwiches, scones with jam and Devonshire cream, an assortment of delectable pastries, and, of course, your choice of tea from more than a dozen blends. Formal gardens just outside offer an opportunity to walk off some of those newly acquired calories and to steal an embrace. On cool winter days, you may want to request the sitting area in front of the fireplace.
*$$$ AE, DC, DIS, MC, V; no checks; breakfast, lunch, afternoon tea, dinner every day; full bar; reservations recommended; www.beverlyhills .peninsula.com.* &

# LUNARIA
◐◐

*10351 Santa Monica Blvd, Los Angeles / 310/282-8870*
Branford Marsalis, Diana Krall, and countless other jazz musicians have
graced the small stage here, though the performers are typically less well
known. But if you are in the mood to snuggle close to your dining companion
and listen to some live jazz, this is a fine choice. At first glance, you might
mistake it for a trendy, overpriced Westside restaurant. However, the open
kitchen turning out French cuisine, Impressionist paintings on the walls,
hand-painted plates, rattan chairs, and cozy lighting create a serene, tender
setting. After 9pm, the partition separating the jazz lounge from the main
restaurant is removed, so diners can linger after eating and enjoy the performance. Your imaginations will soar as you listen to the music. It's also
possible to come just for cocktails or dessert. While enjoying the delicious
French delicacies, you will be able to view the stage. Or you can reserve a
table in the jazz lounge and order a snack there.
$$$ *AE, DC, DIS, MC, V; checks OK; lunch Mon–Fri, dinner Tues–Sat; full
bar; reservations recommended; www.lunariajazzsing.com.* &

---

# MASTRO'S
◐◐

*246 N Canon Dr, Beverly Hills / 310/888-8782*
For the ultimate in Rat Pack cool, visit this wonderfully retro steakhouse,
where portions are large and the music (from Sinatra-era songs to old-fash-
ioned takes on contemporary hits) is hip. There's live music most evenings
in the upstairs dining room, and couples will want to reserve a table by the
window for a view down to the streets of Beverly Hills. For the amorous
sweethearts, table #317 in the corner is the place to be, right up against the
floor-to-ceiling windows. Or request a table in either of the wine rooms,
with a view of the glassed-in treasures from the large list. Lighting is dim
and pleasing, walls are of stacked stone, and a picture of Frank, Dino, and
Sammy hangs behind the bar. Everything, from the hand-cut USDA prime
served with the bone to the spinach side dish, packs heavy garlic, so make
sure both of you indulge. Starters like a potent Caesar salad with optional
anchovies and plump crab cakes are delicious. For the main course, steaks—
from a small filet mignon to an enormous porterhouse—are the draw here,
but there's also a selection of beautifully prepared fresh fish.
$$$$ *AE, DC, DIS, MC, V; no checks; lunch Mon–Fri, dinner every day; full
bar; reservations recommended; www.mastrossteakhouse.com.* &

## MORELS
♥♥

*6301 W 3rd St, Los Angeles / 323/965-9595*
Tucked in The Grove shopping center, Morels is a French bistro downstairs and an American steakhouse upstairs. The best bet for a truly romantic night out is to sit upstairs, in the bungalow on the veranda. It's a quiet little corner set off from the rest of the tables where the two of you can enjoy a succulent steak or fresh seafood. Walk to the corner of the veranda and you can watch the dancing waters in the parklike area down below. Otherwise, request a table in the glass-enclosed private dining room, available when not reserved for a function. Downstairs, lovers can dine on sandwiches, quiche, and salads on the patio and watch the crowds come and go. Don't neglect the cheese course, available wherever you choose to sit, overseen and served by a well-informed fromager and offered with bread and fruit. Though Morels is in the center of town, you'll feel like you're far, far away. After a glass of French wine or maybe a martini, you'll be convinced you're in a Parisian bistro.
*$$ AE, DC, DIS, MC, V; no checks; lunch, dinner every day; full bar; reservations recommended; www.thegrovela.com.* &

## OFF VINE
♥♥

*6263 Leland Wy, Hollywood / 323/962-1900*
You'd never know you're in the heart of Hollywood once you set foot inside Off Vine. Just blocks from the grit of Hollywood street life, this gem is all but hidden from view. A romantic oasis, it offers both indoor and outdoor seating in a small restored Arts and Crafts–style cottage with a lushly landscaped exterior. (Since old homes with hardwood floors don't make for good acoustics, the patio area is a beautiful way to avoid the noise.) Though it's not always open, the upstairs dining room provides a far more intimate setting for trysting. The well-worn wood floors show that many people have passed through here over the years, perhaps just on a first date. The whitewashed walls are punctuated with original artwork, and big, open windows look out to the flower beds and allow the sun to stream in. The style of the cuisine matches the atmosphere. You can choose from a variety of creative pastas, house-made soups, salads, and daily seafood specials. Make sure you order the house specialty, chocolate soufflé, for a decadent finale at this one-of-a-kind Hollywood hideaway.
*$$ AE, DC, DIS, MC, V; no checks; lunch Mon–Fri, dinner every day, brunch Sat–Sun; beer and wine; reservations recommended.* &

## PATINA
✦✦✦✦

*141 S Grand Ave, Los Angeles / 213/972 3331*

When you and your beloved are doing a big night out with an elegant dinner and a concert at the Walt Disney Concert Hall, there's no more romantic spot to dine than this wonderful restaurant manned by master chef Joachim Splichal. Wolfgang Puck may be more famous, but Splichal is widely considered the finest chef in Los Angeles, and his Patina, newly relocated to the ground floor of this impressive music venue in the heart of downtown, supplies the perfect showcase for his talents. Lovers will appreciate the warm, inviting interior, created by architect Hagy Belzberg, featuring walls of undulating walnut. Tables are well spaced, affording privacy (a couple of private dining rooms are available for groups or truly intimate dinners). The menu reflects Splichal's pioneering work in elevating California cuisine to world-class levels. Menus are driven by seasonal ingredients, but alluring selections like sautéed blue prawns with creamy polenta or pheasant with apple-champagne sauerkraut win praise. The superior cheese selection, presented tableside on an elegant cart by the house fromager, is a dream for cheese lovers. The stunning wine list, assembled over the many years of Patina's existence, ensures that you'll have the perfect bottle to complement your meal. Even if you don't make a reservation for dinner, stop in before or after the show for a drink to see this grand dining establishment.

*$$$$ AE, DC, DIS, MC, V; no checks; lunch Mon–Fri, dinner every day; full bar; reservations recommended; www.patinagroup.com.* ♿

## PEARL RESTAURANT & NIGHT CLUB
✦✦

*665 N Robertson Blvd, West Hollywood / 310/358-9191*

Los Angeles has year-round fantastic weather, but few places take advantage of that with large outdoor areas. Come to Pearl (in the space that once housed Moomba and, before that, Luna Park), and you and your sweetie can definitely dine alfresco for a romantic evening under the stars. Large ficus trees separate the patio from the street, and white pleather booths offer comfy seating. Inside, too, can be romantic, as a long, gauzy curtain separates the dining area from the bar. Best of all, if available, are the tables in the semiprivate VIP lounge. These have curtains that open and close at the push of a button, offering maximum privacy. One other pleasing option is a seat by the glassed-in wine cellar. The menu celebrates Americana, with steaks, chops, and great fresh seafood, including signature crab cakes that would please a Maryland native. Ask the sommelier to guide you through the choices on the extensive list or opt for a classic cocktail from the bar. Be sure to dress up, as this place draws a fashionable crowd, both for dinner and the nightly live music.

*$$$ AE, DIS, MC, V; no checks; dinner Mon–Sat; full bar; reservations recommended; www.pearl90069.com.* ♿

## SONA RESTAURANT
●●●●

*401 N La Cienega Blvd, West Hollywood / 310/659-7708*

When the evening calls for a gourmet meal and quiet conversation with the one you love, book a table at this romantic gem. Chef-owner David Myers and his pastry chef wife and partner, Michelle Myers, opened this place to enormous critical acclaim, overcoming whatever bad luck or chi had seemingly cursed previous inhabitants of this restaurant space. The room is understated—no art on the walls, no loud music, no bright colors—as it's all about the food; Michelle designed the minimalist space, from its earth-tone palette to the waiters' charcoal gray suits, to serve as a setting for whatever comes out of the kitchen. Call it modern French or, as they prefer, "seasonally spontaneous" cuisine. Both David and Michelle are artists, and it shows in each and every dish—and in the dishes themselves, which change in shape and size with every course. Couples in search of an outstanding meal should put themselves in the chef's hands and go for one of the multicourse tasting menus, which might include sweetbreads on macaroni or confit of wild Scottish salmon. Wine is elevated to an art form here, too, and bottles are opened and decanted on a 6-ton granite sculpture in the center of the room. Be sure and save room for dessert, as Michelle's creations—like Austrian pulled strudel with black beer ice cream—are the best in town.

*$$$$ AE, DC, DIS, MC, V; no checks; dinner Tues–Sat; full bar; reservations recommended; www.sonarestaurant.com.* ♿

## SUNSET LOUNGE
●●

*9641 Sunset Blvd (Beverly Hills Hotel), Beverly Hills / 310/276-2251*

The Beverly Hills Hotel (see Romantic Lodgings) is a Los Angeles landmark that harks back to the glamorous days of Hollywood. Located adjacent to the lobby, the Sunset Lounge greets you with the sound of live harp music as you're seated in comfortable salmon-colored velvet chairs. Afternoon tea is an ideal way to enjoy this rarefied atmosphere, and at a reasonable cost. A delicious assortment of tea sandwiches, scones, and fruit tarts and truffles accompanies aromatic teas served in Wedgwood china cups. The service is attentive but unobtrusive. This is the perfect way to spend a cozy, intimate afternoon in beautiful surroundings with the one you love.

*$$ AE, DC, DIS, MC, V; no checks; afternoon tea every day; full bar; reservations recommended; www.beverlyhillshotel.com.* ♿

## TABLE 8

*7661 Melrose Ave, Los Angeles / 323/782-8258*
Govind Armstrong has been a chef to watch for years, having started in
Wolfgang Puck's kitchen at the tender age of 13. Today, he has his own
romantic Melrose bôite, which attracts couples in search of a beautiful
room, attentive service, and inventive cuisine. The lighting is dim, and the
mood is set by brasserie-style hanging lamps at this intimate eatery. Tables
are mostly close together, but that doesn't make the mood any less romantic.
Ask for a booth on the wall and order such specialties as Armstrong's signature Kobe beef hanger steak with pea tendrils, or king salmon with charred
escarole. If you can, arrive early and grab a cocktail in the small lounge to
the side of the bar, and you can curl up on oversized chairs while you imbibe
and enjoy the soothing surroundings. For extra privacy, reserve a table in
the tented off, semiprivate area by the entrance.
*$$$ AE, DC, DIS, MC, V; no checks; dinner Mon–Sat; full bar; reservations
recommended; www.table8la.com.* &

## YAMASHIRO'S

*1999 N Sycamore Ave, Hollywood / 323/466-5125*
Yamashiro's (meaning "mountain palace") is a replica of a 600-year-old
pagoda from Kyoto perched on a hill in Hollywood, overlooking the city.
Couples can wind up the narrow road to this hillside perch for an evening
of Asian dining amid a setting that offers breathtaking panoramas. After
you sup on sushi and Asian specialties with your special someone, meander
around the 8 acres of sculptured Japanese gardens for a truly romantic
moonlight stroll. A glass-enclosed bar area offers one of the best vantage
points in town to enjoy the city lights. While Yamashiro's may not serve the
best food in the City of Angels, it's a great place to rendezvous for drinks.
*$$ AE, DC, DIS, MC, V; no checks; dinner every day; full bar; reservations
recommended; www.yamashirorestaurant.com.* &

## ZEN GRILL & SAKE LOUNGE

*1051 Broxton Ave, Westwood / 310/209-1994*
Dark, sexy, and very romantic is the look of this Asian eatery. It's a soaring
space, with a red-carpeted staircase that sweeps up to the quieter second
level. And it's mysterious and seductive on every level, from the "honey-
comb" ceiling with recessed lighting to the black leather banquettes and
Buddha paintings on the walls. Attractive servers sport black tunics, and
sensual textures are everywhere, from the rough-hewn tables to the wine
list, featuring Chinese characters embossed on black leather. Trippy music
sets a certain mood, and it's enhanced by dozens of flickering candles

scattered throughout the cavernous space. Food is a sort of Asian greatest hits, from silky sashimi and satay to phad Thai and spicy soups, with many sexy finger foods among the offerings. There's no hard liquor, but plenty of wine, beer, and sake (more than 75 labels of the latter), as well as cocktails crafted from *shochu*, an Asian lower-proof version of vodka. Sit upstairs, away from the crowds, or at the bar, under a wall of oversized sake bottles, for maximum romantic potential.

$$ *AE, DC, MC, V; no checks; lunch Mon–Fri, dinner every day; beer, wine, and sake; reservations recommended.* ᘓ

# PASADENA AND THE VALLEYS

## ROMANTIC HIGHLIGHTS

Set in the foothills of the San Gabriel Mountains just "over the hill" from Los Angeles and Hollywood, Pasadena and the Valleys (San Fernando and San Gabriel) were once rural regions made up of orange, lemon, and walnut groves and ranches. Today the farms have long since been replaced with largely residential communities, but this scenic area still boasts vast expanses of picturesque countryside, from the hiking paths of Angeles Crest National Forest to equestrian trails in the neighboring foothills. Couples, however, are most often lured to the region's crown jewel: Pasadena. This oasis of style and culture features a beautifully restored historic district, elaborate Victorian mansions, Craftsman-style bungalows, and a sophisticated society with theater, museums, and elegant gardens.

Most of this region's romantic options are found in Pasadena. Perhaps the city's most popular draw is **Old Town** (626/666-4156; www.oldpasadena .com). Bordered by Marengo Avenue on the east, Pasadena Avenue on the west, Holly Street on the north, and Green Street on the south, this 22-block stretch of shops, restaurants, cafes, art galleries, and movie theaters is set in restored buildings from the late 1800s. Start the day with a quick breakfast at **Goldstein's Bagel Bakery** (82 W Colorado Blvd; 626/792-2435), where the two of you can choose from more than 50 different kinds of freshly baked bagels at this Old Town landmark. Then stroll through this bustling district, stopping to browse in such stores as Banana Republic, Crate & Barrel, Sur La Table, and J. Crew. To the east of this historic area, there are more shopping possibilities at **Paseo Colorado** (280 E Colorado Blvd; 626/795-8891), which includes 65 shops, restaurants, and movie theaters.

Just west of Old Town, art lovers will appreciate the vast collection of impressionist works by the likes of van Gogh, Renoir, Degas, and Monet at the **Norton Simon Museum** (411 W Colorado Blvd; 626/449-6840;

www.nortonsimon.org). A lovely rear garden with sculptures by Henry Moore and Barbara Hepworth is a romantic place to rest your feet after gazing at the masterpieces inside. To the east, couples can get a taste of the Far East with a tour of the **Pacific Asia Museum** (46 N Los Robles Ave; 626/449-2742; www.pacificasiamuseum.org), complete with Asian-inspired art, Chinese-style gardens, and koi pond.

Pasadena has hundreds of antique shops for couples who love to search out vintage treasures. Some of the best finds can be had at the **Rose Bowl Flea Market** (1001 Rose Bowl Dr; 626/577-3100; www.rgcshows.com/rose bowl.asp), held the second Sunday of each month at the stadium that also hosts the city's annual January 1 football rivalry. Sure, this gigantic flea market has its fair share of junk, but an antiques annex on the stadium's outer periphery has treasures just waiting to be discovered. However, arrive early so you can beat the antiques dealers who also regularly scour this monthly show.

After an inspired look at period furnishings and accessories at the Rose Bowl, head over to the **Gamble House** (4 Westmoreland Pl; 626/793-3344; www.gamblehouse.usc.edu) for a tour of this Arts and Crafts–style design masterwork. Open for tours, this former home of David and Mary Gamble (heirs to the Procter & Gamble fortune) was built in 1908 by Charles and Henry Greene, and today is an architectural showpiece, known for its craftsmanship and detailed design. You and your betrothed will swoon at the teak woodwork, Tiffany glass and furniture, carpets, light fixtures, and hardware, all custom-designed for the house. It's a great spot to get some fantasy decorating ideas for your own home—or the home you are dreaming about.

The Gamble House isn't the area's only beautiful home. Couples can spend a leisurely afternoon just driving around the posh residential neighborhoods of Pasadena, San Marino, and Arcadia, admiring the Victorian homes and restored Craftsman-style bungalows, many of which were built in the early 1900s for wealthy East Coasters looking to escape harsh winters. These settlers came to enjoy the warm climate and picturesque surroundings of this beautiful Southern California region, just like couples do today.

Lovers who want to get out and enjoy the scenery can take a romantic drive through **Angeles Crest National Forest.** Take Interstate 210 north to the Angeles Crest Highway; follow the highway as it takes a dramatic spin through the Angeles National Forest. As you follow its tendril-like course, each bend in the road exposes an abrupt change in the perspective and dynamics of the landscape. One curve may reveal a deep ravine framed by perilous mountain peaks, while another manifests a procession of massive golden hills weaving their way to eternity. Imagine the fervor you'll feel in the midst of these constant scenic transformations. Your oohs and aahs will be echoed by the smiling person sitting next to you.

Did you remember to bring a basket of goodies? Picnic-planning twosomes can pick up a bottle of wine, a freshly made sandwich, and gourmet snacks at **Pasadena Wine Merchants** (906 Granite Dr; 626/396-9234) or **Village Gourmet** (4357 Tujunga Ave; 818/487-3807) in Studio City. Indeed, mountain picnics have a flavor all their own. The combination of altitude, fresh air, lofty pinery, and stupendous views whet the appetite and the heart. One possible place to spread out a blanket for an afternoon repast is **Charlton Flats** (from Interstate 210 in La Canada, travel north on Angeles Crest Highway for 23 miles), which is set 5,300 feet straight up from sea level. Even during the weekends, this area receives few visitors, so you'll have plenty of privacy to enjoy the food and scenery and to sneak in a few good kisses.

Equestrian-friendly couples can enjoy the beauty of the San Fernando Valley from the saddle with a guided trail tour courtesy of **Bar S Stable** (1850 Riverside Dr; 818/242-8443). Couples can climb onboard one of the stable's quarter horses and take a ride through the northern trails of **Griffith Park** (4730 Crystal Springs Rd; 323/913-4688). If moonlight, margaritas, and horseback seem alluring, a sunset ride that stops at **Viva Fresh Mexican Restaurant** (9000 Riverside Dr; 818/845-2425) for a dinner break beats the heck out of the standard dinner-and-a-movie date night. Or simply just drive into the hills of Griffith Park and find a lookout spot to gaze at the twinkling lights of the city below. It's the perfect spot to steal a kiss or two while enjoying this scenic Los Angeles–area region.

## Access and Information

Located just north of Los Angeles, Pasadena and the Valleys can be accessed from the 101 Freeway, which transitions into the 134 Freeway and the 210 Freeway as it travels east. From the 101 Freeway, you can take Interstate 5 into the north San Fernando Valley, as well as the 170 Freeway, which eventually merges into Interstate 5. In the West Valley, the 405 Freeway serves as the north-south artery. From downtown Los Angeles, the 110 Freeway heads north into Pasadena.

Formerly known as Burbank-Glendale-Pasadena Airport, **Bob Hope Airport** (2627 N Hollywood Wy, Burbank; 818/840-8840 or 800/U-FLY-BUR; www.burbankairport.com) is the area's most convenient airport, and nearby **Los Angeles International Airport (LAX)** (310/646-5252; www.lawa .org) offers travelers more flight options. While the **Metropolitan Transit Authority (MTA)** 800/266-6882; www.mta.net) runs a network of buses and the L.A. subway system, there's nothing like taking a bus to kill an amorous mood, and unfortunately the subway doesn't seem to go anywhere you want to be.

For more information about Pasadena, contact the **Pasadena Convention & Visitors Bureau** (171 S Los Robles Ave; 626/795-9311; www.pasadena cal.com).

# Romantic Lodgings

## ARTISTS' INN & COTTAGE BED & BREAKFAST

❤️🍸

*1038 Magnolia St, Pasadena / 626/799-5668 or 888/799-5668*

An 1895 Victorian farmhouse and neighboring 1909 home form this beautifully and artistically restored inn, complete with flourishing rose garden and white picket fence. Each of the nine guest rooms has its own muse—with a particular artist or artistic period—that is reflected in the decor. For instance, the Van Gogh Room has been outfitted to replicate the tormented master's painting of his own bedroom, while the Expressionist Suite wears the bold, pure colors found in the works of Matisse, Picasso, and Dufy. Couples may want to check in to the Degas Suite, a soft-blue haven with a king-sized canopy bed, a sitting area, and such romantic accoutrements as a fireplace and a whirlpool tub for two. One of five rooms housed in the 1909 cottage, this grand suite is the inn's largest accommodations. B&B traditionalists, however, will enjoy the eighteenth-century English Room, outfitted in frills and cabbage roses. All rooms have telephones and private baths, some with lovely period fixtures. Rooms are also stocked with port wine, so couples can enjoy an after-dinner drink and chocolates in the privacy of their suite. The inn's public rooms are adorned with well-chosen antiques, original art, rich fabrics, and luxurious Oriental rugs. A generous full breakfast is served every morning, and tea and home-baked sweets every afternoon, both of which can be enjoyed on the inn's old-fashioned porch overlooking the blooming gardens. It's a great place to spend a special moment with your special someone on a sunny day. $$–$$$ AE, MC, V; no checks; www.artistsinns.com.

## THE BISSELL HOUSE BED & BREAKFAST

❤️❤️

*201 Orange Grove Ave, South Pasadena / 626/441-3535 or 800/441-3530*

The former home of Anna Bissell McCay (the Bissell vacuum heir), this three-story Victorian mansion on Pasadena's Millionaire's Row is set on a half-acre lot surrounded by 40-foot hedges that keep the world (and the street traffic noise) at bay. Hosts Russell and Leonore Butcher welcome couples to this elegant home, with its mahogany floors, antique-filled rooms, and sweeping veranda. Fresh fruit and flowers await lovers in each of the six guest rooms. All have been individually decorated in a frilly English style and have private bathrooms. With no TVs or phones to intrude, your stay here can be all about enjoying private time with that special someone. The Garden Room is utterly romantic, with an antique, hand-carved queen-sized bed; floral chintz decor; and whirlpool tub for two. The Morning Glory Room, decorated in china blue and white, and the Prince Albert Room, with its double-corner leaded-glass window, boast claw-footed tubs. Gabled ceilings and tall windows that look out onto the exclusive neighborhood make the Rose Room an ideal spot for snuggling up with the one you love. In the mornings, lovers can indulge in a full breakfast, plus afternoon tea and all-day wine and beverages. If the two of you can pull yourselves away from the creative comforts provided within, a small unheated pool and spa sits just behind the house.

$$–$$$ *AE, MC, V; no checks; www.bissellhouse.com.*

## THE GRACIELA
🌹🌹

*322 N Pass Ave, Burbank / 818/842-8887 or 888/956-1900*

This plush boutique hotel is one of the San Fernando Valley's best-kept secrets and provides couples with a quiet retreat in the Burbank Media District, near the Burbank Airport. While many of the guests here are business travelers, the cozy hotel is far from a generic corporate lodging. Its surprisingly luxurious guest rooms decorated with peach hues and warm wood tones provide a perfect lovers' getaway, with such elegant appointments as Italian linens with down duvets, marble bathrooms with oversized tubs, and DVD/CD players for when the two of you want to snuggle up for movies or music. Since the property caters to longer-staying guests, 60 percent of its 100-plus rooms feature kitchenettes, and while there's no on-site restaurant, room service is available if you want someone else to whip you up a midnight snack. The lobby area features a Library Lounge and a full bar for when sweethearts want to linger over a nightcap before returning to their room. A daily afternoon high tea provides a perfect midday respite (though the two of you will need to make a reservation). The lushly landscaped rooftop sundeck is the ideal backdrop for a little sunbathing or soaking under the stars in the Jacuzzi. On a clear night, lovers may even spy the twinkling lights of Hollywood in the distance.

$$$ *AE, DIS, DC, MC, V; no checks; www.thegraciela.com.* ♿

## HILTON UNIVERSAL CITY & TOWERS
🌹

*555 Universal Hollywood Dr, Universal City / 818/506-2500 or 800/ HILTONS*

Location, location, location is the selling point of this hilltop high-rise location just across the street from Universal Studios. Couples who want a convenient place to stay while visiting the theme park and its adjacent shopping and restaurant-filled promenade, Universal CityWalk, will want to reserve a room in this 24-story glass hotel. But be warned: It's perpetually bustling, and there's no real reason to hang out in the busy lobby, though its all-about-glass construction allows views of garden-filled courtyards with trickling fountains from virtually every angle. Still, lovers can find a quiet reprieve in their oversized guest room—decorated in warm tones of

burgundy and green and affording great views of the surrounding hills—or splurge on a room on the club-level Tower Floors, which offer concierge service, a private lounge with complimentary snacks, and excellent views. While evenings might be best spent ordering 'round-the-clock room service and snuggling in your room, there's a lobby lounge where the two of you can listen to live piano music and sip cappuccinos or cocktails, and an all-day cafe-style restaurant just off the lobby serves California-style cuisine. Before heading to the park in the morning, lovebirds can take a dip in the pool or work up a sweat in the exercise room, then board the complimentary tram to the park. An on-site Avis car-rental desk is available for when the two of you want to venture down the hill and explore the surrounding areas of Hollywood, the Valley, and nearby Pasadena.
$$$ *AE, DC, DIS, MC, V; checks OK; www.hilton.com.* &

## THE RITZ-CARLTON HUNTINGTON HOTEL & SPA
❂❂❂❹

*1401 S Oak Knoll Ave, Pasadena / 626/568-3900 or 800/241-3333*
Set on 23 luxuriant acres in the San Gabriel foothills is one of Southern California's most stunning resorts, brimming with romantic possibilities. Originally built in 1906, then reconstructed and reopened as a Ritz-Carlton, it's the kind of place where once you check in, there's no reason to leave. Despite a wealth of modern luxury comforts—including a state-of-the-art 12,000-square-foot spa, salon, and fitness center with signature kur (mud-and-mineral based) body treatments, virtual-reality equipment, and eucalyptus steam—the spectacular grounds retain a timeless charm. Couples can stroll hand-in-hand through the alluring Horseshoe and Japanese Gardens or take a moment to contemplate love as they cross the impeccably restored, rare covered Picture Bridge. While the lure of lounging by the Olympic-sized pool (California's first ever) may sound relaxing, it's hard to leave any of the inviting 418 guest rooms and suites, each gorgeously outfitted in a traditional style that's softened by ultra-pretty English garden textiles and a wonderful palette of celadon, cream, and butter yellow. Indeed, beautifully made feather beds dressed in Frette linens, CD players, big marble baths, and plush terry robes create a truly seductive setting. Couples who want to hole away in their room for the course of their entire stay may want to check into the Club Level, which features five food and beverage presentations in the Club lounge throughout the course of the day—from breakfast and afternoon tea to cordials and after-dinner drinks. However, the promise of a memorable meal in the elegant Dining Room (see Romantic Restaurants) may tempt lovebirds into dressing for dinner. An elegant high tea and alfresco dining in The Terrace are also noteworthy. By the end of your stay, you'll feel so pampered, you'll find it hard to leave.
$$$ *AE, DC, DIS, MC, V; checks OK; www.ritzcarlton.com.* &

# Ogre-the-Top Romance

Sweethearts looking for a unique getaway can check into the **Shrek Honeymoon Suite at the Universal Sheraton** (333 Universal Hollywood Dr; 818/980-1212 or 800/325-3535; www.sheraton.com). A hand-painted heart-shaped doorway serves as the gateway to this forest-like fantasy suite that was designed to resemble the big green ogre's home in the animated film. Inside, sweethearts can chill out and slumber on a king-sized canopy bed decorated with moss and vines and outfitted with green sheets. A breakfast table fashioned from hearty twigs serves as the perfect place for a morning meal à deux, though the two of you will be joined by giant renderings of Shrek, Princess Fiona, and Donkey peeking in through a window. Couples can raise ogre-green flutes (filled with champagne or green punch) and make a toast to Shrek and Princess Fiona's love when they arrive at this romantic hideaway.

Then, take the quick walk over to nearby **Universal Studios Hollywood** (1000 Universal Center Dr; 818/508-9600; www.universalstudios.com) to experience the theme park's "Shrek 4-D" attraction, which takes visitors into Shrek's world with a 12-minute interactive film experience complete with 3-D Ogrevision glasses and 4-D effects, such as theater seats that move during action sequences. Afterward, tour the rest of the park, visiting such attractions as Jurassic Park—The Ride, Terminator 2: 3D, and Revenge of the Mummy—The Ride, before returning to the suite for a night in the faux forest.

Back at the suite, the emerald-colored bathroom features green monogrammed towels, green soap, and environmentally friendly mud bath packets so the two of you can bathe like our big, green hero. And, at turndown, gingerbread cookies are served to finish the Shrekkie day on a sweet note. The whole experience is sure to make other couples green with envy.

—BONNIE STEELE

## SPORTSMEN'S LODGE HOTEL
❂❹
*12825 Ventura Blvd, Studio City / 818/769-4700 or 800/821-8511*
You never know where you'll find an alluring setting worthy of romance, and this San Fernando Valley landmark is a perfect example. While this 200-room hotel is really an upgraded California-style motel, with exterior hallways and an Astroturf deck around the Olympic-sized pool and whirlpool spa, it also boasts lush grounds—with waterfalls, wooden bridges, and a koi-filled lagoon with resident swans—where lovers can gaze into each other's eyes among the foliage. Sure, there's a retro-kitsch element, as this

hotel has been around for more than 50 years, but spacious rooms decorated in country-Colonial style in mauves and blues provide a perfectly comfortable setting for a little getaway. Studio suites even offer extra space for lovers to spread out and make themselves at home. Free shuttle service to and from Universal Studios as well as the Burbank Airport make this a good home base for sightseeing, and an on-site Enterprise car rental desk means that you can avoid crowded airport counters. Food and beverage facilities include a coffee shop, a bar and grill, and a publike lobby bar. There's an exercise room for when the two of you want to work up a sweat, and a petité salon that offers hair, nail, and facial treatments for when you want to look your best for your traveling companion.
$$ *AE, DC, DIS, MC, V; checks OK; www.slhotel.com.* &

# Romantic Restaurants

## BISTRO 45
♥♥

*45 S Mentor Ave, Pasadena / 626/795-2478*
Set on a side street off the beaten path, this stylish bistro offers couples a cool and decadent art-deco-at-the-end-of-the-decade look. Known for its impressive wine list—regularly named one of the top restaurants in L.A. by *Wine Spectator*—Bistro 45 serves up an equally impressive menu of California cuisine, and it changes often. On any given day, couples might enjoy such pleasures as phyllo-wrapped duck confit, an almost-too-beautiful-to-eat Napoleon of scallops and rock shrimp, seared Hawaiian swordfish, and grilled rack of lamb with goat cheese–stuffed zucchini blossoms. Desserts are a major temptation here, especially the chocolate espresso praline cake with cocoa-bean ice cream. More than 20 wines by the glass and plenty of half-bottle choices give wine-lovers a fine selection. Bistro 45 also regularly hosts connoisseur wine dinners, generally built around a particular winery and often attended by the winemakers, which makes for a special night. Couples who want to dine under the stars can feel safe knowing that the outdoor terrace also boasts a retractable roof.
$$ *AE, DC, MC, V; no checks; lunch Tues–Fri, dinner Tues–Sun; full bar; reservations required; www.bistro45.com.* &

## THE BISTRO GARDEN AT COLDWATER
♥♥

*12950 Ventura Blvd, Studio City / 818/501-0202*
Set in a formal European winter garden with skylights, latticework, and ficus trees, the Bistro Garden's dining room oozes romance. Arrive early and you and your significant other can sip martinis in the mahogany bar area, while a piano player makes beautiful music in the background. Although

the menu sticks to the classics, such as French onion soup au gratin, roast rack of lamb with rosemary jus, and filet mignon with three-peppercorn sauce, lovers with a taste for something more modern can sample such selections as the sesame-crusted salmon with soy and wasabi, or chicken curry with mango chutney, chopped bananas, almonds, and shredded coconut. The menu changes with the seasons, but one thing remains a Bistro Garden standard: the decadent chocolate soufflé, baked to order and served with mounds of freshly whipped cream. It's as sweet and rewarding as true love. For couples who'd rather stay in for a night of romance at home, BG to Go, located just next door, offers a fine selection of take-out food; you can also opt to dine in this casual cafe. Open for lunch and dinner every day (and breakfast on weekends), BG to Go offers an enticing selection of fresh soups, salads, sandwiches, pastas, and entrees like rotisserie chicken or poached salmon.
*$$$ AE, DC, MC, V; no checks; lunch Mon–Fri, dinner every day; full bar; reservations recommended; www.bistrogarden.com.* ⅃

## CELESTINO RISTORANTE
🖉🖉🖉

*141 S Lake Ave, Pasadena / 626/795-4006*
Whether you have fond memories of a trip together to Italy or are just dreaming of Italian romance, Celestino Ristorante is the next best thing to being there. The creation of chef Celestino Drago, L.A.'s impresario of Italian cooking, and now owned and run by his brother Calogero, this light and casual cafe serves such regional dishes as Sicilian fish tart with bell-pepper sauce; homemade ravioli stuffed with artichokes, sautéed cherry tomatoes, and shrimp; and salt-encrusted whole striped bass. The menu changes with the seasons, and couples may want to share several selections to sample from this enticing and always satisfying menu. (Think pasta for two, just like *Lady and the Tramp.*) Winemaker dinners, featuring a selection of food and wine pairings, provide the perfect backdrop for a romantic outing, and a four-course prix-fixe menu lets lovebirds indulge without breaking the bank.
*$$ AE, MC, V; no checks; lunch Mon–Fri, dinner Mon–Sat; full bar; reservations recommended; www.celestinopasadena.com.* ⅃

## DELACEY'S CLUB 41
🖉🖉

*41 S DeLacey St, Pasadena / 626/795-4141*
When it's a guy's turn to choose where to dine, DeLacey's may be his pick; it's one of the most comfortable steakhouses around. It's a handsome establishment fashioned after a turn-of-the-century San Francisco chophouse—heavy with wood, glass, and brass—despite the fact that it's only been around since the late 1980s. Spacious booths offer affectionate

couples a place to gaze deep into each other's eyes over oysters Rockefeller, steamed littleneck clams for two, or a perfect Caesar salad. The menu is classic, featuring such Atkins-friendly fare as grilled rib-eye steaks, double-loin lamb chops, prime rib served as rare as you want, and garlicky shrimp scampi. Couples can even make the ultimate carnivore statement by ordering chateaubriand à deux. Grilled sand dabs, spinach salad, and a selection of pastas are also offered for lovebirds who want to save room for such desserts as DeLacey's signature chocolate mousse pie and homemade apple pie. On Friday and Saturday evenings, boogie away the calories with the live entertainment.

$$ *AE, DC, DIS, MC, V; no checks; lunch, dinner every day; full bar; reservations recommended; wwwdelaceysclub41.com.* &

## THE DINING ROOM AT THE RITZ-CARLTON HUNTINGTON HOTEL & SPA
🕭🕭🕭

*1401 S Oak Knoll Ave, Pasadena / 626/577-2867*
If you can't feel the passion in this gorgeous flower-bedecked room in the Ritz-Carlton Huntington Hotel & Spa (see Romantic Lodgings), you won't feel it anywhere. As a pianist plays dreamy standards and show tunes in the background, couples take in the beautiful surroundings of this elegant hotel restaurant, with its wood-paneled walls, crystal sconces, seascape paintings, and a collection of antique carved ships. Amid the refined setting, chef de cuisine Craig Strong serves polished American fare with flair. Couples will find dinner here to be more like a grand romantic gesture than just a meal. It's hard to imagine anything more delicious than a starter of diver scallops and foie gras with artichokes and black truffles. However, main courses such as poached lobster with bok choy, penne, and orange curry sauce or veal brisket with sweetbread schnitzel are equally as memorable. Dessert starts with *la sorpesa*, a predessert teaser compliments of the chef, followed by such innovative sweet treats as candied apple soup served with apple jelly beignet and apple cider ice cream, or warm carrot cake with a liquid center of cream cheese and white chocolate served with fresh ginger ice cream. An impressive wine list of more than 350 vintages ensures the perfect bottle to complement an evening of romance.

$$$$ *AE, DC, DIS, MC, V; no checks; dinner every day; full bar; reservations required; www.ritzcarlton.com.* &

## FIREFLY
🕭🕭🕭

*11720 Ventura Blvd, Studio City / 818/762-1833*
There may be no sign and a velvet rope out front of this vine-covered hot spot, but once you get past the pretentious exterior (and the doorman), this chic little eatery has all the makings for romance. Soft plush sofas, red

walls, book-lined shelves, and cozy dark corners make the cocktail lounge a seductive setting to sip apple martinis and watch the hip crowd. The dining room is actually an open-air covered patio lit by sconces and dozens of flickering candles. A chalet-style fire pit serves as the room's centerpiece, and bungalow-style seating lines the walls. While the small menu changes seasonally, couples can start with such enticing beginners as endive salad, almond-crusted calamari, or a cheese and charcuterie plate. Main courses run the gamut from a decadent hamburger with pancetta, blue cheese, and avocado to crispy red snapper with lyonnaise potatoes. And for couples who believe in togetherness, there's even a unisex bathroom.

$$ *AE, MC, V; no checks; dinner Mon–Sat; full bar; reservations recommended.* &

## FRESCO RISTORANTE
●

*514 S Brand Blvd, Glendale / 818/247-5541*
Located on a major thoroughfare in Glendale, Fresco offers romance seekers a reasonably priced escape at the end of a hectic day. Inside the unassuming stucco structure, vibrant orange walls are punctuated with Roman columns and archways, and a glass-encased wine cellar creates a feeling of elegance. Although the dining room tables may be a little too close for intimacy, recessed alcoves with tables for two provide privacy and quiet. Tuxedo-clad waiters are attentive and serve Northern Italian dishes with an emphasis on fresh, seasonal ingredients. Risotto is the pride of the menu—especially the *risotto a frutti di mare*—but other restaurant highlights include a delightful, thinly pounded and breaded veal chop with capers, garlic, and lemon in a light white-wine sauce; cannelloni stuffed with veal, spinach, and ricotta; and garlicky Caesar salad for two prepared tableside. Chef-owner Antonio Orlando makes his breads, pastas, gelato, sorbetto, and pastries on the premises. For a perfect finale, try the creamy house-made tiramisu. On Friday and Saturday evenings, the soothing tones of a baby grand piano emanate from a softly lit bar. Request your lover's favorite tune, and the night can only get better.

$$ *AE, DC, DIS, MC, V; no checks; lunch Mon–Fri, dinner Mon–Sat; full bar; reservations recommended; www.frescoristorante.com.* &

## JULIENNE
●●●

*2649 Mission St, San Marino / 626/441-2299*
Run by the mother and daughter team of Susan and Julie Campoy, this quaint little French cafe is an alluring spot for breakfast and lunch. Begin the day with a leisurely breakfast of fluffy omelets, bread pudding French toast, thick and creamy steel-cut oatmeal, and a selection of fresh-baked pastries. For lunch, inventive salads and freshly made soups and

sandwiches served on house-made bread rule. (In fact, even the mayonnaise is made on the premises.) The lovely interior features tile floors, windows shaded with lace, and wall mirrors draped in forest green, and on a beautiful day, the flower-strewn patio is unbeatable. After a long day spent exploring the Huntington Library, a cappuccino with a freshly baked muffin or a thick slice of creamy, light quiche can be a lovely finale. Or stop by the gourmet market to pick up such comfort food as Tuscan meatloaf with spicy tomato chutney, homey chicken pot pies, or corn cilantro chowder to take home for a quiet dinner for two.

$ *AE, MC, V; checks OK; breakfast, lunch Mon–Sat (dinner Wed–Fri during summer); wine only; reservations recommended; www.julienne togo.com.* &

## MISTRAL
❂❂

*13422 Ventura Blvd, Sherman Oaks / 818/981-6650*
Ornate crystal chandeliers, wood-paneled walls, rose-colored mirrors from the 1920s, black-and-white tile flooring, and crisp linen tablecloths give this charming French bistro a warm and authentically Parisian feel that's ideal for a stylish interlude. Owner Henri Abergel, a long-standing Valley restaurateur, attracts romancing couples to his cozy dining room with the promise of authentic steak frites (served au poivre with garlic, parsley, and butter and accompanied by a salad), onion soup gratinée, homemade rabbit pâte, and grilled entrecôte. Start with a glass of wine from the award-winning list of French and California selections at the antique cherry wood bar before grabbing one of the small tables against the wall, so you and yours can sit side-by-side and eat cheek-to-cheek. You'll hear both the patrons and the staff speaking French, creating an air of European romance at this chic and cosmopolitan Valley restaurant, which certainly costs a lot less than airfare for two to France. Order a chocolate soufflé and two forks to finish off your meal.

$$$ *AE, DC, MC, V; no checks; lunch Mon–Fri, dinner Mon–Sat; full bar; reservations recommended; www.mistralrestaurant.com.* &

## PANZANELLA
❂❂❂

*14928 Ventura Blvd, Sherman Oaks / 818/784-4400*
There's nothing like Italian ambience to spark the flames of romance, and such is the case at Panzanella, owned and operated by famed L.A.-area restaurateurs Tanino, Calogero, and Giacomino Drago. This talented trio of brothers first charm diners with their irresistible accents and boundless energy, then proceed to dazzle them with delicious Sicilian cuisine. The hosts treat guests like family, and it's a warm, welcoming family you'd want to be a part of. Reserve a cozy booth at this beautifully lit restaurant, so

the two of you can sit close while you enjoy such starters as the namesake Panzanella salad, mushroom soufflé with truffle fondue cheese sauce, and decadent *burrata*. Main courses include signature pastas like *involtini di melanzane* (spaghetti wrapped in eggplant); black tagliolini tossed with fresh tuna, black olives, Sicilian capers, and caramelized red onions; and delicate sea bass with morels (truly addictive). Warm molten Valrhona chocolate cake or silken *panna cotta* with a glass of moscato is a lovely way to end this authentic Italian meal.

$$ *AE, MC, V; no checks; lunch Mon–Fri, dinner Mon–Sat; full bar; reservations recommended; www.giacominodrago.com.* &

## PINOT BISTRO
◐◐◖

*12969 Ventura Blvd, Studio City / 818/990-0500*
The Valley outpost of Joachim Splichal's Patina empire, this elegant French bistro is considered one of the area's finest, with classic bistro fare served amid a cozy setting. The handsome dark interior, with its wood-paneled walls, checkerboard tile floor, hutches displaying fine French china, and candlelit tables, projects an aura conducive to seduction. The main draw, however, is the enticing cuisine. Start with fresh oysters and kick up that romantic mood a notch. However, onion soup with perfectly caramelized onions in a rich beefy stock, topped with bubbling, golden-brown Gruyère, or potato and artichoke terrine are also pleasing appetizers. While the menu changes with the seasons, the two of you might find such tempting entrées as braised lamb shank with Moroccan minestrone, linguine with shellfish, or seared skate wing with wilted *frisée*. And for waist-watching lovebirds, there are also flavorful lighter choices from the daily spa selections. Ask for a table by the fireplace, and you'll enjoy a great view of the entire room. For dessert, order the chocolate croissant bread pudding with rich bourbon crème anglaise; the sinful dessert is perfect to share.

$$$ *AE, DC, DIS, MC, V; no checks; lunch Mon–Fri, dinner every day; full bar; reservations recommended; www.patinagroup.com.* &

## THE RAYMOND
◐◐◖

*1250 S Fair Oaks Ave, Pasadena / 626/441-3136*
The Raymond is, in its own understated way, one of the most traditionally romantic spots in Southern California—a place that doesn't scream romance but subtly lets it get beneath your skin. With the coziness of a mountain lodge and the intimacy of a petite cafe, it's actually the sort of atmospheric restaurant that makes guys feel rather comfortable—all that nice, dark wood paneling and varnished pine floors in a lovingly restored 1930s Craftsman-style California bungalow (formerly the caretaker's cottage at the Victorian-era Raymond Hotel). It's the kind of place that men who spend

their weekends at Home Depot might like. The food is also special without being overly fussy—Long Island roast duckling with fresh pomegranate and cranberry sauce, soft-shell crab with sliced oranges and toasted almonds, rack of lamb chops with fresh rosemary and garlic, and medallions of beef with Stilton cheese in port-wine cream sauce. Lovers may want to try the pancetta-wrapped figs, picked from trees in the restaurant's gardens. (After all, figs are considered the fruit of love.) Tables are scattered throughout the house and quiet garden, with fireplaces, music, wonderful service, and soft lighting only adding to the romantic ambience. The old-fashioned booths in the front two rooms are probably the best choice for an intimate dinner (you can sit close and cuddle), although there really isn't a bad table in the place.

$$$ *AE, MC, V; checks OK; lunch Tues–Fri, dinner Tues–Sun, brunch Sat–Sun; full bar; reservations recommended; www.theraymond.com.*

## RESTAURANT DEVON
❤❤❤

*109 E Lemon Ave, Monrovia / 626/305-0013*
Set in a trio of storefronts that was a hotel in the early 1900s, this respected eatery is a culinary gem in the midst of suburbia. Owners Richard and Gregory Lukasiewicz have created a neighborhood restaurant that dares to be different, with world-class food, a legendary wine list (think 35 wines by the glass and many half bottles), and a romantic atmosphere that features two softly lit dining rooms with views of the glassed-in wine cellar, as well as a sidewalk patio where you and your special someone can watch the comings and goings of trendy downtown Monrovia. Uncork a bottle of wine, sit back, and enjoy this special place. While the menu changes with the seasons, it might include such starters as steamed black mussels, smoked scallops, and homemade soups, and mainstays like prime dry-aged rib-eye steak and fresh fish make for a memorable main course. Lovers with an adventurous palate will appreciate such unusual fare as pan-roasted bear and caribou. Even the delectable desserts push the envelope—caramelized peach slices with blue cheese ice cream, for instance.

$$$ *AE, DC, MC, V; checks OK; lunch Tues–Fri, dinner Tues–Sun; full bar; reservations recommended; www.restaurantdevon.net.* ♿

## TOURNESOL
❤❤

*13251 Ventura Blvd, Studio City / 818/986-3190*
Named for the sunflower, this French country bistro brings a taste of Provence to the Valley with its authentic Gallic fare and charming European atmosphere. Sunflower yellow walls, high-backed chairs, fine china and stemware, and hand-painted wall murals work together to create an utterly romantic atmosphere where lovers can sample escargots, duck à

l'orange, filet mignon, and bouillabaisse chock-full of fresh fish in a fragrant saffron-chardonnay broth. In between courses, diners are presented with sorbet mounded on a silver spoon to cleanse the palate, an elegant touch that only adds to the overall ambience. During the week, the restaurant offers well-priced specials, like lobster on Mondays and steak on Wednesdays. Whatever the two of you order, save room for the house specialty—chocolate Tournesol—a rich chocolate mousse surrounded by a fan of crisp petals shaped like a sunflower. It's almost too pretty to eat, but go for it.

**$$** *AE, MC, V; no checks; lunch Tues–Fri, dinner Tues–Sun, brunch Sun; full bar; reservations recommended; www.tournesolbistro.com.* &

# CATALINA ISLAND

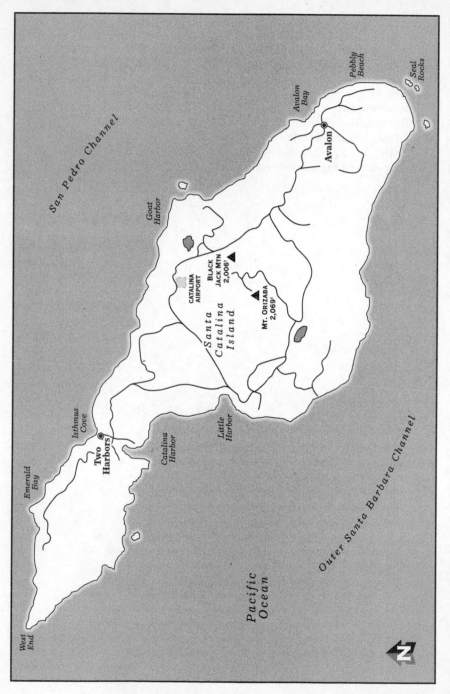

Seal Rocks

Pebbly Beach

Avalon Bay

**Avalon**

San Pedro Channel

Goat Harbor

BLACK JACK MTN 2,006'

CATALINA AIRPORT

MT. ORIZABA 2,069'

*Santa Catalina Island*

Isthmus Cove

**Two Harbors**

Catalina Harbor

Little Harbor

Emerald Bay

West End

*Pacific Ocean*

Outer Santa Barbara Channel

*"A kiss is a course of procedure, cunningly devised, for the mutual stoppage of speech at a moment when words are superfluous."*
—CUPID'S CYCLOPOEDIA

# ♡ CATALINA ISLAND

If you're longing for a romantic island holiday in some relaxing Mediterranean spot like Malta or Capri, take heart: Lovely Santa Catalina Island is located on the same latitude as these faraway gems, and shares many of the same attributes. Bright, sun-filled skies, clean sea air, shimmering azure waters, and friendly locals—it's a seductive recipe for a truly special escape.

Santa Catalina Island is the easternmost of the Channel Islands, a group better known for its five northern members, designated Channel Islands National Park. But Catalina has a more agreeable climate than its sister islands and welcomes visitors by the boatload. While most (86 percent) of the island is strictly protected wilderness, the well-developed town of Avalon makes Catalina the perfect spot where you can enjoy nature in rugged serenity, choose modern comforts, or balance a little of both.

The island was originally inhabited by American Indians, followed by Spanish landowners. In 1919, it was sold to chewing gum magnate and baseball fan William Wrigley Jr. who developed a lifelong love affair with this idyllic retreat and channeled his considerable resources into creating a stylish offshore playground. It was only natural that the island, so close to Hollywood's glamour, would attract celebrities: Cecil B. De Mille, John Wayne, Laurence Olivier, Errol Flynn, and many others were frequent visitors. The biggest names of the Big Band era came over to play the legendary Avalon ballroom in the Casino building, including bandleader Kay Kyser, who performed for a record-breaking crowd of 6,200 dancing fans in 1940.

Today, Catalina is a mecca for outdoor enthusiasts and city-weary solitude seekers, who come to kayak, fish, hike, bike, shop, dine, and breathe in the fresh sea air. Spend your time in charming, historical Avalon. Live out "Gilligan's Island" fantasies in remote Two Harbors. Get to know the unspoiled wilderness of the island's protected interior. Take to the water—

you can scuba dive, snorkel, or just board a glass-bottomed boat—and see the kaleidoscope of sea life teeming beneath the ocean's surface. You'll notice a laid-back island attitude, similar to that in Hawaii, the Caribbean, or anywhere people have better scenery and fewer worries. Take as little or as much time as you can on this offshore jewel; even if the two of you only spend a day, you'll return home refreshed.

# ROMANTIC HIGHLIGHTS

In 1958, the Four Preps sang about Catalina being the island of romance in their classic ballad "Twenty Six Miles (Santa Catalina)." The words ring as true as ever today, as amorous couples seeking an island spark continue to tryst on this speck of land just a few miles—but worlds away—from busy Southern California.

Quaint **Avalon** is the island's only town; it sits in a luxurious amphitheater of green, surrounding busy Avalon Bay, punctuated by clusters of white cottages that house the town's permanent population of around 2,000. Aptly named Crescent Avenue follows the bay's horseshoe curve from the ferry terminal to the landmark art deco Casino building, and all the town's side streets radiate outward. The central portion of Crescent is blocked off for a pedestrian strand; here's where you'll find Avalon's calm, narrow beach and the Green Pleasure Pier, where you can pick up a helpful map at Catalina's Visitor Center. Distances are short in this romantic hamlet and easy to navigate on foot. If you get tired of hoofing it, taxi vans are available, or you can rent bicycles and golf carts along Crescent Avenue steps from the ferry terminal. A great way to escape the crowds is by renting a golf cart then cruising Avalon's narrow hilly streets to find your own perfect viewpoint and sneak a scenic kiss.

Look uphill to the east from the bay, and you'll see two landmark homes. The first is **Holly Hill House**, easily recognized by its Queen Anne frills and prominent striped cupola. It was built in 1888–90 by Peter Gano, who used his blind horse, Mercury, to haul building materials to the site. Legend maintains that Gano lovingly constructed this dream house for his intended bride, who then refused to move to the isolated island and ultimately married another. Gano lived alone in Holly Hill House, never marrying and posting "No Women Allowed" signs at his threshold. The home, listed in the National Register of Historic Places, is privately owned and stands as a sad monument to unrequited passion.

Farther up, on a prime hilltop, sits a home more successfully inhabited by true love. The former Wrigley mansion, now the elegant **Inn on Mount Ada** (see Romantic Lodgings), was named for Mrs. Wrigley when the two were hardly honeymooners (William Wrigley was close to 60 when he purchased the island); they lived out their final years in this lavish home overlooking the harbor. The historic estate is restricted to overnight guests and welcomes a limited number of reservations for breakfast or lunch each day, but you must call ahead. From the house, you can see Avalon's most recognizable landmark: the round, red tile-roofed **Casino**, an elegant art deco masterpiece that houses a still-active movie theater with fabulous vintage murals, as well as a 10th-floor ballroom you can see only by attending a dance event or taking a guided tour. Plan ahead if you want to be a part of the glamorous New Year's Eve celebration in the Casino building's beautiful Avalon ballroom, where nostalgic lovers hold each other close and dance to music of the 1930s, 1940s, and 1950s. At the stroke of midnight, step onto the balcony for a special kiss illuminated only by moonlight's glow on the bay.

The Casino is also home to the tiny—but worthwhile—**Catalina Island Museum** (310/510-2414), which features exhibits on island history and archeology; it also has a contour relief map of the island that helps put it all in perspective. Even the walk to and from the Casino is romantic, as couples stroll hand-in-hand along Via Casino, the waterfront path lined with decorative tiles evoking the heyday of renowned Catalina Island Pottery; vintage original examples adorn the grandiose **Wrigley Memorial** (end of Avalon Canyon Rd; 310/510-2288), a 130-foot-high monument about 1.5 miles from downtown Avalon. The tower's observation deck offers a breathtaking panoramic view across the ocean—as well as plenty of inspiration for a windswept kiss. Wrigley's widow, Ada, personally supervised the botanical gardens that surround the monument, showcasing native plants, many found only on the island.

In 1925, Ada made a gift to the city in the form of the Spanish Moorish–style **Chimes Tower**, high atop Chimes Tower Road across the bay from her home. The mellifluous bells mark each quarter hour and can be rung by hand to commemorate a special event in town. Just below the tower is the adobe-style former home of author Zane Grey, now an inn (Zane Gray Pueblo Hotel; see Romantic Lodgings).

It's difficult to get lost in tiny Avalon, which makes the town perfect for relaxed paramours to explore aimlessly. There's a charming surprise around every corner. Everywhere you'll find the sweet treats that come with seaside vacations, from traditional saltwater taffy pulled in the window of island institution **Lloyd's Confectionary** (315 Crescent Ave; 310/510-7266; www.catalinacandy.com) to **Coldstone Creamery** ice cream shop (120 Sumner Ave; 310/510-8951; www.coldstonecreamery.com). Shoppers will delight in an array of boutiques, gourmet shops, souvenir stands, and even an Internet cafe along Crescent Avenue and side streets. For a hearty breakfast or lunch, stop into **Pancake Cottage** (118 Catalina St; 310/510-0726), the ultimate coffee shop where waitresses tuck pencils behind their ears, balance 10 plates on each arm, and splatter a little coffee while refilling your cup. The menu is a mile long, including a dozen kinds of pancakes and meaty breakfast combos that would satisfy a linebacker.

Much of the most interesting stuff on Catalina Island—rugged back roads, dramatic shorelines, isolated coves, the Casino ballroom, Arabian horses at the Wrigley family's El Rancho Escondido—is either restricted or too remote for the casual visitor. Luckily, there are numerous options for guided excursions, ranging in length from a couple of hours to three-quarters of the day. **Santa Catalina Island Company's Discovery Tours** (310/510-TOUR or 800/626-7489; www.scico.com) offers the greatest variety: In addition to scenic day and night tram tours of Avalon, glass-bottomed boat cruises, and bus trips into the island's interior, they conduct some unusual outings none of the other operators offer. These include the **Undersea Tour of Lover's Cove Marine Preserve** in a semi-submerged boat, nighttime boat trips to see Catalina's famed flying fish, and an exclusive tour of the landmark Casino theater and ballroom.

Though most visitors make the town of Avalon their base for exploring, real nature lovers might prefer remote **Two Harbors**, which can be reached by bus from Avalon—or summer-only ferry service from Avalon and the mainland. Described by island tourist officials as a "rustic village," tiny Two Harbors is wedged on a quarter-mile hourglass of land at Catalina's west end and gets its name from Isthmus Harbor and Catalina "Cat" Harbor, the two pleasure-boat moorings on opposite sides. Isthmus Harbor has a short pier with a friendly **Visitors Center** (310/510-7254) and the **Two Harbors Dive & Recreation Center** (310/510-4272), a complete outfitter for scuba, snorkel, and kayak expeditions. The romantic appeal of this remote location? To start, there are secret emerald coves, scenic ridge hikes, and secluded campgrounds where you can pitch a tent just for two. If the demands of camping will dampen your ardor, try rustically romantic **Banning House Lodge** (310/510-2800), an 11-room clapboard house built in 1910 for the island's pre-Wrigley owners. With sweeping views that encompass both harbors below and the mainland across the channel, Banning House shapes up as an off-the-beaten-path setting to share kisses on a part of the island few will ever see.

## Access and Information

The usual way to reach Catalina Island is via **Catalina Express** (562/519-1212 or 800/481-3470; www.catalinaepress.com), which operates up to 22 daily departures to Avalon from Long Beach and San Pedro. Their high-speed catamarans are equipped with airplane-style lounge chairs, a snack bar, rest rooms, and outdoor deck seating. Service to Two Harbors is also offered, though frequency varies seasonally.

Catalina has very distinct high and low seasons; summers—and holiday weekends—are when crowds are largest and hotel rates are highest.

But Catalina's weather mirrors the mainland, making fall and spring lovely, uncrowded times to visit. If visiting in July or August, be sure to make boat, restaurant, and hotel reservations in advance.

For more information on visiting the island, including New Year's Eve and other events, contact the **Catalina Island Visitors Bureau** (located on the Green Pleasure Pier; 310/510-1520; www.catalina.com).

# Romantic Lodgings

## HOTEL METROPOLE

*205 Crescent Ave, Avalon / 310/510-1884 or 800/300-8528*
When Avalon was in its infancy, around 1887, the Metropole was a destination hotel in classic Victorian style, with distinctive green paint and an elegant facade that dominated early picture postcards. Today's Metropole—a much smaller, modern replacement built on the same spot—evokes the romance of the original grande dame. The hotel is sleek and well appointed, with contemporary, tropical furnishings reminiscent of a Mediterranean villa. There are 48 rooms here, making the Metropole large enough to support a helpful staff who offer the attention of a full-service hotel, yet intimate enough to maintain the ambience of a boutique inn. Every year they up the local ante by adding more pampering amenities, such as in-room DVD players, luxurious Frette linens, and marble bathroom vanities. The hotel is the cornerstone of a stylish open-air shopping plaza, and some balconies overlook its brick pathways, so solitude seekers will prefer the mood of an ocean view or oceanfront room. You'll pay more for the view, but get extra amorous amenities—like a fireplace or whirlpool bath—to complement the bathrobes and minibar that already encourage in-room trysts. On the top floor, there's a wind-shielded rooftop deck and whirlpool overlooking the harbor; downstairs you'll find a cute day spa that offers a surprisingly wide range of exotic treatments, including a candlelit side-by-side couple's massage. Rates include a continental breakfast, and just outside the front door is all of Avalon Bay's activity. It may look touristy from the outside, but the Metropole shapes up as a classy, comfortable retreat perfect for a romantic interlude.
*$$–$$$ AE, MC, V; no checks; www.hotel-metropole.com.* &

## INN ON MT. ADA

*398 Wrigley Rd, Avalon / 310/510-2030 or 800/608-7669*
William Wrigley Jr. purchased Catalina Island in 1918, and by 1921 he had built this ornate Georgian Colonial mansion on the best hillside

property in Avalon. Home to the Wrigley family for 37 years, the house is now an intimate and luxurious bed-and-breakfast that's consistently rated one of the finest small hotels in California. If your particular fantasy is one of wealthy seclusion, this is the place to pretend you're blue bloods, if only for a weekend! The illusion begins when you arrive, as the inn's private shuttle meets the two of you dockside, then whisks you uphill, where refreshments await in the wicker-filled sun-room. Step onto the wide wraparound porch, which still offers the same spectacular vista of Avalon Bay that inspired Wrigley to build on this spot. Upstairs, six superb rooms await you and your beloved—and each features an inspirational view of its own. The best is the Grand Suite, where you can cuddle by the bedroom fireplace or soak in the vintage bathroom's tub. A private terrace is furnished with side-by-side chaises, and a power awning tames the midday sun. If you're morning-shy, early coffee and muffins appear just outside your door on the landing. Each room has its own romantic appeal, from the richly decorated Windsor Room, a corner retreat blessed with a fireplace and exceptional views (even the bathroom overlooks the sea), to the smallest room—Morning Glory—that receives the day's earliest sunbeams. The innkeepers' meticulous attention to detail means you need never leave this hilltop Eden; rates include a hearty hot breakfast, full lunch menu, and an array of evening hors d'oeuvres accompanied by fine wines. Beverages, cookies, and fruit are laid out all day, and nighttime snackers need only raid the butler's pantry, where microwave popcorn and ice cream sundae fixin's await. For lovers who aren't content to merely bask in this pampering solitude, your stay also includes a private golf cart for exploring Avalon.
$$$$ MC, V; checks OK; www.catalina.com/mtada.

## SNUG HARBOR INN
♥♥♥

*108 Sumner Ave, Avalon / 310/510-8400*
This aptly named bed-and-breakfast is the ideal place to drop anchor in Avalon if you're looking for classic B&B service—cozily intimate, personalized, and detailed. The owners spared no expense renovating a once-dark rooming house (circa 1895) into a sky-lit retreat in the heart of the action. Located above shops on a prime bay-front corner, the six bedrooms are light, airy, and impeccably decorated in a relaxing Nantucket theme, with hardwood floors, thick hooked rugs, and the maximum amount of pampering comfort per square inch. Solid new doors and triple-paned windows keep noise out of your boudoir, leaving you to peacefully enjoy the goose-down comforter, flickering gas fireplace, TV, VCR, CD player, whirlpool bathtub, plush terry robe (and slippers!), and custom homemade breakfast-in-bed delivered to your room each morning. When the occasion is extra special, the staff is ready to

arrange flowers, champagne, in-room massages, or whatever will make your sweetie smile. The number-one room for romance is San Nicolas, which boasts a cool blue nautical decor, full frontal harbor view, and a bathroom bathed in sunlight. The sunny, yellow Santa Catalina room has an identical view, along with a smooch-tastic window seat. If you're feeling more sociable than amorous, step into the fireside study for complimentary afternoon wine and cheese before heading out to any of Avalon's restaurants—they're all within walking distance of Snug Harbor.
$$$–$$$$ *AE, DIS, MC, V; no checks; www.snugharbor-inn.com.*

## ZANE GREY PUEBLO HOTEL
🌢🌢

*199 Chimes Tower Rd, Avalon / 310/510-0966 or 800/3-PUEBLO*
Though it's not the most lavish place in town, this historic hilltop home will appeal to lovers of seclusion and scenery. Author and avid fisherman Zane Grey spent his later years in Avalon and wrote many books here, including *Tales of Swordfish and Tuna*, which recounts his fishing adventures off California's coast. His home, named the Pueblo, is perched far above town, with superb sunrise views across the bay. This unfancy house reflects Grey's love of the Arizona desert as well as his frequent South Seas fishing expeditions. Built of teak beams imported from Tahiti, and incorporating Hopi touches like exposed beams, the Pueblo is one of only two hotels in Avalon with a swimming pool—and it's even heated! The most romantic rooms have ocean views, private bathrooms, and tropical ceiling fans. They're simply furnished and correspondingly affordable, since the Pueblo is more about the outdoors. Couples can find many quiet spots here; watch boats meander in and out of the harbor from secluded corners of the home's two large decks, or canoodle indoors on a fireside love seat in the simple, original living room. Complimentary coffee, tea, and morning toast is served, and a shower room is conveniently available if you want to indulge in one last swim after checkout. The hotel also offers complimentary shuttle service to and from town for those hesitant to make the aerobic uphill climb.
$–$$ *AE, MC, V; checks OK; www.virtualcities.com.*

# *Romantic Restaurants*

## CATALINA COUNTRY CLUB
🌢🌢🌢

*1 Country Club Dr, Avalon / 310/510-7404*
The most elegant meals in this typically casual town are found here, where the tiny streets of Avalon rise to meet the foothills' embrace. This

Spanish-Mediterranean clubhouse, built by William Wrigley Jr. during the 1920s, was stylishly restored in 1997 and now has a chic and historic atmosphere, favored by well-heeled golfers and special-occasion diners with a taste for California–Pacific Rim cuisine. Seating is either outdoors, in an elegant tiled courtyard complete with splashing fountain and Mediterranean pottery, or in an intimate, clubby dining room filled with dark woods and polished brass fixtures. Indoors, the walls are lined with black-and-white photos from the club's early days, when Golden Age celebrities flocked to Avalon for sport fishing and spring training. The place truly oozes history, and you can make some history of your own by scoring one of three ultraprivate balcony tables framed by the twinkling lights of town and the harbor beyond. Feed the romantic mood with selections from a menu filled with only organically grown and free-range ingredients and complimented by the island's most comprehensive wine list. Specialties include the club's signature French onion soup, jazzed up with slices of sweet-tart green apple; local sand dabs in a white wine–lemon–fresh-herb meunière sauce; and a classy rack of New Zealand venison, sauced with a rich demi-glace. Share the clubhouse's special dessert, a pastry-wrapped apple "dumpling," bathed in warm pecan–brown sugar syrup and topped with vanilla ice cream. Because the club is a few blocks uphill, shuttle service is available from Island Plaza (on Sumner Ave) on weekends.
$$ AE, DIS, MC, V; local checks only; lunch, dinner every day, brunch Sun; full bar; reservations recommended for dinner; www.scico.com. &

## THE CHANNEL HOUSE

205 Crescent Ave, Avalon / 310/510-1617
With a secluded outdoor patio that's generally agreed to be one of the most romantic dining spots in Avalon, this traditional continental restaurant manages to attract jeans-clad vacationers as well as dressed-to-the-nines islanders. Located harbor-side in the Metropole plaza, the restaurant is in the heart of town and always crowded. The patio is the way to go (put in a request when making a reservation), festooned with twinkling lights and surrounded by vine-covered trellises that obscure the sidewalk traffic along busy Crescent Avenue. Indoor seating is refreshingly quiet, aided by plush carpeting and a pitched, open-beam ceiling; the Channel House projects an aura of elegance without pretension. Dinner always begins with an enormous platter of crisp, fresh crudités and creamy dip, and the menu here is enticing: Local seafood offerings like mako shark, fresh Catalina lobster, or grilled island sand dabs are complemented by meat and poultry that's served with rich accents like foie gras, béarnaise, and butter galore. Lighter fare—like pasta or chicken—can be a wise choice, since meals here include hors d'oeuvres, appetizers, and a range

# More Catalina Kisses

When it's time to literally sweep someone off his or her feet, there's nothing like seeing how the other half lives. **Island Express Helicopter Service** (310/510-2525 or 800/2-AVALON; www.islandexpress.com) has a fleet of executive 'copters and 20-plus years' experience providing the specialty services usually enjoyed only by the wealthy and powerful. Start by eschewing the regular boats *everyone else* takes to Catalina; Island Express flies on demand to Avalon's tiny heliport, where a taxi awaits to whisk the two of you off to town, 3 minutes away. The flight takes just 15 minutes; gaze downward and you can spot the slowpoke ferry that won't even pull into the harbor until long after you've toasted one another with your first island libation! Basic transportation is just the beginning, though, since Island Express also offers high-flying scenic tours of the entire island, complete with pilot narration. Your hearts won't be the only things soaring as you fly over the island's rugged interior, explore the remote west end, and admire the dozens of jewel-like coves that hug the rocky shore. It's a view of Catalina few ever see, and the experience ranks high on our kiss-worthy list. Island Express has two heliports on the mainland—Long Beach and San Pedro—both of which use the same parking lots as the standard ferries. Reservations are required for all flights; at press time the roundtrip fare to the island was $132 per person, and the 30-minute scenic tour cost $113 per person.

—STEPHANIE AVNET YATES

of side dishes that guarantee to leave you both stuffed without depleting your trysting budget. Surprisingly, the restaurant offers just a couple of perfunctory desserts, hardly the lavish selection you might expect. A better post-prandial choice would be to stroll along Via Casino, which begins just outside the front door and is romantically lit each evening to entice lovers to take an intimate bayside promenade.
**$$** *AE, DIS, MC, V; no checks; lunch every day (June–Oct), dinner every day (subject to Mon–Tues closure in winter); full bar; reservations recommended.* &

## LUAU LARRY'S
*509 Crescent Ave, Avalon / 310/510-1919*
Avalon's bar scene is the center of nightlife in this small, virtually car free (no drunk drivers) hamlet, and sooner or later everyone ends up at Luau Larry's, a cozy tropical enclave where fake parrots, puffed-up blowfish,

and shell lanterns swing from the thatched ceiling. Romantic? If you're in a lovingly playful mood, it sure is! And your attention will briefly turn from one another when you discover that Larry's burgers and other pub-style food are among the best eats on the island, a little-advertised fact that fills this small bar from lunch through the wee hours. Everyone's favorite aphrodisiac—oysters—are usually on the appetizer menu, along with popcorn shrimp and other classic noshes, and the house drink is a frightening rum-based concoction called the Wicky Wacker. Stay as long as you're feeling congenial, and when you're ready for just-the-two-of-us, chances are your hotel is just a few swaggering steps away.

$ *AE, MC, V; local checks only; lunch, dinner every day; full bar; reservations not accepted; www.luaularrys.com.* &

## STEVE'S STEAKHOUSE
🖤🖤

*417 Crescent Ave, Avalon / 310/510-0333*
Recommended by many as the best all-around surf and turf steakhouse on the island, this second-floor dining room boasts an exceptional view across Avalon Bay and a gallery-like collection of vintage photographs that evoke the town's historic appeals. You and your sweetie can enhance the romantic and nostalgic quality of the restaurant by ordering the specialty of the house, Steve's harpoon-caught local swordfish, broiled or sautéed to your liking. There's always a catch of the day in addition to a wide range of market-priced fresh seafood, plus true surf and turf combos. If you prefer the "turf," opt for one of five choice beef cuts—there are also saucy teriyaki and BBQ selections, and every meal comes complete with hearty accompaniments that would satisfy even the most hard-working fisherman. Vacationing lovers stream in early to toast one another by the setting sun, so this place hums with activity throughout the night.

$$ *AE, MC, V; local checks only; lunch, dinner every day; full bar; reservations recommended.*

## VILLA PORTOFINO RISTORANTE
🖤🖤🖤

*101 Crescent Ave, Avalon / 310/510-2009*
It's fairly easy to spot the Villa Portofino Hotel, located directly on the bay near the far end of Crescent Avenue. But discerning locals and repeat visitors know the popularity of Villa Portofino's restaurant has far eclipsed that of its lodgings. The restaurant has built a universal reputation for pleasingly authentic Italian cuisine in a quiet, romantic setting. Like many bayfront eateries, this comfortably classy room offers inspirational views across the harbor from many tables, and it's worthwhile for amorous diners to request a front table to bask in the setting.

But the well-delivered seafood and pasta specialties here—accompanied by a nice selection of Italian and California wines—will stoke the flames of romance all by themselves. Of special note are the thin-as-a-wisp beef carpaccio, savory pan-seared scallops, and must-have tiramisu. The granite bar is a fine place for enjoying a glass of wine and hors d'oeuvres, and Portofino's new outdoor seating provides lovers with a beautiful setting to take advantage of balmy summer evenings.

**$$** *AE, DIS, MC, V; no checks; dinner every day (subject to Tues–Wed closure in winter); full bar; reservations accepted only for parties of 6 or more; www.hotelvillaportofino.com.*

# ORANGE COUNTY

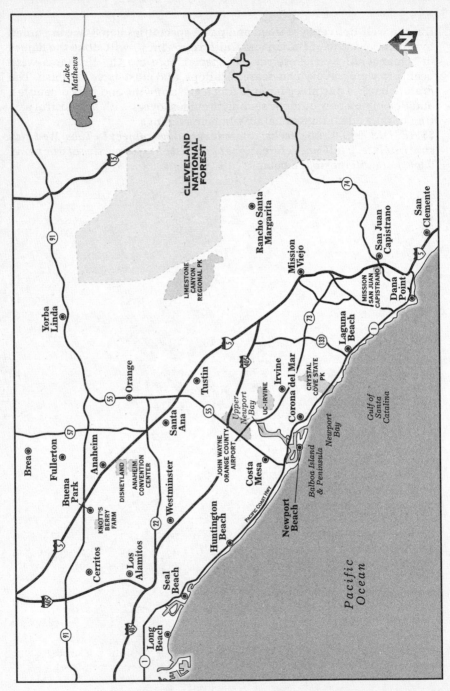

*"I have always found men who didn't know how to kiss. I've always found time to teach them."*

—MAE WEST

# ♡ ORANGE COUNTY

Ever since Fox's "The OC" hit the TV, people's perception of Orange County has changed. Sure, this sunny region of Southern California sandwiched between Los Angeles County to the north and San Diego County to the south features exclusive suburbs and swanky beach resorts by the glistening sea, but most of Orange County is not all glitz and glamour. It's also filled with quiet, nondescript residential neighborhoods, dense woodlands of old oaks, ocher-colored sandstone canyons, and quiet country roads where farmers still sell baskets of just-picked strawberries or jars of homemade honey.

But when it comes to glam, the Orange Coast may be the ultimate romantic destination, with its pristine beaches, charming ocean-side towns, and alluring hideaways. It's the epitome of the California dream, where couples enjoy the fresh ocean breeze, soak up the sun, and frolic on the sandy shoreline. From quaint seaside cottages to five-star resorts, there are plenty of options for making your amorous beach experience simple or grand. Days are for beach going, strolling the boardwalk, browsing specialty boutiques, and lunching at beachside cafes. At night, when the sun sets and the stars come out to play, couples can savor romantic dinners, take moonlit walks on the shore, or soak in the ambience of the area's swank resorts.

Inland Orange County also has its charms. In addition to being home to the world's most famous amusement park, the area boasts charming historic neighborhoods where couples can shop for antiques and tour turn-of-the-century homes. Museums and performing arts complexes provide a little culture for twosomes who feel like viewing priceless artworks or taking in a concert, while professional sporting events and recreational activities are sure to satisfy both enthusiastic spectators and avid action seekers.

While Orange County may have once been thought of as Los Angeles's more conservative and predictable bedroom community, today it is a diverse destination in its own right, offering lovebirds endless possibilities for amour. Whether the two of you opt to spend the day enjoying the sun, sand,

and surf of the Orange Coast, or playing like kids at the happiest place on earth, Orange County is ripe for romance.

# NEAR THE BEACH

## ROMANTIC HIGHLIGHWTS

A string of seaside jewels that have been compared to the French Riviera or the Costa del Sol, the Orange Coast is one of Southern California's most romantic spots—and best-kept secrets. More than 42 miles of premiere shoreline offer pristine stretches of sand dotted with luxury resorts, tide pools teeming with marine life, charming secluded coves that are ideal for kissing, and legendary waves that draw surfers from around the world. From Huntington Beach—also known as Surf City—on the county's northern tip to Spanish-flavored San Clemente at the southern county line, each coastal community—and each separate beach—has a unique character and appeal that makes it a backdrop for bliss.

Indeed, **Huntington Beach** really is all about the surf, and couples in search of the quintessential beach experience should start their tour of Coastal OC here. **Bolsa Chica State Beach** (714/846-3460), which parallels the Pacific Coast Highway (PCH) from the town's northern tip to its most southern edge, is the site of big waves, and surfers come from all over the Southland to experience the pounding surf. Whether the two of you just want to watch the action or get in on it, too, the waves just off Huntington Beach Pier are the epicenter of Surf City. Each summer in August, it's the site of the **U.S. Open of Surfing**, but any day throughout the year, the two of you will be able to watch the riders "hit the lip" and "carve tight cutbacks" from the vantage point of the pier or the sand. For couples who want to learn more about the sport (or indulge their surfing significant other), the **International Surfing Museum** (411 Olive Ave; 714/960-3483; www.surfing museum.org) details the history of this sexy sport. Just down the street at PCH and Main Street, the sport's most famous competitors are immortalized in polished granite stars on the **Surfing Walk of Fame**.

With its glittering harbor and extravagant homes, **Newport Beach** is perhaps the hub of Coastal OC. There's much to do on the sandy shores—from frolicking with your sweetie in the surf to renting a bike from one of the beachfront kiosks and going for a scenic pedal. Newport's **Balboa Peninsula**, a historic area lined with homes and shops featuring vintage clothing, antiques, curios, and eateries surrounding Newport Boulevard, is where the two of you will want to begin the day. Linger over lattes at an outdoor cafe and browse the galleries and boutiques in the waterfront village on

**Lido Isle** (at Balboa Blvd) or the cobblestoned and leafy **Via Oporto**. Then head to nearby Newport Pier and spend some time soaking up the sun and watching the local surfers take on gnarly waves. Just be sure to slather your significant other with plenty of sun block, as this coastal region boasts some pretty intense rays.

While there are plenty of funky beachfront food concessions, sweethearts may want to lunch with the locals at the **Crab Cooker** (2200 Newport Blvd; 949/673-0100). A neighborhood institution, this beachy seafood cafe serves fresh grilled fish and skewered shrimp and scallops on paper plates. And their hearty Manhattan clam chowder is the best around. It may not be fancy, but it's delicious.

If the two of you feel like reverting to childhood, at least for an hour or two, be sure to visit the **Balboa Fun Zone** (600 E Bay Ave at Main St; 949/673-0408; www.thebalboafunzone.com), near the Balboa Pier. Balboa's answer to Coney Island, this is the place to eat cotton candy to your hearts' delight, take silly pictures in the photo booths, or ride the bumper cars or the colorful carousel. After dark, a spin on the ferris wheel will not only afford a spectacular view of the lights along the water, but also will provide a marvelous spot to sneak a few kisses.

Twosomes who want to appreciate the scenic beauty of the Orange Coast from a different vantage point can depart on one of numerous boating excursions from the **Balboa Pavilion** (end of Main St; 949/673-4633), a historic structure built in 1905 that is the city's most famous landmark. From December to March, whale-watching season provides seaborne adventure; sport fishing is a year-round possibility. Both are available through **Davey's Locker** (400 Main St; 949/673-1434; www.daveyslocker.com).

Or for a shorter, yet still beautiful, water-going experience, board the ferry to **Balboa Island** (the ferry landing is off Palm St; 949/673-1070). The charming three-car ferry has been around since the 1920s and transports passengers to the island from the Fun Zone. As you cross the small channel, you can't help but gape at the incredible estates that line the island. The houses seem like an endless potpourri of gingerbread confections, some Cape Cod–style, others right out of a Hans Christian Andersen storybook. Once on the island, the two of you can wander down Marine Street, where you'll find an enticing assortment of diminutive restaurants and specialty shops. Or slip away to the water's edge and plant a kiss or two.

Heading south from Newport Beach and Balboa is **Corona del Mar**, a charming high-rent beach village with rocky cliffs and spectacular beaches for lovers to explore. While **Big Corona Beach** (off Marguerite Ave below Ocean Ave) may attract the area's biggest crowds, its neighboring **Little Corona Beach** (below Pacific Coast Hwy and Ocean Ave at Poppy Ave) is a romantic gem. The secluded cove features rocky tide pools at one end, where you and your sweetheart can poke around and watch sand crabs scurry and sea urchins cling to their perches with each incoming wave.

Couples can continue to marvel at the wondrous beauty of this area at **Crystal Cove State Park/El Moro Canyon** (8741 Pacific Coast Hwy; 949/494-3539). This marvelous 2,200-acre oasis, with 3.5 miles of unbelievably beautiful beaches, provides lovers with a rugged and pristinely preserved spot to camp, hike, bike, and horseback ride. After a hike in the canyon or a romantic stroll on the beach, stop for a creamy date shake at the **Shake Shack** (7703 N Coast Hwy; 949/497-9666), perched on the bluff overlooking Crystal Cove State Beach. It's a charming little beach hut that's been around forever.

Continuing south, the two of you will run into Orange County's crown jewel, **Laguna Beach**. A long-time hangout of the Hollywood crowd (Bette Davis and Judy Garland had vacation homes here, and Heather Locklear is among today's Tinseltown residents), the charming seaside burg may boast gazillion-dollar homes, but it's also an eclectic artist's community, with a quaint downtown village filled with art galleries, boutiques, and cafes. Couples can easily spend the day just browsing the shops and galleries downtown. Stop in the **Fingerhut Fine Art Gallery** (210 Forest Ave; 949/376-6410), which features works by such big names as Pablo Picasso and Dr. Seuss, or visit **Wyland Gallery** (509 S Coast Hwy; 949/376-8000), with its display of nautical and marine life paintings by this famous artist. A great way to tour the galleries—and meet many of the artists in person— is the **First Thursday** program, a city-sponsored art walk held the first Thursday evening of each month from 6pm to 9pm. More than 30 different galleries around town participate, staying open in the evening and offering refreshments. Even the **Laguna Art Museum** (307 Cliff Dr; 949/494-6531; www.lagunartmuseum.org), with contemporary galleries that hold a small but interesting permanent collection, gets into the act with extended hours and free admission.

For couples who want to spend the day marveling at the splendor of the Pacific, Laguna's dazzling beaches are the community's other main attractions. Bustling **Main Beach (Laguna Beach Municipal Park)** provides volleyball and basketball courts, picnic greens, and a winding boardwalk. However, lovebirds who have more of a secluded beach day in mind may want to venture to **1,000 Steps Beach** (entrance on S Coast Hwy at 9th St). There are really only 225 steps down to this idyllic crescent, but couples will find the solitude worth every one. Look up and you'll see houses clinging to the steep cliffs, many with private staircases or electric funiculars that lead to day-use beach houses on the sand.

Farther south, the historic town of **San Juan Capistrano** is the home of the seventh California mission, **Mission San Juan Capistrano** (Ortega Hwy at Camino Capistrano; 949/234-1300; www.missionsjc.com). The beautifully restored structure still stands on the original 10-acre plot. In addition, couples can also visit the ruins of the original stone church, the cool white Serra Chapel (one of the oldest Spanish structures in California), and a museum offering historical insights. But chances are the two of you will be more interested in seeing the annual return of the **swallows**, who instinctively know to come home to this region in March and then leave again in October. Somehow, there's just something romantic about how they return home time and time again.

And perhaps after a captivating getaway to Coastal Orange County, the two of you will follow the lead of these famous birds and make an annual return visit to this picturesque part of Southern California. After all, there's nothing like an ocean-side paradise to bring out the romantic in us all.

## Access and Information

Coastal Orange County is most easily reached by Interstate 405. From Los Angeles, couples can take Interstate 5 south; from San Diego, take Interstate 5 north. Once in the region, Pacific Coast Highway (PCH) serves as a major scenic thoroughfare.

**John Wayne Airport** (949/252-5200; www.ocair.com) is a more convenient airport than LAX. It is centrally located on the borders of Santa Ana, Costa Mesa, and Newport Beach near the 405 Freeway. It's served by many major carriers. Orange County has light-rail service by **Metrolink** (714/636-7433; www.octa.net). **Amtrak** (800/USA-RAIL; www.amtrak.com) trains stop in Fullerton, Anaheim, Orange, Santa Ana, Tustin, Irvine, Laguna Niguel, San Juan Capistrano, and San Clemente.

Most of the beach communities have their own visitor information services. Depending on where you plan to visit, the following organizations may be helpful resources: **Huntington Beach Conference and Visitors Bureau** (417 Main St; 714/969-3492 or 800/SAY-OCEAN; www.hb visit.com), **Newport Beach Conference and Visitors Bureau** (3300 W Coast Hwy; 949/722-1611 or 800/944-COAST; www.newportbeach-cvb.com; 24-hour information center, 949/729-4400), **Corona del Mar Chamber of Commerce and Visitors Bureau** (2843 E Coast Hwy; 949/673-4050; www .cdmchamber.com), **Laguna Beach Visitors Bureau** (252 Broadway; 949/497-9229 or 800/877-1115; www.lagunabeachinfo.com), **San Juan Capistrano Chamber of Commerce** (31781 Camino Capistrano, #306; 949/493-4700; www.sanjuancapistrano.com), **Dana Point Chamber of Commerce's Visitor Center** (24681 La Plaza; 949/496-1555; www.danapointvisitorcenter.com), or **San Clemente Chamber of Commerce** (1100 N El Camino Real; 949/492-1131; www.scchamber.com).

# *Romantic Lodgings*

## THE BALBOA BAY CLUB & RESORT
⚫⚫

*1221 W Coast Hwy, Newport Beach / 949/645-5000 or 888/445-7153*
Couples dreaming of a country-club life can at least pretend they've got a membership to the most exclusive club on the Orange Coast when they check into the Balboa Bay Club & Resort. The former private yacht club opened in 1948 and evolved into a world-class resort in 2003 with the opening of 132 beautifully appointed guest rooms overlooking the yacht-filled bay. Set on 15 acres, the posh resort has a European feel, with its Italian piazza, stone archways, and classic Roman columns. Lovers, however, will find the casually elegant guest rooms distinctly Californian, with rattan furnishings, tropical-patterned drapes, giant marble bathrooms, and plantation shutters that lead to spacious patios overlooking the bay or a lush courtyard. Comfy beds, dressed with sumptuous down-filled gold- and honey-toned duvets and fine linens, encourage sweethearts to sleep late. Suites take the romantic setting one step further with fireplaces for cozying up on a cool night. If the two of you feel inspired to leave your inviting room, you can visit the resort's spa, cruise the bay on a rented yacht, play a game of tennis at the Balboa Bay Racquet Club, tee off at one of several nearby courses, or simply sit by the pool and enjoy the stunning setting. The resort's indoor/outdoor restaurant, First Cabin, is open for breakfast, lunch, and dinner and features such California-inspired cuisine as seafood salads, sandwiches, and pastas at lunch, and grilled fish, steak, and chops for dinner. Duke's Place, named after former Balboa Bay Club member John Wayne, features cocktails and nightly entertainment. Since the Western legend is said to have loved tequila, the drinks menu features a variety of cocktails made with this potent potable in his honor.
*$$$–$$$$ AE, MC, V; no checks; www.balboabayclub.com.* ♿

## BALBOA INN
⚫❦

*105 Main St, Balboa / 949/675-3412 or 877/BALBOA9*
This picturesque Spanish-style inn is a stone's throw from the Balboa Pier and the glistening sea. Though most of the 34 rooms are pretty standard, a couple of enchanting ocean-view suites will stir your heart the minute you cross the threshold. The Master/Honeymoon Suite, complete with gas fireplace, Jacuzzi tub for soaking à deux, wet bar, and private balcony, provides all the makings for a night of romance. From this vantage point, the ocean is so close you can see the waves roll onto the sand, hear the surf lash against the shore, smell the ocean breeze, and taste the salt in the air. The fact that Kareem Abdul-Jabbar was one of the owners of this ocean-side inn in the early '80s may help lure reluctant romance seekers from the couch and the

big game to this alluring spot. If the beach is too crowded, couples can sun worship at the resort's pool and Jacuzzi. However, ask for a room in the back of the inn, as the live bands playing at the popular nightspot across the street on weekends can be heard until the wee hours of the morning. *$$–$$$ AE, MC, V; no checks; www.balboainn.com.* &

## BLUE LANTERN INN
🌂🌂❀

*34343 St of the Blue Lantern, Dana Point / 949/661-1304 or 800/950-1236*
The Blue Lantern Inn is managed by the Four Sisters Inn Corporation, a group that knows everything there is to know about creating romantic accommodations. The other bed-and-breakfasts under this management—such as the Blackbird Inn and Maison Gleurie in Napa and Sonoma, the Green Gables Inn and Gosby House in Pacific Grove, and the Cobblestone Inn in Carmel—are stunning, plush places to get away from it all. The Cape Cod–style Blue Lantern is located on a bluff overlooking the incredible OC coastline. It holds 29 rooms, each with a comfortable bed overflowing with pillows and its own fireplace, Jacuzzi tub, mini-stereo system, fluffy terry-cloth robes, sweeping views, sitting area, and refrigerator stocked with soft drinks. The Tower Suite, with its vaulted ceiling, four-poster king-sized bed awash in floral bedding, and 180° views, is the ultimate place to steal a kiss or two. In between smooching and enjoying the view, you and your honey can use the telescope to try to spot whales in the nearby harbor. In the morning, stroll onto your own private sun deck and linger over a gourmet breakfast of fresh fruits, homemade breads, and freshly made egg dishes. Afternoons can be spent exploring the beautiful coast on bicycles or perhaps lazing around the inn, sipping wine and sampling hors d'oeuvres by the hearth in the library. At night, your bed is turned down and chocolates are left next to a teddy bear with a card that reads, "Good night. Sleep tight. Don't let the bears bite." A little corny for some tastes, but definitely endearing.
*$$$ AE, DIS, MC, V; no checks; www.foursisters.com.* &

## THE CARRIAGE HOUSE
🌂🌂❀

*1322 Catalina St, Laguna Beach / 949/494-8945*
Most bed-and-breakfasts have their charming idiosyncrasies. Given the right touches, nothing is quite as affection-producing as staying in a home where the longings of the heart have been diligently considered. These touches include the morning aroma of freshly baked pastries, downy quilts, antique bibelots and finery, and, of course, a private bathroom. The Carriage House is a perfect, old-fashioned New Orleans–style bed-and-breakfast that can turn just another weekend into a lasting memory. Hosts Andy and Lesley Kettley welcome lovers with a carafe of wine, fresh fruits, and an assortment of goodies in their room. Each of the six suites reflects a different

part of the world, ranging from the English countryside to the Orient; all have their own sitting rooms, and most have kitchens. Suites face a brick courtyard filled with tropical plants and flowers. You won't find a lot of ocean views at the Carriage House—just comfort, privacy, and pleasure. $$-$$$ *AE, MC, V; checks OK; www.carriagehouse.com.*

## CASA LAGUNA
◐◑◖

*2510 S Coast Hwy, Laguna Beach / 949/494-2996 or 800/233-0449*
Entering the grounds of this romantic terraced inn is like stepping back in time to the halcyon days of Laguna Beach's artists' colony. Built in the 1930s, Casa Laguna is an appealing series of California Mission– and Spanish-style structures, comprising 21 rooms and suites all connected by a series of lush and green pathways, stone stairways, and secluded gardens. The entire landscape burgeons with azaleas, hibiscus, bougainvillea, and impatiens, and also with the colorful mosaic of vintage Catalina tile. Most rooms—especially the suites—are downright luxurious, with fireplaces, whirlpool tubs, bathrobes, CD/DVD players, and other in-room goodies. Courtyard and garden rooms are small but endearing, and all are appointed with antique furnishings and private bathrooms. In our romantic opinion, you really should splurge on the Cottage. Here you'll find everything you could want or need for an unforgettable night of romance. Besides providing an incredible ocean view from its private deck, the Cottage also has a fire-place, a living room area, and a fully equipped kitchen for nights when you'd prefer to eat in. Sunsets are best enjoyed from the inn's intriguing bell tower or from the deck above the sparkling pool, which is surrounded by avocado and banana trees. A whirlpool is perched on the hillside directly above the pool, perfect for late-night soaking. Breakfast and afternoon tea and wine are on the house. Couples massages are available in the inn's library. The only distraction that takes this alluring inn down a notch is the constant hum of traffic from the Pacific Coast Highway below. But, chances are the only sounds you'll hear will be the patter of your hearts.
$$$ *AE, DIS, MC, V; no checks; www.casalaguna.com.*

## CASA TROPICANA
◐◑

*610 Avenida Victoria, San Clemente / 949/492-1234 or 800/492-1245*
This unusual inn, set above the San Clemente Pier, is all about adding a little fantasy to your romantic getaway. While it offers a tremendous vista of the sparkling Pacific, the real draw is that each of the nine guest chambers follows a tropical or jungle theme, from the Bogie-and-Bacall-inspired Key Largo to the romantic Out of Africa, complete with a four-poster bed draped in mosquito netting. Several of the rooms carry the theme a little too far: the ceiling of the Emerald Forest is entirely covered with vines, and

the Bali Hai will make you feel like you should be drinking something with an umbrella in it. But maybe there's something to be said for fulfilling those "Me Tarzan, you Jane" fantasies. Most of the rooms have fireplaces and Jacuzzi tubs, and two of the three suites have complete kitchenettes ideal for an extended getaway. If you really want to take a trip to Fantasy Island, consider splurging on the Penthouse. This elaborate fifth-floor suite has its own sun deck and a 180° ocean view. It also features a seductive three-way fireplace that is accessible from the master bedroom, adjoining sitting room, and large step-up tub overlooking the sea. If you wish to leave your car at the inn while exploring San Clemente, you can take the train to a nearby stop. The bad news is that this same train passes right by the hotel hourly, disturbing an otherwise peaceful setting.
$$–$$$$ *AE, MC, V; no checks; www.casatropicana.com.*

## DORYMAN'S OCEANFRONT INN
ʘʘ✿

*2102 W Oceanfront, Newport Beach / 949/ 675-7300 or 800/634-3303*
Located across from the Newport Beach Pier, Doryman's is so enticing you will want to embrace immediately after entering the front door. Everything about this bed-and-breakfast suggests Victorian affluence, starting with the lovely French and American antique furniture and floral bedspreads and wallpaper. The finishing touches are impeccable, from fine linens on the beds to Italian marble and brass fixtures in the bathrooms. Six of the 10 rooms have ocean views and two are luxurious suites with Jacuzzi tubs and spacious sitting rooms. Room 8 may be the most romantic, with its king-sized canopy bed, gas-burning fireplace, and private oceanfront dining table for dinners ordered in. If you can bear to tear yourselves away, you can enjoy sumptuous breakfasts and delightful afternoon teas in the parlor. Or savor a romantic meal at the inn's resident restaurant, 21 Oceanfront (see Romantic Restaurants).
$$$ *AE, MC, V; cashier's checks OK; www.dorymansinn.com.*

## EILER'S INN
ʘ✿

*741 S Pacific Coast Hwy, Laguna Beach / 949/ 494-3004 or 866/617-2696*
Eiler's Inn feels removed from the masses, even though it is in the center of Laguna Beach. The picture-perfect French-Mediterranean–style guest house wraps around a slightly disheveled New Orleans–style brick courtyard overgrown with thick plants and punctuated with comfy white wrought-iron tables and chairs and a tinkling fountain. Inside, lovers can cozy up in a little parlor or sit by the gas-burning fireplace in a more formal but completely casual living room. Bed sizes in the 12 rooms vary from double to king-sized, but all are furnished with an eclectic mix of antiques and individual floral motifs with complementing bedspreads, throw pillows,

and curtains. Couples seeking a little more privacy should request a room upstairs. One such gem is the Larsen Suite (named for long-time greeter Eiler Larsen, whose statue stands out front), which has a large, comfortable sitting room with a gas-burning fireplace for romantic post-beach lounging, a full kitchen, the inn's only TV and VCR, and tremendous ocean views. It also offers easy access to the rooftop patio, where the two of you can hang out under an umbrella-shaded table or sun on cozy chaises. The relaxed atmosphere of this inn is enhanced by the hearty breakfast served every morning. Tea and wine are offered each evening on the patio, and on Saturdays, a classical guitarist serenades guests. With the Pacific Ocean's turbulent surf beckoning at your back door, everything is in order for a sparkling private time together.
**$$–$$$** *AE, DIS, MC, V; no checks; www.eilersinn.com.* &

## FOUR SEASONS HOTEL NEWPORT BEACH
♥♥♥❢
*690 Newport Center Dr, Newport Beach / 949/759-0808 or 800/819-5053*
Located across from Fashion Island, a premier shopping destination, this resort is elegant from start to finish. Couples will feel soothed and pampered from the moment they enter the tasteful, expansive lobby, with its coffered ceilings, gorgeous floral arrangements, and relaxing lounge, which offers plenty of room for conversation. Although we would describe the 285 rooms (including 96 suites) as upscale rather than romantic, their separate living rooms provide the perfect spot for lounging and snuggling. All have terraces with views of the surrounding area and/or the Pacific Ocean in the distance. The rooms on the higher floors are the most sought-after; they offer panoramic views of the coast and Newport's skyline. However, it's hard not to feel regal and loved in even the least-expensive rooms, as the attentive staff provides gallant service. If the two of you can drag yourselves away from your luxurious accommodations, an excellent landscaped pool or a complete spa and exercise facility (including aerobics classes, a lap pool, a Jacuzzi tub, tennis courts, massage services, and a steam room) are sure to entice. Poolside dining and the Garden Lounge and Café provide casual meals, or lovers can savor a memorable dinner in the world-class Pavilion (see Romantic Restaurants).
**$$$$** *AE, DC, MC, V; checks OK; www.fshr.com.* &

## HYATT REGENCY HUNTINGTON BEACH RESORT & SPA
♥♥
*21500 Pacific Coast Hwy, Huntington Beach / 714/698-1234*
When you want to lay low and blend with the crowd, you and your sweetie can check into this massive four-story resort complex, which boasts 517 guest rooms and 51 suites. While the resort caters to a convention crowd and families, its location across the street from the beach makes it a romantic

setting to soak in the Southern California sun and absorb the Surf City charm of Huntington Beach. Opened in 2003, the Spanish-style resort is set among Mediterranean-style courtyards with outdoor fireplaces, reflecting ponds, and gardens with sweeping ocean views. The beautiful, new setting is both sparkling *and* sprawling, so it can be a trek to get to your room. Once you arrive, you'll find spacious accommodations decorated in a palette of rich red, gold, and beige tones, with a cozy pillow-top mattress, large bathroom with natural stone countertop, and a private balcony or patio, where couples can hang out and read the paper together in the morning or enjoy a quiet moment in the evening. Lovebirds may want to splurge and check into a Regency Club Suite, which comes with access to the Regency Club Lounge, where the two of you can enjoy complimentary continental breakfast, afternoon hors d'oeuvres, and dessert. The Regency Club's concierge is also on hand to suggest activities, book spa appointments at the resort's Pacific Waters Spa, or perhaps make dinner reservations at the Hyatt's signature restaurant, The Californian. Specializing in California cuisine like fresh seafood and grilled filet mignon, this elegant eatery serves breakfast, lunch, and dinner every day, as well as a beautiful Sunday brunch. Lovers who'd rather kick off their shoes and enjoy an amorous beach picnic on the nearby sand can pick up all the fixings at Surf City Grocers, also located on the property.
$$$–$$$$ *AE, DC, DIS, MC, V; no checks; www.hyatt.com.* &

## INN AT LAGUNA BEACH
♥♥♥◖

*211 N Pacific Coast Hwy, Laguna Beach / 949/497-9722 or 800/544-4479*
Romance has never been this convenient. The Inn at Laguna Beach is a few steps from the water's edge and an easy walk to the downtown Laguna. Fifty-two of the 70 rooms feature ocean-view terraces, perfect for enjoying the complimentary continental breakfast or watching the sun set at day's end. The rooms are cloaked in the colors of the sea, with walls embellished by the work of local artists. Amenities include feather beds with fluffy duvets, TV/VCRs, robes, and refrigerators. Also, the hotel has air-conditioning, in case the ocean breezes just can't cool those flickering flames of amour. A rooftop sundeck and a beachside pool and spa await lovers who want to soak up the sun, or you can pick up towels, chairs, and shade umbrellas at the front desk and head for Laguna's Main Beach. While the hotel doesn't have a restaurant, Las Brisas (see Romantic Restaurants) is located next door.
$$–$$$ *AE, MC, V; checks OK; www.innatlagunabeach.com.* &

## MANZANITA COTTAGES
◐◐

*732 Manzanita Dr, Laguna Beach / 949/661-2533 or 877/661-2533*
Sweethearts will appreciate the Hansel-and-Gretel charm of this secluded inn, which seems appropriate since the original cottages were built in 1927 by Hollywood producer Harry Greene, who wanted a private compound, close to the beach, so he could invite friends like Joan Crawford for weekend getaways. (Ms. Crawford preferred the Yellow Cottage.) More than 75 years later, the four small cottages and one studio apartment are still serving as a quiet little vacation retreat, perfect for couples in search of a romantic locale. Each cottage has a shingled roof, a gas fireplace, hardwood floors, hand-painted tiles, a fully equipped kitchen, and a private patio just outside French doors in the bedroom. The owners, Debbie and Todd Herzer, renovated the cottages in 1999 and landscaped the grounds with fragrant flowers and vines, which only adds to the amorous allure. Couples who want to stay sequestered for much of their stay can upgrade to bed-and-breakfast status: for an extra $25 per couple, per day, a basket of assorted pastries and a carafe of orange juice will be delivered each morning. Laguna's Main Beach and the center of town are only a 10-minute walk away—but that's if the two of you can find a reason to leave your cottage, which many guests don't.
*$$ MC, V; checks OK; weekly and monthly rates; www.manzanita cottages.com.* ᕦ

## MARRIOTT'S LAGUNA CLIFFS RESORT
◐◐

*25135 Park Lantern, Dana Point / 949/661-5000 or 800/533-9748*
Take an elegant, upscale hotel, mix in a touch of coastal magic, and you've got Marriott's Laguna Cliffs Resort. This Cape Cod–style resort has more than a bit of fairy tale about it. Like a great castle, it is set on a grassy knoll high above the sea, blushing in soft pastels and brimming with bright flowers. Special touches like complimentary lemonade in the lobby keep this expansive resort from feeling too big. Its 350 guest rooms and suites, decorated with a splash of California coastal decor and local artwork, provide sweethearts with such amenities as terry-cloth robes, CD players, and in-room coffee. Most feature patios, from which lucky lovebirds may be able to spy whales in the nearby Dana Point Harbor during whale-watching season. Couples can spend a pleasant afternoon splashing in the pool, strolling the beach and collecting seashells, playing tennis, working out in the extensive fitness center, or enjoying a massage in the grand Spa at Laguna Cliffs. The end to a perfect day, or the beginning of a perfect night, may come when you share a quiet moment on your private seaside terrace and survey the moonlit domain lying before you. The hotel's Regatta Bar & Grill, serving California-inspired cuisine made with fresh local ingredients, is open for

breakfast, lunch, and dinner. In the evenings, lovers can listen to music or dance the night away at Commodore's Bar & Deck.
$$$ *AE, MC, V; checks OK; www.lagunacliffs.com.* ⅋

## MONTAGE RESORT & SPA
◍◍◍◍
*30801 S Coast Hwy, Laguna Beach / 949/715-6210 or 866/271-6953*
Opened in February 2003, this stunning new Craftsman-style five-star resort sits on 30 lushly landscaped acres of prime beachfront real estate a mere 50 feet from the pristine coastline. Couples entering the grand lobby will immediately be swept away by the jaw-dropping views of the Pacific, but once the two of you get past the scenery, there's much to keep your attention, including an impressive collection of plein-air artwork, stunning furnishings and detail work, a mosaic-tiled pool, and lush gardens. The five-story resort has a feel of comfortable sophistication, which carries on its 262 guest rooms, each of which offers an ocean view, an insanely comfortable feather-top bed that will make the two of you want to snuggle until noon, a giant marble bathroom with a deep soaking tub that's impossible to resist (complete with tub pillow, bath salts, loofah sponge, and candles on a silver tray), and a flat-screen TV with DVD player for late-night movie watching. Couples can savor the sound of the surf and the fresh ocean air on their private patio, which features rattan furnishings that are actually comfortable. Or, to get even more relaxed, head to the massive Spa Montage, which boasts indoor/outdoor facilities, an impressive menu of spa treatments, a state-of-the-art fitness room, workout classes like yoga and power walks on the sand, and a beachside lap pool. Afternoons are for lounging by the pool, lunching on fish tacos or giant salads on the patio at the Mosaic Bar & Grille, or strolling hand-in-hand on the ocean lawns. In the evenings, dinner at the magnificent Studio (see Romantic Restaurants) is the perfect way to segue into a night of romance. Or, reserve a table at the more casual but equally appealing Loft, which specializes in farm-fresh salads, grilled meats, pastas, and fresh local seafood. On Sundays, brunch at the Loft is not to be missed. In addition to a spread of sushi, fresh seafood, artisan cheeses, salads, and a made-to-order omelet station, there's a chocolate fountain for dipping strawberries and cream puffs. With an employee-to-guest ratio of three to one, lovers will quickly discover that the attentive staff is going to try their darnedest to meet your every need. Even if you can't afford to stay at this spectacular resort, come enjoy sweeping ocean views and a glass of wine in the chic Lobby Lounge.
$$$$ *AE, DC, DIS, MC, V; no checks; www.montagelagunabeach.com.* ⅋

## PORTOFINO BEACH HOUSE
❍❍❍

*2306 W Oceanfront, Newport Beach / 949/673-7030 or 800/571-8749*
If Doryman's Oceanfront Inn (see Romantic Lodgings) is booked, or if you're just looking for a less expensive option, try this comfortable hotel. Facing the water and just a short walk from the sand, Portofino Beach House offers 15 rooms, located upstairs along a long, carpeted corridor, which is pleasantly spooky (as the best old buildings are). Decorated in earth tones with a blend of genuine Edwardian and Victorian antiques, as well as older, attractive furnishings that aren't quite considered antiques, these cozy guest rooms are equipped with queen-sized beds and marble baths; some have Jacuzzi tubs, ocean views, and gas-log fireplaces. After a night of romance, a complimentary continental breakfast is served each morning in the attractive Bar La Gritta lounge off the lobby, featuring coffee, tea, fresh fruit, muffins, and cereal. Then all the two of you need to do is step outside to soak up the sun and surf. Wine, tea, and treats are offered each afternoon to hold lovers over until dinnertime. The adjoining restaurant, Renato (see Romantic Restaurants), also serves dinner in the hotel's sitting room, which is a great place to curl up in front of the fireplace on comfortable overstuffed chairs. Portofino's only drawback is its proximity to the parking lot for Newport Pier, which is often bustling with wayward surfers and enthusiastic crowds.
$$$ AE, DC, DIS, MC, V; checks OK; www.portofinobeachhotel.com.

## THE RITZ-CARLTON, LAGUNA NIGUEL
❍❍❍

*1 Ritz-Carlton Dr, Dana Point / 949/240-2000 or 800/287-2706*
Royally poised on a tranquil bluff top overlooking the seas, this luxurious resort had been the only game in town for nearly two decades, until the Montage and St. Regis opened their opulent five-star doors. Although it's still swank, the hotel is undergoing some major renovations to keep up with the competition. Still, the romantic possibilities are endless. From the manicured grounds and the two mammoth swimming pools—especially the glittering aquamarine Dana Pool surrounded by towering palms—to the magnificent lobby with its plush carpets, gleaming woodwork, and lavish floral arrangements, this grand resort oozes elegance. The comfortable and pleasant pastel-colored 393 rooms, suites, and Club Suites are spacious, yet cozy and hushed. Every possible concession to comfort has been made, including plush terry robes, marble tubs, and well-stocked minibars. It's worth paying a little extra for an ocean view, since all rooms have French doors that lead to charming, private terraces, perfect for smooching. Lovers who really want to splurge can check in to the exclusive Ritz-Carlton Club Floor, which boasts a private concierge, open bar, all-day light meals, and a secluded after-dinner lounge. If the two of you decide to leave your love

nest, a challenging 18-hole golf course, tennis courts, a top-of-the-line gym, and a gleaming spa offer an array of entertaining options. Or check out beach chairs, towels, umbrellas, and boogie boards and head for the path to the sandy beach. You don't have to be a guest to enjoy the resort's lovely restaurants or to savor afternoon tea in the library filled with rare antique books. Guests and visitors alike can linger over cocktails in the posh lobby area adorned with silk-lined walls, overstuffed couches, and comfortable chairs. From this vantage point, you can take in rousing ocean views, hold hands, and partake in stimulating conversation. The Dining Room (see Romantic Restaurants) more than lives up to its surroundings. It is a kiss-worthy destination for couples ready to splurge on an unforgettable meal. $$$$ *AE, DC, DIS, MC, V; checks OK; www.ritzcarlton.com/resorts/ laguna_niguel.* &

## ST. REGIS MONARCH BEACH RESORT & SPA
🌸🌸🌸❀

*1 Monarch Beach Resort, Dana Point / 949/234-3200 or 800/722-1543*
This grand Tuscan-style hotel set on 172 acres has just about every bell and whistle lovers could dream of: a private beach club; a lagoon-style pool; a 25-treatment room spa and state-of-the-art fitness center; an 18-hole championship golf course; and huge guest rooms with Sony flat-screen TVs (and most have spectacular views of the Pacific). The biggest problem with the St. Regis is that there's no reason for the two of you to ever leave the resort. In fact, the whole palm tree–swaying, bougainvillea-blooming elegance of the place is perfectly summed up in a magnificent reproduction of Maxfield Parrish's *Garden of Allah* painting that you'll find in the Lobby Lounge. The romantic Mediterranean mood is complemented by the groves of olive, pine, and cypress trees, all trucked in from other locales and plopped into the lush landscape to look as if they'd been here forever. Eight on-site eateries cover every conceivable craving, including a poolside bar for post-swim sushi, an on-the-sand beach clubhouse restricted to resort guests, a Euro-style deli/ espresso bar, and a branch of San Francisco's Aqua (see Romantic Restaurants). The state-of-the-art fitness facility has a lap pool and tennis courts for lovers who feel the need to work up a sweat. But when surrounded by this kind of decadence, why not just live it up and worry about your workout when you return home? $$$$ *AE, DC, DIS, MC, V; checks OK; www.stregismb.com.* &

## SURF & SAND RESORT
🌸🌸🌸

*1555 S Coast Highway, Laguna Beach / 949/497-4477 or 800/664-7873*
If you and your sweetheart are looking for a hotel with gorgeous, unob-structed ocean views, it doesn't get much better than this. Surf & Sand holds the distinction of being the Laguna hotel closest to the sea—thanks to the

fact that it was built in the 1950s before zoning laws went into effect. The result: you are practically floating in the water. Tsunami-phobes beware: the only thing between you and the vast Pacific Ocean is about 25 feet of sand. But the views and sounds of the water aren't the only draw for lovers. This elegant, exclusive spot sells out every weekend of the year, with couples flocking here from all over the world. The owners have an eye for the art of love. Each of the 165 rooms is done in a soothing beige and white motif, with plantation shutters that open up to a private patio. Mirrors on the ceiling reflect the waves breaking below. The bathrooms are equipped with giant showers and luxurious spa tubs with direct views to the ocean. While there is really not a bad room in the entire hotel, the newest and most private are in the two nine-story towers. Once you've unpacked and marveled at the views, head down to the beautiful pool area with its marble sundeck and glass walls. The 500-foot-wide beach below is also spectacular, and two giant rock formations on either side keep it relatively uncrowded with foot traffic. After a few hours soaking up the sun and a few piña coladas, it's time to visit the on-site Aquaterra Spa (949/376-2SPA; www.aquaterraspa .com). From hot stone massages to seaweed revitalizers, there are numerous treatments to choose from, but the couples-only "artistic ritual" is not to be missed: You and your sweetie play Picasso and paint each other in different-hued, healing clay. Then you enjoy a colored-Jacuzzi bath and a side-by-side Shiatsu massage. Sounds strange and it is—strangely exhilarating. *$$$$ AE, DIS, MC; V; checks OK; www.surfandsandresort.com.* &

# Romantic Restaurants

## AQUA
●●●
*1 Monarch Beach Resort (St. Regis Monarch Beach Resort), Dana Point / 949/234-3325*
Set in the lobby of the St. Regis Monarch Beach Resort (see Romantic Lodgings) and overlooking the Pacific Ocean, this elegant restaurant is the Southern California outpost of the famed San Francisco eatery. With its warm interior of neutral earth tones, cozy seating, and roaring fireplace, it's an inviting place to celebrate a special occasion or to impress your significant other. While the interior is stunning, an evening at Aqua is more about the innovative cuisine. Chef Bruno Chemel marries French and Asian cooking styles, using fresh local and imported seafood and organic produce. The results are such sophisticated offerings as ahi tuna tartare in lemon olive oil infused with vanilla bean, lobster pot-au-feu, glazed sea bass, hearty Angus filet mignon with crispy *pommes frites*, and sinful soufflé. To best appreciate Aqua's charms, the two of you may want to order the five-course tasting menu and allow wise-beyond-his-years sommelier

Brian Cronin to suggest a draught for every course. It'll be an expensive evening, but the pleasant memory will linger on your palate for a very long time. Afternoon tea featuring fresh-baked scones, dainty sandwiches, and a selection of teas from around the world is served daily in the restaurant's lounge and can be a lovely and leisurely way to while away the afternoon with the one you love. The lounge also serves an abbreviated menu for lunch several days a week.

$$$–$$$$ *AE, DC, DIS, MC, V; no checks; lunch Thurs–Sat, dinner every day, afternoon tea every day; full bar; reservations recommended; www.aqua-sf.com.* &

## THE ARCHES
⊘⊘❶

*3334 W Coast Hwy, Newport Beach / 949/645-7077*
This venerable restaurant, at the beginning of a stretch of the Coast Highway known as Restaurant Row, has been here since 1922. A favorite of the late John Wayne, it's a throwback to another time, as you'll discover when you and your sweetie walk into a main dining room with red leather banquettes and dark hardwood paneling. Start with a martini or a selection from the establishment's impressive wine list of more than 600 vintages, then snuggle into a booth and peruse the giant menu. For dinner, you'll want something thick and juicy, like a hearty steak prepared to your liking or a huge veal chop stuffed with mushrooms and slathered in a rich sauce. Carnivores will love the rack of lamb or beef Wellington, both carved tableside by tuxedo-clad waiters. However, classic seafood selections like lobster Thermidor, sautéed jumbo prawns, and stone crab claws flown in from South Florida (when they are in season) are restaurant specialties. Blue-plate luncheon specials offer dinner-sized portions of favorites like liver and onions, blackened pork chops, and linguine with clam sauce. On Sunday and Monday evenings, The Arches features dinner specials for less than $25. Whatever you order, save room for the decadent bananas Foster; this lush and over-sized dessert is worth every calorie.

$$–$$$ *AE, DIS, MC, V; local checks only; lunch Mon–Fri, dinner every day; full bar; reservations recommended; www.thearchesrestaurant.com.* &

## AUBERGINE
⊘⊘⊘

*508 29th St, Newport Beach / 949/723-4150*
Orange County restaurateurs Tim and Liza Goodell lure lovers to their family of fine eateries with the promise of an amazing meal, and they rarely disappoint. Set in a cozy cottage with slate floors and dark wood cabinets on a quiet Balboa Peninsula side street, Aubergine was their first restaurant and is perhaps their most romantic eatery. Specializing in French-American gourmet fare, the restaurant has a menu that changes daily to make the most

of fresh, seasonal ingredients. Depending on when the two of you visit, you might enjoy such delicious dishes as scallops with tomato vinaigrette, Japanese yellowtail with citrus-ponzu sauce, skate wing fish with green apple and fennel salad, and New York strip steak with glazed root vegetables. Sweethearts feeling a bit adventurous may want to try one of the multicourse tasting menus, which can be a culinary journey. Breads are baked fresh every morning, so forget about counting carbs, and there's an impressive selection of imported cheeses, so your daily fat gram count should go out the window, too. The warm Valrhona chocolate soufflé cake or the brown butter tart make a perfect finale to your perfect evening. An embossed zinctopped bar is a lovely place to enjoy a drink before your meal.
$$$ *AE, DC, DIS, MC, V; no checks; dinner Tues–Sun; full bar; reservations recommended.* &

---

## BASILIC
♥❤

*217 Marine Ave, Newport Beach / 949/673-0570*
There are small romantic restaurants, and then there are really small romantic restaurants. Basilic is an intriguing example of the latter. Squeezed in between shops on the main drag of Balboa Island, the outside alone is enough to provoke your interest. Its facade is reminiscent of a quaint country cabin. A flower box overflows with colorful blossoms, and reflections from the candlelight inside dance on the beveled edges of the cut-glass windows. Inside, you may feel a bit claustrophobic. Don't worry, though. Like a miner in a small cavern, you will quickly feel the thrill of knowing you've uncovered a precious jewel. Floral tapestry banquettes line both sides of the room, divided by an aisle. Small tables dressed in pink linens occupy the space, making it intimate, though not very private. Still, the French-Swiss–inspired food, the candlelight, and the romantic music create the kind of ambience made for whispering sweet nothings. Chef-owner Bernard Althaus serves such tempting dishes as broiled salmon over greens with beets and steamed sea bass with fennel and tarragon jus. On the first Tuesday of the month, he offers Swiss raclette, a decadent cheesy fondue served with cold meats. You and your sweetie can dunk bread in this yummy mass of melted cheese to your heart's content. Just be careful not to extinguish the romantic mood by burning the roof of your mouth.
$$$ *AE, MC, V; no checks; dinner Tues–Sat; beer and wine; reservations recommended.* &

---

## THE BEACH HOUSE
♥♥❤

*619 Sleepy Hollow Ln, Laguna Beach / 949/494-9707*
The Beach House is the perfect choice for couples who want a view of the sparkling Pacific, but would rather don shorts than suits. Linen table-

cloths, fresh flowers, and candlelight create a cozy mood as couples dine on the fruits of the sea and drink in glorious sunsets. Family owned for more than 30 years, the casual restaurant is set in the former home of actor Slim Sommerville and features both indoor and outdoor dining. In addition to a broad selection of seafood, the Beach House also offers steak, lamb, and veal. An early lunch on the sun-drenched patio is a great time to share a coffee-flavored kiss as you make your plans for the day. In the evenings, the two of you can enjoy a leisurely meal in the dining room overlooking the stunning Pacific. The fresh coconut mahi mahi; bouillabaisse chock-full of fresh clams, mussels, and scallops; and Alaskan crab claws, and oven-roasted prime rib with macademia-wasabi mashed potatoes are among the restaurant's specialties. Save room for the cherries jubilee for dessert. It's a showstopper.

$$$ *AE, DC, DIS, MC, V; no checks; breakfast, lunch, dinner every day, brunch Sat–Sun; full bar; reservations recommended; www.thebeach house.com/laguna_beach.htm.* &

## BIBI ANNA'S
**⊘€**

*205 Main St, Balboa Island / 949/675-8146*
After an arduous day of sightseeing, when you're ready for a quiet, romantic dinner but don't want to get dressed up, head to Bibi Anna's. This is one of the few places where candlelight, shorts, and sandals seem to go together. Just down the street from the Newport Pier and around the corner from the playful Fun Zone, this charming little cafe is popular with the suntanned locals. Here the coffee smells of cinnamon, and fresh flowers adorn every table. Though it's not fancy by any means, Bibi Anna's has a sort of underlying refinement. It could be the unexpected quality of the food; you can quickly tell a pro is at work. Offerings are simple but lovingly prepared; pasta, meat dishes, and sandwiches make up the bulk of the menu. In the morning, couples can dine on five different kinds of eggs Benedict, pancakes, or hearty omelets. Lunch is about house-made soups, fresh steamer clams, hearty salads, and sandwiches, while dinner entrées run the gamut from grilled swordfish or mushroom ravioli to roasted rack of lamb or pork tenderloin.

$–$$ *MC, V; checks OK; breakfast, lunch, dinner every day; beer and wine; reservations recommended; www.bibiannas.com.* &

## BUNGALOW RESTAURANT
**⊘⊘**

*2441 E Coast Hwy, Corona del Mar / 949/673-6585*
This Corona del Mar favorite may always be bustling, but soft lighting, a lovely heated garden patio, and a dark cherry wood bar that pours more than 150 wine selections make this a great spot for date night. You and your

sweetie can snuggle into one of the restaurant's intimate, oversized velvet booths and start your meal by sharing a grilled artichoke with lemon-garlic marinade or seared ahi crusted with sesame seeds. Order a bottle of wine from the restaurant's award-winning list, or perhaps try one of the eatery's signature oversized martinis, which range from the classic drink to specialty versions like the pineapple-flavored Tropitini. Steak is the specialty here, and carnivores have a choice of seven different cuts, all of which can be topped with blue cheese, fried onion strings, béarnaise sauce, or sautéed mushrooms. If red meat isn't your thing, hazelnut-crusted Chilean sea bass, risotto with prawns, or a roasted jumbo Australian lobster tail are sure to please. Save room for the chocolate soufflé cake or creamy vanilla crème brûlée.

$$$ *AE, DC, DIS, V; no checks; dinner Mon–Sat; full bar; reservations recommended; www.thebungalowrestaurant.com.* ⅄

## CEDAR CREEK INN
◐◐

*384 Forest Ave, Laguna Beach / 949/497-8696*
Set in the historic Lumberyard Mall in downtown Laguna, this family-owned and -operated restaurant is a Laguna favorite. On warm days, the best tables for canoodling are on the outdoor patio; tables here are shaded by umbrellas, and flower boxes and trees circle the patio. On cold nights, lovers sit inside near the enormous stone hearth while a pianist serenades them with romantic melodies. Brie and pecan chicken, fresh salmon, rack of lamb with cracked pepper, and a variety of pasta entrées include soup or salad, and the menu also offers a large selection of salads and sandwiches. Cedar Creek's popular bar is also an amorous spot to sip cocktails, listen to live music, and order from the grill menu, which includes such sexy fare as oysters on the half shell and crab and scallop cakes. Or simply come for dessert and a nightcap. The restaurant's Toll House cookie pie or Holiday pie (a decadent combination of cranberries, apples, and cream cheese with a streusel topping) are worth the calories. Cedar Creek Inn also has equally charming locations in Brea and San Juan Capistrano.

$$ *AE, MC, V; no checks; lunch, dinner every day, brunch Sun; full bar; reservations recommended; www.cedarcreekinn.com.* ⅄

## THE COTTAGE
◐◐◑

*308 N Pacific Coast Hwy, Laguna Beach / 949/494-8980*
The Cottage is right out of a William Buffet painting: a 1914 beach bungalow filled with pastel-clad lovers enjoying breakfast. On any given weekend, you'll find locals and tourists waiting their turn to do brunch here. And why not? The home-style cooking is hearty and inexpensive, and the tables inside are comfortable and cozy. For more than 35 years, this quaint little

eatery has been serving breakfast, lunch, and dinner. When you are craving something sweet in the morning, try the pancakes or fluffy French toast. However, the corned beef hash with a poached egg is also a brilliant way to start the day. Lunches include homemade quiche, shrimp penne pasta, or a hearty Chinese chicken salad. Evenings on the delightful garden patio are quiet and intimate, with selections like filet mignon, cioppino, or a variety of pastas. But there's something about breakfast here that makes it the most romantic meal of the day. Whatever meal the two of you come to enjoy, stop in the lobby area to have a look at the collection of historic photographs showcasing Laguna's early days.

*$$ AE, MC, V; checks OK; breakfast, lunch, dinner every day; full bar; reservations recommended; www.thecottagerestaurant.com.* &

## DOLCE
☻☻€

*800 W Coast Hwy, Newport Beach / 949/631-4334*
Dolce brings a touch of Italy to the Newport dining scene. The entrance is brightened by pots of colorful flowers, while a canopy overhead keeps the sun at bay. In nice weather, the charming courtyard is the place to be, where comfortable, cushioned iron chairs are placed at small tables adjacent to a central fire pit. Smoking is allowed at the outdoor bar on the far end, so nonsmokers may want to request a table on the opposite side. The interior is more formal, with comfortable upholstered chairs that match the maroon carpet, Italian Renaissance prints on the walls, and live music softly playing in the background. An extensive menu offers a wide variety of choices; among the best are the outstanding pasta dishes. House-made ravioli stuffed with filet mignon, lobster, or mushrooms are truly dreamy. Entrées also deliver, with such selections as fresh fish with herbs; breast of chicken; and veal with prosciutto, mozzarella, and asparagus. Top off your meal with a homemade dessert and a special Dolce after-dinner drink, and the two of you will feel like you're on a regular Roman holiday.

*$$$ AE, DC, DIS, MC, V; no checks; dinner every day; full bar; reservations recommended.* &

## THE FISHERMAN'S RESTAURANT & BAR
☻

*611 Avenida Victoria, San Clemente / 949/498-6390*
A walk on the San Clemente Pier is a must. And while you're there, why not enjoy the relaxed setting of the Fisherman's Restaurant? Blue-and-white-striped umbrellas, wooden tables, and black-and-white photos of fishermen reeling in their catches enhance the nautical theme. The fresh fish of the day is written on a chalkboard, and the rest of the menu lists a wide variety of mussels, scampi, salmon, snapper, and many other mouthwatering choices. Order a couple of beers and nosh on oysters from the fresh oyster bar while

the two of you observe the spectacular sunset, or consider filling up on the hearty Fisherman's Famous Feast. Served for two or more, this family-style meal includes a bucket of clams; a tureen of chowder; warm sourdough bread; a salad; and your choice of clams, crab, swordfish, salmon, or halibut. After all, the couple who breaks bread and cracks crab together may be destined for endless love. The lounge/bar area is located across the pier, so its noise doesn't intrude on diners in search of a quiet, romantic meal.

$$-$$$ *AE, MC, V; checks OK; lunch, dinner every day; full bar; reservations not accepted; www.fishermansrestaurant.com.* &

## FIVE CROWNS
❂❂❹

*3801 E Pacific Coast Hwy, Corona del Mar / 949/760-0331*
This place has tryst written all over it. The dining rooms have cozy corners or banquettes where couples can sit side-by-side. Villeroy and Boch china, classical music, roaring fireplaces, dark wood beams, and long floral curtains contribute to the English formality. In addition, the waitresses are dressed in period costumes, complete with bonnets, aprons, and white stockings. The traditional continental cuisine is quite good—sometimes excellent—and features hearty salads, grilled fish, top-notch beef, and rotisserie chicken. But the specialty of the house at this Lawry's-owned operation is near-perfect platters of prime rib and Yorkshire pudding. With all this red meat on the menu, lovers will want to order a hearty bottle of wine from Five Crowns' award-winning list. Then, sit back and savor your fine—and filling—selections. You can always take a stroll on the nearby beach to walk off your meal.

$$$ *AE, DC, MC, V; no checks; dinner every day, brunch Sun; full bar; reservations recommended; www.lawrysonline.com.* &

## FRENCH 75
❂❂❹

*1464 S Pacific Coast Hwy, Laguna Beach / 949/494-8444*
Housed in a European-style cottage, this swanky Parisian-style bistro, created by Orange County restaurateur David Wilhelm, boasts some of the region's most innovative French fare, served amid a setting of colorful wall art, hardwood furnishings, and leather booths. Sweethearts can start the evening with a glass of bubbly in the champagne bar, with its whimsical mural of monkeys drinking champagne, and watch the hip Laguna crowd congregate. No matter where the two of you are seated in this enticing restaurant, its series of intimate dining rooms definitely sets the mood for romance. Lovers can begin with such affection-inducing starters as oysters on the half shell or French onion soup topped with bubbling Gruyère cheese, then move on to such delicious main courses as flat iron steak with *pommes frites*, roasted chicken, bouillabaisse, or succulent pork tenderloin. Perhaps

the menu highlight, however, is the signature chocolate soufflé, which oozes with gooey high-end Callebaut chocolate. It's so good, the two of you may have to fight over the last bite.
$$$ *AE, DC, DIS, MC, V; no checks; dinner Tues–Sun; full bar; reservations recommended; www.culinaryadventures.com.* &

# HUSH
♥♥♥
*858 S Coast Hwy, Laguna Beach / 949/497-3616*
With its sleek, modern design, Hush seems more like the kind of place you'd find in trendy Los Angeles than in sleepy Laguna Beach. But if you're looking for a restaurant with a super-cool, minimalist design and a highly inventive (and expensive) menu, then this is an impressive and unique spot to take your loved one. Hush becomes a bit of a meat market on weekend nights, so it's best to visit Sunday through Wednesday when the vibe is more intimate and conducive to romance. Choose a table either outside on the patio by the sand fire pit or inside right in front of the fireplace (table 10 to be precise). The wine selection is huge—they offer more than 900 bottles, and the knowledgeable wait staff is happy to suggest wine pairings. Chef Phillip Kaufman has fused Asian, French, and Californian cuisines to create a scrumptious and original menu. The aphrodisiac special—12 oysters with a spicy jelly mignonette—is delicious; so are the scallops served over red beet risotto. You can't go wrong with the seafood or steak entrées: particularly tasty are the salmon with porcini foam and the roasted filet tenderloin. The most popular dessert hands down is the banana strudel with caramel ice cream. Order it and you'll see why. All in all, Hush is an anomaly in Laguna Beach—a world-class restaurant in a small-town beach community. If you want a quaint date, this ain't it. If you want hip, you've hit pay dirt.
$$$–$$$$ *AE, DC, MC, V; no checks; dinner every day; full bar; reservations recommended; www.hushrestaurant.com.* &

# LAS BRISAS
♥♥
*361 Cliff Dr, Laguna Beach / 949/497-5434*
Las Brisas is one of the few restaurants in Laguna Beach with a beguiling ocean vantage point. Sit on the tiled outdoor terrace, where you can order cocktails, like the restaurant's specialty margaritas, and appetizers while watching swirling eddies explode over the rocks below. If you desire quiet and privacy, move to the elegant interior, with its semicircular wall of floor-to-ceiling windows facing the Pacific. This more formal setting features wooden chairs, linen tablecloths, and fresh roses. The menu, inspired by the cuisine of the Mexican Riviera, lists fresh seafood specialties. We recommend favorites such as mesquite-broiled double breast of chicken with tropical fruit salsa; seafood brochettes; and jalapeño fettuccine with

# For Art's Sake

Attracted by the spectacular ocean vistas, hillsides covered with brightly colored wildflowers, and the intense Mediterranean-esque light, artists have flocked to Laguna since the early 1900s. By 1917, the area was recognized as an artists' colony, beckoning such California plein-air impressionists as William Wendt, Edgar Payne, Guy Rose, and Anna Hills. In 1932, the artists formed a cooperative and presented the first **Festival of the Arts/Pageant of the Masters** (949/494-1145 or 800/487-FEST; www.foapom.com), which has become *the* annual event that puts Laguna Beach on the map.

Art lovers from all over the country flock to this magical celebration held every summer on 6 acres of parkland just off Laguna Canyon Road. By day, they stroll through the juried exhibition of original works from dozens of local artists. In the evenings at the adjacent Irvine Bowl, they are treated to the Pageant of the Masters, where live, intricately staged re-creations of classical paintings are presented, accompanied by orchestral music and narration. Under the stars, the audience is wowed by these enchanting picture-perfect stagings. It's a truly unique and ethereal experience—like a painting come to life. In fact, these performances are so popular that tickets sell out months in advance, so purchase tickets early.

The annual **Sawdust Festival** (949/494-3030; www.sawdustartfestival .org), held concurrently with the Festival of Arts and directly across Laguna Canyon Road, provides a venue for local artisans to display and sell their pottery, jewelry, and other crafts amid food booths, entertainment, and hands-on demonstrations. Sharing space with the Sawdust Festival is the annual **Art-A-Fair** (949/494-4514; www.art-a-fair.com) where fine arts—predominantly paintings and sculpture created by artists from around the world—are displayed for sale.

Whether the two of you are serious about appreciating art or just want to enjoy the festive beach gathering, it's a wonderful excuse to spend the day—and night—in Laguna. And, who knows, it may become an annual tradition for you to visit this charming beachside town.

—BONNIE STEELE

shrimp, scallops, mussels, and crab. When sunset nears, a single path of sunlight graces the water's surface; then, slowly, the collage of color crescendos into nightfall while you ponder where the evening will take you next. This is a very popular spot, so the earlier you arrive, the less crowded it will be. $$$ *AE, DC, MC, V; no checks; breakfast, lunch, dinner every day; full bar; reservations recommended; www.lasbrisaslagunabeach.com.* &

## LUCIANA'S
♨♨
*24312 Del Prado, Dana Point / 949/661-6500*
While it's easy to find restaurants with spectacular ocean views in this area, sometimes a romantic interlude calls for simple comforts with few distractions. At Luciana's, you can rediscover the joys of quiet conversation and good food, of holding hands while basking in the glow of candlelight. The interior of this small, quaint brick cottage is modest but elegant, a pleasant contrast of dark woods and crisp green linens. Under the high wood-beamed ceiling of the main dining area, you'll find a scattering of tables arranged within pleasant distance of a cozy hearth. A few feet away, a separate dining area resembles a library. Wednesday through Saturday nights, a pianist and a singer, specializing in seductive Mediterranean songs, serenade guests as they dine on sumptuous, authentic Italian cuisine. While the kitchen specializes in delicious pasta dishes, you can also find a number of fish, veal, and chicken entrées on the menu. Just find a quiet corner or a table by the fire and enjoy yourselves as a heavenly evening unfolds. But be sure to finish the evening with the creamy crème brûlée.
*$–$$$ AE, DC, MC, V; no checks; dinner every day; full bar; reservations recommended.* &

## MIRABEAU BISTRO
♨♨♨
*17 Monarch Bay Plaza, Dana Point / 949/234-1679*
Lovers who want to savor a classic French meal without enduring the oft-pretentious French-restaurant setting can head straight to Mirabeau Bistro. After working at snooty five-star French eateries, chef-owners Katie Averill and David Pratt decided to take what they had learned and open their own French bistro—without the attitude. On a beautiful day, lovers will want to reserve a table on the patio, with its blazing fireplace and gorgeous ocean views. The intimate dining room is also inviting, with its dark wood and granite bar. Wherever you sit, the two of you are sure to enjoy the fine offerings of this friendly eatery. Steak frites, salmon *en papillote*, seared foie gras, rabbit pâte, and cassoulet are among the specialties, and there's also a Special of the Day, like duck à l'orange on Saturdays or beef bourguignon on Tuesdays. Everything is made from scratch, from bread and crackers to ice cream and pastries. The wait staff offers wine by the carafe, poured straight from the barrel in the back, as well as some 40 wines by the bottle. What a great excuse to raise your glass and toast true love.
*$$$ AE, DC, DIS, MC, V; no checks; lunch, dinner Tues–Sun, brunch Sun; full bar; reservations recommended; www.mirabeaubistro.com.* &

## PASCAL
●●◖
*1000 N Bristol St, Newport Beach / 949/752-0107*
There are those who suggest that a proper romantic evening on the Pacific Coast must come with an ocean view. Although a view is nice, there is something to be said for an intimate table in cozy surroundings with excellent food, good wine, and waiters who are savvy enough to be there when you need them and scarce when you don't. Pascal is such a place. Located in a small shopping area, Pascal is a refreshing surprise. Large bouquets of fresh flowers and smaller vases of roses are everywhere you look, and an immense floral mural has been painted onto a white brick wall. Tables are attractively dressed with quilted tablecloths and matching napkins. The decor is French country, and so is the food. The chef-owner, Pascal, and his wife came here from France, bringing all their carefully guarded culinary secrets. Tempting hors d'oeuvres such as herb ravioli in foie gras or marinated salmon with creamy potato risotto are followed by classic fish and steak dishes. The aroma of garlic perfumes the air, and warm feelings abound. It's not unusual for Pascal to leave the kitchen to introduce himself and to make sure you and your sweetie are happy with your meal. While he's visiting your table, you may want to let him know that you are pleased not only with his fine cuisine, but also with the romantic bit of France he has transported to Newport Beach. Epicerie, a wonderful shop next door, is where you can pick up fine wine, French cheeses, quiches, and pastries for a snack or picnic. *$$ AE, DC, MC, V; no checks; lunch Mon–Fri, dinner Tues–Sun; full bar; reservations recommended; www.pascalnewportbeach.com.* &

## PAVILION
●●●
*690 Newport Center Dr (Four Seasons Hotel), Newport Beach / 949/760-4920*
Excellent service and top-notch Cal-Continental cuisine make this lovely, low-key dining room at the Four Seasons Hotel (see Romantic Lodgings) exude romance. Couples who prefer substance over sizzle will appreciate the splendid rose-toned room's understated elegance. Think colossal pillars, oversized floral arrangements, and beautiful artwork. Much of the menu borrows from the Mediterranean, but seasonal changes and daily specials add California touches. Depending on the season, couples might start with such appetizers as beautifully presented ahi tartare with wonton spirals, terrine of foie gras, or sweet corn soup with smoked shrimp. Entrées like salmon with wild rice, grilled veal chop with mushroom strudel, pepper-crusted lamb, or chicken with goat cheese polenta are wonderful main-course selections. A nightly three-course prix-fixe menu can actually be more affordable than ordering à la carte. Whatever you order, a well-thought-out wine list of more than 400 selections is sure to offer the perfect complement to your

meal. Finish off the evening with decadent chocolate fondue cake and two forks. This is a special-occasion spot, when you want to really impress your significant other with a night to remember, so try not to gasp too loudly when the bill arrives.

$$$$ *AE, DC, DIS, MC, V; no checks; breakfast, lunch, dinner every day; full bar; reservations recommended; www.fourseasons.com/newportbeach.* &

## PICAYO
● ● ◖

*610 N Coast Hwy, Laguna Beach / 949/497-5051*
Set in a storefront adjacent to Pavilions supermarket in the north end of town, this enchanting cafe offers couples an alluring setting, with wall murals, romantic lighting, Provençal fabrics, and warm wood accents that create an intimate atmosphere for leisurely meals. Combining the flavor of the Mediterranean with the spirit of Southern France, this attractive cafe seats only 20 guests at a time (dinner is split into two seatings on weekends), creating a totally engaging and intimate ambience. Pretty tables are set in two small dining rooms and also line the outdoor patio. Seafood often dominates the short dinner menu of select starters and entrées. Don't miss the silky lobster bisque accented with orange zest. Also noteworthy are the sautéed sea scallops in lemon chardonnay beurre blanc, the pistachio-crusted halibut, or the charbroiled lamb chops. The predominantly domestic wine list includes a few gems and a few European imports. Service is courteous and subdued, making this one of Laguna's finest hidden treasures.

$$$ *AE, DC, MC, V; no checks; dinner Tues–Sat, brunch Sun; full bar; reservations recommended.* &

---

## RAMOS HOUSE CAFÉ
● ●

*31752 Los Rios St, San Juan Capistrano / 949/443-1342*
Set in San Juan Capistrano's historic Los Rios district, this circa 1881 cottage has all outdoor dining, with tables placed simply on a lush brick patio under a huge oak tree. The small and ever-changing menu of New American and Southern cuisine lets couples choose from a variety of breakfast and lunch favorites. From sweet potato duck hash to a hearty spinach, bacon, and caramelized onion scramble served with sautéed potatoes, spiced applesauce, and a fluffy biscuit, lazy romantic morning meals are all about comfort food here. Lunch might be an ample crock of garden-inspired soup with cheesy bread twists, a robust warm salad, or a pulled pork sandwich. Chefowner John Humphries does great things with collard greens, fried green tomatoes, and other down-home classics. He's also a gifted baker who makes a mean warm berry and banana shortcake. Everything's made by hand on the premises; herbs are grown in the kitchen garden, and the wonderful ice

cream, pastries, and some of the cheeses are made on site. Now if only your sweetie could cook like this!
$ *AE, DC, DIS, MC, V; no checks; breakfast, lunch Tues–Sun; beer and wine; reservations not accepted; www.ramoshouse.com.* &

---

# RENATO
◐◐◖

*2304 W Oceanfront, Newport Beach / 949/673-8058 or 800/571-8749*
Located just off the beach near the Portofino Beach Hotel (see Romantic Lodgings), Renato offers gourmet Italian cuisine in a charming setting. If your heart is set on an ocean view, request one of the two window-side tables; however, all the tables are intimate and beautifully appointed. Classical music sets the mood, and in keeping with the atmosphere, more formal dress is requested: shorts and baseball caps are not permitted. Traditional pasta selections fill the menu, including the house specialty of homemade rotelle pasta rolled with prosciutto and mozzarella. A variety of fish, chicken, and veal dishes are also offered, including a wonderful chicken marsala and filet mignon with peppercorn sauce. Our favorite is the fettuccine with sweet onions, chicken, mushrooms, and sausage. You may want to finish the evening by indulging in a serving of homemade ice cream, rolled in walnuts and light meringue and topped with whipped cream and chocolate sauce. Then take a moonlit stroll on the adjacent shoreline to walk off dinner.
$$$ *AE, MC, V; no checks; dinner every day; full bar; reservations recommended; www.renatoristorante.com.* &

---

# THE RITZ-CARLTON DINING ROOM
◐◐◐

*1 Ritz-Carlton Dr, Dana Point / 949/ 240-2000 or 800/287-2706*
An evening at the Dining Room promises to be a lavish culinary fantasy come true. Under glistening chandeliers, you can dine side-by-side, while the attentive wait staff caters to your every need. Sure, it's wildly expensive and, for most, perfectly impractical, but your taste buds will be eternally grateful, and it is fun to get dressed up and do a big night out. Couples can begin the night with a predinner cocktail in the bar and toast their night of fine dining. Once the two of you are seated, there's much to choose from on the menu, which makes use of the finest ingredients available. Hmm . . . should you order the five- or the seven-course dinner? Do you want to start by sampling from the selection of caviars, or go with the terrine of layered foie gras or the gratin of spaetzle and beef tenderloin paired with duck foie? Decisions, decisions. Chef Yvon Goetz's seasonal menu borrows from Southern France and the Mediterranean with a welcome touch of his native Alsace added. An impressive wine list is sure to provide the perfect selection to accompany your meal. After you've finished your last course, drop by the hotel's Library Room, which overlooks the ocean, for a snifter of cognac in

front of the crackling hearth. A fantasy evening come true just wouldn't be complete without this loving finale.

$$$$ *AE, DIS, MC, V; no checks; lunch, dinner every day; full bar; reservations recommended; www.ritzcarlton.com/resorts/laguna_niguel.* ℥

## THE RITZ RESTAURANT & GARDEN
🌑🌑

*880 Newport Center Dr, Newport Beach / 949/720-1800*
Since it opened in 1977, this classic continental restaurant has been a Newport Beach institution. Elegant, opulent, and, yes, even a bit gaudy, is how we would describe this lavish restaurant. However, the glitz is what has made the Ritz (no relation to the hotel empire) such a popular spot for romantic dining. Bejeweled and bedecked in their finest attire, people love to come here for special occasions to eat rich food, sip expensive wine, and enjoy the restaurant's show-stopping culinary presentations. In the Gallery, dark woods and cozy black leather booths inspire a classically romantic atmosphere; in the Escoffier Room, peach walls, ornate mirrors, and gilded frames create a lighter, more baroque ambience. Meals such as spit-roasted rack of lamb, filet of Lake Superior whitefish, and bouillabaisse with lobster have made this an award-winning restaurant, with attractions for connoisseurs of food and romance alike. Save room for the Ritz's signature Harlequin soufflé, made with Belgian chocolate and Grand Marnier, then head to the elegant bar where the two of you can enjoy an after-dinner drink and listen to live music on Friday and Saturday evenings.

$$$ *AE, DIS, MC, V; no checks; lunch Mon–Fri, dinner every day; full bar; reservations recommended; www.ritzrestaurant.com.* ℥

## ROTHSCHILD
🌑🌑🌑

*2407 E Coast Hwy, Corona del Mar / 949/673-3750*
This is the stuff adoring encounters are made of: an intimate setting, beautiful surroundings, and impeccable service. You and your sweetie will feast on some of the best Northern Italian cuisine around at this old-fashioned eatery, as you also feast your eyes on handsome European antiques and 19th-century paintings in the three cozy dining rooms. Begin your meal with the house specialty of toasted artichokes marinated in herbs and white wine. The pastas are made on the premises and include classic offerings like fusilli bolognese or linguine with clams and shrimp. Rack of lamb with just the right combination of rosemary and garlic or tournedos of beef satisfy carnivorous couples, while a variety of fresh fish selections, like calamari steak or scampi, are also offered. As you share all of this with the one you love, you may just want to top off your evening with a kiss—a chocolate kiss

known as a cappuccino *tartuffo*, a truffle made with cappuccino ice cream, the finest Belgian chocolate, and laced with pralines.

*$$$ AE, MC, V; no checks; lunch Mon–Sat, dinner every day; beer and wine; reservations recommended; www.rothschildscdm.com.* &

## THE SORRENTO GRILLE AND MARTINI BAR
◐◐

*370 Glenneyre, Laguna Beach / 949/494-8686*
Although the interior of this trendy dining spot is exceedingly elegant, it can get excessively crowded and noisy, making it difficult to carry on a conversation or even hear yourselves think. But during less busy times, this can be a romantic and intimate place; just be sure to request one of the small tables on the balcony or one of the booths on the open mezzanine. Wherever you sit, you're sure to enjoy the provocative American bistro cuisine, courtesy of OC restaurateur David Wilhelm. Begin with the barbecued duck spring rolls or grilled artichokes, followed by entrées such as pasta, rare ahi pepper steak, double-cut pork chop, or grilled Delmonico steak with cheddar potatoes. And, since this is a martini bar after all, the two of you can sample from a selection of classic American martinis served in oversized glasses. The room's textured terra cotta and beige stucco walls, wrought-iron chandeliers, rustic tile, and gaslight sconces are merely a backdrop for the floor-to-ceiling windows. The setting creates an amorous ambience that can be great for a special date.

*$$–$$$ AE, DC, DIS, MC, V; no checks; dinner every day; full bar; reservations recommended; www.culinaryadventures.com.* &

## SPLASHES RESTAURANT
◐◐◐

*1555 South Coast Hwy, Laguna Beach / 949/376-2779*
Situated on the first floor of the elegant Surf & Sand Resort (see Romantic Lodgings), Splashes is all about its location—smack dab on the beach. Romance seekers should reserve a table on the bottom terrace, which offers magical views of the waves crashing down on the shore. Just how special a spot is this? The staff estimates four to five marriage proposals happen here a week! On cooler nights, the inside is just as cozy. Reserve a table by the fireplace, settle in, and enjoy the food, which, thankfully, is as good as the setting. Chef Shane Gagnon has trained in Europe and brings a Mediterranean flair to his cuisine. Though his menu changes daily, his seafood dishes are not to be missed—they're so fresh you might wonder if your meal was caught a few hours ago. Begin by sharing the petit plateau appetizer, a delectable collection of tasty shellfish and spicy ceviche. For entrées, go for the swordfish with olive tapenade, the halibut with a vanilla sauce, or whatever fish Gagnon happens to be serving that night. Landlubbers can't go wrong with the 16-ounce Kansas City cut. It's big but great for sharing.

If you find room for dessert, order the apple bread pudding with a caramel sauce that simply melts in your mouth. Then take a few dessert wines out to the beach and have a romantic moonlit stroll.
*$$$ AE, DC, DIS, MC, V; no checks; breakfast, lunch, dinner every day; full bar; reservations recommended; www.surfandsandresort.com.* &

## STUDIO
● ● ● ●

*30801 S Coast Hwy (Montage Resort and Spa), Laguna Beach / 949/715-6000*
While this wonderful restaurant is a part of the Montage Resort and Spa (see Romantic Lodgings), it's set in a separate Craftsman-style cottage on a scenic bluff hovering 50 feet above the beach, creating a setting that's so beautiful, you might almost forget that you've come for the impressive cuisine. Inside, rustic wood beams, rich wood tones, wine vault displays, and sea-green accents create an inviting setting for a perfect night of romance. Esteemed chef James Boyce serves a sophisticated California-Mediterranean menu that changes often, but he sticks with a straight-forward approach that highlights his top-quality ingredients, including fresh-caught seafood, produce grown by local farmers, and farm-raised meats. Starters might include Hudson Valley foie gras, pan-seared skate wing, and light and lemony halibut, while main courses run the gamut from pan-seared New Zealand John Dory and seared swordfish to roasted rack of lamb with shaved artichokes and cannelloni of osso buco. The prix-fixe six-course chef's menu lets you sample a variety of the chef's creations, and if you really want to go all out, have each course paired with wine selections from the restaurant's well-trained sommeliers. Studio's award-winning wine list of 1,800 selections features 50 by-the-glass choices. Desserts are equally impressive. A chocolate–peanut butter Stonehenge is so beautifully presented, you may hesitate to eat it. But one bite will have you quickly toppling over this creamy, crunchy creation and digging in. Chai tea tapioca is also an interesting winner. Overall, the combination of the enchanting setting, near-perfect service, and show-stopping cuisine is sure to make this a romantic night to remember.
*$$$–$$$$ AE, DIS, MC, V; no checks; lunch Sat–Sun, dinner Tues–Sun; full bar; reservations recommended; www.montagelagunabeach.com.* &

## TI AMO
● ● ●

*31727 Pacific Coast Hwy, Laguna Beach / 949/499-5350*
Welcome to seduction, Italian style: the tantalizing smells, the heavenly ocean view. Yes, this is definitely a restaurant after your hearts. The food, like the decor, is inspired by the Italian Renaissance. This means that the house specialty is authentic regional cuisine, made from classic Italian recipes handed down from century to century. The two of you might want

to share a starter of thinly sliced beef carpaccio with roasted peppers, then move on to such selections as honey-and-chile-glazed jumbo scallops or grilled ahi with sun-dried tomato risotto. Homey gnocchi with veal and wild mushroom ragu; ravioli with snow crab, rock shrimp, and orange fennel sauce; or veal scaloppini marsala are among the house specialties. Leave some room for ice cream and berries, or the orange-infused ricotta cannoli, with a house cappuccino to sip on the side. All this is served up in a cozy cottage divided into several rooms. Each dining room is warm and intimate, with gauzy drapes, lots of candles, and fresh-cut flowers. The living room has a cozy hearth, there are two small ocean-view rooms, and a pretty patio features live classical guitar music. As you bask in the golden glow of the sun setting over the ocean, you may realize that you've fallen under the spell of this bewitching restaurant.

$$$ *AE, DC, DIS, MC, V; no checks; dinner Mon–Sat; full bar; reservations recommended.* &

## 21 OCEANFRONT
✪✪❶

*2100 W Oceanfront (Doryman's Oceanfront Inn), Newport Beach / 949/673-2100*

As the sun plays out its final performance of the day, melting into the turquoise sea, 21 Oceanfront prepares for its nightly encore. Time and again, couples in search of romance come to this warm and elegant restaurant, expecting brilliant sunsets, attentive service, and fine cuisine. They rarely leave disappointed. Just a few hundred yards from the crashing waves, seafood and pasta are served in a graceful setting, with black leather banquettes that are perfect for snuggling, mahogany furnishings, green marble, and brass gas lamps. Lovers may want to start with the restaurant's signature dish, lightly breaded abalone, or perhaps Maryland crab cakes chock-full of fresh, sweet crab. Seafood is the specialty for the main course, and fresh fish is flown in daily. Alaskan king crab legs, swordfish, and a succulent filet mignon are favorites for couples celebrating a special night out. An impressive list of California and French wines rounds out this restaurant's offerings, and its lively oceanfront bar features jazz nightly. You may even want to pack a bag for the night: with the exquisite Doryman's Oceanfront Inn (see Romantic Lodgings) right upstairs, you can have everything your hearts need without traveling anywhere else.

$$$ *AE, DC, DIS, MC, V; no checks; dinner every day; full bar; reservations recommended; www.21oceanfront.com.* &

# 230 FOREST
❀❀

*230 Forest Ave, Laguna Beach / 949/494-2545*
This buzzy industrial-style bistro manages to feel cosmopolitan, despite its beachy Laguna locale. It's the sort of place the two of you will want to order drinks from the crowded bar the moment you arrive, and creative martinis like the James Bond (shaken 007 times) and the crème brûlée martini are the way to go. While you are waiting for your table, you can opt to view the eclectic rotating art collection by local artists or the artistic culinary fusion work that's going on in the restaurant's exposed kitchen, courtesy of chef/founding partner Mark Cohen. The dining room is a long, narrow space and can get loud, but seating is comfortable and provides for great people watching, if the two of you can take your eyes off each other, of course. A small heated patio for dining alfresco is also available. If you are in the mood to share, starters like the roasted artichoke crab dip with pita chips or the goat cheese and sun-dried tomato wontons are the perfect starter, followed by winning entrées like smoked baby back ribs, maple-glazed pork chops, and blackened swordfish with carrot ginger. And a variety of pasta bowls such as penne with asiago cream sauce, grilled rosemary-thyme chicken, artichokes, tomatoes, and mushrooms, can be as comforting as a loving glance from your dining partner.
$$$ *AE, DC, DIS, MC, V; no checks; lunch, dinner every day; full bar; reservations recommended; www.230forestavenue.com.* 占

# WIND AND SEA RESTAURANT
❀

*34699 Golden Lantern, Dana Point / 949/496-6500*
If you prefer a casual setting with a harbor view, look no further than Wind and Sea. Nestled at the mouth of the marina, this restaurant boasts close-up views of the passing boats through floor-to-ceiling windows. Or sit outside under blue umbrellas and breathe in the salty ocean air while you and your sweetie sip margaritas and watch the seagulls soar overhead. Splurge on the popular seafood combination for two or choose from the large selection of steaks, fish, sandwiches, and salads. The classic fare includes salmon stuffed with crab, mushrooms, and cream cheese; bacon-wrapped filet mignon topped with béarnaise sauce; and seafood pasta. Comfortable rattan chairs and accents add to the nautical theme. Live entertainment on weekend nights ensures soothing background music throughout your meal. This isn't the most intimate dining experience around, or the most fancy, but it feels very authentic and charming.
$$–$$$ *AE, MC, V; no checks; lunch Mon–Sat, dinner every day, brunch Sun; full bar; reservations recommended; www.windandsea.com.* 占

# POINTS INLAND

## ROMANTIC HIGHLIGHTS

When Walt Disney decided to build his dream park in Anaheim in 1955, the area was nothing more than orange groves and a few ranch homes. Today most of those fields of citrus have been replaced by tract housing, and what was once a land of possibilities has become bustling suburbia. While Inland Orange County might not be as glam as the area's coastal region, this part of OC does have its charms. From the lovely historic neighborhoods of Santa Ana and Old Towne Orange to its splashy newer attributes like the glistening **Crystal Cathedral** (714/54-GLORY; www.crystalcathedral.org) or the cultural offerings of Costa Mesa's **Orange County Performing Arts Center** (600 Town Center Dr; 714/556-ARTS; www.ocpac.org) and **South Coast Repertory** (655 Town Center Dr; 714/708-5500; www.scr.org), Inland Orange County is as diverse as the people who call this area home.

Of course, Inland Orange County is best known as the home of the happiest place on earth, **Disneyland** (714/781-4565 for recorded information; 714/781-7290 to consult with a real person; www.disneyland.com). While a crowded amusement park may not be the first thing that comes to mind when you think about romance, it's surprising how many couples have bonded while whizzing through the Matterhorn in a speeding sleigh or seeing how fast they could spin the famous Tea Cups as a duo. Canoodling with the one you love at this land of imagination can truly be a special day. And for sweethearts who haven't visited Disneyland in a while, there's a whole new theme park right next door. Disney's **California Adventure** offers a new assortment of more sophisticated attractions celebrating the Golden State. While not as big as Disneyland, this amusing venue is broken into three themed areas: the Golden State, Paradise Pier, and Hollywood Pictures Backlot, each offering a distinct flavor of California's fun, diversity, and lifestyle.

If a day at Disneyland just whets your appetite for theme parks, Inland OC is also home to **Knott's Berry Farm** (8039 Beach Blvd; 714/220-5200; www.knotts.com), which started in the early '30s as the roadside restaurant of berry farmer Walter Knotts and his wife, Cordelia. The eatery was so popular that Knotts built an old-fashioned Western ghost town behind the restaurant to entertain guests while they waited in line for Cordelia's famous chicken and biscuit dinners. One thing led to another, and today Knott's Berry Farm has grown into one of Southern California's most popular attractions, complete with thrill rides and shows all reflecting the Old West. (And you can still get an old-fashioned fried chicken and biscuit dinner, too.) In particular, the park has gained a loyal following among couples who enjoy a good fright at Halloween, when it transforms into Knott's Scary Farm for the month of October.

For those who get more of a thrill out of a good sporting event, the area is also home to two professional sports teams: the **Mighty Ducks** National Hockey League team (714/940-2159; www.mightyducks.com) and the American League's **Anaheim Angels** baseball team (714/634-2000; www.angelsbaseball.com). From September through April, hockey fans can take in a game at the **Arrowhead Pond** (2695 E Katella Ave; 714/704-2400; www.arrowheadpond.com), which also hosts big-name musical events. Just across the freeway, you can spend the day at the ballpark, eating hot dogs and peanuts and cheering on the Angels at **Angels Stadium of Anaheim** (2000 Gene Autry Wy). Baseball season runs April through October.

Nearby, sweethearts feeling a little nostalgic can practically step back in time in **Old Towne Orange**. Victorian homes line the streets of this charming little village, but visitors come to check out the more than 50 antique shops and 10 antique malls that are found here in what is often proclaimed the **Antique Capital of Southern California**. Lovers can pick up a brochure of antique shops at most local businesses or at the **Orange Chamber of Commerce & Visitors Bureau** (439 E Chapman Ave; 714/538-3581; www .orangechamber.org) before they set out on a search for vintage finds. After hunting for treasures, a sweet treat can be shared at **Watson Drug and Soda Fountain** (116 E Chapman Ave; 714/633-1050), an old-fashioned soda shop that still looks like it did when it was used as Jimmy Stewart's childhood place of employment in *It's a Wonderful Life*. Sit at the counter and order a milkshake and two straws, and you'll feel transported back to days long gone by.

If modern-day shopping is more what you had in mind, head to Costa Mesa's **South Coast Plaza** (Bristol St at I-405; 714/435-2000 or 800/782-8888; www.southcoastplaza.com). This massive shopping complex features such high-end anchor department stores as Neiman-Marcus, Saks Fifth Avenue, and Nordstrom. Inside the enclosed mall, shops run the gamut from designer boutiques like Gucci and Versace to mainstream favorites like J. Crew and Banana Republic. And with three adjacent complexes— Crystal Court, South Coast Village, and Metro Square—offering plenty of other retail options, it's easy to spend the day spending. When the two of you want to give your feet—and your Gold card—a break, stop in for a Northern Italian lunch and perhaps a glass of wine at **Quattro Café** (near Macy's; 714/754-0300) or sample exotic Asian fare at **Yujean Kang's Asian Bistro** (near Robinsons-May; 714/662-1098). Both are located in South Coast Plaza, so you won't even have to move your car.

A relaxing tour of the art collections of Santa Ana's prestigious **Bower's Museum** (2002 Main St; 714/567-3600; www.bowers.org) is another lovely way to spend the day with your significant other. Exhibiting artwork from around the world, this small museum offers an intimate venue for art lovers to appreciate fine works from a number of noted artists. Once you've let the compelling displays soothe you, head across the street to **Nina Montée Spa** (120 W 20th St; 714/918-8888; www.ninamonteespa.com) to further indulge your senses. Set in a beautifully restored Craftsman-style home, complete with a serene Japanese water garden in the backyard, this rare gem of a spa pampers lovebirds with the Couple's Retreat package, which includes a signature facial, sea-salt body glow, cranial massage with scalp treatment, rainforest rinse, stress-releasing body massage, and a spa meal. It will leave the two of you feeling so mellow, you might need to spend the rest of the day napping, which would be the perfect ending to a visit to Inland Orange County.

## Access and Information

The central point of Inland Orange County is Anaheim, which is about 40 miles south of downtown Los Angeles and 90 minutes north of San Diego. Interstate 5 traverses the region, whether you are coming south from Los Angeles or north from San Diego. Other main thoroughfares include the 55 Freeway, which cuts from Costa Mesa up through Orange and eventually intersects with the east-west 91 Freeway, and the 57 Freeway, which travels south from the San Gabriel Valley.

Orange County's main airport, Santa Ana's **John Wayne Airport** (949/252-5200; www.ocair.com) is about 15 miles from Disneyland, making it much more convenient than LAX, which is about an hour away, depending on traffic. The area is also served by **Metrolink** (714/636-7433; www.octa.net) and **Amtrak** (800/USA-RAIL; www.amtrak.com).

For more information, contact the **Anaheim/Orange County Visitors & Convention Bureau** (800 W Katella Ave; 714/765-8888; www.anaheimoc .org) or **Costa Mesa Conference & Visitors Bureau** (1631 Sunflower West; 714/384-0493; www.costamesa-ca.com).

## Romantic Lodgings

### DISNEY'S GRAND CALIFORNIAN HOTEL
🌑🌑

*1600 S Disneyland Dr, Anaheim / 714/635-2300 or 714/956-MICKEY*
Disneyland isn't just for kids anymore. Indeed, this sophisticated hotel was created with adults in mind, and no expense was spared on the creation of this nostalgic yet state-of-the-art Arts and Crafts–style resort that takes inspiration from California's redwood forests, mission pioneers, and plein-air painters. Couples enter through subtle stained-glass sliding panels to the hotel's six-story living room with a William Morris–designed

marble carpet, an angled skylight seen through exposed support beams, display cases of Craftsman treasures, and a three-story walk-in hearth whose always burning fire warms Stickley-style rockers and plush leather armchairs. Outside, two beautiful swimming pools (one with a waterslide for kids and kids at heart) are nestled in a landscaped garden surrounded by an extensive health club/spa, game room/video arcade, and three dining choices, including the magnificent Napa Rose (see Romantic Restaurants). Guest rooms are spacious and smartly designed, maintaining the Arts and Crafts theme surprisingly well considering the hotel's grand scale. The bathrooms, however, look more like those at the Holiday Inn than a luxury hotel. Couples may want to request a room that overlooks the park (both Disneyland and California Adventure are just steps away), so the two of you can experience the magic of Disney even after the park closes; rooms facing Downtown Disney can be loud in the evenings.
$$$–$$$$ *AE, DC, DIS, MC, V; checks OK; www.disneylandhotel.com.* &

## THE FRENCH ESTATE
☙❦

*2485 Batavia St, Orange / 714/997-5038*
Listed on the National Registry of Historic Places, this former plantation house once served as the estate for the French family. Today, it plays host to numerous weddings in its lovely gardens and welcomes couples to what is now a charming bed-and-breakfast. A dramatic foyer and cozy library serve as inviting public spaces, where lovers can relax and soak in the historic ambience. Upstairs, the inn boasts just one antique-filled guest room, which makes for an intimate stay. Complete with its own entrance, this enticing suite offers a four-poster bed, a separate sitting area, stained-glass windows, and a private bath. The gardens, however, may be the estate's most alluring attribute. The two of you can enjoy a romantic moment in the passion vine–covered pergola, stroll hand-in-hand through the rose garden, or even tie the knot in the wedding arbor. A home-cooked breakfast is served each morning, but if your stay overlaps with a wedding or event at the estate, they will send you off to a local cafe for a complimentary breakfast instead.
$$ *AE, MC, V; no checks; www.thefrenchestate.com.*

## HYATT REGENCY IRVINE
☙

*17900 Jamboree Rd, Irvine / 949/975-1234*
While this 536-room hotel bustles with a primarily business clientele during the week, this AAA four diamond award–winning property becomes a peaceful retreat for lovers who want to get away from it all on weekends. After a recent $15-million renovation, the alluring guest rooms (including 21 suites) welcome couples with soothing colors, blonde woods, luxurious

Egyptian cotton linens, and commissioned artworks. Couples in search of a little extra pampering can check into a room on the Regency Club floor, where complimentary food service is offered throughout the day and a concierge is on hand to assist the two of you with dinner or theater reservations, or in planning a romantic interlude. By day, couples can hit one of three tennis courts, lounge by the pool, indulge in massages at the Massage Center, or work out in the newly equipped fitness center. Or, check out a couple of the hotel's complimentary bikes and take a pedal along the scenic bike trail to Newport. Sweethearts who want to hit the greens can take advantages of preferred tee times at nearby Pelican Hill Golf Club and Oak Creek Golf Club. Or simply sequester yourselves in your room and enjoy a little downtime together. The hotel's The Café restaurant, featuring California cuisine, is open every day for breakfast, lunch and dinner, or couples can grab a quick bite at the walk-up Jamboree Café.
$$$ AE, DC, DIS, MC, V; no checks; www.hyatt.com. &

## THE WESTIN SOUTH COAST PLAZA
♥♥

*686 Anton Blvd, Costa Mesa / 714/540-2500*
When shopping, theater-going, and romancing are on a couple's getaway agenda, they can check into this 392-room hotel in the heart of Costa Mesa. While a pedestrian bridge links the hotel with the exclusive South Coast Plaza for lovers who like to shop and the South Coast Repertory is just a short walk away, sweethearts may find it hard to resist the lure of Westin's signature "heavenly beds," made up with luscious 280-thread-count Egyptian cotton sheets and down comforters. Soothing earth tones, cozy bathrobes, 24-hour room service for a late-night snack, and complimentary Starbucks only add appeal to these comfy accommodations. However, couples that do opt to venture out can play a love match on the hotel's tennis courts, lounge in the sun by the swimming pool, and work up a sweat at the fitness center. For lovers feeling truly indulgent, The Spa at South Coast Plaza pampers with massages, facials, and body treatments. Then, finish up the day with a truly romantic meal amid the Provençal chateau setting of Pinot Provence (see Romantic Restaurants). If Mediterranean fare isn't what the two of you had in mind, you can sup on seafood in Scott's Seafood Bar and Grill, or simply snuggle up together in the Lobby Lounge with a glass of wine and a little snack, and take a moment to toast true love.
$$-$$$ AE, DC, MC, V; no checks; www.starwood.com/westin. &

# Romantic Restaurants

## ANAHEIM WHITE HOUSE
🌑🌑

*887 S Anaheim Blvd, Anaheim / 714/772-1381*
Once surrounded by orange groves, today this 1909 Colonial-style house welcomes lovers for a night of intimate dining. Since 1987, Paris-born Bruno Serato has earned a loyal following by gracefully serving a Northern Italian menu (with a few French items tucked in) to sweethearts in search of a fine meal near Disneyland. Couples enjoy a choice of eight candlelit rooms with Victorian decor. Reserve a table near the fireplace, and the two of you can watch the flames flicker as you dine on steak, veal, lamb, fresh seafood, and pasta. Filet mignon with baked polenta, caramelized shallots, and thyme-scented veal reduction wins over meat lovers; Italian potato dumplings in a silky Gorgonzola sauce is another winning selection. The widely praised wine list features more than 200 California and European vintages, offering top choices for any special occasion. Be sure and save room for the Grand Marnier soufflé with chocolate sauce and chantilly cream; it's worth the calories.
*$$$ AE, MC, V; no checks; lunch Mon–Fri, dinner every day; full bar; reservations recommended; www.anaheimwhitehouse.com.* ♿

---

## ANTONELLO
🌑🌑🌗

*1611 Sunflower Ave, Santa Ana / 714/751-7153*
Gracious owner Antonio Cagnolo adds warmth and style to this lavish Italian restaurant, where couples can enjoy premium service and refined Northern Italian cuisine. The meandering layout and faux palazzo design of the dining room includes many nooks and crannies where couples can enjoy a little privacy for a romantic meal. Specialties like delicate miniature veal ravioli with bolognese sauce from Cagnolo's mother's recipe, creamy risotto with shrimp and champagne, and tender free-range veal chop with porcini and truffles indulge the senses. This utterly upscale yet perfectly endearing and gracious spot is so alluring, the two of you can't help but get caught up in the moment. So, sit back and order a bottle from the noted wine list, which is well supported by a wine-savvy staff, and enjoy all the makings of a special meal.
*$$$ AE, DC, MC, V; no checks; lunch Mon–Fri, dinner Mon–Sat; full bar; reservations recommended; www.antonello.com.* ♿

---

127

## BLACK SHEEP BISTRO
🐑🐑

*303 El Camino Real, Tustin / 714/544-6060*
Finding a slice of European charm in Tustin may be surprising, but why question a good thing? Owners Rick and Diane Boufford lure couples to their laid-back eatery with the promise of Spanish- and French-inspired takes on lamb dishes, including their signature Borrego, Borrego, Borrego, which features an onion stuffed with lamb stew, topped with tender lamb loin, and surrounded by lamb chops. Paella, prepared three different ways, is another specialty, but since it takes an hour to make, lovers will have to be patient. Order a glass of wine from a list peppered with European selections and sample such alluring appetizers as stuffed mushrooms, mussels, or a brilliant cheese plate. (Unless, however, it is a Wednesday evening, when all-you-can-eat paella served on the patio requires no wait.) The restaurant's umbrella-strewn patio is open year-round, and it's the best seat in the house for enjoying a beautiful evening with the one you love. A gourmet market with meats, cheeses, sauces, and spices gives foodies an opportunity to stock up on eclectic edibles, too.
*$$–$$$ AE, MC, V; no checks; dinner Tues–Sat; full bar; reservations recommended; www.blacksheepbistro.com.* &

## CATAL RESTAURANT/UVA BAR
🐑🐑🐑

*1580 Disneyland Dr, Anaheim / 714/774-4442*
After a day at Disneyland, head over to this Mediterranean eatery and tapas bar set in the heart of downtown Disney for a little snuggle time. Upstairs, a series of quiet, intimate rooms provides couples with a place to decompress from the crowds and sample from a menu rich with flavors from the Mediterranean Sea. Think Moroccan-spiced lamb with flaky spinach-feta pie, seared sea scallops with saffron risotto, and osso buco on creamy polenta. Downstairs, the casual Uva Bar (which means "grape" in Spanish) lets lovers stay in the midst of the action while dining on the outdoor pavilion-style patio with its red and white umbrellas. While many of the items offered upstairs in Catal are available here as well, a lighter and more affordable menu features such selections as cabernet-braised short ribs on zesty horseradish mashed potatoes and Andalusian gazpacho with rock shrimp. And, with more than 40 different wines offered by the glass, the two of you can sample a wide selection of vintages and toast your day at the happiest place on earth.
*$$–$$$ AE, DC, DIS, MC, V; no checks; lunch, dinner every day; full bar; reservations recommended Sun–Thurs, not accepted Fri–Sat (Catal), reservations not accepted (Uva Bar); www.patinagroup.com.* &

## THE CELLAR
◖◖◖

*305 N Harbor Blvd, Fullerton / 714/525-5682*
Eating at the Cellar is like being in the French wine country, where you can enjoy classic French-European cuisine in a setting that is so engagingly romantic, it seems unreal. (Note to self: It is. The artistic crew from Disneyland created the restaurant in 1969.) Located below the Villa del Sol shopping center, the Cellar offers three main dining rooms with private, secluded, exclusive booths placed around a room filled with roaring open fireplaces, magnificent statues, crystal chandeliers, and lots of candles. The cavernous stone walls are decorated with silver lanterns, antiques, artwork, and wine casks. The setting is timeless, and the food is classic, with entrées like salmon, Dover sole, New York pepper steak, chateaubriand, and grilled venison medallions with caramelized apple slices among the selections. Be sure to ask your waiter for a tour of the upstairs wine cellars. The restaurant carries more than 1,400 different wines from 15 countries, ranging in price from under $100 to more than $1,500. Wine-tasting sessions occasionally take place in the wine cellars.
*$$$ AE, DC, DIS, MC, V; no checks; dinner Tues–Sat; full bar; reservations recommended.* &

## CHANTECLAIR
◖

*18912 MacArthur Blvd, Irvine / 949/752-8001*
Despite its expansive size, Chanteclair feels intimate. The French country interior is divided into five distinctly different dining rooms, four with fireplaces. The library is filled with small tables encircling a crackling hearth; the garden room, with its tiled floor and hanging plants, feels light and airy. The restaurant's vast wine collection is beautifully displayed in glass cases, and the decor feels homey and comfortable. No matter which room you choose, your evening will be enhanced by classic dishes such as ahi tuna with pan-seared foie gras, succulent steak Diane, Chilean sea bass, and veal shank with grilled forest mushrooms. Cozy up at a table for two by the fire, sip a nice glass of French wine, order something delicious from the traditional French menu, and you'll have all the makings of a magical evening for two.
*$$$ AE, DC, DIS, MC, V; no checks; lunch Mon–Fri, dinner Mon–Sat; full bar; reservations recommended; www.chanteclairrestaurant.com.* &

## CHAT NOIR
◖◖◖

*655 Anton Blvd, Costa Mesa / 714/557-6647*
Oversized leather booths, display wine cellars, and warm red tones with black accents give this Parisian-style bistro the feeling of a sexy supper

club, which is just what Orange County restaurateur David Wilhelm had in mind when he created this chic brasserie. Couples can reserve a cozy corner table indoors for a more intimate meal, or dine in the jazz lounge, where live music can be enjoyed over cocktails or dinner. The lounge also boasts a covered patio, making it possible for couples to dine alfresco or for OC hipsters to smoke like they really are in a Parisian cafe. Whether you opt for a light supper of escargot, caviar, a chilled seafood plate, or mussels, or want something more substantial like steak frites, rack of lamb, or a chicken breast delicately seasoned with herbes de Provence, the traditional French menu plays second fiddle to the musical entertainment. Jazz combos perform nightly, and a DJ plays acid jazz and Verve remixes late into the night. For night owls, a late-night menu makes it possible to enjoy something other than drive-thru food after midnight.

$$-$$$ *AE, DC, DIS, MC, V; no checks; lunch Mon–Fri, dinner every day; full bar; reservations recommends for the restaurant, reservations not accepted for the lounge except for groups of 6 or more; www.culinary adventures.com.* &

## THE HOBBIT
❂❂❂

*2932 E Chapman Ave, Orange / 714/997-1972*
Couples may not find the coveted "ring" here, but they can enjoy the hobbit lifestyle, which advocates enjoying great food and wine and eating no less than six meals a day. Okay, maybe not six meals, but seven courses are served as part of a prix-fixe menu that is served for one seating only each night at this classic European-style restaurant. The extravagant meal takes place over the course of a three- to three-and-a-half hour evening, so lovers should come ready to indulge. Guests begin with champagne and hot and cold hors d'oeuvres in the restaurant's wine cellar and are then seated at a table in the lovely dining room for an appetizer, a fish or fowl course, and a salad. To give diners a little breather, an intermission follows, where you can tour the kitchen, meet the chef, or sneak away for a private moment together on the patio. Upon return, you're served sorbet, the main course (which often includes rack of lamb or stuffed filet mignon), and dessert. The menu changes regularly, so the two of you can enjoy a new dining experience each time you return.

$$$$ *MC, V; no checks; dinner Wed–Sun; full bar; reservations required; www.hobbitrestaurant.com.* &

## LA VIE EN ROSE
❂❂❂

*240 S State College Blvd, Brea / 714/529-8333*
This stunning restaurant, designed to replicate a Normandy farmhouse, succeeds in every regard. The octagonal, steepled ceiling and the small, inti-

mate dining rooms with handsome appointments add to the luxurious effect. Relax near a glowing fireplace in the mansion's lounge, while classic French music serenades you throughout the evening. Owner Louis Laulhere, who hails from Gascony, has created a Provençal menu that reads like a dream. Couples can cozy up in a tapestry-covered booth and order such traditional starters as creamy lobster bisque with puff pastry or the signature lobster ravioli. Winning entrées include poached salmon bathed in beurre blanc, roasted half duckling with orange sauce, or pork tenderloin sautéed with apples and Calvados sauce. For dessert, choose from a tempting selection of fresh-baked pastries wheeled to your table on a three-tiered cart, or go for such decadent classics as custard and strawberry-stuffed crepes or chocolate, raspberry, or Grand Marnier soufflé. After a romantic meal here, the two of you will definitely be living *la vie en rose*.
**$$$-$$$$** *MC, V; no checks; lunch Mon–Fri, dinner Mon–Sat; full bar; reservations recommended; www.lavnrose.com.* &

## NAPA ROSE
◐◑◐◐

*1600 S Disneyland Dr (Grand Californian Hotel), Anaheim / 714/300-7170*
Situated inside the upscale Grand Californian Hotel (see Romantic Lodgings), this sophisticated restaurant boasts a warm and light dining room that mirrors the Arts and Crafts–style of the hotel, down to the Frank Lloyd Wright–stained glass windows and Craftsman-inspired seating throughout the restaurant and its relaxing lounge. On a beautiful evening, couples may opt to sit outdoors, where tables are arranged around a rustic fire pit, gazing out across a landscaped arroyo toward California Adventure's Grizzly Peak. Chef Andrew Sutton personally seeks out California's freshest ingredients, bringing a wine-country sensibility and a passion for fresh, inventive preparations to the Rose's expertly equipped, open kitchen. Begin the evening with the tantalizing Seven Sparkling Sins starter platter for two, which features jewel-like portions of foie gras, caviar, oysters, lobster, and other exotic delicacies. Seasonal main courses are equally impressive, with standouts like grilled yellowtail with tangerine-basil fruit salsa or free-range veal osso buco. Leave room to at least share such inventive desserts as Sonoma goat cheese flan with Riesling-soaked tropical fruit, and gooey chocolate crepes with house-made caramelized banana ice cream. Napa Rose boasts an impressive and balanced wine list, including 45 by-the-glass choices.
**$$$** *AE, DC, DIS, MC, V; no checks; lunch, dinner every day; full bar; reservations recommended; www.disneylandhotel.com.* &

## PINOT PROVENCE
◐◐◐

*686 Anton Blvd (Westin South Coast Plaza Hotel), Costa Mesa / 714/444-5900*
Orange County foodies were positively giddy in 1998 when celebrity chef
Joachim Splichal opened this addition to his Patina empire in the lobby
of the Westin South Coast Plaza Hotel (see Romantic Lodgings). The
Provençal chateau—complete with village antiques, a mammoth fireplace,
and a limestone archway—features comfy yellow-striped banquettes with
pillows where lovers can snuggle close and order from the enchanting bistro's enticing menu. Two cozy garden rooms also make for lovely romantic
patio interludes. Selections run the gamut from Provençal dishes to those
from other regions of France, and dishes make the most of fresh ingredients
gathered from local farmers' markets. Start with a seductive sampling of
seasoned olives, chilly raw oysters, and fritters of brandade (a tasty salt-
cod puree). For the main course, lavender-scented lamb chops, tender rack
of pork with cherries, beef medallions, and lamb shanks with couscous
are winning choices. During lunch, a daily spa menu makes it possible for
sweethearts to watch their waistlines and still eat well.
$$$ *AE, DC, DIS, MC, V; no checks; breakfast, lunch, dinner every day; full
bar; reservations recommended; www.patinagroup.com.* &

---

## TROQUET
◐◐◐

*333 Bristol St, Costa Mesa / 714/708-6865*
Awash in amber lighting, vintage French liquor posters, and fine crystal,
Troquet is a bistro in the finest sense. Neither hectic nor noisy, it's a poised,
seductive room where time slows, and couples can savor the area's best
French cuisine. Owned and operated by famed Orange County restaura-
teurs Tim and Liza Goodell (of Newport Beach's Aubergine), this casual
eatery offers a menu that changes daily, based on what's in season, and
nightly tasting menus that showcase the talents of the chefs. With so many
tempting selections, couples may want to share several dishes, like the
lobster strudel layered with bacon, roasted chicken with crispy *pommes
frites*, bacon-wrapped monkfish, or the decadent sweetbread club sandwich.
While chocolate may seem like a first choice to finish a delicious meal, opt
for the cheese platter instead. It positively seduces.
$$$ *AE, DC, MC, V; no checks; lunch, dinner Mon–Sat; full bar; reserva-
tions recommended.* &

---

## TURNER NEW ZEALAND
◐◐◖

*650 Anton Blvd, Costa Mesa / 714/668-0880*
Not just another steakhouse, this handsome restaurant located around the
corner from the Orange County Performing Arts Center serves free-range,

grass-fed meat from New Zealand's Turner Ranch, which has been one of the area's top meat and seafood purveyors for years. Carnivorous couples can get their red-meat fix in a setting that boasts dramatic archways, high ceilings, tile floors, and lots of windows. The all-natural, hormone-free beef, lamb, and venison selections are simply prepared. Think slow-roasted osso bucco (lamb or beef) or pan-seared venison medallions. And for those who don't do meat, there are plenty of fresh fish selections, like a starter of plump New Zealand mussels in a lemongrass and coconut broth, or entrées such as miso-encrusted orange roughy and crispy king salmon. Whatever the two of you order, be sure and save room for the restaurant's house-made truffles: popping one of three kinds of these chocolatey treats in your mouth is pure bliss.

$$$ *AE, DC, DIS, MC, V; no checks; lunch Mon–Fri, dinner every day; full bar; reservations recommended; www.turnernewzealand.com.* &

# SAN DIEGO AND ENVIRONS

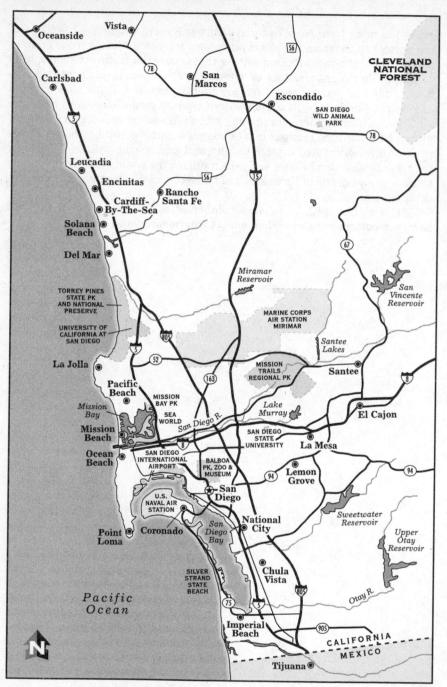

> *"Her lips on his could tell him better than all her stumbling words."*
>
> —MARGARET MITCHELL

# ♡ SAN DIEGO AND ENVIRONS

Set on the beautiful Pacific Ocean, San Diego is fringed by white sand beaches that stretch for 70 miles, attracting outdoor lovers from near and far. The city's constant growth—since its 18th-century founding by Spanish missionaries—has tamed the gentle foothills and deep arroyos (canyons) that define San Diego topography, but those features still amplify the physical beauty that continues to draw modern-day settlers to Southern California. It's a place where palm trees grow like dandelions; the weather is reliably sunny, with warm temperatures moderated by refreshing sea breezes; and small, eclectic beach towns peacefully coexist with a high-tech urban center.

Over the years, San Diego has developed dueling reputations as a convention mecca for business folk as well as a family-friendly vacation spot. But through it all, the area remains a top choice for romantic weekends away. From the laid-back attitudes of Pacific Beach and Carlsbad or the gentrified sophistication of La Jolla and Coronado to the urban vibrance of the red-hot historic Gaslamp Quarter or stylish Hillcrest, each neighborhood has a charm of its own. Indoors and out, intimate moments await discovery: a hot-air balloon ride in Del Mar is a balcony seat to a brilliant sunset, a hike in Torrey Pines State Reserve can be an exquisite way to draw close to nature (and each other), dinner in La Jolla is almost always served with a breathtaking view, and avid baseball fans can even steal a special kiss alone-in-a-crowd at PETCO Park.

Remember not to discount the romantic possibilities of those much-touted tourist spots. The San Diego Zoo may be a famous family draw, but surrounding Balboa Park is one of San Diego's most inspirational places, filled with lush scenery and private glades. An easy excursion across the border, Mexico awaits, redolent with the colorful legacy of Spanish forbearers; a taste of that classical Latin romance can also be found in historic

135

Old Town, where San Diego has its earliest beginnings.

For convenience and diversity, nothing beats the appeal of San Diego as a great place to find togetherness made-to-order.

# NEAR THE BEACH

## ROMANTIC HIGHLIGHTS

Almost everyone comes to San Diego to spend some time at water's edge—who isn't susceptible to the intoxicating romance of a seaside getaway? San Diego's beach neighborhoods are filled with hotels and motels, many of them historic landmarks where romance is layered along with Spanish-inspired stucco and heirloom flowering vines. The grande dame of them all is the Hotel del Coronado (see Romantic Lodgings), a 19th-century masterpiece that holds court over the "island" of Coronado.

Coronado—San Diego's southernmost seaside retreat—isn't really an island, but a bubble-shaped peninsula across the bay from downtown, connected to southern San Diego County by a narrow strand of land so inconvenient that Coronado was reached primarily by ferry before the construction of the soaring Coronado Bay Bridge in 1969. As city-weary couples know only too well, isolation can be a good thing, and for Coronado it led to an aura of exclusivity and the reputation of being an island, figuratively if not literally. To visit Coronado is to step back in time, an opportunity to hold hands and stroll along quiet streets lined with historic Victorian and Queen Anne homes, or enjoy the quaint shops that line Orange Avenue, the main street in town. If you're interested in learning more about the history of this well-preserved early resort community, stop into the **Coronado Historical Museum** (1100 Orange Ave; 619/435-7242; www.coronadohistory .org), which features displays on both the turn-of-the-century "tent city" for vacationers and Coronado's long history of military aviation. Architecture lovers can join up with **Coronado Touring** (619/435-5993), which provides upbeat, informative 90-minute walking tours of Coronado's highlights. Tour leader Nancy Cobb has been doing this for 25 years, so she really knows her stuff; tours leave at 11am on Tuesdays, Thursdays, and Saturdays from the Glorietta Bay Inn (see Romantic Lodgings) and cost $8 per person.

Most of San Diego's beach towns are far more accessible than Coronado. Just north of downtown, Mission Beach lies adjacent to Mission Bay, home of **SeaWorld** (500 SeaWorld Dr; 619/226-3901; www.seaworld.com), the aquatic entertainment park made famous by Shamu the killer whale. Over the years, there have been changes at SeaWorld: Shamu and his tank mates are known by their zoologically correct (and less menacing) name of orca, and SeaWorld has expanded its offerings to include hands-on programs that teach about marine life, a wet-and-wild adventure ride, sophisticated enclosures that mimic climates (such as the frozen Arctic), and magical water-stage acrobatic shows modeled after Cirque du Soleil.

Mission Bay itself is a water playground for all ages, where locals and visitors alike enjoy windsurfing, kayaking, sailing, or jogging and bicycling along the 27 miles of paved bay-front paths. The two of you can rent inline skates (shops abound along Mission Blvd) and glide hand-in-hand past luxury resorts, prime-view condos, and charming marinas. Later, linger over a sunset kiss at Mission Beach, a laid-back surfers' enclave at water's edge. Casual beachfront taverns are plentiful here and in neighboring Pacific Beach, a perfect spot to end the day gazing into each other's eyes—or toward the horizon to catch a glimpse of the rumored "green flash" that occurs as the sun touches the ocean's edge.

During whale-watching season (mid-December to mid-March), take an excursion to **Cabrillo National Monument** (1800 Cabrillo Memorial Dr; 619/557-5450; www.nps.gov.cabr) on Point Loma, south of Ocean Beach. Always an inspirational spot, this windblown tip of land high above the ocean's edge becomes even more romantic when you can observe scores of graceful yet gargantuan California gray whales making their annual migration to warm breeding lagoons in Baja, then returning with their calves to springtime feeding grounds in Alaska. If you miss whale season, there are tide pools to explore, a restored 1855 lighthouse, and beautifully maintained trails for quiet nature walks.

Regardless of what time of year you choose for your seaside rendezvous, in San Diego it's *always* beach season. While it's true that summer offers the warmest temperatures, the fewest chances of rain, and the most plentiful beach vendors, you and your sweetheart will hardly be alone smooching on the sand once June rolls around. Take advantage of the off seasons, even if it means snuggling under a blanket rather than splashing in the surf—we guarantee the privacy will make it worthwhile. Like the San Diegans who flock to them, each beach has its own personality. Ocean Beach has rip currents that make swimming unwise, but it's popular for the off-leash "dog beach" at the northern end. Mission Bay's coves are too calm to really be called beaches, but it's a great spot for beginning kayakers unwilling to brave the waves; Mission Beach is better known for the parade of humanity along its boardwalk. Pacific Beach is a great choice for a winter picnic, since you can easily duck into a pub for warmth. At the north end of Pacific Beach, **Tourmaline Surfing Park** is where the sport's old guard gathers to surf where swimmers are prohibited. La Jolla Cove's calm, protected waters offer the county's best snorkeling; and La Jolla Shores looks like a picture postcard—all wide, flat sand kissed by gentle waves.

La Jolla itself illustrates all the wonderful ways to fall in love with San Diego's coastal neighborhoods. In addition to the abundantly beautiful beaches, La Jolla—whose name, a compromise between Spanish and American Indian derivations, is pronounced "la-HOY-ah" and means "the jewel"—displays scenic perfection. Downtown La Jolla is known as the Village, and aptly so—the breezy criss-crossing streets exude a European ambience and are lined with fascinating shops, fine restaurants, and art galleries displaying works inspired by the physical beauty all around. A tradition of fine seaside hotels prevails, starting with the historic **La Valencia** (see Romantic Lodgings), a fetchingly pink Spanish-style grand hotel; generations of brides have posed in front of the lounge's spectacular picture window overlooking the ocean.

If the two of you stay in La Jolla, you can find all the amorous adventure you want within a six-block radius. Lovers of independent bookstores shouldn't miss **John Cole's Book Shop** (780 Prospect St; 858/454-4766). This wisteria-clad historic cottage is jam-packed with new and used books: cookbooks line the old kitchen, art and architecture flank the fireplace, a selection of harmonicas rounds out the music corner, and garden benches encourage lovers to take a test-read.

Nearby, the **Museum of Contemporary Art** (700 Prospect St; 858/454-3541; www.mcasandiego.org) is known internationally for its collection and exhibitions, which focus on work produced since 1950. Perched on a cliff overlooking the ocean, the galleries and terraces are perfect for a midday kiss against a stunning backdrop; the original building is also historically significant and features a fully restored facade.

If simply breathing in the great outdoors is your favorite aphrodisiac, **La Jolla's Torrey Pines State Reserve** (858/755-2063; www.torreypine.org) features 2,000 acres of nearly pristine land much as it was before San Diego was developed—the chaparral plant community, the rare indigenous Torrey pine trees, springtime wildflower fields, and a lagoon that's visited by migrating seabirds. There are 8 miles of hiking trails, and plenty of solitude. Guided nature walks are offered on weekends and holidays. Lovebirds can reward themselves after a good climb by embracing at one of the many stunning scenic overlooks and celebrating the beauty of this seaside setting.

# Access and Information

Air travelers to San Diego arrive at **San Diego International Airport**, known locally as Lindbergh Field (3707 N Harbor Dr; 619/231-2100; www.san .org). It's conveniently located on the bay adjacent to the heart of town, and just off Interstate 5. The Interstate 5 freeway is the major highway connecting San Diego with points north; it stays within a mile of the coast, veering inland as it bisects downtown, and then continuing to the Mexican border. Most of San Diego's beach neighborhoods are easily accessed from Interstate 5. To reach Coronado, take the Coronado Bay Bridge exit; it's hard to miss this soaring arc built high enough to allow tankers and Navy behemoths to pass underneath. Interstate 8 intersects Interstate 5 north of downtown and provides a direct route to the neighborhoods of Ocean Beach, Mission Beach, and Pacific Beach.

For information on San Diego, including the photo-laden, glossy Visitors Planning Guide, contact the **San Diego Convention & Visitors Bureau** (1040⅓ W Broadway Ave; 619/236-1212; www.sandiego.org). On Coronado, the **Visitors Center** (1100 Orange Ave; 619/437-8788; www .coronadovisitors.com) is located inside the Coronado Museum and dispenses maps, newsletters, and information-packed brochures. Information on La Jolla is distributed by **Promote La Jolla** (7966 Herschel Ave; 858/454-5718; www.lajollabythesea.com).

## *Romantic Lodgings*

### THE BED & BREAKFAST INN OF LA JOLLA
❂❂❂
*7753 Draper Ave, La Jolla / 858/456-2066 or 800/582-2466*
It's easy to miss the ivy-covered entrance to this pleasant hideaway just a few blocks from busy Prospect Street, which makes it all the more alluring for a romantic rendezvous. Once you arrive at the end of the garden path, friendly innkeepers welcome you into a converted home that's captured many hearts since it was built in 1913. This historic treasure boasts a fine pedigree: composer John Philip Sousa lived here in the 1920s, and Kate Sessions, San Diego's grande dame of horticulture, designed the original gardens. Today, the 16 rooms offer a taste of genteel living and cater to couples celebrating a special occasion or much-needed romantic getaway. You'll find plenty of elegant touches—fresh flowers, sherry, and fruit in the rooms, as well as antiques and original artworks that lend the air of a private home. Garden paths lead to a discreet annex that cleverly blends into the vintage property; even the rooms located here feel like they belong in the main house. Lovers may want to check into the spacious Irving Gill Penthouse, named for the prominent local architect who designed the home. The inn's most secluded room, it features a separate private sitting room and small deck, plus a bathtub made for two. If this splurge isn't on the agenda, it's just as easy to evoke romance in the other kiss-worthy rooms, like the Holiday Room, which has a four-poster bed and working fireplace; or the upstairs Peacock Room, with its private balcony for sunbathing. We especially like the Garden Room, a sanctuary with private outside entrance, fireplace, and claw-footed bathtub. Breakfast here completes the effect of an elegant Côte d'Azur pension, served on Royal Albert bone china in the casual-chic dining room or by the patio fountain.
$$$ AE, MC, V; no checks; *www.innlajolla.com.*

## CRYSTAL PIER
❀❀❀
*4500 Ocean Blvd, Pacific Beach / 858/483-6983 or 800/748-5894*
One of beachy San Diego's charms is the way many couples still arrive for "the season," spending a month or more each summer enjoying the shore with a leisure that belies modern pressures. The 26 historic cottages on Crystal Pier are often claimed months in advance by repeat lovebirds who set out barbecue grills, fill the fridge, and hang their beach towels over lounge chairs and wood railings. The scene is more peaceful during the off season, when couples claim the cottages as private escapes. Crystal Pier is a collection of blue-and-white country cottages, complete with shutters and flowering window boxes, built over the ocean on the vintage Crystal Pier right in the heart of Pacific Beach. Each is a self-contained hideaway, with a separate bedroom and fully equipped kitchen, plus a relaxing living room and private patio with breathtaking ocean view. Though the pier is public, only registered guests can drive their cars onto the pier's rumbling boards and claim a precious parking space. During the day, the pier and boardwalk bustle with action, but these cottages face toward the water and offer a wonderful vantage point for watching sunsets and surfers. At night, quiet descends on the beach, and generations of lovers have enjoyed their best night's sleep lulled by the gently splashing surf. Several restaurants are within easy walking distance, and the hotel rents out boogie boards, fishing poles, beach chairs, umbrellas, and other gear. For the best views and most privacy, request one of the farther cottages, and avoid the economical-but-less-charming units near the pier's entry gate.
*$$$ AE, MC, V; no checks; www.crystalpier.com.* ♿

---

## GLORIETTA BAY INN
❀❀◗
*1630 Glorietta Blvd, Coronado / 619/435-3101 or 800/283-9383*
John Spreckels, the sugar baron fond of all things grand and glorious, once lived in this stately mansion on a sloping lawn facing the bay. It's right across the street and somewhat in the (figurative) shadow of the Hotel del Coronado, but this pretty white hotel offers a more personal touch conducive to romance. The original house is a wonder of polished wood, brass, glass, swooping marble stairways, and eye-boggling antiques. Eleven rooms in the main house are our picks for courting with a nostalgic flair. The Penthouse Suite inhabits the home's former solarium, a breezy third-floor retreat with a panoramic view of the island; you'll ride to this private love nest in the home's original two-person brass cage elevator. The bay-view Sunset Room is another oft-requested boudoir, with French doors leading to a private patio and two-person porch swing for afternoon canoodling. The spacious Spreckels Suite will tempt you to sleep in and enjoy breakfast in bed from the efficiency kitchen located in Spreckels' former personal

bedroom suite, while the Crown Room enchants with a decadent blend of rich brocade fabrics, deep jewel-like colors, and a romantic rose theme that extends to the bathroom, which glows with one of the mansion's original skylights. Original tiled bathrooms add to the vintage charm of these main house rooms, and you'll feel like royalty descending the grand staircase for breakfast in the Music Room each morning. Rooms and suites in the hotel's detached annexes—more contemporary motel-style buildings—offer an economical choice; they've been nicely upgraded to match the mansion's classy ambience, but lack the sense of history (not to mention those super-luxe feather beds). Wherever you sleep, though, you'll enjoy the inn's trademark personalized service, including staffers who remember your name and preferences and who happily offer dining and sightseeing recommendations. The hotel offers rental bikes and boat rentals on Glorietta Bay and is within easy walking distance of the beach, shopping, and dining.
$$$ *AE, DC, DIS, MC, V; checks OK (2 weeks in advance); www.glorietta bayinn.com.* &

## THE GRANDE COLONIAL
❤❤❣

*910 Prospect St, La Jolla / 858/454-2181 or 800/826-1278*
Possessing an Old World flair that's more London or Georgetown than seaside La Jolla, the Grande Colonial has garnered accolades for the complete restoration of its polished mahogany paneling, brass fittings, and genteel library and lounge. The choice of discerning couples that long to hide away in a bygone world of privilege and service (albeit with today's modern conveniences and casual lifestyle), this historic hotel a block from the ocean offers elegant romance (and cleverly composed package deals) at surprisingly affordable prices. Numerous historic photos illustrate the hotel's fascinating past, and the reception desk offers a printed sheet with more details of its beginnings as a full-service apartment hotel in 1913. Actor Gregory Peck's father ran Putnam's, the original pharmacy at street level—later a restaurant of the same name—now occupied by the fine Nine-Ten restaurant. Relics from the early days include oversized closets, meticulously tiled bathrooms, and heavy fireproof doors suspended in the corridors. The rooms are an airy joy, outfitted in casually chic traditional decor and easy-to-live-on furniture. To ensure the best inspiration for in-room kissing, we highly recommend the junior suites, which boast refreshing ocean views, convenient dressing areas, and the luxury of a small apartment. All rooms have goose-down comforters and cushy bathrobes, perfect for enjoying a lazy room-service-breakfast morning in your suite. At night, gather in front of the fireplace for a predinner cocktail then proceed to enjoy the market-fresh and inspired cuisine of Nine-Ten, consistently rated one of San Diego's best restaurants. Open for breakfast, lunch, and dinner, the restaurant's chefs who use fresh local produce, fish, and meats, and smoke their own salmon

daily. All the sunny pleasures of La Jolla's village are steps away, as are the delightful sea lions that frolic on Children's Beach around the corner. $$$ *AE, DC, DIS, MC, V; checks OK; www.thegrandecolonial.com.*

## HOTEL DEL CORONADO
◐◐◐◖

*1500 Orange Ave, Coronado / 619/435-6611 or 800/HOTEL-DEL*
Even from "mainland" San Diego, the unmistakable red-roofed turrets of Coronado's enduring treasure are clearly visible and lure lovers just as they've done for over a century. The Hotel Del, as it's fondly known, is the last of California's grand old seaside hotels, a lovingly preserved Victorian confection from the romantic era of serious, steamer-trunk-and-personal-valet travel. The original building, a National Historic Landmark—complete with brass cage elevator, sturdy and oversized proportions, and luxurious beachfront balconies—is our choice for a nostalgic rendezvous; two newer oceanfront towers offer less expensive rooms with the same plush traditional furnishings. With a total of 700 rooms, the Del is hardly intimate, though—be prepared for a bustling resort atmosphere, with two swimming pools, a spa, several restaurants, and a shopping arcade.

The Hotel Del is a beloved landmark, with enough enchanting memories to fill a book. In 1887, it was among the first U.S. buildings with Thomas Edison's new invention, electric light; decades later, author L. Frank Baum wrote several *Wizard of Oz* books in Coronado, modeling the Emerald City's geometric spires after the Del's conical turrets. Romance and intrigue fill the historic halls: In 1920, Edward, Prince of Wales, was the first British royal to visit California. Staying at the Del, his lavish social gatherings were attended by Wallis Simpson (then navy-wife Wallis Warfield), for whom he would later abdicate the throne in one of history's most poignant love stories. The hotel's lower level History Gallery is a treasure trove of hotel memorabilia and stories for couples who want to explore the famous hostelry's past. On the hotel's public level, the Babcock & Story Bar is a great spot for sunset cocktails, followed perhaps by a quiet, romantic meal at the ocean-view Prince of Wales (see Romantic Restaurants). Locals and tourists mob the Crown Room for Sunday brunch—make advance reservations if you'd like to partake of this long-time favorite ritual. The formally laid-out Windsor Garden lies between the hotel and the sand; it's a favorite spot for weddings or a nice place to just enjoy a kiss. $$$ *AE, DC, DIS, MC, V; checks OK; www.hoteldel.com.* ♿

## LA VALENCIA HOTEL
◐◐◐◐

*1132 Prospect St, La Jolla / 858/454-0771 or 800/451-0772*
To many residents and visiting sweethearts, La Valencia Hotel *is* La Jolla, a clifftop landmark that's been the centerpiece of La Jolla society since

opening in 1926. The venerable Mediterranean-style Pink Lady embodies everything about La Jolla: a gracious gentility and a rich patina of history infuse the halls and gathering spaces; bougainvillea-draped walls and wrought-iron garden gates pay homage to the Spanish-Colonial architecture seen around town; and well-heeled locals hobnob with the world's moneyed elite, while welcoming everyone who appreciates the legacy of this grande dame. La Valencia has set a romantic standard for decades, as brides proudly pose in front of the lobby's picture window against a backdrop of La Jolla Cove and the Pacific, grand garden weddings take place every weekend, and nattily dressed couples head up to the ocean-view Sky Room (see Romantic Restaurants) to celebrate special occasions in sumptuously intimate style. The historic Whaling Bar is a clubby setting with a pedigree, once a western Algonquin for literary inebriates, and well-coiffed ladies lunch in the dappled shade of the Mediterranean Room's garden patio.

Couples choose La Valencia for its history, unbeatably scenic location, and time-honored standards of service and style. Each of the hotel's 117 rooms, suites, and villas are comfortably and traditionally furnished, with unique decor, lavish appointments, and all-marble bathrooms with signature toiletries. Rates vary wildly according to view, so if you're trysting on a budget, go for a cheaper room and enjoy the view from one of the many cozy lounges, from a scenic garden terrace, or beside the swimming pool. Lovers with ample discretionary cash opt for one of the 17 smashing villas, where private butlers stock your fridge with your favorite treats—a sampler of pâtes and cheeses, just the right bubbly, or quarts of Ben & Jerry's, if that's your romantic prerequisite. The butlers also unpack your luggage, draw your bath, and generally leave you free to concentrate on sharing kisses you'll remember always.

$$$$ *AE, DC, DIS, MC, V; checks OK; www.lavalencia.com.* &

## THE LODGE AT TORREY PINES
◐◐◐◐

*11480 N Torrey Pines Rd, La Jolla / 858/453-4420 or 800/656-0087*
Combining understated elegance with authentic Arts and Crafts style, this recently built resort is an homage to the Craftsman aesthetic, with peaceful grounds lining the oceanfront Torrey Pines Golf Course. Whether your romantic aspiration is to share a perfect round of golf, indulge in pampering spa treatments, dine on gourmet delights, or simply relax beside the shimmering Pacific, the lodge can make it happen. Guest rooms and public spaces all meticulously re-create the rich woods, sensuous stained glass, low-slung architecture, and organic motifs that characterize the classic Arts and Crafts style of the early 20th century; many are faithfully reproduced from iconic designs by Frank Lloyd Wright, Gustav Stickley, and others. Modestly sized yet fully equipped, the lodge feels like a warm Craftsman mansion, but boasts essential modern amenities and comforts

for couples accustomed to upscale travel. These are hotel rooms where the two of you can really feel at home, whether you're snuggling in front of the fireplace or enjoying the private aromatherapy of the lodge's delectable signature bath products in your sleekly luxurious bath. Couples who want to hit the greens receive preferred tee times at hard-to-book Torrey Pines Golf Course, home of PGA's Buick Invitational and site of the 2008 U.S. Open. The full-service spa features authentic Charles Rennie MacIntosh designs and offers lovers a sleek, chic respite from the cares of the day. Just the tranquil relaxation lounges (snuggly chaises for the ladies, wide-screen TV for men) stocked with tea and snacks are lure enough. However, don't miss the spa's signature Coastal Sage Scrub, a three-part ritual featuring intoxicating custom-blended lemongrass-sage products. For a memorable meal, make reservations at A. R. Valentien, named for the early California artist whose collectible works grace the restaurant. Impeccably prepared fresh regional fare draws foodies from across San Diego County to this well-regarded dining room. The menu changes daily, but couples will want to try such winning selections as white corn soup with black truffle flan, sea bass with chanterelle mushrooms, and the farmhouse cheese plate when they are offered.

$$$$ *AE, DC, DIS, MC, V; checks OK; www.lodgetorreypines.com.* &

## LOEWS CORONADO BAY RESORT
❤❤❤

*4000 Coronado Bay Rd, Coronado / 619/424-4000 or 800/235-6397*
Occupying a private 15-acre peninsula across the bay from San Diego's skyline, this luxury resort is a short drive from downtown Coronado along the whisper-thin Strand. As the two of you make the drive, ocean waves break on one side, while tony harbor-front homes with private docks occupy the sheltered inland side. This is where trysting romantics can indulge their disparate need for seclusion. Even if the two of you opt to never leave the resort, you won't be bored. On arrival, stoke your passions with a twilight gondola ride, where often-smooching couples snuggle under blankets with champagne and hors d'oeuvres while often-singing gondoliers guide authentic Venetian craft through the quiet waterways of the Coronado Cays. Dinner at Azzura Point (see Romantic Restaurants) is a romantic splurge on market-fresh California cuisine accompanied by twinkling city lights from across the bay. During the day, swimming pools and water toy rentals beckon; there's also a pedestrian underpass to Silver Strand Beach, and bike rentals for active couples. Indulge at Sea Spa, the brand-new, full-service spa where sea-derived ingredients will soften you up for whatever comes next. Some of the property's most romantic spots are the oft-missed gardens between the five wings of the hotel. Perfect for a quiet walk and private kiss, each has a

different theme: fragrant culinary herbs, a variety of international palms, an array of citrus trees, or bright flowerbeds.

Be sure to request a room at the end of Loews's fingerlike wings for an uninterrupted bay view from your balcony. Room appointments are stylish and casual, like a freshly furnished beach-house family room—comfy, usable, and nonimposing. You can even customize your retreat with an array of comforts available for the asking, everything from chenille throws and hypoallergenic pillows to Pilates balls and an in-room putting green. Each bathroom features an oversized soaking tub, but before you settle in, check out the room-service bath menu: Four customized bubble baths drawn by an attendant while you wait. The "Relaxation" is a mid-afternoon delight with raspberry iced tea; "Harmony" features bubble bath and soothing eye pillows. However, the two of you will want to go with "Romance," which includes champagne, chocolate strawberries, and candles for tub side. How divine.

$$$$ *AE, DC, MC, V; checks OK; www.loewshotels.com.* &

## PARADISE POINT RESORT
●●●
*1404 W Vacation Rd, Mission Bay / 858/274-4630 or 800/344-2626*
Originally opened by a Hollywood producer in the 1960s as Vacation Village South Seas Paradise, this sprawling resort has been completely upgraded to cater to contemporary tastes. Smack-dab in the center of Mission Bay, the complex is as much a theme park as its closest neighbor, SeaWorld (a three-minute drive). But the well-spaced arrangement of single-story villas across 44 acres of duck-filled lagoons, tropical gardens, and swim-friendly beaches lends a romantic vacation ambience with an island-getaway feel. The rooms all have private lanais (patios), colorful beach-cottage decor, and convenient kitchenettes for assembling an impromptu picnic on the sand outside your front door. You can be as busy or lazy as you like, taking advantage of six swimming pools, an 18-hole putting course, tennis courts, croquet, and sand volleyball; the marina offers water sport rentals, and the activity center provides bikes. On the lazier side, the Indonesian-inspired Spa Terre is a powerful aphrodisiac, offering cool serenity and aroma-tinged Asian treatments in a meditative sanctuary of exotic blossoms, teakwood accents, and scented candles. The Javanese Lulur Royal Treatment is as good as it sounds and appeals to both sexes. The regal ritual begins with a body massage of jasmine oil, followed by a gentle exfoliation, a yogurt massage, and a soak in an Ofuro tub infused with fragrant rose petals. You'll probably be too relaxed to venture far, so why not clasp hands and stroll over to the Baleen (see Romantic Restaurants), the resort's upscale

waterfront restaurant, for some ultrafresh seafood in a colonial island setting (think Tommy Bahama).
*$$$ AE, DC, DIS, MC, V; checks OK (if mailed in advance); www.paradise point.com.* &

## SCRIPPS INN
❂❂

*555 Coast Blvd S, La Jolla / 858/454-3391*
It's not easy to find this meticulously maintained inn, tucked away behind the Museum of Contemporary Art, but you're rewarded with seclusion even though the attractions of La Jolla are just a short walk away. Only a small, grassy park sits between the inn and the beach, cliffs, and tide pools; the view from the second-story inn seems to hypnotize lovers, who gaze out to sea indefinitely. The property is small, and you won't find much intimacy on the grounds, but behind your boudoir door is a private world of white-and-sand, beach-house decor; breakfast-in-bed-worthy luxury linens; and ocean views that range from teasing to tantalizing. Rates vary depending on ocean views—there are no real "clinkers," and you're not to be faulted for being a pragmatic lover and choosing a less expensive room (especially in summer, the high season). But it's worth considering your options: the Vista Ocean Suite is the best in the house, with a separate parlor, kitchen, and private balcony, plus panoramic views from La Jolla Cove to the open Pacific; Deluxe Junior Suites have straight-on sunset ocean views, plus wood-burning fireplaces (our favorites); and the appealing Garden Suite has a lovely courtyard entrance and its own kitchen. In the morning, a complimentary continental breakfast includes fresh-from-the-oven pastries from a local French bakery and trays to carry a wake-up feast back to your slumbering sweetheart. Scripps Inn is one popular love nest, and with only 14 rooms, we strongly recommend booking early.
*$$$ AE, DIS, MC, V; checks OK; www.scrippsinn.com.*

# *Romantic Restaurants*

## AZZURA POINT
❂❂❂

*4000 Coronado Bay Rd (Loews Coronado Bay Resort), Coronado / 619/424-4477*
A perennial contender for most-scenic restaurant in San Diego, this bay-view dining room at the Loews Coronado Bay Resort (see Romantic Lodgings) is a vision of safari chic that reflects the resort atmosphere. If you're feeling amorous, sit side-by-side at a perfectly situated banquette table, where the two of you can enjoy the twinkling city lights across the bay—and maybe a little footsie under the table linens (we won't tell). Toast each other

with a fine wine from the extensive list, carefully chosen to complement Azzura Point's spectacular menu of Pacific Rim, classic French, and Mediterranean flavors blended into a symphony ideal for celebrating a special occasion. Pristine fresh fish and shellfish imported from around the world always sparkle; particular standouts are the oysters splashed with sake vinaigrette, the lobster risotto, and a rare French *loup de mer.* Hearty red meat dishes like beef tenderloin complemented with a heavenly blue cheese tart are also nicely done. Nightly prix-fixe dinners offer multicourse tasting menus that are a signature of this dining room and a fine way to sample the cuisine, while a lighter menu of small plates and appetizers is available in the adjacent bar. The onsite herb garden lends flair to specialty dishes like tangy fennel-mint salad or lavender crème brûlée.

$$$–$$$$ *AE, MC, V; no checks; dinner Tues–Sun; full bar; reservations recommended; www.loewshotels.com.* &

## BROCKTON VILLA
◐◐
*1235 Coast Blvd, La Jolla / 858/454-7393*
Looking for a pleasant change of pace from La Jolla's fancy restaurants? Climb the steep, weathered stairs from La Jolla Cove up to this charming cafe, nestled in a restored 1894 beach bungalow and imbued with the spirit of artistic souls drawn to this breathtaking perch. Named for an early resident's hometown (Brockton, Massachusetts), the funky coffeehouse was rescued by San Diego's trailblazing Pannikin Coffee Company in the 1960s and has now expanded to include romantic (and affordable) candlelit dinners, in addition to morning coffee/tea/breakfast fare and satisfying lunches. A warren of dining spaces—indoors, patio—all overlook the cove, inspiring leisurely mornings made for handholding and enjoying inventive dishes such as soufflé-like "Coast Toast" (similar to French toast) and Greek-flavored "steamers" (eggs scrambled with an espresso steamer, then mixed with feta cheese, tomato, and basil). There are dozens of coffee drinks to coax you and your betrothed from your late-night-sleepy-morning stupor and a convivial atmosphere. At lunch, menu stars include homemade soups and salads plus unusual sandwiches like turkey meat loaf on toasted sourdough with spicy tomato-mint chutney. The constantly expanding dinner menu includes salmon *en croute* (wrapped in prosciutto, Gruyère, and sage, with a grainy mustard sauce), plus pastas, stews, and grilled meats.

$–$$ *AE, DIS, MC, V; no checks; breakfast, lunch every day, dinner Tues–Sun, brunch Sun; beer and wine; reservations recommended for dinner; www.brocktonvilla.com.*

# CHEZ LOMA
◐◐◖

*1132 Loma Ave, Coronado / 619/435-0661*
Couples drawn to Coronado's shingled and turreted Queen Anne cottages will definitely be wooed by this handsome example, a house with all the charm of yesteryear imbuing the nooks and crannies now set with romantic dining tables. Set on a street especially rich in vintage architecture, Chez Loma fits right in—as does chef Ken Irvine's graceful mix of classic and updated French cuisine. The small menu emphasizes seasonal seafood and usually includes stellar preparations of duck, salmon, and filet mignon (including a signature steak in a heady blue cheese sauce). House specialties include a grilled chicken breast enriched with foie gras butter and an earthy mushroom sauce; roasted salmon fillet with a piquant horseradish crust; and a nautical take on classic cassoulet, this one filled with scallops, mussels, shrimp, and salmon sausage in a lobster-based sauce. The servers here are particularly well trained—always available when needed, but never intrusive. Add a carefully chosen wine list, romantic enclosed patio, and very fair prices for the quality, and you've got all the making for a truly amorous dining experience. There's an alcove table-for-two that's often requested for marriage proposals or intimate anniversary celebrations, and we advise saving room for the amazing ginger bread dessert, a spicy-sweet treat bathed in creamy caramel sauce.
**$$–$$$** *AE, DC, DIS, MC, V; no checks; dinner every day, brunch Sun; full bar; reservations recommended; www.chezloma.com.* &

# GEORGE'S AT THE COVE
◐◐◖

*1250 Prospect St, La Jolla / 858/454-4244*
Without a doubt, this three-level property has one of the finest views in the city—a panorama of La Jolla Cove and miles of Pacific coast. But unlike many a view restaurant in town, George's offers some terrific eating, as well. Lovers can unwind with a cocktail in the upstairs bar while waiting for an in-demand window table, then venture downstairs into the quietly elegant dining room, where they specialize in inventive fresh fish dishes that incorporate the flavors of France and the Pacific Rim. The must-have starter is a smoked chicken and broccoli soup (yes, they'll share the recipe so you can re-create it at home). Follow that with the likes of crab cakes with shiitake "hash browns," diver-harvested scallops partnered with lobster risotto, or duck breast paired with buttery foie gras. On the rooftop terrace, the menu is a lower-priced affair featuring excellent seafood salads, a gourmet meat loaf sandwich, very good focaccia, and splendid desserts. Two more reasons to drop by: the ever-changing collection of contemporary art in the main dining rooms, and owner George Hauer's thoughtfully chosen wine list. Reservations aren't accepted on the upstairs terrace, which is open every

day for lunch and dinner, but the open-air setting is so enticing, the two of you are sure to decide it's worth the wait.

$$-$$$ *AE, DC, DIS, MC, V; no checks; lunch, dinner every day; full bar; reservations recommended downstairs; www.georgesatthecove.com.*

## THE GREEN FLASH
🖤

*701 Thomas Ave, Pacific Beach / 858/270-7715*
Known throughout Pacific Beach for its location and hip, loyal clientele, the Green Flash is a terrific place to wind down after a day spent exploring the boardwalk or enjoying the beach. This casual beach front tavern has been a local staple since 1965 and retains the funky charm of a neighborhood hangout. But it's easy to turn your back on happy-hour throngs and enjoy each other's company in this anything-goes atmosphere—most patrons are concentrating on watching for the legendary "green flash" that comes at sunset and for which the place was named. Stake a place on the glassed-in patio for prime viewing—the phenomenon has something to do with the color spectrum at the moment the sun disappears below the horizon, but the two of you may find the scientific explanation becomes less important with every Green Flash cocktail (an appropriately green house concoction blending gin, melon liqueur, and fruit juices). The restaurant serves diner-style fare throughout the day, but raises the bar at dinner to include some decently priced seafood entrées, surf-and-turf combos, and a baker's dozen of finger-food appetizers.

$ *AE, DC, DIS, MC, V; no checks; breakfast, lunch, dinner every day; full bar; reservations not accepted; www.greenflashrestaurant.com.*

## THE MARINE ROOM
🖤🖤🖤

*2000 Spindrift Dr, La Jolla / 858/459-7222*
When anything less than unforgettable simply won't do, reserve a window table at the Marine Room, located at the water's edge in La Jolla Shores. Graceful service and flawless French-Continental cuisine set the mood, but the drama lies in stunning sunset vistas and awesome high-tide waves that splash right up against specially reinforced picture windows (designed by the experts who build tanks for SeaWorld). You can watch the sea from every table, including the central bar, where a cozy buzz of locals gather to gossip over gin and tonics. The dining room has a crisp and formal special-occasion ambience heightened by the impeccably schooled wait staff and the talents of executive chef Bernard Guillas. The French-native chef infuses his brand of Mediterranean-Pacific Rim-California fare with imaginative flavors, from sambuca and fresh lavender to candied shallots and crunchy greens from the sea. Halibut, foie gras, ahi, and sweetbreads are some of the standouts on the menu, which changes according to the season

and the chef's whims. Recent highlights have included halibut poached in pinot noir, dry-aged strip steak with truffle-based potatoes, and goose liver paired with preserved cherries and cognac. Check out the restaurant's dramatic High Tide Breakfasts during winter, complete with a luxurious buffet and waves misting the windows.

$$$ *AE, CB, DC, DIS, MC, V; no checks; lunch, dinner every day, brunch Sun; full bar; reservations recommended; www.marineroom.com.*

## PEOHE'S
◐❨

*1201 1st St, Coronado / 619/437-4474*
With an over-the-top Polynesian decor suitable for Disneyland's Enchanted Tiki Room, Peohe's is in a class by itself—but the awesome view across the bay or the excellent Hawaiian-style seafood and Pacific Rim–accented cuisine lend an air of island romance. Every table in the giant light- and plant-filled atrium has a view; there are even better tables on the wooden deck at the water's edge. Dinner main courses include the signature crunchy coconut shrimp; island-style halibut sautéed with banana, macademia nuts, and Frangelico liqueur; and rack of lamb with Hunan barbecue sauce. Lunchtime options are more casual, including a variety of sandwiches and salads, and the opportunity for a post-meal stroll along the waterfront or through the adjacent Ferry Landing Marketplace. Better yet, before lunch rent bikes in the Marketplace for a self-guided Coronado tour, then return for a well-earned lunch dockside at Peohe's. You might even feel justified in ordering a delectably rich tropical dessert—with two forks, of course.

$$–$$$ *AE, DC, DIS, MC, V; no checks; lunch, dinner every day, brunch Sun; full bar; reservations recommended; www.peohes.com.* ♿

## PRINCE OF WALES
◐◑❨

*1500 Orange Ave (Hotel del Coronado), Coronado / 619/522-8819*
All the glamour of the Hotel del Coronado's (see Romantic Lodgings) past comes to life in this elegant signature dining room, where strains of live jazz piano accompany leisurely and romantic meals. When the weather's fine, choose a table under the stars on the candlelit terrace or cozy up inside where the champagne and gold dining room shimmers in the dimming sun. The view looks out over the perfectly manicured Windsor lawn and swaying palm trees to the Pacific's gently ebbing tide. Reserve a booth for amorous privacy and order slowly to savor this special experience. Start with a flute of imported bubbly with the osetra caviar parfait or oysters with sweet sake sorbet while you study the entrées and consider whether you want to experiment with the wild boar tenderloin or go for the more traditional yellowfin tuna with sautéed foie gras and truffle coulis. While wearing a tie isn't mandatory, it certainly isn't out of place and makes for a nice change of pace in

laid-back San Diego. This is the place to come for a special celebration—or just to revel in the good life for an evening. Impeccable service only adds to the romantic experience, and a wonderful wine selection complements the menu.
$$$$ *AE, CB, DC, DIS, MC, V; no checks; dinner every day; full bar; reservations recommended.* &

## QWIIGS BAR & GRILL
◑◖
*5083 Santa Monica Ave, Ocean Beach / 619/222-1101*
Snag a window table at sunset for the ultimate Ocean Beach dining experience right across from the water. Qwiigs offers spectacular views of surfers, joggers, seagulls, and the Ocean Beach Pier. Couples can start with steamed artichokes, bountiful house salads, fried calamari, and gourmet pizzas in the upper-level cocktail lounge or hover around the busy little sushi bar. The dining room features cozy ocean-view tables with prized window seats and raised U-shaped booths that also face the outdoor spectacle. The place is packed at sunset, naturally. Enormous fresh Cobb salads (we prefer the chicken version over the seafood salad) and thick burgers are good bets at lunch. Dinner specials might include rack of lamb, penne pesto with Japanese breaded chicken breast, fresh fish, or blackened prime rib. A sit-down Sunday brunch includes average-to-good breakfast fare. The ambience and service are fairly low-key, making this a great place for couples to dine after a day at the beach. This is definitely one of those "come-as-you-are" neighborhood haunts. Use the underground parking lot, if possible; street parking spots can be tough to find.
$$ *AE, DC, DIS, MC, V; no checks; lunch Mon–Fri, dinner every day, brunch Sun; full bar; reservations recommended.*

## THE SKY ROOM
◑◑◑◖
*1132 Prospect St (La Valencia Hotel), La Jolla / 858/454-0771*
Saying that the Sky Room is romantic is like calling Placido Domingo a pretty good singer. This ocean-view dining room atop La Jolla's La Valencia Hotel (see Romantic Lodgings) is the place to treat your beloved to an evening of elegance and pomp that will leave the two of you feeling like royalty. Each of the 12 exclusive tables is set with a single long-taper candle; ask for table number 4 or 5, as both are tucked into the front corners overlooking the ocean. Lovers are welcome to step out onto the Sky Room's most charming feature, a tiny twinkle-lit balcony just big enough for two, where the panoramic view has inspired more than a few marriage proposals. Gorgeous flower arrangements, tuxedo-clad servers, Wedgwood china, and long-stemmed roses for the ladies provide a feeling of Old World elegance and a lovely showcase for European-influenced American cuisine.

Selections range from contemporary (free-range chicken with morels, fine Kobe beef imported from Japan) to classic (delicate smoked salmon paired with julienned cucumbers, cream of mushroom soup, velvety foie gras). The special dessert plate is a must-have, a selection of sweets that generally includes tidbits of tiramisu, cookies, and sublime chocolate truffles. Ask the sommelier for assistance with the extensive and fine wine list; this is the place to splurge on a premium French label or vintage champagne.
$$$–$$$$ *AE, CB, DC, DIS, MC, V; no checks; dinner every day; full bar; reservations required; www.lavalencia.com.* &

## THEE BUNGALOW
❷❷❻

*4996 W Point Loma Blvd, Ocean Beach / 619/224-2884*
This old country bungalow stands alone at the edge of Robb Field near the Ocean Beach channel, a romantic hideaway beckoning diners for consistently good Continental cuisine in an unexpected neighborhood location. Solitude-seeking lovers never feel crowded in the four intimate dining rooms, each perfect for a romantic rendezvous. Thee Bungalow is the kind of place that caters to a faithful clientele while always attracting new fans. Some diners stick with the classics: roast duck garnished with green peppercorns, sea bass in a luscious seafood sauce, and rack of lamb. Others are attracted by chef-owner Ed Moore's newer creations, including superb steamed mussels, black-pepper-crusted salmon, and grilled halibut. Your entrée comes with soup or salad (we adored the smoked tomato soup and the tarragon-dressed house salad), so you don't need to order a starter. But if you're extra ravenous, do start with the simple cream-sauced tortellini. Wrap up the evening with a crackle-topped crème brûlée, a Bungalow specialty. The lengthy wine list earns praise for both depth of selection and excellent prices, and the restaurant regularly hosts reasonably priced, heavily attended wine dinners. Although the service and menu are a tad on the formal side, the setting is casual and comfy. Show up in jeans or in jewels—the good people of Thee Bungalow will welcome you just the same.
$$ *AE, DC, DIS, MC, V; no checks; dinner every day; full bar; reservations recommended; www.theebungalow.com.* &

## TOP O' THE COVE
❷❷❷

*1216 Prospect St, La Jolla / 858/454-7779*
With its lushly planted courtyard entrance, piano bar, and several tables overlooking the Pacific, Top o' the Cove is a romantic's dream. This wonderfully preserved cottage is one of La Jolla's earliest (1893), with a centuries-old brick path and original marble fireplace adding historic charm. Ocean-view tables in the back room are the most requested—table 6, in

particular, has gained a reputation for marriage proposals and between-course lip locks—though for post-sunset dining we prefer the cottage's middle room, where a crackling fire stokes intimacy while the two of you enjoy the kitchen's blend of classic French, Pacific Rim, and Mediterranean flavors. An appetizer of risotto and white truffles is exquisite (and should be, for the price). Our top entrée choices are the grilled swordfish or salmon, often sauced with a cabernet sauvignon reduction that's perfect for these full-flavored fish. A rare-roasted Muscovy duck breast is another standout. The restaurant's wine list is breathtaking in depth and price; you can easily drop $100 or more on a bottle. The ultimate lovers' dessert has to be the bittersweet chocolate box, filled with luscious white chocolate mousse and surrounded by raspberry sauce. It's as alluring—and delicious—as true love. $$$–$$$$ *AE, CB, DC, MC, V; no checks; lunch, dinner every day, brunch Sun; full bar; reservations recommended; www.topofthecove.com.* &

## TRATTORIA ACQUA
❶❶❻

*1298 Prospect St, La Jolla / 858/454-0709*
This indoor/outdoor restaurant is nestled on tiled terraces close enough to catch La Jolla's ocean breezes and afford diners ocean views that won't quit. Rustic walls and outdoor tables shaded by flowering vines evoke a romantic Italian villa, and the best view tables are always reserved first. The Mediterranean-influenced menu roams gracefully from Tuscany to Provence to Tangiers, a collection of complementary flavors that elevates this from other San Diego Italian eateries. Start your meal with the complimentary spicy hummus dip while you peruse the lengthy wine list, where notable names from California and Italy are sold at reasonable prices; the restaurant has received *Wine Spectator* accolades for several years running. Acqua's pastas (all available in a smaller appetizer size, too) are as good as it gets—rich, heady flavor combinations like spinach, chard, and four-cheese gnocchi, or veal-and-mortadella tortellini in fennel cream sauce. Other specialties include *saltimbocca con funghi* (veal scaloppini with sage, prosciutto, and forest-mushroom sauce), *cassoulet* (traditional Toulouse-style duck confit, sausage, and braised lamb baked with white beans, tomato, and fresh thyme), and *salmone al pepe* (roasted peppercorn-crusted salmon served over lentils with sherry-shallot vinaigrette). Acqua is an easy walk from most of La Jolla's hotels; if you drive there, validated parking is available in the downstairs garage (enter from Coast Blvd).
$$ *AE, MC, V; no checks; lunch, dinner every day; full bar; reservations recommended; www.trattoriaacqua.com.* &

# IN TOWN

## ROMANTIC HIGHLIGHTS

**D**owntown is San Diego's heartbeat—culturally, economically, historically, and architecturally—and boasts a unique environment where big business and lazy leisure peacefully coexist. If you like your romance spiked with culture and nightlife, San Diego's urban core will fire your passions, and you're guaranteed never to be bored. It all started with the **Gaslamp Quarter** (619/233-5227; www.gaslamp.org), a 16-block historic district that's a San Diego must-see. Scores of wonderfully preserved commercial buildings from the Civil War through World War I line these blocks; during the day, the streets bustle with shoppers, diners, and tourists—as well as a growing community of trendsetters and artists who live in downtown lofts. At night, the area pulses with the energy of stylish restaurants and scene-stopping nightclubs, while horse-drawn carriages impart a 19th-century air of romance to this historic-yet-fresh precinct. Fifth Avenue, downtown's original Main Street, has developed into the hub of the nightlife scene, with gas lamp–style street lamps illuminating hordes of stylish pedestrians. Fourth and Sixth avenues are nearly as crowded, with sidewalk tables spilling from doorways along with infectious rhythms of swing, jazz, and country music.

Couples can shop for souvenirs of their romantic getaway at the quarter's famous **Horton Plaza** (3958 5th Ave; 619/220-6802), a crazy quilt of rambling paths, bridges, towers, fountains, and street performers. Anchored by Nordstrom and Macy's, this unique mall has a movie multiplex and tons of familiar stores like Victoria's Secret (forget to pack anything?).

Downtown may not be blessed with one of San Diego's stunning beaches, but water is never far in this coastal city; a short walk from the Gaslamp Quarter is the **Embarcadero**, a breezy bay-side promenade that celebrates the city's seafaring history, proud Navy lineage, and simple joys of waterfront living. Bay-side diversions include ogling the gargantuan cruise ships that call here, watching fighter jets take off from the Naval Air Station across the water, or riding the 19th-century Looff carousel at nautically themed **Seaport Village** (Harbor Dr at Kettner Blvd; 619/235-4013), an outdoor cluster of shops and restaurants. Couples can stop into **Anthony's Fish Grotto** (1360 N Harbor Dr; 619/232-5103) for an ultra-fresh seafood lunch—or pick up fast and cheap fish-and-chips from the attached Anthony's Fishette—before strolling up to visit the climb-aboard ships of the **Maritime Museum** (1306 N Harbor Dr; 619/234-9153; www.sdmaritime.org). Evoking the days of adventure on the high seas, the museum offers four fine historic vessels (yes, they are all still seaworthy), including the full-rigged merchant ship **Star of India** (1863), whose impressive masts are an integral part of the San Diego cityscape; and the gleaming white San Francisco–Oakland steam-powered ferry **Berkeley** (1898), which worked round the clock carrying people to safety following the 1906 earthquake. In summertime, you can snuggle under the stars on the deck of **Star of India** as you watch nautically themed films projected onto a special outdoor "sail screen."

Or, take your courtship offshore with a bay cruise from **San Diego Harbor Excursions** (619/234-4111 or 800/44-CRUISE; www.sdhe.com), which caters to handholding sweethearts with deluxe harbor tours, winter whale-watching excursions, and romantic dinner or brunch cruises made for gazing at the distinctive San Diego skyline. If you're curious about Coronado, they also run regular ferry service across the bay to the charming Victorian neighborhood anchored by the landmark Hotel del Coronado (see Near the Beach section, Romantic Lodgings); ferry service runs between 9am and 9pm, 365 days a year; it's a kiss-worthy way to enjoy another layer of San Diego's charms.

Landlubbers and avid shoppers will probably want to spend an afternoon in the charming and vibrant uptown neighborhood of **Hillcrest**, another historic enclave that's gained new momentum as a stylish shopping mecca and the heart of San Diego's gay community. Side streets boast an array of lovingly restored homes, ranging from turn-of-the-century bungalows to angular midcentury classics, while the main shopping streets—University, Fourth, and Fifth avenues—offer an always-surprising selection of funky, fancy, and fine wares for home and self. Hillcrest is also the gateway to one of San Diego's most famous, and most captivatingly romantic, landmarks: beautiful **Balboa Park** (with entrances on 6th Ave at Laurel St, and along Park Blvd at President's Wy and Zoo Pl; 619/239-0512; www.balboapark. org). Every love affair is guaranteed a boost inside this magical green oasis, with nearly 1,200 acres encompassing walkways, gardens, historic buildings, the city's best museums, a colorful restaurant, the world's largest outdoor organ, a nationally acclaimed theater company, and the world-famous **San Diego Zoo** (2920 Zoo Dr; 619/234-3153; www.sandiegozoo.org). Even if you don't set foot in a single baroque and ornately tiled building, the wild and groomed landscapes are amorous territory, with quiet corners awaiting discovery. Courting couples are a common sight along El Prado, the park's Spanish-Moorish–flavored main promenade; popular romantic spots include the lushly old-fashioned Botanical Building and its serene pond, the regally classical Spreckels Organ Pavilion, where free outdoor concerts are offered every Sunday at 2pm, and the peaceful and highly symbolic Japanese Friendship Garden. In the evening, El Prado becomes a magical, twinkle-lit haven, perfect for strolling to a relaxed tapas meal at the Prado restaurant (see Romantic Restaurants), then taking in a play at one of the three acclaimed theaters that comprise the park's **Old Globe Theatres** (1363 Old Globe Wy; 619/239-2255; www.theglobetheatres.org), a San Diego tradition centered on an updated replica of Shakespeare's Old Globe in England.

The romance of Mexican-era California—all ruffled skirts and striped serapes—lives on in **Old Town State Historic Park** (4002 Wallace St; 619/220-5422). Old Town is located on the hill where San Diego was founded (now situated near the intersection of I-5 and I-8) where frontier-style barns and adobe cottages (many restored, some replicated) surround a traditional village green, and Spanish flavor isn't far away at **Bazaar del Mundo** (2754 Calhoun St; 619/296-3161; www.bazaardelmundo.com). The meandering passageways and stucco alcoves of the bazaar hold shops and boutiques that carry handicrafts, art, and textiles from Mexico and South America. It's the perfect place for the two of you to get a feel for San Diego's historic roots, so you can appreciate the romance the city holds today.

## Access and Information

**San Diego International Airport–Lindbergh Field** (3703 N Harbor Dr; 619/231-2100; www.san.org) is just 10 minutes from the heart of downtown, a double-edged reminder (visitors adore the convenience, residents abhor the noise) of its early years as a sleepy airstrip. Some major hotels offer free shuttle service from the airport, and taxis also await to whisk you to nearby environs.

Many visitors simply drive to San Diego if they're lucky enough to live in California, but a more old-fashioned—and romantic—choice is **Amtrak** (800/USA-RAIL; www.amtrak.com), which bears the colorful nickname *Pacific Surfliner*. It runs between San Luis Obispo and San Diego, stopping in Santa Barbara, Los Angeles, and Anaheim, as well as numerous smaller stations en route. Portions of the track travel directly on the coast, meaning you and your sweetie can gaze at the sunny surf while sipping a California vintage in true style. In San Diego, you'll arrive at the striking, Mission-style **Santa Fe Station** (at Kettner Blvd and Broadway), built in 1914 and located close to the Embarcadero and downtown. San Diego's **Metropolitan Transit System** (619/233-3004; www.sdcommute.com) runs several dozen routes throughout the county, as well as the bright red **San Diego Trolley**, a light rail network that stretches from Old Town all the way to the Mexican border. The **San Diego International Visitors Information Center** (11 Horton Plaza; 619/236-1212; www.sandiego.org), provides helpful maps and brochures; ask for the biannual **Travel Values** coupon book.

# Romantic Lodgings

## BALBOA PARK INN
❀

*3402 Park Blvd, San Diego / 619/298-0823 or 800/938-8181*
Here's one unusual bed-and-breakfast tailor-made for amorous lovebirds
with a penchant for high drama and theatrical kitsch. The four Spanish
Colonial–style former apartment buildings that comprise the Balboa Park
Inn are united by meandering pathways, a small motel-style office for
check-in, and a flock of flirtatious boudoirs to fulfill any fantasy. This mostly
residential neighborhood is walking distance from Balboa Park and caters
to a straight clientele as well as gay travelers drawn to nearby Hillcrest's hip
restaurants and clubs. About half the inn's 26 rooms are vanilla plain, priced
a few dollars less than the other rooms, but otherwise nothing to write
home about. The rest are Specialty Suites, offering over-the-top themed
furnishings guaranteed to tickle your funny bone and stoke your passions.
One of the most-requested is the Greystoke Suite (as in Tarzan), a jungle-
like retreat with faux animal heads, wild animal prints on the king-sized
bed, a whirlpool tub for two with a simulated waterfall, and *Out of Africa*–
inspired furniture. Your quietest choice would be the Orient Express Suite,
a treasure chest of black lacquer, red silk, and antiques from throughout
Asia, including a stunning four-poster Chinese wedding bed. The Courtyard
Suite is an homage to art deco, all sensuous lines accented with silver leaf,
shimmering ultrasuede, and a sofa Carole Lombard would love. In the bathroom is a double-sized whirlpool tub. Grandiose bathrooms are a recurring
theme; the Park Place Suite's bathroom actually takes up half the room. It's
a fully mirrored space lined in marble, whose elevated whirlpool tub feels
like a stage (ready for your close-up?). Each morning, continental breakfast
is laid out for couples, but service is otherwise impersonal—a boon if, like
Greta Garbo, you want to be left alone.
*$$–$$$ AE, DC, DIS, MC, V; checks OK; www.balboaparkinn.com.* &

## HERITAGE PARK BED & BREAKFAST INN
❀❀❀

*2470 Heritage Park Row, Old Town / 619/299-6832 or 800/995-2470*
Nestled in a cluster of restored Victorian homes overlooking Old Town,
Heritage Park Inn is true to its elegant, old-time roots. Twelve rooms are
contained in two historic homes—the circa 1889 Christian House and the
Italianate Bushyhead House. With a formal Victorian parlor, period antiques,
and stained-glass windows throughout, the ambience is sure to slow your
pace and get you in the mood for romance. Be sure you arrive in time for
afternoon tea in the comfortable vintage parlor, a relaxing space where, if
the two of you are feeling sociable later, you can enjoy the inn's nightly vintage film screening. Take in a spectacular San Diego sunset from the leisure

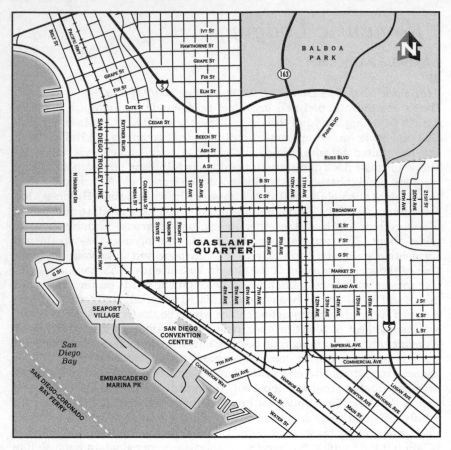

of a veranda rocker, or simply sneak off together and sequester yourselves in the featherbed-and-snuggly-robe luxury of your perfectly appointed room. The hands-down favorite for kissing is the Drawing Room, most often requested for honeymoons and special romantic trysts. Decked out in a regal pale green enhanced by sunlight that streams in the bay window, this room features a whirlpool tub for two in one corner and a secret armoire holding the TV and a mini-fridge. The Grandview Room is also a lovers' choice for the panoramic view you can enjoy from two plush wingback chairs, as well as a lacy burgundy canopy bed straight from the pages of the latest bodice-ripper. A claw-footed whirlpool tub for two completes the fantasy. If you've got your hearts set on a room in the main house—less private than the annex but closer to the wafting good scents of breakfast each morning—climb up to the Turret Room, the elegant original master bedroom with a tower sitting room that overlooks Heritage Park. After you enjoy the inn's romance-inducing candlelit breakfast—a formal seating in the dining room with exquisite gourmet selections—clasp hands for a stroll through the park, or walk to festive Old Town's shops and restaurants. If you're planning a special celebration, the staff can even set up your room with a dozen roses, a box of Godiva chocolates, and a souvenir teddy bear. $$–$$$ *AE, DC, DIS, MC, V; checks OK; www.heritageparkinn.com.*

## HORTON GRAND HOTEL
◐◐

*311 Island Ave, Gaslamp Quarter / 619/544-1886 or 800/542-1886*
The Horton Grand Hotel offers a touch of Victorian-era gentility in the heart of the historic Gaslamp Quarter, and a wonderful treat for couples who love a little historical make-believe. Composed of two historic Victorian hotels, the Horton Grand has quite a colorful history. Wyatt Earp slept here when he lived in San Diego, and the restaurant is named in honor of Ida Bailey, a notorious turn-of-the-century madam whose bordello once occupied this site. Staying at the Horton Grand is a great way to immerse yourselves in the colorful legacy of the surrounding Gaslamp Quarter: horse-drawn carriages even pull up to the front door. Each room is utterly unique; all were renovated with vintage furnishings, gas fireplaces, and bathrooms resplendent with reproduction floor tiles, fine brass fixtures, and genteel appointments. Rooms overlook either the cityscape or the fig tree–filled courtyard. For more space, request one of the 600-square-foot mini suites, located in a newer wing; choosing one means sacrificing historic character for a sitting area and minibar with microwave oven. While the hotel has plenty of its own quirky charm, its location is the real bonus. Couples can live it up at the Gaslamp's many clubs and bars, then stroll or catch a pedicab back to the hotel. The Palace Bar serves afternoon tea Tuesday through Saturday, and there's live music in the evenings. $$$ *AE, DC, DIS, MC, V; checks OK; www.hortongrand.com.* &

## KEATING HOUSE
◐◐

*2331 2nd Ave, San Diego / 619/239-8585 or 800/995-8644*
This grand Banker's Hill mansion, between downtown and stylish Hillcrest, has been meticulously restored by two energetic innkeepers with a solid background in architectural preservation. Doug Scott and Ben Baltic not only know old houses, but also are neighborhood devotees filled with historical knowledge and savvy area recommendations. Over the years, their many labors of love at Keating House have included installing or upgrading private bathrooms for every bedchamber—featuring reproduction fixtures and authentic period design—and nurturing the sumptuous gardens that bloom around all four sides of this local landmark. The house contains a comfortable hodgepodge of antique furnishings and appointments; three additional rooms are in the restored carriage house opening onto an exotic

garden patio. Every room is stunning, especially the Rose Room, upstairs in the main house. This bright and spacious boudoir has a view through original windows to the harbor, a private viewing porch, and a beautifully restored original bathroom with a towel warmer for chilly mornings. The similarly outfitted Yellow Room is another kiss-worthy choice for special occasions. In the carriage house, the Garden Suite is an ideal honeymooner's hideaway, a full private apartment with kitchenette, sitting room, and romantic French garden doors in the bedroom. The inn's parlor and dining room have cozy fireplaces; a better-than-home breakfast is served in a sunny, friendly setting. In contrast to many B&Bs in Victorian-era homes, this one eschews dollhouse frills for a classy, sophisticated approach. $$ *AE, DIS, MC, V; checks OK; www.keatinghouse.com.*

## U.S. GRANT HOTEL
❂❂❂
*326 Broadway, Downtown / 619/232-3121 or 877/999-3223*
In 1910, Ulysses S. Grant Jr. opened this stately hotel, now on the National Register of Historic Places, in honor of his famous father. The San Diego landmark was later purchased by the Sycuan Band of Kumeyaay Indians. The tribe has a special reverence for the hotel's namesake, who as U.S. president in 1875 signed an executive order setting aside San Diego lands exclusively for the Kumeyaay, including the present-day Sycuan reservation. After a $10 million renovation to preserve and enhance the Italianate hotel's grand palatial style and priceless marble, mahogany, and crystal interiors, in 2005 the U.S. Grant will become a member of the Starwood chain's Luxury Collection (putting it in good company with the likes of Kauai's Princeville Resort and San Francisco's Palace Hotel). We predict this treasured landmark will emerge as a top-notch romantic vacation choice for its seductive history, stellar location in the heart of downtown and across the street from the Gaslamp Quarter, and East Coast elegance that remains in its pedigreed bones. Some traditions we hope will remain: afternoon tea in the formal lobby, a genteel gathering with soft piano music as a backdrop, and the clubby Grant Grill, an old-fashioned favorite with theater-goers and a former gentlemen's club that didn't allow women until 1969.
$$$ *AE, DC, MC, V; no checks; www.starwood.com.* ♿

## W HOTEL
❂❂
*421 West B St, Downtown / 619/231-8220*
Are you and your baby like Austin Powers, looking for a shagadelic pad to shimmy away the weekend? When trendy W Hotels opened a branch in conservative downtown San Diego, all the city was abuzz about the cutting-edge decor, alterna-hotel-speak, and why simply *everyone* was flocking to their corner of nearby Little Italy for cocktails around the fire pit on the

sand-covered rooftop bar Beach. The answer is simple: this boutique hotel is funky, with a capital "F" for fun. First, there's the lobby, a huge untraditional living room with a two-story video screen, 24-hour bar, and rows of wicker wing chairs flanking communal tables outfitted with chessboards and other games. Past the bar lies Rice, the groovy, mood-lit restaurant with Asian overtones that carry over to its eclectic Pacific Rim–New American menu. Open for breakfast, lunch, and dinner, Rice features everything from traditional breakfasts and such mainstream fare as New York steak with *pomme frites* and grilled halibut, to more Asian-inspired dishes like summer rolls and tempura. There's a postmodern seaside ambience at W, from the seashells-as-art display downstairs to the playful beach ball pillows and crisp blue-and-white decor in the guest rooms. Sand-colored carpet, wide wood blinds, and stacks of fluffy white towels complete the look. White leather accessories and modern fixtures strike a perfect balance between high-tech demands and laid-back SoCal style. In-room minibar goodies include irresistible W logo toys, and a five-item "intimacy kit" (in case you forgot the Boy Scout creed when packing). We recommend splurging on a corner room (category: Cool), for twice the space plus bathrooms with natural light and deep soaking tubs. Lighthearted and stylish, W shapes up as a fun, grown-up way to tryst in San Diego.
$$–$$$ *AE, DC, DIS, MC, V; checks OK; www.whotels.com/sandiego.* &

## Romantic Restaurants

### BERTRAND AT MR. A'S
❂❂❂
*2550 5th Ave, Downtown / 619/239-1377*
Generations of San Diegans have counted on this 12th-floor restaurant, located near the southern edge of Balboa Park, to deliver sweeping views, formal service, and a special occasion atmosphere that's ripe for romance. But even loyal fans were forced to admit the high-roller temple of Continental cuisine (think Sinatra and pals, red leather booths, etc.) needed a little updating. We got our wish when the restaurant relaunched with a fresh new energy in 2000. The place still remains a stylish rooftop penthouse promising always-special fine dining punctuated by stunning city and bay views through the wall of windows that surrounds the dining room; it just became more modern. Couples can step onto the breezy rooftop terrace for an hors d'oeuvre smooch; the view is panoramic and airy during the day, sparkling and cosmopolitan after sunset. Dishes on the modern French-Californian menu change often, but be on the lookout for standout versions of cassoulet, duck confit, roasted veal, and Maine lobster (the lobster salad with a truffle strudel is to swoon for). The book-sized wine list is heavy on fine Bordeaux and Burgundy, as well as California's top reds, and the skilled bartenders make darn good Cosmopolitans. Although the

restrictive dress code of days past is no more (women in pants and jacketless men were once frowned upon), this is definitely the place to dress fancy and kick the celebration up a notch.

$$$$ *AE, DC, DIS, MC, V; no checks; lunch Mon–Fri, dinner every day; full bar; reservations recommended; www.bertrandatmisteras.com.*

## CASA DE BANDINI

♥♦

*2754 Calhoun St, Old Town / 619/297-8211*
As much an Old Town tradition as the mariachi music that's played here, this Mexican restaurant is well known for giant margaritas and reliable south-of-the-border fare. It fills the nooks and crannies of an adobe hacienda built in 1829 for Juan Bandini, a local merchant and politician. The superbly renovated enclosed patio has iron gates, flowers blooming around a bubbling fountain, and umbrella-shaded tables where couples can dine alfresco year-round. Sidle up to each other with a couple of double Cadillacs on the rocks, and laze away some time in this gracious setting. Casa de Bandini has the distinction of being located inside Old Town State Historic Park, which sets it apart from other fajitas-and-cervezas joints nearby; it's one of our top choices for extra-special ambience and the romance of Old Mexico. If you're staying nearby, make reservations for their enormous Sunday brunch, guaranteed to induce a pleasant Sunday afternoon nap.

$–$$ *AE, DC, DIS, MC, V; no checks; lunch, dinner every day, brunch Sun; full bar; reservations recommended for dinner; www.casadebandini.com.* &

## EL AGAVE TEQUILARIA

♥♥♦

*2304 San Diego Ave, Old Town / 619/220-0692*
Considered the city's top destination for regional Mexican cuisine, this surprising second-floor restaurant on the outskirts of Old Town is a welcome change from the gooey enchiladas and gringo style found nearby. Named for the plant from which tequila is derived, El Agave boasts more than 800 boutique and artisan tequilas from throughout the Latin world—bottles of every size, shape, and jewel-like hue fill shelves and cases throughout the dining room. The two of you can warm yourselves with a selection of tastes; they're all available by the shot for cocktails or for drinking straight, with prices ranging from around $4 for familiar brands to well over $100 for rare aged tequilas smoother than old sippin' whiskey. But this wood-floored and warmly colorful room, accented with handicrafts and antiques from throughout the diverse Mexican states, is about more than tequila. Even teetotalers will enjoy authentically flavored *moles* (rich with peanut, tangy tomatillo, and the familiar dark variety flavored with chocolate and sesame), along with giant shrimp prepared a dozen ways, including marinated and tossed with beans, cactus strips, and orange. El Agave's signature beef fillet

is redolent of goat cheese and dark tequila sauce, while the authentic flan showcases the sweeter side of Latin cuisine.

$$ *AE, MC, V; no checks; lunch, dinner every day; full bar; reservations recommended; www.elagave.com.*

## LAUREL RESTAURANT & BAR
❂❂❂
*505 Laurel St, Downtown / 619/239-2222*
Laurel is so sophisticated, you might think you're on a date in some chic spot in San Francisco or New York. Live piano music adds to the glamour of dining in this swank room on the ground floor of a high rise adjacent to Balboa Park; playgoers flock here for preshow sustenance and take advantage of shuttle service to the Globe Theaters. While it's true that many sweethearts come to Laurel simply for the panache of pricey furnishings, flattering light, and exquisite martinis, many more are drawn by the masterful Provençal and classic French cuisine paired with an outstanding 800-item wine list that emphasizes Rhône vintages and that has garnered praise each year from *Wine Spectator*. Longtime Laurel fans still enjoy signature standouts such as the Provençal chicken stewed in a pot with fragrant herbs, a masterful duck confit with silken meat and crackly skin, long-simmered osso buco, and an appetizer tart flavored with Roquefort and caramelized onions. Laurel's wait staff is polished and professional, and genial bartenders are legendary for setting the service standard here. If you and your special someone are short on time or funds, follow the example of savvy locals and drop by for a quick, intimate bite at the bar.

$$$ *AE, DC, DIS, MC, V; no checks; dinner every day; full bar; reservations recommended; www.laurelrestaurant.com.*

## PARALLEL 33
❂❂
*741 W Washington St, Mission Hills / 619/260-0033*
Inspired by a theory that all locales along the 33rd parallel of the globe share the same rich culinary tradition, Chef Amiko Gubbins presents a cuisine that beautifully combines flavors from Morocco, Lebanon, India, China, and Japan. The restaurant is eclectically modern, with a multiethnic Indian-African-Asian decor throwing soft shadows throughout, inviting lovers to engage in conversation and intimate, leisurely dining. Set the mood by sipping a "Tears of the Prophet" cocktail (an intoxicating concoction of mandarin vodka, pomegranate juice, and fresh mint leaves). Then the two of you can begin your culinary travels in Morocco with the chicken b'stilla (a flaky phyllo pie filled with chicken, almonds, cinnamon, and currants and topped with preserved lemons and confectioner's sugar), or in Japan with the ahi *poke* (a mixture of raw tuna, Asian pear, mango, and wasabi dressing). Jet over to Shanghai to eat the *panko* and black-sesame-seed-crusted soft-shell crabs with soba noodles in a spicy

coconut-chile sauce, or to India for Goan shrimp curry with coconut basmati rice and fried shallots. The dessert menu is short: Medjool date madeleines, a deliciously warm rhubarb and strawberry concoction, and the ubiquitous chocolate cake. All come with homemade gelato (vanilla-rose, coconut, and roasted banana) and taste great with one of the carefully chosen sherries and dessert wines.

**$$–$$$** *AE, DIS, MC, V; no checks; dinner Mon–Sat; full bar; reservations recommended; www.parallel33sd.com.* &

## PRADO RESTAURANT
❂❂

*1549 El Prado, Balboa Park / 619/557-9441*
For too many years, this prime piece of real estate in Balboa Park housed a mediocre eatery and rather dusty bar. Then the Cohn family—proprietors of the Gaslamp District's Blue Point Coastal Cuisine and the dim sum/New Mexican–inspired Kemo Sabe eateries, among others—took over, and one of San Diego's most appealing (and romantic) dining destinations was born. Set off a lush courtyard in the House of Hospitality, Prado has a spacious, multileveled dining room, a separate bar, and a lovely garden view patio, all done up in modern hacienda decor. Couples can start out with a trendy Mojito or pisco sour to set the Latin tone, then choose just about anything on the ambitious Mexican- and California-cuisine–influenced menu. A few of the standouts include chicken-tortilla soup, pork prime rib, and a clever combo of lemon-thyme grilled swordfish with butternut squash (prepared two different ways) and red beet–truffle puree. With its charming location, fun ambience, and consistently good food and drink, the Prado is great for a leisurely lunch, a relaxed dinner date, or a pretheater dinner before heading across the plaza to a performance at the Globe or Cassius Carter. The restaurant also offers catering and is the site for numerous weddings.
**$$** *AE, DC, DIS, MC, V; no checks; lunch, dinner every day; full bar; reservations recommended; www.cohnrestaurants.com.*

## STAR OF THE SEA
❂❂❂

*1360 Harbor Dr, Embarcadero / 619/232-7408*
San Diego's Embarcadero is a flourishing bay-side district by day, but nighttime brings a slowdown in traffic and a change in the crowd. Tourists, fishermen, and joggers recede into the background, making way for romance-minded diners heading to the upscale star of wharf-side dining, the aptly named Star of the Sea. Designed with sensuous lines inside and out that include plush seashell-inspired booths, curvaceous flatware, and an undulating deck, the Star's modern decor and fine cuisine are a fine partner to seductive sunset views through the floor-to-ceiling windows. After you step across the dramatic over-the-water entry, take your place for a parade

of seafood jewels that begins with aphrodisiac oysters and other exquisite shellfish. Specialties include a dazzling lobster with basil gnocchi, Norwegian salmon garnished with feta cheese and saffron sauce, and succulent scallops arranged on a bed of truffle risotto. For dessert try the puffy Belgian chocolate soufflé garnished with three sauces (but order it at least 20 minutes before you'd like to dig in). The wide-ranging wine list offers lots of fish-friendly sauvignon blancs and chardonnays. Not up for a full dinner? Grab a seat in the bar or the over-the-water patio and graze on appetizers. $$$–$$$$ *AE, DC, DIS, MC, V; no checks; dinner every day; full bar; reservations recommended; www.starofthesea.com.* ♿

## TOP OF THE MARKET
♥♥♥

*750 N Harbor Dr, Embarcadero / 619/232-3474*
The panoramic views of San Diego Bay are as much an attraction as the huge menu of fresh catches at the Fish Market Restaurant and its upstairs, upscale sister, Top of the Market. Downstairs you'll find a full-service cocktail bar, a busy oyster bar, and friendly, casual service. But upstairs is a much better place to kiss: the same top-notch seafood from local and imported waters is presented with more refinement—and the bay views inspire romance. Situated on a waterfront promontory and turning its back on downtown San Diego lurking just blocks behind it, the Top resembles a broad riverboat, with walls of windows and wooden decks. Ask for an intimate two-seater on the enclosed balcony directly over the water, where seagulls swoop by at sunset and even the bustle of the Top's popular bar fades into the background. The list of menu offerings is astounding; you can tour the Seven Seas with Norwegian salmon, Alaskan halibut, New Zealand mussels, and Mississippi catfish, all flown in daily and all given the signature mesquite-grill treatment. The linen and candlelight setting is soothing, and after twilight the view transforms to one of twinkling lights on boats floating in the bay.
$$$ *AE, CB, DC, DIS, MC, V; no checks; lunch, dinner every day; full bar; reservations recommended for large groups; www.thefishmarket.com.* ♿

# NORTH COUNTY COAST

## ROMANTIC HIGHLIGHTS

Just 20 minutes north of downtown lies a progression of pretty beach towns—Del Mar, Cardiff-by-the-Sea, Encinitas, and Carlsbad—so alluring even resident San Diegans make North County a popular destination for a romantic rendezvous. Here you can devote your time to each another, filling the days with low-key, mainly outdoor activities that offer plenty of inspiration for relaxed, midday kisses.

Del Mar is a quiet and insular upscale community that explodes each summer during racing season at the famous **Del Mar Racetrack and Fairgrounds** (I-5 at Via del la Valle, main entrance on Jimmy Durante Blvd; 858/792-4252, 858/793-5555 for 24-hour event hotline; www.delmarfair. com), which still glows with the aura of Hollywood celebrity dating back to when actor Bing Crosby opened the thoroughbred club and sang "Where the Surf Meets the Turf," which is still played each season before the first race. You and your sweetie can don your race-day finest (women wear fancy hats, still a beloved tradition) and hobnob with horse lovers from around the country at this elegant, Spanish-inspired racetrack. Nearby, a stretch of picture-perfect beach beckons—you can enjoy the view from a table at beachside **Jake's Del Mar** (see Romantic Restaurants), or spread your towels on the sand in front of the adorable beach cottages that line the shore and inspire envy in mere mortals.

One of North County's most intimate beach parks can be found in Solana Beach, just north of Del Mar. **Fletcher Cove Beach Park** (at the foot of Lomas Santa Fe Dr; 858/755-1569), a secluded gem for safe swimming and beach walking, is sheltered by tall cliffs. At low tide, you and your sweetheart can walk a mile or more in either direction and find layers of fossilized oyster shells, a reminder of a time when most of the San Diego coast lay at the bottom of an ancient sea.

After appreciating these relics from the past, couples can unearth modern treasures at Solana Beach's nearby **Cedros Design District** (Cedros Ave between Via de la Valle and Lomas Santa Fe; www.cedrosdesigndistrict .com), an extra-long block containing some of San Diego's best sources of home furnishings, from antique warehouses to garden boutiques to furniture showrooms and even designer textiles. When you're feathering a love nest, Cedros is a terrific resource.

Encinitas is a charming, neighborly town best known for the local nursery industry. At the edge of Encinitas, the **Self-Realization Fellowship** (939 2nd St; 760/436-7220) shimmers like an Eastern mystic's vision with its lotus-blossom-shaped towers and mysterious inner gardens. Couples are welcome, and the gardens provide a serene setting for quiet introspection. Each spring the nearby **Carlsbad Ranch** (Palomar Airport Rd, east of I-5; 760/431-0352; www.theflowerfields.com) explodes in a rainbow of color, blanketing the hillside with brilliant ranunculus visible from the freeway. The fields are open to the public, and they sell flowers, bulbs, and gardeners' gifts. Even if you don't visit during the spring bloom—or during December, when the nurseries are alive with holiday poinsettias—there's plenty of floral beauty for lovers to enjoy throughout the year.

Second to Carlsbad Ranch in popularity is **Weidner's Gardens** (695 Normandy Rd; 760/436-2194; www.weidners.com), where a field of tuberous begonias blooms June through August; fuchsias and impatiens are colorful between March and September; and the holiday season (beginning November 1) brings an explosion of poinsettias and the opportunity to dig your own pansies. Couples also might want to devote an afternoon to **Quail Botanical Gardens** (230 Quail Dr; 760/436-3036; www.qbgardens.com), a serene compound crisscrossed with scenic walkways, trails, and benches; this nonprofit garden is dedicated to the conservation of rare plants from around the world and displays the country's largest bamboo collection along with 30 acres of California natives, exotic tropicals, palms, cacti, and other unusual species. It's the perfect place for a romantic stroll.

Carlsbad might be the best-known North County destination, a chic grown-up beach town that welcomes lovebirds to two first-class spa and golf resorts: the Four Seasons Resort–Aviara and La Costa (see Romantic Lodgings), in addition to preserving its charming historic village near the beach. Spas were a part of the town's earliest history, starting with the original mineral spring that led to the town's namesake—the spa town of Karlsbad, Czechoslovakia. Today's **Carlsbad Mineral Water Spa** (2802 Carlsbad Blvd; 760/434-1887; www.carlsbadmineralspa.com) is housed in the Alt Karlsbad Haus, site of the original well that was discovered by retired sea captain John Frazier in the 1880s as he was drilling away on his homestead. Guests still luxuriate in carbonated mineral-water baths said to soothe all sorts of ailments, and the water is bottled for local markets and home delivery.

**Carlsbad State Beach** parallels downtown and is a great place to stroll with your loved one along a wide concrete walkway that's also popular for jogging and inline skating. For more solitude, wait until after dark and take a romantic moonlight stroll on the sand; the night-lit boardwalk offers a sense of security.

Nearby **State Street** is a popular prowl for antique hunters, and the **Carlsbad Visitors Center** (400 Carlsbad Village Dr; 760-434-6093; www.carlsbadca.org) is housed in the restored 1887 Santa Fe train depot. Serious discount shoppers head to the other side of the freeway, where the **Carlsbad Company Stores** (on Paseo del Norte, off I-5 between Palomar Airport and Cannon Rds; 760/804-9000) sprawl in a Mediterranean-inspired complex housing everything from Crate & Barrel and Royal Doulton to Gap and Donna Karan outlets. If you get hungry, try the surprisingly chic **Bellefleur Winery and Restaurant** (see Romantic Restaurants), a Tuscan-style outpost that anchors the mall.

If a vacation with your beloved tickles the child inside, you may want to visit Carlsbad's premiere family attraction, **Legoland** (1 Legoland Dr; 760/918-LEGO or 877/534-6526; www.legolandca.com). This colorful theme park is literally built from the well-loved interlocking blocks and features a gravity coaster ride (don't worry, it's made of steel) through a LEGO castle, in addition to a life-sized menagerie of tigers, giraffes, and other animals, and scale models of international landmarks (the Eiffel Tower, Sydney Opera House, and so on)—all constructed of real LEGO bricks. Even grown-up visitors will appreciate "Mini-Land," a 1:20 scale representation of American achievement, from a New England Pilgrim village to Mount Rushmore, complete with moving parts. It's a wonderful spot to spend a fun, whimsical day with the one you love.

# Access and Information

San Diego's North County beach towns are strung along Interstate 5, beginning with Del Mar to the south, and ending with tiny Oceanside, gateway to the U.S. Marine base Camp Pendleton. If the responsibility of driving will spoil the romantic mood, join San Diego's working folk aboard the **Coaster** (800/COASTER; www.gonctd.com), a friendly commuter rail line that runs between downtown's Santa Fe Depot and Oceanside, with stops in Solana Beach (near Del Mar), Encinitas, and Carlsbad.

If, on the other hand, you'd rather take life in the slow(er) lane behind the wheel, hook up with the scenic pre-interstate route that literally hugs the coastline, known along the way as Camino del Mar, Pacific Coast Highway (PCH), or Old Highway 101—all depending on what town you're in.

For more information on all of San Diego's northern destinations, contact the **North County Visitors Bureau** (800/848-3336; www.sandiegonorth.com).

# Romantic Lodgings

## CARDIFF BY THE SEA LODGE
♥♥♥

*142 Chesterfield Dr, Cardiff-by-the-Sea / 760/944-6474*
The romance of this North Coast town will engage you before you even arrive, merely upon hearing its name. Cardiff-by-the-Sea was named after an English seaside village, its streets followed suit (Manchester, Birmingham, Liverpool), and residents do their best to preserve that small-town feeling despite being a mere 25 minutes from downtown San Diego. There's not a whole lot here, though, other than a wonderful sandy beach and a few sunset-view restaurants, which makes the Cardiff by the Sea Lodge a special reason to visit. Frequent guests praise this lovingly hosted bed-and-breakfast, even though its Cape Cod–inspired exterior offers little sense of the lavish every-day's-a-honeymoon rooms that await the amorous adventurer. Not for the faint of heart—but definitely for the sentimental at heart—is the inn's most-requested Sweetheart Room. It's every honeymoon suite cliché, all wrapped up in one spectacular ocean-view boudoir tucked in the contemporary inn's centerpiece turret. A symphony of pink and bur-

gundy, it features a bed that embraces you with giant hand-carved hearts, ornate scrolled beam ceiling, pink leather loveseats, and a heart-shaped whirlpool tub facing the fireplace. Other themed rooms, like the Country French, Santa Fe, or Southwest, also feature kiss-worthy amenities like fireplaces, whirlpool tubs, and ocean views, but without the fanfare; there's something for everyone in the lodge's 17 rooms. Breakfast is made to order and served on an ocean-view terrace, and more sociable guests are welcome to savor sunsets around an open pit fire ring on the rooftop.
$$$ *AE, DIS, MC, V; checks OK; www.cardifflodge.com.* ὃ

## FOUR SEASONS RESORT–AVIARA
♥♥♥♥

*7100 Four Seasons Pt, Carlsbad / 760/603-6800 or 800/332-7100*
The Four Seasons is sleek, swank, and serene, with fluffy cloud-like beds that will make the two of you want to sleep in all day. Situated on a prime bluff overlooking a nature preserve with the ocean beyond, the resort offers every over-the-top comfort with the never off-putting ease that sets Four Seasons resorts apart. When not wielding clubs or racquets, couples can lie by the pool serenaded by Peruvian pipes, relax in a series of delightfully landscaped gardens, or luxuriate in the full-service spa, where treatments incorporate regional flowers and herbs. The ambience here is one of both privilege and comfort; rooms are decorated with soothing neutrals and nature prints that evoke the spirit of the surrounding Batiquitos Lagoon. In fact, the name Aviara is a nod to the egrets, herons, and cranes that are among the 130 bird species nesting in the protected coastal wetlands. Each room has a furnished balcony or terrace, where you can enjoy your room-service breakfast or a sunset cocktail (while clad in the snuggly bathrobe provided by the hotel). Somehow, the staff manages to make every guest feel specially cared for, even when all 329 rooms are full, and it's that personal touch that will make the two of you Four Seasons's devotees. The hotel's spa is among the county's finest, offering classic pampering treatments, indoor and outdoor treatment rooms and cabanas, and in-room massage for the reclusive. You can also book their indulgent couple's suite, featuring an intimate lounge area with marble fireplace and shower for two, an attached treatment room with side-by-side massage tables, and a private patio with whirlpool. Nature lovers might prefer a romantic walking excursion to the wilderness of the lagoon on a nature trail with several different access points; the hotel's staff will gladly point you in the right direction. When you return, plan to dine at the resort's stellar Northern Italian restaurant, Vivace, winner of the AAA four-diamond award (see Romantic Restaurants).
$$$–$$$$ *AE, DC, DIS, MC, V; checks OK; www.fourseasons.com.* ὃ

## LA COSTA

●●●(

*2100 Costa del Mar Rd, Carlsbad / 760/438-9111 or 800/854-5000*
Sitting on 400 rolling acres just five minutes from the beach and freeway, La Costa was a trailblazer in the world of hospitality. Opened in 1965, it was the first U.S. resort to offer a full-service spa and quickly gained a reputation as the premiere destination resort for tennis, golf, and rejuvenating treatments. Recently, the famous resort underwent some major rejuvenation of its own, as $140 million was spent to completely rebuild, refine, and re-imagine a La Costa for today's vacationer. After all, tastes change, and when the stellar Four Seasons–Aviara went in down the street, La Costa found itself behind the times, with sterile spa attendants in antiquated pink aprons, and rooms that had seen better days. Now that it's been completely transformed, La Costa is once more one of San Diego County's most romantic and luxurious destinations. The five-star treatment begins on arrival, as a cadre of fresh-faced attendants take your car, your luggage, and your worries away, leading the two of you into the Rancho California–style lobby/clubhouse to check in. A smart new design clusters all the public spaces—restaurants, boutiques, health spa, etc.—around a central courtyard, while guest rooms are generously spread around to provide maximum privacy and enjoyment of the lovely pedestrian-friendly grounds. Our favorite rooms overlook the golf course; they're nicely proportioned, with easy-to-live-on furniture and high-quality tailored bedding, all in attractive Pottery Barn colors and accented by rich dark woods. Hammocks and wind chimes dot the landscape along the walk to the swimming pool—a portrait of Grecian glamour, complete with hooded lawn chaises—the tennis courts, the spa, or the Chopra Center (the new headquarters of feel-good guru Deepak Chopra). Daily yoga and meditation are offered at the center, along with transcendent ayurvedic treatments; at the other, more traditional spa, pampering lies beyond an intoxicating water-therapy suite fragranced with the resort's signature coco-mango bath products. *Aaah!* The two of you will be so relaxed, you'll have to fight to stay awake for some romantic time together.
$$$–$$$$ *AE, DC, DIS, MC, V; checks OK; www.lacosta.com.* 占

## L'AUBERGE DEL MAR RESORT AND SPA

●●(

*1540 Camino del Mar, Del Mar / 858/259-1515 or 800/505-9043*
This deluxe 120-room resort may be right on Del Mar's main drag, but you'll find ample privacy for any romantic rendezvous. Small and wonderful, L'Auberge has all the elements of a great getaway, starting with its location in the exclusive little beach town that's rich in charming cafes, pricey-but-fun boutiques, and a fervent sense of seclusion. L'Auberge is the town's centerpiece public spot, built on the site of the historic Hotel Del Mar (1909–69). Favored by the horsey set that flocks here during summer racing season, the

hotel is also known for stylish intimate weddings and impromptu getaways for stressed-out couples. Guest rooms exude the elegance of a European country house, complete with marble bathrooms, architectural accents, well-placed casual seating, and the finest bed linens and appointments; each has a private balcony or patio. For the most privacy, request a top-floor corner room from which you can gaze at the treetops and glimpse the Pacific. Bring your swimsuit, because the inn has two pools—one for lounging, another for lap swimming—and the beach is a short stroll away. There are also tennis courts and a terrific little spa where the two of you may want to indulge in a treatment or two. L'Auberge's central location means you can explore Del Mar's shops and restaurants on foot—but you'll also want to save a night for J. Taylor's (see Romantic Restaurants), a Mediterranean dining room that easily stands alone as one of Del Mar's finest restaurants. At the very least, don't miss its legendary breakfast of huevos rancheros. $$$ *AE, DC, DIS, MC, V; checks OK; www.laubergedelmar.com.*

# Romantic Restaurants

## AMERICANA
◐◐

*1454 Camino del Mar, Del Mar / 858/794-6838*
Located across the street from L'Auberge Del Mar on the town's best corner—well, at least the most centrally located—this versatile little dining room occupies one of the original structures from Del Mar's early Tudor-style village. During the morning hours, this farmhouse-chic spot feels like a bright and welcoming coffee shop, perfect for lovers who want to linger over the paper and enjoy just-baked muffins, challah bread French toast, omelets, and pancakes with granola or chocolate chips. Lunch brings an equally homey lineup: egg salad sandwiches, a classic BLT, turkey burgers, and attractive salads. At dinnertime, however, Americana takes on a much more sophisticated aura, dressed up with candlelight, white tablecloths, and artful gourmet cuisine. It's cozy and intimate, a romantic choice that's also easy on the wallet. You don't need to know that chef-owner Randy Gruber has an impressive resume of local kitchens to appreciate the way he evokes an American brasserie, with food that's somehow both inspired and comforting at the same time. Don't miss the quickly seared scallops with red lentils, the silken sliced duck breast paired with perfect green beans and pearly couscous, or the salmon perched on a clever succotash of beans and vegetables. For dessert, lemon tart brûlée or the unusual banana tarte Tatin are best shared with your special someone. $$ *AE, DC, DIS, MC, V; no checks; breakfast, lunch every day, dinner Tues–Sat; full bar; reservations recommended; www.americana restaurant.com.* &

## ARTERRA
✪✪✪
*11966 El Camino Real Dr (Marriott Del Mar), Del Mar / 858/369-6032*
Couples who find romance in farm-fresh dining will swoon for Arterra. Though the atmosphere of this hotel restaurant across the freeway from the beach may be a bit generic, the cuisine of chef Carl Schroeder, under the guidance of restaurant co-owner and mentor chef Bradley Ogden, make Arterra one of North County's most enticing eateries. Each morning, Schroeder visits nearby Chino Farms to stock up on fresh organic goods before he composes the day's menu. Start with one of his salads made with the farm's fresh micro greens that might include red pears and Gorgonzola soufflé, baby beets and blood oranges, or heirloom tomatoes strewn with fresh corn kernels. Main courses are equally impressive, such as sautéed day boat scallops with wild pink prawns, sweet pepper rouille, and fresh peas; or alderwood-smoked duck breast with roasted sweet potato–apple puree. The wait staff is well trained and can help the two of you navigate the menu or pick the perfect wine to complement your meal. A berry sampler, which includes miniature strawberry shortcake, blueberry crisp, and a boysenberry float, is the perfect way to finish off your memorable meal.
*$$$ AE, DC, DIS, MC, V; no checks; breakfast, lunch, dinner every day; full bar; reservations recommended; www.arterrarestaurant.com.* ♿

## BELLEFLEUR WINERY & RESTAURANT
✪
*5610 Paseo del Norte, Carlsbad / 760/603-1919*
Looking sort of like a beautiful fish out of water, this upscale restaurant/bar anchors one end of an outlet-store mall (the Carlsbad Company Stores). It's a welcome presence among the fast-food joints, discount shoe stores, and displays of last year's fashions. Boasting the "complete wine country experience," Bellefleur's cavernous, semi-industrial dining room, coupled with the wood-fired and wine-enhanced aromas emanating from the clanging open kitchen, do somehow evoke the casual yet sophisticated ambience of California wine regions like Santa Barbara or Napa. The place can be noisy and spirited, drawing shopping-weary couples for cuisine that ambitiously introduces Pacific Rim, Italian, French, and classic American styles to each other. Fancy wood-fired pizzas and Tuscan white bean soup rub elbows with cheeseburgers, grilled lamb loin, and steamed local mussels in a yellow curry sauce; on the bar menu, you'll find smoked salmon, presented sushi style, alongside French onion soup. At lunch, the place has a casual feeling; a dressier, older crowd shows up at night. Affordable table wines are sold under the Bellefleur label, but the extensive wine list also features better-known California brands.
*$$$ AE, DIS, DC, MC, V; no checks; lunch, dinner every day; full bar; reservations recommended; www.bellefleur.com.* ♿

# IL FORNAIO
◐◖

*1555 Camino del Mar, Del Mar / 858/755-8876*
This ever-growing chain dazzles couples with stunning decor and interesting takes on gourmet pasta, pizza, and bread. The elegantly designed dining rooms are an instant transport to Italy with plenty of Carrara marble, terra-cotta flooring, vaulted ceilings, hand-painted trompe l'oeil friezes, and an open oven where meats and signature breads are baked to perfection (breads, pastries, and all food items are available for takeout). At times, the food doesn't live up to the ambience and prices, but the saving grace is a wind-kissed view of the Pacific that enhances your romantic dining experience. During the day, or on late-sunset evenings, lovers can ask for a table on the terrace, order a glass of wine, and quickly settle into the European-style relaxation of it all. Most of the pasta dishes are good (*ravioli di verdura al funghi* is filled with Swiss chard, pine nuts, basil, parmesan, and mixed mushrooms, topped with fresh tomatoes and artichokes), and the pizzas are nearly perfect (try pizza *capricciosa* with prosciutto cotto, kalamata olives, artichokes, and mushrooms). Other specialties include well-executed renditions of veal, steak, chicken, and lamb. For dessert, the tiramisu is a must, accompanied by a perfect espresso or cappuccino.
$$ *AE, DIS, DC, MC, V; no checks; lunch, dinner every day, brunch Sun; full bar; reservations recommended; www.ilfornaio.com.* ♿

# J. TAYLOR'S OF DEL MAR
◕◕

*1540 Camino del Mar (Auberge Del Mar Resort and Spa), Del Mar / 858/259-1515 or 800/505-9043*
Couples staying at L'Auberge Del Mar (see Romantic Lodgings) will want to reserve a night for dinner at the resort's elegant restaurant. When the weather is nice, ask for a table on the outdoor terrace, where lush gardens and waterfalls add an air of romance, or snuggle indoors at a fireside table, as sweeping cathedral ceilings create a wonderfully spacious feel. Chef Tom Atkins, who has cooked at the James Beard House, serves up such decadent starters as pan-seared Hudson Valley foie gras with blackberry balsamic glaze and grilled white asparagus with raspberry vinaigrette and roasted pine nuts. Entrées, such as the oregano butter–poached swordfish with fresh spinach pasta or pork medallions with garlic mashed potatoes and port mushroom sauce, are flavored with fresh herbs from the kitchen's garden. After the two of you share the old-fashioned butterscotch pudding topped with Myer's rum and chantilly cream for dessert, you can enjoy live jazz and a nightcap in the lounge on weekend nights.

Even if you don't have time for a big romantic dinner, the restaurant serves breakfast and lunch every day.

$$$–$$$ *AE, DC, DIS, MC, V; checks OK; breakfast, lunch, dinner every day, brunch Sat–Sun; full bar; reservations recommended; www.lauberge delmar.com.*

## JAKE'S DEL MAR
❤️❤️

*1660 Coast Blvd, Del Mar / 858/755-2002*
A magical combination of sea, sand, and sky kisses the dining room and outdoor terrace at Jake's Del Mar. The same attributes create the perfect setting for a romantic meal. Jake's is casual and vaguely tropical, a nod to its seaside location as well as restaurant cousins, the Duke's chain of Hawaiian eateries. The restaurant's classic waterfront grill menu showcases California coastal cuisine, an amalgam of fresh fish and seafood in simply classic preparations, along with Asian, Latin, and even Mediterranean menu standards. Try the mussels in herbed saffron broth, mirin-glazed mahimahi accented with Asian-French ginger butter, giant scampi sautéed with Italian flavors, or beef tenderloin with rich mushroom béarnaise sauce. Everything is big and colorful, including the bar menu of inventive appetizers, perfect to share for a light dinner accompanied by tropical drinks. For sunset reservations, call early: prime tables near the breaking waves are in high demand at dusk. At meal's end, share a piece of hula pie, the Hawaiian import that combines coffee ice cream, chocolate cookie crust, and macadamia nuts into a gooey treat.

$–$$ *AE, DIS, MC, V; no checks; lunch, dinner every day, brunch Sun; full bar; reservations recommended for dinner and brunch; www.jakes delmar.com.* ♿

## PAMPLEMOUSSE GRILLE
❤️❤️❤️

*514 Via de la Valle, Solana Beach / 858/792-9090*
High rollers, socialites, business folk, trophy spouses, and trysting lovers abound at this stylish bistro across from the Del Mar racetrack. While many are no doubt drawn by the ambience—a chic, sophisticated take on French country—others come for the imaginative fare. The food isn't always Triple Crown material, but the kitchen delivers artfully garnished, creatively conceived variations on nouvelle American and classic French cuisine. The foie gras is always outstanding, as are the grilled fish specials prepared with your choice of a half dozen sauces. Lamb stew, a very tender pork prime rib, and a roasted tomato fennel soup are also perennial favorites. Salads and side dishes make fine use of the vegetables from Chino's produce farm (favored by chefs from L.A. and San Francisco) just down the road, and desserts—especially the semibaked, melting chocolate truffle cake or the trio of crème brûlées—are guaranteed to top off a romantic meal in style. Pamplemousse is busy during

the racing season (linger in the bar and the two of you might get a hot tip), but the prosperous mood and society gossip stay in the air year-round.

**$$$** *AE, CB, DC, DIS, MC, V; checks OK; lunch Wed–Fri, dinner every day, brunch Sun; full bar; reservations recommended; www.pgrille.com.* ♿

---

# VIVACE
◐◐◐◐

*7100 Four Seasons Pt (Four Seasons Resort–Aviara), Carlsbad / 760/603-6800*

The elegant dining room of this fine Italian restaurant in the Four Seasons Resort–Aviara (see Romantic Lodgings) oozes amour. Velvet-covered banquettes, beautiful flower arrangements, fine crystal, and soft lighting create an ambience for sweethearts to revel in romance as they savor classic Northern Italian fare. Start with such antipasti selections as beef tenderloin capriccio or lobster and heirloom tomato salad. Then the two of you may want to share a pasta course like house-made shrimp and spinach ravioli or penne with sun-dried tomatoes, baked eggplant, artichoke, and buffalo mozzarella, before moving on to such winning entrees as balsamic-glazed salmon with polenta or a double lamb chop with gnocchi. On a warm evening, the two of you can dine under the stars on Vivace's outdoor patio, but indoors by the fireplace with floor-to-ceiling windows overlooking the Pacific Ocean and Batiquitos Lagoon is surely romantic as well. Save room for the warm chocolate tart with apricot sauce or one of the restaurant's house-made gelatos. Both are worth every calorie.

**$$$–$$$$** *AE, DC, DIS, MC, V; checks OK; dinner every day; full bar; reservations recommended; www.fourseasons.com.* ♿

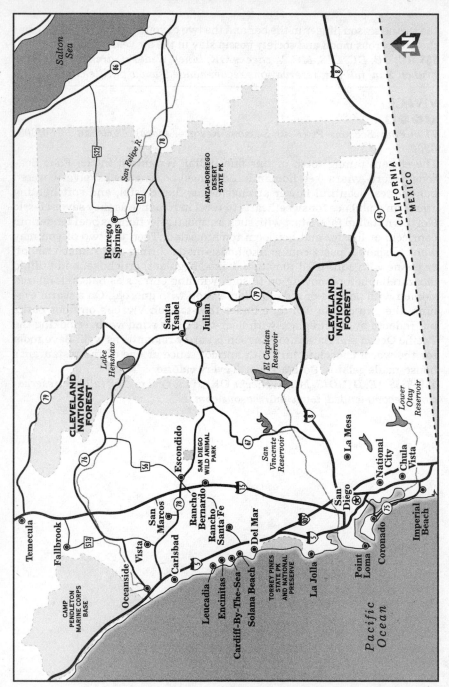

*"There is nothing in kissing once; it's the second time that counts."*

—MAURICE HEWLETT

# ♡ SAN DIEGO MOUNTAINS, VALLEY, AND DESERT

While the city of San Diego and the county's tony coastal communities may get the most hype, there is a whole other lesser known—but equally magnificent—lover's oasis to the northeast that is just ripe for exploration. Romance seekers will have no problem finding memorable and exciting things to see and do here. In fact, you may be overwhelmed by all the choices. The climate is so diverse—from the arid and tranquil desert to the historic mountain towns to the lush wine country of the inland valley—that the hardest part about vacationing here is deciding exactly what kind of romantic adventure you want to have.

The rolling green hills and valleys of inland San Diego offer a multitude of activities, perfectly tailored for the kiss-seeking set. To the south, the ultra-affluent communities of Rancho Santa Fe and Rancho Bernardo pamper visitors with exclusive inns, restaurants, and boutiques. Less expensive but just as enchanting are the cities and villages to the north—such as Escondido, Vista, and Valley Center. Here it's all about discovering the breathtaking hiking trails and lakes, the wineries, the arts center, and the awe-inspiring wildlife park.

To the east, the sleepy mountain town of Julian is where you and your sweetheart can pick delicious apples in the expansive orchards; go antiquing, wine tasting, or horseback riding; or take a tour of the old gold mines. There are four seasons here, and in the spring, the blossoming daffodils dot the landscape like a floral fireworks show. Farther north, you'll discover the village of Santa Ysabel, which is all about the arts. This is an enchanting spot to get cuddly and cultural by taking in a few galleries and museums.

If you travel past the verdant mountains, where the oaks and pines slowly give way to ocotillo blooms and desert dust, you soon find yourself in the badlands of the Anza-Borrego Desert. The climate may be dry, but the love doth overfloweth in this otherworldly oasis. The warm days are perfect for hand-in-hand hikes, and the cool nights offer some of the most jaw-dropping stargazing sessions you will ever experience. Temperatures soar to the triple digits in the summer, so the best time to visit is during the spring months, when the wildflowers are in full bloom.

# INLAND NORTH COUNTY

## ROMANTIC HIGHLIGHTS

It's almost unfair that a place can be blessed not only with perfect weather—temperatures average 70°F with low humidity—but also with scenic beauty and big-city sophistication. Inland San Diego possesses all those qualities—you just have to know where to look. In the past few decades, rich agricultural farmland and cattle ranches have given way to a massive suburban sprawl. But beyond the generic gated communities and ugly strip malls, the old charm and rustic flavor of times past still thrive here.

**Rancho Santa Fe** is as good a place as any to warm up your lips. Steeped in history, the town used to be the property of the Santa Fe Railroad Company, who bought the land to grow eucalyptus trees for their railroad tracks. Lucky for us, eucalyptus turned out to be too soft, so the forests remain, as do many of the Spanish Colonial Revival buildings built by architect Lillian Rice in the 1920s. **La Flecha House** (6036 La Flecha; 858/756-5600) is the town's first residential home and headquarters of the Historical Society. It's got a cute little museum and walking maps of the village—which is only three tiny streets. While the Census Bureau has tagged this the wealthiest community in the nation, the only sign of Benjamins seems to be the Mercedes SUVs parked along the road. The town itself is surprisingly low-key, with family-owned boutiques, wine stores, and antiques shops, the best being the **Country Friends Shop** (6030 El Tordo; 858/756-1192). After a morning of light shopping, be sure to have lunch at the **Inn at Rancho Santa Fe's Dining Room** (see Romantic Restaurants), which has delicious food and a precious garden patio. Less pricey but equally charming is **Thyme in the Ranch** (16905 Avenida de Acacias; 858/759-0747).

Head farther east, and you'll soon be smack-dab in the middle of another exclusive community, **Rancho Bernardo**—or "RB" as the locals call it. Unlike Rancho Santa Fe, this village has no main street to speak of. What it does have is the **Rancho Bernardo Winery** (13330 Paseo del Vernao Norte; 858/487-1866), an absolutely adorable re-creation of an Old West town that also just happens to be the site of an old vineyard founded in 1889. Aside from a tasting room, you'll find tiny streets lined with old vintage horse carriages and antiques, craft galleries, glass blowers, and fragrance shops. Grab a seat for two on the little white tree swing that hangs on the side of the road, then visit **Hope Aesthetics Boutique** (858/673-0404), a happy little shop that is nationally famous for its healing body creams and lotions. We highly recommend the grilled salmon BLT at **Café Merlot** (858/592-7785).

North up Interstate 15, you'll find **Escondido**, the region's largest city and a vibrant cultural hub. The downtown area here is fairly industrial and unattractive, but surprisingly there are a few gems on Grand Avenue that make it worth your visit. The **Escondido Antique Mall** (135 W Grand Ave; 760/743-3210) has a terrific collection in 60 separate shops. Right next door, the **Mingei International Museum** (155 W Grand Ave; 619/239-0003) showcases beautiful Japanese origami and paintings. The **California Center for the Arts** (340 N Escondido Blvd; 760/839-4123) is just a block and a half away. This massive concert hall and theater attracts world-class symphonies, dance troupes, and operas. Hopeless romantics would be wise to check out the schedule before visiting. *Carmen* anyone?

To truly appreciate Escondido and its neighboring cities to the north and west, you must take a detour from the overly developed strip-mall hell and discover the area's stunning natural beauty. There are several natural habitat preserves, filled with endangered Engelmann oak woodlands, wild flowers, and 300 species of wildlife. **Daley Ranch** (3024 La Honda Dr; 760/839-4680) is home to 19 hiking trails, some easy and some tough, but all gorgeous. Trek 1 mile to the Ranch House, built in 1928, and enjoy a picnic in the shade. Also nearby is **Lake Dixon**, where you can rent rowboats and paddleboats and float away into paradise. **Felicita County Park** (742 Clarence Ln; 619/694-3366) is the former site of one of the oldest Indian villages in the county. It has 53 green acres of woodlands and meadows—the perfect place to picnic in the shade of an oak tree and get some serious smooching in. Be warned: all these parks get very crowded in the summer. For some quality private time, it's best to visit in the spring or fall, or even in the winter when the weather is good—which is pretty much always.

Escondido is also home to the area's largest and best-known winery, **Orfila Vineyards** (13455 San Pasqual Rd; 877/727-9463). This enchanting property, nestled perfectly at the foot of the San Pasqual Mountains, has a cavernous tasting room decorated with hundreds of old barrels of wine. Order a few glasses of their esteemed syrah and wander out to the grape arbor, which has great views of the valley. Be sure to ask for a self-guided tour map, which takes you on a pretty little walk past the vines, rose bushes, and the crush pad (how appropriate!).

Travel several miles east farther into the valley, past the ostrich farms, and suddenly you've entered another continent. **San Diego Zoo's Wild Animal Park** (15500 San Pasqual Valley Rd; 760/747-8702; www.wild

animalpark.org) is a giant open-air animal preserve and home to hundreds of endangered species, such as rhinos, giraffes, elephants, and zebras. The animals all roam about in vast fields that have been designed to look like the African bush. A train takes you around the park's periphery, but the best way to get up-close-and-personal is to pay a little extra and reserve a Photo Caravan Tour; safari trucks take you right into the heart of the animal enclosures. Giraffes will walk up to you and eat animal crackers out of your hand. To ensure maximum *oohing* and *ahhing*, visit the park in the spring, when the animals have their babies.

## Access and Information

Inland San Diego is best accessed by car. Interstate 15 takes you to exits for Escondido and Rancho Bernardo. For areas farther west, such as Vista, San Marcos, and Rancho Santa Fe, use Interstate 5. One slower but far more scenic route is Highway 101, which runs right along the coast. Highway 78 will get you from areas west to those farther inland. To get from Rancho Santa Fe to Escondido, we highly recommend Del Dios Highway, a beautiful road that cuts through a valley and past pristine Lake Hodges. For more information about the area, contact the **San Diego North Convention and Visitors Bureau** (800/848-3336; www.sandiegonorth.com).

## Romantic Lodgings

### CAL-A-VIE
❂❂❂❈
*29402 Spa Havens Wy, Vista / 760/945-2055 or 866/SPA-HAVENS*
Provençal romance meets California cool at this beautiful and ultraprivate spa. The owners hail from New Orleans, and the French influence can be felt from the moment you walk in the front door. Antiques and fresh flowers fill the rooms, fleur-de-lis doormats are at each door, and the rooms are marked by little French signs with such titles as Salon D'Beautie or L'Asoptherapie. Even the menu has French flair, via the bayou. Three healthy meals are included in the price of your stay, and most guests are put on 1,200-calorie-a-day menu plan. Who knew low-cal gumbo could be so delicious? The grounds are impeccably maintained, with little paths and wood bridges that wind through waterfalls. There are also more than 200 acres of walking trails that snake through the surrounding hills. The setting is so private and conducive to kissing, you might be asked to "get a room." And rooms they have—24 of them, all with comfy, country inn furniture and decks. The best is room 11, which comes with a private deck, but we also recommend rooms 12–15 for their perfect views of the mountains. In years past, the spa

required only single occupancy, but fortunately for health-seeking lovers, they've recently relaxed their policy, and now couples can stay here whenever they please. You can choose from 10 to 16 spa treatments, ranging from hot stone massages to seaweed wraps. There is also a fitness center; exercise classes; tennis courts; a pool; and the Labrynth, a fun, meditative stone maze you can wander together. If you just want to veg out, the breakfast room is a cozy place to nuzzle and watch DVDs on a big-screen TV, while you sip a tasty tomato concoction called the Revitalizer. The good news: you're both guaranteed to leave this place feeling 10 times healthier than when you arrived. The bad news: it's *gonna* cost you.

$$$$ *AE, DC, DIS, MC, V; checks OK; 3-, 4-, and 7-night packages only; www.cal-a-vie.com.*

## CASTLE CREEK INN
🌀🌀

*29850 Circle R Wy, Vista / 760/751-8800 or 800/253-5341*
Attractive grounds, comfortable accommodations, and four hot, cascading soaking pools are the draw to this simple roadside inn. While this may not be a spot to plan your whole vacation around, it's a very pleasant and private place to stay for a day on your way to somewhere else. Just off Interstate 15, but far enough away to be quiet and bucolic, the inn offers tastefully decorated rooms with high ceilings, Bavarian antiques, and little paintings of puppies that may seem tasteful to some, but borderline tacky to others. The large minisuites, with decks overlooking the pool or the golf course across the street, are your best bets for privacy. Although the Castle Creek no longer operates a restaurant, there is one at the country club just across the street that serves breakfast, lunch, and dinner. What it *does* have is a spa, which offers facials and massages, and the four hillside outdoor soaking pools are connected by cascading little waterfalls. Not the most private place to kiss, but certainly a joy to lounge in and relax.

$$-$$$ *AE, DC, DIS, MC, V; no checks; www.castlecreekinn.com.* ♿

## THE INN AT RANCHO SANTA FE
🌀🌀🌀

*5951 Linea Del Cielo, Rancho Santa Fe / 858/756-1131 or 800/843-4661*
History buffs and romantics alike will find numerous reasons to love this beautiful, magical inn. Located in the heart of the tony village of Rancho Santa Fe, the Spanish Colonial landmark was designed by architect Lillian Rice in 1923 as the town's first guesthouse. The property has expanded over the years to a sprawling 23-acre inn with 87 guest rooms, but thankfully the owners have stayed true to the original architecture, and Rice's guesthouse is still here as the main building. The lobby is a sight to behold—massive wood beams, comfy leather couches, and the largest fireplace in town. Perched on the walls, you'll find a collection of large, wooden ship models that are said

to be just as valuable as the inn itself. Like a fine old wine, the rooms here are often delicious but unpredictable. Every one comes in a different shape and size, though they are all furnished impeccably with rustic, Monterey-style furniture. Thanks to a grandfather clause, many rooms come with actual wood-burning fireplaces, not the gas-powered ones now required by the state. For maximum privacy, ask for a garden cottage with a private patio. Room 133 is called the Honeymoon Suite, and though it's been compared to a small dollhouse, you and your sweetie probably won't mind being in such close proximity to each other. The property boasts pretty Spanish piazzas with fountains and miles of horse trails that the two of you are welcome to walk on (just watch your step). Our favorite spot for kissing, however, is in the rose garden just outside the The Dining Room restaurant (see Romantic Restaurants). Visit it during the spring and summer when the roses are in full bloom, and you'll swear you've entered paradise.

$$$–$$$$ *AE, DC, MC, V; no checks; www.theinnatsf.com.* &

## MORGAN RUN RESORT & CLUB
🌀🌀🌢

*5960 Cancha De Golf, Rancho Santa Fe / 858/756-2471 or 800/378-4653*
Romance and horsing around go hand-in-hand at Morgan Run. Modeled after Churchill Downs, the crisp white buildings and bell tower here make it feel more like a racetrack than a resort. Even the hotel is named after a thoroughbred. The lobby is decorated with traditional English Victorian furniture, equestrian paintings, and large racing trophies. But while the horse theme dominates, the only real horse you'll see is at the nearby Del Mar Racetrack. This is primarily an exclusive country club with 89 guest rooms thrown in for good measure. The main attraction is golf, but you'll also find 11 tennis courts, a pool and Jacuzzi, a fitness center, and spa services (couple's in-room massages are a must). The guest rooms are tasteful and understated and mirror the resort's equestrian motif. Couples will want to reserve the suites or the executive kings, which come with mahogany furniture and cozy gas fireplaces. There is a pretty restaurant, The Morgan Grille, which is open only to guests and serves nonspectacular but hearty breakfast, lunch, and dinner. We recommend reserving a table out on the deck, where the two of you can relax by the fire pit in wicker chairs and stare out at rolling Bermuda fairways. A word of warning: 60 percent of the resort's weekday business is corporate events. Be sure to stay here only on weekends or during holidays, or else you may find yourself sharing the dining room with 50 executives wearing suits and nametags—not very conducive to romance.

$$–$$$ *AE, MC, V; no checks; www.morganrun.com.* &

# QUAILS INN HOTEL
❤❤
*1025 La Bonita Dr, Lake San Marcos / 760/744-0120 or 800/447-6556*
Set on a lake (albeit a man-made one), this quiet hotel is a nice family-owned alternative to the cookie-cutter Ramada and Hampton Inns that crowd the area. It is part of the massive, 250-acre San Marcos Resort, which also consists of a country club, shopping area, and private homes. The real draw, however, is Lake San Marcos, and no romantic retreat here should even be considered if you do not secure one of the four lakefront cottages. Inside these tastefully decorated suites, you'll find a big bedroom and a cozy lounge area with L-shaped couches, high A-framed ceilings, and a full kitchen. A deck overlooks the lake, where in the early morning you'll be able to see—and hear—all the ducks, swans, and pelicans (but, ironically, no quails) that also vacation on the property. In the summer, the hotel can arrange a private boat ride à deux on one of the hotel's duffys—electric-powered riverboats. Equipped with nothing but your honey and a bottle of complimentary wine, you can motor down 1 mile to the lake's dam, a remote spot that can only be accessed via the water. Kiss here and the only living creatures that will spot you are a few local frogs. Back on land, you'll find four pools for leisurely sunbathing, a recreation room, and tennis courts. The Quails Inn Dinnerhouse (760/744-2445) was recently renovated and serves lunch and dinner. Order their special sun-dried cherry–crusted salmon and feast while you overlook the moon's reflection on the lake.
$$ *AE, DC, DIS, MC, V; no checks; www.quailsinn.com.*

# RANCHO BERNARDO INN
❤❤❤
*17550 Bernardo Oaks Dr, Rancho Bernardo / 858/675-8400 or 800/770-7482*
The main building of this hacienda-style inn is romance central. Couples will find lots of cozy armchairs and couches around roaring fireplaces. Antiques and artifacts fill the halls, giving the building an old California hunting lodge feel. FYI: the best smooching spot is by the fireplace with the elk antlers, or out back on the deck at night by one of the three outdoor fireplaces. Unfortunately, the unique, Old World charm of the main building is not replicated in the 287 rooms that surround the property. They're more akin to the cookie-cutter interiors you'd find in any big corporate hotel. Nevertheless, the hotel offers a plethora of activities and amenities to keep you both happy, including five golf courses, twelve tennis courts, two pools, seven hot tubs, and a spa. The main restaurant, El Bizcocho (see Romantic Restaurants), serves extraordinary food fit for gods, and the restaurant downstairs, the Veranda, is also quite tasty (and far less expensive), serving salads, sandwiches, and entrées like fresh grilled fish, free-range chicken, and braised lamb shanks. For maximum privacy, be sure to book a room on the second floor, which overlooks the golf course—otherwise you

183

may find yourself sharing your back patio with a golfer.
$$$–$$$$ *AE, DC, DIS, MC, V; checks OK; www.ranchobernardoinn.com.* &

## RANCHO VALENCIA
●●●●
*5921 Valencia Circle, Rancho Santa Fe / 858/756-1123 or 800/548-3664*
This is heaven on earth for lovers. The only drawback? You actually have
to leave. The brain trust behind this Spanish-Mediterranean rustic resort—
hidden on a 40-acre plateau surrounded by exotic flowers and eucalyptus
trees—seems to have thought of every last trick in the romance playbook.
It's no wonder the place draws some of the wealthiest couples in the world,
including Bill and Melinda Gates and Celine Dion and Rene Angelil. There
are 49 beautiful suites decorated tastefully with whitewashed wood beams,
ceilings fans, stucco walls, two plasma TVs, and tile fireplaces. The bath-
room is home to a walk-in closet larger than most one-bedroom apartments,
as well as a hot tub and steam shower. French doors lead you to your own
private patio, which has another larger bubbling hot tub—perfect for sip-
ping wine under the stars. Little touches—like fresh orange juice and the
newspaper outside your door in the morning, and turndown service at
night that includes little slippers by the side of your bed and the next day's
weather forecast—make you realize how much attention has been given to
detail. If you should choose to leave the cozy confines of your suite, there are
myriad options, including tennis courts, swimming pools, hikes, a gourmet
restaurant (Rancho Valencia Restaurant; see Romantic Restaurants), and,
in spring 2005, a brand new spa. Ask about the romantic getaway package,
which includes champagne upon arrival, spa treatments, and candlelit
dinner served in your room by the fireside. Whether you come here to hon-
eymoon, to propose, or just to vacation, a stay here is guaranteed to be a
romantic experience you won't soon forget.
$$$$ *AE, CB, DC, MC, V; checks OK; www.ranchovalencia.com.* &

## THE WELK RESORT—SAN DIEGO
●●
*8860 Lawrence Welk Dr, Escondido / 760/749-3000 or 800/932-9355*
Founded in the 1960s by bandleader/accordion player Lawrence Welk, this
sprawling 1,000-acre resort caters primarily to mature couples. It is defini-
tively anti-hip, which many might find refreshing in our fad-mad culture.
And with a little advance planning and knowledge, romance can easily be
found here. A few important facts to know: First, the resort is divided into
hotel rooms and rentable villa suites. Avoid the hotel rooms, which are faded
and dated, and opt for the one-bedroom villa suites. They are relatively new,
come with full kitchens, nice bathrooms, fireplaces, and decks that overlook
the golf course and surrounding mountains. Second, avoid the summer
months and holidays, when families invade the resort and the noise level

quadruples. By day, play golf on two championship courses, swim in one of six pools, play tennis, or investigate the mini Lawrence Welk museum. By night, dine at Mr. W's pub (which serves such classic fare as chicken and dumplings, filet mignon, and country-fried chicken), sing a little karaoke, and then take in a Broadway musical at the on-site 340-seat theater. $$–$$$ *AE, DC, DIS, MC, V; no checks; www.welkresort.com/Sandiego.* &

# Romantic Restaurants

## DELICIAS
❡❡❡❡

*6106 Paseo Delicias, Rancho Santa Fe / 858/756-8000*
From the decor to the cuisine, everything about this elegant eatery is romantic. Huge vases of beautifully arranged flowers, high ceilings, and large skylights give the main dining room an airy, joyous feel, though it tends to get a bit noisy on busy nights. We prefer the tables outside in the flower-filled back patio, with a huge outdoor wood-burning fireplace. Wolfgang Puck designed the original menu here and, though he was replaced by the extraordinary Barry Layne, his influence can still be felt in the eclectic menu, which is California meets France by way of China and Italy. For appetizers, share the calzones with lobster and the scrumptious egg roll with shiitake mushrooms and mascarpone. For an entrée, you can't go wrong with the goat cheese–encrusted rack of lamb. Top it all off with the chocolate "baby cake" with a cream cheese center. If the quality of a restaurant can be judged by its repeat customers, then Delicias is off the charts. Seventy percent of the clientele here are the extremely affluent locals, who know a good thing when they see—and eat—it.
$$$ *AE, CB, DC, DIS, MC, V; no checks; dinner every day; full bar; reservations recommended.* &

## THE DINING ROOM
❡❡❡

*5951 Linea Del Cielo (Inn at Rancho Santa Fe), Rancho Santa Fe / 858/756-1131*
The main restaurant at the Inn at Rancho Santa Fe (see Romantic Lodgings) was recently renovated to match the elegance and old-school charm of its host hotel. And they've done a terrific job. One can only imagine that this is what it must have felt like to dine in splendor in the roaring '20s. The best tables are in the library, a pretty room with high ceilings, a toasty fireplace, and great views of the flower-laden piazza just outside. On weekend nights, a flamenco band gathers here to play wonderful live jazz. If the library's all booked, ask for a main dining-room booth—they're as comfy as they are intimate. Unlike the traditional decor, the food is fresh and original. Chef A. J. Voytko calls his cooking Rancho Cuisine, and he mainly uses

ingredients from local organic farms—many considered the best in the country. You'll find a variety of different culinary influences, from Mexican to Asian, prepared simply but tastefully. Voytko offers a harvest menu and a low-carb menu, which change weekly. But your best bet is going with the four-course tasting menu, which changes every day. If you're really lucky, he'll be serving the calamari salad with apples or the duck confit and black-olive smashed potatoes. But pretty much everything on the menu is a winner.

$$$–$$$$ *AE, DC, DIS, MC, V; no checks; breakfast, lunch, dinner every day, brunch Sun; full bar; reservations recommended; www.innatrsf.com.* &

## EL BIZCOCHO
♥♥♥♥

*17550 Bernardo Oaks Dr (Rancho Bernardo Inn), Rancho Bernardo / 858/675-8500*
Step inside this luxurious and stately dining room and suddenly the two of you will feel like you're entering a different era—wrought-iron chandeliers hang from the grand ceilings, the waiters wear tuxedos and carve your food at the table, and the customers are all dressed to kill (gentlemen are required to wear jackets). This is a setting fit for a king and queen—or even better, two people who absolutely adore each other and want to celebrate that love in a special way. It's no surprise that the restaurant is one of the area's most sought after places for marriage proposals. Who could possibly say "no" after feasting on one of Chef Gavin Kaysen's superb tasting menus? We recommend the James Beard House Dinner, a mouth-watering five-course meal, which received the stamp of approval from one of the world's top chefs. The menu changes every three months or so, but you can be assured to find fresh and innovative takes on traditional French fare: a foie gras and smoked eel Napoleon, venison medallions with chocolate sauce, and a chestnut mousse in the shape of a pyramid, for example. Hands down, the most romantic table in the restaurant is table 65, a cozy booth that overlooks the 18th hole of the Rancho Bernardo Inn golf course, though the furthest thing from your mind will be putting.

$$$–$$$$ *AE, CB, DC, DIS, MC, V; checks OK; dinner every day, brunch Sun; full bar; reservations recommended; www.ranchobernardoinn.com.* &

## MILLE FLEURS
♥♥♥

*6009 Paseo Delicias, Rancho Santa Fe / 858/756-3085*
This exquisitely delicious and stupendously expensive restaurant is hidden in a quiet courtyard in the center of town. It is consistently rated one of the top restaurants in San Diego County, and for good reason—this place is a little slice of culinary nirvana. Decorated like a French country inn—with tiles on the walls, two fireplaces, and antique furniture—and frequented

by San Diego's wealthy elite, the main dining room is as glamorous a spot to feast as you will ever find. We prefer it to the relatively sedate candlelit tables outside on the patio. But the main attraction here is the food, which is so fresh, you'll feel as though the ingredients have been picked individually for you. The restaurant's award-winning chef, Martin Woesle, trained in Europe and has a flair for infusing his classic French and German cuisine with California's freshest local produce. As a result, the menu changes every day according to what's in season. Order anything with asparagus in the spring or tomatoes in the summer. Woesle's ahi with avocado or swordfish with farm green vegetables are not to be missed, nor is the wine list, which boasts a stunning 700 selections. The only drawback here is the attitude of the staff. While obviously proud to be working at such an exclusive restaurant, it's a pity they have to act so stuffy. **$$$-$$$$** *AE, DC, MC, V; no checks; lunch Mon–Fri, dinner every day; full bar; reservations recommended; www.millefleurs.com.* &

## 150 GRAND CAFÉ
♦♦♦
*150 W Grand Ave, Escondido / 760/738-6868*
With its fast-food chains and strip malls, downtown Escondido is not the place you'd expect to find a charming and flavorful restaurant modeled after an English country library. But 150 Grand is just that—a cheery little place to cuddle amid large colorful murals, green slate floors, and white shelves lined with cookbooks. The owners are from the UK and have brought the coziness of the countryside to the room, but all other comparisons to England stop there. The food is distinctly California fresh (you won't find fish-and-chips here), and American chef Carlton Greenawalt changes the menu every day, depending on what produce is in season. There are no heavy sauces or rich, cardiac arrest–inducing items on the menu. This is all about subtle flavors and lightness. Settle in at the table for two by the fireplace and order the Dungeness crab salad or the ahi sushi taco. If you're lucky, Greenawalt will also be serving the blueberry–pinot noir salmon. A surprisingly tasty dessert is his avocado ice cream. Who knew? **$$-$$$** *AE, DC, DIS, MC, V; checks OK; lunch, dinner Mon–Sat; full bar; reservations recommended; www.150grandcafe.com.* &

## RANCHO VALENCIA RESTAURANT
♦♦♦
*5921 Valencia Circle (Rancho Valencia), Rancho Santa Fe / 858/759-6216*
This restaurant's warm and inviting ambience reflects Rancho Valencia's (see Romantic Lodgings) dedication to all things romantic. The dining room is formal (you may even want to wear a suit or dress), but the attitude is laid-back. You'll feel like you're sitting in your own little secret garden—with plants and flowers everywhere you look. Reserve a table by the back

windows that overlook the lush gardens and tennis courts. On cool nights, another wonderful option is to sit outside on the patio by the wood-burning fireplace. A jazz trio plays out here in the summer. In keeping with the decor, the food here is traditional classic French, but it's infused with a little California creativity. Chef Steven Sumner is a local who has spent quite a bit of time in Japan and Hawaii, and he brings those influences to his menu. Start with the Hawaiian sashimi crisps, which are mini tacos filled with papaya-mango salsa and tuna. (Warning: this is not first-date food, as it can be a bit messy). Other satisfying choices include the white truffle–dusted diver scallops and the mesquite-fired rack of lamb. The chef's dessert sampler is not to be missed. Don't even think twice about it—how often in your life do you get to dine like this?
$$$–$$$$ *AE, DC, MC, V; no checks; breakfast, lunch, dinner every day; full bar; reservations recommended; www.ranchovalencia.com.* &

# TEMECULA VALLEY AND FALLBROOK

## ROMANTIC HIGHLIGHTS

Located where Riverside and San Diego counties meet, this glorious stretch of land is one of the Southland's best-kept secrets for lovers. The warm, dry days and cool, crisp evenings, coupled with the sea breeze that blows into the valley via the Rainbow Gap, make this the perfect spot for vineyards—and for couples who savor the good life. Consider this Napa Valley lite. It has most of the amenities of its more famous counterpart in the north, but fewer crowds. The wining and dining is top notch here. Add to the mix beautiful rolling hills, sweeping vistas, and plenty of private hideaways to kiss until your heart's content, and you have the perfect ingredients for love.

Upon arriving in **Temecula**, there are only two words you need to know: balloons and wine. Your adventure begins early in the morning, as you rise with the sun aboard a colorful, seven-story-high hot-air balloon. Snuggling together in a basket, the two of you will sweep just above the treetops, giving you, literally, a bird's eye view of the green and red vineyards below. There are five balloon operators in the area. One of the best is **A Grape Escape** (40335 Winchester Rd; 888/7HO-TAIR), which offers sweetheart flights for just two people plus the pilot. Be warned, the operators report at least three marriage proposals a week aboard these flights. For true balloon aficionados, don't miss the **Balloon and Wine Festival** (www.tvbws.com) the first weekend of June. There's food, wine, entertainment, and the true spectacle of being aboard one of the 50 balloons that take off each morning.

After your balloon ride, you'll want to head straight to the vineyards, which is the area's main attraction—and deservedly so. There are 22 wineries that line a 3-mile stretch along Rancho California Road. They are opened year-round and offer wine tastings to the public for a nominal fee. Most are family owned, giving the entire area a warm and welcoming vibe. All are beautifully situated and landscaped and offer special secluded spots to hide away. Because the wine country is small, you can literally begin on the west end of the road, head east, and hit every single winery in one or two days. However, you'll probably want to choose a designated driver, or, even better, book a ride on the **Grapeline Wine Country Shuttle** (888/8-WINERY; www.gogrape.com) and let someone else do the driving.

While all the vineyards offer spectacular views, the best place to stop and take in the scenery (not to mention the wine) is **Falkner Winery** (see "A Toast to Romance"). It not only boasts the best view (it is the highest vineyard at 1,000 feet), but also has the odd distinction of being the only winery with an outdoor tasting bar. Stop for lunch of **Allie's at Callaway** (see Romantic Restaurants), which has tasty Mediterranean food and a romantic patio that overlooks the rolling hills to the west. FYI: local couples consider this the best place in town for a champagne brunch. For more information on the wineries, contact the **Temecula Valley Winegrowers Association** (909/699-6586; www.temeculawines.com).

Just south of wine country, you and your honey will find another attraction certainly worth visiting—or at least driving through. **Old Town Temecula** (take I-15 south and exit at Front St) is a quaint, Old West town (circa 1859), lined with antique stories, ice cream parlors, craft shops, and a few authentic historical buildings. While much of the real Old Town was destroyed years ago, the street has gone through a recent facelift and is now picture perfect—if not a tad corny—with its boardwalks and reconstructed saloons.

Each Saturday, the festive **Farmers' Market** comes to town—featuring local fruits, vegetables, and baked goods, as well as local craftsmen and massage therapists, who will ease out your knots for a nominal fee. For some authentic, albeit kitschy, Old West flavor, be sure to stop by the **Swing Inn Café** (28676 Front St; 909/676-2321) and order the 99-cent biscuits and gravy. At night, the **Temecula Stampede** (28721 Front St; 909/695-1761) has live country-western music, line dancing, and a mechanical bull. Yee-haw!

For a little R&R, head 5 miles south to less-traveled **Fallbrook**. Here, you will find a lot fewer tourists and an abundance of avocado orchards—the area has been dubbed the "avocado capital of the world." Play a round of golf on the gorgeous 18-hole **Pala Mesa Resort** championship course (2001 Old Highway 395; 760/728-5881; www.palamesa.com). Or spoil yourself rotten at **Los Willows** spa (see Romantic Lodgings), which offers both half- and full-day spa packages. There is a dreamy, private hike along the **Santa Margarita River Trail** (San Dia Creek Rd), which snakes 2½ miles along the river bank. Local naturalists claim that this trail boasts the most species of flowers of any trail in Southern California. Pick a few for your lover, then climb along the big boulders that jut out into the river. You'll feel a million miles away from civilization, which is sure to bring out a little romance.

## Access and Information

The best way to reach Temecula Valley is by car via Interstate 15, which cuts through the heart of the region. The valley is 50 miles north of San Diego and 90 miles south of Los Angeles. For wine country, take the Rancho California Road exit and head 4 miles east. All of the vineyards are either on this road or just off it. To get to Fallbrook, exit Interstate 15 at Mission Road and head south. For more information, contact the **Temecula Chamber of Commerce** (26790 Ynez Ct; 909/676-5090; www.temecula.org) or the **Fallbrook Chamber of Commerce** (233 E Mission Rd, Ste A; 760/728-5845; www .fallbrookca.org).

## Romantic Lodgings

### THE INN AT CHURON WINERY
♥♥♦

*33233 Rancho California Rd, Temecula / 909/694-9070*
Beautiful gardens and fountains surround this French-style chateau B&B in the heart of wine country. With its grand circular entrance lined with floral wallpaper and filled with antiques, the inn might strike some as a tad pretentious for casual Temecula, but it's still fun to play make-believe king and queen here. There are 25 rooms, but you'll want to reserve a gigantic luxury suite with gas-burning fireplace, Jacuzzi tub for two, and a private balcony with scenic views of the vineyards. If you get up early enough, you'll be able to see the hot-air balloons floating across the morning sky. Our favorite room is the Cabernet Suite, which is fittingly decorated with wine-red carpets and tasteful, if not austere, classical French furnishings. In the evening, guests are invited to partake in the private wine reception downstairs in the tasting room. Take a few glasses of merlot outside in the gardens and find a private spot to sip and smooch.
$$$-$$$$ *AE, DIS, MC, V; no checks; www.innatchuronwinery.com.*

# A Toast to Romance

What better place to squeeze your honey then where they squeeze grapes? With 22 fully operating vineyards all within 10 minutes of each other, Temecula wine country is the perfect getaway for amorous couples looking for a satisfying day of wine sipping. Most vineyards have gift shops and tasting rooms open to the public, and many now offer jazz concerts in the summer months. A word of advice: with some exceptions, the area is not known for its chardonnay. For the tastiest selections, stick with the reds like merlot and sangiovese. The sparkling wine is also excellent. The best time to visit is from the end of August to October, when the green and red grapes are on the vine and the smell of wine is in the air.

Start at **Callaway Coastal Vineyard & Winery** (32720 Rancho California Rd; 909/676-4001; www.callawaycoastal.com). This is the largest, oldest, and most famous winery in the area and home to an award-winning chardonnay. It also happens to be home to the scrumptious Allie's at Callaway (see Romantic Restaurants). Just across the street, you'll find **Thornton Winery** (32575 Rancho California Rd; 909/699-6961; www.thorntonwine.com), which is known for its seven varieties of champagne. Stroll over to the bar and ask for the lip-red cuvée rouge, which tastes like liquid raspberry and chocolate. **Falkner Winery** (40620 Calle Contento; 909/676-8231; www.falknerwinery. com) boasts a lovely, ranch-style building and outdoor tasting bar. Try their Luscious Lips syrah as you take in a free Sunday-afternoon jazz concert. Also offering a "Jazz in the Vines" series is **Wilson Creek Winery** (35960 Rancho California Rd; 909/699-9463; www.wilsoncreekwinery.com), which wins lots of awards for its almond champagne (sounds strange, we know, but you gotta try it). **Ponte Winery** (35053 Rancho California Rd; 909/694-8855; www.ponte winery.com) adds a little Italian flare to the region. The winery is owned by two Italian brothers, who named their best wines after their daughters Isabel and Juliet. This is a pretty spot with high ceilings and large wood beams. Be sure to feast on the delicious wood-fired pizzas they serve on their outdoor patio. One of the nicest rooms for tasting can be found at **Mount Palomar Winery** (33820 Rancho California Rd; 909/676-5047; www.mountpalomar. com). It's a rustic, Spanish-style winery with adobe and wood that came from an old barn in Washington. Order some sherry or port and sit outside in the picnic area, which offers beautiful views.

At this point in your adventure, it should be difficult for both of you to stand, but no romantic trip to Temecula is complete without a visit to **Miramonte Winery** (33410 Rancho California Rd; 909/506-5500; www.mira montewinery.com). Besides offering a hardy Bordeaux called Opulante, this

*Continued on next page*

winery specializes in hand-etched bottles for any occasion. Starting at $45 and going all the way to $275, bottles can be designed for you and your loved one, with any message you see fit—just keep it PG-13. For more information on these etchings, log on to www.celebrationcellars.com.

—JONATHAN SMALL

## LOMA VISTA BED & BREAKFAST
❂❂❂
*33350 La Serena Wy, Temecula / 909/676-7047*
Perched up on a hill surrounded by grapefruit trees, this Spanish-style 10-room inn is as charming as it is private. The location doesn't get any better—smack dab in the middle of wine country and overlooking the sprawling vineyards to the south and west—and the ambience here is cozy country casual. The two of you can relax by the fireplace in the living room decorated with pine furniture and flowers, or sip complimentary wine on the outdoor patio. There are no TVs or phones to distract you, just the quiet comfort of a warm fire and the sounds of birds singing. Inside, guests will find complimentary fresh fruit and sherry waiting for them upon their arrival. Each room is named after a type of wine and decorated in a different motif. The most romantic rooms are the Cabernet Sauvignon (which has a log cabin–chic theme with its dark wood and red-brick fireplace) and the Sauvignon Blanc (which has a canopy bed, Southwestern-style furnishings, and a terrace). Every morning, owner Shelia Kurczynski prepares a home-cooked champagne breakfast that includes such tasty delights as fresh grapefruit from the garden, crepes, and eggs Benedict. There's also a wine and cheese hour on weekend nights, when guests get to sample local vino. Book your rooms at least two months in advance, as demand is high and supply is low.
*$$–$$$ MC, V; no checks; www.virtualcities.com.*

## LOS WILLOWS
❂❂❂
*530 Stewart Canyon Rd, Fallbrook / 760/731-9400 or 888/731-9400*
The ultimate in pampering can be experienced at this super-remote spa. Tucked away in a canyon and surrounded by 44 acres of avocado trees, palms, and a private vineyard, this all-inclusive inn is so private, hardly anyone knows about it. This is a good thing. Space is limited—there are only eight rooms—and you want to make sure to take advantage of all the divine spa treatments. There are two buildings: a spa and main lodge. The lodge is a cheery place, with murals of bucolic scenes on the walls and little snacks left out for the guests to nibble on. Each room is impeccably decorated and

comes with a balcony and a Jacuzzi tub. While all the rooms are charming, the best is the Waterfall Room, which overlooks a man-made waterfall in the back garden. Start your day by taking a 2-mile hike in the lush surroundings (a picnic breakfast can be packed upon request). Then, get ready for some serious relaxation: Down at the spa, couple's Swedish-style massages are available, as well as numerous body-care treatments from the gods. We like the avocado crème wrap, in which you are wrapped in the nourishing oils of avocado, transforming your skin into butter. Top it all off in the sauna or steam room, which, rather conveniently, is only big enough for two, or cuddle up in the outdoor Jacuzzi under the stars. The inn serves a healthy, low-fat breakfast, lunch, and dinner, but unlike some spas, you won't leave the place famished.
$$$–$$$$ *AE, DIS, MC, V; checks OK; www.loswillows.com.* &

# OAK CREEK MANOR
♥♥♥♥
*4735 Olive Hill Rd, Fallbrook / 760/451-2468 or 877/451-2468*
It doesn't get much more romantic—or decadent—than this. Austrian-born innkeepers Johannes and Ingrid Zachbauer have taken a southern plantation replica of Thomas Jefferson's Monticello estate and infused it with European elegance. The result is a four-room, museum-like B&B that feels like it's from another time. With its marble floors and high ceilings, the manor is decorated with art from all over the world. Because the manor sits near a sleepy creek and is surrounded by fountains and gardens, the mood here is completely conducive to long naps and lots of kissing. Privacy is the main objective here. All the rooms are spread far apart from each other and have private gardens, as well as whirlpool tubs and fireplaces. You could stay here the entire weekend and never see another guest. The main house is home to the Rose Room, inspired by an English rose garden, with its pink carpets and floral furnishings. For those who really want to splurge, there is also the gargantuan Manor Suite, with a full bar and entertainment center. The very private Carriage House is also available at a relatively reasonable price. While breakfast is included with all rooms, we strongly suggest you arrange for lunch or dinner with Johannes, a classically trained chef. He will prepare a private meal that rivals the elegance and quality of top European inns. It's just that good.
$$$–$$$$ *AE, MC, V; checks OK; www.oakcreekmanor.com.*

# PALA MESA RESORT
♥♥♥
*2001 Old Highway 395, Fallbrook / 760/728-5881 or 800/722-4700*
Pala Mesa has a lot going for it: a gorgeous location, a top-rated golf course, and romantic chalet-style guest rooms. The recent $9-million renovations can be seen in the handsome new main lodge and restaurant, with its stone

and wood trimmings, as well as in the beautifully tended grounds, overflowing with citrus and avocado trees and fragrant white roses. There are quite a few choice spots to wander off and seek some privacy, including the garden pavilion with its waterfalls and the private benches near the manicured yoga lawn. The rooms themselves are private and cozy—albeit a tad generic—and nicely furnished with comfy pillow-top beds and a country-ranch decor. You'll want to reserve one of the hillside suites, which have extra-large patios for soaking in some rays and taking in the panoramic views of the nearby mountains. Some of the suites also have hot tubs. The resort offers day trips to the nearby Los Willows spa, as well as extremely relaxing in-room treatments. There's a large pool, tennis courts, croquet, bocci, a fitness center, and a dramatic 3-mile hike around the mountains. $$ AE, DC, DIS, MC, V; no checks; www.palamesa.com. &

## TEMECULA CREEK INN
❀❀❀
*44501 Rainbow Canyon Rd, Temecula / 909/694-1000 or 877/517-1823*
If golfing and smooching are your things, this resort is definitely the place to play and stay. It has three different nine-hole courses surrounded by the breathtaking boulders and brush of the San Jacinto Mountains. If that isn't beautiful enough for you, the canyon in which it sits gets its name from the rainbows that frequently appear on either side of the valley. As you drive down the long entranceway and glimpse the inn, don't let the gray, fading '70s-style buildings throw you. Inside are lovely rooms with large furniture and American Indian–inspired designs. Each of the 130 rooms has a deck and a view; the junior suites are particularly roomy. For those who don't play golf, fear not. There is still plenty of fun to be had here—swimming in the outdoor pool, playing tennis, biking, and indulging in in-room massages. The inn is also strategically located between the Temecula Valley vineyards to the north and the Pechanga and Pala casinos to the south, perfect for day and night trips. Add to the mix an on-site gourmet restaurant, Temet Grill (see Romantic Restaurants), with spectacular views of mountains and fountains, and you have the perfect recipe for a romantic getaway. $$$ AE, DC, DIS, MC, V; checks OK; www.temeculacreekinn.com. &

# Romantic Restaurants

## ALLIE'S AT CALLAWAY
❀❀❀
*32720 Rancho California Rd, Temecula / 909/694-0560*
Here's a wonderful chance to be romantic and philanthropic at the same time. Owner Steve Hamlin donates a large portion of his proceeds to various charities, so not only are you eating fine food, but you're also contributing

to a good cause. Named after Hamlin's wife, the restaurant sits up on a hill next to the Callaway Coastal winery. There are two spacious outdoor decks (fear not—they're heated in the winter), which offer some of the best views of all the surrounding wineries. The sunsets here are particularly gorgeous, so to add to the enchantment quotient, you might want to book a table around that time. The restaurant isn't as formal as some of the others in the area, but once you settle in under the green awning and rustic chandeliers you'll feel as if you've been transported to the Italian countryside. The food is Mediterranean inspired and uses lots of avocado, citrus, and herbs. The shrimp Mai'ai is a guilty pleasure—jumbo shrimp sautéed with macademia nuts, bananas, and hazelnut liqueur. Our only complaint is that this place isn't open for dinner during the week.
*$$$ AE, DC, DIS, MC, V; no checks; lunch Mon–Sat, dinner Fri–Sat, brunch Sun; wine only; reservations recommended; www.alliesat callaway.com.* &

## AQUA TERRA
◐◐

*2001 Old Highway 395 (Pala Mesa Resort), Falbrook / 760/728-5881 or 800/722-4700*
Located off the main lobby of the Pala Mesa Resort (see Romantic Lodgings), this surf-and-turf restaurant offers a pleasant diversion from the area's classic wine-country cuisine. Here, it's all about the raw bar and the extensive martini selection. Before entering the main dining room, couples should settle down at the bar and enjoy a few oyster shots, then wash them down with a sky-blue concoction called an Aquatini, which comes with a gummy shark candy. The bar area is quite noisy and crowded, so it's best to continue the more intimate conversation in the back of the restaurant, on the terrace that overlooks the golf course. The dining room is pleasant enough, though a tad bland, with high ceilings and yellow tablecloths. The food isn't particularly creative either, but that doesn't mean it isn't good. Start with the scallops wrapped in bacon and topped with pesto sauce. The steak and lobster is by far the best entrée on the menu. Though the restaurant is opened for breakfast, lunch, and dinner, romance seekers should come here only at night, long after the raucous golfing crowd has put away their clubs and gone to bed.
*$$$ AE, DC, DIS, MC, V; no checks; breakfast, lunch, dinner every day; full bar; reservations recommended.* &

## CAFÉ CHAMPAGNE
◐◐◐

*32575 Rancho California Rd, Temecula / 909/699-0088*
Just outside the front door of this gourmet restaurant at the Thornton Winery, you'll find a quaint herb garden. A sign tells you that all the herbs

grown here are used in the tasty food—a not-so-subtle reminder that you are about to partake in a deliciously fresh meal, seasoned with local ingredients and local TLC. Inside you will discover romance central, a charming space designed by winery co-owner Sally Thornton. The decor is a hodgepodge of French country inn meets Asia, but it works. Toward the front, there are stunning views of the Callaway winery and the fountain in the courtyard. In keeping with the whimsical, multicultural surroundings, the menu is also a fusion delight. If you do one thing together in Temecula, you must order the ahi avocado tower appetizer and two forks. Stacked high and surrounded by pickled shiitake mushrooms, it's simply scrumptious. The duck entrée with a ginger-lavender honey sauce will also put you in the mood for love. Thornton Winery is known for its sparkling wine, so don't hold back. Sample a few of their best—including the cuvee rouge, a sinful blend of raspberry and syrah.

$$$ *AE, DC, DIS, MC, V; no checks; lunch, dinner every day, brunch Sun; beer and wine; reservations recommended; www.thorntonwine.com.* &

## GOURMET ITALIA
🌣🌣

*27499 Ynez Rd (Tower Plaza), Temecula / 909/676-9194*
Granted, you wouldn't usually expect to find a romantic eatery in a shopping mall next to a Starbucks, but this sleeper Italian restaurant is an adorable alternative to the crowded and expensive restaurants in the wine region. Not much larger than a hole in the wall, the narrow main room has yellow walls, candlelit tables, and a large colorful map of Italy—just in case you forget where the food comes from. The best tables are by the windows or in the secret back room, which only accommodates a few couples. There is also a lounge next door that serves wine and a special house martini. Live jazz can be heard on weekends. While the restaurant may be small, the food makes a big impression. In fact, this is where many of the area's best chefs come to eat on their nights off. The pizzas are all yummy with thin, crunchy crust and fresh ingredients. The pastas are also authentic and delicious. Try the angel hair pasta with fresh tomatoes, garlic, and basil. For carnivores, the veal scaloppini is also excellent. If the food doesn't put a smile on your face, the bill will. It's nice to know that sometimes love don't cost a thing—well, at least not very much.

$$ *AE, DIS, MC, V; no checks; lunch, dinner Tues–Sat; beer, wine, and martinis; reservations not required.* &

## TEMET GRILL
🌣🌣🌣🌣

*44501 Rainbow Canyon (Temecula Creek Inn), Temecula / 909/587-1465*
With its large iron chandeliers and American Indian artifacts covering the walls, Temet Grill at Temecula Creek Inn (see Romantic Lodgings)

seems more like a meat-and-potatoes hunting lodge than a gourmet restaurant—but looks can be deceiving. Chef Tim Stewart's menu is one of the most imaginative in the region. He calls it "wine country cuisine," and it's designed to complement the many different vinos from nearby vineyards. Ask for a romantic table near the windows, which overlook a beautiful stone fountain, then order some local wine, settle in, and prepare for a little culinary heaven. For starters, the crab cakes in a Nantua lobster sauce literally melt in your mouth. Another delicious appetizer is the spinach salad with Brie and poached pear. Winning entrées are the pistachio-encrusted pork medallions and the salmon in vanilla sauce, which is so rich you won't need dessert. Well, maybe just one. Order the brownie stuffed with peppermint patty and ask for two forks. If there's anything remaining on your plate at the end of the meal, you have a tremendous amount of willpower.
*$$$ AE, DC, DIS, MC, V; no checks; breakfast, lunch, dinner every day; full bar; reservations recommended; www.temeculacreekinn.com.* &

# JULIAN

## ROMANTIC HIGHLIGHTS

When people think of Julian, the first image that comes to mind is apples. Undeniably, this mountaintop town is famous for its fruit and fruit pies, but Julian's dedicated preservation of its historic Western roots and its woodland surroundings make a visit to this romantic frontier retreat an experience to savor. Upon arriving at the diminutive town—situated at 4,235 feet—it's impossible to resist deeply inhaling the crisp, fresh mountain air lightly tinged with the homey aroma of just-baked apple pie. If you could bottle the fragrant air like a perfume, you'd have a jar filled with the blended scents of fruit and pine trees, fragrant cinnamon and allspice, and smoky musk from a blazing hearth. On the main thoroughfare—aptly named Main Street—charming stores, cafes, and bed-and-breakfasts occupy historic buildings (or replicas of them), where visiting couples will typically find an old-fashioned wood fire burning and a proprietor standing by with a warm greeting and a welcoming smile.

Julian's original claim to fame was gold, the first flecks having been discovered in 1869. After 60 years of what was San Diego County's first and only gold rush, the mines became depleted, so those who remained in the town turned to farming the rich soil instead of digging below it. Apples soon became the crop of choice, and every fall the harvest is celebrated when Julian is a blossom with roadside fruit stands offering everything from the most succulent fruits to the tastiest ciders.

# Love and Marriage and a Horse and Carriage

Jaunting down a country road in a horse-drawn carriage while you snuggle next to your sweetie is the ultimate romantic fantasy. But dreams do come true in Julian when you and your significant other take a trip with **Country Carriages** (760/765-1471). Proprietors (and drivers) Suzanne and Wayne Moretti whisk guests out of town, along Farmer Road, to the peaceful countryside. The 20- to 30-minute tour is about $25 per couple. During the 2-mile tour, you can hold hands under a blanket as your hosts point out local landmarks and proffer sightseeing tips. If you are heading out for dinner in town, the couple will also make buggy pick-ups at many of the area's lodgings to transport you to an enchanting meal. A carriage ride is also the ultimate time to pop the big question and pop champagne (if the answer is "yes," of course). The Morettis, who have witnessed many a marriage proposal, are happy to customize the ride with champagne if prior arrangements are made. And, in case you were wondering, it *is* possible to get married aboard the authentic horse-drawn carriage. During a 1½-hour trip, a non-denominational minister joins couples in holy matrimony at a serene spot just out of town at the turnaround. A simple flower arrangement, champagne, and a "Just Married" sign are included in the package. The horse and carriage can often be found at the corner of Main and Washington streets, but it's best to call ahead for reservations—especially during the busiest season, from September to December.

—BARBARA WERNIK

When you pack your suitcase for a trip to Julian, bring your heels as well as your hiking boots, since a day here can include everything from touring **Eagle and High Peak Mine** (end of C St; 760/765-0036) and fruit picking at **Calico Ranch U-Pick Orchard** (4800 Highway 78; 858/586-0392) to a stage performance at **Pine Hills Lodge and Dinner Theater** (2960 La Posada Wy; 760/765-1100). Though the Cedar Fire of 2003—the largest fire in the history of San Diego County—burned hundreds of homes and a number of favorite hostelries in the Julian area, the tourist-friendly gold mining town remained intact, and rebuilding is ongoing for the outlying areas. On a happier note, romantic vacationers won't have to contend with huge, impersonal resorts on a getaway to Julian. Instead, they'll receive lots of personal attention at historic lodges and hotels, one-of-a-kind (and even one-room) bed-and-breakfasts, and cozy cabins in the townsite and nestled in the surrounding hills. Contact the Julian Bed-and-Breakfast Guild (880/765-4333; www.julianbednbreakfastguild.com) for complete information on all accomodations in the area.

A year-round destination with four distinct seasons, Julian's climate can range from snow-kissed days in the winter to spectacular sun-drenched springs, when 3 million (!) daffodils, as well as lilacs, lilies, peonies, and blossoming fruit trees embellish the town. Fall, with its profusion of color and bountiful harvest, is the busiest time of year. During autumn weekends, expect to find throngs of visitors; consider arriving midweek if the thought of crowds puts a damper on your romantic mood. No matter what the season, however, nighttime brings about a brilliant explosion of stars. The best evening show in town is absolutely free, since there are no city lights to interfere when nature's own twinkling treasures illuminate the sky. Make a wish on a falling star (or meteor shower, if you get lucky) or join **Observer's Inn Sky Tours** (3535 Highway 79; 760/765-0088; www.observersinn.com) for a professional astronomer's explanation of outer space.

Back down to earth, couples keen for a bit of quiet contemplation and one-on-one time have miles of luxuriant wilderness to explore, ideal for hiking, bird watching, or mountain biking. Pack a picnic basket and a blanket and head to nearby **Volcan Mountain Wilderness, William Heise County Park**, or **Laguna Mountain State Park** for a daylong trek. Or, if your motto is "Why walk when you could ride?" head on over, partners, to **Julian Stables Trail Rides** (760/765-1598; www.julianactive.com) where you can pony-up for a trail adventure that you'll never forget. For sweethearts seeking a peak experience, **Sky Sailing** (31930 Hwy 79; 760/782-0404) will send you soaring over the mountains and valleys on a glider for a bird's-eye view of the land down under. Lovers of the outdoors can catch bass while basking in the beauty of **Lake Cuyamaca** (15027 Hwy 91; 760/765-0515 or 760/765-8123), which is also stocked with 40,000 rainbow trout and offers motorboats, paddleboats, and rowboats for waterside exploration.

For a romantic reminiscence of days gone by, saunter around the town into candle, candy, crafts, and collectibles shops, many housed in old Western-style buildings dating back to the 1870s. Purchase past treasures at several antique stores or more recent artwork at local galleries offering sculptures, paintings, and stained glass crafted by local artists. Annually, the town hosts a self-guided **Open Studios Tour** (www.julianstudios.org). Refreshments anyone? Take a break at **Miner's Diner & Soda Fountain** (2130 Main St; 760/765-3753), featuring a 1930s-style soda fountain, where you can sit on a stool and sip a sarsaparilla or ice cream soda or pucker up for a gargantuan pickle from the colossal counter-top barrel. At the **Julian Pioneer Museum** (2811 Washington St; 760/765-0227), imagine what days were like in Julian circa 1869 and see the best lace collection in California. Next door to the museum is the **Grosskopf House**, where you can peek at a reconstructed blacksmith's home.

Just outside the town, along lovely, winding Julian Orchards Drive, is **Menghini Winery** (1150 Julian Orchards Dr; 760/756-2072), home of premium varietal wines and the **Grape Stomp & Art Music Fest** in September. Smack-dab in the middle of an apple orchard, the winery offers complimentary tastings of their wines that are made on site—from white wines aged in stainless steel to reds aged in French oak barrels.

Speaking of sampling, a day in Julian wouldn't be complete without tasting at least one of the famous apple pies, too. Choose your favorite one from such fine pie palaces as **Mom's Pie House** (2119 Main St; 760/765-2472), **Julian Café & Bakery** (2112 Main St; 760/765-2712) or **Julian Pie Co.** (2225 Main St; 760/765-2449 or 760/765-2400). Local folks and tourists are sure to give you their opinions of which bakery makes the best pastry in town, but you'll have to decide for yourself. Just make sure you purchase plenty of pies to take home—a sweet reminder of your golden, delicious days spent in Southern California's own Big Apple.

## Access and Information

Just 60 miles northeast of San Diego, Julian is bordered by Mount Laguna to the south, Volcan and Palomar mountains to the north, and the Anza-Borrego Desert State Park to the east. From Interstates 5 or 15 southbound, turn east on Highway 78 to Julian or turn east on Highway 76, then turn right on Highway 79 to Julian. From Interstate 8 east or west, turn north on Highway 79 (Sunrise Hwy) to Julian. If you take Sunrise Highway on a clear day, you can't see forever, but you'll get a winsome view of the desert, the Salton Sea, and perhaps Baja California in Mexico. Along your journey, keep an eye out for deer and pheasants on the road and eagles and hawks in the sky. For more information, contact the **Julian Chamber of Commerce** (2129 Main St; 760/765-1857; www.julianca.com).

## Romantic Lodgings

### EAGLENEST BED & BREAKFAST
🖤🖤🖤

*2609 D St, Julian / 760/765-1252 or 888/345-6378*
It's always the right season for love at Eaglenest Bed & Breakfast, since each of the suites in this large Victorian home on D Street (one block above Julian's Main Street) are named after a special time of year. Winter's Room lends itself to snuggling, with a wood-burning fireplace, private patio, and personal hot tub; the Autumn Room, decorated with fall's more somber colors, has a red-brick gas fireplace and a private hot tub—perfect for cou-

System Julian

ples who want to stay in and nest. There's a seductive view from the Spring Room, as well as an iron canopy bed and sumptuous claw-footed bath. The Summer Room is country at heart and light and bright in spirit. Homey touches here include an always-present platter of brownies or cookies for guests to munch, games and videos to keep lovers entertained, and four friendly, frolicking golden retrievers. Each morning, a full country breakfast is served family style on the second floor, and when weather permits, couples can dine outdoors on a deck overlooking the inn's swimming pool and Jacuzzi. Owners Jim and Julie Degenfelder are happy to arrange itineraries and will also welcome guests' dogs during the week. For the ultimate amorous getaway, Eaglenest pulls out all the romantic bells and whistles as part of a two-night romance package. Champagne, fresh flowers, balloons, and chocolates will be ready and waiting in whichever seasonal room sparks your romantic whim. The two of you can also enjoy a one-hour horse-drawn carriage ride, followed by dinner at one of Julian's top restaurants and a full-body massage for two. If the package seems like romantic overkill, couples can pick and choose from among these amorous options.
$$$ AE, DIS, MC, V; checks OK; www.eaglenestbnb.com.

## JULIAN HOTEL
◐◐
*2032 Main St, Julian / 760/765-0201 or 800/734-5854*
The doorway to the Julian Hotel is not your ordinary entryway. For once it is opened, lovers cross over the threshold and are transported back 100 years in time. If the walls could talk at this hotel, they'd reveal how the inn was the dream come true for former slave Albert Robinson and his wife, Margaret. The site where the hotel now sits—right in the heart of Julian's historic district—was once the Robinson family's popular restaurant and bakery. Folks attracted by the Robinsons' famous hospitality clamored to stay overnight when the property expanded and became Hotel Robinson. Today, owners Steve and Gig Ballinger lovingly preserve the history and integrity of the inn. The Julian Hotel is now listed in the National Register of Historic Places and is a State of California Point of Historical Interest. Couples staying at the Julian Hotel can make history of their own—since there are no televisions or telephones to interrupt their privacy. Guest rooms have been authentically restored and have private baths. Of the 16 rooms at Julian Hotel, the most romantic is the Honeymoon House. The two-room house is a veritable Victorian sanctuary with a canopied bridal bed, a ladies' vanity room, and an oversized antique claw-footed bathtub. On nights when the brisk mountain air settles around the town, honeymooners at heart can cozy up by the classic cast-iron fireplace. The hotel's Patio Cottage also offers a secluded haven for two, with a fireplace and veranda, perfect for gazing out at the gardens or at a multicolored sunset. In the morning, guests ease into the day with a full breakfast in the parlor, an intriguing room suggestive of

System201

a Masterpiece Theatre mystery show, with traditional lace curtains, antique furnishings, rich brocade rug, and clusters of greenery. A hosted afternoon tea, with scones, cookies, and beverages (no alcohol), is a welcome break after a busy day. This genteel hotel is truly a reminder of an age when there were railroads instead of rockets and couriers instead of computers. $$ *AE, MC, V; checks OK; www.julianhotel.com.*

## ORCHARD HILL COUNTRY INN
✪✪✪✪

*2502 Washington St, Julian / 760/765-1700 or 800/71-ORCHARD*
When you stay at Orchard Hill Country Inn, the very thought of leaving your suite is enough to send you diving back under the down covers of your featherbed. Outside adventures might be waiting, but more irresistible temptations are inside: you can soak à deux in a Jacuzzi tub, read poetry to your amour by a blazing fire, or sip some bubbly out on the private veranda. Comfy California-country rooms at the inn—all individually decorated— offer serenity, solitude, and such tasteful touches as home-baked cookies, Belgian chocolate truffles, and complimentary beverages. No wonder there are so many "Do Not Disturb" signs hanging outside room doors. Situated just under the stars atop a pine-studded hill overlooking Julian, the Orchard Hill Inn is small enough to be called intimate, but spacious enough to guarantee privacy. Expect a warm greeting from proprietors Darrell and Pat Straube and their family upon arriving at the inn. They and their staff treat guests like extended family—apparent by the number of guests (50 percent!) who return for a replay of their romantic getaway. Guests can choose to stay at one of ten rooms in the main lodge, or in one of a dozen deluxe accommodations in five California Craftsman cottages nestled around the property. The most romantic room is the Cortland Deluxe Spa Suite, with a superb spa tub oh-so-close to a warming fireplace. Then again, each guest room has some distinctive feature: a window seat, a dual-sided fireplace, a sublime view, or an intriguing color scheme. The property's Massage Service Suite is on hand, so to speak, to provide everything from a Swedish massage to foot reflexology. The lodge's great room, with its massive stone fireplace, is a splendid setting for predinner wine and cheese hors d'oeuvres or a postdinner snuggle with your sweetie. (It's also a picturesque spot to marry or renew wedding vows, as many couples choose to do.) Hearty breakfasts are served every morning, and include the inn's signature scones, fruity jams, positively addictive granola, and a cooked-to-order hot entrée. (A smoked salmon omelet with caviar, diced potatoes, and sausage is definitely worth getting up for.) On selected nights, a four-course meal is also served (see Romantic Restaurants). Orchard Hill's 4 acres offer territory for twosomes to explore—a continental picnic lunch is packed in a keepsake tote, upon request.
$$$ *MC, V; checks OK; www.orchardhill.com.* ✤

## SHADOW MOUNTAIN RANCH
❀❀
*2771 Frisius Road, Julian / 760/765-0323*
Shadow Mountain Ranch bears a striking resemblance to Hansel and Gretel's storybook cottage, but the inn's Gnome Home is truly the next best thing to gingerbread. A favorite with guests who prefer the fanciful to the practical, the Gnome Home looks like a tree stump topped with a mushroom cap. Inside the hut, which was inspired by the works of artist and sculptor Tom Clark, is a round living room with hand-carved furnishings and a round wooden ceiling. Pass through the round archway to the bedroom, which is—shocker—also round. A stone shower, which is roomy enough for two and turns into a cascading waterfall when turned on, and a stone sink, in the shape of a face, completes the theme. The ranch also offers five more magical rooms, among them the cozy Grandma's Attic that's reached by crossing a wooden bridge, and the Victorian Rose, which is outfitted with an antique vanity and a slipper tub. For the young and adventurous, the Tree House room is positioned up in a centuries-old oak tree. From this room, the view of the 15-acre ranch is majestic, but couples will have to rough it a bit with the acorn-sized bathroom (a shower built for two is available in the main house). Shadow Mountain Ranch is the oldest B&B in Julian, lovingly created and cared for by Loretta and Jim Ketcherside. The main lodge, where afternoon tea is served every day, has an upscale Old Western sitting area, complete with a Remington sculpture, a generous fireplace, and an adjacent game room with a pool table. The Western theme extends to the grounds, where three buggies, one chuck wagon, and a backboard lend authentic atmosphere. A full breakfast is served family style in the very retro Apple Pantry. (Check out the old-fashioned phone on the wall.) Here, couples mingle by the toasty fireplace while awaiting one of Loretta's famous specialties—sometimes marinated steak and eggs or zucchini pancake and cheese. After breakfast, it's time to feed the leftovers (if there are any!) to the on-site horses and cows, which are as mellow and contented as the guests who stay at Shadow Ranch.
$$ *No credit cards; checks OK; www.shadowmountainranch.net.*

## VILLA DE VALOR
❀❀
*2020 3rd St, Julian / 760/765-3865 or 877/96-VILLA*
Intimate and romantic, Villa de Valor bed-and-breakfast is like a valentine wrapped in lace, from the red front porch and surrounding white fence, to the angels, candles, and billowing curtains that adorn shelves, tables, and windows. An artist, nondenominational minister, inn owner, and true romantic at heart, Valorie Ashley has created a retreat as captivating as her pencil drawings and sketches that grace the parlor wall. Known as Hildreth House at the turn of the century, the graceful Victorian dwelling

was owned by the town's beloved doctor, H. L. Hildreth. Since taking ownership, Ashley has passionately transformed the rooms into individual love nests with private entrances, fireplaces, and bathrooms. For the final touch, a video or two of Hollywood's great love-themed movies can be found in every room. The accommodations—Suite Harmony, Suite Peace, and Suite Serenity—have such unique furnishings as period antiques, elevated beds with crib-like frames, and even pull-down stairs that lead lovers to a loft where they can gaze dreamily at the stars (sigh). In the morning, Ashley serves guests a four- to five-course candlelit breakfast at individual tables in the art gallery–like parlor. After dining, guests can enjoy a quiet moment in the garden or watch Ashley hand feed a wild scrub jay that flies by for breakfast. The property also boasts an outdoor wet/dry aromatherapy sauna for two and a gazebo, where Ashley can officiate at a ceremony that includes those famous words, "I do."
*$$$ AE, MC, V; checks OK; www.villadevalor.com.*

# Romantic Restaurants

## THE JULIAN GRILLE
● ● ●

*2224 Main St, Julian / 760/765-0173*
Ask anyone who lives in Julian what the best restaurant is and they'll invariably recommend the Julian Grille. Just a short stroll from any point on Main Street, the Grille offers couples a choice of dining in the country cozy cottage restaurant or out on the patio under the arbor or umbrellas. It's a tough decision. The outdoor area overlooks the town's main thoroughfare, and has a lovely fountain that serenades couples as they look deeply into each other's eyes. Inside, however, the lights are low and passions are high for hungry lovebirds who peruse menus at fireside tables or on the glassed-in veranda. Start your meal with an appetizer sure to please: baked spice Brie, roasted garlic shrimp, or stuffed mushrooms Rockefeller. Succulent salads, served with garlic-cheese bread, include a crab Louis, chicken on greens, and grilled salmon over spinach. Save room for such entrées as roast prime rib of beef au jus or boneless chicken breast breaded with pecans, sautéed and topped with peaches for a winsome twist on a traditional dish. For dessert, indulge in chocolate wipeout cake or Bailey's cheesecake while you sip Julian Gold Muscat Canelli dessert wine. A glorious morning with your beloved and a bit of bubbly is the ultimate way to welcome the start of a brand new Sunday, so be sure to try the Sunday brunch. The Grille scramble is certain to tempt, with its sausage, ham, bacon, and veggies, or stay with traditional favorites like French toast and pancakes.
*$$ AE, DIS, MC, V; checks OK; lunch every day, dinner Tues–Sat, brunch Sun; full bar; reservations recommended.* &

# THE JULIAN ROOM AT ORCHARD HILL COUNTRY INN
❂❂❂
*2502 Washington St (Orchard Hill Country Inn), Julian / 760/765-1700 or 800/71-ORCHARD*
Visitors to Julian who haven't stayed at the Orchard Hill Country Inn (see Romantic Lodgings) may be missing out on one of the best dining spots in town. On four evenings of the week, the inn serves its guests a four-course gourmet dinner featuring seasonal specialties. A hand-painted floor-to-ceiling mural of the local landmarks decorates the main dining room, and an adjacent veranda gives diners a bird's-eye view—via oversized windows—of the historic district below. For those seated in the early part of the evening, a striking sunset is a first course like no other; later arrivals will sup among the stars. A roasted vegetable soup is a sumptuous starter, followed by a salad of mixed greens, roasted walnuts, Gorgonzola, and a creamy mustard vinaigrette. Entrées might include pork tenderloin with a port wine and Gorgonzola reduction, veal cutlet stuffed with sun-dried tomatoes and feta, blackened Creole shrimp, and grilled portobello mushrooms stuffed with spinach and squash. Impossible to think of dessert? Not when it's the specialty of the house—bread pudding with lemon sauce and chantilly cream or coffee ice cream with a yummy coffee sauce. Cap off the meal with a glass of port, and you have all the makings of an enchanted evening.
*$$$ MC, V; checks OK; dinner Sun, Tues, Thurs, Sat; beer and wine; reservations required; www.orchardhill.com.* &

# JULIAN TEA & COTTAGE ARTS
❂❂
*2124 3rd St, Julian / 760/756-0832 or 866/765-0832*
Is it possible to fall in love with a teashop? Yes, if it's as adorable and charming as Edie and Jim Segers's Julian Tea & Cottage Arts. Every detail of the emporium says "romance," from the floral tablecloths and shelves full of patterned tea cozies to the bouquet-like rugs and delicate china settings gracing each table. This is the ultimate retreat from a hectic world, a place that harkens back to a gentler time, when there were enough moments in the day to sit down and languor over a cup of tea and nibble on tasty treats. The building was once known as King House, built in 1898 for Clarence King, son of the noted gold miner George Valentine King (founder of the Golden Chariot Mine). Refreshments are served every day, during seatings at noon, 1:30pm, and 3pm. Afternoon tea consists of finger sandwiches, scones, dessert, and tea. These are elegantly served in courses, not just plunked down on the table on a tray. Couples can also choose a cream tea, dessert tea, snack tea, or sweet tea. Lunch choices include soups, sandwiches, salads, and cheeses. The house tea is Yorkshire Gold from Taylor's of Harrogate, and you can drink as much of it as you like. Before or after sitting down, explore the shop's other enticements: a room displaying baby clothes, cards, gifts,

international foods and teas, and, of course, beautiful tea sets. Why not have one packaged to go, so you can re-create your own tea for two?

*$ AE, DIS, MC, V; checks OK; afternoon tea every day; no alcohol; reservations recommended weekdays, reservations required weekends; www.juliantea.com.* ⅃

## ROMANO'S DODGE HOUSE
●●

*2718 B St, Julian / 760/765-2265*
Red-and-white-checkered tablecloths topped with glowing hurricane lamps and watercolors on the walls by local artist Sally Snipes set the romantic ambience at Romano's Dodge House. The food is Italian, the music is classic, and the mood is mellow in the two rooms that serve a clientele made up of loyal locals and tourists-in-the-know. Owner Carole Sansregret will tell you about the restaurant's history: It was a house originally owned by Mr. Dodge, a miner from Texas. The Romano's bought the home in the late 1970s and converted into a restaurant in 1982. Request a table for two by the blazing fireplace and enjoy service by the warmest wait staff this side of the Mississippi. Before perusing the extensive menu, request a refreshing *appletini*. Now you're ready to decide between the house's signature dish, pork Juliana (chops simmered in a whisky apple cider–cinnamon–garlic cream sauce), or chicken cacciatore à la Sicilian. Can't decide? Then go with the Chef's Choice, with *brasciole* (stuffed rolled beef), chicken cacciatore, and sausage. Just be sure to save room for the garlicky mashed potatoes and home-baked rolls. For dessert, take turns feeding each other the sinfully delicious Sicilian torte (layers of ricotta cheese, nuts, and chocolate) or the tiramisu. Ah, that's amour!

*$–$$ No credit cards; checks OK; lunch, dinner Wed–Mon; full bar; reservations recommended; www.romanosjulian.com.* ⅃

# ANZA-BORREGO DESERT STATE PARK

## ROMANTIC HIGHLIGHTS

Located on 600,000 sweeping acres, the Anza-Borrego Desert State Park is the largest desert state park in the contiguous United States. *Anza* is derived from the name of Spanish explorer Juan Bautista de Anza, who first came across this region in 1774 while seeking an overland route from Sonora, Mexico, to Monterey, California, while *borrego* is the Spanish word for bighorn sheep, which can still be seen today in this isolated desert habitat that lies mainly in San Diego County. In addition, it's not uncommon for visitors to spy roadrunners dashing across the street as golden eagles soar overhead. There are also kit foxes, mule deer, desert iguanas, and four species of rattlesnakes that slither about this desert floor.

With a varying terrain that ranges in elevation from 15 feet to more than 6,000 feet above sea level, Anza-Borrego is a diverse landscape, with more than 600 kinds of desert plants, and fossils and rocks dating back some 540 million years. The stark backdrop can be both haunting and awe-inspiring, creating an extraordinary setting to celebrate love.

While the area boasts 360 days of sunshine throughout the year, this Colorado Desert region is known for its blooming display of native wildflowers and cacti from late February through early April. Call the **wildflower hotline** (760/767-4684) for an update on the status of the blooms. It's a gorgeous time to visit the park area, since temperatures are mild compared to the 110°F-plus summer days.

Throughout the year, however, outdoor enthusiasts come to enjoy the park's 110 miles of riding and hiking trails. Walking past palm groves fed by year-round springs, sandstone canyons, granite mountains, washes, and scenic vistas may sound enticing, but the desert can be a dangerous place. You'll want to plan ahead by stopping for a map at the **Anza-Borrego Desert State Park Visitors Center** (200 Palm Canyon Dr; 760/767-4205; www.anzaborrego.statepark.org) or consider taking a guided free hike with one of the park's volunteer naturalists.

Before heading out for a day in the desert, stop in at the **Badlands Market & Café** (561 Palm Canyon Dr; 760/767-4058) to pick up picnic goodies. This gourmet spot features daily specials, as well as plenty of exotic teas, tempting desserts, and snacks for the sophisticated palate. And, don't forget to pack plenty of water. Staying hydrated is important in this dry, hot desert region.

A good starter hike, known as the **Borrego Palm Canyon self-guided hike**, starts at the campgrounds near the visitors center. Just a mile and a half each way, this simple trek leads to a waterfall and massive fan palms, which offer a serene stop that's ideal for a picnic lunch or just a quick photo op. Best of all, it only takes about half an hour to reach this breathtaking spot.

If exploring the area via jeep sounds a bit more enticing, call **San Diego Outback Tours** (619/980-3332 or 888/BY-JEEPS; www.desertjeeptours.com). The air-conditioned four-wheel-drive excursions cover both the desert and the mountains, always with a well-versed guide. The two of you will see ancient American Indian sites, caves, fossil beds, and the region's most spectacular view from Fonts Point, which overlooks the Badlands—named by the early settlers because it was an impossible area for moving or grazing cattle. And, along the way you'll learn plenty about the area's history and geology.

Another way to tour the desert is on horseback, and somehow riding an Arabian horse through this desert landscape seems like a truly romantic gesture. **Smoketree Arabian Horse Rentals** (1560 Rango Wy; 760/767-5850) takes couples on guided tours of the area, so the two of you can play cowboy for the day in this rural setting. Once you climb in the saddle you'll see the desert from a whole different vantage point.

Adventure-seeking lovers will want to head to the **Ocotillo Wells** area of the park, which is the hub of off-road vehicle activity. While riding dirt bikes and dune buggies may not seem all that alluring to some, the adrenaline rush it provides is sheer bliss to others.

Set in the midst of the park is **Borrego Springs**, a tiny, eclectic desert town that boasts art galleries, Western shops, and an overall small-town feel. While it doesn't take long to stroll through town along the main drag of Palm Canyon Drive, there are plenty of stops for browsing. **Caldwell's** (540 The Mall; 760/767-3300) features local art, jewelry, and gemstones, and couples can suit up for the desert with Western wear and T-shirts from **Desert Robin** (590 Palm Canyon Dr; 760/767-5560) or browse for antiques, Western wear, and clothing at **Tumbleweed Trading Co.** (526 The Mall; 760/767-4244).

Romantics with a sweet tooth will want to pick up a treat at **Olde Homestead Fudge Company** (590 Palm Canyon Dr; 760/767-5404), where handcrafted fudge is made on the premises. If you buy a pound in the store, they'll give you a free half pound. Can you say, "Midnight snack?" Be warned, however: this decadent goodie has been known to melt pretty quickly in the desert heat.

The last weekend of October, Borrego Springs kicks off its tourist season with **Borrego Days.** It's a fun time to visit this funky desert town, when the festival has the streets abuzz with a classic car show, a parade, an arts show, and lots of live music. Locals mix comfortably with visitors, and you can get a true feel for this funky desert retreat. In fact, many of the area's visitors are regulars who come to enjoy the relaxed atmosphere of this charming resort town. Who knows, it could end up becoming a special place for the two of you as well.

## Access and Information

Located on the eastern side of San Diego County, the Anza-Borrego Desert State Park is approximately a two-and-a-half hour's drive from Los Angeles and about two hours via car from San Diego, Palm Springs, and Riverside. From San Diego County, take Interstate 8 east to the Highway 67 exit and head north toward Ramona. Go through Ramona to Santa Ysabel and turn left to Highway 79. (Visitors coming from Los Angeles County take Interstate 15 through Temecula to Highway 79.) From Highway 79, turn right onto Highway S-2 and travel to Highway S-22. Follow Highway S-22 through the town of Ranchita for approximately 12 miles, then turn right at the stop sign, which will take you to downtown Borrego Springs.

Displays detailing the desert landscape and guidebooks on the region can be found at the **Desert Natural History Association** (652 Palm Canyon Dr; 760/767-3098; www.abdnha.org), while more information about dining, lodging, and golf is available from the **Borrego Springs Chamber of Commerce** (786 Palm Canyon Dr; 760/767-5555 or 800/559-5524; www.borregosprings.org).

# *Romantic Lodgings*

## BORREGO SPRINGS RESORT & COUNTRY CLUB
◐

*1112 Tilting T Dr, Borrego Springs / 760/767-5700 or 888/826-7734*
If a round of golf, a game or two of tennis, or just lounging around a palm tree–lined pool sound like the makings for a romantic getaway, check out this reasonably priced, AAA three-diamond 100-room resort nestled between the Santa Rosa Mountains. While guest rooms are a tad generic, they feature oak cabinetry, refrigerators, microwaves (suites have full kitchenettes), and pink grapefruit–scented bath products that pay homage to the locally grown fruit. Each room has it own terrace, but couples may want to request a second-story room for the best mountain views. The resort's beautifully landscaped 27-hole championship golf course is, perhaps, its main draw for lovebirds who want to spend the day on the links. The only full-service golf facility in Borrego, this course gets busy on weekends, so you'll need to book your tee time when reserving a room. Six lighted tennis courts provide another option for outdoor activity, and the two of you can cool off later in one of two swimming pools. For a casual meal, couples can dine at the resort's Borrego Springs Country Club, which offers casual fare like salads, sandwiches, grilled chicken, and steaks for lunch and dinner Monday through Saturday, as well as a Sunday brunch. However, during the summer months when the temperatures heat up, the restaurant is closed.
$$ AE, DIS, MC, V; no checks; www.borregospringsresort.com. &

## BORREGO VALLEY INN
◐◐◖

*405 Palm Canyon Dr, Borrego Springs / 760/767-0311 or 800/333-5810*
Set on 10 acres, this 14-room bed-and-breakfast offers a slice of Santa Fe in the California desert. New York transplants Grant and Allisen Rogers have created a charming adobe-style inn, complete with hanging dried red pepper strands and Hopi ladders. Standard, deluxe, and premium guest rooms vary in size, but all are decidedly Southwestern with Satillo tile floors, fireplaces, private patios, and walk-in showers. Couples in search of privacy and a little extra space may want to check into the El Presidential suite, which features a separate living room and bedroom, a full kitchen, and a huge patio with a barbecue and an outdoor kiva fireplace, which

creates a perfect setting for snuggling up by the fire under the stars. Mornings start with a spread of homemade breads and muffins, fresh fruit, and freshly ground coffee from Ecuador Estates in the guest lounge. In the afternoons, the lounge serves as a cozy retreat where guests can mingle while sampling wine and snacks by the roaring fireplaces. The innkeepers leave the lights on in the two pools until midnight, so you can swim under the stars. For couples feeling a bit frisky, one of the pools is clothing optional. $$–$$$ DIS, MC, V; no checks; www.borregovalley.inn.com. ⅙

## LA CASA DEL ZORRO
❁❁❁
*3845 Yaqui Pass Rd, Borrego Springs / 760/767-5323 or 800/824-1884*
There's no need to suffer and sweat in the desert. Instead, book a room or casita at this lush oasis, buried in date palms set against a mountain backdrop. The tile-roofed casitas with one to four bedrooms are spread about in clusters throughout the 42-acre property, and all have kitchen facilities and living and dining rooms. Two-story white buildings with tiled roofs house the large guest rooms, most with fireplaces to keep the two of you warm on a chilly desert night. However, couples who want to pull out all the stops should splurge for one of the casitas with a private pool or spa. Five pools—one reserved for adult-use only—are scattered about the gardens, and a river flows over boulders between the buildings. After lounging by the pool, hit one of six lighted tennis courts or laze away the afternoon with a game of bocci ball or chess on a life-sized board in the garden. Couples can also make appointments for relaxing in-room massages. The resort will arrange for jeep and hiking tours, and courtesy carts transport guests around the lushly landscaped grounds. The resort's Butterfield Room restaurant (see Romantic Restaurants) offers the most formal dining in the area. Rates here drop considerably in summer. $$$–$$$$ AE, DC, DIS, MC, V; no checks; www.lacasadelzorro.com. ⅙

## THE PALMS AT INDIAN HEAD
❁❁
*2220 Hoberg Rd, Borrego Springs / 760/767-7788 or 800/519-2624*
Originally opened in 1947 then rebuilt after a fire in 1958, this art deco–style hilltop lodge was a favorite hideaway for such movie stars as Bing Crosby, Clark Gable, and Marilyn Monroe. Today, owners David and Cynthia Leibert are slowly restoring the charming 12-room property to its original grandeur. Shaded by palm trees and adjacent to the state park, the inn occupies one of the most envied, quiet sites in the valley—complete with a panoramic view across the entire Anza-Borrego region. For couples in need of a little pool time, the selling point of this romantic hideaway is a completely restored 42-by 109-foot pool, which features a subterranean grotto bar where you can watch swimmers frolic underwater in the deep end. Two poolside bungalow

suites with direct access to the pool are perhaps the most coveted rooms for romance. Each is complete with tile floors, a wet bar, and a fireplace. Lovebirds who forget their swimwear can stop in at the resort's gift shop, Tumbleweed West, which also offers Southwestern art, as well as kitschy souvenirs. A complimentary continental breakfast is offered each morning, and lunch and dinner are served every day in the Krazy Coyote Saloon & Grille (see Romantic Restaurants).
$$–$$$ *DC, DIS, MC, V; checks OK; www.palmsatindianhead.com.*

# Romantic Restaurants

## BUTTERFIELD ROOM
♥♥❬

*3845 Yaqui Pass Rd (La Casa del Zorro), Borrego Springs / 760/767-5323 or 800/824-1884*
After a casual day in the desert, couples can shower off the dust and sweat and dress for a refined dinner (gentlemen are required to wear jackets) at this formal restaurant inside the La Casa del Zorro resort (see Romantic Lodgings). Overlooking the rose garden, the elegant eatery boasts linen tablecloths, beautiful place settings, and original paintings by Marjorie Reed depicting the 19th-century Butterfield stagecoach line, which once ran through this desert region. Lovers can order a nice selection of wine from the resort's 6,000-plus bottle cellar and savor such dishes as cedar-plank king salmon, poached Chilean sea bass, and succulent rack of lamb. After dinner, stop in at the resort's casual Fox's Den lounge, which features live music on weekends.
$$$ *AE, DC, DIS, MC, V; no checks; lunch Sat–Sun, dinner every day; full bar; reservations required; www.lacasadelzorro.com.* &

## KRAZY COYOTE SALOON & GRILLE
♥♥

*2220 Hoberg Rd (The Palms at Indian Head), Borrego Springs / 760/767-7788*
Located in the Palms at Indian Head (see Romantic Lodgings) overlooking the resort's massive swimming pool, this casual eatery offers perhaps the best views in the Anza-Borrego region—and the food is good, too. The lunch menu includes brunch items for late-rising lovebirds, or the two of you can order juicy burgers, gourmet pizzas, or extra cheesy quesadillas as you dine on the sunny patio. In the evenings, prime steak, grilled seafood, and a respectable wine list combine with the setting to create all the makings for a romantic meal. Indeed, it's hard not to feel amorous as the sparse lights of Borrego Springs twinkle on the desert floor below.
$–$$ *AE, MC, V; no checks; lunch, dinner every day; full bar; reservations not necessary; www.thepalmsatindianhead.com.*

# CALIFORNIA'S CENTRAL COAST

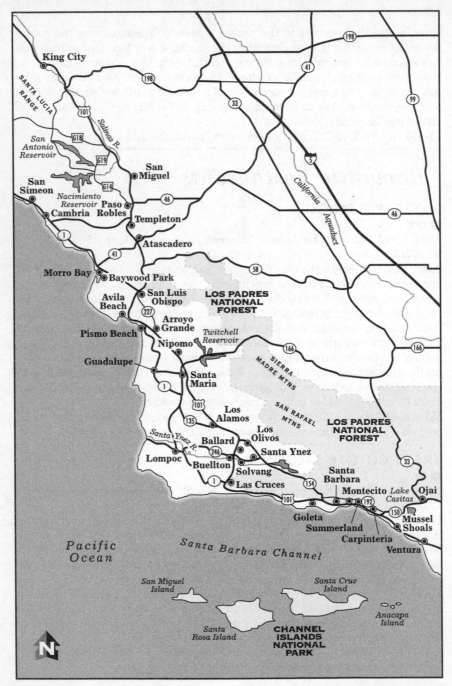

King City

SANTA LUCIA RANGE

198

41

99

Salinas R.

101

618

San Antonio Reservoir

619

614

San Miguel

San Simeon

Nacimiento Reservoir

Cambria

Paso Robles

Templeton

5

California Aqueduct

46

46

1

Atascadero

41

Morro Bay

58

Baywood Park

Avila Beach

San Luis Obispo

LOS PADRES NATIONAL FOREST

227

Arroyo Grande

Pismo Beach

Nipomo

Twitchell Reservoir

166

166

Guadalupe

Santa Maria

SIERRA MADRE MTNS

1

101

Los Alamos

SAN RAFAEL MTNS

135

Los Olivos

LOS PADRES NATIONAL FOREST

Santa Ynez R.

Ballard

246

Santa Ynez

33

Lompoc

Buellton

Solvang

Santa Barbara

1

Las Cruces

154

Montecito

192

Lake Casitas

Ojai

101

Goleta

Summerland

Carpinteria

150

Mussel Shoals

Ventura

Pacific Ocean

Santa Barbara Channel

San Miguel Island

Santa Cruz Island

Anacapa Island

Santa Rosa Island

CHANNEL ISLANDS NATIONAL PARK

N

*"Kisses are a better fate than wisdom."*
—E. E. CUMMINGS

# ♡ CALIFORNIA'S CENTRAL COAST

The dramatic landscape of California's Central Coast unfolds like an accordion of picture postcards: pristine beaches, windswept cliffs, cow-studded pastures, historic mission towns, and tree-shaded country roads. The area's diversity is part of its continued appeal. Couples can bask in sunshine at the ocean's edge, bicycle through lush vineyards, ride horses along rural back roads, and shop a boulevard of chic boutiques—all in one day.

Glorious—and romantic—vacation destinations are sprinkled throughout the beachfront towns. The coastline itself has a distinct personality: sunny white-sand beaches segue into rocky, cliff-lined shores, then give way to calm, picturesque bays. Quintessential Californian beach towns reflect the influence of the American Indian tribes who first lived here, and residents of upscale suburbs retain something of the frontier flair of pioneer ranchers.

Though "Central Coast" refers primarily to the coastline between Cambria on the north and Ventura County on the south (and the region is best known for attractions such as the opulent tourist mecca Hearst Castle and the wealthy beach city of Santa Barbara), some equally intriguing destinations are tucked into the inland mountains and valleys, where citrus orchards and vineyards beckon twosomes in search of bucolic beauty. Agriculture is the economic mainstay of both Santa Barbara and San Luis Obispo counties. Everywhere you drive, you'll see roadside stands peddling fresh-from-the-fields strawberries, apples, oranges, avocados, corn, tomatoes, cucumbers, and more. The weekly farmers' market is a tradition in San Luis Obispo and many neighboring towns, and is a perfect way for couples to enjoy the area's bounty on the cheap.

Central Coast residents are as diverse as the region itself. Well-heeled urban escapees co-exist with lifelong farmers who still work the land; bohemian artists inspired by their surroundings are juxtaposed with college students who bring an up-to-date presence. Yet all share an appreciation for this laid-back collection of old-fashioned communities, close to—yet a world apart from—the state's bustling metropolises eager romance-seekers race to escape every weekend of the year.

# VENTURA

## ROMANTIC HIGHLIGHTS

Nestled between gently rolling foothills and the sparkling blue Pacific, Ventura is romantically endowed with the picturesque setting and clean sea breezes typical of the California coast. Since most of the city's development has taken place inland and to the south, there's a charming small town character to the historic district, known nostalgically by its Spanish mission name, San Buenaventura. The town grew up around **Mission San Buenaventura** (225 E Main St; 805/643-4318; www.sanbuenaventuramission.org), which was founded in 1782 as one of the California mission chain. Still in use for daily services, the current buildings date from 1815 and have been restored to depict the everyday mission life of the 19th century. Touring the interior garden, couples will see the antique water pump and olive press once essential to survival and get a look at the whitewash-and-red-tile architecture whose influence can be seen throughout town. Across the street is the **Ventura County Museum of History and Art** (100 E Main St; 805/653-0323; www.vcmha.org), which couples will find worth a visit for its rich Native American Room, filled with Chumash treasures, and its enormous archive of historical photos depicting Ventura County from its origin to the present time. History lovers should stop by the majestic **San Buenaventura City Hall** (501 Poli St; 805/658-4726), which presides over town from a hillside at the end of California Street. Built in 1912 to serve as the county courthouse, this neoclassical landmark is filled with architectural detail, inside and out. The two of you can look for the carved heads of Franciscan friars whimsically adorning the facade and maybe steal a kiss while admiring the detailed carvings. In the summertime, the city hall can be fully explored by escorted tour.

Antique hounds have been flocking to Ventura for many years, and even casually browsing couples can spend the better part of a day shopping for collectible treasures along Main Street. Start with one of the mall-style places, where dozens of different sellers present a mind-boggling selection that ranges from Hawaiian aloha shirts to antique armoires, from fine china to art deco lithographs, or even *Star Wars* lunch boxes and Nancy Drew first editions. Our favorites are **Heirlooms Antiques** (327 E Main St; 805/648-4833); **Times Remembered** (467 E Main St; 805/643-3137); **Nicholby Antiques** (404 E Main St; 805/653-1195); and **Portobello Antiques**

(494 E Main St; 805/641-1890), an antique furniture warehouse. If the weather's nice—and it usually is—lovers can stroll along the **Ventura Promenade**, a paved ocean-side pathway wide enough to accommodate bicyclists and inline skaters. On the weekends, **canopied surreys** are available for rent in front of the Holiday Inn (450 E Harbor Blvd, at California St; 805/648-7731) at the boardwalk; you'll see romantically inclined couples leisurely pedaling up and down the beach, an old-fashioned vignette straight out of Ventura's Victorian past.

Part of Ventura's quiet metamorphosis from a sleepy farm town to a chic coastal charmer has been the embracing of a wine country aesthetic, a natural in this region so dominated by agriculture in general and wine in particular. The favorite new pastime, and one suited to lovebirds in a convivial mood, is strolling between the wine bars setting up shop in the vintage storefronts on Main Street. After catching the last rays of sunset over the ocean, head to **Alegria Wine Bar** (321 E Main St; 805/643-3323), where local and imported vintages are poured among Ventura's favorite home accessory showroom. Or you can sample the trailblazer **Wine Lovers** (1067 E Thompson Blvd; 805/652-1810), Ventura's first wine bar, where romantic lighting, plush loveseats, and elegant ambience create a cozy place to cuddle while you enjoy complimentary wood-fired pizzas that turn a wine tasting into a small meal.

Wherever you drive in Ventura County—even on busy Highway 101—orange groves and strawberry fields dominate the landscape, offering a seductive inducement to stop and explore the farmers' fresh produce stands scattered throughout the countryside. A short drive south of old San Buenaventura lays picturesque **Ventura Harbor**, headquarters of Channel Islands National Park. The Channel Islands are unspoiled and uninhabited gems where nature lovers and outdoor adventurers can taste what coastal California was like 400 years ago, before the influence of European settlers. There are a variety of day excursions, kayak and dive outfitters, and camping programs that let you choose how to explore the five distinct islands. The best place to start is at the **Channel Islands National Park Visitors Center** (1901 Spinnaker Dr; 805/658-5700; www.nps.gov/chis), where maps and displays will help you get acquainted with the various programs and individual personalities of the islands. Nearby is **Ventura Harbor Village** (on Spinnaker Dr off Harbor Blvd; 805/642-8538; www.ventura harborvillage.com), a vaguely Mediterranean-style shopping/entertainment complex spread along the length of the marina. In addition to waterfront restaurants, gift shops, and paddleboat rentals, there's a small carousel to amuse the kid inside us all, and a fresh fish market if you're planning to cocoon for a little dinner à deux. Sport fishing and dive charters operate nearby, and a narrated harbor cruise departs from the village aboard the **Bay Queen** (805/642-7753). If you're here during the annual gray whale migration season—from late December through March—consider taking a

CALIFORNIA'S CENTRAL COAST

whale-watching cruise to observe the graceful leviathans up close. **Island Packers** (1867 Spinnaker Dr; 805/642-1393; www.islandpackers.com) offers half- and full-day excursions.

Inland from the harbor lies the historic **Olivas Adobe** (4200 Olivas Park Dr; 805/644-4346). Built in 1847 as the showplace of prosperous Rancho Miguel, the restored two-story house is filled with antiques and surrounded by tranquil, century-old gardens; one grape arbor dates to the 1840s, and a tiled Spanish-style fountain forms the gateway to a stunning rose garden. Though the adobe is open only on weekends, the grounds are a designated historical park and worth a visit for a glimpse into California's romantic Spanish past.

## Access and Information

Coastal Ventura is located along Highway 101, the main highway that leads from Los Angeles all the way up the Central Coast. To reach old downtown and the mission, take the California Street exit from Highway 101 northbound, or the Main Street exit from southbound Highway 101. The harbor is just down the coast; the most convenient freeway exit is Victoria Avenue.

Most visitors simply drive to Ventura, but a more old-fashioned—and romantic—choice is to ride the **Amtrak** (800/USA-RAIL; www.amtrak .com) *Pacific Surfliner*. It runs between San Luis Obispo and San Diego, stopping in Santa Barbara and Los Angeles, as well as many smaller stations en route. Portions of the track travel directly on the coast, meaning you can gaze at the sunny surf while sipping a California vintage in true style; in Ventura, you'll arrive at the town's tiny train platform nestled between the ocean and downtown.

To learn more, make the **Ventura Visitors and Convention Bureau** (89-C S California St; 805/648-2075 or 800/333-2989; www.ventura-usa.com) your first stop, since their office is in the heart of old downtown.

## Romantic Lodgings

### BRAKEY HOUSE BED & BREAKFAST
◐◐

*411 Poli St, Ventura / 805/643-3600*
Visit Brakey House and you'll soon discover why this quirky little inn draws romantics seeking a European-style lodging experience. Most obvious are the colorful foreign flags flying outside this 1890 Cape Cod–style house, whose perch near Ventura's imposing neoclassical City Hall is within convenient walking distance of San Buenaventura's historic district and the beach. The distinctive mark of German proprietors is evident everywhere,

despite a recent change in ownership and name (though the previous name, La Mer, is still found around the property and on the website). Charming Old World furnishings grace the five guest rooms, each named for the off-shore Channel Islands and decorated (with very fine antiques) to evoke a different theme. Whether the two of you choose the Victorian-style Santa Barbara chamber with its wood-burning stove and Jacuzzi tub for two, the Americana-themed Anacapa hideaway with its sunken antique bathtub and Mission-style furniture, the San Miguel room with its nautical theme and cabinlike wood paneling, or the rosy-hued Santa Rosa room, you'll enjoy a private entrance, a private bath, and complimentary wine in your room. The best kisses are rumored to take place in the Santa Catalina penthouse suite, which boasts a native-inspired decor and ocean views from the sitting room, private deck, and even the two-person whirlpool. There's a spectacular coastal view from three of the five guest rooms, as well as the cozy parlor where breakfast is served. Brakey House's Bavarian-style breakfast features muesli and Black Forest ham, in addition to cakes, breads, cheeses, fresh fruits, and plenty of strong coffee. The staff can arrange concierge services such as gourmet candlelight dinners, cruises to Anacapa Island, country carriage rides, therapeutic massage/mineral baths . . . or all of the above. *$$–$$$ MC, V; no checks; www.lamerbnb.com.*

---

## THE CLIFF HOUSE INN
💋💋

*6602 W Pacific Coast Hwy, Mussel Shoals / 805/652-1381 or 800/892-5433*
This small hotel perched cliff-side is often booked solid by intrepid lovers seeking a dramatic vantage point for watching winter storms while cozy and protected in ocean-view rooms—though it has plenty of appeal during the calm warmer months, as well. Located between Ventura and Santa Barbara where Highway 101 snakes right alongside the rocky beach, the Cliff House punctuates an isolated strip of beach houses overlooking an artificial reef. The inn makes the most of its dramatic surroundings: every room has a spectacular Pacific view, as does the impressive swimming pool, which is surrounded by deck lounges and graced by an enormous Chilean wine palm whose fronds rustle seductively. Guest rooms are just large enough to hold a few basic pieces of white wicker furniture with cheerful floral upholstery, and bathrooms are equally utilitarian. The location, though untouristy, is a good one: decent beaches and surfing are close by, as are Santa Barbara's restaurants and attractions, and even Ojai is only a short jaunt inland. These quiet accommodations are tailor made for contemplation and romance, not to mention sunset watching, table tennis, and ringside seats for passing porpoise and whales. In the evening, the two of you can lounge on the poolside chaises that make a perfect vantage point for stargazing, and the night sky is brilliant—far from any city lights. The hotel's Shoals restaurant boasts the same stunning ocean view—they even serve poolside in pleasant weather.

Open for lunch and dinner every day, the dining room is simple and sparsely adorned, but the restaurant does a good job of creating a mood with subdued lighting and polished service. Not surprisingly, seafood figures prominently on a seasonally composed menu that highlights fresh local ingredients and familiar California cuisine. A diverse Sunday brunch menu features traditional breakfast selections, salads, sandwiches, and fresh seafood entrées. $$ DC, DIS, MC, V; local checks only; www.cliffhouseinn.com. &

## PIERPONT INN
♠€

*550 Sanjon Rd, Ventura / 805/643-6144 or 800/285-4667*
One of those places you see from the freeway but never learn about, the Pierpont is a landmark property well worth further investigation, and one consistently voted "most romantic" in local reader polls. Inside the main building—a 1908 California Craftsman—the Arts and Crafts style reigns, and photos from the inn's rich and colorful past adorn the warm wood-paneled walls. When it was built, the hotel enjoyed unobstructed views of and access to the beach, but Highway 101 rudely intruded in 1962. Today, clever landscaping manages to obscure the highway without hiding the Pacific, and double-paned windows help preserve the romantic ambience—indoors, at least. Though the property is no longer the pinnacle of luxury, it doesn't take long to appreciate the sense of history, style, and dedication to hospitality here. The newly renovated guest rooms are spacious but otherwise unremarkable, and the hotel's suites offer more room to spread out. Many have terrific (freeway notwithstanding) ocean views, and the best also have fireplaces for evening snuggling. But for the most romantic punch, we suggest booking one of two utterly darling, English Tudor–style cottages; surrounded by climbing roses, they lay a short stroll from the main hotel and are happily insulated from the freeway. A classic kidney-shaped swimming pool welcomes couples who don't feel like venturing to the beach, and massage and spa services are available on the premises. Room rates include a continental breakfast in the Pierpont's dining room, the ocean-view Austen's restaurant. Open to the public for lunch and dinner, this relaxing spot is best appreciated by sitting at a window table so you and your sweetie can gaze over the large, sunny lawn dotted with Adirondack chairs to the sea beyond. Recommended dishes are soup (gazpacho, clam chowder, and French onion are always on the menu), fresh and crisp main-course salads, seafood shepherd's pie, and traditional bouillabaisse. $$ AE, DC, DIS, MC, V; checks OK; www.pierpontinn.com. &

## THE VICTORIAN ROSE
☙

*896 E Main St, Ventura / 805/641-1888*
Owners Richard and Nona Bogatch are just the people to make your romantic
fantasy come true; the couple have taken a 19th-century church—complete
with soaring steeple—and created a truly unique five-room bed-and-breakfast that nearly defies conventional description. Indulging their passions
for religious paraphernalia, antique clocks, and Victorian knickknacks, the
Bogatches have filled literally every corner of their theatrical creation with
so many items, it's often precarious just navigating from the formal breakfast table—elevated on the former altar—through the large chapel (now
filled with velvet settees and antique armchairs) to the guest rooms. Often
requested by honeymooners and anniversary celebrants looking for something truly special, the rooms are also dramatically decorated, thankfully
less busy than the public areas, but each adheres to a chosen theme. Each
room is meticulously outfitted in period style with impressive antiques.
Paneling and other architectural features from the church's remodel were
also salvaged and re-used in crafting private bathrooms for each room. Welcoming comforts like turndown service with chocolates, plus fireplaces and
balconies in select rooms, add to the romantic ambience. If the two of you
love poking through vintage collections, appreciate ecclesiastical artifacts,
and don't mind a little clutter, the Victorian Rose is for you. It's situated
just a few blocks from the heart of old downtown, in a stretch filled with
art galleries.
$$–$$$ *AE, DIS, MC, V; checks OK; www.victorian-rose.com.*

---

# *Romantic Restaurants*

## CAFE FIORE
☙☙❀

*66 California St, Ventura / 805/653-1266*
Stroll with your beloved to this Italian gathering spot in the heart of
downtown and enjoy coastal breezes along the way to what promises to
be a night of romance. The front of the restaurant is dominated by a warm
Italian hearth and a grand three-sided bar. Either is a nice spot to relax with
a cocktail or a glass of wine from Fiore's varied list. Combining fine food
and a casual cozy-up-to-the-fireplace kind of atmosphere that encourages
couples to sit and stay a while, the restaurant sports stained concrete floors
and banquette booths. It all serves to reinforce a speakeasy atmosphere,
accented with exposed brick and ceiling crossbeams from the building's
industrial past. In the afternoons or on warm evenings ask for a table on the
romantic patio; if you desire a more snuggly atmosphere, request a booth,
where you and your sweetie can also enjoy live jazz each evening. Fiore's

chef boasts impressive stints at three-star restaurants in Italy and some of the coolest kitchens in L.A., so you really can't go wrong ordering off this appealing menu that specializes in the traditional regional dishes of Italy, as well as some nouveau Italian cuisine. There's everything from the caponata of Sicily to osso buco that's just like Mom's. The spaghetti is enlivened with traditional veal-ricotta meatballs; creamy risotto is tossed with its classic *fruitti di mare* accompaniment of clams, mussels, scallops, and calamari; grilled Italian sausage takes center stage atop mashed potatoes and sautéed broccolini; and authentic wood-fired pizzas are available with a staggering 14 different topping combinations. For dessert, it can only be Sicilian cannoli, stuffed with sweet ricotta cream.
$$ *AE, MC, V; no checks; lunch, dinner every day; full bar; reservations recommended.* &

## DECO
◐◑◖

*394 E Main St, Ventura / 805/667-2120*
Couples who are fans of Santa Barbara's sublime Sage & Onion will want to reserve a night for a romantic meal at this stylish restaurant opened by successful Santa Barbara restaurateur Norbert Furnée. Deco offers a sophisticated yet accessible menu—the seamless blending of fresh regional ingredients, Mediterranean and Asian accents, and thoughtful presentation often referred to as "wine country cuisine"—that raises the bar for Ventura's chefs, as well as a wait staff often unaccustomed to wine pairings and amuse bouches. Deco's historic storefront has been reclaimed as a gallerylike space, where fine paintings and dining couples are equally well lit by flattering indirect light and flickering votives. The balance is warm and cozy, yet modern and chic. From the seasonally composed menu, the two of you may enjoy dishes like Asian-style Dungeness crab cakes sweetened by vanilla-wasabi cream; pork tenderloin glazed with Kahlua and served with aromatic green tea–jasmine rice; pinot noir–braised lamb shank atop a roasted garlic risotto cake; and desserts that highlight market-fresh fruit and premium chocolate. The handsome bar attracts its own wine-tasting clientele each evening and is a nice choice for a quick snack, should you have other plans for the night.
$$$ *MC, V; no checks; lunch Mon–Fri, dinner every day; wine only; reservations recommended; www.decorestaurant.com.*

## 71 PALM RESTAURANT
◐

*71 N Palm St, Ventura / 805/653-7222*
Inside a charmingly restored 1910 Craftsman home just a block off Main Street, this ambitious restaurant may not always be perfect, but it is always enchanting enough to make any afternoon or evening rendezvous

*très romantique.* Though the well-composed French country-style menu sometimes promises more than the kitchen can deliver, the delightful setting helps make 71 Palm a pleasant change of pace in a town of relatively few dining options. The two-story house was once a showplace home, and you can still see the ocean from the airy upstairs dining room. Downstairs, simple bistro tables are arranged around the original tile fireplace, where a fire crackles pleasantly during nearly every meal. The inviting decor features the warm woods and rich muted colors associated with the Arts and Crafts period, and the home's original moldings and built-in features have been expertly preserved. As a rule, dinner is more thoughtfully prepared than lunch, and couples won't go wrong sticking with bistro basics like steak *au poivre* with crispy *pommes frites*, Provençal lamb stew, or Santa Barbara mussels *marinière.* Authentic French appetizers shine at both lunch and dinner; coarse country pâte is served with crusty bread and tangy cornichons, the charcuterie sampler is sized for two, and the onion soup gratiné is rich and cheesy—just the way it should be. Be sure to visit the antique-filled original rest rooms upstairs.
$$ AE, DC, DIS, MC, V; no checks; lunch Mon–Fri, dinner Mon–Sat; full bar; reservations recommended; www.71palm.com. &

## TABLE 13
◐◐

*185 E Santa Clara St, Ventura / 805/648-1462*
For dressed up dining with a chic, retro flair, you and your sweetie can put on your cocktail nation duds and head over to the newly reincarnated Table 13. This warm and modern dining room is virtually unrecognizable from its previous life as Pastabilities, once a Ventura mainstay for traditional Italian fare. Proprietors Giovanni and Alessandro Tromba have done a masterful job of nudging the place into the 21st century, dressing it with a stylish decor of deep burgundy draperies, tuxedo-gray walls, and oversized paintings that lend further drama to a room already sporting a sophisticated supper club atmosphere. If you're celebrating, request the fabled table 13, long considered bad luck in the restaurant business; the Trombas decided to turn tradition on its head and not only designate a table 13 but also literally elevate its status, and now the cozy padded booth offers the best seats in the house. Champagne is already iced in anticipation of toasting twosomes, and strains of jazz provide a romantic backdrop wafting in from the bar's intimate stage. The menu offers mainly haute Italian with a few surprising Asian touches, like grilled albacore with a fruity mango-ginger-mint sauce. Classic oysters Rockefeller are redolent of Pernod liqueur, and risotto *pescatore* is studded with calamari, scallops, and shrimp. One appetizer rich enough to share is marinated eggplant rolled with proscuitto and ricotta then glazed in a tomato cream sauce. Purists will enjoy Giovanni's Specials, a page of favorites from the old Pastabilities menu like Penne 13,

enlivened by tiny veal meatballs and vegetables then topped with buffalo mozzarella.

$$$ *AE, MC, V; local checks only; dinner every day; full bar; reservations recommended.* ☙

# OJAI

## ROMANTIC HIGHLIGHTS

**O**jai sits in a secluded crescent-shaped valley, where the natural beauty has inspired Hollywood filmmakers, artists, and free spirits for decades. Lovers with a sense of the dramatic, the bucolic, and the magical will surely find romance in this pretty spot. In fact, the area once captivated movie producer–director Frank Capra who, when scouting locations for *Lost Horizon* in 1936, selected sleepy little Ojai to stand in for legendary utopia Shangri La. To see the spectacular vista admired by Ronald Colman in the movie, drive east on Ojai Avenue, continuing uphill until you reach the gravel turnout near the top; a stone bench provides the perfect spot for leisurely kisses and quiet contemplation. Another phenomenon praised by residents and visitors alike is the so-called pink moment, when the brilliant sunset over the nearby Pacific is reflected onto the Topa-Topa Mountains, creating an eerie and beautiful pink glow. If it sounds like the perfect setting for a proposal, rest assured, you're hardly the first to think of it!

Still blanketed with citrus groves stretching toward wild, rocky foothills, the Ojai Valley can trace its popularity back to the 1870s, when journalist Charles Nordhoff praised its ideal climate, natural mineral baths, and spectacular setting. The valley's name, Ojai, is a Chumash word that can mean either "nest" or "moon." Bohemian artisans, well-heeled equestrians, camera-shy celebs, New Age gurus, and sweethearts in search of romance have all embraced idyllic Ojai and left their mark on the valley.

Ojai's downtown is both charmingly rustic and pleasantly sophisticated, thanks to the influence of urban émigrés from Los Angeles and Santa Barbara. There is no shortage of couple-friendly activities here, enough to fill a romantic day trip, weekend, or even longer. Shops, galleries, and cafes are concentrated in the Arcade, whose Mission-revival arches shade pedestrians from the midday sun. Across the street is Libbey Park, centerpiece of the community and home to open-air Libbey Bowl, where musical notes enhance many summer evenings and sunset picnics for two. Classical music fans throughout the state look forward to June's **Ojai Music Festival** (805/646-2094; www.ojaifestival.org), which has been drawing worldclass performers since 1947. Past appearances by Igor Stravinsky, Aaron

Copland, the Juilliard String Quartet, and others of their caliber ensure sold-out crowds—and sold-out lodgings—each year, so make arrangements early if your rendezvous will coincide with the festival.

There's no understating the powerful influence of the visual arts on Ojai. The town is home to more than 35 well-regarded artists working in a variety of media. Most have home studios and are represented in one of Ojai's many galleries. Every October, visiting lovebirds get a chance to enter the private studios of many area painters, sculptors, potters, and wood-carvers during the two-day **Ojai Studio Artists Tour** (call the Chamber of Commerce at 805/646-8126 or log onto www.ojaistudioartists.com for ticket information). This unique event makes a wonderful weekend for trysting art aficionados, and it's also a great way to bring home an original piece without paying the gallery markup.

You can't visit Ojai without hearing about local legend Beatrice Wood, an internationally acclaimed ceramic artist responsible for putting Ojai on the art world's map. Wood, who was declared a California Living Treasure, worked up until her death in 1998 at 104 years of age. Her luminous luster-ware pottery and whimsical sculpture are occasionally displayed in local galleries but are more commonly found at museums such as New York's Whitney or San Francisco's Craft & Folk Art. You can learn more about Wood and her Ojai studio online (www.beatricewood.com). Numerous galleries represent other Ojai artists, including **HumanArts** (310 E Ojai Ave; 805/646-1525; www.humanartsgallery.com), specializing in jewelry and smaller pieces (they have a home accessories annex several doors away); **Grand Dames Gallery** (1211 Maricopa Hwy; 805/640-1252), showcasing the work of Ojai's female painters and sculptors along with a token male artist now and then; and **Primavera** (214 E Ojai Ave; 805/646-7133), featuring an eclectic collection of glass, jewelry, wood, ceramics, and paintings.

Any bibliophile who's been to Ojai knows about used-book purveyor **Bart's Books** (302 W Matilija St; 805/646-3755), a quirky local institution where books are displayed in every nook and cranny of a converted cottage, including the patio, the garden shed, and even along the sidewalk outside the entrance gate. After hours, these sidewalk racks are on the honor system; if you decide to purchase a book from the racks while returning from a romantic dinner, simply drop your money into a little payment box.

When you're ready to emerge from your love nest to stretch your legs and enjoy Ojai's legendary embracing climate, you and your sweetie can pedal off together on rented bikes from **Bicycles of Ojai** (108 Canada St; 805/646-7736) or gallop toward the sunset on a pair of horses (the Ojai Valley Inn offers guided horseback rides; 805/646-5511), both on the Ojai Valley Bike & Equestrian Trail, which winds scenically for 8.8 miles, most of it parallel to Ojai Avenue. Even more recreational activities are available at sparkling **Lake Casitas** (follow Hwy 150 northwest from Ojai until signs direct you to Lake Casitas; 805/649-2233), hidden just minutes uphill from the valley floor. Site of the 1984 Olympic rowing events, the lake boasts a shoreline full of coves and inlets. Swimming is not allowed because the lake serves as a domestic water supply, but you can rent rowboats and small motorboats from the boathouse (805/649-2043).

Long before "New Age" was a national buzzword, Ojai was home to several esoteric sects with various metaphysical and philosophical beliefs. Even if you're not normally drawn to spiritual sites, those in Ojai help calm the senses and open your heart to appreciate the romantic intentions that brought you here. One of the oldest is the **Krotona Institute of Theosophy** (46 Krotona Hill; 805/646-2653; www.theosophical.org/centers/krotona/index.html), which moved here from Hollywood in 1924. The center is notable for its natural beauty, metaphysical research library, bookshop, adult education school, and the architecture of its buildings. The noted philosopher Jiddu Krishnamurti stayed at Krotona before founding the **Krishnamurti Foundation** (1070 McAndrew Rd; 805/646-2726; www.kfa .org), named for the theosophist who first visited in 1922. Though he traveled the world speaking on his philosophy, Krishnamurti always returned to Ojai, the place he called a "vessel of comprehension, intelligence, and truth." The foundation includes a research library, historical archives, and a retreat center. For some self-guided enlightenment in a stunning natural setting, head to **Meditation Mount** (805/646-5508; www.meditation.com), several bucolic acres located at the east end of the valley on Reeves Road (about 2½ miles off Ojai Ave). This nonprofit organization encourages and facilitates meditation on the laws and principles of humanity and nonsectarian spirituality, believing that doing so will serve humanity by spreading light and energy between souls. They invite visitors to use their meditation room, which is open every day from 10am till sunset, though we sometimes prefer traipsing along their grassy knoll to discreet outdoor seating overlooking the valley.

## Access and Information

The Ojai Valley has the unique quality of being romantically secluded yet conveniently accessible by car. The drive from Los Angeles takes about 90 minutes, and it's less than an hour from Santa Barbara. From Highway 101 in Ventura, exit to Highway 33, which winds through eucalyptus groves and several tiny towns before joining Highway 150, which becomes Ojai Avenue, the town's main street. From the north, two-lane Highway 150 intersects Highway 101 near Carpinteria—just south of Santa Barbara—and provides a curvaceous and stunning jaunt through ranchlands and then along a ridge above sparkling Lake Casitas before descending into downtown Ojai.

Once in town, it's easy to find your way around; Libbey Park is the town's center, located on Ojai Avenue at Signal Street (until recently the town's only stoplight). The **Ojai Valley Chamber of Commerce and Visitors Center** (150 W Ojai Ave; 805/646-8126; www.the-ojai.org) is two blocks away, on the corner of Blanche Street. Make this your first stop for a colorful **Visitors Guide**, featuring a map of valley streets and businesses and plenty of other helpful information and advice.

# *Romantic Lodgings*

## EMERALD IGUANA INN
♦♦♦

*End of Blanche St, Ojai / 805/646-5277*
This intimate hideaway is so exclusive, and offers such a complete sense of solitude, that couples must register at the Emerald Iguana's more conventional sister property, the Blue Iguana Inn on Ventura Avenue just at the entrance of town. Once given the key to whimsically named cottages like Grasshopper, Raven, and Lilypad, you and your sweetie can proceed to this serene enclave just a few blocks from downtown Ojai, confident you won't be disturbed for the balance of your stay. A mosaic-tiled iguana fountain welcomes you to the property, where 12 enchanting and luxurious cottages hide within a magical garden setting. Flowering vines trail across each trellis and climb every fence, while stately eucalypti shade the property and shelter visiting birds and butterflies. This lovers' haven is really something out of a storybook, achieving an old and well-nestled ambience through the work of local stone masons, wood carvers, and copper artisans to create one-of-a-kind lodgings furnished with colorful furniture, rugs, and accessories from around the world. Think Cost Plus Imports goes upscale—way upscale—but at prices Cost Plus devotees can still enjoy. All guest quarters are equipped with full kitchens, comfy bathrobes, and high-quality amenities, and many offer extras like private patios or balconies, wood stoves, and whirlpool tubs. For guaranteed romance, we can recommend one of the three bilevel one-bedroom cottages: Peacock has a charming claw-footed tub and cozy wood-burning stove; Cricket boasts two private upstairs balconies and a whirlpool tub for two; and Frog has a deluxe living room with wood stove and a whirlpool tub in the bathroom. There's a small lily pad of a swimming pool on the grounds, and tiny lanterns light the pathways after dark. Breakfast/dinner packages and in-room massage are available to customize your stay.
*$$$ AE, DIS, MC, V; checks OK; www.emeraldiguana.com.*

## THE MOON'S NEST INN
🖤🖤
*210 E Matilija St, Ojai / 805/646-6635*
Ojai's oldest building—a former schoolhouse (circa 1872)—has been reborn as a romantic bed-and-breakfast that's charmingly historic while offering every modern comfort. This old-fashioned clapboard building, located within easy walking distance of downtown shopping, dining, and attractions, was fully renovated in 1998 by innkeepers Rich and Joan Assenberg, who carefully preserved, replaced, or complemented the inn's historic details. Five of the seven guest rooms now boast private bathrooms, and several also enjoy private balconies. In addition to being greeted by an afternoon wine reception, couples will appreciate such extras as bottled water and chocolates in each room. Throughout the house, from the cozy fireplace parlor to the sunny breakfast room, dramatically painted walls highlight architectural features like crown molding, and the entire inn is furnished with a mix of carefully chosen antiques and quality contemporary pieces. A once-neglected side lawn has been transformed into a restful tree-shaded garden, complete with a rock-lined pond and a large trellised veranda where breakfast is served on pleasant days. The most romantic room is the Classic Revival, a slightly naughty boudoir painted in bold red and furnished in a *Moulin Rouge* style with an antique French iron bed and secluded balcony overlooking the garden. A cottage on the grounds houses an intimate beauty-and-massage salon (in-room massages are also available), and, for a nominal fee, guests enjoy full day-use privileges at the Ojai Valley Athletic Club.
*$$ AE, MC, V; checks OK; www.moonsnestinn.com.* &

## OJAI VALLEY INN & SPA
🖤🖤🖤
*905 Country Club Rd, Ojai / 805/646-5511 or 800/422-OJAI*
Travelers with a sense of romance have been sojourning at this genteel resort since 1923, when Hollywood architect Wallace Neff designed the clubhouse that's now the focal point of the quintessentially Californian, Spanish Colonial-style complex. Guest accommodations on the sprawling ranch can be individual cottages, low-rise buildings, or modern condos. The unusually spacious rooms have kiss-enhancing features like fireplaces, premium bed linens, and secluded terraces or balconies that open onto picturesque views of the valley and mountains. A beautiful oak-studded Senior PGA Tour golf course ambles through the property, adding to the stunning setting and making the inn a popular destination for golf lovers. At press time, the inn was in the midst of an extensive renovation and expansion, expected to further enhance its unique sense of place and design. The work is scheduled for completion in 2005, when the inn will unveil a cluster of new luxury suites and several new restaurants, while maintaining its trademark "some-

thing for everyone" philosophy. It features tennis courts, complimentary bicycles, horseback riding, and your choice of swimming pools for outdoor recreation. Next to the golf course, the jewel of the resort is the pampering Spa Ojai, where stylish spa treatments—many modeled on American Indian traditions—are administered inside a beautifully designed and exquisitely tiled Spanish-Moorish complex. Mind/body fitness classes, art classes, nifty workout machines, and a sparkling outdoor pool complete the relaxation choices; it's easy to spend an entire splendid day at this rejuvenating spot. The inn's dining choices are scheduled to include an informal pub, a scenic terrace cafe, and a formal dining room for those special-occasion splurges. Details were still under wraps as we went to press, but the Ojai Valley Inn will undoubtedly continue its tradition of top-quality, inspired cuisine, one that's made its restaurants favorite dining destinations for valley residents as well as trysting guests.

$$$$ *AE, DC, DIS, MC, V; checks OK; www.ojairesort.com.* &

## ROSE GARDEN INN
💋

*615 W Ojai Ave, Ojai / 805/646-1434 or 800/799-1881*
Romance and frugality mix well at this classic ranch-style motel that's been well maintained and thoughtfully updated to present an attractively low-key alternative to the pricey country club around the corner. Situated a few blocks from the heart of town, with rose-filled gardens that border the Ojai equestrian and walking trail, this inn has a lazy, nostalgic feel. Despite being set back from the main road into Ojai, the Rose Garden's ample grounds provide many unexpectedly intimate spots where two can woo. Cedar log bench swings and hammocks are strategically placed in a tree-shaded yard that gazes onto the inn's best feature, an enormous heated swimming pool and Jacuzzi nicely hidden behind mature hedges. Rooms are small in size but big in appeal, with knotty cedar vaulted ceilings, cute kitchen alcoves, fine-quality beds, and a mismatch of functional furniture that reflects this place's rustic and inexpensive nature. Choose a deluxe fireplace cottage toward the back of the property for privacy and quiet, and you'll be that much closer to the two-person redwood sauna that beckons from the pool house. In the morning, head to the lobby for a complimentary continental breakfast spread; if you've got the munchies come afternoon, snacks are laid out here, as well.

$ *AE, DC, DIS, MC, V; checks OK; www.rosegardeninnofojai.com.*

## THEODORE WOOLSEY HOUSE
💋

*1484 E Ojai Ave, Ojai / 805/646-9779*
Built in 1887 by Theodore S. Woolsey, attorney and Yale University dean, this grand American Colonial stone and clapboard home was converted into

a bed-and-breakfast exactly 100 years later by innkeeper Ana Cross. Don't expect a perfectly restored "museum" of a house, though. The Woolsey-Cross home displays many idiosyncrasies, ranging from an incongruous (but refreshing) 1950s kidney-shaped swimming pool to a curious mix of antique furniture and modern tchotchkes throughout. A virtual backyard playground also includes a fishpond, putting green, horseshoe pit, volleyball court, and croquet lawn, all scattered amongst 7 acres of countryside near Ojai's citrus orchards. The five guest rooms are decorated in an old-fashioned lace-and-floral fashion, each with equally frilly private bath (although some baths aren't en suite). Be sure to get all the specifics when booking, since there are rooms offering fireplaces, claw-footed tubs, or other extras. The best choice for courting couples is Elizabeth's Room, a secluded boudoir located downstairs with a private entrance and garden terrace (plus the inn's only king-sized bed); another good choice is the two-story woodsy cottage with oversized whirlpool tub and kitchenette, placed discreetly among the oaks a few steps from the main house. A large European-style breakfast buffet is served each morning, and a special "celebration package" will enhance your stay with a welcome basket of champagne and snacks, private sit-down breakfast, and late checkout for lazy lovebirds. This house has a storied history of ownership by some of Ventura County's early movers and shakers, and oozes the romance of bygone days; what the inn lacks in polish, it makes up for in character, with a virtually unchanged living room and plenty of corners for some discreet snooping.

$$ *No credit cards; checks OK; www.theodorewoolseyhouse.com.* &

# Romantic Restaurants

## AZU
○○◐

*457 E Ojai Ave, Ojai / 805/640-7987*
After only a couple visits to Ojai, even casual day-trippers get caught up in the village's history and sense of community. So it's no surprise everyone held their breath when venerable Bill Baker's Bakery, a mainstay for generations, closed its doors. New owner Laurel Moore painstakingly restored the landmark building and quickly turned the apprehensions of locals and visitors alike to pleasure with her inspired and romantic result: a Mediterranean tapas bar, delicatessen, restaurant, and bakery. She created a place with warmth and an authentic Spanish ambience inspired by Ojai's climate, lifestyle, and landscape—so similar to the Iberian embrace of Moore's well-remembered travels there. During renovation, workers uncovered the building's original, century-old bread baking oven and left it exposed so today's diners can see and enjoy it. Azu is, in fact, known for its breads, each made from organic seeds, flours, and grains—including a luscious sourdough from

a 100-year-old starter. Whether you're in the mood for a full meal featuring braised lamb shank with roasted tomatoes; pan-roasted salmon with blood orange–wine sauce; or traditional Spanish paella with chicken, duck, mussels, and shrimp, or simply want to enjoy a small tapas selection before heading off to more private romantic destinations, Azu is well-located and a breath of fresh air. Blue Mediterranean tiles, a rich wood bar and counters, and small, round, traditional tapas tables make for a congenial atmosphere at lunch or dinner. Either way, be sure to save room for their inspired pastry chef's seasonally rotating creations like lemon tart with pistachios, or fresh fig and almond tarts.
**$$** *AE, MC, V; no checks; lunch, dinner Tues–Sun, brunch Sun; beer and wine; reservations recommended on weekends.*

## BOCCALI'S
❤❤

*3277 Santa Paula–Ojai Rd, Ojai / 805/646-6116*
You'll find this small wood-frame restaurant set among citrus groves, in a nostalgic pastoral setting that hasn't changed for decades. Sit together at one of the outdoor picnic tables shaded by umbrellas and twisted oak trees, or inside where the tables are covered with red-and-white-checked oilcloth. Like an old-style roadhouse, Boccali's has a complete lack of pretension, coupled with excellent home-style Sicilian grub, including lasagne that could win a statewide taste test hands down. An equally delicious meatless version is available, with spinach filling and marinara sauce. Their pizzas run a close second, even though they can be topped with suspiciously trendy ingredients like crab, whole garlic cloves, shrimp, and chicken. A large garden behind the restaurant provides summer produce including tomatoes, basil, eggplants, peppers, onions, squash, garlic, and melons—and that farm-fresh flavor asserts itself in Boccali's family legacy recipes from Lucca, Italy, by way of two generations in the Ventura–Santa Barbara area. Fresh lemonade, squeezed from fruit plucked off local trees, is the usual drink of choice. Come hungry and plan on sharing with your beloved, for portions are truly generous.
**$** *No credit cards; local checks only; lunch Wed–Sun, dinner every day; beer and wine; reservations recommended.*

## DEER LODGE TAVERN
❤❤

*2261 Maricopa Hwy, Ojai / 805/646-4256*
Amorous cowpokes and fillies will love sharing a rollicking kiss at this rustic landmark saloon nestled in the Ojai Valley's gorgeous foothills. The building dates back to the Depression, when it served as a country store with bait and hunting supplies for local sportsmen. Several generations later, it's still the favorite watering hole of Ojai hippies, bikers, and anyone with a taste for

stick-to-your-ribs tavern fare and rockin' live music in the never-empty bar. Couples exploring the north valley on Highway 33 can swing by for lunch, drawn by the savory aromas of Deer Lodge's outdoor weekend pig roast with all the traditional fixin's. It's also a great place for a romantic dinner coupled with a fun night of dancing in an anything-goes atmosphere that's about as far from city living as it gets. The lodge is reminiscent of a different era, with rough-hewn wood construction, potbelly stoves, a roaring river-rock hearth, and antler chandeliers that combine in a cozy tavern style. New owners have been busy sprucing up the place and expanding to include enclosed outdoor dining, a nice list of local wines, and a hearty lodge menu with enough contemporary touches to bring in an upscale—yet adventuresome—clientele. Be on the lookout for game dishes that go way beyond the buffalo burger to include boar, elk, antelope, or pheasant. There's a zesty seasoned "cowboy's" tri-tip roast, delicious baby back ribs, and a full complement of salads, pasta, and finger-lickin' appetizers for smaller—or less carnivorous—appetites. Big, country-style omelets kick-start the day at breakfast, and ooey-gooey good desserts are too yummy to pass up.

$–$$ *AE, MC, V; no checks; breakfast, lunch, dinner every day; full bar; reservations recommended on weekends; www.ojaideerlodge.com.*

## L'AUBERGE
◔◔

*314 El Paseo, Ojai / 805/646-2288*
Often touted as the most romantic restaurant in Ojai, L'Auberge is a swank holdover from the days when classic French cuisine was the epitome of fancy dining. Far from outdated, though, it remains an excellent choice for special occasion dining and well regarded by the cosmopolitan crowd who weekend and vacation in Ojai. Housed in a 1910 mansion with fireplace and ornate chandeliers, a short, pleasant walk from downtown, the restaurant has a charming terrace with a marvelous view of Ojai's "pink moment" at sunset. For proposals, celebratory toasts, or just stealing a lover's kiss between courses, choose a table by the hearth or on the outdoor terrace, which is shaded by lattice work and massive oak trees reminiscent of a Renoir painting. The French-Belgian menu is unswervingly traditional, and L'Auberge is known for its exceptional escargots and sweetbreads. Among the other selections are scampi, frogs' legs, poached sole, tournedos of beef, and duck à l'orange. The weekend brunch menu offers a selection of perfectly prepared crepes. This kind of place may have gone seriously out of style, but if you love classic French, you'd do well to take advantage of this still-excellent grande dame.

$$ *AE, MC, V; no checks; dinner every day, brunch Sat–Sun; full bar; reservations recommended.* ♿

# THE RANCH HOUSE
❶❶❶

*S Lomita Ave, Ojai / 805/646-2360*
If you're going to have only one meal in Ojai, have it here. The name may suggest steaks 'n' spuds, but the reality of this Ojai Valley gem couldn't be more different. Originally conceived in 1949 by Alan and Helen Hooker—two Krishnamurti followers drawn to Ojai's natural beauty—the restaurant began life as a vegetarian boarding house. The Hookers were hippies before hippie was hip, and it wasn't long before they turned their ranch house into a full-fledged restaurant, adding meat dishes and exceptional wines to a menu that continues to emphasize the freshest vegetables, fruits, and herbs in what is now ubiquitously known as California cuisine. Freshly snipped sprigs from the lush herb garden will aromatically transform your simple meat, fish, or game dish into a work of art, and couples are encouraged to stroll hand-in-hand through this splendid kitchen garden during their visit. From an appetizer of Cognac-laced liver pâte served with its own chewy rye bread to leave-room-for desserts like fresh raspberries with sweet Chambord cream, the ingredients always shine through. With guests driving in from as far as Los Angeles just for a Ranch House meal, everything has to be perfect, and this peaceful and friendly retreat never disappoints. Equally impressive are the polished yet friendly service and magical setting, with alfresco dining year-round on a wooden porch facing the scenic valley as well as in the romantic garden amid twinkling lights and stone fountains. $$$ *AE, DC, DIS, MC, V; checks OK; dinner Tues–Sun, brunch Sun; beer and wine; reservations recommended; www.theranchhouse.com.* ♿

# SUZANNE'S CUISINE
❶❶❶

*502 W Ojai Ave, Ojai / 805/640-1961*
Ojai's roster of exceptional restaurants includes this understated charmer a few blocks from the center of town where every little detail bespeaks a preoccupation with quality. Each ingredient is as fresh and natural as it can be, and these recipes—a blending of California cuisine with Italian recipes from chef-owner Suzanne Roll's family—show them off to full advantage. Every meal begins with a basket of home-baked rolls served with butter squares, each accented by a single pressed cilantro leaf. Vegetables are al dente, and even the occasional cream sauce tastes light and healthy. A highlight of the lunch menu is the Southwest salad: wild, brown, and jasmine rice tossed with smoked turkey, feta, veggies, and green chiles. At dinner, pepper-and-sesame-crusted ahi is served either sautéed or seared (your choice). Suzanne's covered outdoor patio should be your first seating choice, especially for couples seeking a bewitching backdrop to match the seductively delicious food. Its marble bistro tables are shaded in summer by lush greenery and warmed in winter by a fireplace and strategically

placed heat lamps. When it rains, a plastic cover unfurls to keep water out while maintaining an airy garden feel—about as kiss-inspiring as it gets. This is the kind of restaurant that makes you long for decadent three-hour lunches and romantically unhurried dinners, so sit back, enjoy, and—by all means—don't skip dessert.

*$$ DC, DIS, MC, V; local checks only; lunch, dinner Wed–Mon; full bar; reservations recommended; www.suzannescuisine.com.* &

# SANTA BARBARA AND ENVIRONS

## ROMANTIC HIGHLIGHTS

To many Californians—and an even higher percentage of romance-seeking couples—Santa Barbara is simply the only place to go for the perfect vacation getaway. It's often called America's Riviera, and with good reason: Nestled in a picturesque curve of the Southern California coastline, Santa Barbara is fringed with palm-lined, white-sand beaches, while the green sloping foothills of the Santa Ynez Mountains form a scenic backdrop. The city's distinctive Mediterranean architecture—a Spanish-Moorish-Mission Revival mosaic of whitewashed stucco, red-tile roofs, and oak-shaded courtyards—is its most memorable feature. Santa Barbara grew up around the Spanish presidio (military fortress) at the heart of today's downtown. When a 1925 earthquake and resulting fire destroyed much of "modern" Santa Barbara, city planners mandated that all new construction would mimic the historic style; those regulations are still in place, resulting in a charmingly consistent citywide "look" that's often cited as one of the town's most romantic attributes. Even couples on a lazy lovers' weekend might have enough spare time to soak up the atmosphere, and there's no better way than the appropriately named **Red Tile Tour**, a self-guided walking tour of the city's historic core (maps are available at the visitor center; allow one to three hours to complete). Encompassing 12 blocks, the tour begins at the lovely **Santa Barbara County Courthouse** (1100 Anacapa St; 805/962-6464), a grandiose 1929 example of flamboyant Spanish Colonial Revival architecture. If you have time for only one activity in town, ride the elevator up to the fourth-story clock tower, where you can see from the mountains to the bay. Helpful signs will assist the two of you in identifying the buildings and gardens you're eyeing; you might even glimpse one of the many weddings held in the garden throughout the year.

Santa Barbara's most distinctive—and most visited—landmark is the elegant **Santa Barbara Mission** (at Laguna and Los Olivos Sts; 805/682-4149; www.sbmission.org), a 1786 masterpiece known as the Queen of

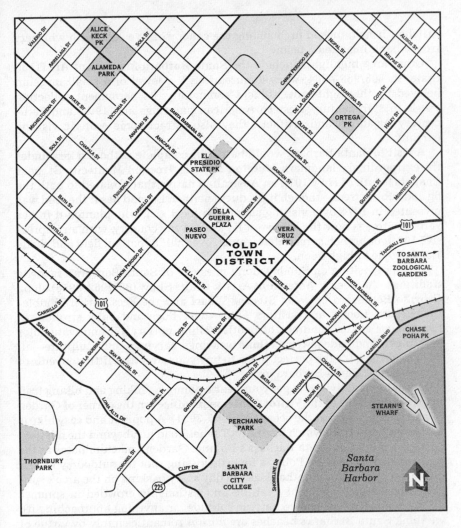

the Missions for its Greco-Roman Revival grandeur and stunning hillside setting with commanding ocean views. Couples can tour the old padres' quarters (now a small museum), the eerily beautiful cemetery, the fragrantly landscaped inner courtyard, and the still-active parish church—the only one of the mission chain with twin bell towers. A short drive uphill from the mission is the 65-acre **Santa Barbara Botanic Garden** (1212 Mission Canyon Rd; 805/682-4726; www.sbbg.org), where more than 5 miles of paths meander through a landscape of indigenous California plants arranged in representational habitats (redwood forests, canyon woodlands, meadows, deserts, and the like). A perfect kissing spot within the gardens is the

Pritchett bench, tucked high among the canopy of live oaks with whispers from a babbling stream below.

Other area highlights include the **Santa Barbara Museum of Art** (1130 State St; 805/963-4364; www.sbmuseart.org), a jewel of a small museum beloved by this tight-knit, affluent community. Its permanent collection excels in 20th-century Western American paintings and 19th- and 20th-century Asian art and artifacts; they also attract some esoteric visiting exhibits.

A visit to Santa Barbara would hardly be complete without a kiss under the extraordinary landmark **Moreton Bay Fig Tree** (on Montecito St, near Chapala, south of Hwy 101), an Australian native that's related to both the fig and rubber trees—though it produces neither. Legend has it the seed was presented in 1874 by a visiting sailor to a local girl, who planted it in her yard; the tree is now the largest of its kind in the country, with an impressive 160-foot branch spread that would cover half a football field and shade 1,000 people at high noon.

If you're visiting on Sunday, don't miss one of Santa Barbara's favorite traditions, the weekly **Waterfront Arts & Crafts Show** (805/962-8956) along Cabrillo Boulevard between Stearns Wharf and the Fess Parker/Doubletree Resort. Locals and visitors alike—with dogs and baby strollers in tow—linger at the hundreds of booths selling pottery, oil and watercolor paintings, handmade jewelry, ethnic weavings, carvings, and sculpture—all by local artists. It's the perfect place to buy your sweetie a little souvenir of your romantic Santa Barbara visit.

For outdoor activities to get your hearts pumping, hiking and biking trail maps are available at the **Visitor Center main office** (on the corner of Garden St and Cabrillo Blvd at the ocean; 805/965-3021). A popular and easy hike is the **Seven Falls Trail**, which begins on Tunnel Road just beyond the mission; it skirts the edge of Santa Barbara's Botanic Garden and culminates at the aptly named Inspiration Point, a favorite kissing spot for outdoorsy lovers.

Many couples would rather laze the day away basking on the area's sun-kissed beaches. Though they can be unquestionably crowded in summer (off season is the best choice for true solitude, or anything approaching it), we think Santa Barbara's beaches are *always* romantic simply by virtue of their astounding beauty. The broad stretch of beach hugging the ocean from Stearns Wharf to Montecito is **East Beach**, the city's most popular beach; along it are places to fish, swim, and play volleyball, plus some grassy areas for sitting and a small playground. Rest rooms, showers, a playground, and volleyball courts are scattered in the area, and the **Cabrillo Pavilion Bathhouse** (1118 Cabrillo Blvd; 805/965-0509) provides lockers and use of their weight room for a minimal fee. **West Beach**, on the other side of Stearns Wharf, includes the Santa Monica Harbor and offers a gentle-wave lagoon that's perfect for nonswimmers. **Leadbetter Beach**, between West Beach and Shoreline, is sheltered by a high cliff and is good for swimming and beginning surfers. At **Shoreline Park** (Shoreline Dr, north of the harbor), take the steps down to the secluded white-sand beach to escape the crowds, or for an even more remote spot head to **Mesa Lane Beach** (north, at Mesa Ln, off Cliff Dr), a very private strip of sand hidden by bluffs, which is also a good surf spot. Also off Cliff Drive is the beach locals refer to as **Hendry's Beach** (Arroyo Burro Nature Reserve; 2981 Cliff Dr; 805/687-3714), with good picnic areas, snack bars (such as the Brown Pelican), and excellent swimming, fishing, and surfing.

Some of us are eager to find a romantic pastime more active than sunbathing, but less strenuous than hiking, and Santa Barbara provides a wonderful setting for prowling the shops and galleries that line its tree-shaded streets. There are specialty stores and boutiques in historic **El Paseo** (State St, above de la Guerra St) and **La Arcada** (State St, above Figueroa St) and the beautiful, modern mall **Paseo Nuevo** (State St at de la Guerra St) with Spanish Colonial facades and faux balconies, which holds anchor stores Macy's and Nordstrom, boutiques, and a cinema. While State Street is the main shopping area and the prime destination for antiques and vintage clothing, some of the best shops are on side streets, a perfect opportunity to explore at your leisure. The **Italian Pottery Outlet** down near the beach (19 Helena St; 877/496-5599; www.italianpottery.com) has a huge selection of Italian serving dishes, plates, vases, and bowls for a third less than elsewhere. For shopping with a truly antique flavor, head to **Brinkerhoff Avenue** (1½ blocks west of State St between Cota and Haley Sts). Several of the well-preserved Victorian homes on this single historic block have opened their doors as antique shops, rare booksellers, and collectibles stores.

Shopping is also the primary pastime in nearby **Montecito**, an exclusive suburb whose name means "little mountain" in Spanish; gentry horse farms, mansions, and tennis courts characterize this lushly wooded little mountain. Activity is centered around several well-heeled blocks of Coast Village Road, where upscale but affordable boutiques share the sidewalk with all-day cafes and wonderful dinner spots, all caressed by clean sea breezes.

Santa Barbara is the seat of a county increasingly regarded for its excellent wines, and no romantic interlude here is complete without visiting some of the many wineries where this nectar is grown and produced. The stunningly beautiful wine region of the **Santa Ynez Valley** is about 30 minutes from downtown Santa Barbara and is discussed in detail in the next chapter.

# Access and Information

The **Santa Barbara Municipal Airport** (500 Fowler Rd; 805/967-7111; www.flysba.com) is located in Goleta about 15 minutes north of downtown Santa Barbara, and boasts the same red-tiled Spanish Colonial charm and million-dollar seaside location that makes the rest of the city so appealing. It's small enough to easily navigate, but large enough to offer direct flights to most major hubs in the west, including Denver, Dallas/Fort Worth, Las Vegas, Los Angeles, Phoenix, Seattle, San Francisco, San Jose, and Salt Lake City. Most major car rental companies are conveniently located at the airport, and the **SuperRide** (805/683-9636 or 800/977-1123; www.superride .net) shuttle service provides passengers with advance-reservation rides to and from the airport.

Santa Barbara is 92 miles from Los Angeles and 332 miles from San Francisco, on Highway 101. Highway 154, through the San Marcos Pass, joins Highway 101 from the Santa Ynez Valley to the north. Many visitors simply drive to Santa Barbara, but a more old-fashioned—and romantic— choice is the **Amtrak** (800/USA/RAIL; www.amtrak.com) *Pacific Surfliner.* It runs between San Luis Obispo and San Diego, stopping in Goleta, Ventura, and Los Angeles, as well as numerous smaller stations en route; in Santa Barbara, you'll arrive in the heart of busy State Street, a great place to catch a taxi or trolley.

State Street is Santa Barbara's main commercial thoroughfare, an always-crowded, tree-shaded avenue of shops and cafes; it runs perpendicular to the waterfront. A 25-cent electric shuttle runs regularly along Cabrillo Boulevard and up and down State Street; it's a convenient way to traverse the most popular part of town without having to hunt for parking. For more information on events and activities in town, contact the **Santa Barbara Visitors Bureau** (1 Santa Barbara St; 805/966-9222 or 800/927-4688; www.santabarbaraca.com) or visit their walk-in center on Cabrillo across from the beach.

# Romantic Lodgings

## BACARA RESORT & SPA
✪✪✪✪

*8301 Hollister Ave, Goleta / 805/968-0100 or 877/422-4245*
Couples can be the stars of their own glamour vacation in a setting seemingly dreamt up by a Hollywood cinematographer: 78 ocean-side acres of sandy beaches and breathtaking bluffs, isolated from the bustling world but gifted with the finest in service and amenities. The newest resort around Santa Barbara for the sleek and chic is Bacara Resort & Spa, with more than 350 luxurious guest rooms and suites, all with stunning views from

private patios or balconies—and nightly rates starting at $400 and soaring to $2,500. The resort was obviously built to appeal to the movie star and mogul crowd from L.A.—the 225-person screening room ensures that no one will miss seeing the rushes of their latest film project—who never hesitate to indulge in the very best when it comes to paparazzi-free, amorous getaways. The lodgings are in one-, three-, and four-story Mediterranean villas, each graced with Frette linens, plush robes, and Spanish dark wood furniture with blue and white fabrics. Located 20 freeway minutes from downtown Santa Barbara, the resort is designed with a nod to Spanish Colonial and Mission architecture in a villagelike setting, with tile roofs, splashing fountains, covered archways, and wooden trellises. Adjacent is the resort's own 1,000-acre Ranch of Bacara, a lemon and avocado ranch where you can hike, ride mountain bikes, or have a picnic. The three-level spa offers a full menu of treatments, including a citrus-avocado body scrub, Thai massage, and an ultimate body blitz (if you have to ask, you don't need one). Three zero-edge swimming pools with cabanas keep the two of you from being bored paddling in circles. There are also three restaurants: Miró, a fine dining restaurant named after Spanish artist Joan Miró; the Bistro, a relaxed cafe with Mediterranean food for lunch and dinner; and the informal Spa Café for light, healthful meals and snacks. On a bluff over the ocean, Miró specializes in Basque-Catalonia cuisine, and offers a fine wine list. The restaurant also features a lounge area where couples can enjoy a light dinner of tapas and fresh-made sangría. All restaurants make use of produce and herbs grown in the resort's 1,000-acre garden. Booked for weddings even before its official opening day, Bacara is a natural choice for over-the-top romance, so don't be afraid to make special requests for your beloved. For example, the off-season Bacara Amour package stacks the deck with a welcoming bottle of bubbly, dinner for two in Miró, breakfast in bed the next morning, and a day of wine tasting followed by a candlelit in-room massage for two.
$$$$ *AE, MC, V; checks OK; www.bacararesort.com.* &

## EL CAPITAN CANYON
♦♦♦
*11560 Calle Real, Santa Barbara / 866/352-2729*
Think camping sounds romantic? Sleeping on twigs, cooking over a flame, bathing with cold water, and fending off insects? Naw, we don't either! Which is why we—along with scores of savvy Californians and (moderately) adventurous young Hollywood types—are so enamored of the recently revamped El Capitan Canyon, located along the coast sufficiently north of Santa Barbara to feel really rustic yet close enough to SB's dining and shopping. This is camping "lite," or "comfort" camping. You don't need a tent. You don't need a sleeping bag. You don't even need to pack supplies for s'mores. Yet you'll enjoy possibly the most carefree camping experience of your life, with plenty of opportunity for warm, private, cozy, and bug-free

kisses. Surrounded by the oaks and sycamores of this scenic canyon that descends gradually to the beach below, safari tents and cedar cabins are positioned in and around the meadows, streams, and woods of this environmentally protected natural paradise. Choose a king cabin in the Meadow area, the most conducive to romance, where the song of creek-side frogs will lull you to sleep until the sun rises behind the regal mountain range. American Indian symbols that speak of early canyon inhabitants adorn the threshold and furnishings of these comfortable cabins, which are warmed by gas-powered cast-iron stoves and include full electricity and plumbing in private bathrooms with Jacuzzi tubs and functional little kitchenettes. Take the short hike down to the compound's Canyon Market, a congenial store/deli where you can pick up breakfast or lunch, outdoor essentials, and souvenirs, as well as wine and pre-measured barbecue kits that include everything you need for a cookout on the fire pit next to your cabin. Toast the moon with after-dinner s'mores (there's a kit for that, too) and we're certain the sleep you enjoy in your king-sized bed will be among the best ever. Throughout the year, guests can explore the beach, hiking trails, and bike paths, or lounge by the heated swimming pool. Bikes and water gear are available, wine-tasting excursions can be arranged, and spa-quality massages are offered in rustic yurts that dot the property. Yeah, now *this* is camping.
$$$–$$$$ AE, MC, V; checks OK; www.elcapitancanyon.com.

## EL ENCANTO HOTEL AND GARDEN VILLAS
❀❀❁
*1900 Lasuen Rd, Santa Barbara / 805/687-5000 or 800/346-7039*
For those who want to revel in the old Santa Barbara resort style, this famous romantic retreat's 84 cottages are perched on 10 lushly landscaped acres high above town. Some were built as early as 1912 in the popular Craftsman style, and others have a Spanish Colonial sensibility, but all are set among tropical foliage, waterfalls, arbors, a Japanese garden, and lawns rolling down to views of the ocean beyond. By the 1920s, when railway lines brought East Coast families to spend an entire season here, El Encanto had opened as a resort hotel. Today, many of the cottages have wood-burning fireplaces, porches, and French doors; they're all so different, it pays to spend a moment with your reservation agent to choose the one right for your romantic rendezvous. The intimate main building houses an airy lounge, a bar, and the acclaimed El Encanto restaurant (see Romantic Restaurants), whose million-dollar views have always been its main draw. For many years, the local buzz has been about this grande dame's much-needed renovation, planned for "next year" since Clinton was in office. When the furnishings, amenities, and service here finally live up to the historic charm of these cottages and gardens, El Encanto will be a world-class retreat for an exclusive,

upscale clientele. Until that time, take advantage of their pre-rehab rates to enjoy one of the most exquisite settings in Southern California. *$$$$ AE, DC, MC, V; checks OK; www.elencantohotel.com.*

## FOUR SEASONS BILTMORE
●●●●

*1260 Channel Dr, Montecito / 805/969-2261 or 800/332-3442*
This elegant 236-room property, loaded with the luxury associated with the Four Seasons chain, is one of the state's most beautiful Old World–style hotels. The regal main Spanish Revival building, built in 1927, stands amid towering palms overlooking the Pacific, creating the ideal backdrop for romance. Magnificent wrought-iron gates lead into a pale-hued lobby with hand-decorated archways, bowls of orchids, and polished antiques resting on waxed terra-cotta tiles. Rooms are tastefully furnished in soft tones with beds of the utmost comfort, plantation shutters, botanical prints, and marble bathrooms with fluffy towels and robes. Heat lamps, hair dryers, book lights, and bowls of candy are some of the extra amenities, and at the touch of a button, earplugs, hot water bottles, non-allergenic soap, and even that toothbrush you forgot will magically appear. For more privacy, book one of the green-trimmed California bungalows, many of which have fireplaces and patios. They're first class, with a tariff to match, but memories of this romantic splurge will sustain you for some time after your stay. In addition to the pool and tennis courts, the expansive lawn area behind the main building is home to croquet, shuffleboard, and an 18-hole putting green. The gym is fully equipped, and bikes are at the ready—along with a map of local bike paths—for when you and your sweetie want to get out and explore. Complimentary day passes to the exclusive Coral Casino Beach and Cabana Club across the street are available for guests who want to swim in an Olympic-sized pool or try some surfing—this perk is one of the most excellent hotel amenities we have discovered and a powerful romantic incentive to choose the Biltmore in summertime. La Marina is the Biltmore's elegant restaurant, a conservative favorite where refined and artistically composed cuisine is presented for dinner beneath soaring wood beams that embody the resort's Spanish Colonial flavor. Open for breakfast, lunch, and dinner, The Patio restaurant, with its retractable glass roof, offers casual fare like pastas, salads, and seafood, and also hosts a famous Sunday brunch, when chefs man food stations and serve everything from roast beef to custom omelets. In the La Sala lounge, afternoon tea by the fire gives way to live jazz nightly, with dancing on Friday and Saturday evenings. After listening to the soothing strains of the band, take a moonlit stroll, and you have all the makings for a memorable night of romance.
*$$$$ AE, DIS, MC, V; no checks; www.fshr.com/santabarbara.* &

## HOTEL OCEANA
◐◐◖

*202 W Cabrillo Blvd, Santa Barbara / 805/965-4577 or 800/965-9776*
This is a sister property to Santa Monica's Oceana, a sophisticated and upscale boutique hotel, and one familiar to romantic vacationers from Los Angeles. Here, they've kicked it down a notch, eschewing ultra-service and amenity-laden suites for a lighter, more beach-friendly feel that still offers a more upscale experience than the surrounding budget motels—but without the four-star price tag. The Oceana compound—a low-rise amalgam of four formerly independent motel properties—deftly maintains its vintage-era architecture and charm (including splendid original tile work) while injecting contemporary comforts and a breezy, colorful coastal style. Chic Italian linens, in-room CD players, and designer furniture unify the diverse layouts of all completely remodeled rooms and provide a serene counter-point to the bustle of Cabrillo Boulevard and East Beach outside the front door. (You'll also be walking distance from State Street, Stearns Wharf, and the harbor.) If gazing at the big blue from the privacy of your boudoir is essential, ocean-view rooms come at a premium; many couples prefer the quieter garden- or poolside rooms, happy to trade views for serenity. A full European-style breakfast is served each morning (for a nominal charge), and Oceana even has a minispa on the property where massages, facials, and body treatments will soften you and your betrothed up for a special date together. With swimming pools, the beach, and hotel packages that combine lodging with everything from jeep tours to kayaking, Oceana is well suited for active romantic adventures.
$$$–$$$$ *AE, DIS, MC, V; checks OK; www.hoteloceana.com.* ⛐

---

## INN OF THE SPANISH GARDEN
◐◐◐

*915 Garden St, Santa Barbara / 805/564-4700 or 866/564-4700*
Because Santa Barbara is a conservative, low-growth city, frequent visitors were delighted to welcome, in 2002, the rare appearance of a brand-new boutique hotel in the heart of the city's historic center. Newly constructed to blend seamlessly with the surrounding low-rise Spanish Colonial offices—all white stucco, graceful arches, and distinctive red-tiled roofs—this romantic 23-room inn is imbued with creative spirit from the colony of artists' studios that once stood on this site. Frette linens, fireplaces, and French press cof-feemakers are the hallmarks of sophisticated service that includes a bed-and-breakfast–style encyclopedia of local menus, complimentary gourmet continental breakfast and espresso bar, and the overall sensation of staying at a wealthy friend's villa. The ambience is pure Santa Barbara, with mean-dering gardens and bubbling fountains; interiors blend Mediterranean style (golden sponge-painted walls, terra-cotta floor tiles) with authentic Spanish Colonial flavor (rustic wooden doors, colorful woven rugs) and Asian accents

(raw silk upholstery and Chinese vases). No detail is overlooked: there's a well-equipped exercise nook, quiet lap pool surrounded by gardens, and a path to the historic artist cottages, some converted to house workshops with noted Central Coast artists. The hotel's over-the-top Romance Package is perfect for a marriage proposal or other extra-special event. It includes a bottle of wine, two in-room massages, breakfast in bed, a special romance guide to the city, and lots of extra touches like heart-shaped bath confetti and a rose-scented candle.
$$$$ *AE, DC, DIS, MC, V; no checks; www.spanishgardeninn.com.* &

## INN ON SUMMER HILL
♥♥♥
*2520 Lillie Ave, Summerland / 805/969-9998 or 800/845-5566*
Located just a quick freeway blast (five minutes, tops) south of Santa Barbara, tiny Summerland is both a suburb of its big sister and a charming resort town on its own, where well-heeled residents are busy building quaint hillside cottages and restoring decrepit Victorian houses. The town is a great place for couples to browse antique shops and boutiques along Lillie Avenue, have a seaside lunch, and enjoy Summerland's tiny beach, secluded Lookout County Park. If it weren't for the convenient—but well-trafficked—highway that passes fairly close to the New England–style inn, we would have given it three lips without a second thought. This enchanting Craftsman-style inn may look as vintage as the town of Summerland, but inside it's brand-spanking new, with all the modern amenities. If you simply can't live without a fireplace, VCR, and whirlpool bathtub, this luxury bed-and-breakfast is for you. Each of the 16 rooms also has a balcony or patio. Decor is heavy-handed English country (think layers and layers of fabric prints and frills, romantic canopy beds, fluffy down comforters). If you'd like an ocean-view room, ask when you book, but remember that you'll have to look across Highway 101, which stretches the length of Summerland like an inescapable concrete-and-steel river. Inside the inn, however, pampering is taken to the highest level. Rooms have instant hot water taps for coffee or tea, small refrigerators, and even bathroom phone extensions. A video library is available for those who want to cocoon in their room. Rates include a lavish gourmet breakfast each morning, as well as hors d'oeuvres and wine in the afternoon. Before bedtime, the dining room is sweetened with complimentary desserts. A variety of celebration packages, custom gift baskets, and a breakfast-in-bed option make this B&B a popular anniversary getaway.
$$$$ *AE, DIS, MC, V; no checks; www.innonsummerhill.com.* &

## SAN YSIDRO RANCH
○○○○

*900 San Ysidro Ln, Montecito / 805/969-5046 or 800/368-6788*
Lodgings like the San Ysidro Ranch make us question our four-lip rating system—this very special destination goes above and beyond our romantic expectations and deserves at least 10 kisses. Imagine a summer camp for the wealthy, with quaint winding trails overgrown with flowers and trees, and peaceful rolling hills beyond. Here, quiet seclusion has been elevated to an art form, and two devoted souls can be as reclusive here as they choose. Upon arrival, you'll be escorted to a private cottage already bearing your name, impeccably outfitted in country luxury, with wood-burning stove or fireplace, outdoor terrace, goose-down comforter, cozy Frette robes, fresh flowers, and dozens of other luxuries to pamper every aspect of your being. Folks have been replenishing themselves here for years, including Laurence Olivier and Vivien Leigh—who were married here—and honeymooners John and Jackie Kennedy. The hotel's verdant 540 acres have been compared to the city's botanic garden. Visiting couples have the run of the ranch, including tennis courts, swimming pool, bocci ball court, driving range, and wilderness hiking trails. The Stonehouse Restaurant (see Romantic Restaurants), a rustic but pricey regional American eatery set amongst all this natural beauty, is considered by some the best in the county. Dogs are welcomed, too, and are greeted on check-in with biscuits and a doggie bed. For those that can afford the best money can buy, the ranch is a slice of heaven on earth.
$$$$ *AE, MC, V; checks OK; www.sanysidroranch.com.* &

## SIMPSON HOUSE INN
○○○◖

*121 E Arrellaga St, Santa Barbara / 805/963-7067*
If you were rich and had a very good *majordomo,* life would be like this. The Simpson House is the only B&B in North America that's earned AAA's five-diamond rating, and it's well deserved. This imposing Victorian estate is an elegant world of its own, despite being near the heart of downtown. Guest rooms in the main house feature period detailing, color-coordinated with Oriental rugs and plush upholstery and complemented with brass beds, European goose-down duvets, and fine antiques. In back, beyond the stone patio and lawn (the domain of Bella, the most petted black Lab in town), vacationing lovebirds enjoy more privacy in old barn suites and two-story cottages with courtyards and stone fountains, tucked between tall oaks and magnolias. Each is stylishly modern country-cottage in decor, with open-beamed ceiling, river-rock fireplace, whirlpool tub, and wet bar. Service is pampering, practiced, and discreet, and includes a complete gourmet breakfast—with china and silver—delivered to your room or secluded patio. Wine and a lavish array of hors d'oeuvres are served nightly in the sitting area

or can be enjoyed on the main house's wisteria-draped porch. A facial or a massage can be arranged, and a game of croquet on the lawn is most civilized entertainment. Bicycles and beach equipment are also offered, along with an extensive collection of videos. The only difficult part of staying at the Simpson House is knowing that you'll eventually have to return home. Fortunately, you will leave with a new appreciation for the finer things in life—including each other.
**$$$** *AE, DIS, MC, V; checks OK; www.simpsonhouseinn.com.* &

## THE UPHAM HOTEL AND COUNTRY HOUSE
●●

*1404 de la Vina St, Santa Barbara / 805/962-0058 or 800/727-0876*
The Upham combines the intimacy of a bed-and-breakfast with the service of a small hotel. Built in 1871, it contains 50 rooms in the main building and garden cottages. Still, feather duvets, botanical prints, plush settees, louvered wood shutters, and grand armoires make this feel like a vintage country house where lovers can relax and unwind. The real finds here are the 14 cottage-style guest rooms, set along a path that meanders through flower gardens and verdant lawns. Each simple country room has a private entrance, a large four-poster bed, mahogany antiques, and a small bath. Some rooms have private porches, secluded patios, and gas fireplaces. However, the Master Suite may be the most enticing retreat for vacationing sweethearts, with its wet bar, whirlpool tub, and a private yard with swinging hammock. A walkway with trellised arches and a gazebo weaves its way around the pretty garden and into the main building, where continental breakfast, afternoon cheese and wine, and evening milk and cookies are served. The Upham also boasts its own highly regarded bistro-style eatery, Louie's, which serves lunch and dinner every day. Specializing in fresh seafood, pastas, and California cuisine, the restaurant boasts a sunny veranda for couples who want to enjoy the weather. It fills up with more than just hotel guests, so be sure to make a reservation. The hotel also owns the former Tiffany Inn down the street, a restored seven-bedroom Victorian offering the classic B&B experience, with loads of antique details and a full-service breakfast.
**$$$–$$$$** *AE, DIS, MC, V; checks OK; www.uphamhotel.com.*

# Romantic Restaurants

## BEACHSIDE BAR CAFE
●●

*5905 Sandspit Rd, Goleta / 805/964-7881*
Goleta Beach Park is a romantic picture postcard of the quintessential California beach scene: grassy bluffs behind a white-sand, crescent-shaped

cove, palm trees waving in the breeze, a friendly wooden fishing pier, and the promise of glorious sunsets to share at day's end. In the middle of it all sits Beachside Bar Cafe, a come-as-you-are crowd pleaser, where sandy-toed surfers, book-toting students, lunch-hour professionals, early-dining retirees, and, of course, hungry lovebirds comingle over an all-day menu of chowders, salads, and sandwiches (including a zesty ahi burger), as well as an extensive raw shellfish bar and cocktail-hour noshes. Come sunset, it's standing room only, and everything from oysters and ceviche to Yucatán seafood skewers or outstanding crab cakes—as well as tropical cocktails that enhance the island vibe—sports Happy Hour prices. The two of you will enjoy an ocean view from nearly every indoor seat as well as the wind-shielded covered patio (with heat lamps in case of chill). The restaurant is done up in a beachy blend of gray clapboard, island rattan, and nautical paraphernalia. The food here is good and satisfying, served up by a youthful wait staff who occasionally point out a pelican offshore diving for *its* meal.
**$–$$** *AE, MC, V; checks OK; lunch, dinner every day; full bar; reservations not necessary.*

## BOUCHON
❍❍❍
*9 W Victoria St, Santa Barbara / 805/730-1160*
Although the name is French for "wine cork," almost all of the corks are coming out of local bottles at this chic restaurant serving Wine Country cuisine. Owner Mitchell Sjerven and chef Charles Fredericks worked at many of the town's finer eating establishments before teaming up in 1998, and their expertise is reflected in the restaurant's culinary offerings, as well as the simple but elegant setting that invites quiet passion between sweethearts. The list of local wines by the glass is impressive, as is the wine list in general, including such selections as an excellent sangiovese from the Cambria region and a viognier from Santa Ynez. The well-informed staff loves to help with menu selections; recommended seasonal dishes might include pan-roasted bluefin tuna with roasted tomato tapenade, lemon confit, and Santa Barbara olives; lime-seared sea scallops with sweet corn risotto; or rosemary- and garlic-marinated lamb loin with sweet potato gnocchi. Don't miss the Meyer lemon pudding cake or the warm chocolate cake with homemade banana ice cream. The warm and hushed dining room is adorned with paintings by Paul Brown (a respected local painter of wine labels), the kitchen is in view beyond beautiful etched glass panels, and the garden patio is heated. If the two of you just want to drop in for the ambience and a glass of fine local wine, an adjoining wine bar is open on weekends.
**$$$** *AE, DC, MC, V; checks OK; dinner every day; beer and wine; reservations recommended; www.bouchonsantabarbara.com.* &

# BROPHY BROS CLAM BAR & RESTAURANT
✪✪❶

*119 Harbor Wy, Santa Barbara / 805/966-4418*

Though it may not be romantic in the conventional sense—despite unrivaled harbor views, Brophy's is casual and boisterous—even the most ardent suitors will happily step out for this eatery's famous clam chowder. However, there are plenty more treasures from the sea served amid the ocean breezes: cioppino; the cold combo platter of shrimp, crab, oysters, clams, and ceviche; or its hot counterpart with steamed clams, oysters Rockefeller, and beer-boiled shrimp. The fresh fish menu changes daily; the two of you may find Hawaiian ahi breaded with roasted cashews, served with tarragon mustard cream sauce; local thresher shark marinated in olive oil, citrus, garlic, cilantro, and red onion; traditional lobster; fresh mahimahi; or succulent swordfish steak grilled and topped with tarragon-crab cream sauce. Meat eaters, however, needn't be disappointed; the burgers here aren't bad either. Lunch outside on the balcony and absorb the sights and sounds (and sometimes smells) of the fisherman's world around you, or in the evening join regulars at the inside bar as they trade tales of the sea over draught beer and steamers. Expect a wait, as this in one of Santa Barbara's well-known treasures.

*$$ AE, MC, V; no checks; lunch, dinner every day; full bar; reservations recommended.*

# CITRONELLE
✪✪✪

*901 Cabrillo Blvd, Santa Barbara / 805/963-0111*

Tucked away inside the oceanfront Santa Barbara Inn—a respectable small hotel overlooking East Beach—Citronelle's reputation always precedes it. Not only is executive chef Michel Richard one of the culinary world's most respected statesmen (known for his Washington, D.C., flagship Citronelle as well as L.A.'s chic Bastide), but also the restaurant's name is invariably mentioned in discussions of Santa Barbara's best and most romantic dining settings. Richard composed the menu and chose the restaurant's prime site for its panoramic beach and sunset view. A Provençal blue-and-yellow color scheme nicely invokes the sea and sunshine found outside Citronelle's ocean-view windows; it's a peaceful atmosphere and perfect backdrop for the well-honed California-French bistro menu, featuring meats and fish with often-rich sauces. Request a window-side table, order a bottle from the fine wine list, and choose from such outstanding specialties as "porcupine" shrimp with Japanese *shiso* and goat cheese dressing; sautéed sea bass with shiitake risotto and chardonnay sauce; leek-crusted chicken pot-au-feu; or braised lamb shank with black olive sauce. Richard's forte has always been dessert, and you'll kick yourself if you don't leave room for favorites like crème brûlée layered with caramelized phyllo dough. Just ask for two forks and make sure the romantic mood isn't spoiled over who gets the last bite. $$$–$$$$ *AE, MC, V; no checks; dinner every day; full bar; reservations recommended; www.santabarbarainn.com.* ♿

## COLD SPRING TAVERN
♥♥

*5995 Stagecoach Rd, Santa Barbara / 805/967-0066*
The summit of Highway 154, about halfway between Santa Barbara and Santa Ynez, has been well-traveled for hundreds of years by American Indians, pioneers, and today's wine country seekers who choose the scenic alternative to Highway 101. Stagecoach Road traces the original pathway through the pass, and until a bridge was built in 1963, this winding and rugged road served as the only way across 400-foot-deep Cold Spring Canyon near the top of the pass. These days, more car tires than horse hooves kick up dust along the road, but little else has changed about the former stagecoach stop. Housed in a charming moss-covered shingle cabin with gingham-draped windows and romantic fireplace nooks, nestled among the trees next to a babbling brook, the restaurant and bar have dark interiors furnished with mounted animal trophies, rusty oil lanterns, and memorabilia from the tavern's 100-plus years of service. The lunch menu is simple and hearty, featuring burgers of buffalo, ostrich, or beef, plus sandwiches, salads, and Cold Spring's renowned chili. Dinner is more elegant than you might expect; excellent-quality cuts of meat and fresh vegetables abound. Look for stuffed chicken with sherry–sour cream sauce, barbecued baby back ribs, or rack of lamb with champagne-mint glaze. Venison sausage–stuffed mushrooms in garlic butter is the house appetizer, a tasty but rich artery-clogger best shared. Weekends and nights, especially during summer, the saloon-style bar next door is packed with revelers singing along to Wurlitzer classics or dancing to local bands. In addition to visiting the rustic restaurant and bar, you can roam around the remaining outbuildings and namesake artesian springs that made this spot an ideal watering stop. Don't miss the resident 19 cats, all named George. It'll take you 20 minutes to drive here from downtown, but the incredible coastline views along the way make the romantic trip worthwhile. $$ *AE, MC, V; no checks; breakfast Sat–Sun, lunch, dinner every day; full bar; reservations recommended.*

## EL ENCANTO
♥♥♥

*1900 Lasuen Rd (El Encanto Hotel and Garden Villas), Santa Barbara / 805/687-5000*
El Encanto restaurant, part of the historic hilltop hotel of the same name (see Romantic Lodgings), is indisputably one of the best places in Santa

Barbara to watch the sun set, which immediately qualifies it as a Best Place to Kiss. It's set in an area of Santa Barbara known locally as "the Riviera," and the mountain-to-ocean views from this restaurant's rambling perch are second to none. Whether you're enjoying lunch on a sunny afternoon or dinner under the stars, the food just makes the view seem even grander. Although the stunning tableau might momentarily distract you from your lover's conversation, your taste buds will be concentrating on the cuisine. El Encanto is popular with a crowd that includes many of Santa Barbara's conservative old guard, so they offer a fairly consistent menu that may include appetizers such as carrot cream soup or imported caviar served with buckwheat blini; main courses include paella brimming with local black mussels, Manila clams, chorizo, rock shrimp, chicken, and cilantro. A grilled veal chop arrives with braised endive and red wine–cranberry sauce; rack of lamb is redolent of Provençal herbs; beef tenderloin is enriched by shallot-morel sauce; and vegetarian entrées like grilled asparagus risotto cakes are frequently offered. Superb desserts—such as classic floating island—are served as the stars compete with the harbor lights.
*$$$ AE, DC, MC, V; checks OK; lunch, dinner every day, brunch Sun; full bar; reservations recommended; www.elencantohotel.com.*

## EMILIO'S RISTORANTE AND BAR
◐◐◖

*324 W Cabrillo Blvd, Santa Barbara / 805/966-4426*
At this romantic Italian restaurant, arched windows open to Pacific breezes on warm nights and candles provide the only light as evening sets in. As if that weren't enchanting enough, add whitewashed walls, exposed wood beams, soft jazz, and clinking wineglasses and you've got yourself one romantic dining room. Situated on the water, Emilio's feels like a secret sanctuary in an obscure Italian village, and it's just a short evening stroll away from harbor-front hotels like Hotel Oceana (see Romantic Lodgings). Soulful dishes include oak-grilled salmon and the signature Oscar's Paella, created by longtime staff member Oscar Garcia and overflowing with mussels, clams, and spicy sausage. As you feast, enjoy the ever-changing display of works by local artists. Emilio's also offers great vegetarian selections like a truffle-laced portobello spring roll with sweet pea puree and whipped curry potatoes, house-made sun-dried tomato–goat cheese raviolis topped with braised spinach, or butternut squash tortellini bathed in sage butter and walnuts. Whatever your choice, arrive with a good appetite; the beautiful painted Italian plates bear hefty portions.
*$$ AE, MC, V; no checks; dinner every day; full bar; reservations recommended; www.emiliosrestaurant.com.*

# EPIPHANY
●●

*21 W Victoria St, Santa Barbara / 805/564-7100*
Kevin Costner is one of the partners (with husband-wife team Alberto and Michelle Mastrangelo) in this sparse and elegant new restaurant just off State Street, but there's no Hollywood attitude here. Located in the former 1892 home and office of Santa Barbara's first female doctor, it has a stylish romantic feel, with hardwood floors, and banquettes and couches in striped silk with lots of brushed silk pillows. There are some surprises on the menu, particularly the signature raw bar, made possible because all the fish is sushi grade. Raw bar appetizers include crusted tuna, ceviche, and opa (moonfish) tartare. Main courses include vodka-cured salmon, cured in-house and served with Yukon gold potatoes; Atlantic salmon served with morels, braised leeks, and sauce foie gras; and amberjack (in the tuna family) with fingerling potatoes and heirloom tomatoes. Chef Michael Goodman also offers a roasted beet salad with citrus vinaigrette, quail egg, and brioche toast. The decor throughout is what Michelle calls "urban elegance," with the walls in the bar painted Ralph Lauren red behind the mahogany and marble counter, and the restaurant's walls in a khaki color. The welcoming foyer has a Victorian brick fireplace crowned with a stained-glass window, and candles glow from every corner. If you want to cuddle and smooch, step into Epiphany's seductive lounge, where you can indulge in a specialty martini or sip champagne, nosh on an eclectic bar menu, or enjoy an after-dinner drink on the garden patio.

*$$$ AE, DIS, MC, V; no checks; dinner every day; full bar; reservations recommended; www.epiphanysb.com.* &

# SAGE AND ONION
●●●

*34 E Ortega St, Santa Barbara / 805/963-1012*
A consistent favorite among vacationing couples since it opened in 2000 (and a culinary spawning ground for chefs who've since moved on to other prestigious kitchens), Sage and Onion is located in a beautifully renovated downtown Spanish storefront. The understated room is as stylish and comfortable as a favorite cashmere sweater, with a high ceiling, an elegant wood bar, and chic white table settings that set the mood for a romantic meal. It's an effect one might call classic, aided by a Mediterranean undertone that perfectly suits the "American Riviera." Chef Steven Giles fuses his English heritage, French training, and passion for American food into a contemporary cuisine that's creative without being ostentatious. The kitchen "brigade" (Giles gets high marks for crediting his cooks on the menu) delivers impeccably groomed platters, served by an equally dedicated wait staff. Giles is a farmers' market devotee, always utilizing the region's best and freshest ingredients; menu standouts include quail ravioli in a tangy

gooseberry reduction, Hawaiian ono atop coconut-infused jasmine rice; sea bass bathed in saffron-mussel cream; and the Sage and Onion potpie, a British-inspired crust filled with braised rabbit, sweet onion, and slow-roasted root vegetables. Dessert lovers won't want to miss the perfect version of a liquid center chocolate cake, served here with house-made roasted banana ice cream. For a nostalgic flavor, try the butterscotch pudding, all dressed up with toffee and chantilly cream.

$$$ *AE, MC, V; no checks; lunch Tues–Fri, dinner every day; full bar; reservations recommended; www.sageandonion.com.*

## STONEHOUSE RESTAURANT
ΘΘΘ(

## PLOW & ANGEL BISTRO
ΘΘΘ

*900 San Ysidro Ln (San Ysidro Ranch), Montecito / 805/969-4100 or 800/368-6788*

Though regarded by many as Santa Barbara County's finest gourmet dining, the Stonehouse Restaurant at the exclusive San Ysidro Ranch (see Romantic Lodgings) has a low-key, welcoming atmosphere. The romance starts along a winding tree-lined road in the Montecito foothills and continues when you behold the bucolic setting—the restaurant is housed in the Ranch's 1889 stone-walled citrus packing house, where a warren of small dining spaces lends an intimate feel. Downstairs, the more casual Plow & Angel Bistro occupies the former wine cellar, now warmed with a broad fireplace. One kitchen does dual-duty for both eateries, capitalizing on local seafood and premium meats—as well as produce from the Ranch's own organic garden—to supply a well-crafted menu of American regional cuisine. Sweethearts may want to begin with such tempting starters as phyllo-wrapped baked Brie surrounded by sweet-tart honey-fig-balsamic syrup or Hudson Valley foie gras perfectly accented with peppery and fruity flavors. Main courses range from citrus-braised local lobster accompanied by corn-crab risotto and enhanced with musky truffles to fruit- and fontina-stuffed chicken breast. Lovers trying to reduce those love handles will appreciate the menu's vegetarian, Atkin's, and Zone diet selections. At the equally romantic Plow & Angel, economy-minded twosomes can feast on hearty bistro fare like saffron steamed mussels in Pernod broth, Asian-style pan-seared salmon, expertly grilled steaks and chops, and a prosciutto-laced mac 'n' cheese that's out of this world. In addition, anything from the Stonehouse menu can be served downstairs, allowing the two of you to mix and match flavors (and prices). The wine list is superb, and desserts are worth saving room for.

$$$$ *(Stonehouse)* $$$ *(Bistro) AE, MC, V; checks OK; breakfast, lunch, dinner every day (Stonehouse), dinner every day (Bistro); full bar; reservations recommended; www.sanysidroranch.com.* &

## WINE CASK
✪✪✪✿
*813 Anacapa St, Santa Barbara / 805/966-9463*

While the two of you may consider yourselves the perfect pairing, this sleek and sophisticated restaurant specializes in ideal matches of a different type. As the name implies, the Wine Cask is the place to go for an extensive wine list; and they began pairing fine wines and foods long before it became trendy. Informal elegance in the tradition of great European restaurants has been captured within these stucco walls, which are accented by a stunning hand-stenciled ceiling and a grand stone fireplace. Owner Doug Margerum, who also runs a small adjoining wine shop, presides over a vast cellar of more than 2,000 labels and ensures they will beautifully complement the restaurant's cuisine, a sophisticated repertoire of dream-worthy dishes such as delicate, tangy duck spring rolls; grilled foie gras with apple risotto and blackberry sauce; porcini-crusted salmon; lamb sirloin with mint-infused cabernet sauce; or filet mignon on a bed of truffle-laced potatoes. The best dessert choice is warm peach-caramel napoleon—with a vintage port or Madeira accompaniment. We also recommend the Sunday or Monday prix-fixe tasting, which includes six courses and five wine pairings. An outdoor patio offers a charming alternative to the main room; with trumpet vines twined overhead, hummingbirds, and dappled sunlight under the umbrellas, it couldn't be more romantic, and even more so when star-lit on warm evenings. Aspiring oenophiles might be interested in the Cask's special wine tasting/dining events, which usually include fine hors d'oeuvres and lively conversation, where the perfectly matched two of you can discover excellent vintages in a cordial, polished atmosphere.

$$$ *AE, DC, MC, V; no checks; lunch, dinner every day; full bar; reservations recommended; www.winecask.com.*

# SANTA YNEZ VALLEY WINE COUNTRY

## ROMANTIC HIGHLIGHTS

The beautiful Santa Ynez Valley sits just a short drive from downtown Santa Barbara, but this rural corner of the county offers a completely different flavor from the coastal cool—both literal and figurative—of its close neighbor. When you approach by car, the valley first reveals itself in a tableau of sensuous mountain ranges and a dramatic landscape that evokes the essence and romance of what "old" California was all about. There are three towns—Santa Ynez, Solvang, and Los Olivos—nestled in this fertile triangle, where days are warmer and sunnier than on the coast.

Begin your romantic exploration in **Santa Ynez**, which offers the most authentic look at the valley's 19th-century cattle ranching past, as well as some of its newest shopping and dining. But Santa Ynez remains a farm town whose centerpiece is the historic Santa Ynez Feed & Mill, which still supplies hay, grain, and tack to valley ranchers and cowboys. Spanning just two blocks, downtown Santa Ynez sports false-front Old West façades and down-home hospitality. For a look at conveyances of yesteryear, visit the **Parks-Janeway Carriage House** (corner of Sagunto and Faraday Sts; 805/688-7889), operated by the Santa Ynez Valley Historical Society. This small but exceptional museum comprises the largest collection of horse-drawn vehicles west of the Mississippi, featuring rare examples of stagecoaches, covered wagons, a horse-drawn hearse, personal surreys, and more. Tour-bus groups are common in the valley, drawn to nearby Solvang and to Santa Ynez's **Chumash Casino** (on Hwy 246 in Santa Ynez; 805/686-0855 or 800/728-9997; www.chumashcasino.com), where high-stakes bingo, video gaming, and spirited card games entertain 24 hours a day while adhering to state guidelines that permit gaming on American Indian lands. While the bright lights and noisy clamor of a Las Vegas–style casino aren't everyone's romantic cup of tea, if you're a twosome that loves a full house, you'll be happy to know the Chumash Casino will also boast a hotel and spa by late 2004.

A completely different experience awaits nature lovers who follow Highway 154 south; you'll soon see picturesque **Cachuma Lake** (805/686-5054). The reservoir, created in 1953 by damming the Santa Ynez River, is the primary water source for Santa Barbara County and the centerpiece of a 6,600-acre county park with a flourishing wildlife population and well-developed recreational facilities. Migratory birds—including bald eagles, rarely sighted in these parts—abound during the winter months, and full-time residents include blue herons, osprey, red-tailed hawks, golden eagles, deer, bobcats, and mountain lions. Make a date for one of the naturalist-led eagle or wildlife cruises (805/686-5050) offered year-round on the lake (in winter, bring along a fleecy wrap big enough to snuggle under) and you can appreciate all this bounty together. Camping, boating, and fishing are all popular activities centered around a small marina.

Nearby **Solvang** is one of our state's most popular tourist stops and would probably look out-of-place cutesy if everyone weren't so accustomed to it. Here, everything that can be Danish is Danish: You've never seen so many windmills, cobblestone streets, wooden shoes, and gingerbread trim—even the sidewalk trash cans look like little Danish farmhouses with pitched-roof lids. At night, though, the village truly does radiate a romantic storybook charm, as twinkling lights in the trees illuminate sidewalks free of the midday throngs. Solvang ("sunny field") gets a lot of flak for being a Disney-fied version of its founders' vision, but it does possess a genuine Old World lineage, which the two of you can learn about with a quick visit to the small **Elverhøj Museum** (1624 Elverhoy Wy; 805/686-1211). Set in a traditional, handcrafted Scandinavian-style home, the museum consists of fully furnished typical Danish rooms and artifacts from Solvang's early days. Most intriguing are promotional pamphlets distributed in Nebraska and Iowa nearly 100 years ago to lure more Danes to sunny California.

Solvang can be easily explored on foot, but couples might like to pedal their way around town the old-fashioned way, in a fringe-top surrey from **Surrey Cycles** (Mission Dr and 1st St, on the park; 805/688-0091), which also offers 18-speed bikes suitable for exploring the surrounding hills and wine country. In the center of town, upstairs from the Book Loft and Kaffe Hus, you'll find the **Hans Christian Andersen Museum** (1680 Mission Dr; 805/688-2052), which is more interesting than it sounds. The gallery is filled with memorabilia pertaining to Andersen, father of the modern fairy tale and Danish national hero. In addition to rare and first editions of his works, displays include manuscripts, letters, photographs, and a replica Gutenberg printing press.

But most folks come to Solvang to enjoy Danish smorgasbords; sample delectable Old World pastries, such as those found at the best storefront, **Olsen's Bakery** (1529 Mission Dr; 805/688-6314); and shop in town for gifts and souvenirs—or for bargains at Solvang Designer Outlets.

Every September, the town hosts **Danish Days,** a three-day festival of Old World customs and pageantry; it features a parade, demonstrations of traditional Danish arts, dancing by the Solvang Dancers, and a raffle to win a trip to Denmark. Of course, plenty of *aebleskiver* (Danish apple fritters) are served up along with the fun. February's **Flying Leap Storytelling Festival** (805/688-9533) grows in popularity each year, with events ranging from nationally renowned storytellers to local folks swapping impromptu tales in the park or ghost stories in the school barn.

On the edge of town is an historic building *without* windmills, roof storks, or other Scandinavian embellishment—the **Spanish Mission Santa Ines** (1760 Mission Dr; 805/688-4815; www.missionsantaines.org), built of adobe by American Indians in 1804, destroyed by the earthquake of 1812, partially rebuilt, and then burned in 1824 in a violent American Indian revolt. Santa Ines never regained its initial prosperity or its harmonious existence. Today, little of the original mission remains, but the structures painstakingly replicate the originals. The chapel, still in use for daily services, features the ornate painting and tile work typical of Spanish missions. The grounds also include the well-restored and well-maintained monks' garden, an ideal spot for a brief stroll to regain your romantic composure after all that Danish kitsch!

Farther north, **Los Olivos** is a charming village that looks exactly like the movie set for a small town, complete with a giant flagpole instead of a traffic light to mark its main intersection. Along the town's three-block business district, a wooden boardwalk contributes to the Wild West atmosphere. Although this tiny dot on the map has starred as a backwards Southern hamlet in such TV shows as "Return to Mayberry," Los Olivos sits squarely at the heart of Santa Barbara County's wine country—and it boasts all the upscale sophistication you'd expect from a place that attracts big-city transplants and cosmopolitan tourists. Next to wine touring and dining, the favorite pastime here is shopping, and Los Olivos has more than its share of art galleries and antique shops. **Gallery Los Olivos** (2920 Grand Ave; 805/688-7517) is for serious collectors of regional artists, while **Judith Hale Gallery** (2890 Grand Ave; 805/688-1222; www.judithhalegallery.com) showcases paintings and Navajo-crafted silver jewelry—and there are many more shops awaiting your leisurely discovery.

Since kisses taste better with a drop of the noble grape upon your lips, we wholeheartedly recommend touring the many Santa Ynez Valley wineries, each of which offers a unique experience and a chance to stock your home wine cellar. You might think of Santa Barbara County as a "new" wine region, but winemaking here is a 200-year-old tradition, first practiced by Franciscan friars at the area's missions. In the past 20 to 30 years, area vintners have been gaining recognition, and today wine grapes are one of the top crops in the county. Pick up a copy of the widely available **Winery Touring Map** and let the adventure begin. If you'd like to sample wines without driving around, head to **Los Olivos Tasting Room & Wine Shop** (2905 Grand Ave; 805/688-7406; www.losolivoswines.com), located in the heart of town, or **Los Olivos Wine & Spirits Emporium** (2531 Grand Ave; 805/688-4409; www.sbwines.com), a friendly barn in a field half a mile away. Both offer a wide selection, including wines from vintners who don't have their own tasting rooms.

## Access and Information

The Santa Ynez Valley sits neatly in the triangle created by Highways 101, 246, and 154. Highway 101 is the major freeway through the area, traveling north from Santa Barbara through the valley. Highway 154 is the alternate, more scenic route from downtown Santa Barbara, climbing the San Marcos Pass and skirting Lake Cachuma before descending to the town of Santa Ynez and continuing on a northern loop to intersect Highway 101 near Los Olivos. Highway 246 links the two, serving as the main route from Santa Ynez to Solvang, and then on to Buellton where it intersects Highway 101.

For more information on this region of Santa Barbara County, contact the **Santa Barbara Conference & Visitors Bureau** (805/966-9222 or 800/927-4688; www.santabarbaraca.com); you can also pick up a glossy **Destination Guide** at the **Solvang Visitor Bureau** (1511 Mission Dr; 805/688-6144 or 800/GO-SOLVANG; www.solvangusa.com). There's a comprehensive **Santa**

Ynez Valley Visitors Association (800/742-2843; www.santaynezvalley visit.com), and the Santa Barbara County Vintners' Association (805/688-0881 or 800/218-0881; www.sbcountywines.com) produces a winery touring map that's widely available throughout the county at visitor centers, lodgings, stores, and, of course, wineries.

# Romantic Lodgings

## ALISAL GUEST RANCH & RESORT
🌸🌸
*1054 Alisal Rd, Solvang / 805/688-6411 or 800/4-ALISAL*
Part of a working cattle ranch, this rustic yet quietly posh retreat is ideal for the couple seeking the romance of the Old West. But you certainly won't be asked to pitch hay or groom horses—it might interfere with your horseback riding, golfing, poolside lounging, or general amorous pursuits. Alisal is Spanish for "alder grove," and the ranch is nestled in a vast, tree-shaded canyon, offering 73 guest cottages equipped with wood-burning fireplaces, refrigerators, and covered brick porches ideal for sitting and smooching amid the scenery. There aren't any TVs or phones to spoil your togetherness, but restless lovers will never tire of the resort's activities, which include hiking, playing tennis or croquet, bicycling, and fishing in the Alisal's private lake, where sailboats, paddleboats, and canoes sit ready for use. Wildlife abounds on the ranch's 10,000 acres, so don't be surprised by your audience of eagles, hawks, deer, coyotes, and mountain lions. Golf here is top-notch, with two championship 18-hole courses, both of which offer impeccably maintained fairways accented by mature oak, sycamore, and eucalyptus trees. The River Course, which is also open to the public, winds along the Santa Ynez River and offers spectacular mountain vistas. Resident PGA and LPGA pros are on hand for instruction. As if a visit here weren't sybaritic enough, a breakfast buffet and sit-down dinner, featuring fresh local ingredients and a wide range of choices like grilled steaks, chicken, ribs, and fresh local seafood, are included, and during the day a poolside snack bar and a golf-course grill make it entirely possible to never leave this peaceful getaway. In the evening, the upscale ranch-style Oak Room lounge features live entertainment in a comfortable setting the perfect way to end a romantic day. Once you have settled into life at the Alisal, you'll have a whole new appreciation for the concept of "home on the range," and the easygoing atmosphere and slower pace is truly something you easily could get used to. However, families flock to the Alisal during spring break, winter vacation, and summer recess, so lovers should time their visit for when the kids are in school in order to enjoy a more adult-oriented romantic ambience.
$$$$ *AE, MC, V; checks OK; www.alisal.com.* ♿

# THE BALLARD INN
❂❂❂

*2436 Baseline Ave, Ballard / 805/688-7770 or 800/638-2466*
Occupying just a few square blocks, Ballard is the Santa Ynez Valley's smallest community, but its strong romantic appeal seduces many who flock here for its popular gourmet restaurant and the valley's most charming bed-and-breakfast. Situated midway between Los Olivos and Solvang, Ballard is surrounded by apple orchards and horse farms kept with as much care as any Kentucky breeding farm. Built to look as though it had been standing proud for 100 years, this two-story gray-and-white inn is actually of modern construction, offering contemporary comforts to gentleman farmers and city-weary lovebirds alike. Charming country details lend a romantic air, from the wicker rocking chairs that decorate the inn's wraparound porch to the white picket fence and the carefully tended rosebushes. Step inside and the first thing you'll notice is a fire warming the giant hearth that serves both the lobby and the inn's reception desk. The downstairs public rooms, including an enormous sunny parlor, are tastefully furnished with a comfortable mix of hand-hooked rugs, bent-twig furniture, and vintage accessories. A grand oak staircase leads to the authentic Americana guest rooms that are each decorated according to a theme from the valley's history or geography and range in style from Western to country-elegant to grandmotherly. Seven of the rooms have wood-burning fireplaces to snuggle beside, and several boast private balconies for surveying the countryside. The most romantic (and most expensive) is the Mountain Room, a minisuite decorated in rich forest green, with a fireplace and a private balcony. Other favorites are the Vineyard Room, with a grapevine motif and a large bay window, and Davy Brown's Room, whose tall stone fireplace, wood paneling, and hand-stitched quilt lend a log-cabin appeal. Included in the rate are a gracious wine and hors d'oeuvres reception each afternoon, evening coffee and tea, and a delicious full breakfast each morning; be forewarned, however, that a 10 percent service charge is added to your bill. The Ballard Inn Restaurant, tucked into a cozy room downstairs by a crackling fire, has recently been reinvented by heavy hitter San Francisco chef Budi Kazali, who plans to marry the quiet exclusivity of the small restaurant with his signature East-meets-West fusion cuisine. Still in the works at press time, the gourmet menu will include Sonoma duck breast with sweet potato puree and balsamic reduction, spicy grilled quail on arugula Thai salad, and pan-seared scallops atop lemongrass risotto. We expect the restaurant's trademark mood lighting, impressive wine list, and intrinsic intimacy not to change a bit. The restaurant is open for dinner Wednesday through Sunday.
$$$–$$$$ *AE, MC, V; checks OK; www.ballardinn.com.* ♿

# FESS PARKER'S WINE COUNTRY INN & SPA

🌸🌸

*2860 Grand Ave, Los Olivos / 805/688-7788 or 800/446-2455*

With an elegance (and a price) that comes dangerously close to being out of place in this unpretentious town, the newest holding in the wine-country dynasty of Fess Parker is still worth considering for a very memorable romantic getaway: the state-of-the-art pampering will make you and your sweetheart feel special. After taking over the former Los Olivos Grand Hotel, Parker inaugurated a deluxe spa featuring French treatments that use ocean products such as seaweed, algae, and mud in a variety of exfoliating and soothing therapies. For the ultimate in private pampering, a trio of scrubs, baths, and other rub-on potions can be placed in your room—complete with bathrobes, extra towels, and detailed instructions for self-application (or applying to one another). Each of the spacious guest rooms is luxuriously appointed, with a fireplace, oversized bathroom (some have Jacuzzi tubs), wet bar, and cozy down comforter. A turndown fairy leaves Godiva chocolates on your pillow. The inn's decor conjures up the feel of a tasteful French country home of a Parisian dignitary. Staying in the main building will make the two of you feel more like a country-house guest, but the annex across the street has easier access to the heated outdoor swimming pool and whirlpool. A warm lobby/sitting room woos romance seekers with its fire roaring in the main hearth; there's also a quiet cocktail lounge and a pretty back garden often used for weddings or small luncheons. After a day of touring the Santa Ynez Wine Country, the Vintage Room provides an idyllic place for a romantic repast. The formality of the dining room may seem out of place at first, but candles flickering at every table and dimly lit wall sconces set a relaxed, romantic mood. Warm color tones create a sense of intimacy and complement the antiques and fresh flowers placed around the plush dining room. Aiming high, Parker brought in some culinary heavy hitters for the Vintage Room and created a polished spot that wouldn't be out of place in one of L.A.'s or San Francisco's choicer hotels. Breakfast and lunch are a notch above average, but dinner is the best, with choices like pan-seared scallops glazed with pinot noir served atop potatoes whipped purple with beets, pan-seared venison medallions with a couscous flan accented with Asian pear-molasses chutney, or herb-crusted halibut alongside Dungeness crab dumplings bathed in tamari-ginger jus. $$$$ *AE, DC, DIS, MC, V; checks OK; www.FessParker.com.* ᦞ

# SANTA YNEZ INN

🌸🌸🌸

*3627 Sagunto St, Santa Ynez / 805/688-5588 or 800/643-5774*

Wine lovers who savor the good life now have a luxurious hotel to bed down in after a romantic day of "swill and chill." Set in the up-and-coming Western-rich outpost of Santa Ynez, this 14-room Victorian-style

inn features Frette linens, DVD/CD systems, beautiful extensive gardens, an on-site minispa, and personalized white-glove treatment. Each guest room sports a richly dramatic decor—some have balconies with valley and vineyard views—and it's all done up in a bygone style of elegance and opulence orchestrated by owners Douglas and Christine Ziegler, whose attention to detail is astounding. Though the inn is newly built, the Zieglers were determined to replicate the style prevalent 100 years ago when Santa Ynez was a major overnight coach stop. They painstakingly sought reproduction antique fixtures with modern technology, including Victorian-style lamps with dimmers, remote-control gas hearths behind grand mantels, and authentic-looking door handles with microchip security. The all-marble bathrooms are royal in size and scope, featuring dual steam showers, oversized vanities, completely addictive apricot bath products, and innovative Ultra Tub whirlpools, which use powerful air jets (thus eliminating some people's concerns about recirculated water). You can make a faux-dramatic grand entrance down the main staircase each morning to the formal dining room, where breakfast is a multicourse treat straight from the pages of an Edith Wharton novel (but scaled down for today's palates), and the inn offers enough day-long munching that guests need never leave: afternoon tea and snacks, evening wine and hot hors d'oeuvres, and a scrumptious dessert hour before bedtime. Room service is also available from the Cal-American restaurant next door, the Vineyard House (3631 Sagunto St; 805/688-2886; www.thevineyardhouse.com); this converted Victorian landmark shares ownership and ambience with the Inn—plus some of the same breathtaking cross-valley views. Open for lunch and dinner, the Vineyard House features such signature dishes as crispy buttermilk chicken and salmon with spinach.
$$$$ AE, DIS, MC, V; checks OK (30 days prior to arrival); www.santaynezinn.com. &

## UNION HOTEL & VICTORIAN MANSION
♦

*362 Bell St, Los Alamos / 805/344-2744 or 800/230-2744*
Seemingly destined to slide quietly into ghost-town status with the construction of Highway 101, the former stagecoach stop of Los Alamos reinvented itself as an authentic Old West attraction, complete with wooden boardwalks and an enormous antique showcase in the former train depot, plus the historic Union Hotel & Victorian Mansion. This lodging duo, a fantastic time-travel fantasy, simply must be seen to be believed. The partially original Union Hotel has boardinghouse-style rooms upstairs and a dining room and saloon below—much like it did back when it was built in 1880. In 1972, the late Dick Langdon began painstakingly restoring the hotel to 19th-century authenticity, using old photographs to ensure an exact re-creation. Walk through the front door, and it's like walking on the set of

the "Wild Wild West TV" series. Overstuffed velvet wing chairs adorn the front parlor, gilded wrought-iron grating frames the bell desk, and swinging saloon doors lead into the adjacent barroom. Upstairs, where fading carpet runners and creaky hardware reinforce the illusion, most of the rooms share a common bath (although they're equipped with in-room sinks). A single shower room is the hotel's only concession to modernity; the few rooms with private baths are best suited for romancing overnighters, but they have only a tub—claw-footed, of course. Even though the double beds overwhelm the simple, tiny bedrooms, the charm of this place is truly infectious. Breakfast—a generous family-style feast—is included, and diversions like billiards, shuffleboard, and card tables provide entertainment. The hotel's period-style dining room also serves dinner on weekends, offering steaks, seafood, and a nightly family special.

Next door stands the Victorian Mansion, an ornate Queen Anne built around 1890 in nearby Nipomo. Langdon moved it here, then spent nine years creating over-the-top B&B theme rooms that simply scream "tryst" to anyone with a theatrical sense of humor. Each has a fireplace, a hot tub, a chilled bottle of champagne upon arrival, and a secret door through which breakfast appears each morning. Sleep in the '50s Room and you'll bed down in a vintage Cadillac at a drive-in movie, watching *Rebel Without a Cause*. The Pirate Room is a schooner's stateroom where lanterns sway gently and the sound of seagulls provides the backdrop for the 1938 film *The Buccaneer*. The Egyptian Room, a tapestry-laden sheik's tent, boasts a hieroglyphic-papered bathroom entered through a mummy's sarcophagus while *Cleopatra* plays onscreen—you get the idea. If you choose the Victorian Mansion for its privacy, be sure to stop into the Union Hotel—or its saloon—just to say you've been there.

$$ *(Union Hotel)* $$$$ *(Victorian Mansion) AE, DIS, MC, V; no checks; www.unionhotelvictmansion.com.* &

---

# Romantic Restaurants

## BROTHERS RESTAURANT AT MATTEI'S TAVERN
🌣🌣🌣

*2350 Railway Ave, Los Olivos / 805/688-4820*
Share a dinner experience that deftly combines the romance of the Santa Ynez Valley's colorful frontier past with the delicious wine-country cuisine that's grown from its current appeal. Mattei's Tavern is a Los Olivos landmark, a rambling white Victorian that's submerged in wisteria and history: Italian-Swiss immigrant Felix Mattei built the roadside tavern in 1886 to accommodate stagecoach travelers preparing for the mountainous journey to Santa Barbara. Although the tavern stopped accepting overnight guests in the 1960s, Mattei's has always been known throughout the county for fun,

good food, and even romance, a reputation that continues now that brothers Jeff and Matt Nichols—two creative L.A.-trained chefs—have reinvented the kitchen while keeping the rest of Mattei's thankfully intact. Couples might find themselves seated in one of several downstairs dining rooms: in the Mattei family's formal dining room, on the white-wicker enclosed sun porch, or inside the former water tower, looking up through the skylight at owls nesting atop the structure. The brothers' seasonal California-international menu emphasizes the bounty of the fertile surrounding valley and is composed to pair well with the abundant local wines. Grill selections include Scottish salmon on vegetable rice, accented with roasted bell pepper salsa. A tender rack of lamb is fanned over mashed potatoes studded with tangy black olives on a rich rosemary sauce. Desserts, often as numerous as main course choices, include a fudge brownie with house-made roasted banana ice cream, warm chocolate truffle cake, and fresh sorbets served with Mom's oatmeal cookies.

$$$ *MC, V; local checks only; dinner every day; full bar; reservations recommended.* &

# CABERNET BISTRO
❤❤

*478 4th Pl, Solvang / 805/693-1152*
There's a little pocket of France ensconced in the otherwise Danish town of Solvang, and it's been steadily praised by even the most worldly of gourmands. Chef-owner Jacques Toulet comes from a family of restaurateurs in the Pyrenees and developed a fine reputation in Los Angeles when he and his brother opened their own restaurant, Les Pyrenees, in Santa Monica in the 1970s. A decade ago, Jacques and his wife, Diana, moved to the Santa Ynez Valley and opened Cabernet Bistro. Open beams, antiques, and light pink tablecloths make the dining room elegant but relaxed, an all-around romantic choice whether you're celebrating a special occasion or simply sharing an intimate dinner for two guaranteed to flirt with your palates. The menu offers veal Escoffier with morel mushrooms, T-bone steak, and fresh swordfish, as well as quail and rack of lamb. The signature dish is duck; you can order duck à l'orange, duck amaretto, duck with peppercorn sauce, duck with cherries, and duck cassis, and those aren't the only duck options. In fact, they sell 2,000 orders of duck a year, even in this town known for Danish pancakes. Honeymooners might be especially drawn to the provocatively named Wedding of Neptune entrée, but this marriage of tender whitefish and salmon inside a delicate puff pastry with a creamy tarragon sauce is also a house specialty. For dessert with an extra romantic punch, order the creamy almond praline cake, invented by Jacques for Diana for their wedding anniversary.

$$-$$$ *AE, DIS, MC, V; no checks; dinner Thurs–Tues; beer and wine; reservations recommended; www.cabernetbistro.com.* &

## CHEF RICK'S
🏵️🏵️

*1095 Edison St, Santa Ynez / 805/693-5100*
For couples who love a party almost as much as they love each other, this new casual dining spot is a festive addition to the wine-country savvy core of otherwise rustic Santa Ynez. Chef Rick's just feels jovial, with bright colors splashed everywhere, from the purple-and-red table linens and clusters of fresh flowers brightening every corner to the bold ethnic artwork that adorns the simple walls of this large and welcoming restaurant. Rough-hewn Mexican furniture evokes the feel of a sun-splashed patio south of the border, and it's a perfect backdrop for the eclectic world cuisine of chef Rick Manson, which fans have grown to love at his original eatery in Santa Maria. This nearly identical sister branch is in the heart of Santa Ynez Valley action and is wooing a whole new crowd of wine-country trysters eager for an international take on California cuisine, spiced up with a zesty southern flair. Highlights of the lip-smacking menu include such well-honed crowd pleasers as crunch-tastic coconut beer shrimp; fried green tomato salad (served with one of Manson's four patented and bottled dressings, in this case, green onion); Cajun meatloaf po'boy sandwich with spicy "fire" fries; black bean raviolis with Yucatán-inspired chile sauce; and shrimp-crusted sea bass with sweet potato crisps. Desserts follow the same more-is-more philosophy, ensuring that no one leaves hungry. Though this bright and open room—and the highly visible patio dining outside the front door—won't do much for intimate conversation, Chef Rick's creations will add another kind of spice to your romantic evening.
$$ *AE, DIS, MC, V; checks OK; lunch, dinner every day; beer and wine; reservations recommended; www.chefricks.com.* ♿

---

## HITCHING POST
🏵️❤️

*406 E Hwy 246, Buellton / 805/688-0676*
Would you believe the *New York Times* and *Gourmet* magazine have praised this steak house in sleepy Buellton, calling it one of the best in the country? Looking for all the world like an ordinary roadhouse, it offers oak-fired barbecue steaks, lamb, pork, turkey, seafood, and smoked duck, not to mention grilled artichokes with smoked tomato mayonnaise. These robust meals are served to meat lovers with the restaurant's own label of pinot noir, made and bottled at local Au Bon Climat/Qupe winery. The bar also functions as a tasting room for house-produced wines. By the time you smell the wood-burning fire pit from outside, you're helpless to resist being lured inside by the promise of regional fare that harkens back to the valley's earliest ranching days. Plenty of arm-in-arm couples file in alongside the local ranchers and well-heeled horsey folk who appreciate good value and a full plate, for this is an old-style joint where one price includes your appetizer,

side dishes, and even dessert—for those who still have room. The restaurant is dark and rustic, a real man's kind of place, with photographs of actual and would-be cowboys on a trail ride in the 1940s. Owner Frank Ostini's family has been in the business of serving up Santa Maria–style grilled meats since they bought the original Hitching Post in Casmalia, the year he was born—50 years ago. His brothers now run that one. Frank has had the Buellton version, which he thinks of as "Hitching Post 2," for 15 years. If the two of you get hooked on the steaks, you can later order and have them sent to you in Central or Southern California, already seasoned and grilled, via two-day UPS. The staff cooks them rare, packs them up, and ships them overnight, with instructions on how to reheat them and re-create your memorable meal at this Central Coast landmark.

**$$** *AE, MC, V; checks OK; dinner every day; full bar; reservations recommended; www.hitchingpostwines.com.* &

---

# NUUVA RESTAURANT & CAFE AT THE BALLARD STORE
❤❤

*2449 Baseline Ave, Ballard / 805/686-2430*

The tiny town of Ballard has long been anchored by the historic Ballard Store, a one-time farmers' grocery and supply outpost that's become a beloved landmark in the Santa Ynez Valley. It's been years since livestock feed, tractor parts, and gingham bolts have stocked the shelves, but the Ballard Store has kept pace with the times, preserving its vintage country exterior in keeping with the built-to-look-historic Ballard Inn directly across the street. Surprisingly, the small market out front has always hidden a well-regarded restaurant entered from the adjacent side street, but that dining room has just traded its homemade checked curtains and folksy farmhouse ambience for a big-city sophistication. Taken over in mid-2004 by trendy Santa Barbara restaurateurs, the interior now sports a low-lit and stylish blend of moss-colored walls, chic black napkins, modern black-and-white photography, and indirect lighting along with the well-weathered original wood floors. Candles and soft jazz provide an after-dark romantic accent, especially at the kiss-encouraging tables around their gently flaming hearth. The black-clad service staff still stumbles over some new haute cuisine lingo like "nage" and "coulis," while carrying out platters of Nuuva's highlights: Mediterranean-flavored roasted mussels, rich lobster risotto with caviar and tangy lemon, salmon over a rice-couscous pilaf bathed in a coconut curry sauce, and a respectable New York steak with tempura onions and green peppercorns. The front store has been reborn as a breakfast/lunch cafe and coffee bar, with happy outdoor tables for watching the world go by.

**$$–$$$** *AE, MC, V; no checks; breakfast, lunch every day, dinner Tues–Sun; full bar; reservations recommended.* &

# SAN LUIS OBISPO AREA

## ROMANTIC HIGHLIGHTS

**P**retty San Luis Obispo can't be seen from Highway 101 and, as a result, many motorists think the Madonna Inn, a perpetually pink roadside honeymoon haven (see Romantic Lodgings) is all there is to the place. But nothing could be further from the truth; with its beautiful surrounding countryside, charming neighborhoods of historic cottages, and developing wine region nearby, SLO—as the locals call it—is a romantic destination packed with excellent kissing spots just far enough off the beaten path to lend an exhilarating air of discovery to your amorous exploration. Of course, the big-city transplants who live in this relaxed yet vital college town might argue that everything's already been discovered, but even with the influx of new residents and commerce, SLO's downtown is wonderfully compact and perfect for exploring on foot, while the county's sparkling coastline communities—including Pismo Beach and Avila Beach—are only minutes away.

Like several other charming Central Coast towns, this one began life as a Spanish mission outpost. Founding friar Junípero Serra chose this valley in 1772, based on reports of friendly natives and bountiful food, and established **Mission San Luis Obispo de Tolosa** (782 Monterey St; 805/781-8220; www.oldmissionslo.org), whose well-restored mission church, padres' quarters, and colonnade are in the heart of town, fronted by the pedestrian-friendly Mission Plaza, a pretty park that serves as SLO's town square for festivals and other events. Spend a relaxing day hand-in-hand, simply strolling, shopping, and exploring SLO's compact downtown; start with a visit to the **San Luis Obispo Chamber of Commerce** (1039 Chorro St; 805/781-2777; www.visitslo.com), where you can pick up the colorful, comprehensive **Visitors Guide** and the self-guided **Mission Plaza Walking Tour**.

On Thursday nights, everyone comes out for the **Farmers' Market** (Higuera St, between Osos and Nipomo Sts; 6:30–9pm), a beloved local tradition. Emptied of auto traffic, Higuera Street fills with a colorful and festive assemblage of vendors and entertainers. Shoppers stroll through, clutching bags of luscious fruits and vegetables, fresh flowers, locally made arts and crafts, and warm baked goods. The sounds of Peruvian street musicians, old-fashioned brass bands, or lively dance troupes fill the air as the tantalizing aroma of oak barbecue wafts from sidewalk grills. For an affordable romantic adventure, come hungry and graze your way through a classic SLO evening that won't break the bank.

Lovers of fresh air and outdoor activity might want to explore on two wheels; SLO County is a terrific region for bicycling, with scenic terrain for riders of all levels. Pick up the **San Luis Obispo County Bike Map**, a color-coded guide that includes mileage, terrain descriptions, and a list of local bike shops, available at the chamber of commerce.

Whether you and your sweetie venture out by bicycle or car, try a short excursion to **Avila Beach**, where half the fun is in getting there; from San Luis Obispo, scenic San Luis Bay Drive leads toward the ocean, a quiet country road embraced by lush foliage and unfolding vistas. During the late summer and fall harvest seasons, take a romantic detour into woodsy, sun-dappled See Canyon, where makeshift roadside fruit stands and U-pick signs mark this apple-producing region. Continuing on, you'll come to **Sycamore Mineral Springs**, a 100-year-old therapeutic hot springs that's long been regarded as a quintessentially sexy rendezvous for its secluded hillside hot tubs and magical **Gardens of Avila** dining room (see Romantic Lodgings and Romantic Restaurants). San Luis Obispo Bay is as lovely as ever, with its azure, crescent-shaped natural harbor filled with bobbing sailboats. Follow its natural curve to the Old San Luis Pier for a day's sport fishing or a hearty fresh-caught meal. Avila Beach is a little bit like Rip Van Winkle, just waking from a period when it was effectively asleep for several years. After an environmental tragedy from the seepage of underground crude oil, the waterfront was essentially leveled to allow for complete cleanup. At press time, the still-bare town was starting to flourish with attractive bay-front seating and landscaping, the resurgence of local businesses—like the casual **Custom House Restaurant** (404 Front St; 805/595-7555; www.oldcustom house.com) overlooking the bay—and plans call for Avila Beach to spring back to the sunny and popular resort it once was, though perhaps a little less funky. No amount of soil contamination could destroy the charm of Avila's picture-perfect cove, surrounded by mountains and dramatic ocean cliffs. One enduring pleasure is the **Pecho Coast Trail**, a 3½-mile hike leading to the Point San Luis Lighthouse. The landmark lighthouse, built in 1889 in the Prairie Victorian style, is the only remaining example of its type on the West Coast. Organized by the Land Conservancy, docent-led hikes ascend steep cliffs to attain stunning views. The entire hike takes about half a day, departing about 9am. For schedule and reservations, call 805/541-8735.

About 15 minutes south of downtown SLO lies **Pismo Beach**—and its upscale neighbor **Shell Beach**—where vacationers have been heading for the romance of a classic beach town since the dawn of SoCal surf culture in the 1950s. The native Chumash, who lived here as far back as 9,000 years ago, named Pismo Beach for the abundance of *pismu*, or tar, found in the sand—and you might still find gray traces on your feet after a day on the beach (hence the "tar-off" wipes provided in most local hotel rooms). Today's Pismo is a time-warp shrine to days when California beach towns were unpretentious places meant for just goofing off: Surfers roam the sands year-round, drawn by the timeless song of that siren, the perfect wave, and upscale weekenders come to let it all hang out (even though the

263

new beachfront resorts are the height of luxury). Here is where you'll find the acclaimed Pismo clam, which reached near extinction in the mid-1980s due to overzealous harvesting. If you'd like to get your feet wet digging for bivalves, you'll need to obtain a license and follow strict guidelines. But it might be a little more romantic to simply come for the annual **Clam Festival**. Held at the pier each October since 1946, the weekend celebration features a chowder cook-off, a sand-sculpture contest, the Miss Pismo Beach pageant, and a competitive clam dig. If you're around between October and March, don't miss a kiss amid the **monarch butterfly preserve** (on Pacific Coast Hwy in nearby Grover Beach). The brilliantly colored monarchs nest in a grove of eucalyptus and Monterey pine, where an information board tells you about their unique habits. During cold weather (below 40°F), they remain densely clustered on tree branches, but on warm days you'll see their stately orange-and-black wings fluttering throughout the area as they search for flower nectar.

The nectar that's been drawing increasing numbers of lovebirds to San Luis Obispo County, though, is fine wine produced by the area's 20 or so wineries. Often overshadowed by the Central Coast wine regions in Paso Robles and the Santa Ynez Valley, the **wineries in the Edna Valley**—in the foothills between San Luis Obispo and the town of Arroyo Grande—are slowly but surely coming into their own. Though the best known, Corbett Canyon Vintners, is not open to the public, most of the others are, and they offer a uniquely personal tasting experience that's scenic and unpretentious. Pick up a winery map, pack a picnic lunch, and take your sweetheart on a relaxing country excursion that's perfect for wine neophytes as well as experienced imbibers.

# Access and Information

Highway 101 runs right into San Luis Obispo, skirting the downtown area despite tall trees that keep the freeway well hidden from view and muffle any traffic noise. Marsh Street and Higuera Street—both one way, in opposing directions—are the town's main drags for commerce, and the centrally located Mission Plaza is at the corner of Higuera and Broad Streets.

Though there is a small commercial airport about 3 miles south of town, SLO's convenient location—a 3½ hour drive from Los Angeles—means most visitors arrive by car. The city's charming, old-fashioned train station is served by two **Amtrak** (800/USA-RAIL; www.amtrak.com) trains, one that runs as far south as San Diego and another that travels north to Seattle. It's a slower but much more romantic way to travel and enjoy the scenery—and time alone together. The San Luis Obispo station is about six blocks from downtown.

For more information on what to see and do, contact the **San Luis Obispo Chamber of Commerce** (1039 Chorro St; 805/781-2777; www.visitslo.com) or visit the **San Luis Obispo County Visitors & Conference Bureau** (1037 Mill St; 805/781-2531 or 800/634-1414; www.sanluisobispocounty.com). At the coast, the **Pismo Beach Chamber of Commerce** (581 Dolliver St; 805/773-4382 or 800/443-7778; www. classiccalifornia.com or www.pismochamber .com) can provide additional lodging and event information. If you're planning a winery excursion, contact the **San Luis Obispo Vintners & Growers Association** (5828 Orcutt Rd; 805/541-5868; www.slowine.com) for a map and helpful tips.

# Romantic Lodgings

## APPLE FARM INN
❤❤
*2015 Monterey St, San Luis Obispo / 805/544-2040 or 800/255-2040*
Don't let the location of this inn, set on the edge of San Luis Obispo's business district, deter you from venturing inside. Although the inn is run like a hotel and the 103 rooms do have some hotel-like characteristics, this ultra-popular frilly getaway is remarkably quiet and always booked well in advance by couples who know there's enough country charm to make the Apple Farm definitely kiss worthy. The entire complex—which includes a restaurant, gift shop, and working cider mill—exhibits an over-the-top Victorian-style cuteness, with floral wallpaper, fresh flowers, and sugar-sweet touches. No two guest rooms are alike, although each has a gas fireplace, a large bathroom with plush terry robes, canopies over queen- or king-sized beds, and lavish country decor. Some bedrooms open onto cozy turreted sitting areas with romantic window seats, while others have wide bay windows overlooking the creek that rambles through the property. Extra-special occasions call for a stay in one of two Millhouse suites, which feature balconies and private hot tubs, and where the two of you can drift off to sleep to the sound of the gently splashing waterwheel. Sparkling cider and chocolate kisses are part of the welcoming package, and complimentary coffee and tea can be delivered to your room; sleepyheads can also opt for breakfast in bed (for an additional cost). Rooms in the motel-style Trellis Court building have the same amenities as those in the main inn (including fireplaces and cozy decor); they cost less but also appeal more to families (something to consider when you're looking for tranquil grown-up time). The hotel also has a heated outdoor swimming pool and Jacuzzi, and there's unlimited hot apple cider on hand in the lobby. If you want not only the convenience of staying in town and the amenities found in full-service hotels, but also

country hospitality and a little romance, then you'll surely be happy at the Apple Farm Inn.
*$$$ (Main Inn) $$ (Trellis Court) AE, DIS, MC, V; checks OK; www.applefarm.com.* &

## THE CLIFFS AT SHELL BEACH
◐◐

*2757 Shell Beach Rd, Shell Beach / 805/773-5000 or 800/826-7827*
What it lacks in personality, this efficiently luxurious cliff-top resort hotel makes up for in comfort, and a boutique style of personalized service that belies its 165-room size. Guest rooms are light and airy, stylishly redone to sport a business-goes-to-the-beach decor of warm sand and water tones, sleek Euro-modern light wood furniture, and pale, creamy marble bathrooms outfitted with hair dryers and irons that make a carefree romantic getaway that much easier. Private balconies make the most of oceanfront breezes, and though most rooms gaze *toward* the Pacific, those with uninterrupted views are a sublime splurge that virtually guarantees a passionate return on your investment. Poolside beverages and snack service give more reason to recline by the heated swimming pool and whirlpool, which are shielded from the wind and situated to capitalize on the bay views. The Cliffs has its own spa, so a massage or facial are a convenient conclusion to a day of sightseeing or wine touring. If the two of you are feeling lazy, a more leisurely treat is to hit the beach, accessible via a private staircase that zigzags down to a prime, albeit small, strip of sandy beach. (However, be forewarned that high tide comes nearly to the base of the cliffs.) The adjacent Sea Cliffs Restaurant features an eclectic menu of grilled meats and fish accented by international flavors—a little Caribbean here, a little Pacific Rim there. Asian cioppino and Texas BBQ half chicken are among the diverse menu options. Open for breakfasts and dinners, the ocean-view restaurant is more formal than it ought to be considering the area. However, it does have a terrific wine list featuring Central Coast labels reasonably priced and available by the glass. The only Sunday brunch more extensive and formal than the one served here is down the coast at Santa Barbara's Four Seasons.
*$$$–$$$$ AE, DC, DIS, MC, V; no checks; www.cliffsresort.com.* &

## GARDEN STREET INN
◐◐

*1212 Garden St, San Luis Obispo / 805/545-9802*
The prettiest accommodations in town are here in this gracious Italianate– Queen Anne bed-and-breakfast near downtown. Built in 1887 and fully restored in 1990, the house is a romantic monument to Victorian gentility and to the good taste of owners Dan and Kathy Smith. At the Garden Street Inn, nostalgic twosomes can indulge the fantasy of being well-to-do gentry

with a turn-of-the-century townhouse a short stroll from downtown SLO's own historic landmarks. That's certainly how Dollie McKeen must've felt, tending this mansion for four decades; a luxury suite named for her is the inn's finest boudoir, with gilded crown molding, fine rich furnishings, and an ornate antique fireplace. Each bedroom and suite is decorated with well-chosen antique armoires, opulent fabric or paper wall coverings, and vintage memorabilia. Choose your romantic fantasy, whether it includes a claw-footed tub, fireplace, Jacuzzi tub, or private deck—there's one to suit every fancy. Most honeymooners and amorous celebrants can't help but select The Lovers, a flowering English garden of a suite named after Picasso's famous painting and embellished with a gorgeous canopy bed, whirlpool tub, and serenely private balcony. Breakfast is served in the morning room as the sun filters through original stained-glass windows, and each evening wine and cheese are laid out for guests. When all you want to do is cocoon here with your sweetheart, choose a literary inspiration from the inn's well-stocked library and while away the hours.
*$$$ AE, MC, V; checks OK; www.gardenstreetinn.com.* &

## MADONNA INN
♠

*100 Madonna Rd, San Luis Obispo / 805/543-3000 or 800/543-9666*
The Madonna Inn loudly entreats lovers with a sense of humor to take a break from good taste and have a memorably tacky experience to giggle about for years to come. Conjured from the fertile imaginations of local icons Alex and Phyllis Madonna (Alex, who passed away in 2004, was a lifelong Central Coast resident responsible for much of the local construction boom), this eccentric hotel is a wild fantasy world where faux-rock waterfalls, velvet-flecked wallpaper, marbled mirrors, and deep shag carpeting are just the beginning. The only consistent element of the decor is Phyllis Madonna's favorite color, a ubiquitous pink that pops up even on the bath product labels. The 109 rooms are individually decorated in themes so unusual the Madonna Inn sells 109 different postcards—just in case your friends can't believe you slept in digs reminiscent of "The Flintstones." Everybody's kiss-and-don't-tell favorites include the all-rock Caveman rooms, featuring waterfall showers and giant animal-print rugs. Other over-the-top options include Swiss Chalet and English Manor, which look like they sound. Many guests of this Disneyland-for-adults request their favorite rooms annually, celebrating anniversaries or New Year's Eve, and the Madonna Inn has hosted hundreds of honeymooners each year. Although it's best known for its outlandish features, the inn pays attention to guests' comfort—after all, it takes more than kitsch to keep 'em coming back. The rooms are spacious and very comfortable; if the loud decor doesn't keep you up, there's a very good night's sleep to be had. A surprisingly good coffee shop adjoins a delectable European bakery. Don't miss the formal Gold Rush dining room, an

eyeful beyond description that's flaming with fuchsia carpet, pink leather booths, and gold cherub chandeliers. Even those checking out early are treated to coffee and tea in the registration office.

$$–$$$ *AE, MC, V; checks OK; www.madonnainn.com.* ♿

## PETIT SOLEIL BED & BREAKFAST
◐ ❶

*1473 Monterey St, San Luis Obispo / 805/549-0321 or 800/676-1588*
Petit Soleil is one of our favorite "ugly duckling" stories with a happy ending: a delightful bargain within walking distance of downtown San Luis Obispo. From the bare bones of a once-plain motel on busy Monterey Street, innkeepers John and Diane Conner have created a European style pension with an authentic flair. Step inside the cobblestone courtyard and find yourself transported to the rustic, colorful charm of Provence. By the time you stroll past potted geraniums, vintage stone fountains, and over-turned vintage French *bicyclettes* to enter the inn's tiny office, you'll have left the street bustle far behind. If you're lucky, coffee cakes or muffins from the oven will give you an olfactory preview of the next morning's breakfast, a hearty spread featuring fresh goods from the weekly farmers' market and delicious house specialties the Conners are only too willing to share their recipes for. The couple traveled throughout Europe and has strived to recreate a feeling of Old World comfort and ease with delightful touches of whimsy. That style is reflected in the sunny breakfast room, which looks simultaneously thrown together and perfectly coordinated, with farmhouse furniture and a colorful splash of traditional Provençal fabrics. Petit Soleil's 15 unique guest rooms are standard sized, but distinguished by the same well-considered decor that makes each feel extra special. For the most romantic kisses, we advise one of the three king-bedded—and extra spacious—rooms: The Rendez-vous Room evokes an intimate Parisian loft, the Chanticleer Room features a country ambience with the whimsical theme of roosters and hens, and the soothing green Le Jardin Room will lull you to sleep within the peaceful surrounds of a French garden. Seafood lovers will rejoice to know, at press time, an inland branch of Pismo Beach's chowder heaven Splash Cafe (see Romantic Restaurants) was getting ready to open just across the driveway.

$$$ *AE, MC, V; checks OK; www.petitsoleilslo.com.* ♿

## SEAVENTURE RESORT
◐ ◐ ❶

*100 Ocean View Ave, Pismo Beach / 805/773-4994 or 800/662-5545*
Pounding waves, beautiful sunrises, scintillating sunsets, and the sheer majesty of the ocean provide the perfect setting for a romantic interlude at this heavenly beachfront resort, where exceptional pampering is offered without a trace of pretentiousness. Each room is decorated in a soothing blend of

deep greens, with thick carpeting, white plantation-style furnishings, and a gas-burning fireplace. With the beach directly below, private balconies or decks are welcoming enough, but in addition, almost all rooms have irresistible private hot tubs. Whether the night is foggy or clear, slide into the spa tub and the invigorating yet ethereal experience is worth the entire cost of the room. It's almost as enticing to release your cares without leaving your feather bed as the two of you loll in terrycloth robes, splurge on refreshments from the well-stocked wet bar, or slip into mindlessness with a movie from the hotel's video library. At morning wake-up time, a continental breakfast basket is delivered to your door, so you can enjoy pastries in bed before another soothing soak in your tub for two. For another relaxing indulgence, schedule a visit to SeaVenture's on-site therapeutic massage center. Make a celebration out of dinner by heading upstairs to SeaVenture's romantic restaurant, a small and well-regarded dining room with an emphasis on seafood and international flavors that often get upstaged by solid-gold sunsets. Think Greek shrimp with orzo pilaf or filet mignon seared with roasted garlic potato gratin. Live jazz Wednesday through Saturday only adds to the romantic ambience. If you can't stand to leave your love den, they also offer room service, and there's a special Sunday brunch, as well. Additional amenities include free use of cruiser bikes and beach pedal-surreys. During the off-season, take advantage of lower rates, special romance packages, and the lack of crowds—and enjoy your romance to the fullest. $$-$$$$ *AE, DC, DIS, MC, V; checks OK; www.seaventure.com.* &

## SYCAMORE MINERAL SPRINGS RESORT
◐◐

*1215 Avila Beach Dr, San Luis Obispo / 805/595-7302 or 800/234-5831*
First discovered in 1886 by prospectors drilling for oil, these natural bubbling mineral springs nestled in the foothills between San Luis Obispo and nearby Avila Beach provide relaxation and rejuvenation in an idyllic natural setting. Until the mid-1970s, the spa facility was a therapeutic center staffed by doctors and nurses. Today, no one feels obliged to plead medical necessity in order to enjoy the sensuousness of Sycamore Springs, and the resort has gained a reputation for re-lighting romantic sparks for even the most stressed-out pair. There are close to 75 private mineral baths on the property—one on each room's private deck or balcony, with two dozen more tucked away on the wooded hillside above the spa. Hot tub rentals for nonguests are available 24 hours a day, and a half-hour soak is included with massage and facial services. The spacious guest rooms, many of which have fireplaces, are in contemporary condo-style two-story buildings. During the monarch butterfly nesting season (October to March), you can spot hundreds of the splendid orange-and-black insects around the property's dense sycamore trees. The resort's Gardens of Avila restaurant (see Romantic Restaurants) is an amorous destination in its own right, and

269

there are some fantastic midweek packages that reward couples with meals, spa treatments, and other amenities.

$$$–$$$$ *AE, DIS, MC, V; local checks only; www.sycamoresprings.com.* &

# Romantic Restaurants

## BIG SKY CAFE

●◖

*1121 Broad St, San Luis Obispo / 805/545-5401*
This casual, almost boisterous all-day restaurant is such a delicious local institution we'd be remiss not to include it. Anyone who's familiar with L.A.'s Farmers' Market knows funky Kokomo Cafe and its cousin, the Gumbo Pot, and will recognize some signature recipes on the menu of this eclectic, imaginative restaurant opened by a former Kokomo chef. At breakfast, they serve the same red-flannel turkey hash, a beet-fortified ragout topped with basil-Parmesan glazed eggs to hungry lovebirds who want to start the day with a hearty meal. And, the Cajun-Creole influence spices up the menu at almost every turn. In fact, Big Sky might be the only place on the Central Coast where you'll find decent jambalaya, gumbo, or authentically airy beignets. The menu is self-classified "modern food," a category that here means a dizzying international selection including Caribbean shrimp tacos with chipotle-lime yogurt; Thai curry pasta tossed with sautéed tiger shrimp; Moroccan pasta with spicy tomato-cumin-peanut sauce; and Mediterranean broiled chicken infused with garlic, rosemary, and olive oil. The setting is comfy casual; creative paint treatments and weathered furniture create a vaguely Southwestern ambience accented by local art and a blue, star-studded ceiling. Big plush booths and small wooden tables coexist happily and complement the long counter/bar. Big Sky is well known and well liked, as evidenced by the benches thoughtfully placed outside for hungry sweethearts who encounter a wait.

$ *AE, MC, V; local checks only; breakfast, lunch, dinner every day; beer and wine; reservations not accepted; www.bigskycafe.com.* &

## BUONA TAVOLA

●●◖

*1037 Monterey St, San Luis Obispo / 805/545-8000*
Situated next to the art deco masterpiece Fremont Theater, this upscale dining room and its charming outdoor patio offer Northern Italian cuisine in a setting that's fancy enough for romantic special occasions but welcoming enough for casual meals. Checkerboard floors and original artwork adorn the warm, intimate interior, while lush magnolias, ficuses, and grapevines lend a garden atmosphere to terrace seating out back. Sweethearts can begin by choosing one of the traditional cold salads on the antipasti list,

then proceed to a main course menu that highlights delicious homemade pastas. Favorites include *agnolotti di scampi allo zafferano* (half-moon purses pinched around a scampi filling then smothered in saffron-cream sauce) and *spaghettini scoglio d'oro* (a rich pasta dish overflowing with lobster, sea scallops, clams, mussels, shrimp, diced tomatoes, and saffron sauce). The balance of the menu can be equally tongue twisting, filled with rich, intense sauces and satisfying meat dishes. The wine list is a winner, with traditional Italian offerings complemented by stellar choices from the surrounding wine region. A second location recently opened in nearby Paso Robles (943 Spring St; 805/237-0600).
*$$ AE, DIS, MC, V; local checks only; lunch Mon–Fri, dinner every day; beer and wine; reservations recommended; www.btslo.com.* &

## GARDENS OF AVILA
◐◐◐◖

*1215 Avila Beach Dr (Sycamore Mineral Springs Resort), San Luis Obispo / 805/595-7365*
Romance is the focus at this contemporary restaurant, set on a wooded hillside of the Sycamore Mineral Springs Resort (see Romantic Lodgings). As a prelude to dinner, couples often start with a glass of wine near the glowing fireplace in the small, cozy lounge, which features an immense mahogany bar. In the dining room, towering palm trees frame a handful of tables topped with white linen tablecloths and fine dinnerware. A cathedral ceiling with a massive wrought-iron chandelier and beautiful hanging ferns complete this picture, while tall windows allow a view of the rock wall and landscaped garden outdoors. Because both the resort and restaurant are renowned for attracting the romance-minded, they not only won't mind if you indulge in an extra-long smooch, but they also go the extra mile to provide suitable intimate corners for celebrating, proposing, and between-course kissing. If you've got a flair for the dramatic, request the balcony table, a table for two elevated on a Juliet balcony overlooking the dining room. You can even dim the lights to control your private ambience, a feature employed for so many marriage proposals the restaurant has actually lost count! Another romantic choice is the dining room's back booth, a spacious upholstered hideaway that's obscured from public view. The restaurant's lighting is magical inside and outside, where garden tables luxuriate against a backdrop of tropical foliage, just waiting for whispers of love to rustle their fronds. The substance of dining is here, too, as the California eclectic menu is often hailed as one of the Central Coast's finest. Seafood is prepared especially well, so you can't go wrong with one of the fresh-catch specials. Other offerings include duck confit with artisan goat cheese and cherry compote, pistachio-crusted rack of lamb with a Mediterranean vegetable ragout, a Thai red-curry shellfish medley over soba

noodles with garden-fresh cilantro and mint, and a selection of desserts guaranteed to send you away with a blissful smile.

$$$–$$$$ *AE, DIS, MC, V; local checks only; breakfast, lunch, dinner every day, brunch Sun; full bar; reservations recommended; www.sycamore springs.com.* &

## GIUSEPPE'S CUCINA ITALIANA
◐◑

*891 Price St, Pismo Beach / 805/773-2870*
Go ahead and give in to temptation . . . the enticing aroma wafting from this always-crowded standout on Pismo Beach's Italian restaurant row is enough to lure carb-conscious lovers inside. Known countywide for consistently good home-style food, generous portions, and a friendly, casual ambience, Giuseppe's can get a little too boisterous for comfortable kissing, but it retains a classy touch just a notch above the usual family-style pizza joint. Paso Robles vintner Gary Eberle even chose to have one of his famed winemaker dinners in Giuseppe's private rear cottage—a 40-minute drive from the winery itself, so that's really saying something. White linen rather than red-checked tablecloths set the stage for a menu that offers both traditional Southern Italian–style fare (pizza, lasagne, veal parmigiana), and trattoria-influenced California cuisine (peppercorn-seared ahi tuna, grilled portobello mushrooms in an arugula-tomato salad, and individual gourmet pizzas). Dinners come with soup or salad; try the highly recommended "alternate" salad, butter lettuce with creamy Gorgonzola. Appropriately, given its seaside location, Giuseppe's menu includes plenty of ocean fare—favorites include an appetizer of clams stuffed with shrimp, scallops, and lox, baked in the wood-fired oven and served with aioli.

$$ *AE, DIS, MC, V; local checks only; lunch, dinner every day; full bar; reservations not accepted; www.guiseppesrestaurant.com.* &

## OLDE PORT INN
◐◖

*Port San Luis, Avila Beach / 805/595-2515*
You can drive all the way out onto the pier, but if the handful of parking spaces are filled you'll have to park on shore and stroll out past sport-fishing outfitters and snack stands to reach this unique seafood restaurant. While not everyone will find the brisk, fishery-scented walk conducive to romance, your reward lies within once you enter this longtime institution and, for many, the *only* reason to drive to Avila Beach. In the mornings, the wooden platform bustles with commercial fishermen unloading their daily catch of rock cod, halibut, crab, and the like, while pelicans and seagulls vie with sea lions for undersized fish. You can count on the family-run Olde Port Inn to serve the absolute freshest seafood, from their hearty, fresh-catch cioppino (a house specialty) to fresh scallops and shrimp tossed in pasta. (There are

also filet mignon and chicken piccata for any landlubbers tagging along.) They make clam chowder, of course, and also offer fish-and-chips, scallops and chips, and shrimp and chips. Dinners, sized for hungry dock workers, include soup or salad, potatoes, vegetables, and plenty of warm sourdough bread. Though the upstairs dining room has a nice bay view through picture windows, request one of the glass-topped tables downstairs if you want a straight-down view of the churning waters below. Gooey, decadent desserts include a homemade peach cobbler that's well worth the extra calories. **$$** *AE, MC, V; no checks; lunch, dinner every day; full bar; reservations recommended; www.oldeportinn.com.* &

## THE PARK RESTAURANT
✿✿❤

*1819 Osos St, San Luis Obispo / 805/545-0000*
San Luis Obispo has a new fine-dining player on the scene, and it's a great prelude to a romantic after-dinner kiss. Located in an old-fashioned neighborhood across from the city's quaint train depot, the Park Restaurant inhabits a historic storefront with ornate turn-of-the-century architecture and frontier-style wood boardwalks outside. But inside, all is sleek and modern, with clean lines, simple furniture, and a sophisticated timelessness that suits special celebrations as well as impromptu midweek dinners out. Chef Meagan Loring's "California rustic" cuisine is a short list of seasonally changing, world-influenced culinary delights, thoughtfully presented and heavily influenced by available produce and artisanal foods from the surrounding region. The signature appetizer is a seductive concert of goat cheese with farm-made honey and earthy black truffle oil; follow this with an eclectic selection like mushroom moussaka in a delicate béchamel with roasted Swiss chard, Oaxacan chicken mole with a creamy polenta-yam cake, or rich Spanish paella with Portuguese linguiça sausage, shellfish, and market-fresh vegetables. If the weather's fine, choose an outdoor table on the Park's side patio, an intimate spot sheltered by decades-old pines. **$$$** *AE, MC, V; no checks; dinner Tues–Sun; beer and wine; reservations recommended.*

## SPLASH CAFE
✿

*197 Pomeroy Ave, Pismo Beach / 805/773-4653*
You might expect Pismo Beach restaurants to sell a lot of clam chowder, and you'd be right—although the bivalves are actually imported, since Pismo's famous clams aren't sold commercially. But that doesn't stop Splash from serving up a darn good bowl of the stuff. Although Splash is a beachy burger stand with a short menu and just a few tables, locals agree that its creamy, New England–style chowder is the best in town, which explains why the place makes 10,000 gallons annually. If you like, you can order it in a

sourdough bread bowl. If that's not enough of a meal, the menu also includes fish-and-chips, hamburgers, hot dogs, and other sandwiches. Come as you are: sandy feet and damp swimsuits are common attire here. Where's the romance? Though your meal at Splash may be a short but delicious break in the amorous tone of your romantic vacation, you can relive every moment of your special getaway later, at home, by ordering up flash-frozen pints and quarts of their memorable chowder. The restaurant ships overnight on dry ice and will even include sourdough bowls for super-simple at-home meals. If that doesn't evoke pleasant memories of the beach, then nothing will. At press time, a second location was getting ready to open in San Luis Obispo.

$ *No credit cards; local checks only; lunch, dinner every day; beer and wine; reservations not accepted; www.splashcafe.com.* &

# MORRO BAY

## ROMANTIC HIGHLIGHTS

Close enough to San Luis Obispo to qualify as a bedroom community, Morro Bay has still preserved much of the rustic seafaring ambience that gives it romantic appeal. Surrounded by wild land and abundant wildlife, the harbor is a working one, always alive with the clatter of fishing boats and the pungent odors of daily hauls. Denounced in the past as an unredeemable collection of bare motels and seafood shacks, Morro Bay has reaped the rewards of urban flight by welcoming upscale shopping, dining, and kiss-friendly romantic lodgings into town.

The city itself is named for scenic Morro Bay, a vast, sheltered inland body of water filled with sea mammals. The bay itself was in turn named for the peculiarly shaped **Morro Rock**, a prehistoric sentry anchoring the mouth of the waterway. This ancient towering landmark, whose name comes from the Spanish word for a Moorish turban, is a volcanic remnant inhabited by the endangered peregrine falcon and other migratory birds. Across from the rock, a monstrous oceanfront electrical plant mars the visual appeal of the otherwise pristine bay. The Embarcadero runs along the water's edge and is Morro Bay's main thoroughfare.

At the foot of Morro Bay Boulevard, by the Fisherman's Memorial, sits the town's giant chessboard, inspired by open-air boards in Germany. Three-foot-tall redwood pieces—each weighing over 20 pounds—stand on an *Alice in Wonderland*-sized board, and countless couples have posed with this whimsical landmark. If you'd like to challenge each other's wits—not to mention your biceps—you can reserve match time for a small fee by contacting the **City Park & Recreation Department** (805/772-6278; www.morro-bay.ca.us). As you stroll farther down the Embarcadero, the two of you might be intrigued by the barking of harbor seals emanating from the **Morro Bay Aquarium** (595 Embarcadero; 805/772-7647). This modest operation with its tanks displayed in a dank and grim basement-like room won't be putting Sea World out of business any time soon, but it is officially sanctioned to rehabilitate injured and abandoned sea otters, seals, and sea lions. During their stay, all the animals learn to perform tricks for a morsel of fishy food (50 cents a bag). If it doesn't sound romantic yet, you haven't gazed into the irresistible eyes of a spotted baby seal.

Next, it might be time to share the rush of sea breezes and the exhilaration of salty spray kissing your face. Water recreation is a mainstay in the bustling marina, and couples can venture out on a kayak tour from **Kayak Horizons** (551 Embarcadero; 805/772-6444; www.kayakhorizons.com), which offers two-person boats (so you needn't part even for an hour). Landlubbers can keep their feet on the ground at the 8,400-acre **Montana de Oro State Park** (Pecho Valley Rd; 805/528-0513), which is located 6 miles southwest of Morro Bay and encompasses sand dunes, jagged cliffs, coves, caves, and reefs. Named "mountain of gold" by the Spanish for the golden poppies that carpet the hillsides each spring, the park contains trails for hiking, biking, and horseback riding, as well as rest rooms and picnic facilities. One easy and satisfying route is the 4.4-mile **Bluff Trail**, with a trailhead at the park's visitor center; take a breather atop wildflower-strewn bluffs, where you can share a kiss or perhaps even glimpse sea otters in the waves below. The park's eucalyptus groves are also the best place for observing the golden monarch butterflies that nest here from October through March.

Roughly 5 miles north of Morro Bay and just 15 miles south of Cambria lies **Cayucos**, a small town that has retained its Old West feel and remains an authentic California beach town. A boardwalk and old-style storefronts give it a look of a Ponderosa on the Pacific. People come here for the beach, night fishing on the pier, or a meal at renowned **Hoppe's Garden Bistro** (see Romantic Restaurants). The 940-foot Cayucos Pier was built in 1875, and the Pacific Steamship Company's ships stopped here to pick up dairy products. Later, abalone and sea lettuce were shipped from the pier. It's a great place for a private walk or a quiet moment on one of the benches, contemplating the Pacific—or each other. There's picnicking in a wind-protected area next to the pier. Cayucos Beach is reached by nine different stairways placed along Pacific Avenue between First Street and 22nd Street. Cayucos State Beach (at Ocean Dr and Cayucos Rd) is great for surfing and boogie boarding. It has a third of a mile of sandy beach, excellent for swimming, wading, sunning, and surfing.

Every year on New Year's Day at noon, on the south side of the pier, 3,000 to 5,000 people take part in the **Cayucos Polar Bear Dip.** Some dippers go in and immediately retreat, but others even swim around the pier. The water is icy cold, and maybe that's why people dress in costume to, er, bear it. If you'd rather celebrate when it's warmer, plan to visit on the Fourth of July for the town's celebration that draws 10,000 to 15,000 people and includes an old-time parade, a street fair, and fireworks from the pier.

## Access and Information

Morro Bay is located on Highway 101, a short 20- to 30-minute drive from downtown San Luis Obispo. Morro Bay Boulevard is the main route into town from the freeway; it will drop you at the Embarcadero, which runs parallel to the bay shore and is home to most of the town's dining and shopping. Main Street is more utilitarian, providing most of the services required by locals; follow Main Street south and you'll pass through the heavily forested Morro Bay State Park before finding yourself in the "back bay" community of Baywood Park. Tiny Cayucos is located north of Morro Bay and seaward of Highway 101; it's delightfully insulated from any sights or sounds of the freeway, and all the town's businesses are concentrated on the one main street, Ocean Avenue.

If you're new to town, stop in at the **Morro Bay Visitors Center** (845 Embarcadero Rd, Suite D; 805/772-4467 or 800/231-0592; www.morrobay .org) for helpful information and a map of the 25-cent trolley that ferries locals and visitors around town, with convenient stops along the Embarcadero and at Morro Bay State Park. For more information on Cayucos, contact the **Cayucos Chamber of Commerce** (158 N Ocean Ave; 805/995-1200; www.cayucoschamber.com).

## Romantic Lodgings

### BACK BAY INN
●

*1391 2nd St, Baywood Park / 805/528-1233 or 877/330-2225*
Nestled in one of the southernmost inlets of vast Morro Bay, the tranquil little community of Baywood Park is popular with sweethearts who like to explore nearby Montana de Oro State Park or quietly launch their kayaks from the small wooden landing right across the street from this affordable yet romantic bed-and-breakfast. A formerly unremarkable motel, the remodeled inn still features a simple layout and compact rooms, though each one is now oriented to take advantage of stunning cross-bay views. A Nantucket-Americana decor adds character to the otherwise basic rooms, and the inn even boasts its own cute bay-front boardwalk (too short for a lengthy amorous stroll, it nevertheless adds ambience to the property). The Back Bay Inn sits directly across the street from the Baywood Inn Bed &

Breakfast (see following listing), attracting a similarly romantic clientele. However, the Back Bay lures lovers who might prefer less theme-oriented rooms and the more affordable rates here. Couples will pay slightly more for the upstairs rooms, since they offer more privacy and views uninterrupted by other lovebirds who might be strolling across the lawn. But every guest can look forward to the sweet, simple breakfast that's included in the room rate. Each morning a basket with juice, baked treats, and fresh fruit is delivered to your door. There's even an in-room fridge and coffeemaker for cocooning lovers unwilling to walk to the adjacent espresso bungalow for their morning fix. Baywood Park has a quiet serenity going for it, since local businesses max out one city block—a few eateries, a couple of boutiques—but the surprisingly fine Mare Blu (see Romantic Restaurants) is directly across the street.

$$–$$$ *AE, MC, V; no checks; www.backbayinn.com.* &

## BAYWOOD INN BED & BREAKFAST
◐◖

*1370 2nd St, Baywood Park / 805/528-8888*
You may be skeptical the first time you lay eyes on this bed-and-breakfast. The two-story gray inn facing out onto Morro's "back" bay looks like a garden-style office building, and though, indeed, the 1970s building was constructed for business tenants, its spacious interiors lent themselves perfectly to a remodel into B&B suites. Each of the 15 theme rooms is an exploration of style and romance and provides an overnight escape to various romantic destinations. From the knickknacks and ruffles of Granny's Attic to the pale pastels of California Beach or the rough cedar beams and stone fireplace of Appalachian, there's a room for every taste and preference. Our favorite is Quimper, a French country-style room with a tiled hearth and vaulted ceiling illuminated by a clerestory window. Every room has a separate entrance, fireplace, microwave oven, coffeemaker, and refrigerator stocked with complimentary snacks and nonalcoholic beverages; many have bay views. Wine and cheese are served on the mezzanine overlooking the tranquil bay across the street, a friendly reception highlighted by a tour of many of the rooms. A nice continental breakfast is delivered to your room in the morning. A night in one of these rooms may even inspire the two of you to plan your next vacation to the part of the world your room depicts. If you're looking for solitude, the Baywood Inn fits the bill; and there are a couple of decent restaurants on the block, so you never really have to wander far. At press time, the Baywood Inn was set to begin building an additional eight bay-front rooms, as well as a separate Baywood Village annex two doors away. Check with them for discounts during construction, or be one of the first to sample the new rooms once they're completed.

$$ *MC, V; checks OK; www.baywoodinn.com.* &

## THE INN AT MORRO BAY
●●
*60 State Park Rd, Morro Bay / 805/772-5651 or 800/321-9566*
Though its sleek brochure hints at a snooty, ultra-glamorous resort, low-key romance seekers will be pleasantly surprised by this exceedingly comfortable and affordable place where the splendid natural surroundings are the focus of attention. Two-story Nantucket-style buildings have contemporary interiors tempered by blond-wood cabinetry, polished brass-framed feather beds, and reproduction 19th-century European furnishings. Rates vary wildly according to the view; the best rooms enjoy unobstructed views of Morro Rock plus convenient access to a bay-front sun deck, while those in back face the swimming pool, gardens, and eucalyptus-forested golf course at Morro Bay State Park. You might prefer to choose based on the in-room amenities you'll be enjoying together; nearly every room has a cozy fireplace for late-night cuddling, and about two-thirds of the 97 rooms have private hydrotherapy spas. The waterfront cottage has two fireplaces, a private deck with outdoor whirlpool, a bathroom with a Roman soaking tub, and a big-screen TV (we prefer to think you'll watch romantic movies, not the playoffs). Bliss is only a few steps away at the Spa & Wellness Center, which offers an array of pampering treatments and value-added packages, including a "couples" option to experience any treatment side-by-side. Complimentary beach cruiser bikes are at the ready for an invigorating harbor-side ride. The Orchid is the Inn's romantic bayside restaurant, featuring a California/Continental menu of fresh seafood and grilled meats with a distinct Pacific flair. Seafood paella, rack of lamb, and fresh pasta are among the restaurant's specialties. The tableside panorama progresses from serene sun setting over the water to the twilight parade of fishing boats returning to harbor, followed by the moon rising over the ocean. The adjacent Bay Club piano lounge is a romantic spot to enjoy intimate cocktails, appetizers, and live entertainment with the same stunning seaside view. Guests hardly need to leave the premises, since the Orchid also serves a full breakfast Monday through Saturday, as well as Sunday brunch.
$$–$$$$ *AE, DC, DIS, MC, V; checks OK; www.innatmorrobay.com.* ᕦ

## MARINA STREET INN
●
*305 Marina St, Morro Bay / 805/772-4016 or 888/683-9389*
This warm and pleasant inn in a yellow old-fashioned captain's-style house is run by former teachers Vern and Claudia Foster, who themselves were captured by the romantic air of Morro Bay's azure sunsets, glimmering gold on the bay, and the dark green of the surrounding hills. The Fosters thoughtfully tend to lovely gardens and cozy seating areas that encourage their guests' relaxation and shared words of love. There are great views from the home's bay windows, and each of four rooms is decorated differently, all

special. Our favorite is the Dockside Room, which has a four-poster bed, a matching bureau, nautical antiques, and an attached patio. In case the two of you forget you're near the water, you can hear the foghorns from here—it's a soothing extra that reinforces a sense of yesteryear. From the window, you can see a bit of the ocean and bay, plus a fantastic view of Morro Rock. Another favorite, the Rambling Rose Room, is decorated in warm reds and greens, with Battenburg lace curtains and bedspread. A four-poster bed, armoire, and English writing desk add to the charm, and the attached patio looks out over the garden. The Garden Room has a romantic four-poster bed made of willow. Each morning, a full gourmet breakfast is served in the dining room, and every afternoon wine and cheese are laid out by the crackling fireplace. Ever the gracious hosts, Vern and Claudia are happy to share advice for your daily excursions, make helpful dinner reservations, and set up romantic wine-country tasting trips.
$–$$ *AE, MC, V; checks OK; www.marinastreetinn.com.* &

# Romantic Restaurants

## HARBOR HUT
◆
*1205 Embarcadero, Morro Bay / 805/772-2255*
Tiki heads and taxidermied swordfish beckon diners to the best choice among several seafooders that, together with sport-fishing outfitters, dot Morro Bay's Embarcadero and lend the air of a New England seaside village right here in California. The Polynesian vibe inside is reminiscent of all the Trader Vic's clones in the world, but the subdued lighting and cozy feel of the hut, coupled with a terrific view of the sun setting over Morro Rock on the bay, make this standard fare more of a romantic trip. Serenaded by the gentle clang of fish-boat rigging, the place is nice enough for special meals, but also casual enough to stroll in wearing sailing duds. Oysters top the plentiful list of appetizers, followed by an extensive menu of seafood (prawns, steamers, king crab, swordfish, bouillabaisse, and so on) and surf-and-turf combos. Landlubbers can go for baby back ribs, New York brandied pepper steak, charbroiled teriyaki chicken, and even a few pasta dishes. Dinners here include appetizers (clam chowder, anyone?) and baked potatoes, making the Hut popular with local early-bird bargain hunters, sweethearts looking for an affordable meal, and anyone who appreciates good value.
$$–$$$ *AE, MC, V; local checks only; lunch, dinner every day; full bar; reservations recommended.*

## HOPPE'S GARDEN BISTRO
♥♥€

*78 N Ocean Ave, Cayucos / 805/995-1006*
Chef Wilhelm Hoppe brought his Culinary Institute of America (CIA) training
and well-developed, European-honed style to tiny Cayucos in late 2000, and
the town's surprise romantic dining destination was born. His originality
shows in unexpected touches, like the garlicky house-made hummus that
accompanies each basket of focaccia, croissants, and baguettes, or the
surprising herbal sweetness of Mediterranean lemonade. Set in a vintage
downtown building—once the turn-of-the-century Cottage Hotel—Hoppe's
offers intimate seating in the simple, airy dining room or tucked outside
among decades-old gardens, where some bricks date to the original hotel
oven and morning glories climb across romantic trellises. The menu begins
with a shellfish bar, daily selection of artisan cheeses, and impressive list of
reasonably priced local wines (Hoppe's adjoining wine shop has a similar
selection of hard-to-find boutique wines for toasting true love later, back in
your hotel room). The lunch menu offers such dishes as a goat cheese and
red pepper omelet with chives, a warm salmon terrine with garlic aioli, or
applewood-roasted brisket with horseradish sauce. At dinner, choose from
the likes of seared king salmon glazed with honey and sesame, fresh local
swordfish with a mussel-curry broth with Dungeness crab, or the signature
dish, sautéed Cayucos red abalone in hazelnut-mango butter. After your
meal, indulge in exotically flavored house-made sorbet and ice cream that
accompany luscious desserts composed of local products, and a short-but-
sweet list tempts with ports and dessert wines.
*$$ AE, DIS, DC, MC, V; checks OK; lunch, dinner Wed–Sun, brunch Sun;
beer and wine; reservations recommended; www.hoppesbistro.com.* ⅋

---

## MARE BLU RISTORANTE
♥♥€

*1346 2nd St, Baywood Park / 805/528-1271*
The name means "blue sea," and that's just what the two of you will see from
the tiny pocket of Baywood Park that reveals this surprisingly sophisticated
charmer just steps from the town's two appealing romantic lodgings. It's
easy to imagine the idyllic lifestyle enjoyed in this vintage cottage just three
doors from the edge of the bay, since much of its original character remains
despite being artfully transformed into an Italian restaurant that attracts
gourmands from around the county. Ask for a seat in the front room, where
couples can take advantage of a mood-enhancing fire and catch a glimpse of
the sunset's glow over flowering shrubs in the front garden. The cozy hearth
warms the simple room, where tables are dressed in ivory linen to match the
clean, beach-white walls and airy open-beam ceiling. Casual diners make
up most of Mare Blu's clientele, but the sophistication of service and cuisine
can easily inspire you to make a special romantic evening here. You'll know

you're close to wine country from the wine list; select something to toast with from the well-selected but affordable list of some Italian, but mostly Central Coast, bottles. From a menu that seamlessly marries authentic Italian techniques, inventive Mediterranean flair, and a love of the region's freshest ingredients, we recommend the classic saltimbocca, a thinly pounded pork loin in rich prosciutto-sage-Marsala sauce; tender grilled quail with polenta and mission fig sauce; creamy gnocchi with forest mushrooms and smoked duck; and the tangy-sweet dessert of laurel-infused risotto pudding with dried cherries and caramel sauce.
*$$$ MC, V; no checks; breakfast, dinner every day, brunch Sun; beer and wine; reservations recommended.*

## WINDOWS ON THE WATER
♥♥❀

*699 Embarcadero, Morro Bay / 805/772-0677*
If you're looking for a special dinner in Morro Bay, there's nowhere better suited to an upscale, romantic celebration than this respected restaurant overlooking the waterfront and distinctive Morro Rock. An airy, high-ceilinged, multilevel space that takes full advantage of bay views, the bistro has Tuscan golden-ochre walls complemented by dark wood accents. But the cuisine—a California-French-pan-Asian hybrid incorporating local fresh seafood and produce—is the main attraction, and it's presented with a welcome level of sophistication. On any given evening, the menu might boast local abalone served with tangy Japanese cucumber salad; cedar-planked salmon with cilantro pesto and citrus-scented rice; crustacean-rich Pacific bouillabaisse; or oak-fired steaks with garlicky jus. The wine list is composed of the choicest Central Coast vintages and selected French wines. All in all, Windows is one class act.
*$$-$$$ AE, DC, DIS, MC, V; local checks only; dinner every day, brunch Sun; full bar; reservations recommended; www.windowsonthewater.net.* ♿

# PASO ROBLES

## ROMANTIC HIGHLIGHTS

Although its Spanish name means "pass of oak trees"—and majestic trees dot the landscape of this romantic and bucolic inland region—Paso Robles is today better known for the grapevines that blanket its rolling hills and country lanes. Part of the up-and-coming Central Coast wine country, Paso Robles currently boasts almost 40 wineries. The town is also proud of its faintly checkered past: It was established in 1870 by Drury James, uncle of outlaw Jesse James (who reportedly hid out in these parts). In 1913, pianist Ignace Paderewski came to live in Paso Robles, where he planted zinfandel vines on his ranch and often played in the Paso Robles Inn (see Romantic Lodgings), which today maintains a small exhibit in his honor.

Paso Robles is blessed with a well-preserved, turn-of-the-century downtown that could have leapt from the play *The Music Man*. Sadly, though, the town's iconic clock tower was one of several core historic buildings destroyed in a deadly 2003 earthquake, which also devastated the cellars of some local wineries, but the loss hasn't even dented the charming ambience downtown. At the center of town is **City Park** (at Spring and 12th Sts), a green gathering place—complete with festival bandstand—anchored by the 1907 **Carnegie Historical Library** (805/238-4996), a Classical Revival brick masterpiece that today houses an exhibit of area maps, early photographs, and historical documents. Several downtown side streets are lined with splendid historic Victorian, Craftsman, and Queen Anne homes, all shaded by grand trees. Couples can drive along Vine Street between 10th and 19th streets for a superb peek into the past, including the **Call-Booth House** (1315 Vine St; 805/238-5473), a carefully restored Victorian on the National Register of Historic Places that now houses an art gallery featuring local painters and artisans. The **Paso Robles Pioneer Museum** (2010 Riverside Ave, near 21st St across the railroad tracks; 805/239-4556; www.prpioneermuseum.org) is worth a visit for couples interested in the heritage of a working frontier town. The small museum is filled with donated artifacts presented as a series of life-size dioramas illustrating the town's history, ranging from American Indian settlements and vintage ranching equipment to a primitive turn-of-the-century medical-surgical office.

Lovers with a love for antiques have been flocking to Paso Robles since long before the wine-country explosion, and downtown still proves fertile hunting ground for treasure seekers. The best are the giant mall-style stores representing dozens of dealers; the two of you can easily spend hours in just one building. Two reliable choices are **Antique Emporium Mall** (1307 Park St; 805/238-1078) and **Great American Antiques Mall** (1305 Spring St; 805/239-1203).

Along with the Santa Ynez Valley, the Paso Robles **wine country** has been steadily gaining a respected reputation that's beginning to rival that of California's *other* wine country—you know, the one north of San Francisco. Although vines have been tended in Paso Robles's fertile foothills for 200 years, the area has until recently been overlooked by wine aficionados—even though it was granted its own appellation in 1983. But some time around 1992, wine grapes surpassed lettuce as San Luis Obispo County's primary cash crop, and now the whole character of the area has shifted into wine-country mode—albeit without the pretension and stifling crowds of California's more established Napa Valley region. **Wine touring** in Paso Robles is reminiscent of another, unhurried time; here it's all about enjoying a relaxed rural atmosphere and taking romantic drives along country roads from winery to winery. The region's friendly ambience and small crowds make it easy to learn all about the winemaking process, often from the winemakers themselves.

The **Paso Robles Wine Festival** each May started out in 1983 as a small, neighborly gathering but has grown into the largest outdoor wine tasting in California. Nearly a dozen events make up the three-day weekend, including winemakers' dinners with guest chefs, a golf tournament, a 5K run, a 10K bike ride, concerts, and winery open houses and tastings, plus the carnival-like festival itself in City Park. Call the **Paso Robles Chamber of Commerce** (805/238-0506) for ticket information.

But any time of year is fine for a romantic day of touring the friendly wineries of "Paso"; just bring along a helpful winery map and set out on your adventure. Remember that the eastern side of town (east of Hwy 101) is known for hot and dry conditions that nurture bold red grapes, while the cool hills to the west offer a unique microclimate where white varietals and more delicate reds flourish.

If the two of you are teetotalers, follow the enticing fragrance emanating from **Sycamore Farms** (2485 Hwy 46 W; 805/238-5288; www.sycamorefarms. com), a completely nonalcoholic destination where hundreds of herbs are grown for culinary, medicinal, and decorative purposes. Learn about them at the farm's walk-through garden; Sycamore also sells fresh-cut and dried herbs, nursery seedlings to transplant at home, and a bevy of herbal vinegars and other gourmet treats. It may just inspire you to start a little garden at home.

## *Access and Information*

Paso Robles is located on Highway 101 just 29 miles north of San Luis Obispo and a half-hour drive inland—via Highway 46—from seaside Cambria. Spring Street is the town's main drag, and freeway exits are clearly marked. You'll find the area's abundant wineries snaking out from Highway 46, to the east and west of town.

Unless you fly into San Luis Obispo, Paso Robles is primarily a driving destination. An old-fashioned and romantic travel choice is the *Coast Starlight*, an **Amtrak** (800/USA-RAIL; www.amtrak.com) route that runs between Los Angeles and Seattle, including a stop in Paso Robles.

The **Paso Robles Chamber of Commerce** (1225 Park St; 805/238-0506 or 800/406-4040; www.pasorobleschamber.com) publishes a small but helpful **Visitors Guide** and operates a staffed visitor center. For a complete map of local wineries and tasting rooms, contact the **Paso Robles Vintners and Growers Association** (805/239-8463; www.pasowine.com).

# *Romantic Lodgings*

## INN PARADISO
●●●

*975 Mojave Rd, Paso Robles / 805/239-5892*

Innkeeper and professional chef Rochelle Harringer is living her dream on five stunning acres, and you can join in for a romantic and culinary getaway at this extraordinary property. You'll know something is different when you turn your back on Paso's busy downtown and mushrooming suburbs, driving just a few minutes to the edge of town where open ranches and centuries-old oaks take over. Harringer's property is one-of-a-kind, anchored by a main house whose reclaimed wood beams, hand-hammered ironwork, and whimsical carved accents create a unique frontier-meets-wine-country welcome. Inn Paradiso is the palatial guest house, located a few steps away, overlooking a refreshing swimming pool. Three luxurious and ultra-private master suites are available, each outfitted with a hillside balcony, brocade bedding, antique and custom furnishings, elegant marble bathrooms, and every creature comfort of a fine estate. They all adjoin a guests-only great room, where picture windows flank an oversize stone hearth and comfy leather armchairs encourage you to sit back and listen to tunes from the CD library—or played on the corner piano. In the morning, Harringer works her magic as an experienced chef to present a full, personalized breakfast in the group dining room, then welcomes guests from a day of wine-tasting with homemade hors d'oeuvres in the afternoon. Upon request, she can compose a candlelit four-course dinner for two, following her personal style of rustic and simply prepared food, using the best of farmers' market ingredients paired with fine wines. Just a few hours in this peaceful retreat, surrounded by timeless lodge architecture and flower-strewn hillsides, bring a tranquility that leaves no doubt why so many romance-seekers and honeymooners pledge to return to this paradise.
**$$$$** *AE, DIS, MC, V; checks OK; www.innparadiso.com.*

## JUST INN
●●●

*11680 Chimney Rock Rd (Justin Vineyards and Winery), Paso Robles / 805/238-6932*

Originally designed as overnight accommodations for visiting wine-industry executives, these three private suites at Justin Vineyards & Winery are perfectly suited for romantic getaways. An English country garden fronts the Tuscan-style two-story cottage, which coordinates with the Italianate winery and tasting room on the property, one of Paso's most renowned wine success stories. In the spacious guest suites, a combination of French-country and Italian influences creates an atmosphere that is both stylish and cozy. Richly glazed walls, vaulted ceilings with exposed beams, antiqued

pine furnishings, and wrought-iron touches lend rusticity, while polished hardwood floors, plush upholstered chairs, marble baths with two-person spa tubs, and corner fireplaces add comfortable elegance to each guest room. Charming hand-painted murals adorn each boudoir, where the elevated bed (complete with tiny stepstool) gains added drama from the poufy featherbed and down comforter that entice sleepyheads and lovebirds to dive in for the best night's sleep ever. Fresh floral bouquets and a stereo stocked with classical CDs set the mood for romance. But sumptuous interiors are just half the story; the inn is surrounded by 72 acres of hillside vineyards, and there is no more romantic setting for a stroll through the vines, up the road past rural farmland, or simply to the Justin tasting room for a sip of their superlative and award-winning Bordeaux-style Isosceles blend. In warmer weather, bring along a swimsuit for the outdoor swimming pool with whirlpool spa. A full gourmet breakfast is served each morning in Deborah's Room, the inn's intimate dining room that's also become an insider's destination for outstandingly personalized prix-fixe dinners (if you're interested in adding this special treat to your celebration, be sure to book in advance). Two differently composed four-course menus are available each evening, either with or without Justin wine pairings, and might include seared duck with braised endive, followed by pan-roasted veal filet with heirloom potatoes and Cabernet essence. The restaurant also serves a bistro lunch featuring endive salads, gourmet burgers, and prosciutto and arugula pizzas on its Wishing Well patio on Saturdays and Sundays.
$$$$ *AE, DIS, MC, V; checks OK; www.justinwine.com.*

## PASO ROBLES INN
❤

*1103 Spring St, Paso Robles / 805/238-2660*
Lovers attracted to the retro 1940s look of this sprawling downtown inn will enjoy learning about the *first* El Paso de Robles Hotel, a grand landmark favorably compared to the finest hotels in San Francisco. Designed by famed architect Stanford White and built in 1891, the "absolutely fireproof" structure burned to the ground in 1940, leaving only the ballroom wing that sits, boarded up and off limits, behind the hotel. Many photographs and relics of the old hotel are on display in the lobby, whose Spanish-style architecture and tile reflect the passion for Mission Revival that was in full swing when this replacement was built just two years later. A stroll through tranquil, lovely grounds leads visiting sweethearts to a footbridge over the creek meandering through this oak-shaded property and to the original two-story hotel units with convenient carports. Well shielded from street noise, these rooms are simple but boast creature comforts (shiny new bathrooms, gas fireplaces, and microwaves in many rooms) added in a massive 2000 update that, unfortunately, removed much of their nostalgic charm. Insider tip: avoid room numbers beginning with 1 or 2—they're in a less

desirable building near the street. The best rooms here are worth the extra bucks: newly built Spa Rooms provide couples with fireplaces and privacy-shielded outdoor whirlpools supplied by the property's mineral springs. A large heated pool near the creek makes for great afternoon dips, and the Paso Robles Inn Steakhouse (with its Cattleman's Cocktail Lounge) serves Harris Ranch beef, fish, ribs, and pastas either on its patio overlooking the garden or indoors by the fire. Coffee shop fare is served in the inn's recently restored Coffee Shop, which opens at 5:45am every day. $$-$$$ AE, DC, DIS, MC, V; no checks; www.pasoroblesinn.com. &

## THE SUMMERWOOD INN
♦♦
*2130 Arbor Rd, Paso Robles / 805/227-1111*
Across from Summerwood Winery about a five-minute drive from the center of town, this elegant bed-and-breakfast is a favorite with honeymooners because of its splendid setting and luxurious hospitality. Though the main building—a white-clapboard cross between Queen Anne and Southern plantation style—looks old, it was actually built in 1994. This means that guest rooms are extra-spacious and bathrooms ultramodern, though the entire inn is furnished with formal English-country antique reproductions. The inn and its nine guest rooms are decorated in formal English style with polished mahogany furniture and nicely tailored fabrics, but expansive windows and high ceilings help keep the atmosphere bright and airy. Summerwood's vine-planted acres are just steps from the inn's back patio and visible from every room's private balcony. Each of the nine rooms is named for a wine (Syrah, Bordeaux, Chardonnay, etc.) and has a gas fireplace, TV, terry bathrobes, and bedside bottled water. Luxury is achieved through small, thoughtful touches; you'll find fresh flowers accompanying everything from the chocolate on your pillow with turndown service to the morning coffee tray left discreetly outside your door. The room rate includes a full breakfast, afternoon wine and hors d'oeuvres, and late-night cookies. If you're looking for a romantic splurge, the Moscato Allegro room features an in-room whirlpool for two, and the top-floor Cabernet Suite is as rich and decadent as an aged wine, with sumptuous furnishings, a seven-headed shower, and an ultra-private patio with a view. $$$-$$$$ MC, V; checks OK; www.summerwoodwine.com. &

## VILLA TOSCANA
♦♦♦
*4230 Buena Vista Dr (Martin & Weyrich Winery), Paso Robles / 805/238-5600*
Martin & Weyrich Winery has raised the bar for wine country bed-and-breakfasts with this eight-room sanctuary at its winery just 10 minutes from downtown Paso Robles. It's well-suited for wine lovers and lovers

in general. Just as their tasting room—nearby along Highway 46—reflects a passion for all things Tuscan, this spacious inn could hardly do more to re-create Italy's sun-drenched countryside in the rolling hills of Central California. Italian music wafts through the courtyard and bistro, where a daily hors d'oeuvres spread features Italian nibbles like buffalo mozzarella, marinated green beans, imported cheese, warm asparagus sprinkled with tuna and fresh herbs, and a selection of Martin & Weyrich wines served in Speigelau stemware. The entire compound is done up in rich shades of sunflower gold, terra cotta, and elegant jewel tones, and every corner makes the most of a never-ending view across vineyards and the oak-dotted plains beyond. No detail was spared in the guest rooms, whose size and appointments replicate an Italian palazzo rather than an earthy Tuscan villa; each is high tech and ultraluxe, with deliciously cozy Italian 700-thread-count bed linens, spa-style bathrobes, a state-of-the-art satellite TV/VCR/DVD hidden in a remote-controlled cabinet, environmentally sensitive bath products, a fireplace, a private stone balcony, and a discreet and superbly stocked minikitchen. Gourmet breakfast is served each morning in the bistro, and at press time Villa Toscana was adding an infinity-style swimming pool overlooking the adjacent vineyard.
$$$$ AE, DIS, MC, V; checks OK; www.myvillatoscana.com. &

# Romantic Restaurants

## ALLORO
⊘❶
*1215 Spring St, Paso Robles / 805/238-9091*
Newly arrived in constantly improving historic downtown Paso, Alloro is the brainchild of chef-owner Fabrizio Iannucci, who offers a taste of Southern Italy and specialties of his native Sardinia. Already a recipient of *Wine Spectator's* Award of Excellence, this unassuming eatery knows how to showcase area wines along with their cuisine and is a popular local favorite. Set in a renovated storefront across the street from City Park, Alloro boasts a sunny interior, simply furnished with colorful paintings and solid bistro seating, and attracts as big a crowd for their affordable lunch specials as for relaxed and romantic dinners. Fresh Mediterranean flavors star on an authentic menu that includes the whimsically named *strozzapreti* (priest stranglers), spinach-ricotta dumplings with grilled sausage in tomato sauce; mushroom-filled *agnolotti* sautéed in prosciutto-mushroom cream sauce; macademia-crusted salmon in a picatta sauce; and the surprising addition of bubble and squeak, the English cabbage-potato mash. After a day of

seeing the sights, it's the perfect place to relax with your significant other, soak up the local ambience, and enjoy a leisurely meal.

**$$ AE, DC, MC, V; no checks; lunch Tues–Fri, dinner Tues–Sun; full bar; reservations recommended.** &

## BISTRO LAURENT
●●

*1202 Pine St, Paso Robles / 805/226-8191*
Although it was inevitable that fine dining would follow on the heels of fine wine, chef Laurent Grangien nevertheless created quite a stir when he opened this cozy yet sophisticated bistro in a town unaccustomed to innovations like a chef's tasting menu. With his extensive French cooking background and his Los Angeles restaurant experience, Grangien offers a California-tinged style of French cuisine, while maintaining an unpretentious atmosphere that locals—and visiting couples—have come to love. Banquette-lined walls make virtually every table in the historic brick building a cozy, private booth, and there's alfresco dining on a romantic patio. While you peruse Bistro Laurent's impressive list of Central Coast wines, you'll enjoy a complimentary hors d'oeuvre (goat cheese toasts, perhaps). Menu highlights include traditional bistro fare such as roasted rosemary garlic chicken, pork loin bathed in peppercorn sauce, or ahi tuna in a red-wine reduction. If the two of you are feeling daring, choose the four-course tasting menu, which changes nightly to reflect the chef's current favorite ingredients or preparations. During lunchtime, the shady patio magically becomes its own separate restaurant, dubbed Petite Marcel, and serves a simple Provençal menu that changes weekly.

**$$ MC, V; no checks; lunch Mon–Sat (spring–fall only), dinner Mon–Sat; beer and wine; reservations recommended.** &

## MCPHEE'S GRILL
●●◖

*416 Main St, Templeton / 805/434-3204*
Inside what used to be Templeton's general mercantile store (circa 1860), chef-restaurateur Ian McPhee has created an eatery that manages to perfectly balance the town's rural Americana with the big-city culinary eclecticism he honed so successfully at Cambria's much-missed Ian's. An old-fashioned pressed-tin ceiling complements the sponge-painted walls adorned with English livestock prints and stenciled barnyard animals. Through the open kitchen, dining sweethearts can watch chefs garnishing McPhee's most popular plates. Chewy ancho-chile strips adorn the Mexican tortilla soup, and baby orange wedges frame the rustic bread salad—country bread draped with warm Dubberke cheese and topped with vinaigrette-tossed mesclun. Main courses range from lighter fare, like shiitake-mushroom ravioli in macadamia-nut butter dotted with sun-dried tomatoes, to hearty peppered

filet mignon in a cabernet-olive reduction over tangy blue cheese potatoes. Fresh fish specials always reflect McPhee's innovative style, and wife June presents delectable desserts. An impressive list of Central Coast wines, many available by the glass, ensures a perfect match for your meal.
*$$ MC, V; checks OK; lunch Mon–Sat, dinner every day, brunch Sun; beer and wine; reservations recommended; www.mcphees.com.* &

## PARIS
🖤🖤
*1221 Park St, Paso Robles / 805/227-4082*
*Ooh la la . . .* there's a romantically authentic touch of the City of Lights here in downtown Paso Robles, and local Francophiles are flocking in by the score. We don't know what made Claude and Chrystel Chazalon relocate to Paso from their native France, but we're delighted they brought this cheerful eatery with them. At lunchtime, Paris offers a wonderful break from sightseeing and wine tasting, or perhaps just a serene precursor to that vacation staple, the afternoon nap. In the evening, couples lazily stroll in, knowing that, though relatively casual, this boîte will deliver a languid meal worth cherishing. The restaurant's European decor of sunshine-colored walls, traditional checked tablecloths, vintage art deco posters, and Parisian-style fixtures provides the ideal stage for classic brasserie fare with just a *petit* California twist. Favorites include classic onion soup gratiné, house-made pâte with tangy cornichons and crusty baguette, escargots sharing space with mushrooms in a creamy garlic sauce, rabbit fricassee in white wine–tarragon sauce, and Hudson Valley duck in zesty pepper-cream sauce. Lunch is a lighter version of the same fare, though couples can still enjoy lovely, jewel-like desserts made with European touches like sugary fruit syrups, buttery pastry cream, and grainy chocolate sauce.
*$$ AE, MC, V; no checks; lunch, dinner Tues–Sat; beer and wine; reservations recommended.* &

## VILLA CREEK
🖤🖤🖤
*1144 Pine St, Paso Robles / 805/238-3000*
There's no better way to end a twilight stroll across downtown Paso Robles's historic park square than with a zesty and romantic meal at this cornerstone restaurant directly across the street. When Villa Creek opened in 1998, the town's limited dining scene welcomed the bright newcomer, whose refreshing Latin-influenced menu was built around local ingredients and paired well with the bold Paso wines gaining prominence in the region. Regional vintners quickly became regular diners, and before long Villa Creek's owners were steeped in the winemaking culture and producing their own varietals for the restaurant and local connoisseurs. Now there are many fine and varied choices in local dining, but Villa Creek remains among the

best. Step inside, and the glare of the street disappears in this moody and rustic early-California setting, like a frontier saloon that's grown up into a fine restaurant. Villa Creek's menu blends the traditional flavors of Central America with Mediterranean wine country traditions, creating a cuisine that's both fiery and sophisticated. The restaurant's specialties include chile-seared ahi with Asian salsa, sautéed shrimp in spicy garlic–red wine broth, crab cakes with lime cilantro crema over local greens, and polenta-crusted calamari with chipotle aioli. Couple these fine selections with a nice wine, and you have the makings of a special meal for two.

$$–$$$ *AE, DIS, MC, V; no checks; dinner every day; beer and wine; reservations recommended; www.villacreek.com.* &

# CAMBRIA AND SAN SIMEON

## ROMANTIC HIGHLIGHTS

Many vacationing sweethearts discover **Cambria** only when they visit Hearst Castle for the first time, but after that, they're hooked on the sophisticated little village that combines the best elements of both Northern and Southern California: a sense of isolation with practical access routes that make an impromptu tryst easy to achieve. The town's name reportedly compares the natural beauty of the area with the lush, rolling countryside of Wales, whose ancient name was Cambria; townsfolk prefer the Welsh pronunciation, with a long *a* ("CAYM-bria").

However you pronounce it, Cambria truly has a split personality. The main part of town is known as the "village," a charming enclave of restored Victorians, art galleries, antique stores, boutiques, and exceptional restaurants nestled among pine-blanketed hills. Across the highway, however, **Moonstone Beach** (named for the translucent stones that wash ashore) is lined with inns offering couples an opportunity to sleep alongside the breaking surf and to take amorous strolls on windswept beaches populated by seals and sea lions. Keep in mind that Cambria is also an excellent base for a romantic exploration of the bucolic wine country in nearby Paso Robles, especially the wineries that dot the rolling hills along Highway 46, less than 30 minutes away (see Paso Robles).

Shopping is a major pastime in Cambria village; boutique owners are hyper-savvy about keeping their merchandise current—and priced just a hair lower than in L.A. or San Francisco. This close-knit community has always attracted artists and artisans of the highest quality, so listen when you hear phrases like "important piece" and "museum quality" bandied about. Combine a sweet hand-in-hand stroll through town with a window-shopping excursion that might just net you an extra-special memento of your romantic getaway. The finest handcrafted glass artworks, from affordable jewelry to investment-scale sculpture, can be found at **Seekers Collection & Gallery** (4090 Burton Dr; 805/927-4352; www.seekersglass.com). Nearby, at **Moonstones Gallery** (4070 Burton Dr; 805/927-3447; www.moonstones .com), you'll find a selection of works ranging from woven crafts to jewelry to woodcarvings and other crafts. If a visit to the nearby Paso Robles wine country has inspired you, **Fermentations** (4056 Burton Dr; 805/927-7141) has wines, wine accessories, and gifts, plus wine-country gourmet goodies to sample. Across the street, **Heart's Ease** (4101 Burton Dr; 805/927-5224 or 800/266-4372; www.hearts-ease.com) is located inside a quaint historic cottage and is packed with an abundance of garden delights, apothecary herbs, and custom-blended potpourris. Women who appreciate casual style and ease of care can drag their significant other along to **Leslie Mark** (801 Main St; 805/927-2234; www.lesliemark.com) with its deceptively simple line of versatile cotton and rayon separates.

About 10 minutes east of town, on a rambling country road whose landscape is reminiscent of a romantic painting, sits **Linn's Fruit Binn** (east of town on Santa Rosa Creek Rd; 805/927-8134; www.linnsfruitbinn.com), a family farm known statewide for freshly baked pies and other goodies. The Linn family's cash crop is the olallieberry, a tart blackberry hybrid used in pies, preserves, salsas, teas, mustards, candies, and anything else they dream up. Their most popular pies are apple-olallieberry and rhubarb, which are even sold frozen for easy transport home. You and your sweetie can set out on a quiet adventure with a rambling drive to Linn's—where you can share kisses in the dappled sunlight of the farm—followed by an afternoon snack at their in-town restaurant **Linn's Main Binn** (2277 Main St; 805/927-0371). This casual all-day restaurant also carries decorative housewares, gifts, and a selection of Linn's food products; in addition to slices of warm pie served with ice-cold milk or steaming fresh coffee, they feature homemade daily soups, hearty sandwiches, and fresh-from-the-farm salads.

Though it started out as a Portuguese whaling port, the town of **San Simeon** today is synonymous with **Hearst Castle** (750 Hearst Castle Rd; 805/927-2020 reaches the information center; 800/444-4445 for information on tour schedules, prices, and advance ticket purchases [recommended]; www.hearstcastle.org) and the stretch of highway-side motels catering to the 1-million-plus tourists who flock here annually. Though kissing might be considered inappropriate during your tour, the castle is unquestionably fascinating. The fantasies ignited by sharing a glimpse at this real-life Xanadu will last a lifetime. The lavish palace that publishing magnate William Randolph Hearst referred to as "the ranch" sits high above the coastline. It's opulently and almost haphazardly furnished with museum-quality treasures purchased by Hearst, a collector with indiscriminate taste and inexhaustible funds who spent years traveling to Europe buying up complete interiors and art from ancestral collections. Touring the house, you'll see carved ceilings from Italian monasteries, fragments of Roman temples, lavish doors from royal castles, and a breathtaking collection of Greek pottery scattered among equally priceless volumes in the library. The estate boasts two swimming pools—one indoor, one outdoor—whose grandiose opulence must be seen to be believed. Besides viewing the palatial grounds and interiors, visitors learn about Hearst's Hollywood connection and the countless celebrities who were weekend guests. Now operated as a State Historic Monument by the Department of Parks and Recreation, the landmark Hearst Castle can be seen only by guided tour; four separate itineraries cover different areas of the estate.

If you've got a few spare minutes and want to see the other side of San Simeon's history, cross Highway 1 to the sheltering bay where Hearst's father in the 1880s built a wharf, a pier, and Mission-style warehouses for the operation of what was then a massive cattle ranch. His son would later use the port to bring in the voluminous building materials and furnishings for the castle, including crates of exotic animals for his private zoo (the zebras you see grazing with cattle alongside the highway are remnants of that short-lived endeavor). Near the end of San Simeon Point, stop into **Sebastian's General Store** (442 San Luis Obispo–San Simeon Rd; 805/927-4217; www.sebastians.com); the rustic country store, which has been in operation since 1852, dispenses basic groceries and souvenirs and operates a small snack bar.

One of the most spectacular natural attractions along this stretch of rugged coast is its abundance of marine mammals. Seals and sea lions are often spotted along Cambria's Moonstone Beach, but the area most popular with elephant seals is the rocky shoreline below **Piedras Blancas Lighthouse** (about 12 miles north of Cambria). These enormous creatures are practically year-round residents, allowing visitors the opportunity to eavesdrop on their always intriguing—and frequently noisy—society. The most active time is mating season in December, when females who have just given birth to the pups conceived the previous year almost immediately conceive again. Mothers and pups hang out on shore for several months. Meanwhile, other seals return for molting, and younger seals are nearly always present, as they need to reach maturity before they're able to spend long periods out at sea.

Along Highway 1 just a few minutes south of Cambria lies **Harmony**, a town whose big reputation belies its tiny size. You couldn't find a better name for this small country town that takes up less space than a city block and has a population of only 18 people. Highway 1 used to pass right through the center of town along what's now known as Old Creamery Road, named for the once-vital dairy operation; William Randolph Hearst even used to stop in to stock the weekend larder on his way up to San Simeon. The old creamery building now houses a few gift shops and a postal station. Sweethearts can take home a souvenir Harmony snow dome or even get married in the town's tiny wedding chapel, which is fashioned from a massive wine barrel and makes an exceptionally unusual place to say "I do."

Like its neighbor Cambria, Harmony also has an arts and crafts movement, and most visitors stop off here to shop at one of three serious galleries, all on the same street. Inside the barnlike **Phoenix Studios** (10 Main St; 805/927-0724), you can watch the resident glassblowers create superbly designed vases, lamps, and bowls. Their organic patterns and smooth, iridescent colors have a sophisticated art nouveau style. Next door is **Backroads** (2180 Old Creamery Rd; 805/927-2919), a gallery displaying mainly small items like jewelry, glassware, and handmade paper goods made by regional artists. Across the street, the cavernous **Harmony Pottery Studio/Gallery** (Old Creamery Rd; 805/927-4293) displays ceramic artwork ranging from inexpensive painted bathroom accessories to elegant glazed platters and vases, with hundreds of pieces in between.

# Access and Information

Cambria is a destination for drivers, since there is no convenient air or public transportation to this part of the coastline. It's easily accessible, though: From downtown San Luis Obispo, the drive along Highway 1 (the Pacific Coast Highway) takes less than an hour, a scenic jaunt with sea cliffs to one side and scenic ranchland on the other. From Highway 101 in Paso Robles, take Highway 46 west; it's an equally scenic 45-minute drive through rolling hills of vineyards and bucolic farms.

The **Cambria Chamber of Commerce** (767 Main St; 805/927-3624; www.cambriachamber.org) welcomes visitors seven days a week. You can pick up free map/guides to the area or purchase Hearst Castle tour tickets (on a walk-in basis). For a virtual stroll around town, visit www.cambria-online.com, a comprehensive Web site with links to many local shops, restaurants, and lodgings. Tourist information—mostly pertaining to Hearst Castle—is also available from the **San Simeon Chamber of Commerce** (9255 Hearst Dr; 805/927-3500; www.hearstcastle.org/visitors_center/san_simeon_history.asp).

# Romantic Lodgings

## BEACH HOUSE BED & BREAKFAST
◆◆

*6360 Moonstone Beach Dr, Cambria / 805/927-3136*
If you've ever envied friends with vacation homes and wished for your own casual, comfy cabin or beachfront cottage, this is the place to live out your fantasy. Reconfigured as a B&B, this three-story, A-frame wood house still has the vibe of a 1950s vacation flop, happily sporting unchic decorative

touches and a communal kitchen and living room. Each afternoon guests gather around the main fireplace or on the seaside deck for wine and appetizers and use the telescopes and binoculars provided for bird-, dolphin-, seal-, and whale-watching. All six quirky rooms have full or partial ocean views, private baths, and cable TV. Consider splurging on an ocean-view room (worth every penny) with a fireplace to chase the evening chill away. Hosts Penny and Tom Hitch own the Moonstone Beach Bar & Grill a few doors down, where full breakfast is provided each morning. Open for breakfast, lunch, and dinner, the restaurant specializes in beachy cuisine like oysters, steamer clams, mussels, and chowder, as well as a variety of salads, pastas, and surf-and-turf selections. It is also a great place to end a sunset stroll or enjoy a nightcap on the heated oceanfront patio before returning to snuggle in your boudoir. $$–$$$ *MC, V; no checks; www.cambria-online.com/thebeachhouse.* ♿

## THE BLUE WHALE INN
♥♥♥

*6736 Moonstone Beach Dr, Cambria / 805/927-4647 or 800/753-9000*
Every detail of this contemporary Cape Cod–style bed-and-breakfast tends to matters of the heart. Expansive floor-to-ceiling windows make the living room a fabulous place from which to survey the panoramic ocean view. Relax, watch for whales (a telescope is provided), and savor the setting sun while enjoying the complimentary wine, cheese, and appetizers served here each evening. The inn's six guest rooms are set behind the front reception area, and as a result enjoy only partial ocean views across the parking spaces, so they are laid out as inward-oriented luxury retreats perfect for lovers who want to cocoon away from the rest of the world. Each room is a country-elegant minisuite boasting the most romantic accoutrements: canopied four-poster beds, designer decor, gas-log fireplaces, comfy loveseats, and duo-sized whirlpool tubs in classic marble bathrooms. High ceilings, white shutters, and muted color schemes lend an airy ambience without compromising an ounce of coziness. A delectable gourmet breakfast is served in the front dining room beside those wonderful water-facing windows, and features such away-from-home treats as gingerbread pancakes with lemon sauce, orange-pecan French toast, and aromatic fresh pastries. $$$–$$$$ *AE, DIS, MC, V; checks OK; www.bluewhaleinn.com.*

## FOGCATCHER INN
♥

*6400 Moonstone Beach Dr, Cambria / 805/927-1400 or 800/425-4121*
This contemporary hotel's faux Tudor style—featuring thatched-look roofing and rough-hewn stone exteriors—fits right into the architectural mishmash along funky Moonstone Beach, even though the hotel is one of the area's newest properties. It's that welcoming Old English personality

and the thoughtful room features that make the FogCatcher a fine romantic choice for the most kisses per vacation dollar. Its 60 rooms are contained in a U-shaped building situated so that many rooms have unencumbered views of the crashing surf across the street, while some gaze toward the ocean over a sea of parked cars, and others are hopelessly landlocked. Rates vary wildly according to the quality of view, but all rooms have identical amenities. Inside you'll find a surprising attention to comfort, especially considering the FogCatcher's rates, which can drop dramatically midweek and off season. Rooms are immaculately maintained and furnished in a comfy cottage style with oversized pine furniture, floral accents, and stylish fixtures. Each is made cozier by a gas fireplace and also boasts a microwave oven, coffeemaker, and stocked refrigerator; the rate also includes a continental breakfast buffet. Unlike many comparably priced Moonstone Beach lodgings, the FogCatcher also has a heated outdoor swimming pool and whirlpool, which elevate the romantic possibilities year-round.
**$$–$$$** *AE, DIS, MC, V; checks OK; www.fogcatcherinn.com.* &

## J. PATRICK HOUSE
⚫⚫
*2990 Burton Dr, Cambria / 805/927-3812 or 800/341-5258*
Hidden in a pine-filled residential neighborhood overlooking Cambria's east village, this picture-perfect B&B is cozy, elegant, welcoming, and intensely romantic. The main house is an authentic two-story log cabin, where each afternoon innkeepers John and Ann host wine and hors d'oeuvres next to the living room fireplace, and each morning serve breakfast by windows overlooking a garden filled with hummingbirds, Chinese magnolias, fuchsias, white and pink Japanese anemones, flowering Jerusalem sage, primrose, and bromeliads. The eight guest rooms, most of which are in the adjacent carriage house, are named for Irish counties; couples vie for the Clare Room (the only suite located in the main house), so reserve early if you want to treat your sweetheart to the best room here. Secluded upstairs, its country elegance is enhanced by lovely antiques and the same luxurious amenities found in all the rooms: private bath, wood-burning fireplace, feather duvets, and bedtime milk and cookies. The inn has always been popular for honeymoons, anniversaries, and proposals, so the innkeepers have a few romantic tricks up their sleeves: Be sure to inquire about arranging chilled wine or champagne on arrival, personalized floral bouquets, or in-room massage (for one or two). Every morning John prepares a lavish breakfast that begins with fresh-squeezed juice and homemade granola, breads, and muffins and includes house specialties like cheese blintzes with berries, chile-corn soufflé, or stuffed French toast. You'll be well fortified for your day, whether you plan outdoor pursuits, wine touring, or simply napping with your sweetheart under the pines.
**$$** *DIS, MC, V; checks OK; www.jpatrickhouse.com.* &

## MCCALL FARM BED & BREAKFAST
◆

*6250 Santa Rosa Creek Rd, Cambria / 805/927-3140*
Most Cambria bed-and-breakfasts are situated either in the village (near shopping and dining) or on Moonstone Beach, with the ocean just across the street, but McCall Farm offers neither of those conveniences. That doesn't mean you should cross it off your list, though, for the bucolic pleasures of this restored farmhouse and the surrounding Santa Rosa Creek Valley are a romantic treat well worth the 15-minute drive to town or the beach. You can't get any more country than the original 1885 clapboard home and 20-acre working farm the McCall family has called home for two generations. In between harvesting their bountiful fruit orchards and vegetable plots for local farmers' markets and tending the flowers and herbs that fringe the gracious porch, the McCalls manage to welcome weekend guests to two upstairs rooms. The romantic Rose Room features namesake pink hues, Victorian lace, and an en suite bathroom; the cheerful Yellow Bird Room is furnished with simple period pieces and has a private bath (the home's charmingly remodeled original) at the end of the hallway. It's the perfect escape for city-weary couples who can enjoy a hearty gourmet breakfast each morning and spend a lazy day exploring the grounds, strolling to nearby Linn's farm for their legendary pies and preserves, or simply enjoying some quiet time together until wine and hors d'oeuvres appear downstairs at sunset.
$$$ *MC, V; checks OK; www.bbonline.com/ca/mccallfarms.*

## OLALLIEBERRY INN
◆◆◀

*2476 Main St, Cambria / 805/927-3222 or 888/927-3222*
Cambria's bed-and-breakfasts are standard-setters for aspiring innkeepers, and this charming nine-room B&B is one of the best in town. This lovingly maintained 1873 Greek Revival house—a convenient two-block stroll from the heart of Cambria's east end of the village—has recently received a face-lift from new owners, who made the downstairs public rooms more spacious, expanded on the berry theme throughout with artisan-made stained-glass windows and berry-dotted lace drapes, and honed their skills with the legendary breakfast and hors d'oeuvres recipes that were the legacy of the previous innkeepers. Stepping through the front door is like stepping back into time, where an old-fashioned aesthetic meets new-fangled hospitality. Like the home's entry hall and breakfast room, guest quarters are a tasteful blend of antiques and contemporary touches, with fresh carpeting and less lace than before. Six rooms are in the main house; though all have private baths, three of the baths are across the hall rather than en suite. The renovated carriage house has three spacious rooms overlooking the picturesque creek that trickles through the home's backyard and nourishes a lovely English garden with plenty of seating nooks for whispered words of love. Seven rooms have

fireplaces. The most charming room is Room at the Top, a sunny nook where the two of you can relax fireside or soak in the antique claw-footed tub. Ask about off-season packages with local restaurants.

$$–$$$ *AE, MC, V; checks OK; www.olallieberry.com.* &

---

## RAGGED POINT INN & RESORT
### UNRATED
*19019 Hwy 1, San Simeon / 805/927-4502*

The number-one reason to stay here—make that the only reason—is the breath-takingly dramatic setting. Perched on a grassy cliff high above the ocean, this little 20-room motel offers views as spectacular as any farther north in pricey Big Sur. Part of an upscale rest stop complex that includes a gas station, minimart, gift shop, snack bar, and the Ragged Point Inn restaurant (see Romantic Restaurants), the motel itself is folksy and basic—and reminds many of Alan Alda and Ellen Burstyn's secluded ocean-side tryst in *Same Time, Next Year*. Each spacious room features an oceanfront balcony or patio, along with separate heating controls for getting cozy on blustery nights. The furnishings are contemporary and comfortable; bathrooms are small but serviceable; and the motel is set back a ways from the other roadside facilities, so you can count on silence and seclusion. Take long walks along the shore, enjoy the moonlight over the water, and cherish the alone time that keeps the spark of love afire. Foxes and raccoons are often spotted scurrying around the grounds, and the entire place feels surprisingly wild, especially considering Highway 1 is just a few steps away. San Simeon and Cambria are a 25-minute drive south, but the restaurant is so good, you *could* eat all your meals here. Ask for an upstairs room to get the best view—and the most privacy. Two new luxury rooms (6 and 7) get our vote for romance, featuring cozy fireplaces, whirlpool tubs, and kitchenettes in case you'd rather laze away the day.

$$ *AE, DIS, MC, V; checks OK; www.raggedpointinn.net.* &

---

# *Romantic Restaurants*

## BISTRO SOLE
◑◑◖

*1980 Main St, Cambria / 805/927-0887*

Nestled against the creek that runs through Cambria's east village, this unassuming bistro is a consistent winner with locals and visitors alike and a frequent pick for casual romantic dining. Occupying a restored cottage, the simply furnished and relaxing cream-hued dining room is joined by a lighter enclosed patio overlooking the garden, where—on pleasant evenings—tables are set next to heat lamps for pleasant alfresco dining. The menu showcases seasonally fresh ingredients in casual wine country Cal-Med fare, ranging from pasta (the house specialty is penne with chicken-apple sausage and

spinach in a creamy marsala sauce) and bistro-style steaks to Asian-tinged seafood specials like sesame-encrusted salmon glazed with citrus or blackened catfish with ginger-orange salsa. A vast and well-priced selection of Central Coast wines includes many fine vintages available by the glass.
*$$ AE, MC, V; local checks only; dinner every day, brunch Sun; wine only; reservations recommended; www.bistrosole.com.*

## THE BLACK CAT
❤❤❤

*1602 Main St, Cambria / 805/927-1600*
Back in the days when culinary bible *Zagat Guide* was rating Central Coast restaurants, there were precious few qualifiers in the stretch between Santa Barbara and Santa Cruz—but the standouts were all concentrated in pretty Cambria, whose strategic position midway between Los Angeles and San Francisco meant an influx of romance-seeking gourmands with big-city standards. This recent addition to the village restaurant scene follows that trend by providing a casually elegant spot with forward-thinking and professionally executed cuisine that could easily hold its own in the hippest L.A. 'hood. The Black Cat is an intimate 42-seat room where warm, subdued decor lets diners concentrate on the food and on each other: White table cloths stand out against Tuscan yellow walls, anchored by a burnished wood floor and wood-burning fireplace. Down-pillowed benches decorate the room, and fresh red roses on candlelit tables enhance the romantic mood. The menu is traditional American with an eclectic European influence that includes traditional tapas such as veal-stuffed fried green olives, chorizo-stuffed quail, and prosciutto-grape bruschetta. The seasonal menu changes frequently but might include savory main courses like New Zealand lamb on goat cheese polenta, seared ahi with melted leeks and citrus butter, or duck with farm-fresh cherries. Fine china complements the efficient service, and Riedel stemware showcases the carefully selected wine list that's heavy with Paso Robles vintages. The 20-seat wine bar is a livelier scene, where you and your sweetie can stop in for pre-dinner tapas or to dine informally.
*$$$ AE, MC, V; no checks; dinner Thurs–Mon; beer and wine; reservations recommended; www.blackcatbistro.com.*

## THE BRAMBLES DINNER HOUSE
❤

*4005 Burton Dr, Cambria / 805/927-4716*
Looking at the exterior of this Old English cottage-style lodge, it's easy to predict the menu: prime rib, of course, and Continental-American specialties reminiscent of the 1950s, when the Brambles first opened. But the Greek influence of owner Nick Kaperonis is everywhere, as *dolmades* and *saganaki* share billing with oysters Rockefeller, chicken cordon bleu, and rack of lamb. Since the dining room's romantic retro atmosphere alone isn't enough to com-

pete with the culinary excellence elsewhere in town, Brambles stays on the top with the freshest fish and beef, expert preparation, and fair prices; they've also augmented the menu with some lighter Mediterranean fare. To do it right, however, forget the diet for a night and order sour cream for your baked potato, extra butter for your lobster, and one of the restaurant's tempting chocolaty desserts. The Brambles recently added an outdoor patio ensconced in the trees, which becomes a magical starlit forest after the sun sets. Locals grouse that the place is too popular with busloads of tourists, whose package deals often include the restaurant's early-bird dinner, so it's wise to dine later—unless scoring a bargain will make your date that much better.
$$ *AE, DIS, MC, V; checks OK; dinner every day, brunch Sun; full bar; reservations recommended; www.bramblesdinnerhouse.com.* ⅃

## RAGGED POINT INN
◕◕
*19019 Hwy 1, San Simeon / 805/927-5708*
Located 15 miles north of Hearst Castle, Ragged Point Inn shares a million-dollar view and a dramatic cliff-top location with its adjacent motel (see Romantic Lodgings). Indeed, the view is so inspiring that it compels many couples to embrace while gazing to sea. The dining room is classic California-redwood architecture with plenty of view windows, and there's a partially enclosed patio for alfresco dining when the weather allows. There really isn't an unromantic table in the place, and the window-side tables even afford a view of the starlit sky after night falls. Ragged Point's menu is California cuisine, with hearty American favorites and gourmet European touches. Recommended choices include herb cheese–stuffed mushrooms, baby back ribs in ginger-barbecue sauce, and homemade ravioli in orange-sage sauce. At lunchtime, there are a variety of gourmet sandwiches. Come here during daylight to enjoy the scenery; plan on lunch or a reasonably early dinner (the dining room serves lunch until 4pm; dinner starts at 5pm) and make a point of strolling the well-landscaped, Japanese-inspired gardens. Ragged Point also serves up a hearty and satisfying breakfast, a boon to those who spend the night at this isolated and appealing outpost.
$$ *AE, DIS, MC, V; local checks only; breakfast, lunch, dinner every day; beer and wine; reservations recommended; www.raggedpointinn.net.* ⅃

## ROBIN'S
◕◕
*4095 Burton Dr, Cambria / 805/927-5007*
"Home Cooking from Around the World" is the slogan at this eclectic cafe that's been a local favorite for many years. Located on the east side of Cambria's still-expanding village, Robin's has a cozy, casual, almost hippie-esque sambience, and a menu that runs the gamut from exotic Mexican-, Thai-, or Indian-tinged recipes to simple vegetarian salads, pastas, and sandwiches. The robust flavors

of extremely fresh ingredients shine through every dish, and the food manages to taste well composed yet distinctly homemade. Best bets include the soup of the day; the "black bean surprise," a tortilla dip appetizer of beans, cheese, guacamole, salsa, and sour cream; salmon fettuccine in cream sauce with fresh dill sprigs; and *roghan josh*, a Northern Indian lamb dish in a richly spiced nutty yogurt sauce accompanied by sweet-tangy chutneys. Much of the menu is somewhat health oriented, giving couples the justification to indulge in one of Robin's to-die-for desserts, like vanilla custard bread pudding in Grand Marnier sauce. If you choose to sit outside on the glassed-in deck, which is embraced by meandering trumpet vines, the well-spaced heat lamps and glowing lanterns will keep you as warm as your betrothed's words of love.

$$ *MC, V; local checks only; lunch, dinner every day; beer and wine; reservations recommended; www.robinsrestaurant.com.* ⅋

## SEA CHEST OYSTER BAR & SEAFOOD RESTAURANT
◗◖

*6216 Moonstone Beach Dr, Cambria / 805/927-4514*
This gray clapboard cottage is festooned with brass portholes, anchors, fishing nets, buoys, and virtually anything else to accentuate the seaside atmosphere. Warm and welcoming, the Sea Chest even has a game-filled lounge where you and your honey can play cribbage, checkers, and chess while waiting for your table. Once you're seated at a table for two—either gazing out at the waves rolling ashore or sitting beside a cozy pot-bellied stove—choose from an extensive menu of fresh seafood from local and worldwide waters. Oysters (the most touted of all aphrodisiacs) are the main attraction: oysters on the half shell, oyster stew, oysters Casino, oysters Rockefeller, or devils on horseback (oysters sautéed in wine and garlic, then topped with bacon and served on toast). The menu also features steamed New Zealand green-lipped mussels, steamed clams and other clam preparations, halibut, salmon, lobster, and scampi, plus whatever looked good from off the boats that morning. There's a respectable list of microbrews and imported beers, along with a selection of Central Coast wines.

$$ *No credit cards; checks OK; dinner Wed–Mon (open Tues May–Sept only); beer and wine; reservations not accepted.* ⅋

## THE SOW'S EAR CAFE
◗◗◖

*2248 Main St, Cambria / 805/927-4865*
If it were in Los Angeles or San Francisco, the Sow's Ear would cost twice as much and you'd never get a reservation—it's that good. One of Cambria's tiny old cottages has been transformed into a warm, romantic hideaway right on Main Street. The best tables are in the fireside front room, lit just enough to highlight its rustic wood-and-brick decor. Pigs appear in oil paintings, small ceramic or cast-iron models adorning the shelves, and the Americana

woodcut sow logo. Though the menu features plenty of contemporary California cuisine, the most popular dishes are American country favorites given a contemporary lift, including a warmly satisfying chicken-fried steak with outstanding gravy, chicken and dumplings any grandmother would be proud of, and zesty baby pork ribs. Other standouts are salmon prepared in parchment and grilled pork loin glazed with chunky olallieberry chutney. Although dinners come complete with soup or salad, do share one of the outstanding appetizers—the calamari is melt-in-your-mouth, and marinated goat cheese perfectly accompanies the restaurant's signature marbled bread baked in terra-cotta flowerpots. The wine list is among the area's best, featuring outstanding Central Coast vintages, many available by the glass. If you have only one nice dinner in town, make this the place for your rendezvous.

**$$** *AE, DIS, MC, V; local checks only; dinner every day; beer and wine; reservations recommended; www.thesowsear.com.* &

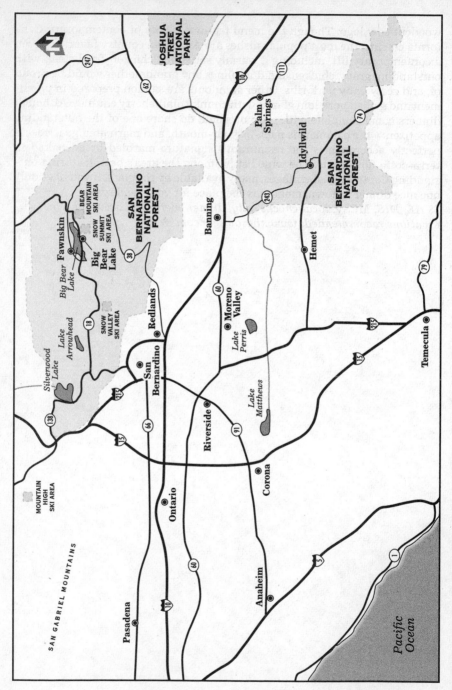

*"A kiss has often proved a more potent arouser than any storm."*

—E. M. MOORE

# ♡ INLAND EMPIRE AND MOUNTAIN REGION

Just east of Los Angeles lies a vast land of 28,000 square miles known as the Inland Empire. Made up of the western areas of Riverside and San Bernardino counties (as well as parts of eastern Los Angeles County), it consists of wide palm-lined streets presenting original turn-of-the-century residences, antique stores, sleepy main streets, and orange groves—miles and miles of them thanks to Eliza and Luther Tibbets. The couple managed to plant the first seedless orange tree in California in 1875. Theirs was a coupling that bore fruit and literally begat an empire. If that's not romantic, what is?

Orange groves brought prosperity to the region, but today those endless acres of citrus have made way for urban sprawl. The air still wafts with the scent of orange blossom, however, in towns like Riverside and Redlands. But that air is stilled by two mountain ranges that flank the area and create an inversion layer of smog, which makes Redlands and Riverside, for all their charm, the sad recipients of some of the L.A. Basin's worst air. Still, there are enough days to be counted when the wind works its powers, and the sky gives way to a blue horizon and views of the snow-capped mountains that lie within errand-driving distance.

The 11,000-foot San Bernardino Mountains guard the empire as a chimera against the expanse of the Mohave Desert that lies on the other side and extends to Arizona. The climes of the Inland Empire may have more rain and coolness attached, but temperatures can still climb in the summer months.

Romance in the Inland Empire is about driving, sightseeing, taking your time, and taking a step back—about half a century—to a simpler time. It is within these distances that you can pick apples at lush orchards, ride a hot-air balloon over the orchards and scenic rock formations, or hike a scenic forest trail in the San Bernardino National Forest or San Jacinto Mountains.

# RIVERSIDE AND REDLANDS

## ROMANTIC HIGHLIGHTS

In 1900, just 25 years after the first navel orange trees were planted in **Riverside**, the city was California's richest per capita and home to half the state's production of oranges. The wealth didn't stay buried behind the cottonwoods. The town's Main Street is full of Victorian splendor and maybe even some Gothic refinements when you count the Mission Inn (see Romantic Lodgings).

Today, nearly 300,000 people call Riverside home. Lovers will find hip restaurants and clubs, a happening central pedestrian mall, a well-respected university, an arts community, wine-tasting shops, coffee houses, and lots of antique stores.

If art museums are your thing, the **Riverside Art Museum** (3425 Mission Inn Ave; 909/684-7111) is particularly romantic. The circa 1929 building was designed by Julia Morgan, who designed the Hearst Castle, and it features atmospheric touches like verandas, wrought-iron fixtures, turrets, and large sunlit spaces. Permanent collections include works by well-known California artists such as William Keith, Ralph Love, Rex Brandt, and Robert Wood. Up the street, the **California Museum of Photography** (3824 Main St; 909/787-4787), run by the University of California at Riverside, is contemporary and provocative, with photo exhibits that explore the works and their relationship to society. Whether or not the dark spaces and track-lighted walls prove to be good places to kiss, the museums will at least give you and your honey plenty to talk about.

For couples drawn more to architecture than art, a visit to **Heritage House** (8193 Magnolia Ave; 909/689-1333) lets lovers see the inside of the outer showings of wealth in this city. The Queen Anne Victorian dates from 1891 and was built by the Bettner Oranges fortune with a no-budget plan. Catherine Bettner found no better way to employ her profits than to build the finest house in Riverside on an estate shaded by palms, magnolias, rose bushes, and fruit trees. Take the tour and you'll glimpse a different time, when grand interior staircases, Persian rugs, delicate gas light fixtures, marvelous tile fireplaces, and plenty of art pieces were the period decor of the day.

Riverside is awash in antiques, whether in a living museum or grand stores such as the **Mission Galleria** (3700 Main St; 909/276-8000). This is one massive city block of antiques and accessories, which fill nook after nook of concession corners selling everything from love potions, aromatherapy, and bath powders to bubble glass, grandfather clocks, aged rattan, and china closets. One boutique is all about chocolate, while another sells vintage lingerie. You'll find old mirrors and an Enchanted Cottage area in a British garden tea setting. It's a great place to browse hand-in-hand, discovering all sorts of odds and ends in paths that lead to fascinating moments to share.

A pedestrian mall adjacent to the Mission Inn cuts through the center of Riverside, providing plenty of cafes, coffee houses, antique shops, art galleries, and boutiques. One cool shop, **Dragonmarsh** (3744 Main St; 909/276-1116), features employees that greet you costumed in Renaissance garb (think Guinevere and Lancelot). But the themed staffers are only part of what's in store. There are shelves of special stones, candles, spell kits, charms, essences, jewelry, and amulets—everything one could want to attract luck and love and temporarily be transported back to the Middle Ages. Don't miss the "toadly frogs" corner, especially if you are looking for a prince.

Art lovers will like **First Thursdays in Riverside** (909/684-7111; www.riversideartscouncil.org/artwalk.htm), when 17 area galleries and museums open their doors from 6pm to 9pm for a moveable feast of paintings, ceramics, and food between Lemon and Market streets along Mission Inn and University avenues. If you happen to visit in April, but sure to take part in the **Sunkist Orange Blossom Festival** (909/715-3400). The two-day event celebrates Riverside's citrus heritage with a parade, a circus, live entertainment, an antique train, and trolley rides in downtown Riverside.

Just northeast of Riverside, lovers will find the sleepy town of **Redlands**, which features a small, charming old downtown area with a generous presence of well-preserved homes and mansions dating from the city's orange empire days. Lovers of history can stop in at the **A. K. Smiley Public Library** (125 W Vine St; 909/798-7565), a hauntingly beautiful Moorish establishment built in 1984 with carved friezes, stained glass windows, and gorgeous woodwork, which is a terrific resource for couples who want to learn more about historic Redlands.

Nearby, **State Street** is a page right out of small-town California, a lazy ficus-shaded street with brick sidewalks and stores selling all manner of rubber stamps and stickers, antiques, and comic books. A good place to stop and take note is **Redlands Galleria** (17 E State St; 909/793-2204), a contemporary warehouse-style restaurant with skylights and well-placed wall art, where the two of you can indulge in grilled Brie with sun-dried tomatoes and portobello mushrooms, or pesto chicken paired with a Napa wine.

Follow your way down to broad, palm-lined **Olive Street**, where the citrus fruit folks embedded their fortunes with homes so elaborate and enduring the neighborhood still stands today. Here, you'll see places like

**Holt House** (405 W Olive) and **Burrage House** (1205 Crescent), which is rumored to have the town's only glassed-in swimming pool, and **Morey House** (140 Terracina Blvd) that's easily recognized from its constant use in films and photographs. Or tour the **Kimberly Crest House & Garden** (1325 Prospect Dr; 909/792-2111; www.kimberlycrest.org), a fairytale-style 1897 castle with three stories of turrets and winding staircases and, no doubt, a secret passageway or two. This is where you ooh and ahhh at French Revival gilt furniture and silk damask wall coverings. Terraced Italian gardens, orange groves, and ponds surround this historic landmark home. The lily ponds with koi and papyrus offer some romantic respite.

Wander down **Orange Street**, and you'll feel like you've stepped more into the Depression Era, though it's still charming and has a preserved atmosphere. Your travels will take you to the old Redlands Santa Fe Line train depot, now a shaded sitting area with its outdoor Mission Revival design waiting area. The **Jazz & Java** (349 Orange St; 909/792-8083) coffee house and frilly chocolate and sweets shop fronts the depot, if sweets for your sweetie with a java jolt are in order.

If the historic train station gets you curious about the region's past, visit the **San Bernardino County Museum** (2024 Orange Tree Ln; 909/307-2669 or 888/BIRDEGG; www.co.san-bernardino.ca.us/museum), which depicts the region's heritage and natural history with three floors of exhibits on anthropology, archaeology, history, birds, mammals, reptiles, fossils, and fine art.

However you plan to spend your time in Redlands and Riverside, the two of you are sure to enjoy the timeless feeling of this history-rich area. It's a great place to slow down and enjoy a little romantic quiet time together where you can appreciate the past and look toward the future.

## Access and Information

**Ontario International Airport** (south of I-10 between Haven and Vineyard Aves; 909/937-2700; www.lawa.org/ont/ontframe.html) is the area's most convenient airport and is served by numerous commercial airlines. By car, Riverside is about an hour's drive east of Los Angeles. Couples take Interstate 10 east to San Bernardino County. From San Diego, travelers enter Riverside County via Interstate 15. Redlands is on most maps about an hour's drive east of Los Angeles via Interstate 10, just east of the Interstate 215 interchange and about 15 miles northeast of Riverside.

Contact the **Riverside Convention and Visitors Bureau** (3750 University Ave; 909/684-4636; www.riversidecb.com). In Redlands, the **Redlands Chamber of Commerce** (1 E Redlands Blvd; 909/793-2546; www.redlands chamber.org) is also a helpful resource, but the best source of information is www.redlandsweb.com, which is overflowing with background about the preserved mansions, festivals, area motels, and anything else a visitor might want to locate in town.

# Romantic Lodgings

## THE MISSION INN
●●●

*3649 Mission Inn Ave, Riverside / 909/784-0300 or 800/843-7755*
A National Historic Landmark built in stages between 1902 and 1931 by hotelier Frank Miller, the Mission Inn began as a modest two-story adobe home and eventually evolved into one of the West's most exquisite hotels. One of the architects hired by Miller was Arthur B. Benton, who seized upon Miller's love of the dramatic and proceeded to riff on a number of architectural themes. Consequently, the inn is part Mission-style Revival, part castle, part church. The Innkeeper Suite (also known as the Ronald Reagan Suite since the nation's 40th president spent several nights here) is located high up on a patio known as "Spanish Row"—the place to find a room (numbers 420–435) if cost is no limit. Each suite has unique architectural touches, such as special fabrics, furnishings, views, patios, balconies, window seats, coffered ceilings, and tall, arched leaded windows. However, all of the 238 guest rooms in this grand hotel are quaint and indescribably of another era. For example, the hallways were built wide enough for "wintering" guests of yore, who came with enormous steamer trunks. A key antiquity on the grounds is the St. Cecelia Chapel, which is often occupied on weekends for weddings. Lots of incredible amenities include a large pool and Kelly's Spa, a new full-service facility. The locals will tell you that without a guided tour of the Mission Inn (which takes about an hour and 15 minutes), you're missing the Riverside experience. The tour allows you to amble through most of the public areas and up to the topmost parapets (yes, parapets: the hotel's architecture is highly eclectic). And there is no other hotel within the Inland Empire with three top-flight restaurants—the Mission Inn Restaurant, Las Campanas, and Duane's Steak and Seafood (see Romantic Restaurants).
*$$$–$$$$ AE, DC, DIS, MC, V; checks OK; www.missioninn.com.* &

# Romantic Restaurants

## BACK TO THE GRIND
●

*3575 University Ave, Riverside / 909/784-0800*
Conveniently located in historic downtown Riverside, Back to the Grind is part espresso bar, part cafe juice bar. Exposed brick, high molded

ceilings, and cozy couch nooks with real books on the shelves give this healthy hangout the feel of an artist's loft. The lovely outside patio, filled with the work of local artists and photographers, is a splendid place to kiss. Settle back with a cup of exquisitely ground coffee or a fresh juice drink. Smoothie selections like "Brain Power," "The Workout," and "Raspberry Radical" include a selection of seven dietary supplements like ginkgo biloba, Chinese ginseng, soy protein powder, bee pollen, multivitamin powder, vitamin C, and kava. Four kinds of espresso are sure to give you a jolt and get your romantic day off to a grand start.

**$$** *MC, V; no checks; breakfast, lunch, dinner every day; no alcohol; reservations not necessary.* &

## DUANE'S PRIME STEAK & SEAFOOD
♥♥♥

*3649 Mission Inn Ave (The Mission Inn), Riverside / 909/341-6767*
Set inside the historic Mission Inn (see Romantic Lodgings), Duane's is simply a class act. It's not necessarily a very large restaurant, but it has a grand scale, with high ceilings, huge wall hangings, big chairs, big tables, and, thankfully, big portions. Ringing the room are arched windows and ornate balconies—faux and real. These, in an odd way, focus attention on the centerpiece of the restaurant's decor: a hugely vibrant and colorful Old West painting that totally dominates the restaurant's rear wall. (The maitre d' will regale you for 10 minutes on both the historical events it depicts and the painting's own colorful history.) Devotees of this traditional steakhouse are distinctly the let's-start-with-a-martini kind of crowd. Much of the restaurant's excellent reputation is about its beef. Flash-cooked steaks are rare, juicy, and tender. There's an extensive array of wines and desserts for you and your sweetheart to savor with your meal.

**$$$$** *AE, DIS, MC, V; no checks; lunch Mon–Fri, dinner every day, brunch Sun; full bar; reservations required; www.missioninn.com.* &

## LAS CAMPAGNAS
♥♥

*3649 Mission Inn Ave (The Mission Inn), Riverside / 909/341-6767*
One of three restaurants located within the Mission Inn (see Romantic Lodgings), Las Campagnas ("the bells") offers a much more casual setting than the inn's other dining establishments. The restaurant is totally alfresco (outdoor heaters will keep lovers adequately warm on chilly days or brisk evenings), and couples dine on a terra cotta–tiled patio amid a true garden setting, which includes lush, varied foliage in festive flowerboxes and planters and a serene central fountain. The decor gives the impression this restaurant has been part of the Mission Inn from the beginning, even though it's a relatively new offering. Couples dine on authentic Mexican fare—fresh salsa and guacamole, and entrées like Veracruz snapper, chicken

Vallarta (don't ignore that sweet but smoky chipotle-apricot sauce), and mahimahi tacos—washed down with the restaurant's refreshing signature margaritas. Sit back in this lovely setting; sip a papaya, kiwi, or Midori margarita; munch on chips and salsa; and you have all the makings of a romantic repast.
$$$ *AE, DC, DIS, MC, V; no checks; lunch, dinner Mon–Sat; full bar; reservations recommended; www.missioninn.com.* &

## MARIO'S PLACE
♥€
*3646 Mission Inn Ave, Riverside / 909/684-7755*
On Saturday nights in Riverside, this charming Italian restaurant is a showcase for the best jazz in the Inland Empire. Just across the pedestrian mall from the Mission Inn, Mario's resides in a restored 1895 building with exposed brick, dark mahogany wood, and soft lights. Dinners range from rustic to refined—fusilli with ragù of wild boar, sweet pea tortellini with truffle butter and asparagus, ostrich served with celery root puree and sun-dried tart cherries, or Scottish salmon cooked in a parchment envelope with citrus, ginger, and coriander. The wine list wins awards for its inventory of California and European varietals, and waiters know how to pair the wine with your dinner selections. For couples who've already had dinner, this is also the place to wind down with a cognac and gentle ambience. Find a schedule of performers, wine tastings, and other notable happenings on the Web site.
$$$ *AE, DIS, MC, V; no checks; lunch Thurs–Fri, dinner Mon–Sat; full bar; reservations recommended; www.mariosplace.com.* &

## MISSION INN RESTAURANT
♥♥€
*3649 Mission Inn Ave (The Mission Inn), Riverside / 909/341-6767*
Step into the courtyard of this restaurant just off the Mission Inn's (see Romantic Lodgings) inimitable lobby, and you'll find yourself in a Moroccan desert dream. A massive tile fountain in which three Mayan-inspired frog sculptures frolic blithely sits under a Vatican-like lighted dome that, as darkness approaches at dinnertime, seemingly hangs in midair. Tier upon tier of windows, most arched, rise on every wall, and giant lanterns of cast concrete incredibly top the flying buttresses above. Birds fly freely, as if in a prelude to the swallows' return to Capistrano. The fragrance of bursting blooms fills the air. Talk about an atmosphere for romance. On top of all this, the service is attentive, and entrées—like the double pork chop with superb garlic mashed potatoes, tender filet of beef, or prime rib—are sumptuous.

Lighter alternatives include seared salmon and spinach fettuccine with grilled shrimp.
$$$ *AE, DC, DIS, MC, V; no checks; breakfast, lunch, dinner every day; full bar; reservations recommended; www.missioninn.com.* &

## THE RESTAURANT OF JOE GREENSLEEVES
♥♥♠

*220 N Orange St, Redlands / 909/792-6969*
The Restaurant of Joe Greensleeves makes its home in a narrow historical building in the heart of downtown Redlands. Beautiful, romantic, and spirited—but more in a brassy than intimate way—this is a restaurant where diners are clearly enjoying themselves, partaking in the overall buzz. Beveled glass windows and a row of green library lamps give the restaurant an elegant feel, and interesting interior touches include a wooden half-shell of a vessel embedded into the left side of the building. On the opposite wall, there's a large fireplace that warms couples at nearby tables. The cuisine artfully falls between gourmet and chophouse, rendering prime cuts of beef and fresh fish equally superb. Traditional game dishes, such as venison, boar, ostrich, bison, and elk, often grilled on chef Umberto Orlando's orangewood fire, are the specialty here. And couples can watch the chef at work in his stunning open kitchen. House-made soups like red bell pepper purée and the black bean tureen are a delicious way to start your meal. And save room for dessert, which includes decadent tortes and cheesecakes. Look up and you'll see a ceiling bestrewn with thousands of wine corks—it's a reminder that Joe Greensleeves has won numerous awards from *Wine Spectator*.
$$$ *AE, DIS, MC, V; no checks; lunch Mon–Fri, dinner every day; full bar; reservations recommended.* &

## TABLE FOR TWO
♥

*3600 Central Ave, Riverside / 909/683-3648*
Do salads that resemble flower arrangements sound romantic? If so, you and your loved one may well discover that Table for Two is a splendid place to kiss. Despite its location in an office building, this small but impeccably appointed eatery boasts an incredible spicy-smelling Thai kitchen and loads of modern decor. This is a place of brilliant feasts, including ground chicken and shrimp salad with grilled Japanese eggplant, stir-fry standards such as cashew chicken (in this case, with roasted curry paste), and conventional Thai soups and curries. Dishes are presented with an eye for color; stalks of broccoli are piled generously on large, white bistro-style plates, like river logs outside a sawmill. While couples can savor an intimate moment or two between courses, they'll appreciate the neighborhood presence, which

consists of retired teachers from the nearby University of California—Riverside, young couples, and families.

$ *MC, V; no checks; lunch, dinner every day; beer and wine; reservations not necessary.* &

## TOAD IN THE HOLE
🐸🐸🐸

*3737 Main St, Riverside / 909/369-8792*
Despite its name, Toad in the Hole can be quite romantic. It offers dark booths with white cotton table dressings, a long bar with low lights delivered from hanging Tiffany lamps, and a contemporary setting that would make a fine place to share wine and quiet conversation. Outside, a terraced Italian garden with cascading fountains, artistic stonework, and a curved stairway provide the perfect setting for a pre- or postdinner stroll. The specialty of the house, called the King's Feast, features aged prime rib, slow roasted in au jus, with horseradish; Lord Whitby's corn chowder; salad; creamed spinach; Yorkshire pudding; and baked potato or pilaf. If that sounds like a bit much, try the fried artichokes to start, or order a beef Wellington for two. But try to save room for the tart and sweet peach cobbler, which is worth every calorie. Thursdays through Saturdays, a jazz combo entertains lovers while they dine in this quiet setting. On Sundays, a champagne brunch offers a generous selection, including lox and bagels, made-to-order omelets, chicken cordon bleu, and delicate pastries all prepared by the restaurant's French-trained chef.

$$ *AE, DIS, MC, V; no checks; breakfast, lunch, dinner every day, brunch Sun; full bar; reservations recommended.* &

# IDYLLWILD

## ROMANTIC HIGHLIGHTS

Hemmed into a hamlet in the rocky San Jacinto Mountains a mile high in the alpine flora, the tiny resort town of Idyllwild feels miles from the urban onslaught. Flatlanders in search of crisp mountain air swell the place on weekends, but there is plenty of room for everyone. Bed-and-breakfasts offer a romantic hideaway for couples in search of peace and quiet, and there are plenty of great pancake cafes for feeding them and fun notion shops to keep them busy. In the winter, there is snow, and in the summer, Idyllwild offers a cool, dry respite.

Couples will know they've arrived in Idyllwild when they see the rustic log prefab cabin-style buildings along **Circle Drive**, signaling a sudden burst of coffee houses and restaurants and a certain "walkability" that makes you want to park. The village has enjoyed its heyday as an artist colony, then as a getaway for the hip and famous in the early 1900s. Today, Idyllwild still draws art lovers with more than a dozen art galleries and an **Art Alliance** (866/439-5278; www.artinidyllwild.com) that sponsors Sunday Mornings Art Cafe, when each gallery takes a turn hosting a Sunday morning coffee open house.

Stop at the **Town Crier Visitors Center** (54295 Village Center Dr; 888/659-3259; www.idyllwild.com) to pick up a visitors guide of the area. For $2, a large map put out by the Chamber of Commerce also lists and describes services and attractions and shows that the village is a compact spread negotiated by South Circle Drive at one end, North Circle Drive in the middle, and Pine Crest Avenue at the north end, with pines, trails, hidden cabins, and coves fanning from this hub.

In the heart of town, couples can browse through cafes, shops, boutiques, and galleries. There's **88 Far East International** (54225 N Circle Dr; 909/659-5066) for Korean blankets, dim sum mixes, and mini Egyptian mummy replicas. **Florist in the Forest** (54585 N Circle Dr; 909/659-4143) offers tropical blooms and silk roses, while **Faux Ever After** (54210 N Circle Dr; 909/659-9511; www.fauxeverafter.com) is chock-full of stained glass, architectural ornaments, sculptures, and gifts. At the center of town, **Country Farms** (25980 Hwy 243; 909/659-3434) sells canned and jarred goods, local fruit, honey and confections, and manzanita jelly. The manzanita tree is one of the village's signature treasures with its smooth red bark, tiny pink blossoms, and delicate red berries that apparently turn delicious when cooked in a pressure cooker and boiled with sugar.

Also at the center of town is the **Idyllwild Tree Monument**, a 50-foot totem poll created by chain-saw artist Jason La Benne. La Benne, who dedicated the piece to the Cahuilla Indians (who summered in Idyllwild), started out with a bald eagle, to which he added a mountain lion, a squirrel, a raccoon, an Indian chief, a butterfly, and a coyote. Surely you will find some other things in there if you look hard enough, as it's a little like one of those "find these items" puzzles in a children's *Highlights* magazine.

**Tahquitz Rock**, which juts out in white boulders above town, is one of Southern California's premier rock-climbing sites and has a story that will entertain you and your lover over a fire on a cold night. Apparently, the spirit of Chief Tauquitch, a benevolent-turned-malevolent leader who once ruled over all the American Indians in the San Jacinto Valley, resides in a cave covered by the great rock. He was banished to the cave long ago after his people condemned him, and locals claim to still hear him rattling around today.

While Tahquitz Rock is a popular hike, Idyllwild presents an abundance of other hiking options from easy to difficult, shaded to open, and scenic to serious. For example, the **Pacific Crest Trail**, which extends 2,600 miles from Mexico to Canada, passes through the San Jacinto district. It begins a quarter mile east of the junction of Highways 371 and 74 in Garner Valley and winds through the wilderness, exiting north of Cabazon Peak near Interstate 10 in the desert by Palm Springs. A hiking permit is required for travel through the wilderness section.

Lovers more interested in an easy scenic stroll can take the **Ernie Maxwell Scenic Trail**, a 2.6-mile hike that leaves from Fern Valley Road, just before Idyllwild's densely forested **Humber Park**, where the sun filters through the pines, creating the perfect spot to stop for a kiss. Beginning at an altitude of 6,100 feet, it crosses streams along the way as it descends 600 feet. For permits and information and maps, contact the **Mt. San Jacinto State Park & Wilderness office** (909/659-2607); the **Idyllwild Ranger Station** (corner of Hwy 243 and Upper Pine Crest in the village; 909/659-2117), or the **Idyllwild Nature Center** (located about a half mile north of town on Hwy 243; 909/659-3850; www.idyllwildnaturecenter.net).

Couples looking for a special picnic site may want to check out **Fuller Mill Creek** (about 7 miles north of town on Hwy 243). This scenic spot has tables for lovers to spread out their gourmet goodies, grills for those who want to barbecue, and, most importantly, rest rooms. **Idyllwild County Park** (on County Park Rd) and **Lake Fulmor** (Hwy 243, about 10 miles north of Idyllwild) are other lovely locales for an afternoon of picnicking. (Lake Fulmor is also stocked with rainbow trout, but fishing permits are required.)

In June, Idyllwild hosts the **Timber Festival** (Idyllwild County Park, off Hwy 243; 909/659-4936). This country festival features logging contests, a barn dance, music, food, and an arts and crafts fair. It's the perfect spot for you and your sweetheart to soak up small-town ambience and appreciate country life.

## Access and Information

Idyllwild is approximately a two-hour drive from Los Angeles, or about an hour's drive from Palm Springs. Couples can reach Idyllwild by going east from Interstate 15 on Highway 74 through Hemet to Highway 243, making the final tortuously curved climb into the pines (total distance about 40 miles). The drive takes you through rough and rolling landscapes with a few odd stops available at roadhouse cafes, general stores, and psychic reading abodes.

For help planning your trip, call **Idyllwild Chamber of Commerce** (54295 Village Center Dr; 909/659-3259 or 888/659-3259; www.idyllwild chamber.com).

# *Romantic Lodgings*

## ATIPAHATO LODGE

*25525 Hwy 243, Idyllwild / 888/400-0071*
*Atipahato* is an American Indian expression meaning "at the top of the hill." That's a perfect description, of course, for the Atipahato Lodge in Idyllwild. It's set on a hillside overlooking the San Jacinto State Forest. But another apt name might conceivably be the Antipasto Lodge, because it's like an appetizer for the meal that is Idyllwild. The lodge abuts the forest's 10,000-acre nature center. A seasonal stream and waterfall course through the lodge's 5 acres, which are perfect for walking, hiking, and even cross-country skiing when there's snow on the ground. The Atipahato recently has been renovated by its new owner, a former hotel executive. Guest rooms can be romantic with their vaulted, open-beamed ceilings and knotty-pine interiors. Each features a television, a complete kitchenette with coffee maker, and a private balcony with a forest view.
**$$** *AE, DIS, MC, V; no checks; www.atipahato.com.*

## IDYLLWILD INN

*54300 Village Center Dr, Idyllwild / 909/659-2552 or 888/659-2552*
Any place that has been family owned for 100 years must be pretty special. Set smack in the middle of town, the Idyllwild Inn features 15 cabins scattered through an open pine forest like a gracious little Tyrolean village. Cabins are neat with a simple mountain decor; each has a wood-burning fireplace, kitchen, and deck, creating the perfect atmosphere for a romantic getaway. Some were built as early as 1910, others in the 1930s and 1950s, newer duplexes in the 1980s, and some funky theme rooms opened in 1990—although it's obvious all have been carefully maintained and upgraded. The bustle of Idyllwild is literally outside the front gate, but once you're inside this compound you'll really feel you're in a mountain town. Although asphalt paths allow you to drive right up to your digs, unfortunately, the asphalt tends to dominate the landscape a bit; but you can park your car throughout the duration of your stay and just take Idyllwild on foot. When you reserve, request a cabin far from the entrance.
**$$** *DIS, MC, V; checks OK; www.idyllwildinn.com.* &

## STRAWBERRY CREEK INN

*26370 Hwy 243, Idyllwild / 909/659-3202 or 800/262-8969*
One of the first bed-and-breakfasts in the region and long one of the best, Strawberry Creek has a location just far enough outside town (about a quarter mile) to grant romance seekers the peace and quiet they crave. Yes,

there is a Strawberry Creek, and a walking path follows it all the way into town. The inn was fashioned by owners Diana Dugan and Jim Goff from a large shingled cabin built in 1941. Five rooms in the main cabin put you and your sweetie closest to the large living room/recreation room/library downstairs—the true heart of the house and a great place to snuggle around a fire on chilly days. Four rooms out back on the courtyard are newer but feel a bit less cozy, and there's a small single cabin close to the creek for couples in search of privacy. Decor elements include a range of window seats, antique bed frames, wood-burning fireplaces, and skylights; all rooms have private baths. A full breakfast is served out on a big glassed-in porch.
$$ *DIS, MC, V; checks OK; www.strawberrycreekinn.com.* ⅙

# Romantic Restaurants

## ARRIBA
♦♦

*25980 Hwy 243, Idyllwild / 909/659-4960*
Although this Mexican eatery shares its log-walled space with the Squirrel's Nest (a burger, beer, and shake joint), Arriba feels cozy and spacious, with a fireplace and windows overlooking a tree-shaded path. Couples can order beef burritos doused in piquant red sauce, chimichangas, and fish tacos made with grilled red snapper. A combo dish of chile relleno and chicken enchilada, served with rice and beans, salad, or *albondigas*, comes with fresh guacamole for a dollar more. While the food isn't exactly romantic, the outdoor patio is: it comes alive at night with twinkly lights, rock music, and a young crowd who come to sip Arriba's secret, homemade frosty margaritas. If there is a night scene in Idyllwild, this is probably it. But with soft lights around you and a sky full of stars shining through the pine tops, it is a scene worth seeing in this sleepy town.
$ *AE, DIS, MC, V; no checks; breakfast, lunch, dinner every day, brunch Sun; full bar; reservations not required.*

## CAFÉ ROMA
♦

*54750 N Circle Dr, Idyllwild / 909/659-5212*
Café Roma is a cozy refuge to relax and unwind after a day in this mountain town. As with many Idyllwild hangouts, it's something of a mix of the conventional and the rustic. A river-rock fireplace warms the room, while windows overlook the lush pine trees outdoors. In warmer weather, you can even migrate to a corner table on the enclosed sun porch for a little romance. The food is simple, but healthy. A choice of salads, pastas (such as one with roasted eggplant and sun-dried tomatoes), pizza, and a wide variety of desserts, brought out on a creaky cart to tempt the unsuspecting, are the bill

of fare here. The cafe also prepares picnic lunches and other provisions for romantic getaways into the lovely woods outside.

$ *AE, DIS, MC, V; no checks; breakfast, lunch, dinner every day; beer and wine; reservations not necessary.* &

## GASTROGNOME
● ●

*54381 Ridgeview Dr, Idyllwild / 909/659-5055*
Known to the local yokels simply as "the Gnome," this chic but rustic country inn is replete with cedar panels, lace curtains, and two huge stone fireplaces beneath a lovely landscape painting. Floor-to-ceiling wine racks, polished copper panels, and brick and wood walls give the eatery a cozy feel for couples who want to enjoy a hearty meal after a long day of hiking the mountaintops high above the hamlet. Dinners feature rack of lamb or a selection of seafood dishes, which are prepared simply. Skewered shrimp, broiled salmon, halibut, and even lobster are among the fresh choices. For the carnivores, there are tournedos of beef capped with mushrooms and béarnaise. Lunch is more informal and features a respectable hamburger, which you can enjoy outdoors on one of the Gnome's two newly remodeled decks.

$$ *AE, DC, DIS, MC, V; no checks; lunch Mon–Sat, dinner every day, brunch Sun; full bar; reservations recommended; www.thegnome.com.* &

## MOZART HAUS
● ●

*264345 Hwy 243, Idyllwild / 909/659-5500*
This is a full-fledged restaurant, but the Bavarian bakery is fragrant and, admittedly, a diet buster. There's Black Forest strudel (filled with chocolate, cherries, and cream cheese), classic crepes Salzburg, and a light breakfast menu with strudel, Incan porridge, and organic coffees. The modest A-framed cottage has a high apex and ample windows that bathe the hospitable natural wood and native Bavarian bric-a-brac and decor with generous forest-filtered light. The Bavarian motif carries as far as flower-painted porcelain and china, and a staff that, weather permitting, would be equally happy in dirndls or lederhosen. Mozart Haus's cozy dining rooms best lend themselves to snowy winter dinners, featuring bratwurst, knockwurst, or bockwurst, all served with plenty of classic German side fare such as potato salad, spaetzle, sauerkraut, or cucumber salad. Mozart's garden is a lovely place to down its selection of German, Austrian, and Czech beers, especially Weteberger Dark, a favorite from Germany's oldest brewery. The garden is also where local patrons come the last week of September to kick off the Harvest ritual known as Oktoberfest.

$$$ *AE, DC, DIS, MC, V; checks OK; lunch, dinner Thurs–Mon; beer and wine; reservations recommended.*

## OMA'S EUROPEAN BAKERY & RESTAURANT
♥
*54241 Ridgeview Dr, Idyllwild / 909/659-2979*
Located on the outer rim of Idyllwild's village area away from the busy weekend bustle, Oma's is ground zero for a romantic morning. When the moment calls for something light, low key, and fattening, stop in at Oma's for an amazing array of forbidden confections to sweeten the experience. Large, thick, and soft scones are the thing to have here, with hazelnut-flavored coffee. The scones break like cake in your hand and are best enjoyed with Oma's homemade honey butter or fig jam. Jumbo cinnamon rolls also have made a reputation for themselves in these parts, and day-old pastry is not wasted here, but rolled into today's bread pudding. If you want to sit down for a complete breakfast, try the cheese blintzes—the real thing—served with sour cream and cherry preserves. Belgian waffles topped with in-season fruit, homemade granola, hot oatmeal, and homemade yogurt with fresh fruit and muffins are other winning selections. Have your morning refreshment in the "living room," where tables for two collect around a corner hearth filled with antique ceramic animals, a cuckoo clock, a gnome under a mushroom, and a bookshelf of rescued hardcovers from earlier eras. Cupids on the window add a touch of romance. Lunch also is served every day, and the food gets heavier with selections like wurst platters or Black Forest ham on generously stacked sandwiches.
*$ AE, DIS, MC, V; checks OK; breakfast, lunch every day; wine; reservations not necessary; www.omabakery.com.* &

# BIG BEAR AND LAKE ARROWHEAD

## ROMANTIC HIGHLIGHTS

Crisp mountain air, towering pines, and a quaint Bavarian setting lure lovers to the resort towns of Big Bear and Lake Arrowhead. Set high in the San Bernardino Mountains, these bucolic alpine villages sit on the shores of two manmade lakes, surrounded by the San Bernardino National Forest, and provide a pristine and relaxed backdrop for romance. From the rustic cabins of Big Bear to the exclusive vacation homes of Lake Arrowhead, these mountain burgs are the ultimate settings for hiking, skiing, mountain biking, or simply relaxing with the one you love.

**Big Bear** was first discovered in 1845 by Benjamin Wilson, the onetime mayor of Los Angeles and namesake of Mount Wilson, during an expedition to the Mojave River. Wilson reported back that this wilderness was "alive with bear." Today the only bears you'll likely find in the area are of the carved variety; still the region is rich with a history of the miners, loggers, and dam builders who first developed the resort town. Tourism began in the region shortly after a 45-foot dam was built in 1884 to harness the winter run-off, creating Big Bear Lake. Entrepreneur John Metcalf built the first resort hotel on the south shore a few years later, and Angelenos in search of some peace and quiet quickly began making the trek up the mountain.

Today the south shore is Big Bear's most densely populated region, with log-cabin cottages, B&Bs, pancake cafes, firewood outlets, and a busy gas station or two surrounded by tall, century-old pines. Indeed, Big Bear Lake is not so sleepy, with more than 15,000 residents calling the community home. And that number increases greatly with the growing number of tourists making the ascent into the San Bernardino Mountains to enjoy a bounty of activities, including skiing, snowboarding, mountain biking, hiking, camping, four-wheeling, horseback riding, sailing, and simply kicking back.

Highway 18 passes through the town of Big Bear Lake and its **main village**, which keeps its early 20th-century sensibility with Victorian cottages leading off the main street, and weathered wooden façades fronting the stores and cafes. Whatever the season, couples can easily spend an hour or two ambling from bookstore to jewelry boutique and sports clothing outlet to sweets shop.

Couples who want to explore the forested trails of this breathtaking area should make their first stop the **Big Bear Discovery Center** (located on North Shore Dr between Fawnskin and Stanfield cutoff, next to the U.S. Forest Service Ranger Station; 909/866-3437). Friendly staffers will provide maps of the local trails and point couples toward the best paths for their hiking ability—whether that means an easy stroll through the shady forest or a power climb up a rocky façade. The center also offers hands-on learning activities, outdoor adventure-tour information, and souvenir shopping.

**Big Bear Lake**, which measures 6 miles in length and has 23 miles of shoreline, comes alive during the summer with swimming, boating, and weekend residents who come to enjoy the season at various summer retreats. Couples wanting to see the shore from the lake's vantage point can board the **Big Bear Queen** (909/866-3218; www.bigbearmarina.com). The paddle-wheeler makes hour-and-a-half-long narrated lake tours and runs every day during the summer months. Lovers can book a romantic, moonlit dinner cruise on Tuesday and Thursday evenings.

Or, get up before the sun, head for Pleasure Point Marina, and hit the lake for a day of fishing with **Big Bear Charter Fishing** (909/866-2240; www.bigbearfishing.com). Whether the two of you are serious anglers or just want to get out on the lake and pretend you are, these friendly fishermen will provide all your gear and will help you hook a trout or two. The two of you just have to show up and cast out a line.

A moonlit mountain trail ride can also be an amorous way to spend the evening in this alpine resort town. **Rockin' K Riding Stables** (731 Tulip Ln; 909/878-4677) has 90-minute rides when the moon is waxing half or better. They also offer sunset rides and trail rides for up to four hours. Experienced riders can even take to the trails and camp out under the stars with your horse, your honey, and a couple of doting camp staffers who'll fix your coffee and grub—and strum campfire songs while you look for Orion.

Nearby, **Lake Arrowhead** sets the mood for mountain romance, though it is more of an exclusive retreat with beautiful lakefront mansions than neighboring laid-back Big Bear. Named for an arrowhead-shaped rock rooted in American Indian folklore, the area has a storied history as a 1920s resort town, when the Hollywood elite flocked to the alpine retreat to escape city life. Back in those days, the **Lake Arrowhead Village**, located on the south shore at the end of Highway 173, was the hub of activity. It was the site of the community dance hall, where couples gathered to listen to big band music and dance the night away. While the dance hall's original steeple still stands, today the village has become a cluster of faux-Swiss offices, outlet shops, a perennial Christmas shop, and restaurants, all housed in a newer structure that was rebuilt in 1979, after the original village was burned down in a fire department drill. Fronting the beautiful lake, the village is still a fun place to stroll and take in the mountain ambience.

Near the village, a marina joins the picturesque lake. Since this pristine body of water is restricted to use by residents, the only way to experience this alpine jewel is to embark on a romantic tour aboard the **Arrowhead Queen** (purchase tickets dockside at Leroy's Sports; 909/337-3814). The 60-passenger paddle-wheeler passes historical landmarks and sites along the lake with a narrating script and makes hourly departures from the village from 10am to 6pm every day during the summer months.

During the winter months, downhill skiing and snowboarding may be the main attraction in this neck of the woods, but for lovers who want to enjoy the peace and quiet of the forest—and get a good workout—cross-country skiing is another option. **Rim Nordic Cross Country Skiing** (Highway 18, five miles east of Running Springs; 909/867-2600; www.rimnordic.com) takes groups out to traverse the snow-covered meadows of this beautiful setting. Once the two of you have tried this sport, you may never want to strap on downhill skis again.

Ice skating is another winter activity that can bring out the romantic in us all. In nearby Blue Jay, the **Ice Castle** (401 Burnt Mill Rd; 909/337-0802; www.icecastle.us) lets couples skate the day away. The facility serves as a training center for Olympic figure skaters. You won't find hockey boards here. Rather, you have an open, spacious skating area with views into the surrounding woods, and ballet-style mirrors across one end of the floor so you can monitor your form and style. And you won't have to wait until "couples' skate" to hold hands while you glide across the ice together.

While winter sports are a fun way to spend the day, just driving around the scenic forests of this mountain resort can be romantic during any season. You can cruise the Rim of the World Highway, which provides marvelous airy views of the surrounding high desert—stark, rocky, and bare with verdant pockets—while the pines seem to get thicker with the altitude. Along the way, find a number of romantic spots to check out and take your time. The mountain can wait: the scenery is gorgeous and life seems to go on as it always has as you pass little mountain hamlets like Crestline, Lake Gregory (the best summer lake swimming in the area, as the water temperatures are near perfect), and Twin Peaks—all framed by dense forest and quiet, narrow roads. Before you start your trek, the two of you may want to stop in at the **Alpine Deli** (27226 Hwy 189; 909/337-1776) in Blue Jay and pick up snacks for the road. After all, you never know when you'll round a twisty mountain bend and come upon the perfect spot for an impromptu alpine picnic.

As you drive, you'll see haunting reminders of the fire of 2003 that burned nearly a million acres, stopping just short of Big Bear. Charred relics, robbed of branches and needles, stand stumped and stunned on hills they had shaded for possibly a hundred years. Perhaps these remains can serve as a reminder to make the most of every day, starting with your romantic journey to this charmingly beautiful mountain resort.

## Access and Information

Highway 18 leads into the Big Bear and Lake Arrowhead mountain resort region. To reach Big Bear Lake from Interstate 10, drive Highway 30 and Highway 330 into the mountains, where Highway 330 connects with Highway 18 in Running Springs. To reach Lake Arrowhead, bypass Highway 330; Highway 30 also connects with Highway 18 about 25 minutes south of Lake Arrowhead, providing a more direct route. If you're heading east on Interstate 10, Interstate 215 is a shortcut to Highway 30 (for either lake).

There are several good first stops for information. The **Big Bear Resort Chamber of Commerce Visitors Center** (630 Bartlett Rd; 909/866-7000 or 800/4-BIG BEAR; www.bigbear.com) offers brochures and maps and has people to answer your questions. You can pick up a free, detailed map of the area at the **Lake Arrowhead Communities Chamber of Commerce** (in Lake Arrowhead Village, lower level; 909/337-3715 or 800/337-3716; www.lakearrowhead.net).

# Romantic Lodgings

## ALPENHORN BED & BREAKFAST
🌣🌣🌣

*601 Knight Ave, Big Bear Lake / 909/866-5700 or 888/829-6600*
The exterior of the eight-room Alpenhorn is reminiscent of a quaint Adirondack cabin, while the interior seems every inch a country manor house. Couples can prepare for an apron-adorned staff to minister to their every need—from serving gourmet evening hors d'oeuvres to turning down the bed at night in the elegant style of the world's swankiest hotels. A blend of antiques, gorgeous textiles, plush hypoallergenic mattresses, romantic fireplaces, and updated bathrooms all contribute to the refreshing semiformal ambience. The inn is surrounded by beautifully landscaped gardens, and a rambling stream lies just beyond the rear deck. In the design, construction, and operation of the facility, owners-innkeepers Robbie and Chuck Slemaker have clearly emulated the five-star comfort, service, and convenience of some of California's best-known wine country bed-and-breakfasts. As the locals say, breakfast alone is worth the visit to this chic inn. Why? Because this multicourse meal, presented on Villeroy and Boch fine china with gleaming Oneida silverware, includes such delicious treats as cheese strata, custom-cooked eggs, sweet grapefruit brûlée, creamy banana-swirled oatmeal, and homemade granola with yogurt. Yum!
*$$$ AE, DC, DIS, MC, V; checks OK; www.alpenhorn.com.* ♿

## CHATEAU DU LAC BED & BREAKFAST
🌣

*911 Hospital Rd, Lake Arrowhead / 909/337-6488 or 800/601-8722*
This inn has been called everything from "Hansel and Gretel on the outside, Hans Christian Andersen on the inside," to an "undeniably special attraction." Its most important cache, however, is that it looks down onto the lake, making it one appealing—even dignified—place indeed. Chateau Du Lac lacks pretense but maintains its elegance and romance, and does so without losing subtlety in the equation. Each of its five rooms is elegantly decked out; fancy pillows and an occasional teddy bear keep things warm and comfy. All rooms feature a mesmerizing view of the lake, but the premium Lakeview Suite features the ultimate romantic vantage point. This enticing suite sets the stage for love with a private balcony, fireplace, sound system, and an expansive bathroom with Jacuzzi, which has its own lookout onto the lake. Breakfast at the inn includes quiches, scones, omelets, and other entrées, which make the morning lavishly enjoyable. In fact, so is the afternoon, thanks to afternoon tea.
*$$$ AE, DC, DIS, MC, V; checks OK; www.chateau-du-lac.com.*

## GOLD MOUNTAIN MANOR
🍯🍯

*1117 Anita Ave, Big Bear City / 909/585-6997*
Gold Mountain lies along Big Bear Lake's north shore in an area that features large rustic cabins with a solid architectural lineage. If you're looking for seclusion, this is not really the place, since neighboring cabins surround the inn. But not to worry; the inn remains nothing if not a grand old log mansion, set back beyond a front lawn bestrewn with pines. Built in 1928 with sturdy timbers and strong architectural details, the historical inn has been expertly and lovingly restored to its former glory by owners-innkeepers Trish and Jim Gordon. At most bed-and-breakfasts, there's often a tradeoff between finding yourself amid multigenerational clutter and enjoying modern amenities. It's a dilemma that the Gordons have solved rather well. All seven rooms range in size from the Lucky Baldwin, a modest themed retreat of red and black flannel that's perfect for snuggling, to the large and alluring Ted Ducey Suite, which sports a wood stove, private whirlpool tub, a glassed-in-porch-turned-bedroom, and an Old West motif. Couples can while away the afternoon on the inn's shady wraparound porch or curl up in the cozy and wonderfully romantic living room, complete with its mammoth stone fireplace, which is the perfect setting for a cold, snowy night. Each morning, the Gordons (who possess formal culinary training) present a full gourmet breakfast, along with hors d'oeuvres and beverages in the afternoon.
*$$$ AE, DC, MC, V; no checks; www.goldmountainmanor.com.*

## GRAY SQUIRREL INN
🍯

*326 S Hwy 173, Lake Arrowhead / 909/336-3602*
There are bound to be plenty of gray squirrels, as well as Steller's Jays, on hand to greet couples checking in for a romantic getaway at this nine-unit hideaway. Nestled amid great oaks, prestigious pines, soothing cedars, and the magnificent dogwoods that bloom in the spring, the Gray Squirrel Inn is within walking distance of the Lake Arrowhead Village and the lake itself. All rooms are individually decorated and have a unique appeal. Some have frilly floral bedding, while others feel more rustic. Two honeymoon suites are the slam-dunk best places to kiss—each has an incredible forest view—but couples who desire extra space may want to check into a family suite, which has a kitchenette, living room, bedroom, and bathroom. If the two of you are planning to enjoy the great indoors instead of the mountain setting, you may want to reserve the executive suite, which features a 52-inch big-screen TV, two couches in the living room (one is a remote-control massage couch), a bedroom equipped with a queen-sized bed, and a kitchen with an icemaker and microwave.
*$$ MC, V; no checks; www.graysquirrelinn.com.* &

# Romance on the Slopes

A beautiful setting, fresh mountain air, towering pines, and swooshing down the slopes with the one you love can make for a truly romantic day. Whether you and your sweetie are beginner skiers more concerned with where you'll savor hot chocolate in front of a roaring fire after a day on the slopes, or die-hard snowboarders ready to take on the most challenging halfpipe, the Big Bear–Lake Arrowhead area is Southern California's winter playground. Set high in the San Bernardino Mountains, this alpine region serves as home to several major ski resorts where lovers can enjoy the beauty of a snowy mountain day together. Ski season usually runs from November to April, depending on Mother Nature.

The **Snow Summit Ski Resort** (880 Summit Blvd; 909/866-5766; www.bigbearmountainresorts.com) is the area's most popular ski resort and was designed to attract skiers of all levels. Eleven chair lifts take skiers up the mountain. And snowmaking machines ensure that the well-groomed terrain provides enough snow for a great day on the slopes. There are also freestyle areas for adventurous skiers and snowboarders.

Nearby **Bear Mountain** (4310 Goldmine Dr; 909/585-2519) has been transformed into **The Park at Bear Mountain**, a 195-acre snowy expanse devoted entirely to freestyle terrain. Within the park, daredevils will find jumps, jibs, and halfpipes, which provide plenty of opportunities to impress your significant other.

Combined, both areas offer 430 skiable acres, with 55 runs for everyone from beginners to black diamond skiers. Twenty-three chair lifts, including four high-speed quads, whisk you and your sweetheart to the top. Lift tickets are good for runs and shuttles at both resorts, which reside about a mile apart. It's best to call ahead and reserve tickets (909/866-5766; www.bigbearmountainresorts.com).

In nearby Running Springs, **Snow Valley** (35100 Hwy 18; 909/867-2751; www.snow-valley.com) offers 35 ski trails set on 240 acres of skiable terrain. While there is a ski and snowboard school for beginners, this resort also offers a designated Snow Play area, where couples can sled and frolic in the snow without having to brave the steep mountain. Bring a gourmet lunch and the two of you can even enjoy a picnic amid this winter wonderland.

During the summer months, Snow Summit opens its **Scenic Chair Lift** for rides up to the top of the mountain. Whether you come to enjoy the view of the tree tops and the surrounding mountain caps or to ascend the summit as a starting point for an alpine hike, this romantic two-seater ride will make your hearts flutter.

—LARK ELLEN GOULD AND BILL BECKER

## MOOSE LODGE
❤❤

*39328 Big Bear Blvd, Big Bear Lake / 909/866-2435 or 877/585-5855*
This fine and funky lodge, located within 2 miles from almost everything
in Big Bear, is a great place for couples to live out that rustic-cabin-in-
the-woods fantasy. Twenty separate cabins with kitchens or kitchenettes
and wood fireplaces are spread out on 2 acres under some of the oldest and
tallest pines in Big Bear. Several cabins have Jacuzzi tubs for added warmth.
Couples in search of an amorous spot will want to check out Cabin 5, which
is particularly romantic with its French country decor, queen-sized bed,
and full kitchen. Here, lovers can soak in the indoor Jacuzzi, which boasts
a view of the fireplace. Most cabins have some theme attached—whether it's
fishing and sailing, bears, beach, deer, skiing, or the Shenandoah—and all are
simple, well heated, clean, and furnished with dining tables, televisions, basic
bathrooms, and very comfortable queen-sized beds. There is no maid service
unless requested, which can be a blessing for couples who like to hibernate.
Many of the cabins feature a screened-in porch, which is a good place to sit
and watch the wind in the trees on temperate days and starry evenings. In
the summer, lovers can compete in ping-pong and horseshoes or work on their
tans at the pool. Or add a little heat to your romantic retreat with a visit to the
barrel-shaped wooden sauna, which is available at all hours.
$$$ *AE, MC, V; checks OK; www.majesticmooselodge.com.*

## NORTHWOODS RESORT
❤❤

*40650 Village Dr, Big Bear Lake / 909/866-3121 or 800/866-3121*
Located less than two blocks from the lake and only steps away from the
Big Bear Village, this 147-room resort is the area's closest thing to a conven-
tional hotel. Inside the main lobby, a giant river-rock fireplace is aglow with
a blazing fire and log trim lines the comfy room, creating the feeling of a
rustic mountain lodge. Guest rooms may be on the newer side, but they have
been decorated with custom-designed wood furnishings by local artisan Tim
Holland to give the feel of a mountain retreat. Guest rooms facing the hotel's
lush courtyard have balconies overlooking the resort's year-round heated
pool and spa, perfect for couples who want to open the door and enjoy the
fresh mountain air. Lovebirds may want to splurge and check into one of the
resort's 10 suites, which sport fireplaces, kitchenettes, wet bars, stand-alone
whirlpool tubs, and VCRs and DVD players so the two of you can snuggle in
for movie night. A well-equipped fitness room provides a place to work out,
but on a beautiful day, the nearby hiking trails seem much more appealing.
Northwoods Trading Company, the resort's gift and sundry shop, features
many items created by local artisans. The hotel's restaurant, Stillwells (see
Romantic Restaurants), serves breakfast, lunch, and dinner.
$$$ *AE, DIS, MC, V; no checks; www.northwoodsresort.com.* ♿

# ROSE GABLES VICTORIAN BED AND BREAKFAST
◐◐

*29024 Mammoth Dr, Lake Arrowhead / 909/336-9892*
Leave it to the English to give us the most pristine Victorian-themed inn in Lake Arrowhead. In their "retirement," English couple Meryl and Don Jacks have fashioned a three-room inn from a former single-family house high on a hilltop with breathtaking views of the mountains and desert beyond. Only half the pair—Meryl—is truly English, but she has clearly remade the little house into an inn by applying extraordinary elements of English decor, such as antiques, wallpaper, bric-a-brac, and paintings. As a complement to Meryl's design skills, Don is an expert craftsman who has fashioned all of the wood floors, stone fireplaces, and ceramic tile throughout the house. Consequently, the rooms here are delightful (all come with his-and-her cotton robes). The top room, known as Pearls and Lace, is decidedly romantic and features a forest view, step-up king-sized bed, a big bath tub, and a fireplace in both the bedroom and the bathroom. Sound like a great place to kiss yet? As for common areas, inside a cozy den features a fireplace, dartboard, and private sauna/steam chamber. Outside, an enchanted front garden produces flowers throughout the year. Meryl's breakfasts revolve around her delicious waffles with fresh fruit, omelets, or fresh-baked quiche. Indeed, her cooking is top-flight. Pop enough of her generous hors d'oeuvres in the evening, and the two of you might very well decide that dinner in town will not be necessary. After all, a lovely night in might do just as well.
**$$** *MC, V; checks OK; www.rosegables.com.*

# STARGAZERS INN & OBSERVATORY
◐◐

*717 Jeffries Rd, Big Bear Lake / 909/878-4496, 909/878-4067, or 866/482-7827*
Most lovers don't know that there's really an observatory—albeit a solar one—in Big Bear. A big former CalTech Jet Propulsion Laboratory sungazing station sits on a jetty in the middle of the lake, off the north shore. You can also spot the heavens from the Stargazers Inn & Observatory's computerized telescope. A heavenly retreat in its own right, this romantic inn boasts five alluring rooms with private spa tubs, fireplaces, fresh-cut flowers, evening turndown service, lavish terry cloth robes, soft down comforters, featherbeds, complimentary bath salts and aromatherapy, and VCRs and DVD players. A romance package features candlelight in your room; rose petals strewn on your bed; piquant incense in your whirlpool-equipped bathroom—you get the picture. For those who want to gaze to the skies, this B&B features a spectacular gallery of space photos and an evening astronomy program. (Don't worry, you and yours will suffer no demerits for some deft kissing on the sly between slides.) While the night skies are spectacular to even the naked eye, couples can peer into the telescope for

views of the earth's moon, planets, galaxies, star clusters, nebulae, comets, lunar eclipses, meteors, and satellites. The inn's living room boasts multiple fireplaces, a TV, videos, bookshelves, board games, billiards, and darts. Thinking of serenading your sweetheart? A small baby grand piano and karaoke machine are on hand for any such romantic gestures. The inn's three outdoor decks offer great views of the night skies, the surrounding mountains, and area wildlife. Breakfast comes in two sizes here: an early bird version is served at 7am for skiers, fishermen, and others who want an early start; and a full breakfast begins at 8am for "the rest of us." Hors d'oeuvres and beverages are served during the evening social hour, and there's also a 24-hour refreshment center with soda, coffee, and tea.
$$$ AE, DIS, MC, V; checks OK; www.stargazersinn.com.

## STORYBOOK INN
◔

*28717 Hwy 18, Skyforest / 909/337-0011 or 877/337-0011*
This charming and romantic B&B, which claims a history more than six decades long, sits pretty on the enchanting Rim of the World Highway, with its breathtaking views (some say you can see all the way to the Pacific Ocean on a clear day). Innkeepers Richard and Patty Teachout welcome guests to their themed guest rooms, perhaps the most romantic of which is the Tom Sawyer Suite, which features its own entrance, a sun porch with breathtaking views, a wood-burning stove, and a Jacuzzi tub. All rooms, however, boast down feather beds and pillows for long, lazy mornings, and TVs with VCRs (there's a complimentary video library) for quiet evenings. The hotel's View Restaurant, featuring simple presentations of classic continental cuisine, is open on weekends and holidays and will provide a candlelit in-room dinner for two. Complimentary buffet breakfast and evening libations are served each day. A bocci ball court, archery range, hiking trails, and mountain bikes provide lovers with plenty of activity. Or simply stake out one of the inn's hammocks and laze the day away.
$$ AE, MC, V; checks OK; www.storybookinn.com. ઙ

## WILLOW CREEK INN
◔◔

*1176 N Hwy 173, Lake Arrowhead / 909/336-4582 or 877/MNTN-AIR*
Unlike the rustic historic cabins you might associate with a casual mountain resort, the Willow Creek Inn is more like a supersized B&B. Set in a modern and grandiose contemporary showcase home, this gray-and-white Cape Cod–style estate sits on the north side of Lake Arrowhead, and it's a class act all the way. Its manicured front lawn sweeps up toward the entry porch. Inside, a sunken living room sports a river-rock fireplace, and extra-large windows frame the wooded rear of the house. Innkeeper Letty Cummings is clearly a perfectionist, though she does not let that interfere with

her gracious and congenial personality. She may be watching every detail, but at the same time, she makes couples feel like cherished family friends. The four upstairs guest rooms are decked out with designer floral fabrics, classic crown moldings, and chair rails, which add an air of distinction to the newer home. Each has its own thoughtfully outfitted private bath, the most spectacular of which is in the enormous Celebration Suite that boasts a bay-window spa tub for two. In the morning, the scent of Cummings's fresh cinnamon rolls is enough to get anyone out of bed.
**$$** *AE, DIS, MC, V; checks OK; www.arrowheadbandb.com.*

## WINDY POINT INN
❂❂❂
*39015 North Shore Dr, Big Bear / 909/866-2746*
This contemporary architectural showpiece B&B, plunked down right on the shore, has the best view in the San Bernardino Mountains, which creates an amazing backdrop for kissing. While you may be tempted to stay in your room all day—luxuriating in front of a fire, soaking in the two-person tub (most guest bathrooms have them), or sliding open a door to gentle breezes and a 300° view of open water and distant peaks—the welcoming great room is also a wonderful place to snuggle up with the one you love and gaze out the floor-to-ceiling windows overlooking the lake. If there's any inn in Big Bear with feng shui or Zen to it, it's this one, with its varied collection of art and sculptures and eclectic furnishings. In the evenings, the two of you can make use of a telescope for stargazing or take a moonlit stroll down to the inn's private dock and beach. Innkeepers Val and Kent Kessler know about hospitality—especially when it comes to breakfast. Lounge back on the tree-fringed lakefront deck and partake of 1 of their 24 gourmet breakfast menus. Or better yet, have breakfast served in your room.
**$$$$** *AE, DIS, MC, V; checks OK; www.windypointinn.com.*

# *Romantic Restaurants*

## CASUAL ELEGANCE
❂❂
*26848 Hwy 189, Agua Fria / 909/337-8932*
Jan Morrison is a local legend. The self-taught chef is known as Lake Arrowhead's Ms. Congeniality, and her restaurant, Casual Elegance, holds the unofficial title of Lake Arrowhead's best and most romantic. Set in a modestly redone, little 1939 house just five minutes from Lake Arrowhead Village, Casual Elegance was founded in 1991, expanding on Morrison's successful catering business by offering her signature dishes at this dinner-only eatery. Eclectic mountain-rustic rooms feature just a few tables each, giving couples an intimate dinner setting. Each night, Morrison whirls

away in her kitchen, but without fail comes out to greet her guests. Her extremely creative menu includes Maryland-style crab cakes with a ginger-papaya cream sauce, pork medallions with tart cherries, flame-broiled rib-eye and New York steaks, and New Zealand rack of lamb encrusted with either honey-hazelnut or roasted garlic. For dessert, couples will want to save room for lascivious ice cream pies, including fudge and butterscotch. Morrison's daughter, Jackie, has assembled an impressive wine list to pair with her mother's creations, including both lesser known and boutique California labels—exquisite when sipped from Morrison's top-flight Riedel crystal stemware.

$$$ *AE, DC, DIS, MC, V; no checks; dinner Wed–Sun; beer and wine; reservations required.*

---

## EVERGREEN INTERNATIONAL SEAFOOD & STEAK RESTAURANT
✿

*40771 Lakeview Dr, Big Bear Lake / 909/866-7675*

This cavernous wood-wrought restaurant overlooking the lake is ready for romance, from the twinkle lights strung from the moldings to the faux-rose trellised altar and pergola in the front corner. Windowside tables in the far reaches of the restaurant offer privacy with a view. At night, candlelight makes up for the darkened lake view, but couples may want to start their evening with sunset cocktails and relax with a panorama of sparkling lake water and pines under a multicolored sky. Dinner begins with warm bread and homemade Bavarian sweet butter that melts in your mouth. Appealing entrée choices include diamond-cut slow-roasted prime rib au jus, presented with a fresh rose on top (served on weekends only); New York steak *au poivre* with cognac peppercorn sauce; rack of veal with mushroom sauce; and grilled and marinated passion fruit chicken served over rice. Or order filet of beef Wellington à deux that is crowned in a delicate mushroom sauce and baked in flaky pastry crust for a mouthwatering meal. The restaurant doubles as a wedding hall when you say the word, and owner Dr. Jerry Lemke, a pastor of the Baptist faith, is a fun man to have around to manage the vows.

$$$ *AE, DIS, MC, V; no checks; lunch Sat–Sun, dinner every day, brunch Sun; full bar; reservations not necessary.* ♿

---

## FRED AND MARY'S
✿✿✿

*607 Pine Knot Ave, Big Bear Lake / 909/866-2434*

From the just-folks sound of its name, you might expect Fred and Mary's to be a homey little comfort-food joint. You'd be wrong. Though the interior is unremarkable—a vaguely Tuscan motif of sponge-painted walls and majolica fruits, with curiously contrasting Western-style wood chairs—it's the impressive California cuisine emerging from talented chef Colin

Colville's small kitchen that lures lovers to this atypical mountain eatery. While some locals don't quite know what to make of the inventive menu, which features bluefin tuna, pork tenderloin, and duck confit (accented with oven-roasted leeks, spicy fennel, and chipotle), foodies are thrilled to have a gourmet eatery in this unadventurous dining region. The bill is modest compared to similar meals in L.A., and the portions are abundant, but dinner here will prove to be one of the more expensive meals in town. Service can be unpredictable, but if gourmet fare adds to the amour of the evening, this restaurant definitely will take your love quotient up a notch.

$$$ *AE, DIS, MC, V; no checks; dinner Thurs–Mon; beer and wine; reservations recommended.* ᴋ

## MADLON'S
⌀❹

*829 W Big Bear Blvd, Big Bear City / 909/585-3762*
This fairy-tale country cottage just across the Big Bear city line comes highly recommended from local innkeepers. Restaurant namesake Madlon is a magnanimous matriarch who loves to stop by her customers' tables, and otherwise fills her lace-curtained, storybook-like eatery with warmth and friendliness. Since founding Madlon's in 1987, she has put together an appealing menu of favorites sure to entice the taste buds of even the most finicky lovebirds. Couples can settle in to one of the restaurant's deep comfy booths and order such perennial favorites as chardonnay-poached salmon, ahi Florentine, braised lamb shanks in white bean stew, goat-cheese stuffed chicken, or a traditional filet mignon. A signature appetizer of jalapeño cream soup, with just enough cream to subtly suffocate the peppers' searing heat, is a brilliant way to start your meal. Just ask for two spoons, and the two of you can share this warm and comforting treat.

$$$ *DC, DIS, MC, V; no checks; dinner Tues–Sun, brunch Sat–Sun; beer and wine; reservations recommended.*

## PAOLI'S NEIGHBORHOOD ITALIAN RESTAURANT
⌀

*40821 Village Dr, Big Bear Lake / 909/866-2020*
Paoli's is the kind of place you are grateful to see on a cold winter afternoon when the snow is beginning to bear down. Warm and cozy, this traditional Italian place does the trick with red-and-white-checkered tablecloths and windowside booths. The two of you can warm each other's hands, then warm your hearts with some of Mama Paoli's rich minestrone or thick pasta e fagioli soups. The casual comeliness of the place allows for puffy jackets, muddy boots—whatever you have on—and it's more about old-fashioned charm than quiet and serene fine dining. Four-cheese lasagne in a rich meat sauce is the specialty of the house and comes with soup or salad and garlic bread. Other authentic Italian entrées include chicken piccata and

shrimp scampi, or simply go casual and order a large pizza. The service is quick and polite, and couples won't break the bank on this no-frills hearty meal.

$ AE, DIS, MC, V; no checks; lunch, dinner every day; beer and wine; reservations not necessary. &

## STILLWELLS
●●

*40650 Village Dr (Northwoods Resort), Big Bear Lake / 909/866-3121*
Located in the Northwoods Resort (see Romantic Lodgings), Stillwells is an antler-trophy-and-pine kind of place. A large stone fireplace and exposed beamed ceiling give it an alpine, après-ski atmosphere. Knotty pine chairs, log cabin–like walls, cozy booths, and large tables, as well as an outdoor carp and turtle pond, complete the rustic picture. The menu includes creatively presented seafood, such as Ritz cracker–coated crab cakes, smoked trout salad, shrimp scampi, and blackened salmon. However, prime aged filet mignon, New Zealand rack of lamb, and venison osso buco style (which arrives steaming in the night air, with asparagus spears set upright around it) provide a hearty meal sure to help you and your sweetie sustain the chilly mountain air. For dessert, the two of you may want to share s'mores, which you can roast over a fire and assemble right at your table. Isn't that much better than campfire cooking? The rest of the dessert menu is equally tantalizing, with fruit cobblers and several cheesecakes. On Sunday mornings, a champagne brunch features a variety of breakfast and lunch creations, including a cooked-to-order pasta station. There is live music on weekends and on the patio during the summer.

$$$ AE, DIS, MC, V; no checks; breakfast, lunch, dinner every day, brunch Sun; full bar; reservations recommended; www.northwoodsresort.com. &

## SUSHI ICHIBAN
●

*42151 Big Bear Blvd, Big Bear Lake / 909/866-6413*
If you're one of those people who can't imagine ordering seafood at a mountain location, you needn't worry about finding a sushi bar in Big Bear. If, on the other hand, you and your partner are craving sushi during your mountain visit, head straight for Sushi Ichiban. Besides providing a cozy, romantic ambience, it's the only sushi bar around and offers commendable sushi, too. Whether in the city or the country, behind every great sushi bar is a great sushi chef. In this case, it's sushi master Abe-san, an L.A. transplant who has set up shop in a highly visible corner in the midst of a residential shopping corridor, across the street from Big Bear's K-Mart. At least three days a week, Abe-san personally heads down the mountain to find the freshest fish available. Admittedly, his place is tiny—only six sushi bar seats and a few simple dinette tables along the front window—but that just

makes the find rarer. Abe-san is mainly a purist, though a few "designer" rolls, like California and spider, show up on the hand-lettered special board. He also offers teriyaki, sukiyaki, katsu, and udon-noodle bowls (a great, if unorthodox, après-ski warm up).

**$$** *AE, MC, V; no checks; lunch, dinner Thurs–Tues; beer and wine; reservations not accepted.*

# THE PALM SPRINGS DESERT RESORT AREA

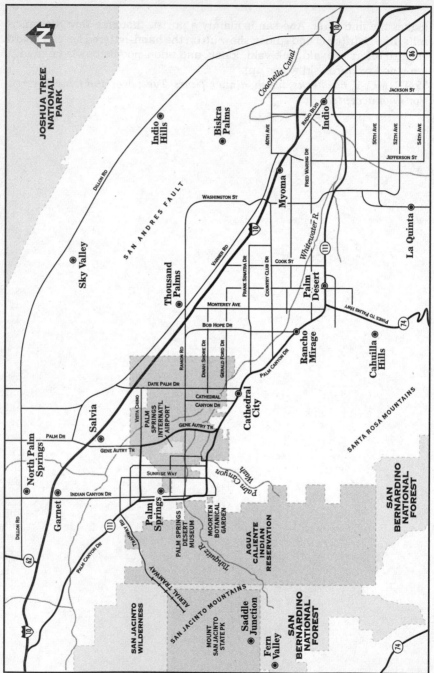

# ♡ THE PALM SPRINGS DESERT RESORT AREA

**H**ugged by sensuously sloping foothills and bisected by the snaking Interstate 10, Southern California's desert resort cities have lured pleasure-seeking couples for more than a century. After all, who could resist the intoxicating blend of relaxing sun-kissed days, star-kissed balmy evenings, and the small-town pace that persists despite the area's phenomenal growth over the decades?

The Coachella Valley stretches from the San Gorgonio Pass, gateway to Palm Springs (where fields of towering, wind-driven turbines herald your arrival), west toward Arizona, and encompasses about a dozen little communities. Movement along the San Andreas Fault over the millennia lowered this area and also lifted the adjacent mountains to 10,000 feet or more. These ranges, the San Jacinto and San Gorgonio, frame the valley with slopes purple in summer and enticingly snowcapped in winter. Although runaway development of the flat valley floor has created a patchwork of emerald golf courses, gleaming luxury communities, and vast stretches of auto-friendly pavement, there is plenty of wild terrain for exploring, and the telltale perfume of smoky mesquite and fragrant creosote reminds anyone who steps outdoors this is truly a distinctive environment.

This magical oasis is only two hours by car from Los Angeles and San Diego and has always evoked a sense of romance. In the city of Palm Springs, intimate inns and secluded hideaways far outnumber traditional hotels, a testament to the amorous intentions of your fellow vacationers. Lazy days spent swimming, sunbathing, and shopping together are what the desert is about, followed by low-key evenings of fine dining, entertainment, and often moonlit soaking in the ubiquitous hot tub. Weather is definitely the desert's calling card, since the mercury is already approaching shorts-and-tanks weather while most of the country shovels late spring snowfalls. Even in Southern California, coastal dwellers get a jump on summer by heading to the desert. All this makes Palm Springs—and its neighboring resort towns—unique in the otherwise year-round destination of California. The desert has very distinct "high" and "low" seasons, which affect hotel rates dramatically. The high season is in winter, from January through April: although the weather mimics the rest of Southern California, visitors from around the country are escaping the chill, and always-full hotels get to charge full price. Spring and fall are "shoulder" seasons, when the desert begins to warm into the 80s; this is the most wonderful time to visit and take advantage of reasonable rates. In summer, usually from Memorial Day through mid-September, sizzling temperatures attract bargain hunters, since room rates are slashed by as much as 50 percent. For couples who can take the heat, it's the perfect time to celebrate romance amid the beauty of the serene desert region.

# PALM SPRINGS

## ROMANTIC HIGHLIGHTS

For many couples in search of romance, the city of Palm Springs *is* the desert. This grown-up little frontier town was originally inhabited by the American Indians who understood how to live, soaking in the valley's natural hot spring baths during winter, then fleeing to its cool and verdant canyons to escape the summer heat. In the 1920s, bungalow courts and small motels sprang up, and Hollywood's Golden Age celebrities swept in to vacation in the glorious, dry winter sunshine, sparking illicit romances that made their way back to Los Angeles gossip columnists. Through the 1950s and '60s, Frank Sinatra, Bob Hope, President Eisenhower, and a host of other big names—including honeymooners Elvis and Priscilla Presley—kept Palm Springs in the limelight. Today, Palm Springs is in the midst of an unprecedented revival that has it gracing the covers of style and leisure magazines around the world. Hollywood celebrities are back in droves; a stylish gay community has embraced the town; and hipster baby boomers have discovered Palm Springs as an enclave of classic midcentury architecture, much of it by internationally acclaimed Southern California design masters like Richard Neutra, Rudolph Schindler, and Palm Springs's most defining architect, Le Corbusier disciple Albert Frey.

But before golf courses and Cadillacs, before movie stars and socialites, there was the Agua Caliente band of **Cahuilla Indians**. The tribe settled here more than 1,000 years ago, living a simple life amid the beauty and spirituality of the open desert. Today, the Cahuilla still own half the land on which Palm Springs is built and actively work to preserve the area's American Indian heritage. Four miles south of Palm Springs is the entrance to their reservation and three spectacular palm canyons open to couples in the mood to explore (South Palm Canyon Dr; 760/325-5673; www.indian-canyons .com). **Andreas, Murray**, and **Palm Canyons** offer huge granite formations, water-polished rock, rushing streams and quiet pools, and surprisingly dense groves of indigenous *Washingtonia* palms—they survive on snowmelt and underground water supplies. In 2001, nature-loving couples thrilled to the re-opening of the Agua Caliente–owned **Tahquitz Canyon** (500 W Mesquite Ave; 760/416-7044; www.tahquitzcanyon.com), a sacred place filled with American Indian legend and stunning natural scenery. Tahquitz's famous waterfall was featured in Frank Capra's 1936 film *Lost Horizon*, but the canyon later became a refuge for hippies, transients, and squatters, who vandalized the natural environment and left mounds of trash behind. In 1969 the tribe closed the canyon to outsiders. Today, there's a modern new visitor center, and two-hour ranger-led tours take couples who like to hike as far as the waterfall.

Tucked into the same mountainside plain as the Indian Canyons lies a man-made paradise of desert flora perfect for a quiet rendezvous for the botanically inclined couple. **Moorten Botanical Gardens** (1701 S Palm Canyon Dr; 760/327-6555) offers a quick tour of deserts around the globe in the span of a half-hour's walk. Rather than brilliant flowers and lush greenery, this otherworldly acreage boasts 3,000 varieties of hardy desert plants and features a stunning variety of local flora as well as imports collected by the Moortens on trips abroad. Clasp hands and follow the self-guided walking tour, where you'll pass succulents, smoke trees, agave, and ocotillos, as well as spiky plants, fuzzy plants, fragrant plants, and alien-looking plants. Don't miss the greenhouse-like "cactarium," where hundreds of rare, weird, and wonderful cacti flourish. Moorten Gardens offers cuttings for sale, and the entire grounds are often reserved for wedding parties—especially in spring, when the succulents flower in a brilliant display of color and shapes.

Couples can learn about the desert in its natural state through other outdoor activities, like the four-wheel-drive eco-tours offered by **Desert Adventures** (760/324-JEEP or 888/440-JEEP; www.red-jeep.com). Experienced naturalist guides man the company's fleet of red Jeeps, taking sweethearts into the rugged Santa Rosa Mountains, through untouched desert to learn about native wildlife, or through picturesque ravines that hug the San Andreas Fault.

Downtown Palm Springs is centered on **Palm Canyon Drive**, a wide, one-way boulevard that's designed to be pedestrian friendly—with tree-shaded benches, brick-paved sidewalks, and hidden courtyards. Each Thursday night, in fact, the street is closed to vehicles between Amado and Baristo

Roads for the pedestrian-only **VillageFest**. This popular street fair draws much of Palm Springs out to stroll and schmooze; crafts vendors and tempting food booths compete for your attention with wacky street performers and even wackier locals shopping at the mouthwatering fresh produce stalls. Couples can partake in such services as chair massage, acupressure, or even advice: we've seen tarot card readers and financial advisors as well as an "Ask the Rabbi" booth. The event is as much a neighborhood social as a chance to shop—and a huge part of Palm Springs life today. Though present-day Palm Canyon is lined with scores of art galleries, antique stores, souvenir shops, restaurants, and hotels, the street has managed to retain a nostalgic, small-town charm reminiscent of 1930s Palm Springs. The historic **Plaza Theatre** (128 S Palm Canyon Dr; 760/327-0225; www.psfollies.com) hosts the long-running **Fabulous Palm Springs Follies**, a vaudeville-style show filled with lively production numbers—the entire cast are "retired" showgirls, singers, dancers, and comedians who range in age from 50-something to 85-plus. Their energy is an inspiration, though the old-fashioned revue is mostly popular with an older crowd. Couples won't want to miss the **Plaza** (open between Palm Canyon Dr and the parallel, other-direction Indian Canyon Dr), one of the town's original shopping arcades, which sports the low-rise Spanish style—stucco archways, red-tile roofs, bougainvillea-draped railings—that characterizes much of old Palm Springs. Local fixture **Desmond's** (160 S Palm Canyon Dr; 760/325-1178) has occupied a prime Plaza space since 1936, long enough for their once-stodgy "mature resort wear" to gain new popularity among today's hipsters, who now shop alongside Palm Springs retirees for brightly patterned sport shirts, polyester golf duds, and pastel trousers. Shopping developments on Palm Canyon Drive include the **Desert Fashion Plaza**, anchored by Saks Fifth Avenue, and the upscale **Vineyard** (corner of Baristo Rd and Palm Springs Promenade). But couples won't want to overlook the dozens of charming and fascinating individual shops that line Palm Springs's main streets; within one block, the merchandise can vary from estate jewelry to antiques to 1950s memorabilia, original paintings, beauty supplies, tacky souvenirs, and designer clothing.

Toward the mountains, the **Heritage District** (known locally as the Tennis Club district after the celeb-frequented hotel that used to anchor the neighborhood) features a concentration of historic homes and hotels. It's a time capsule of the '30s, '40s, and '50s, and many vintage motels and inns have been swept up in the current madness for mid-century style and reincarnated as nostalgic versions of their own past. It seems that Palm Springs, once the town that progress forgot, is now a treasure trove of midcentury relics; they continue to emerge from 1950s-era vacation homes and often find their way to the desert's established vintage stores like **Modern Way** (2755 N Palm Canyon Dr; 760/320-5455; www.psmodernway.com), which deals in 1950s and '60s furniture, lighting, accessories, rugs, and art. One whole section of Palm Canyon has become known for antiques, vintage furnishings, and art galleries, and they're showcased once a month during the **First Friday street promenade** (N Palm Canyon Dr, between Tachevah Dr and Amado Rd; 4pm–9pm). All the boutiques stay open late, with entertainment, food, and fun rounding out this little sibling to VillageFest.

In town, couples can spend an hour or two viewing the paintings, sculpture, and American Indian artifacts, as well as the natural sciences, showcased at the big-city-sophisticated **Palm Springs Desert Museum** (101 Museum Dr, at Tahquitz Canyon Wy; 760/325-7186; www.psmuseum.org), which rests in a deep well of landscaped sculpture gardens set up against the mountainside. The Annenberg Theater on the museum's ground floor hosts concerts, drama, film, and dance. Near the airport, the **Palm Springs Air Museum** (745 N Gene Autry Trail; 760/778-6262; www.air-museum.org) takes advantage of the dry desert air to preserve some of the world's last examples of still-operable World War II aircraft, including the famous **Flying Fortress** with its ball turret nose. It's definitely a guy's place, but gals may be happy to accompany their significant other for a look at these historic aircrafts. After all, spending time together is what a romantic visit to Palm Springs is all about.

---

# Access and Information

Palm Springs has a wonderful airport—small and sweet, it boasts a vintage airstrip ambience that's amplified by the Air Museum (see Romantic Highlights) nearby. About eight major airlines fly into **Palm Springs International Airport** (3400 E Tahquitz Canyon Wy; 760/318-3800; www.palm springsairport.com) and provide direct service from dozens of West Coast destinations as far away as Vancouver, British Columbia, as well as national hubs like Chicago, Dallas/Fort Worth, Salt Lake City, and Denver. Car rentals are available on site.

Palm Springs is 120 miles east of Los Angeles and 140 miles northeast of San Diego. Most visitors drive to the desert from points west; from Interstate 10 eastbound, take the Highway 111 turnoff and you'll breeze into town along North Palm Canyon Drive, the main thoroughfare. As you do, you may want to stop in at the **Palm Springs Visitor Information Center** (2781 N Palm Canyon Dr; 760/778-8416 or 800/34-SPRINGS; www.palm-springs.org), which is located in an architectural landmark at the corner of Tramway Road. Pick up a copy of *Palm Springs Life* magazine's monthly **Desert Guide**, a somewhat biased but extremely helpful resource packed with phone numbers, maps, and restaurant and hotel information. The **Palm Springs Desert Resorts Convention & Visitors Authority** (70-100 Hwy 111; 760/770-9000 or 800/41-RELAX; www.palmspringsusa.com) is a terrific source of information on Palm Springs and the entire Coachella Valley.

These brochures reflect a real understanding of the desert's hip and romantic appeals, and you can get after-hours information and events listings on the 24-hour recorded hotline (760/770-1992).

# Romantic Lodgings

## ANDALUSIAN COURT
◖◖◖◖

*458 W Arenas Rd, Palm Springs / 760/323-9980 or 888/94-ROOMS*
Looking like a vintage Mission-style estate, the newly built Andalusian Court blends perfectly with its fashionable neighbors and offers the heady taste of exclusivity for sweethearts who want to celebrate romance just a few blocks from Palm Canyon Drive's shopping and fine restaurants. Everything is premium quality at this beautiful Spanish-themed cluster of eight lavish minivillas, each boasting a private whirlpool, a fully equipped kitchen, and over-the-top comforts for couples accustomed to the very best. Landscaped pathways, secluded gardens, tile-framed fountains, and a sparkling pool provide a magical setting that suits privacy-minded, romance-seeking sophisticates. Every villa rates four lips on our kissing scale, none less romantic than any other, but there are subtle differences that might help you choose your love nest. The higher numbers—villas 6, 7, and 8—lie closer to the pool, which is a plus in the convenience factor (but the intimate whispers of others could distract your own flirtations). Villa 4, tucked in the back corner, offers quiet seclusion; but its private whirlpool is located in the surrounding gardens—though most guests judge that lack of complete privacy is more than compensated by the glowing fire pit next to the tub. If you'd like your whirlpool-for-two well hidden behind your villa's outer wall, select villas 1 through 3, and prying eyes will never know what's happening amid the bubbles. Discreet, almost telepathic service is the special gift of Andalusian's innkeepers, who arrange for everything from in-room massages or post-swim alfresco hors d'oeuvres to activities throughout the valley, for those able to tear themselves away from all this pampering. In the morning, freshly prepared breakfast is brought to each villa, laid out where you desire: in the kitchen, on the patio, or even on breakfast-in-bed trays. The sky's the limit when it comes to special requests: a poolside professional outdoor kitchen is available, as is an on-call chef to throw some shrimp on the barbie—or whip up a gourmet meal in the privacy of your suite's professional kitchen.
*$$$$ AE, DIS, MC, V; no checks; subject to midweek closure in Aug; www.andalusiancourt.com.* ⚘

## KORAKIA PENSIONE
✪✪¢

*257 S Patencio Rd, Palm Springs / 760/864-6411*

Located on a quiet side street within walking distance of downtown, Korakia's overwhelming sense of romance immediately transports trysting visitors to a Moroccan oasis. Scottish artist Gordon Coutts built the white-walled, wedding cake–like house in 1924 as a retreat and salon for his many artistic and intellectual friends. Today, it's a darling of the superchic fashion/entertainment world, equal parts rustic and luxurious. The absence of alarm clocks and TVs encourages couples to venture outside, reviving the art-compound ambience of old. A fine choice for lovers is the upstairs Artists Studio, a light, airy suite where Winston Churchill once painted; windows gaze mountainward, and a full kitchen will help you settle right in. Downstairs, the Library is our pick for most romantic room (and the competition was tough in this magical place)—the combination of a stately four-poster bed, a secluded private patio, and stocked bookcases will have you hearing strains of chamber music and erudite conversation from a time when this room's high-beamed ceiling presided over a local cultural mecca. Owner Doug Smith virtually invented the term "restorative designer" and has a knack for balancing vintage character (well-worn wood floors, stucco arches, '40s bathroom tile) with modern features like Chinese slate showers and discreetly mounted air conditioners. The decor reflects his frequent worldwide jaunts and may include giant, hand-carved four-poster beds draped in mosquito netting, British campaign furniture, and African and Balinese influences. Numerous fireplaces lend magical warmth on cold winter nights. Continental breakfast is served in the walled entry patio to the full-throated accompaniment of 15 lovebirds and parakeets. A Mediterranean villa directly across the street with cocoa-brown walls, tile roof, and palm-fringed eaves has also joined the Korakia ensemble; the grounds boast a garden massage hut draped with gauzy sheers and several secluded cottages fresh from the patented Korakia makeover. In season, kitchenettes for light cooking are stocked with Häagen-Dazs ice cream, baguettes, and Brie.

*$$$–$$$$ MC, V; checks OK; subject to midweek closure in Aug; www.korakia.com.* &

## ORBIT IN
✪✪✪

*562 W Arenas Rd, Palm Springs / 760/323-3585 or 877/99-ORBIT*

Fun, sun, romance, and an obsessive love for all things modern inspired the visionary owners of the Orbit In's two classic restored properties in Palm Springs's chic Tennis Club district. Known as the Oasis and the Hideaway, this duo is a cozy homage to midcentury motifs; a cocktails-by-the-pool Rat Pack lifestyle; and the individual architects, photographers, and designers

# Take Romance to New Heights

It's been a desert "peak" experience for generations, and it may be just the thing to "elevate" your affair to new heights. It's the **Palm Springs Aerial Tramway** (Tramway Rd off Hwy 111; 760/325-1391 or 888/515-TRAM; www.pstramway.com), offering a bird's-eye perspective on the entire Coachella Valley and the chance to make memories in a scenic spot hidden from view to those on the desert floor. Originally opened in 1963—the harrowing tales of building the tramway's towers and upper station are worth the trip—and then renovated in 2000 with state-of-the-art revolving cars from Switzerland, this ride is a perfect splurge for lovers. Climb aboard at day's end, so you can appreciate the glorious sunset sky during the 2½-mile ascent up Mount San Jacinto. It takes only 14 minutes, but deposits you in a different world. At 8,500 feet, temperatures are usually around 40°F cooler than on the desert floor, and the mountain is blanketed with snow in winter. The tramway's Ride 'n' Dine package includes a casual barbecue meal in the lodge-style **Top of the Tram cafeteria**—not so romantic, but it'll do in a pinch. For a much better date, make dinner reservations at **Elevations** (760/327-1590), the new gourmet restaurant set at the top of the tramway that offers a breathtaking view of the desert along with excellent California-fusion cuisine. Enjoy a bottle of wine as you watch the sky begin to darken and the twinkling lights of Palm Springs dot the desert floor; later, you can use the upper elevation chill as a nice excuse to snuggle on your ride back down the mountain.

The tramway is a treat during daylight hours as well, since the upper station is the gateway to **Mount San Jacinto State Park** (909/659-2607; www.sanjac.statepark.org), with trails for hiking, cross-country skiing, or snowshoeing. You can rent equipment at the Nordic Ski Center in the tramway's upper station, which also offers trail maps and safety recommendations. If you're feeling less active, plenty of well-placed benches offer a side-by-side respite for gazing across the valley skyline, into the evergreen forest, or simply into each other's eyes.            —STEPHANIE AVNET YATES

responsible for Palm Springs's reign as a mecca of vintage modernism. It's ultragroovy in a sophisticated way . . . imagine the chic 1956 living room of your parents' swinging, childless friends, and you won't be far off. Savvy connoisseurs of collectibles will dig the museum-quality furnishings in each carefully themed room (Martini Room, Bertoia's Den, Atomic Paradise, and so on), while the rest of us enjoy tripping down memory lane with amoeba-shaped coffee tables, glowing rocket-ship lamps, Eames recliners, kitschy Melmac dishware, and strappy vintage chaises on every room's private patio. Requisite modern comforts range from superluxe bedding and lounge-music CDs for creating the right in-room mood to a fleet of complimentary Schwinn cruiser bikes, a secluded Jacuzzi, and poolside misters to cool even the worst summer scorcher. Restored fixtures, original built-ins, and pristine tiles grace kitchenettes and bathrooms. At the Oasis, guests gather at the poolside boomerang-shaped bar, or in the Albert Frey lounge (homage to the late, great architect whose unique home sits midway up the mountain backdrop). In 2003, the Orbit In expanded to include the Hideaway, another architectural gem just a block away that's been given the same impeccable facelift, but with a more secluded ambience equally suited to high-style lovebirds. The Hideaway's swimming pool floats in a sea of lawn, with a poolside massage room that lures couples from vintage chaises and a glowing fire pit. The emphasis here is slightly less social than the Oasis; though there's a convivial fireplace lounge, guests seeking more head to the Oasis for cocktail hour—leaving the amorous to court in solitude. $$$–$$$$ *AE, DIS, MC, V; no checks; subject to midweek closure in Aug; www.orbitin.com.* &

## THE SPRINGS OF PALM SPRINGS HOTEL & SPA
◐€

*227 N Indian Canyon Dr, Palm Springs / 760/416-1388*
Proving—once and for all—that you can't put a price tag on true love, this new sister to the ultraluxe Andalusian Court (see review) is a great place to kiss without breaking the bank. The Springs possesses the same Spanish-Moorish flair, attention to detail, and personal service of its sister, but this stylishly restored courtyard property sits between downtown's two main boulevards and features its own day spa. In fact, a healthful philosophy prevails here, from the poolside juice bar and property-wide nonsmoking policy, to water exercise classes and complete spa getaway weekend packages. For indulgent lovers unconcerned with such vagaries, the Springs's 25 individually designed suites are made for romance, boasting richly textured residential quality furniture; dreamy pillow-top mattresses; raw marble bathrooms with steam showers (about half also have whirlpool tubs); snuggle-up fireplaces; a deco-meets–Spanish Revival style that perfectly suits Palm Springs; and surprising rates that start at $149 in season (including a continental breakfast buffet in the lounge). A large swimming pool/whirlpool combo occupies the center courtyard, overlooked by a mezzanine terrace whose open hearth is a social draw each evening. Honeymooners and other amorous overnighters frequently request Room 221: this spacious boudoir showcases an extra-large, sky-lit bathroom with duo-sized Jacuzzi tub, a sensually curved fireside loveseat, and a "Juliet" balcony overlooking Palm Canyon Drive (this is the best seat in the house

for Thursday's VillageFest). The runner-up is Room 225, where theatrical arches frame a grand oval tub open to both the bedroom and bathroom. Take the pampering to another level by visiting the adjacent Rituals spa, which specializes in couple's treatments performed in a serene duo treatment room with a fireplace and whirlpool. Their signature is the Raindance Therapy, a relaxing sensory adventure that simulates a tropical rainforest. Paired with a massage for each of you, it's a splurge you won't want to miss.
$$–$$$ *AE, MC, V; no checks; www.thespringsofpalmsprings.com.* &

## VICEROY PALM SPRINGS
●●●
*415 S Belardo Rd, Palm Springs / 760/320-4117 or 800/237-3687*
Chic lifestyle magazines like *Condé Nast Traveler* have been lining up outside this flavor-of-the-moment boutique hotel to write about its snappy style, shoot photos of its precisely manicured grounds, and play paparazzi to the countless young Hollywood hipsters who are making this the desert retreat *du jour*. Indeed, Viceroy is so picture-perfect, the two of you will feel like you've stepped into the pages of a magazine fashion spread—impeccably posed on poolside chaises—and when you add that to the Viceroy's other attributes conducive to *l'amour*, it shapes up as the perfect trysting destination. Formerly four or five (it's difficult to tell anymore) separate bungalow and motel properties situated side-by-side a block from Palm Canyon Drive, the new Viceroy compound has been seamlessly united by lavish garden pathways, gleaming white exteriors trimmed with elegant black, and an over-the-top Hollywood Regency style that simply screams 1968. Think lots of marble, inside and out; Grecian urns and classical statues; a crisp black, white, and lemon yellow color scheme that really pops; mirrored accessories everywhere; and a fanciful blend of neoclassical and modern furniture: the net effect looks like an old *Life* magazine layout of Joan Crawford at home in Beverly Hills. The most requested rooms, and best for couple's getaways, are the villas that cluster around one of Viceroy's stunning lawns. They're worth the splurge for space, solitude, and available extras like romantic candlelit meals served in your private dining room. Throughout the property, which offers three separate swimming pools, toga-like canvas shields private lanais, poolside cabanas, and the outdoor dining terrace of Citron, the hotel's bright yellow-on-white gourmet restaurant (as hot a ticket as the rooms). Open for breakfast, lunch, and dinner, this chic eatery serves innovative takes on meat, chicken, and seafood, and pours wines from an all-West Coast wine list. When you're done pampering each other, traipse through the bougainvillea to the Estrella Spa, an intimate hideaway resurrected from two former villas. In one, luxurious locker rooms have built-in steam showers, and a serene relaxation parlor features healing tea elixirs and "spa lite" snacks; the other holds state-of-the-art treatment rooms. Nature-loving couples choose the privacy-draped outdoor cabanas

for side-by-side massages, but we're stuck on the facial room, an enveloping black den with its sparkling crystal-bed fireplace.
$$$–$$$$ *AE, DIS, MC, V; checks OK; www.viceroypalmsprings.com.* &

## VILLA ROYALE INN
♥♥❤

*1620 Indian Trail, Palm Springs / 760/322-3794 or 800/245-2314*
Villa Royale is an oasis—in the middle of an oasis—guaranteed to make your hearts beat faster and refresh your city-weary minds. This charming inn, five minutes from the hustle and bustle of downtown Palm Springs, evokes a Mediterranean cluster of villas, complete with climbing bougainvillea and rooms with decor that combines rural grandeur with eclectic European flair. The property dates back to Palm Springs's early heyday, when it was the home of ice-skating starlet Sonja Henie, and has always enjoyed a "hidden secret" reputation. Recently, a new cadre of celebrity owners—including Tony Shalhoub of "Monk"—carefully renovated the property, enhancing what worked and fixing the rest. The result is an enchanting, Old World experience that combines the friendly, personal attention of a bed-and-breakfast with the knowledgeable and professional staff of a fine hotel. Guest rooms front a series of inner courtyards enhanced by meandering brick paths, vine-covered stone arches, urns filled with flowering bushes, and bubbling stone fountains. Rooms vary widely in size and ambience; larger isn't necessarily better, as some of the inn's most appealing rooms are in the smaller, more affordable range. They all boast pampering touches like fluffy down duvets and cushy bathrobes; some have fireplaces, private patios with Jacuzzis, full kitchens, and a variety of other amenities. Talk to the reservationists about your special romantic needs, and they'll match you with the right bedchamber. If you want a tried-and-true choice, Room 101 is the recommended "honeymoon suite," a secluded one-bedroom fireplace suite tucked in a corner at the end of its own rosebush path. The hotel's regal outdoor whirlpool is a few steps away, and it'll feel like yours alone when you lay back and admire the perfect mountain view. In the daytime, you may find yourself napping in the dappled shade beside one of two swimming pools; at night, see why Europa (see Romantic Restaurants) restaurant is truly the romantic favorite of longtime devotees.
$$$ *AE, DC, DIS, MC, V; checks OK; www.villaroyale.com.*

## THE WILLOWS HISTORIC PALM SPRINGS INN
♥♥♥❤

*412 W Tahquitz Canyon Wy, Palm Springs / 760/320-0771*
Everything glorious about Palm Springs's past lives on at the Willows, definitively a best place to kiss, to luxuriate, and to elegantly indulge your senses. The eight-room inn was built in 1927 as a private estate, and today the house snuggles against Mount San Jacinto, its Tuscan-yellow walls,

red-tile roofs, and multiple terraces tangoing in and out of a grove of tall palms, fringed willows, and the stone mountainside itself. The owners have lovingly returned the home to elegant perfection, redolent of the Golden Age when Albert Einstein spent weeks visiting, when Clark Gable and Carole Lombard hid away here, and when, in the 1950s, Marion Davies, mistress of William Randolph Hearst, owned it and converted the only kitchen into a bar. Today, every surface and every furnishing has been restored, from door hinges to flagstones. The large rooms, tastefully furnished with fine antiques, inspire romantic interludes with just a glance. The Marion Davies room is a classic 1930s boudoir, with an elaborately carved bed, Romeo and Juliet balcony, and marble-trimmed bathroom. The spacious Library is the most requested honeymoon room, a mahogany coffered retreat with a private garden patio and rich leather furnishings. Throughout the house, each terrace reveals a view of gardens and the ragged curtain of mountains beyond; a 50-foot waterfall burbles down the mountainside into the breakfast patio. The inn's full-time staff serves a glorious breakfast (the bread pudding with walnut and berry sauce is heaven, accompanied by scrambled eggs with chèvre and chives) and provides intuitive, unobtrusive service. No visitors are allowed to roam the grounds (although many ask). At twilight, as the desert cools, guests gather in an open veranda room beneath a Moroccan-arched ceiling to sip wine and enjoy hors d'oeuvres. It's the perfect relaxing way to end the day in this romantic paradise.

$$$$ *AE, DC, DIS, MC, V; checks OK; subject to closure during Aug; www.thewillowspalmsprings.com.*

## Romantic Restaurants

### THE CHOP HOUSE
### THE DECK
❷❷❻

*262 S Palm Canyon Dr, Palm Springs / 760/320-4500 (Chop House) or 760/325-5200 (Deck)*

There's nothing that says "red-blooded American lover" like a well-aged, perfectly grilled steak, and the desert is where steakhouse-as-art-form never went out of style. Of the dozens in the valley, we like the Chop House for catering to a new, hip meat-and-martini set who've taken the Sinatra-era inspiration and run with it. Located on a chunk of prime Palm Canyon Drive real estate in the heart of downtown, this fairly new restaurant cultivates an established look with distressed brick, weathered stone walls, and a dark, woody atmosphere accented with postmodern touches. You'll know you're in the right place just by reading the cocktail menu, which includes such savvy libations as the Metropolitan. The Chop House is the dining room of choice for well-heeled desert couples and cleaned-up gentlemen

golfers, both of whom know to request one of the high-backed, crescent-shaped booths that line the front room. You should follow suit, for these cushy banquettes are best for smooching over crab legs, oysters, calamari, or a classic blue cheese Wedge salad. Though it's hard to tear your attention from the list of prime, aged, juicy steaks—especially when nightly specials offer rich extras like foie gras and truffle-infused reduction sauces—seafood is another forte, like the Hawaiian mahimahi crusted with macademia nuts and laid atop lobster mashed potatoes with a lemongrass-coconut sauce. Upstairs from the Chop House, the Deck sky bar and restaurant overlooks the street (there's no better people-watching perch when Thursday's VillageFest is in full swing), with spectacular mountain views from the open-air deck. Romantic fireplaces warm desert breezes at night and misters cool couples in the daytime. Their "global foods of the sun" menu, with Caribbean, Mediterranean, Latin, and Pacific Rim influences, is a terrific choice for a leisurely lunch; when cocktail hour rolls around, join the locals who congregate at the fiber-optic sky bar, watch sports on wide-screen TVs, and, later in the evening, dance to live jazz.
**$$–$$$** *AE, MC, V; no checks; dinner every day (Chop House), lunch, dinner every day (Deck); full bar; reservations recommended (Chop House), reservations not necessary (Deck); www.palmsprings chophouse.com, www.the-deck.com.* &

---

## EUROPA
🖤🖤🖤

*1620 Indian Trail, Palm Springs / 760/327-2314*
Long advertised as the "most romantic dining in the desert," Europa is a sentimental favorite of both gay and straight clientele. This European-style hideaway exudes charm and ambience. As you approach Europa's vintage garden house—on the grounds of equally enchanting Villa Royale Inn (see Romantic Lodgings)—the starlit courtyard and glowing swimming pool set the stage for a memorable experience. Whether the two of you sit together under the stars on Europa's garden patio or in subdued candlelight inside this French country cottage, you'll savor dinner prepared by one of Palm Springs's most dedicated kitchens and served by a discreetly attentive staff. If you're celebrating a special occasion, or just want to sneak some between-course kisses, the best table in the house is positioned close to the crackling hearth and next to a fountain-view window. Longtime staffers say they've lost count of all the marriage proposals joyfully accepted by lovers seated there. Every detail will make your darling feel whisked off to a splendid Gallic chateau, where fine meals arrive on heirloom-quality blue toile platters, and Mediterranean flavors blend in time-honored Europa recipes. Start by sharing a Hunter's Terrine, country pâte with saffron-garlic crisps and a tart orange-cranberry relish; next you might enjoy the escargot, served shelled and warm, bathed in buttery garlic broth and ladled over

lemony field greens. Main course favorites range from the always-perfect filet mignon marinated in olive oil and Armagnac, to a superior duck confit sweetened with honey and Grand Marnier, or the show-stopping salmon baked in parchment and served with crème fraîche and dill. Whatever you do, don't skip Europa's aphrodisiac desserts, including the Royale chocolate torte with gooey molten center and their signature chocolate mousse.
*$$$ AE, DC, DIS, MC, V; checks OK; dinner Tues–Sun, brunch Sun; full bar; reservations recommended; www.villaroyale.com.*

## JOHANNES
◍◍◍
*196 S Indian Canyon Dr, Palm Springs / 760/778-0017*
When romance means treating your true love to only the very best, head to the place where talented chef-owner Johannes Bacher blends the comfort of a friendly neighborhood boîte with some of the most up-to-date cuisine in the desert. Located in a plain, low storefront steps away from Palm Canyon Drive, the place oozes casual sophistication. Two boxy rooms—one with tangerine walls, a quieter one avocado green—have sparse furnishings, colorful accessories, and an open, industrial flavor, while the open kitchen hums behind a pale birch counter stacked with gleaming white plates at the ready. Bacher melds flavorful California cuisine with European flair and international accents, including dishes from his Austrian youth. Roasted beets paired with grapefruit and goat cheese in a tasty salad; meatballs braised in a Malayan blend of yellow curry and kaffir lime; seared scallops bathed in an anchovy-sage-balsamic sauce; crispy duck in a fruity peach-plum sauce; and always Wiener schnitzel with traditional parsley potatoes or spaetzle are among the eclectic menu's highlights. A selection of multi-course tasting menus is always available (in summer, it's a $29.99 bargain!). Johannes perennially wins *Wine Spectator* accolades for an encyclopedic wine list, an achievement extending to an enticing selection of after-dinner spirits, dessert wines, and inventive elixirs.
*$$$ AE, DIS, MC, V; no checks; dinner Tues–Sat; full bar; reservations recommended; www.johannesrestaurant.com.* ⅙

## LAS CASUELAS TERRAZA
## LAS CASUELAS NUEVAS
◍
*222 S Palm Canyon Dr, Palm Springs / 760/325-2794*
*70-050 Hwy 111, Rancho Mirage / 760/328-8844*
The sights and sounds of Mexico—colorfully painted tile framed by tropical plants, white stucco walls, and lively mariachi music—has made Las Casuelas a romantic tradition since 1958. They started in a hole-in-the-wall up the street, but instant popularity meant expanding to this central location, where the Delgado family converted a 1920s *casa* into the first of many

indoor and outdoor dining areas that form this desert oasis. Las Casuelas Terraza draws its energy from the heavy foot traffic of Palm Canyon Drive, and a big palapa-fringed bar and patio opens to the street. In the evenings, live music pumps out from here as strongly as the straight shots of aged tequilas from their ever-expanding menu. The menu is filled with generous and delicious platters that are mostly attuned to the mild "gringo" palate; one item that captures a sense of authenticity is the Oaxacan-style black bean "pizza" (really a tostada) with chicken. But the long menu of burritos, enchiladas, tostadas, fajitas, and chimichangas—not to mention *magnifico* margaritas—satisfy couples in search of a traditional Mexican food fix. In nearby Rancho Mirage, Las Casuelas Nuevas is a slightly more upscale version of Terraza, located along Restaurant Row in a romantic hacienda-style building with seating indoors or on a large, Spanish-style patio. Like the original, it attracts a sizzling nightlife scene with live music and flowing bar, but still offers a fine ambience for low-key lovers to enjoy the generations-old Mexican recipes of the Delgado family.
**$$** *AE, DIS, MC, V; no checks; lunch, dinner every day, brunch Sun (Nuevas only); full bar; reservations recommended; www.lascasuelas.com, www.lascasuelasnuevas.com.* &

---

## LE VALLAURIS
❍❍❍
*385 W Tahquitz Canyon Wy, Palm Springs / 760/325-5059*
Named for the small town in the south of France where Picasso took to making pottery, Le Vallauris exudes uncompromising elegance in both fine, contemporary French-Mediterranean cuisine and the practiced, formal manner in which it's served. The restaurant occupies a historic ranch-style house not far from the hubbub of Palm Canyon Drive (but seemingly a world apart), its ficus-shaded exterior understated but for the fleet of valet-parked luxury sedans outside the front door. Step inside the equally understated foyer and glimpse the old-school cocktail lounge and classically decorated chain of small rooms that provide indoor seating. Draped alcoves, fine paintings, and crisp traditional linens and china lend a romantic air to these tables, but Le Vallauris has built its reputation on the magical outdoor patio that twinkles seductively through every window. There's a warm hearth at one end, and the trees—almost as numerous as the tables—weave a full canopy that lets in dappled sunlight in daytime and glows with tiny lights after dark. The songs of vintage French crooners waft gently from hidden speakers, and the air is subtly cooled on warmer days and heated for cool evenings. This special setting says amour like no other, and the food is equally as extravagant. Start with beluga caviar for two; terrine of foie gras; or light, crisp crab cakes with whole-grain mustard sauce. Lamb lovers will yield willingly to a perfectly roasted rack, classically seasoned with garlic and thyme, or, at lunch, to the more exotic marinated grilled lamb loin

with sesame sauce. The veal chop with *pommes soufflées* is one of Southern California's best. Fish is often seared or sautéed, accented with inventive sauces. And if your sweetie has a sweet tooth, this is the time to forget any dieting and splurge on some of the best desserts we've ever tasted.
**$$$** *AE, DC, DIS, MC, V; checks OK; lunch, dinner every day, brunch Sun (closed July–Aug); full bar; reservations recommended; www.levallauris.com.* &

## SPENCER'S
♥♥€

*701 W Baristo Rd, Palm Springs / 760/327-3446*
Snuggled up against the base of Mount San Jacinto and surrounded by the vintage homes of the Tennis Club district, Spencer's boasts a romantic, country-club ambience just a few blocks from the heart of Palm Springs. Stunning mountain views from the outdoor patio, friendly atmosphere, a fresh and delicious menu, and modern-yet-clubby decor by renowned L.A. restaurant designer Dodd Mitchell create an enticing setting for romance. Inside Spencer's, smooth beige furnishings and dark wood accents are soothing either day or evening, made more so by soft piano accompaniment at lunch and dinner. The menu is California-Continental, offering plenty of big salads and savory small plates at lunch, and dinner choices that range from pumpkin-lobster soup or wild mushroom fettuccine to grilled fish and hearty steaks. The outdoor patio is choice seating for romantic interludes, with soft lighting accenting seductive, balmy evenings. Look up and you'll see the cascading hillside that forms a lovely backdrop for Spencer's and is the wedding choice for many a couple. Whether you're in tennis whites or leisure duds, the two of you may want to stroll around the neighborhood before or after your meal; it's Palm Springs's most charming area.
**$$$** *AE, MC, V; no checks; lunch, dinner every day, brunch Sun; full bar; reservations recommended for dinner; www.spencersrestaurant.com.* &

## ST. JAMES AT THE VINEYARD
♥♥♥

*265 S Palm Canyon Dr, Palm Springs / 760/320-8041*
Palm Springs's most interesting dinner menu fuses Pacific Rim, French, Indian Ocean, and American steakhouse cuisines in a unique style born of owner James Offord's love of travel. Set behind a small courtyard but still visible from the hopping action of Palm Canyon Drive, this iconic gathering place is laid out like a series of over-the-top ethnically decorated dining salons, where couples can indulge their fantasies of Far East travel by settling in next to a larger-than-life Shiva to share an appetizer like coconut-milk steamed mussels or spicy beef satay with green papaya salad. Warm spices, found throughout the eclectic menu, will complement your amorous mood (they say spices stimulate the heart). St. James remains rightfully

famous for its signature made-to-order curries—lamb, chicken, shrimp, or vegetable—served with traditional condiments and basmati rice. Other standouts include a stir-fried lobster tail over couscous, grilled lamb rack, or a fabulous bouillabaisse Burmese that immerses a bounty of seafood in an enlivened sauce. Service is attentive but unhurried; couples should be ready to enjoy a meal that will last several hours. The bar, featuring almost a hundred folk-art masks on the walls, is downtown's most sophisticated watering hole, and the restaurant's wine list boasts a *Wine Spectator* Award of Excellence.

$$$ *AE, DC, DIS, MC, V; no checks; dinner every day (subject to midweek closure in summer); full bar; reservations recommended; www.stjames restaurant.com.* ⟵

# THE OTHER DESERT RESORTS

## ROMANTIC HIGHLIGHTS

If you're not in Palm Springs, you must be "down valley," which is how locals refer to the resort communities that have developed east of Palm Springs proper. As a rule, they attract trysting lovebirds with their spread-out, upscale, country-club atmosphere. Whether the two of you are serious about golf, or yearn for the complete abandon offered by enormous all-inclusive resorts, chances are you'll find your bliss in Rancho Mirage or Palm Desert. Home to a well-heeled, sporting crowd, this area fills to capacity during major annual events like the Bob Hope Chrysler Classic golf tournament in January, the Kraft Nabisco Championship for the Ladies Professional Golf Association (LPGA) (formerly the Nabisco Dinah Shore) in March, and the star-studded Pacific Life Open tennis tournament, also in March. If that's not your game, acres of sparkling swimming pools lie in wait for you and your sweetie; plus, some of Southern California's very best healing and pampering spas can be found at the big-ticket resort hotels that rule valley tourism.

Eleven miles from Palm Springs, quiet **Rancho Mirage** is perhaps best known to outsiders as the home of the Betty Ford Center, as well as the residences of former presidents Gerald Ford and Dwight Eisenhower. It's a wealthy, low-profile town with a peaceful nature that is broken only by a self-proclaimed Restaurant Row that occupies a stretch of Highway 111, accompanied by several glitzy shopping malls.

But couples on a shopping quest pass right through on their way to **Palm Desert** to visit the equivalent of Beverly Hills's Rodeo Drive: **El Paseo** (running parallel to Hwy 111). This glamorous, palm-lined street boasts almost a hundred boutiques, gift and antique shops, and galleries and restaurants of the highest quality. Simply walking up one side of the divided street and down the other gives the two of you about a mile of nonstop window shopping and browsing. Whether it's for entertainment, a fun souvenir of a playful vacation, or a piece of serious jewelry to mark the occasion, El Paseo is a shopper's paradise.

Lovers who want to get in touch with nature can visit the best attraction in town, the zoo and botanical garden named the **Living Desert** (47-900 Portola Ave, about 4 miles south of Hwy 111; 760/346-5694; www.living desert.org). Look for directional signs in town and along Highway 74 (the Pines-to-Palms Highway leading into the mountains), following them to reach this fascinating collection of gardens and more than 130 animal species. Established in 1970 as a nonprofit educational and conservation center, the Living Desert has morphed into a fun place to learn about desert environments and ecology, and to see native bighorn sheep gamboling over their own mountainside, mountain lions in a realistic stone grotto, plus eagles and kit foxes and imported exotics such as cheetahs, zebras, meerkats, and Arabian oryx.

Night owls won't find too much to crow about in Palm Desert, but for couples craving a cultural fix, look to **McCallum Theatre for the Performing Arts** (73-000 Fred Waring Dr, in the Bob Hope Cultural Center on College of the Desert campus; 760/346-6505; www.mccallumtheatre.com) for Broadway shows and performances by national dance companies, jazz greats, and pop superstars. It's the only big-name entertainment spot in the region and can be the perfect way to spend a special night with the one you love.

As befits a community where a household's second car is often a golf cart, the annual parade starring the carts moonlighting as Rose Parade floats is a big deal. Started in 1964 as a bit of a joke, the **November Golf Cart Parade** (760/346-6111; www.golfcartparade.com) has grown to a well-publicized event attracting an estimated 25,000 spectators and more than 100 whimsically transformed carts. During past parades, giant slot machines, oversized golf bags, a spectacular Noah's Ark, and a champagne bottle have all motored majestically up one side of El Paseo and down the other. If you and your sweetie are in town in November, don't miss this event.

Further east, **La Quinta** has a romantic reputation that was clinched early in the 20th century, when the seductive, Spanish-style **La Quinta Resort & Spa** (see Romantic Lodgings) opened in a previously remote corner of the desert. Palatial homes and elite golf courses now surround the still-enchanting resort, making La Quinta the valley's newest growth boomtown. Artists from throughout the world converge here each March for the **La Quinta Arts Festival** (77-865 Avenida Montezuma, held at Frances Hack Park; 760/564-1244; www.lqaf.com), a four-day art show and sale. In addition to juried art displays and wares that span every artistic medium, the event includes live entertainment, wine tasting, and plenty of good food.

More of a blue-collar community than its resort brethren just up valley, **Indio** supports a thriving date-palm industry that goes back to the early 1900s. As the story goes, the president of the railroad, C. P. Huntington, carried back some date shoots from a vacation to Algeria during the 1880s. Sensing a great opportunity, the U.S. Department of Agriculture got into the act; date palms were planted throughout the area, and by 1914 growers had formed the Coachella Valley Date Growers' Association. Like a big county fair, the **National Date Festival** takes over **Desert ExpoCentre** (46-350 Arabia St; 760/863-8247; www.datefest.org) every February for 10 days. Concerts and classic carnival rides are joined by exhibit halls crammed with fruits, vegetables, art exhibits, industrial arts, fossilized blue-ribbon pies—you know, all that great fair bric-a-brac. The town is still known for acres of date farms and shops selling the ever-popular date shake. Couples craving this sweet concoction can stop at the popular **Shields Date Garden** (80-225 Hwy 111; 760/347-0996 or 800/414-2555) for a creamy shake.

No mystery surrounds the naming of **Desert Hot Springs**, which lies north of Palm Springs off Highway 10. Most people know Desert Hot Springs only as home to **Two Bunch Palms** (see Romantic Lodgings), a luxurious retreat whose trademark mud baths played a prominent part in the Robert Altman film *The Player*. But the town is also home to about 15,000 people and about 40 hot-springs spas, which devotees swear have medicinal properties. Most commonly touted as a remedy for arthritis and rheumatism, the steaming mineral water bubbles up at an average of 140–150°F, perfect for filling the various pools, soaking tubs, and private bathtubs offered at the local motels and resorts. Couples who want to soak in the goodness of these healing waters just need to book an appointment. Most of these local havens offer day rates for those who just want to drop in for a few hours, as well as treatments such as massage, facials, body wraps, and aromatherapy.

While there isn't much else to do in Desert Hot Springs—or the Palm Springs Desert Resorts, for that matter—that's just the point. This desert region is a place to slow down and reconnect with each other, and find as many places to kiss as you can.

## Access and Information

The resort cities down valley from Palm Springs are strung like jewels along Highway 111—from west to east they are Cathedral City, Rancho Mirage, Palm Desert, Indian Wells, La Quinta, and Indio. Desert Hot Springs is northwest of Palm Springs; Gene Autry Trail leads away from the airport, and after crossing Interstate 10 becomes Palm Drive, Desert Hot Springs's main commercial thoroughfare.

The **Palm Springs Desert Resorts Convention & Visitors Authority** (70-100 Hwy 111; 760/770-9000 or 800/41-RELAX; www.palmspringsusa.com)

is your best source of information on all the destinations throughout the Coachella Valley. Their brochures reflect a real understanding of the desert's hip and romantic appeals, and you can get after-hours information and events listings on the 24-hour recorded hotline (760/770-1992). In addition, you can get specific information from several local agencies, including **Rancho Mirage Chamber of Commerce** (42-464 Rancho Mirage Ln; 760/568-9351; www.ranchomirage.org); **Palm Desert Visitor Information Center** (72-990 Hwy 111; 760/568-1441 or 800/873-2428; www.palm-desert.org); and the **Indio Chamber of Commerce** (82-503 Hwy 111; 760/347-0676 or 800/44-INDIO; www.indiochamber.org).

# Romantic Lodgings

## LAKE LA QUINTA INN
●●

*78-120 Caleo Bay, La Quinta / 760/564-7332 or 888/226-4546*
A hidden secret hideaway that'll make lovers feel like invited guests at a ritzy European villa, this 13-room Norman-style bed-and-breakfast lies on the shores of man-made Lake La Quinta, surrounded by equally luxurious homes. It's just blocks from the legendary La Quinta Resort—but a world of privacy away—and around the corner from gourmet haven Omri & Boni (see Romantic Restaurants). Your pulse will slow the moment you enter the inn's foyer and glimpse the shimmering lake through picture windows across the house. Time it right and arrive just for the afternoon wine and hors d'oeuvres shared by the other lucky couples having their own romantic experiences here. Each uniquely decorated and exquisitely outfitted room has a fireplace, and some rooms have private outdoor hot tubs for intimate stargazing. Whether you bed down in the nautical Captain's Quarters, spacious Tuscan Suite, Oriental Lotus Suite, regal La Mancha Suite, or the wild Safari Suite, you'll awaken to the tantalizing aroma of a gourmet breakfast (choose the Tuscan Suite, and they'll even serve it on your private balcony). One afternoon, if the two of you can tear yourselves away from admiring the lakefront view, head to the inn's on-site massage room for a rejuvenating body treatment (massages can also be performed in your room upon request). Pampering options, like a 24-hour pool and Jacuzzi, and staffers eager to help compose the perfect amorous getaway, help complete the fantasy.
$$$-$$$$ *AE, MC, V; checks OK; www.lakelaquintainn.com.* ♿

## LA QUINTA RESORT & CLUB
◘◘◘◖
*49-499 Eisenhower Dr, La Quinta / 760/564-4111 or 800/598-3828*
The valley's second-oldest resort (it dates back to 1926) is the very definition of the classic Palm Springs experience. Set against a towering mountain backdrop, it boasts rambling oasis-like grounds and subdued elegance, with a Hollywood Golden Era feel (Mary Pickford was a frequent guest). To this day, no other desert resort approaches its grand sense of place coupled with understated charm—the ultimate backdrop for romance. Originally a cluster of 56 tile-roofed guest casitas widely spaced on lawns, the resort has grown into a large town-size complex of golf courses, a tennis club, new rooms, bungalows, ballrooms, and a spa—yet without losing intimacy. From the moment the two of you drive down the long entry road between towering columnar cypresses, you'll feel as though you're leaving the real world's hubbub behind and entering a Spanish village. The casitas have early California hacienda decor and furnishings, with white-walled simplicity, rich leather, and colorful textiles. Color abounds outside, where billows of bougainvillea spill over the rooftops and colorfully glazed tiles adorn fountains and terraces. Almost all have porches for sitting in the deep shade and listening to the mariachi music float over from the Adobe Grill. Three fine restaurants make it possible to never leave the grounds: Azur (see Romantic Restaurants), Morgans (a steakhouse open every day for breakfast, lunch, and dinner that also features a fine breakfast buffet), and Adobe Grill (featuring regional Mexican cuisine with live mariachi music and *muchas* margaritas, open for lunch Thursday through Saturday during high season and dinner every day). Named one of *Tennis* magazine's top 10 U.S. resorts, La Quinta offers one of the most beautiful settings in the country, along with 23 courts. Add plenty of gardens for private contemplation, championship tournament golf courses, and a heavenly 23,000-square-foot spa that includes a large fitness center (with yoga and other activities and spa treatments ranging from the golfer's massage to open-air showers, warm-stone therapy, and an outdoor aromatherapy tub) and you've got a gracefully aging Eden that continues to attract bliss-seeking lovers to the desert.
$$$ *AE, DC, DIS, MC, V; checks OK; www.laquintaresort.com.* &

## THE LODGE AT RANCHO MIRAGE
◘◘
*68-900 Frank Sinatra Dr, Rancho Mirage / 760/321-8282 or 866/518-6870*
The only major resort hotel in the Coachella Valley region that's actually on the mountainside, the uber-luxurious lodge was the site of Trista ("The Bachelorette") and Ryan's much-publicized wedding. It's perched high above Highway 111, and in contrast to the towering mountains, the hotel's architecture is linear, modern, and horizontal—a broad U shape that opens it to the fantastic cross-valley vistas that make couples' hearts beat a

little faster. The exterior may be all about the spectacular desert setting, but inside the two of you will find yourselves in a French country palace with gleaming marble floors, crystal chandeliers, brocade armchairs, baroque oil paintings, and long halls. You might find yourself indulging fantasies of being lord of your own baronial retreat. But the staff's dedication to service personalizes the otherwise formal environment. Accommodations are spacious—all have private balconies with views of the pool, mountains, valley, or all three—with elegant stone finishes, fabrics, and crisp linens. A club floor offers couples added amenities: a private lounge, a personal concierge, and complimentary food and beverage service during the day. It's a worthwhile expense to make your rendezvous as carefree as possible. Available romantic enhancements include the can't-miss rose-petal bed turndown, an on-call bath butler to fill a tub with aromatic and fun extras, a chef's dinner for two served in a private hilltop gazebo, and the SoCal resident package that starts with a luxury Mercedes delivered to your door—at home—so you can make the drive in style. The lodge's cabana-fringed swimming pool and outdoor hydro-spa, perched on the rim of the property, have outstanding views of the entire valley. Couples are treated well in the first-class Avanyu Spa, where a tantalizing menu of healing and beauty treatments includes Pancha karma, a two-therapist massage designed to cleanse and rejuvenate, and couple's massages performed in a private poolside cabana.
$$$–$$$$ *AE, DC, DIS, MC, V; checks OK; www.lodgeatranchomirage.com.* &

## MARRIOTT'S RANCHO LAS PALMAS RESORT & SPA
❤❤❤

*41000 Bob Hope Dr, Rancho Mirage / 760/568-2727 or 800/I-LUV-SUN*
Located in a part of the valley best known for enormous, all-inclusive resorts that are more family playgrounds than romantic hideaways, Rancho Las Palmas's low-rise hacienda style and strikingly intimate grounds make this Marriott a surprisingly kiss-worthy choice for lovebirds who want to have it all—full service and recreation options in a setting that also inspires passion. The hotel's cozy and rustic lobby belies the nearly 500 rooms scattered across its grounds, but a fleet of bright red golf carts (designed to resemble mini-woodie wagons) stands ready to whisk you and your bags to the far corners of the property. Request a room in buildings 1 through 5, which are closest to the quieter adults-only pool the two of you will prefer using and an equally easy walk to the spa and restaurant. Guest rooms are decorated with the same early California charm found outside, featuring Mission-style furnishings and French doors opening onto private patios and balconies. Rancho Las Palmas is also a golfer's paradise, and two of the 27 Ted Robinson–designed holes are woven throughout the resort, their lakes and greens forming part of the lush landscaping. A 25-court tennis club completes the sporting scene. More languid luxury is offered at the 20,000-square-foot European-style health spa, which features 26 treatment rooms,

saunas, steam, hydrotherapy, two fitness centers, and a menu of globally inspired exotic treatments. Meet up after your treatment at the spa's coed outdoor pool, where super-plush chaises will encourage duo napping. We think Spa Las Palmas is the desert's best full-service spa—and their delightfully tempting spa boutique is tops, too. In the evening, the two of you can walk across the street and take advantage of The River, a modern outdoor "anti-mall" built around dramatic water features; its five big restaurants, Borders bookstore, and multiscreen theater complement the resort's offerings and ensure that you can happily eschew your car for the duration of your romantic getaway.

$$$–$$$$ *AE, DC, DIS, MC, V; checks OK; www.rancholaspalmas.com.* &

## MIRAMONTE RESORT & SPA

*45-000 Indian Wells Ln, Indian Wells / 760/341-2200 or 800/237-2926*
When you're weary of *la vida loca* and need some together time, head for *la dolce vita* at this totally Tuscan boutique resort with Old World grace that embodies the classic definition of romance. Recently remodeled and reinvented to cater to a sophisticated and well-traveled crowd, Miramonte resembles a Mediterranean oasis, where small guest-room villas named for Italian towns share space with pretty landscaping, gurgling fountains, discreetly placed hammocks, and brilliantly flowering bougainvillea. The diversions that pass for "activities" here are of the relaxing variety: carry a cocktail to the second-story piazza, take a seat at the grand outdoor hearth, and gaze toward the pink-hued Santa Rosa Mountains. If that's too taxing, simply take in the same view from Miramonte's oasis-like swimming pool or enormous outdoor whirlpool. The hotel recently opened a 12,000-square-foot spa, the Well, where lovers can sample the outdoor relaxation rooms, paint-it-on mud bars, submerged river benches, and fitness classes like Hydro Yo-Chi, which blends yoga and tai chi in a water environment. Help make your stay extra special by reserving a Dolce Suite, where extra-large marble bathrooms and a separate living area feel more residential than hotel-like. The color palette throughout is inspired by Tuscany, where colors are soft yet rich, fabrics are as wonderful on the skin as the eyes, and Old World furnishings make Miramonte feel like it's been here for decades. The lobby, cocktail lounge, and Italian-inspired Ristorante Brissago all share an open communal space, often abuzz with golfers drawn by Indian Wells's excellent courses and the hotel's own golf packages and convenient shuttle service. Open for breakfast, lunch, and dinner, Brissago specializes in Italian-inspired fare. During the summer season, the restaurant's high iced tea, featuring a giant cool beverage and finger sandwiches, doubles as a light and refreshing meal.

$$$–$$$$ *AE, DC, DIS, MC, V; checks OK; www.miramonteresort.com.* &

## MOJAVE
⬡⬡

*73-721 Shadow Mountain Dr, Palm Desert / 760/346-6121 or 800/391-1104*
It used to be there weren't many lodging options in Palm Desert; couples either rented private condos or settled in at the self-contained playgrounds-for-all-ages offered by the megaresorts. Then a savvy boutique hotel group bought this low-slung vintage motel—perfectly situated on a residential street just one block from stylish El Paseo—and transformed it into the retro-chic Mojave. Combining three elements Palm Desert's known for (chic decor, lazy relaxation, and top-notch amenities) with three it definitely isn't (nostalgia, seclusion, and reasonable prices) really works here. Each of the 24 rooms, arranged around a sparkling pool and Grecian-draped whirlpool, exudes 1940s glamour in shades of persimmon, saffron, and the grapefruits that grow along meandering pathways outside. Filled with reproductions of iconic period furniture and accented with vintage black and white photos of desert landscapes, the rooms are all surprisingly unique; some feature kitchenettes, some deluxe bathtubs—and the two most romantic choices have fireplaces to keep you toasty on chilly desert evenings. Despite rates that can plunge as low as $89 in summer, Mojave doesn't skimp on the details: poolside chaises upholstered in the hotel's signature orange sit ready with neatly rolled towels; creamsicle-fringed umbrellas shade tables perfect for alfresco enjoyment of the nicely composed continental breakfast each morning; bathrooms feature imported bath potions in spa-style pump jars; and the in-room honor bar tempts with '40s treats like grape Nehi and Necco wafers. This little property is perfect for hiding away from it all, but should you venture out, Mojave offers complimentary access to a nearby health club and a discount program with El Paseo merchants and restaurants. Now that's romance we can all afford.
$$–$$$ *AE, DC, DIS, MC, V; no checks; www.hotelmojave.com.* ♿

---

## TWO BUNCH PALMS
⬡⬡⬡

*67-425 Two Bunch Palms Trail, Desert Hot Springs / 760/329-8791*
Hollywood glitterati weren't the first to discover how great it feels to soak in the desert's hot springs; native Cahuilla Indians gathered here hundreds of years before Chicago mobster Al Capone allegedly hid out in the 1930s-era stone buildings that form the core of today's resort. Two Bunch Palms is annually voted one of the world's top-ten resorts by *Travel + Leisure* and *Condé Nast Traveler* magazines, drawing lovers seeking relaxation, rejuvenation, and the pure sigh-inducing pleasure only a health spa can deliver. Despite being a celeb magnet, it's still a friendly and informal haven offering renowned spa services, quiet bungalows nestled on lush grounds, and trade-mark lagoons of steaming mineral water. Service is famously discreet, and the outstanding spa treatments (10 varieties of massages, mud baths, body

wraps, facials, salt rubs, and more) will heal you mentally and physically. Two Bunch is a summer camp for grown-ups, where the rich and famous pad about in bathrobes, forbidden by gentle but insistent signs from using cell phones or speaking above a whisper. If you saw the movie *The Player*, this is where Tim Robbins whisked Greta Scacci away for some desert canoodling; it worked for those fictional lovebirds, and it'll work for you, too. Lodgings range from guest rooms equipped with minifridges and cable TVs (some with private patios) to spacious suites and villas with separate dining areas, minikitchens, and whirlpool spas. The pond area is shaded by large trees and encircled by a manicured lawn dotted with chairs that invite you to curl up and soak in the serenity of your surroundings. At twilight, guests often spot adorable white-tailed rabbits hopping about this area. Room rates all include an exceptional buffet breakfast with coffee, fresh-squeezed juices, pastries, cereals, and fresh fruit in the Casino Dining Room, a stained-glass setting for culinary and interpersonal magic. It's also open for lunch and dinner, serving a slightly "lite" cuisine (translation: there's no cream in the soup, but you can still get rack of lamb or filet mignon and a glass of wine for dinner). Fresh salads, hearty sandwiches, and entrées like Two Bunch chicken enchiladas make up the lunch menu, while dinners include low-sodium, low-fat entrées like banana leaf–wrapped sea bass, beef medallions, and shrimp pasta.
$$$–$$$$ *AE, MC, V; no checks; www.twobunchpalms.com.*

# *Romantic Restaurants*

## AZUR BY LE BERNARDIN
◐◐◐◖

*49-499 Eisenhower Dr (La Quinta Resort and Spa), La Quinta / 760/777-4835*
The classic hacienda lines of the original dining room at historic La Quinta Resort and Spa (see Romantic Lodgings)—high, open-beamed ceiling, thick adobe walls, rustic ranch-inspired chandeliers—haven't changed much over the years, but now serve as a familiar backdrop to cuisine the likes of which staid La Quinta has never seen, unless they're frequent visitors to the Big Apple, that is. New York's acclaimed Le Bernardin has partnered with the resort to create a culinary destination worth driving for. Couples should try to arrive early and step into the warm cocktail lounge for an aperitif or, if you're lucky, a chance introduction to chef Jasper Schneider, who's taken the Le Bernardin model of exquisitely presented seafood and run with it to create his own signature cuisine. His fish is flown in daily from Hawaii, Spain, the Atlantic coast—wherever Schneider knows he can get prime product on a given day. Some creations are classic Le Bernardin, like the light-as-air skate wing bathed in lemon brown butter and toasty hazelnuts, or the rich saffron bouillabaisse topped with a floating aioli crab

cake. Schneider's inventiveness shines through in an outstanding appetizer of progressive fluke ceviches, a quartet of tender whitefish that starts with a perfectly simple citrus-onion marinade; each of the four ceviches is complex, subtly (and not so subtly) surprising your taste buds. It's not all seafood, though. There's a sublime duck accented with the sweet-savory tang of apples and fennel, and a slow-roasted rib chop *au poivre* with rich and savory accompaniments that satisfy like three meals in one. Take time to savor your meal, a fine wine served in exquisite stemware, and the polished service that makes it all seem effortless. Choose from a list of utterly unique desserts to end the meal in style. The romance of Azur is in sharing these artistic culinary treats; and if you're staying at La Quinta, only a gentle walk through subtly lit gardens stands between this culinary palace and your sweet slumber.

$$$$ *AE, DIS, MC, V; no checks; dinner Tues–Sat (subject to closure during Aug); full bar; reservations recommended; www.laquintaresort.com.* &

---

## CUISTOT
◐◐◐◖

*73-111 El Paseo, Palm Desert / 760/340-1000*

Driving down Highway 111, lovebirds won't be able to miss Cuistot (pronounced "qwee-stow") restaurant, a stone-clad French-style farmhouse that flirts with hungry passersby from the prominent corner where stylish El Paseo intersects the valley's main thoroughfare. Cuistot has always been regarded as the valley's consistent choice for fine French dining, and, in 2003, it moved to this grand location and instantly became the place to be in Palm Desert. The main room is anchored by a giant romantic hearth, creating a warm and congenial atmosphere where red crescent-shaped booths line rustic stone walls, and couples sit close together, praising their robust and creamy wild mushroom soup in tones no louder than a whisper. Another dining room affords a ringside seat just outside the glassed-in kitchen, and yet another occupies the semiprivate wine room, where wines and stemware are stored; it can be closed off for intimate groups. The most romantic seating is outdoors, where patio seating allows you to see the lights of the desert through the fronds of swaying palms and flames from a warm hearth at the terrace's edge. In addition to that much-recommended mushroom soup, the California-French menu wows couples with skillet-roasted veal chop, beef chop with bordelaise sauce, Chinese-style duck in mango-Madeira-ginger sauce, and quail stuffed with sweetbreads over black rice. For dessert, share the floating island served in a 2-foot-tall martini glass; its traditional flavor is the perfect foil for such a whimsical presentation.

$$$–$$$$ *AE, MC, V; no checks; lunch Tues–Sat, dinner Tues–Sun (closed late July–early Sept); full bar; reservations recommended.* &

---

# JILLIAN'S
● ● ●
*74-155 El Paseo, Palm Desert / 760/776-8242*

Beauty without pretension makes Jillian's a real find amid desert resort bistros that cater to the well-heeled crowd, and it's particularly popular with couples. Whether the expressions of bliss on so many faces are from amorous inspiration or from decadent desserts like whisky-spiked and butterscotch-glazed pudding made with local Medjool dates, we can't say for sure. But we're getting ahead of ourselves: the Jillian's experience begins the moment you leave your car and step through an arched gateway to be greeted by trickling fountains and a private garden straight from a storybook. Once a rustic hacienda-style home built around an inner courtyard, the restaurant's been transformed into a supremely welcoming set of intimate dining rooms that open onto a magical patio where twinkling palms stand like pillars holding up the night sky. Always request an outdoor table when reserving. Proprietors Jay and June Trubee are well known in the desert, and to this day Jay does the honors in the kitchen—assisted by longtime sous chef Jorge Barajas (he's the one with his own date orchard—but that's jumping ahead *again*). Their style is robust Americana, with a strong emphasis on home-made pastas, including their acclaimed cannelloni. Colorado rack of lamb is crusted with seasoned breadcrumbs while whitefish dijonnaise arrives on a bed of mashed potatoes. All desserts are made on the premises, and they're too good to skip. In addition to Jorge's trademark steamed pudding, there's Jay's luscious Hawaiian cheesecake, a symphony of pineapple, coconut, and crunchy macadamia nuts that's been featured in *Gourmet* magazine. Choco-holics crawl in for a fix of the triple chocolate layer cake.
$$$ *AE, DC, MC, V; local checks only; dinner every day in season (closed Jun–early Oct); full bar; reservations recommended.* ₺

---

# OMRI & BONI
● ● ◖
*47-474 Washington St, La Quinta / 760/777-1315*

Chef Omri Siklai and his wife Boni lend their names to this La Quinta hot spot, an angular, modern sculpture of a building that's a far cry from the nearly hidden space in Palm Desert they recently outgrew. Romance seekers and devotees have been waiting years for this new restaurant, a 21st-century monument to modern materials and geometric lines that nevertheless caters to desert denizens with that most-valuable attribute: a big back parking lot. Inside, a picture window showcases the nearby mountains' stately silhouette, while gossamer curtains and halogen chandeliers soften the interior's stark lines, creating an alluring setting for amour. It also provides a fitting backdrop for self-taught Omri's inventive cuisine, one that meshes bold cooking techniques with original recipes and creative flavors. Gaze into the open kitchen and you'll see meats sizzle on the grill and ducks turn golden on the rotisserie. Try house specialties like mesquite-roasted quail on a pool of chimichurri; Maine lobster filled with calamari, shrimp, and garlic; or Omri's popular pancetta-seared veal chop with black morels. Desserts offer an international sweetness, from Italian *panna cotta* to French mousse and Bavarian strudel. After years spent as the valley's best-kept secret, Omri & Boni have traded their low profile for a spotlight where flavor meets architecture, and it makes an ideal choice for a special dinner for two. **$$–$$$** *AE, MC, V; no checks; dinner Wed–Mon (subject to Mon closure in summer); full bar; reservations recommended.* &

## SHAME ON THE MOON
◗❮

*69-950 Frank Sinatra Dr, Rancho Mirage / 760/324-5515*
With a convenient just-off-Highway 111 location in Rancho Mirage, and a warmly dim classic dining room, Shame on the Moon is the kind of Palm Springs restaurant couples have been enjoying for generations. The American-continental menu has been discreetly updated for contemporary tastes, as has the decor in the main dining room, where nearly every table is a smooch-tastic booth, and window tables look out on spotlit tropical foliage on the temperature-controlled terrace. The effect is something like a terrarium, but these patio tables are among the most requested by dreamy-eyed romantics. Dinners here are a comfortable mix of standards like stuffed chicken breast, rack of lamb, and the restaurant's acclaimed orange-glazed Long Island duck, plus creative interpretations like veal meat loaf and horseradish-crusted salmon. On any given night, most diners appear to be repeat customers, drawn by Shame on the Moon's consistent service, quality, and affordability: complete dinners, including appetizer, usually stay below the $20 mark. Add plenty of off-street parking, a practiced bartender, and genial maitre d', and it's easy to see why this mainstay is equally popular among old and young, gay and straight, local and tourist. **$$–$$$** *AE, MC, V; no checks; dinner every day; full bar; reservations recommended; www.shameonthemoon.com.* &

## TASTEBUD TANGO
◗◗

*73-675 Hwy 111, Palm Desert / 760/568-9799*
If the tango is the dance of love, then amorous types will naturally gravitate to this evocatively named gourmet-style bistro, where lively colors and flavors will entice your taste buds to join you in this romantic dance. Tucked away next to Casuelas Cafe (whose neon sign is a better landmark to find your way), Tastebud Tango is the brainchild of former caterers who correctly guessed how to strike a chord with local diners. Amid a dining room of tomato red, lemon yellow, and mango orange hues, the vivid flavors of California fusion cuisine—fresh ingredients with Latin, Pacific,

and Mediterranean accents—are perfectly matched with an affordable and user-friendly wine list. Choose a window-side table for deep gazes between courses, and plunge right in with an appetizer like oysters Tango, baked with spinach, bacon, and Cognac butter. The house specialty is deep-fried green olives filled with goat cheese and sausage, served with a fennel-spiked dipping sauce. For a main course, try Mexican-style flank steak that's been tenderized in tequila and lime for 24 hours, then grilled and served with sweet corn-cheddar gratin; or tapenade-crusted rack of lamb atop a creamy chèvre-potato puree. Though the atmosphere is classy-casual, and more bustling than intimate, Tastebud Tango is an insider's choice that will please any flavor-seeking couple.

**$$–$$$** *AE, DC, MC, V; no checks; dinner Wed—Sun; full bar; reservations recommended.*

# HIGH DESERT DESTINATIONS

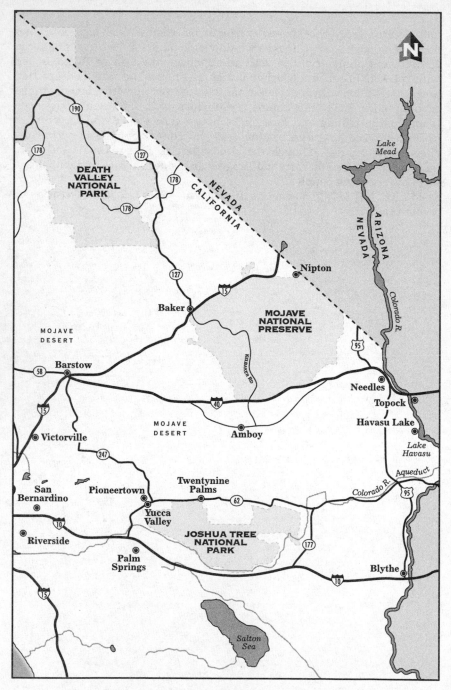

*"It is not the kiss endured, but the kiss returned that lives."*

—EDITH WHARTON

# HIGH DESERT DESTINATIONS

Southern California's High Desert regions may be the antithesis of—as well as the antidote for—the human rat race. Approximately 25 million acres of hauntingly serene desert landscape offer a romantic respite from the hustle and bustle of daily life.

Scarecrow-like Joshua trees, serving as sentries to the stillness of a lost world, stimulate the imagination. Picture embracing your significant other at sunset, when nature's palette paints an awe-inspiring canvas filled with reds, oranges, and magentas. Or perhaps kiss in the crispness of the evening air, while overhead a galaxy of stars brightens the vast desert skies.

Couples who crave privacy will find wide-open spaces in gratifying abundance. Hiking and camping summon introspective adventurers, while such remarkable geographic phenomena as Racetrack Valley in Death Valley, where rocks the size of boulders mysteriously appear to move themselves in the dead of night, and the 6,000-year-old Amboy Crater, which rises 285 feet above the flat expanse of desert below, pay homage to the might of Mother Nature.

There is a great deal of diversity in California's High Desert, from its hearty terrain to its adaptive wildlife. The Joshua tree, which proliferates in Joshua Tree National Park, was named by Mormon pioneers who thought the largest of the yuccas resembled the biblical prophet Joshua beckoning them to their own promised land. In Death Valley, 11,000-foot mountain peaks rise majestically over alkali flats, piñon woodlands, and flowing sand dunes.

The Mojave National Preserve, bordered by Interstate 15 on the north, Interstate 40 on the south, and Highway 95 on the east, is nicknamed "the Lonely Triangle." How lonely is it? The Kelso Dunes, arguably its most popular attraction, are visited by less than a couple dozen people a day. Talk about an isolated place to share a kiss!

Because of the vast distances that encompass California's High Desert, a reliable vehicle is essential. Snuggle up, keep your eyes open, and enjoy an ascetic panorama that will gratify your senses and inspire your imagination. It's otherworldly, but then again, so is true love.

# JOSHUA TREE NATIONAL PARK

## ROMANTIC HIGHLIGHTS

Secluded, stark, and beautiful, Joshua Tree National Park is a place where lovers can really get away from it all. The park achieved national monument status in 1936 and became a national park in 1994. Today, Joshua Tree, or JT as the rock climbers call it, remains nearly as pristine as it was back in the days before the government took measures to protect it.

With its remote locale, Joshua Tree isn't exactly a mecca for fine dining, so lovers will want to pack a cooler filled with plenty of water and picnic supplies for a day in the park. There's nothing worse than being thirsty and hungry in the middle of the desert.

Start your exploration with a stop at one of Joshua Tree's best-kept secrets, **Cottonwood Spring Oasis** (located 7 miles from the park's southern entrance). The spring was formed by earthquakes centuries ago and was frequented by the Cahuilla Indians. Later, prospectors used the spring for gold processing, and the ruins of three gold mills are still in the vicinity. Couples arriving early may spy bighorn sheep drinking from the nearby **Cottonwood Wash**, and small tracks indicate the presence of other animals. There are only 158 desert fan palm oases in North America, and the Cottonwood Spring Oasis is one of five in Joshua Tree National Park. Several hikes begin at Cottonwood Spring, and the trails reveal spectacular views.

While some couples come to Joshua Tree to enjoy its serene beauty, others arrive in the park ready to **rock climb**, a sport which has increased in popularity here, sometimes making it difficult to find a campsite from November through May, when the temperatures are cool. Even if the two of you aren't ready to try scaling the park's rocky monoliths, it can be fun to watch the rock climbers grapple their way up the steep inclines.

However, hiking may be a more accessible activity for couples who want to get out and enjoy the beautiful setting. **Black Rock Canyon** (situated in the northwest corner of the park) offers several moderate hiking trails. The road leading up to the canyon dead-ends at a lovely campground, and the hills behind the camp contain a number of hiking trails that wind their way through Joshua trees, junipers, cholla cacti, and desert shrubs. The best time to hike here is from February through May, when the Joshuas, shrubs,

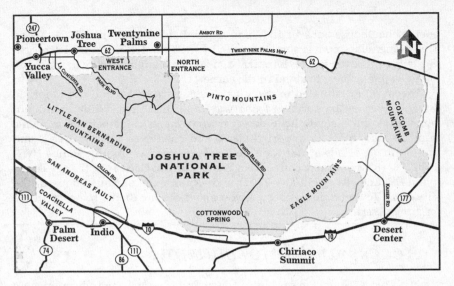

and annuals bloom. Armchair outdoor enthusiasts—who prefer to stay in camp—may spot such common wildlife as jackrabbits, cottontails, and squirrels, while Gambel's quail, great horned owls, scrub jays, and cactus wrens fly overhead. **Barker Dam Trail**, near **Hidden Valley Campground**, offers another easy path through boulders that leads to a rockbound pool built at the turn of the century. It's a beautiful hike and proves that not all water in the desert is an oasis.

There's more than just stark desert terrain in the area. The easternmost gateway into the park, **Twentynine Palms**, is home to more than 28,000 desert dwellers who enjoy wide-open vistas, crystal-clear skies, and a casual style of living. Named for the number of trees at the **Oasis of Mara** (located at the park's northeastern entrance point), this little desert town has myriad galleries run by the city's active art colony. After a day in the park, you and your sweetie can stop in at **Twentynine Palms Artists Guild Art Gallery** (74055 Cottonwood Dr; 760/367-7819) to view some of the area's local desert artwork, then step outside and appreciate nature's large-scale masterpiece. The city's **Oasis of Murals**, found on buildings throughout the town, now number 20. One of the most recently painted murals is called *Iraqi Freedom,* which commemorates the events that transpired on March 21, 2003, when the First Marine Division crossed Kuwait and began Operation Iraqi Freedom. Some of those U.S. forces that participated in the military action were trained at the Twentynine Palms Combat Center, giving this a local connection. Other murals depict a variety of scenes from the city's history.

Also in town is the **Old Schoolhouse Museum** (6760 National Park Dr; 760/367-2366), which started out as a *Little House on the Prairie*-style one-room schoolhouse back in 1927 and which held classes until 1954. Today this former classroom is a museum run by the Twentynine Palms Historical Society. Admission is free. Be warned: if you get caught kissing in the classroom, you may have to stand in the corner!

**Yucca Valley**, situated midway between Los Angeles and the Colorado River, serves as the northwest doorway to Joshua Tree. While there's not much to do in this cute little desert town, couples can stock up on picnic supplies ranging from imported meats and cheeses to artisan breads and freshly made salads at **Rattler Fine Foods** (61705 Twentynine Palms Hwy; 760/366-1898) or grab a coffee from **Water Canyon Coffee Co.** (55844 Twentynine Palms Hwy; 760/365-7771) and explore the antique shops in the city's Old Town section. After all, you may need a caffeine fix, even in the pristine desert.

## Access and Information

Joshua Tree National Park is best reached by car, so you can fully appreciate the stunning desert scenery. The park lies 140 miles east of Los Angeles and can be approached from the west via Interstate 10 and Highway 62 (Twentynine Palms Hwy). The north entrances to the park are located at Joshua Tree Village and the city of Twentynine Palms. The south entrance at Cottonwood Spring Oasis, which lies 25 miles east of Indio, can be approached from the east or west, also via Interstate 10.

**Palm Springs International Airport** (3400 E Tahquitz Canyon Wy; 760/318-3800) is the area's closest airport. It's about 94 miles from Palm Springs to Twentynine Palms, and 50 miles from Twentynine Palms to Amboy.

For more information, contact the **Joshua Tree National Park** (75585 National Park Dr; 760/367-5500 or 800/365-2267; www.nps.gov/jotr). Other helpful information centers include **Black Rock Nature Center** (in Black Rock Canyon at the northwest corner of the park; 760/367-3001; open Oct–May), and **Oasis Visitor Center** (74485 National Park Dr, corner of Utah Trail before you enter the park; 760/367-5500).

## Romantic Lodgings

### THE OASIS OF EDEN INN & SUITES
⬡⬡

*56377 Twentynine Palms Hwy, Yucca Valley / 760/365-6321 or 800/606-6686*
This funky 40-room hotel offers 14 cleverly decorated theme rooms for couples seeking to add a touch of the exotic to their Joshua Tree getaway. They say nature inspires passion, so the two of you may want to check into the Jungle Room, where you'll be immersed in tropical greenery, with cheetahs,

toucans, and jaguars pictured on the walls. An in-room spa and waterfall and his-and-hers rock showers add to this faux outdoor experience. The nostalgic Rockin' '50s Suite has a bed that resembles a 1959 Cadillac, and you and your honey can soak in the suite's spa while looking at a wall mural of Mulholland Drive. (It's Inspiration Point, without the curfew.) The Roman Suite is perfect for modern-day Antonys and Cleopatras, with its marble flooring and columns, while the Plantation Room is something out of *Gone with the Wind*. The inn's basic rooms are just that—basic—with garden views, kitchenettes, and VCRs so you can snuggle in for movie night after a day of outdoor adventure. A sparkling pool and whirlpool provide lovers with a place to cool off from the desert heat, and in-room spa services, like the Tropical Journey's Couple's Spa package (two hours of massage and pampering), provide the ultimate way to relax and unwind. A complimentary continental breakfast is provided each morning as well as dessert and tea in the evening; romance baskets (complete with champagne or sparkling cider, chocolates, snacks, and bath goodies), dinner packages, and lunches for hikers are also available.
$$–$$$ *AE, DC, DIS, MC, V; checks OK (in advance); www.oasisofeden.com.* ♿

## RIMROCK RANCH CABINS
♥♥♥

*PO Box 313, Pioneertown / 760/228-1297*
The slogan used by this charming rustic hideaway is, "the high desert getaway for stressed-out city dwellers." However, it could just as easily be called, "the high desert getaway for lovers." Located 4,500 feet above sea level with temperatures about 20° cooler than nearby Joshua Tree National Park, Rimrock contains all the requisite elements for a romantic escape—rustic cabins, fresh air, magical sunsets, and star-filled skies. The Rimrock Ranch was the first homestead in the area, built in 1947 at the snow line above Yucca Valley. A few other cabins were added during the 1950s to house actors and directors of the dozens of cowboy movies shot in Pioneertown. Today, Rimrock's four cabins retain its heritage, boasting an eclectic mix of lodge-style elements and antique furnishings. Each knotty-pine cabin has a cozy bed made with a fluffy down comforter and pillows (perfect for snuggling), a fully equipped kitchen, a bathroom stocked with such thoughtful touches as peppermint and lavender soap, and a private patio with outdoor fireplace to keep the two of you warm while you enjoy the desert night. Sunsets and stars are best viewed around the Rimrock's giant timber observation deck, and there is a rock-lined campfire pit for when nothing will beat a gooey s'more. After a day of rock climbing, hiking, or biking, lovers can return for a cooling dip in Rimrock's mineral water plunge pool. Or, to really relax, book an in-room massage for two. While there's much to see and do here, many couples opt to never leave their cabins.
$$ *AE, MC, V; checks OK; www.rimrockranchcabins.com.*

## ROUGHLEY MANOR BED & BREAKFAST
◐◑◖

*74744 Joe Davis Rd, Twentynine Palms / 760/367-3238*
In 1924, desert pioneers Elizabeth and Bill Campbell turned a once-primitive campsite into an elegant Colonial-style three-story stone-walled mansion. Today, a rustling oasis of mature Washington palms, cypress trees, rose gardens, and trickling fountains surrounds this former homestead dream of the young lovers. Located near the northeast edge of Joshua Tree National Park, Roughley Manor has aged well, and dedicated innkeepers Jan and Garry Peters share the original owners' attributes of industriousness and imagination. The main house has smooth Vermont maple floors and a relaxing wood-paneled great room that's an ideal place to hang out by the fire. Upstairs are two grand suites, including the romantic Campbell Suite, which was the original owners' master bedroom and today houses a four-poster bed, a fireplace, a separate reading room, and deep-set windows that look out into the treetops and surrounding desert landscape. Other rooms (all are air-conditioned) are housed in a cozy cottage, a charming farmhouse, a stone building next to the property's original 1930s reservoir, and a newly converted bar with sunset-facing porches and brand-new everything. Couples get a hearty gourmet breakfast, evening desserts, coffee, and tea—plus a stunning sky full of stars to inspire romantic dreams.
*$–$$ AE, MC, V; checks OK; www.roughleymanor.com.*

## THE 29 PALMS INN
◐◑

*73950 Inn Ave, Twentynine Palms / 760/367-3505*
These rustic adobe bungalows and historic wood-frame cabins have been a romantic getaway since 1928. Sprawled over 35 acres, the setting is pure eye candy, with fan palms, palo verde, mesquite, and an oasis lagoon making the grounds seem like something conjured from an *Arabian Nights* tale. Each accommodation is unique; bungalow rooms with sun patios are housed in a 1929 adobe, while wood-framed cottages and several houses and cabins provide lovers with their own private retreats. Couples may want to reserve Forget-Me-Not, a 1934 adobe bungalow that sits in the shade of the desert vegetation right next to the inn's enchanting spring-fed pond. Decorated with the works of local artists, the bungalow has a queen-sized bed, fireplace, and private sun patio with a picture-perfect view of the desert and oasis. Thick adobe walls provide insulation during the warm desert days and cold nights. Built in 1930 for local artist Irene Charlton, Irene's Adobe is another romantic hideaway. This beautiful little adobe house boasts a separate bedroom and living room with a cozy fireplace, a fully equipped kitchen, and a very private large courtyard with a covered patio, perfect for couples who want to while away a lazy afternoon enjoying the desert setting. In the mornings, complimentary homemade sweet breads and coffee

are served around the pool patio. Adjacent to the pool, the inn's restaurant (see Romantic Restaurants) serves grilled steaks, seafood, and chicken, complemented by seasonal vegetables from the inn's year-round garden. $$ *AE, DC, DIS, MC, V; checks OK; www.29palmsinn.com.* &

# *Romantic Restaurants*

## PAPPY & HARRIET'S PIONEERTOWN PALACE
◆

*53668 Pioneertown Rd, Pioneertown / 760/365-5956*
After spending the day amid the quiet serenity of Joshua Tree, couples can crank things up a notch with a lively night at this friendly neighborhood honky-tonk in nearby Pioneertown, which was originally built as a Western movie set in the 1940s. Resembling an old Western saloon, this restaurant/nightspot is a fun place for casual meals, drinks, and live music. During the day, couples dine on such simple fare as burgers, hot dogs, chicken sandwiches, and salads. In the evening, they stoke up the outdoor mesquite grill and also serve steaks, ribs, tri-tip, and chicken. Whether the two of you want to just throw back a couple of icy long-necks and listen to live music or two-step the night away, Pappy & Harriet's is sure to provide ample opportunities for country-western-inspired kissing. Once a favorite watering hole for the likes of Gene Autry and Mick Fleetwood, this local hangout has attracted such big-name performers as Lucinda Williams and Concrete Blonde's Johnette Napolitano (who lives nearby); their soulful songs about love and heartbreak can only add to your night of amour. $-$$ *AE, DIS, MC, V; no checks; lunch Mon–Sun, dinner Thurs–Sun; full bar; reservations recommended; www.pappyandharriets.com.*

## THE RESTAURANT AT 29 PALMS INN
◆◀

*73950 Inn Ave, Twentynine Palms / 760/367-3505*
Adjacent to the pool at the 29 Palms Inn (see Romantic Lodgings), this charming little restaurant serves the best meals in the area. On a beautiful evening, couples can dine outdoors at a poolside table and perhaps be serenaded by the barn owls that live in the nearby palms. The menu favors a hearty Continental approach to grilled steaks, seafood, and chicken, including such highlights as garlicky shrimp scampi, succulent lamb chops, and perfectly seasoned rosemary chicken. Winning starters include the hickory-smoked salmon (marinated and smoked on the premises), and spinach salad tossed with raisins and sunflower seeds. All seasonal vegetables come from the inn's year-round garden, and the crusty sourdough bread is baked fresh each day. Order up two of the best margaritas this side of Palm Springs and toast each other and your time in the desert. If the two

of you have room for dessert, the old-fashioned chocolate sundae is perfect to share.

**$$** *AE, DC, DIS, MC, V; no checks; dinner every day; full bar; reservations recommended; www.29palmsinn.com.* ⅙

# MOJAVE NATIONAL PRESERVE

## ROMANTIC HIGHLIGHTS

There are some who think this 1.6 million-acre parcel of parched desert property, bypassed if not ignored by civilization and its compulsive preoccupation with construction, is located in the middle of nowhere. They're wrong. The Mojave National Preserve, the third-largest national park after Yellowstone and Death Valley, is actually at the end of nowhere—or perhaps the beginning of it.

This desert park remains as it always has been: a stark contrast to the modern world. It is an ideal escape for the true romantic who believes that precious solitude is the ultimate aphrodisiac. From its rose-colored sand dunes to its intriguing limestone caverns, there is romance in the simple beauty of this land, which ranges in elevation from less than 1,000 feet to nearly 8,000 feet. The best time to visit the preserve is from October to May, when temperatures are mild and more than 300 species of animals roam the expansive desert.

Couples approaching Mojave National Preserve from the southwest will first spy the **Granite Mountains**. These grand monoliths, with their pink spires and pinnacles, rise hundreds of feet above the ground and once formed the core of a volcanic mountain range. Another volcanic remnant, **Cima Dome**, is famous for its smooth dome shape that rises nearly 1,500 feet above the desert floor and covers more than 75 square miles. This large, rounded rock isn't barren, however. It is covered with Joshua trees, making it a most unusual forest.

Volcanic rock formations make **Hole-in-the-Wall** (20 miles northwest of I-40 via Essex and Black Canyon Rds) a fascinating place for couples to explore. This area began to take shape more than 18 million years ago, when volcanic eruptions from nearby Woods Mountains spewed layers of lava and ash. Holes were formed in the rock as a result of gases captured during the eruption, along with uneven cooling. Over the course of countless centuries, erosion has enlarged these holes to create amazing caverns. The oxidation of iron in this volcanic material lends a contrasting reddish color to the gray background.

Lawrence of Arabia never wandered through the **Kelso Dunes**, but if he

# *Sleeping Under the Stars*

For some, there's nothing like camping under the stars with a significant other. This is back to basics, where communing with nature takes center stage. Since there are few hotels in the area, many couples visiting Mojave National Preserve opt to bring their sleeping bags and tents and call the outdoors home for a couple of days.

There are three campgrounds in the preserve where lovers can set up camp and toast marshmallows by moonlight. However, spaces are available on a first-come, first-serve basis, so make sure to arrive early.

The **Hole-in-the-Wall Campground** (20 miles northwest of I-40 via Essex and Black Canyon Rds; 760/733-4040) sits at 4,400 feet above sea level and is surrounded by sculptured volcanic rock walls, creating serene surroundings for setting up camp. It has 35 campsites with areas large enough for motor homes and trailers, and two walk-in tent sites. Facilities include pit toilets, picnic tables, fire rings, trash cans, and drinkable water on a limited basis. There are no utility hookups, but there is a sanitary disposal station. The **Black Canyon Equestrian & Group Campground** (760/928-2572) located at Hole-in-the-Wall, has no water, so camping couples should bring their own or at least bring along containers for transporting water from the nearby campground.

**Mid Hills Campground** (30 miles northwest of I-40 via Essex and Black Canyon Rds), nestled in piñon pine and juniper trees 5,600 feet above the desert floor, is a cool place to camp—literally. Temperatures are generally 10 to 15 degrees lower here. The 26 campsites include such facilities as pit toilets, picnic tables, fire rings, trash cans, and drinkable water on a limited basis. The road leading to the campground is not paved, making it treacherous for motor homes or trailers, so most campers pitch tents. Several trailheads can be found near this site, making it an ideal starting point for a day of hiking and taking in nature's beauty.

As vegetation in the desert is sparse, collecting firewood is not permitted, so lovers who want to build a warm, romantic campfire will need to bring their own firewood. Backpackers and hikers are allowed to camp within the national preserve by going at least half a mile from any developed area or road and a quarter mile from water sources. While privacy is a dream for outdoorsy couples, there is no official registration system, so the two of you may want to make sure that someone knows where you are. Backcountry camping is limited to a 14-day stay. Since only a few trail signs exist, it's a good idea to take

*Continued on next page*

a reliable map and become familiar with the area.

Roadside camping, also known as car camping, is permissible within the national preserve. However, it is limited to areas that have been traditionally used for this purpose. Camping tramples vegetation, so selecting sites that have already been used helps protect the desert from further damage.

—KEITH TUBER

had he may have felt right at home. The Eastern Mojave's main attraction, these delicate wind-blown sculptures soar as high as 600 feet, with the bulk of the sand deposits blown here from the Mojave River sink east of Afton Canyon. Their creation was a mystery until recently, when geologists figured out the puzzle by studying the wind patterns and mountain formations. The sand grains themselves are mostly quartz and feldspar, the result of erosion. It takes about two hours to climb the dunes, for those who accept that challenge. From the top, lovers can share an intimate moment as they look out on the timeless landscape.

Railroad buffs, and those who love the allure of the West, also can visit the nearby historic **Kelso Depot**, built in 1924. The town of Kelso itself grew up around this Union Pacific Railroad stop, with nearly 2,000 people residing in the desert community during its 1940s heyday. The town later experienced hard times with the decline of steam locomotives. Today, the once-elegant structure is in the process of being restored.

Another Mojave highlight is the **Mitchell Caverns** (760/928-2586). First owned by silver miner Jack Mitchell, these limestone caves contain a wide variety of formations, including *El Pakiva* (the Devil's House) and *Tecopa* (named for a Shoshone chief). The two of you can huddle close as you marvel at the prominent stalactites and stalagmites during a 90-minute guided tour, but be sure to call ahead and make a reservation.

Just to the south of the preserve, **Amboy** was once a bustling whistle stop on Route 66 before Interstate 40 was built less than 20 miles away. Today, the small town remains frozen in time, bleached by the desert sun. Couples can stop in at **Roy's Café & Motel** (Rt 66; 760/733-4263; www.rt66roys.com), built in the 1930s, which calls itself "the crustiest, dustiest gas stop on all of Route 66," for a cool drink before heading to **Amboy Crater**, which lies just southeast of the town. Formed 6,000 years ago by a volcano that spewed lava over 24 square miles, the crater features two trails—one easy, the other more difficult—for couples who feel inspired to experience the wonders of this 246-foot basalt cinder cone. After all, kissing in a crater can be a memorable event—perhaps the ultimate Kodak moment.

To the northwest of the preserve, Baker boasts the **world's largest thermometer**, symbolic of the highest temperature ever recorded in the United States—134°F in nearby Death Valley. The thermometer sits just above the **Mojave Desert Information Center** (72157 Baker Blvd; 760/733-4040). While

Baker may appear to be a dusty little settlement in no man's land, dreams have come true in this tiny town. A few lucky prospectors recently found their riches not in dusty gold mines, but by taking a chance on the California Lottery. **Wills Fargo Country Store** (72129 Baker Blvd; 760/733-4477) has the distinction of having sold five winning Super Lotto tickets, with jackpots ranging from $4.2 million to $14 million. So, you and your sweetie may want to invest in the dream.

Only 63 miles west of Mojave National Preserve, **Barstow** sits at the junction of Interstate 15, Interstate 40, and Highway 58. Mainly just a resting spot for travelers in need of gas, food, and rest rooms, this glimpse-of-the-past drive-thru town's Main Street is the only remaining section of Route 66 to still be designated "Main Street."

# Access and Information

Mojave National Park is best reached by car. Interstate 15 traverses the preserve's northern boundaries, while Interstate 40 skirts its southern perimeter. Within the preserve, one primary north-south route, Kelbaker Road, splits the region between the interstates. Road conditions vary inside the preserve, from paved two-lane highways to rugged four-wheel-drive roads.

The nearest airports are **Ontario International Airport** (140 miles from the western boundary of the national preserve; 909/975-5360; www.lawa .org/ont/ontframe.html) and Las Vegas's **McCarran International Airport** (60 miles from the national preserve's eastern boundary; 702/261-5211; www.mccarran.com).

General information can be obtained from the National Park Service's **Mojave Desert Information Center** (72157 Baker Blvd; 760/733-4040). The **Hole-in-the-Wall Information Center** (20 miles north of I-40 on Essex and Black Canyon Rds; 760/928-2572) also provides information on the region.

# Romantic Lodgings

## HOTEL NIPTON
🌑🌑

*72 Nipton Rd, Nipton / 760/856-2335*
Couples choosing to enter the preserve from Interstate 15 can make the 1885-founded gold mining town of Nipton home base for exploring. The whistle-stop of a town, population 70 (give or take a few), is just a few miles from the Nevada state line. Opened in 1996, Hotel Nipton feels more like an Old West movie set than a tiny bed-and-breakfast. The historic adobe hotel, built in the Spanish territorial style with a wrap-around wooden porch, has four guest rooms decorated in period style, three with double beds and the

other with twin beds. Couples may want to check into the Clara Bell Room, named in honor of silent movie star Clara Bow and her husband, cowboy Rex Bell, who once operated a nearby ranch. An inviting parlor features a collector's case of old bottles and memorabilia unearthed during the restoration of the mining town, as well as scrapbooks and decanters of sherry. It's a wonderful place for the two of you to curl up with a good book or to chat about your day exploring the desert. In the evening, lovers grab a towel and head outdoors for a soak in the hotel's heated whirlpools alongside the railroad tracks, where it's possible to enjoy nature's astrological show in the dark desert sky. In the mornings, continental breakfast is brought to your room—kind of like breakfast in bed. Guests do have to rough it a bit, though, by sharing two bathrooms located down the hall.
*$$ DIS, MC, V; checks OK; www.nipton.com.*

## WILLS FARGO MOTEL
◉

*72252 Baker Blvd, Baker / 760/733-4477*
If clean and convenient are what the two of you had in mind, book a room at this 30-room motel, where guest rooms in the newer wing (circa early 1990s) feature king-sized beds and tub/shower combinations. It might not be the Four Seasons, but it's better than camping. Named for one of its former owners, Will Herron, this tiny motel has one big selling point—a 10-foot-deep pool—where lovers can plunge in to cool off from the desert heat.
*$ AE, DC, DIS, MC, V; no checks.* ♿

# *Romantic Restaurants*

## THE MAD GREEK
◉

*72155 Baker Blvd, Baker / 760/733-4354*
Family-owned and -operated for more than a decade, this desert landmark lures lovers in transit for an authentic Greek meal. A statue of Hercules decorates the dining room, where such tasty Mediterranean fare as sizzling shish kebab, eggplant salads, hummus, baklava, and gyros are served to hungry couples exploring the desert. Or, for those who feel more comfortable chowing down on an old-fashioned American hamburger or sandwich, that's possible, too. Strawberry shakes made with real strawberries or icy margaritas will cool you off after a day in the desert heat. Couples can start the day here with a hearty breakfast before heading out for a day of desert hiking and touring. While this may not exactly be the Greek Islands, the Mad Greek offers far more ambience than the nearby Denny's.
*$ AE, DIS, MC, V; no checks; breakfast, lunch, dinner every day; full bar, reservations not necessary.* ♿

## IDLE SPURS STEAKHOUSE
❀

*690 Old High, Barstow / 760/256-8888*
Set in a historic house, this old-fashioned steakhouse has been luring steak-loving lovers since it first opened back in 1950. Couples can have a predinner cocktail in the rustic Get-Away Lounge, with its old-fashioned barstools and vintage decor. Then, sit down to dinner on either the patio—an indoor atrium filled with plants, trickling fountains, and a giant skylight—or in the garden room, which boasts an impressive collection of antiques and looks out on to the lights of Barstow. Slow-cooked prime rib, sumptuous USDA choice steaks, chicken, lobster, fresh fish, and giant salads are served by a friendly, efficient wait staff. And each entrée comes with such classic accoutrements as soup or salad, garlic cheese toast, vegetables, and a fluffy baked potato. One thing's for sure: no one is going to go hungry here.
**$$** *AE, MC, V, DIS; no checks; lunch Mon–Fri, dinner Mon–Sun; full bar; reservations recommended; www.idlespurssteakhouse.com.* W

## PEGGY SUE'S NIFTY FIFTIES
❀

*35654 Yermo Rd, Yermo / 760/254-3370*
Nostalgia reigns supreme at this time-warped eatery. Open for breakfast, lunch, and dinner, this '50s-style diner serves lovers such old-fashioned fare as juicy burgers, succulent steaks, homemade chili, and hearty soups. There's even a soda fountain/ice cream parlor, so the two of you can dig into a jumbo banana split or share a thick and rich shake with two straws, all while listening to '50s music on the jukebox. Built in 1954 and restored and expanded in 1987, this roadside diner also offers a five-and-dime store, where you can pick up hokey curios and souvenirs as reminders of the great time you had together. And, of course, old-fashioned candies are a must for the road trip home.
**$** *AE, MC, V; no checks; breakfast, lunch, dinner every day; beer and wine; reservations not necessary.* ♿

# DEATH VALLEY

## ROMANTIC HIGHLIGHTS

**A**s you depart the glittering lights, honking cars, and frenetic energy of the city and settle into the drive to Death Valley, something rather exquisite and surprising happens along the way. The suburban strip malls, massive billboards, and neon fast-food restaurant signs slowly seep away, and before you realize exactly what's happened, balmy blasts of desert air start rolling over you, lulling you into languid relaxation. Miles and miles of empty road open up, and the landscape changes to craggy mountain red rocks and towering cacti as far as the eye can see. For couples heading to Death Valley for a romantic sojourn, renting a convertible for this otherworldly drive is definitely the way to go. Be sure to pack a dozen seductive CDs since few radio stations tune in on this seemingly endless road toward one of the hottest places on earth. Certainly the name "Death Valley" does not immediately suggest rocketing romance, but don't allow that intimidating label to dissuade you from experiencing this land of exotic extremes.

Death Valley earned its name when the first explorers and immigrants entered the area, looking for what they thought was a shortcut from the Midwest to California, only to find nearly unlivable conditions right smack in the middle of the desert. Big oops. Today, Death Valley gives all-new meaning to the word "extreme." It sits 282 feet below sea level—the nation's lowest point here bottoms out at an astonishing 11,049 feet below sea level. Winters in this desert destination are mild, with temperatures in the 60s and 70s, making it conducive to exploring **Death Valley National Park**'s many natural attractions. Summer days can reach temperatures in the 120°F-plus range, and ground temperatures have reached 201°F—that's just 11°F shy of the boiling point for water. Needless to say, on a hot summer day, it's possible to only stand outside your air-conditioned automobile or hotel room for a few minutes and gasp. Hemmed in by nine mountain ranges, Death Valley is cut off from rainfall or cooling Pacific winds, which makes it one of the driest places in the world. It averages less than 2 inches of annual rainfall. Talk about extremes.

Death Valley National Park's size is no less intense: it sprawls across 3.4 million acres, which makes Death Valley the largest national park in the contiguous United States, almost five times larger than its glamorous California counterpart, Yosemite. Good news for all lovers, but most especially nature lovers: all but a tiny fraction of that expanse is federal wilderness, which means this Connecticut-size chunk of unique topography will always be preserved for its rugged animal inhabitants and the brave adventurers among us.

If you think solitude and "getting away from it all" are synonymous with high romance, this secluded hot spot (and we do mean *hot*) is the ultimate lovers' getaway. Pack comfortable clothing, well-built walking shoes, and a broad-brimmed hat that provides sun protection. (Hint: this is the place to pack a pup tent for two, not your Jimmy Choo stilettos.) Whether you voyage around for an extended weekend or trek the unique eco-region for a few hours, Death Valley is awe-inspiring in its own *Lost in Space*, desolate kind of way. It squats at 6,433 feet in elevation—more than a mile and a quarter below the valley floor—and the rugged red rocks are sunny, dry, and clear throughout the year.

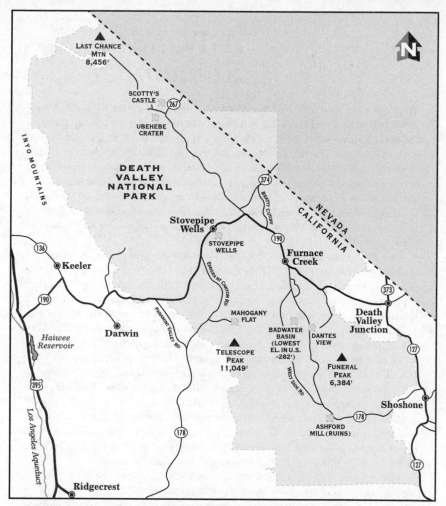

Believe it or not, Death Valley is also a land of subtle but inescapable beauties: morning light creeps across the eroded badlands of **Zabriskie Point** to strike **Manly Beacon**; the setting sun casts lengthening shadows on the sand dunes at **Stovepipe Wells**, and myriad wildflowers color the golden hills above **Harmony Borax** on a warm spring day. Death Valley contains an astonishing array of natural attractions and more than 900 kinds of diverse plants and wildlife you cannot find anywhere else on earth.

One of the area's few man-made must-sees is **Scotty's Castle**, built in 1924 by Chicago tycoon Albert Johnson at a cost of $2.5 million and now administered by Grapevine Ranger Station (760/786-2313). This Moorish mansion with its four towers opens every day for tours of its rooms (the grounds are

# A Walk to Remember

More than just cracked terrain and miles and miles of sand, Death Valley National Park offers a variety of diverse landscapes that create the ideal backdrop for everything from a romantic stroll to a sweat-inducing uphill climb. The two of you can pack up the car with snacks and plenty of water, lace up your hiking boots, and head out for a day of exploration. Order a boxed picnic lunch (roasted rosemary chicken, grilled vegetables, and lemon bars, perhaps) at Furnace Creek Inn and strike out on your own to drive and discover Death Valley's multitudinous natural wonders. Be sure to bring along maps, driving routes, and extra water bottles. It's a big old country out there.

One desert oasis worth a visit is **Darwin Falls** (just west of Panamint Springs off Hwy 190 on Wildrose Canyon Rd). Lovers can reach the creek-side trail by taking a beautiful drive through the Panamint high country, which snakes past dozens of vista points, ghost towns, forests, and hiking territory. Shade from the surrounding forest, combined with the high elevation, makes this one of Death Valley's coolest spots. Located 5 miles behind the Panamint Springs Resort (you can't miss the signage) at the 3,000-foot level, this 2-mile hike wanders past a year-round stream and cascading 30-foot waterfalls. Fed by nearby artesian wells, this seemingly out-of-place oasis provides welcome relief to desert wildlife and hikers alike, since it's the only water source for miles around. (However, stick to drinking your bottled water, as the artesian wells are not safe for drinking.) Nothing like smooching under a private waterfall on a torrid day! Hiking beyond the first set of falls is steep and the rocks can be slippery, so be careful. A twisted ankle (or worse) is a quick way to end a day of outdoor amour.

For couples feeling a little more ambitious, consider taking a romantic ramble up the **Telescope Peak Trail**. Starting from the Mahogany Flat Campground, this 7-mile trail follows the rough, steep road after Charcoal Kilns to upper Wildrose Canyon Road. Hike this strenuous trail to the highest peak in the park (11,049 feet) with a 3,000-foot elevation gain. Ancient bristlecone pines appear just above 10,000 feet, and the summit rewards you with spectacular views ranging from Badwater, the lowest point in the Western Hemisphere, to Mount Whitney, the highest point in the Lower 48. Don't forget that the high altitude may slow you down, so save the champagne for later and drink plenty of bottled water.

—NICOLE DORSEY

open for self-guided touring). The stories of the unlikely friendship between Johnson and con man Walter Scott (Scotty)—who both pursued a secret gold mine—are as tasty as the mansion's opulent interiors.

However, the natural wonders of this vast desert expanse are just as rich as the Scotty's Castle's opulent architecture. Indeed, the two of you could easily find a dozen majestic hikes and long lovers' lane drives. For example, you can expect a stiff, cool breeze on the edge of **Ubehebe Crater**, located in the northern section of the park. A spectacular remnant of a violent volcanic explosion that occurred 3,000 years ago, the crater sinks 462 feet below the west rim, with the bottom reachable by a trail that starts at the parking lot. It's an easy five-minute hike down, but you'll huff 'n puff climbing back up the loose cinder trail. Climb two steps up and slide one step back down all the way back up to the rim. Also a short hike away is **Little Hebe Crater**, a series of three craters within a crater. With cavernous volcanic craters on either side, this scenic spot offers plenty of extraordinary photo opportunities, if you can tear your eyes off each other, that is. **Desolation Canyon, Hells Gate**, and the **Badwater Salt Flats**, to name just a few, are also spectacular park sights worth visiting. (Kudos to the turn-of-the-century miners who so descriptively, and dramatically, named these particular sights.)

Other Death Valley attractions that will give the two of you a glimpse of the area's wealth of history include the **Borax Museum** at Furnace Creek Ranch (see Romantic Lodgings; 760/786-2345) and **Harmony Borax Works** ruins—complete with the original 20-mule-team wagons on display—and the one-of-a-kind **Amargosa Opera House** (at the intersection of Hwy 190 and Hwy 127; 760/852-4441; www.amargosaoperahouse.com) at Death Valley Junction.

## *Access and Information*

Approximately 120 miles northwest of Las Vegas and 275 miles northeast of Los Angeles, Death Valley National Park is about a two-and-a-half-hour drive from Las Vegas or a five- to six-hour drive from Los Angeles, depending on the traffic, of course. From Las Vegas, take Interstate 15 south to Highway 160 and proceed toward Blue Diamond/Pahrump. Four miles from the first stoplight, turn left on Belle Vista Road and proceed to Death Valley Junction and turn right. A left on Highway 190 leads into the park. From Los Angeles, take the 405 Freeway to Highway 14 and proceed north to Highway 395. From Highway 395, go to Searles Station Road and turn right, proceeding to Trona Road. Turn right on to Highway 178 and travel to Panamint Valley Road (do *not* take Wildrose Canyon); this leads to Highway 190, which takes you into the park.

Prefer to fly? Couples lucky enough to have access to a private or chartered aircraft can land at Furnace Creek Resort's 3,040-foot by 70-foot lighted airstrip. Otherwise, the nearest airport is **McCarran International Airport** (702/261-5211; www.mccarran.com) in Las Vegas.

As you enter the park, check in at the **Death Valley National Park Visitor Center** (on Hwy 190, 15 miles inside the park boundary; 760/786-2331; www. nps.gov/deva) or with a park ranger for current back-country road conditions. For general information or specific park brochures, you can write to the **Department of the Interior, National Park Service, Office of Public Inquiries** (PO Box 37127, Room 1013, Washington, DC 20013-7127 [include a SASE]; or call 760/786-2331).

Since Death Valley is a national park, a $10 vehicle entrance fee is charged to incoming visitors. Campground fees range from $10–$16 per night if you have an RV or a camper. Since winter is the park's most popular season, be sure to reserve your accommodations in advance.

---

# Romantic Lodgings

## FURNACE CREEK INN
♥♥♥(

*On Hwy 190, 1 mile south of visitor center, Death Valley  / 760/786-2345 or 800/236-7916*

When you and your sweetie first motor up the long, welcoming driveway to this magnificent oasis set among the towering mountains, panoramic canyons, and gleaming salt flats of Death Valley National Park, this lush sanctuary seems more like a mirage than a hotel. Almost tucked into the mountainside, the three- to four-story inn is a complete contrast to the desolate desert landscape. This quixotic haven receives plenty of water from a natural spring, so it's surrounded by lush vegetation, including palm trees, flower beds, and a garden with cobblestone walking paths. While the historic AAA four-diamond inn is just one of two distinctly different hotels that make up the Furnace Creek Resort, you'll definitely want to hang your hats at this more private and tranquil inn, pard'ner. The 66-room inn is a unique lovers' getaway because there really are no distractions. You may choose to have a massage at the small but well-equipped fitness center or maybe spend a lazy day at the pool. Evenings are all about lounging and gossiping around the swimming pool, a veritable Furnace Creek tradition. Originally built in the 1920s for guests of the Borax Mining Company, the Mediterranean Arabian–style inn has recently been renovated. Decorated in subdued earth tones, each room has comfortable chairs, a small refrigerator, and lazy ceiling fans. Couples, however, may want to spring for one of the few lodgings with a wood-burning fireplace or a private spa tub. Although the bathrooms are small, they have been spruced up with brass fixtures and decorative ceramic tiles. Bathrobes are provided and are especially appreciated after a dip in the naturally warm (82°F) spring-fed swimming pool.

Request a room with a terrace overlooking the garden, and the two of you can sit in the late-afternoon sun and enjoy the desert vista while sipping an aperitif. The deck off the first floor (below the lobby) is open to all guests, and also has a good vantage point for couples to gaze romantically off into the distance (and into each other's eyes). A beautiful gazebo for sudden "pop the question" romantic urges is one of the highlights of the inn's perfectly manicured grounds.

$$$$ *AE, DIS, MC, V; local checks only; closed from mid-May–mid-Oct; www.furnacecreekresort.com.* &

## FURNACE CREEK RANCH
❂❂

*On Hwy 190, 1 mile south of visitor center, Death Valley / 760/786-2345 or 800/236-7916*

If the prices at the Furnace Creek Inn are beyond your budget, Furnace Creek Ranch, just adjacent to the inn, offers more affordable rooms in a Western-style setting. The ranch caters mostly to large groups, but lovers will find the rooms are clean and simple—but not luxurious, so you won't be able to rely on this setting alone to spark your amorous inclinations. Once a working alfalfa ranch that harvested as many as nine crops a year to feed the Borax mine livestock (those 20-mule teams got hungry!), this 224-room complex is like a small city, complete with a post office, a country store, a coffee shop, a swimming pool, stables, four lighted tennis courts, and a Borax Museum dating back to the old mining days. An oasis-like golf course at one end wins the moniker of "the world's lowest 18-hole course," with tees at 214 feet below sea level. Couples will want to be careful not to scare the often-pregnant coyote that sunbathes at the fourth hole. During its early years, the course was leased to cattle ranchers off season, and the fairways were kept neatly mowed by a small flock of very fat sheep! Summer visitors can save up to 20 percent off regular rates.

$$$ *AE, DIS, MC, V; local checks only; www.furnacecreekresort.com.*

# *Romantic Restaurants*

## FURNACE CREEK INN DINING ROOM
❂❂❂

*On Hwy 190 (Furnace Creek Inn), 1 mile south of visitor center, Death Valley / 760/786-2345 or 800/236-7916*

Surrounded by stunning views of mountain ranges and desert saltpans so close you can almost reach out and touch them, the 100-seat Furnace Creek Inn Dining Room is dark and decadent, and tables are spaced well apart so you have plenty of privacy. The elegant atmosphere is softened by flickering candlelight, overstuffed armchairs and rich tapestries, and each window-side table overlooks the inn's well-kept gardens. Service is low-key but impeccable, and they offer a fabulous desert-derived menu. If you're not too busy playing footsie under the table, you'll notice the dining room's accent is on meat, lively game dishes, and true south-of-the-border spices. Snappy appetizers that highlight the area's unique cuisine include rattlesnake empanadas with guacamole, crispy cactus *napolitos*, and Mojave chicken with green chiles. For the fainter of heart (especially those lovers who don't want their eyes watering during a romantic tête-à-tête), more mainstream options include braised lamb shanks, grilled quail, and pork tenderloin, or seafood selections like chile-dusted wild Alaskan salmon with chipotle-vinaigrette greens and mesquite-smoked corn. For more relaxed dining, The Lobby Oasis Lounge is a sexy alternative, though you can still order from the dining room menu—and wear jeans or whatever you prefer for the evening. Trimmed in native Death Valley rock to match the original fireplace, the granite bar counter is crowned by a glass etching that depicts the now famous 20-mule teams that traversed Golden Canyon during the old mining days. The walls of the bar are made of embedded native rock and crystals of borax from the nearby mines, and the massive ceiling supports are actual timbers taken from the trestles of the old Death Valley Railroad. Who would have thought you'd find all this elegance and old-style romance in the middle of the desert? **$$$** *AE, DIS, MC, V; local checks OK; lunch and dinner every day (closed mid-May–mid-Oct); full bar; reservations recommended; www.furnacecreekresort.com.* ♿

## WRANGLER STEAKHOUSE AT THE FURNACE CREEK RANCH
♥♦

*Hwy 190, Death Valley / 760/786-2345 or 800/236-7916*
This 150-seat steakhouse offers some of the heartiest carnivorous dining in the desert. Barbecue ribs, fried chicken, a soup and salad bar, and a variety of specialty steaks are on the menu at this casual eatery. Breakfast and lunch are served buffet style, while evenings are for ordering off the menu. Chef's favorites include the 16-ounce charbroiled porterhouse and the New York strip. Order a selection from the clever list of California varietal wines and toast your day in the desert while the two of you snuggle on one of the restaurant's overstuffed couches. But most importantly, save room for dessert and ask for two spoons to share such sumptuous desserts as brownie à la mode or chocolate indulgence cake. Sunday brunch boasts house specialties of thinly sliced smoked salmon and freshly baked pastries. A casual daily afternoon tea is also a great way to unwind after a day of exploring. **$$** *AE, DIS, MC, V; local checks OK; breakfast, lunch, afternoon tea, dinner every day, brunch Sun; full bar; reservations not accepted; www.furnacecreekresort.com.*

# Wedding Index

# Pet Index

## INLAND EMPIRE AND MOUNTAIN REGION

### BIG BEAR AND LAKE ARROWHEAD
Gray Squirrel Inn
Moose Lodge
Storybook Inn

## THE PALM SPRINGS DESERT RESORT AREA

### THE OTHER DESERT RESORTS
La Quinta Resort & Club
The Lodge at Rancho Mirage

## HIGH DESERT DESTINATIONS

### JOSHUA TREE NATIONAL PARK
Rimrock Ranch Cabins
The 29 Palms Inn

Marina del Rey
description of, 3
lodgings, 11
restaurants, 14–15
Marina Street Inn, 278–79
Marine Room, The, 149–50
Mario's Place, 309
Maritime Museum, 154
Marmalade Café, 25
Marriott's Laguna Cliffs
Resort, 100–101
Marriott's Rancho Las
Palmas Resort & Spa,
354–55
Mastro's, 56
McCall Farm Bed &
Breakfast, 296
McCallum Theatre for the
Performing Arts, 350
McCarran International
Airport, 373, 380
McPhee's Grill, 288–89
Meditation Mount, 224
Melisse, 19
Menghini Winery, 200
Mesa Lane Beach, 235
Metrolink, 93, 124
Metropolitan Transportation
Authority, 37, 63, 156
Michael's, 19–20
Mid Hills Campground,
371–72
Mighty Ducks, 123
Mille Fleurs, 186–87
Millennium Biltmore Hotel
Los Angeles, 44
Miner's Diner & Soda
Fountain, 199
Mingei International
Museum, 179
Mirabeau Bistro, 113
Miramonte Resort & Spa,
355
Miramonte Winery, 191–92
Mission Bay
description of, 137
lodgings, 145–46
Mission Galleria, 305
Mission Hills, 163–64
Mission Inn, The, 307
Mission Inn Restaurant,
309–10
Mission San Buenaventura,
214

Mission San Juan
Capistrano, 92–93
Mission San Luis Obispo de
Tolosa, 262
Mistral, 72
Mitchell Caverns, 372
Modern Way, 336
Mojave, 356
Mojave Desert Information
Center, 372–73
Mojave National Preserve
access to, 373
highlights of, 370–73
information about, 373
Mom's Pie House, 200
Monrovia, 74
Montage Resort & Spa, 101
Montana de Oro State Park,
275
Montecito
description of, 235
lodgings, 239, 242
Moon's Nest Inn, The, 226
Moonstone Beach, 290
Moonstones Gallery, 291
Moorten Botanical Gardens,
335
Moose Lodge, 324
Morels, 57
Moreton Bay Fig Tree, 234
Morey House, 306
Morgan Run Resort & Club,
182
Morro Bay
access to, 276
highlights of, 274–75
information about, 276
lodgings, 276–79
restaurants, 279–81
Morro Bay Aquarium, 275
Morro Bay Visitors Center,
276
Mount Palomar Winery, 191
Mount San Jacinto State
Park, 340
Mozart Haus, 316
Mr. Marcel, 36
Mt. San Jacinto State Park
& Wilderness Office, 313
Muscle Beach, 3
Museums
Bower's Museum, 123–24
California Museum of
Photography, 304

Catalina Island Museum,
79
Coronado Historical
Museum, 136
Getty Center, 36
International Surfing
Museum, 90
Julian Pioneer Museum,
199
Laguna Art Museum, 92
Los Angeles County
Museum of Art, 36, 39
Malibu Lagoon Museum,
3
Mingei International
Museum, 179
Museum of Contemporary
Art, 36, 138
Museum of Latin
American Art, 22
Pacific Asia Museum, 62
Riverside Art Museum,
304
Santa Barbara Museum
of Art, 234
Mussel Shoals, 217–18

**N**

Napa Rose, 131
Naples, 23
Neiman Marcus, 34
Newport Beach
description of, 90–91
lodgings, 94, 97–98, 102
restaurants, 105–6, 109,
114–17, 120
Newport Beach Conference
and Visitors Bureau, 93
Nicholby Antiques, 214
Nico's, 31
Nina Montée Spa, 124
Nipton, 373–74
Northwoods Resort, 324
Norton Simon Museum,
61–62
Nuuva Restaurant & Cafe at
the Ballard Store, 261

**O**

Oak Creek Manor, 193
Oasis of Eden Inn & Suites,
The, 366–67
Oasis of Mara, 365
Oasis Visitor Center, 366

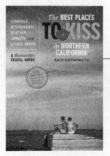